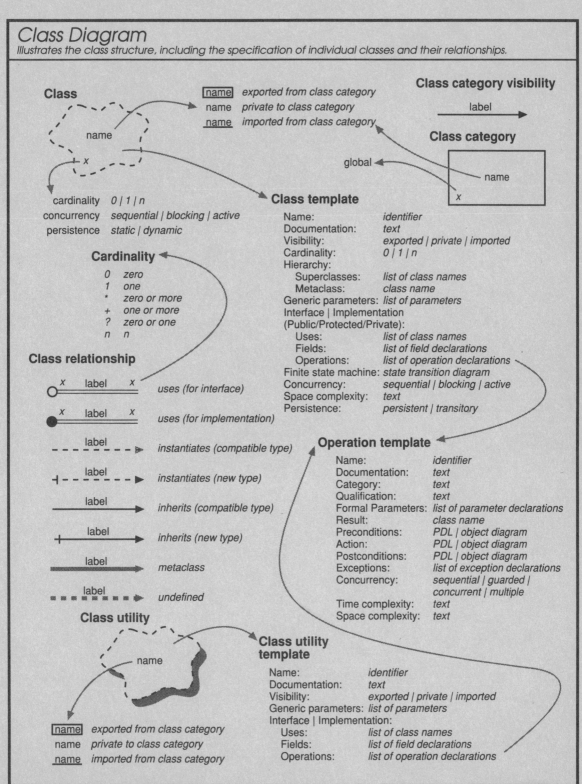

Class Diagram
Illustrates the class structure, including the specification of individual classes and their relationships.

Class

name

x

Class category visibility

label

[name] *exported from class category*
name *private to class category*
name *imported from class category*

Class category

name

x

global

cardinality   *0 | 1 | n*
concurrency   *sequential | blocking | active*
persistence   *static | dynamic*

Cardinality

0   *zero*
1   *one*
*   *zero or more*
+   *one or more*
?   *zero or one*
n   *n*

Class relationship

○ *x* label *x*   *uses (for interface)*
● *x* label *x*   *uses (for implementation)*
- - - label - - →   *instantiates (compatible type)*
-|- - - label - - →   *instantiates (new type)*
—— label ——→   *inherits (compatible type)*
—|— label ——→   *inherits (new type)*
══ label ══→   *metaclass*
■■■ label ■■■→   *undefined*

Class utility

name

Class template

Name:	*identifier*
Documentation:	*text*
Visibility:	*exported	private	imported*
Cardinality:	*0	1	n*
Hierarchy:	
Superclasses:	*list of class names*
Metaclass:	*class name*
Generic parameters:	*list of parameters*
Interface	Implementation	
(Public/Protected/Private):	
Uses:	*list of class names*
Fields:	*list of field declarations*
Operations:	*list of operation declarations*
Finite state machine:	*state transition diagram*
Concurrency:	*sequential	blocking	active*
Space complexity:	*text*
Persistence:	*persistent	transitory*

Operation template

Name:	*identifier*
Documentation:	*text*
Category:	*text*
Qualification:	*text*
Formal Parameters:	*list of parameter declarations*
Result:	*class name*
Preconditions:	*PDL	object diagram*
Action:	*PDL	object diagram*
Postconditions:	*PDL	object diagram*
Exceptions:	*list of exception declarations*
Concurrency:	*sequential	guarded	concurrent	multiple*
Time complexity:	*text*
Space complexity:	*text*

Class utility template

Name:	*identifier*
Documentation:	*text*
Visibility:	*exported	private	imported*
Generic parameters:	*list of parameters*
Interface	Implementation:	
Uses:	*list of class names*
Fields:	*list of field declarations*
Operations:	*list of operation declarations*

[name] *exported from class category*
name *private to class category*
name *imported from class category*

OBJECT ORIENTED DESIGN

WITH APPLICATIONS

The Benjamin/Cummings Series in Ada and Software Engineering
Grady Booch, Series Editor

Booch, *Object-Oriented Design: With Applications*

Booch, *Software Components with Ada: Structures, Tools, and Subsystems*

Booch, *Software Engineering with Ada, Second Edition*

Gonzales, *Ada Programmer's Handbook*

Gonzales, *Ada Programmer's Handbook with Language Reference Manual*

Miller/Petersen, *File Structures with Ada*

Other Titles of Interest

Conte/Dunsmore/Shen, *Software Engineering Metrics and Models*

DeMillo/McCracken/Martin/Passafiume, *Software Testing and Evaluation: A Report*

Elmasri/Navathe, *Fundamentals of Database Systems*

Hewlett-Packard, *The Ultimate Guide to the* vi *and* ex *Text Editors*

Kelly/Pohl, *A Book on C: Programming in C, Second Edition*

Kelly/Pohl, *C by Dissection: The Essentials of C Programming*

Kerschberg, *Expert Database Systems*

Luger/Stubblefield, *Artificial Intelligence and the Design of Expert Systems*

Pohl, *C++ for C Programmers*

Pohl, *C++ for Pascal Programmers*

Sobell, *A Practical Guide to the UNIX System, Second Edition*

Touretzky, *Common Lisp: A Gentle Introduction to Symbolic Computation*

OBJECT ORIENTED DESIGN

WITH APPLICATIONS

Grady Booch

Rational

The Benjamin/Cummings Publishing Company, Inc.

Redwood City, California • Fort Collins, Colorado • Menlo Park, California
Reading, Massachusetts • New York • Don Mills, Ontario • Wokingham, U.K.
Amsterdam • Bonn • Sydney • Singapore • Tokyo • Madrid • San Juan

To Jan
my friend, my lover, my wife

Sponsoring Editor: Alan Apt
Associate Editor: Mary Ann Telatnik
Production Supervisor: Brian Jones
Cover and Text Designer: Gary Head

Copyeditor: Nicholas Murray
Proofreader: Ellen Kurek
Cartoonist: Tony Hall

Camera-ready copy for this book was prepared on a Macintosh II using Microsoft Word and Adobe Illustrator. All Smalltalk examples were developed using Objectworks by ParcPlace Systems. All Object Pascal and C++ examples were developed using translators from Apple Computer running under the Macintosh Programmer's Workshop. All CLOS examples were developed using a translator from Franz, Incorporated. All Ada examples were developed using the Rational Development Environment.

The notation described in this book is in the public domain, and its use is encouraged for all (but please acknowledge its source).

Library of Congress Cataloging-in-Publication Data

```
Booch, Grady.
     Object oriented design with applications / Grady Booch.
        p.   cm.
     Includes bibliographical references.
     ISBN 0-8053-0091-0
     1. Object-oriented programming (Computer science) I. Title.
     QA76.64.B66 1991
     005.1--dc20                                    90-34884
                                                        CIP
```

3 4 5 6 7 8 9 10 DO 9594939291

The Benjamin/Cummings Publishing Company, Inc.
390 Bridge Parkway
Redwood City, California 94065

Preface

Mankind, under the grace of God, hungers for spiritual peace, esthetic achievements, family security, justice, and liberty, none directly satisfied by industrial productivity. But productivity allows the sharing of the plentiful rather than fighting over scarcity; it provides time for spiritual, esthetic, and family matters. It allows society to delegate special skills to institutions of religion, justice, and the preservation of liberty.

HARLAN MILLS
DPMA and Human Productivity

As computer professionals, we strive to build systems that are useful and that work; as software engineers, we are faced with the task of creating complex systems in the presence of scarce computing and human resources. Over the past several years, object-oriented technology has evolved in diverse segments of the computer sciences as a means of managing the complexity inherent in many different kinds of systems. The object model has proven to be a very powerful and unifying concept.

Goals

Because object-oriented design is a relatively young practice, a discipline for effectively applying the elements of the object model has not yet emerged. This book provides practical guidance on the construction of object-oriented systems. The specific goals of this book are

- To provide a sound understanding of the fundamental concepts of the object model

- To facilitate a mastery of the notation and process of object-oriented design
- To teach the realistic application of object-oriented design within a variety of problem domains, using Smalltalk, Object Pascal, C++, the Common Lisp Object System (CLOS), and Ada

The concepts presented in this book all stand on a solid theoretical foundation, but this is primarily a pragmatic book that addresses the issues of industrial-strength software engineering.

Audience

This book is written for the computer professional as well as for the student.

- For the practicing software engineer, we show you how to effectively use object-based and object-oriented programming languages to solve real problems.
- In your role as an analyst or architect, we offer you a path from requirements to implementation, through the use of object-oriented design. We develop your ability to distinguish "good" object-oriented designs from "bad" ones, and to trade off alternate designs when the perversity of the real world intrudes. Perhaps most important, we offer you fresh approaches to reasoning about complex systems.
- For the program manager, we provide insights on how to allocate the resources of a team of developers, and on how to manage the risks associated with complex software systems.
- For the tool builder and the tool user, we provide a rigorous treatment of the notation and process of object-oriented design as a basis for computer-aided software engineering (CASE) tools.
- For the student, we provide the instruction necessary for you to begin to acquire several important skills in the science and art of developing complex systems.

This book is suitable for use in undergraduate and graduate courses as well as in professional seminars and individual study. Since it deals primarily with a method of software design, it is most appropriate for courses in software engineering and advanced programming, and as a supplement to courses involving specific object-based and object-oriented programming languages.

Structure

This book is divided into three major sections – Concepts, The Method, and Applications – with considerable supplemental material woven throughout.

Concepts

The first section examines the inherent complexity of software and the ways in which complexity manifests itself. We present the object model as a means of helping us manage this complexity. In great detail, we examine the fundamental elements of the object model: abstraction, encapsulation, modularity, hierarchy, typing, concurrency, and persistence. We address basic questions such as What is a class? and What is an object? Because the identification of meaningful classes and objects is the key task in object-oriented design, we spend considerable time studying the nature of classification. In particular, we examine approaches to classification in other disciplines, such as biology, linguistics, and psychology, then apply these lessons to the problem of discovering classes and objects in software systems using the techniques of domain analysis and conceptual modeling.

The Method

The second section presents a method for the development of complex systems based on the object model, which we call simply object-oriented design (OOD). We first present a graphic notation for object-oriented design followed by its process. We also examine the pragmatics of object-oriented design – in particular, its place in the software development life cycle and its implications for project management.

Applications

The final section offers a set of five complete, nontrivial design examples encompassing a diverse selection of problem domains: process control, scientific tools, information management systems, artificial intelligence, and command and control. We have chosen these particular problem domains because they represent the kinds of complex problems faced by the practicing software engineer. It is all too easy to show how certain principles apply to simple problems, but since our focus is on building useful systems for the real world, we are more interested in showing how the object model scales up to complex applications. Since every reader may not be familiar with the problem domains chosen, we begin each application with a brief discussion of the fundamental technology involved (such as database design and blackboard system architecture). We also use these applications to show how object-oriented design can be used with a variety of object-based and object-oriented programming languages, namely, Smalltalk, Object Pascal, C++, the Common Lisp Object System

(CLOS), and Ada. The design of software systems is rarely amenable to cookbook approaches; therefore we emphasize the incremental development of applications, guided by a number of sound principles and well-formed models.

Supplemental Material

A considerable amount of supplemental material is woven throughout the book. Most chapters have sidebar boxes that provide information on important topics such as the mechanics of method dispatch in different object-oriented programming languages. We also include an appendix on object-oriented programming languages, in which we consider the distinction between object-based and object-oriented programming languages and the evolution and essential properties of both categories of languages. For those readers who are unfamiliar with the languages used in the applications, we provide a summary of the features of each language, with examples. We also provide a glossary of common terms and an extensive classified bibliography that provides references to source material on the object model. Lastly, the endpages provide a summary of the notation and process of the object-oriented design method.

The software for the applications described in Chapters 8 through 12 are available from the publisher.

Using This Book

This book is designed to be read from cover to cover as well as in less structured ways. If you are looking for a deep understanding of the underlying concepts of the object model or the motivation for the principles of object-oriented design, you should start with Chapter 1 and continue forward in order. If you are primarily interested in learning the details of the notation and process of object-oriented design, start with Chapters 5 and 6; Chapter 7 is especially useful to managers of projects using this method. If you are most interested in the practical application of object-oriented design to a specific problem domain, select any or all of Chapters 8 through 12.

Acknowledgments

This book is dedicated to my wife, Jan, for her loving support.

Through many face-to-face discussions as well as exchanges of electronic and real mail, a number of individuals have shaped my ideas on object-oriented design. For their contributions, I especially thank Sid Bailin, Daniel Bobrow, Dick Bolz, Dave Bulman, Dave Bernstein, Brad Cox, Tom DeMarco, Mike Devlin, Adele Goldberg, Tony Hoare, Michael Jackson, Ralph Johnson, James Kempf, Norm Kerth, Phil Levy, Barbara Liskov, James MacFarlane, Masoud

Milani, Harlan Mills, Steve Neis, Dave Parnas, Bill Riddel, Kurt Schmucker, Ed Seidewitz, Dan Shiffman, Bjarne Stroustrup, Dave Thomas, Mike Vilot, Tony Wasserman, Peter Wegner, Lloyd Williams, Niklaus Wirth, and Ed Yourdon.

A large part of the pragmatics of this book derives from my involvement with a number of very large software systems being developed around the world at companies such as AT&T, Autotrol, Boeing, Computer Sciences Corporation, Contel, Ericsson, Ferranti, General Electric, GTE, Holland Signaal, Hughes Aircraft Company, IBM, Lockheed, Martin Marietta, NTT, Philips, Rockwell International, Shell Oil, and TRW. I have had the opportunity to interact with literally hundreds of professional software engineers and their managers, and I thank them all for helping to make this book relevant to real-world problems.

A special thanks goes to my editor, Alan Apt, for his encouragement during the life of this project. Thanks also to Tony Hall, whose cartoons brighten what would otherwise be just another stuffy technical book. Finally, thanks to my three cats, Camy, Annie, and Shadow, who kept me company on many a late night of writing.

Brief Contents

Contents

Chapter 11: Common Lisp Object System: Cryptanalysis 407

Chapter 12: Ada: Traffic Management System 443

Concepts

Sir Isaac Newton secretly admitted to some friends: He
understood how gravity *behaved*, but not how it *worked!*

LILY TOMLIN
The Search for Signs of Intelligent Life in the Universe

CHAPTER 1

Complexity

A physician, a civil engineer, and a computer scientist were arguing about what was the oldest profession in the world. The physician remarked, "Well, in the Bible, it says that God created Eve from a rib taken out of Adam. This clearly required surgery, and so I can rightly claim that mine is the oldest profession in the world." The civil engineer interrupted, and said, "But even earlier in the book of Genesis, it states that God created the order of the heavens and the earth from out of the chaos. This was the first and certainly the most spectacular application of civil engineering. Therefore, fair doctor, you are wrong: mine is the oldest profession in the world." The computer scientist leaned back in her chair, smiled, and then said confidently, "Ah, but who do you think created the chaos?"

1.1 The Inherent Complexity of Software

The Properties of Simple and Complex Software Systems

A dying star on the verge of collapse, a child learning how to read, white blood cells rushing to attack a virus: these are but a few of the objects in the physical world that involve truly awesome complexity. Software may also involve elements of great complexity; however, the complexity we find here is of a fundamentally different kind. As Brooks points out, "Einstein argued that there must be simplified explanations of nature, because God is not capricious or arbitrary. No such faith comforts the software engineer. Much of the complexity that he must master is arbitrary complexity" [1].

We do realize that some software systems are not complex. These are the largely forgettable applications that are specified, constructed, maintained, and used by the same person, usually the amateur programmer or the professional developer working in isolation. This is not to say that all such systems are crude and inelegant, nor do we mean to belittle their creators. Such systems tend to have a very limited purpose and a very short life span. We can afford to throw them away and replace them with entirely new software rather than attempt to reuse them, repair them, or extend their functionality. Such applications are generally more tedious than difficult to develop; consequently, learning how to design them does not interest us.

Instead, we are much more interested in the challenges of developing what I will call *industrial-strength software.* Here we find applications that exhibit a very rich set of behaviors, as, for example, in reactive systems that control some physical process and for which time and space are scarce resources; applications that maintain the integrity of thousands of records of information while allowing concurrent updates and queries; and systems for the command and control of real-world entities, such as the routing of air or railway traffic. Software systems such as these tend to have a long life span, and over time, many users come to depend upon their proper functioning. In the world of industrial-strength software, we also find applications that model intricate phenomena, such as scientific tools for planning optical experiments and programs that mimic some aspect of human intelligence. Although such applications are generally tools of research, they are no less complex, for they are the means and artifacts of exploratory development.

The distinguishing characteristic of industrial-strength software is that it is intensely difficult, if not impossible, for the individual developer to comprehend all the subtleties of its design. Stated in blunt terms, the complexity of such systems exceeds the human intellectual capacity. Alas, this complexity we speak of seems to be an essential property of all large software systems. By *essential* we mean that we may master this complexity, but we can never make it go away.

Certainly, there will always be geniuses among us, people of extraordinary skill who can do the work of a handful of mere mortal developers, the software engineering equivalents of Frank Lloyd Wright or Leonardo da Vinci. These are the people whom we seek to deploy as our systems architects: the ones who invent innovative mechanisms that others can use as the architectural foundations of other applications or systems. However, as Peters observes, "The world is only sparsely populated with geniuses. There is no reason to believe that the software engineering community has an inordinately large proportion of them" [2]. Although there is a touch of genius in all of us, in the realm of industrial-strength software we cannot always rely upon divine inspiration to carry us through. Therefore, we must consider more disciplined ways to master complexity. To better understand what we seek to control, let us next examine why complexity is an essential property of all large software systems.

Why Software Is Inherently Complex

As Brooks suggests, "The complexity of software is an essential property, not an accidental one" [3]. We observe that this inherent complexity derives from four elements: the complexity of the problem domain, the difficulty of managing the developmental process, the flexibility possible through software, and the problems of characterizing the behavior of discrete systems.

The Complexity of the Problem Domain. The problems we try to solve in software often involve elements of inescapable complexity, in which we find a myriad of competing, perhaps even contradictory, requirements. Consider the requirements for the electronic system of a multi-engine aircraft, a cellular phone switching system, or an autonomous robot. The raw functionality of such systems is difficult enough to comprehend, but now add all of the (often implicit) nonfunctional requirements such as usability, performance, cost, survivability, and reliability. This unrestrained external complexity is what causes the arbitrary complexity about which Brooks writes.

This external complexity usually springs from the "impedance mismatch" that exists between the users of a system and its developers: users generally find it very hard to give precise expression to their needs in a form that developers can understand. In extreme cases, users may have only vague ideas of what they want in a software system. This is not so much the fault of either the users or the developers of a system; rather, it occurs because each group generally lacks expertise in the domain of the other. Users and developers have different perspectives on the nature of the problem and make different assumptions regarding the nature of the solution. Actually, even if users had perfect knowledge of their needs, we currently have few instruments for precisely capturing these requirements. The common way of expressing requirements today is with large volumes of text, occasionally accompanied by a few drawings. Such documents are difficult to comprehend, are open to varying interpretations, and too often contain elements that are designs rather than essential requirements.

A further complication is that the requirements of a software system often change during its development, largely because the very existence of a software development project alters the rules of the problem. Seeing early products, such as design documents and prototypes, and then using a system once it is installed and operational, are forcing functions that lead users to better understand and articulate their real needs. At the same time, this process makes developers more expert in the problem domain, enabling them to ask better questions that illuminate the dark corners of a system's desired behavior.

Because a large software system is a capital investment, we cannot afford to scrap an existing system every time its requirements change. Planned or not,

The task of the software development team is to engineer the illusion of simplicity.

large systems tend to evolve over time, a condition that is often incorrectly labeled *software maintenance*. To be more precise, it is *maintenance* when we correct errors; it is *evolution* when we respond to changing requirements; it is *preservation* when we continue to use extraordinary means to keep an ancient and decaying piece of software in operation. Unfortunately, reality suggests that an inordinate percentage of software development resources are spent on software preservation.

The Difficulty of Managing the Development Process. The fundamental task of the software development team is to engineer the illusion of simplicity, to shield users from this vast and often arbitrary external complexity. Certainly, size is no great virtue in a software system. We strive to write less code by inventing clever and powerful mechanisms that give us this illusion of simplicity, as well as by reusing existing designs and code. However, the sheer volume of a system's requirements is sometimes inescapable and forces us either to write a large amount of new software or to reuse existing software in novel ways. Just two decades ago, assembly language programs of only a few thousand lines of code stressed the limits of our software engineering abilities. Today, it is not unusual to find delivered systems whose size is measured in hundreds of thousands, or even millions of lines of code (and all of that in a high-order programming language, as well). No one person can ever understand such a system completely. Even if we decompose our implementation in meaningful ways, we still end up with hundreds and sometimes thousands of separate modules. This amount of work demands that we use a team of developers, and ideally, we use as small a team as possible. However, no matter what its size, there are always significant challenges associated with team development. More developers means more complex communication and hence more difficult coordination, particularly if the team is geographically dispersed, as is often the case in very large projects. With a team of developers, the key management challenge is always to maintain a unity and integrity of design.

The Flexibility Possible Through Software. A home-building company generally does not operate its own tree farm from which to harvest trees for lumber; it is highly unusual for a construction firm to build an on-site steel mill to forge custom girders for a new building. Yet in the software industry such practice is common. Software offers the ultimate flexibility, so it is possible for a developer to express almost any kind of abstraction. This flexibility turns out to be an incredibly seductive property, however, because it also forces the developer to craft virtually all the primitive building blocks upon which these higher level abstractions stand. While the construction industry has uniform building codes and standards for the quality of raw materials, few such standards exist in the software industry. As a result, software development remains a labor-intensive business.

The Problems of Characterizing the Behavior of Discrete Systems. If we toss a ball into the air, we can reliably predict its path because we know that under normal conditions, certain laws of physics apply. We would be very surprised if just because we threw the ball a little harder, halfway through its flight it suddenly stopped and shot straight up into the air.[*] In a not-quite-debugged software simulation of this ball's motion, exactly that kind of behavior can easily occur.

Within a large application, there may be hundreds or even thousands of variables as well as more than one thread of control. The entire collection of these variables, their current values, and the current address and calling stack of each process within the system constitute the present state of the application. Because we execute our software on digital computers, we have a system with discrete states. By contrast, analog systems such as the motion of the tossed ball are continuous systems. Parnas suggests that "when we say that a system is described by a continuous function, we are saying that it can contain no hidden surprises. Small changes in inputs will always cause correspondingly small changes in outputs" [4]. On the other hand, discrete systems by their very nature

---

[*] Actually, even simple continuous systems can exhibit very complex behavior, because of the presence of chaos. Chaos introduces a randomness that makes it impossible to precisely predict the future state of a system. For example, given the initial state of two drops of water at the top of a stream, we cannot predict exactly where they will be relative to one another at the bottom of the stream. Chaos has been found in systems as diverse as the weather, chemical reactions, biological systems, and even computer networks. Fortunately, there appears to be underlying order in all chaotic systems, in the form of patterns called attractors.

have a finite number of possible states; in large systems, there is a combinatorial explosion that makes this number very large. We try to design our systems with a separation of concerns, so that the behavior in one part of a system has minimal impact upon the behavior in another. However, the fact remains that the transitions among discrete states cannot be modeled by continuous functions. Each event external to a software system has the potential of placing that system in a new state, and furthermore, the mapping from state to state is not always deterministic. In the worst circumstances, an external event may corrupt the state of a system, because its designers failed to take into account certain interactions among events. For example, imagine a commercial airplane whose flight surfaces and cabin environment are managed by a single computer. We would be very unhappy if, as a result of a passenger in seat 31D turning on an overhead light, the plane immediately executed a sharp dive. In continuous systems this kind of behavior would be unlikely, but in discrete systems all external events can affect any part of the system's internal state. Certainly, this is the primary motivation for vigorous testing of our systems, but for all except the most trivial systems, exhaustive testing is impossible. Since we have neither the mathematical tools nor the intellectual capacity to model the complete behavior of large discrete systems, we must be content with acceptable levels of confidence regarding their correctness.

The Consequences of Unrestrained Complexity

"The more complex the system, the more open it is to total breakdown" [5]. Rarely would a builder think about adding a new sub-basement to an existing 100-story building; to do so would be very costly and would undoubtedly invite failure. Amazingly, users of software systems rarely think twice about asking for equivalent changes. Besides, they argue, it is only a simple matter of programming.

Our failure to master the complexity of software results in projects that are late, over budget, and deficient in their stated requirements. We often call this condition the *software crisis*, but frankly, a malady that has carried on this long must be called normal. Sadly, this crisis translates into the squandering of human resources – a most precious commodity – as well as a considerable loss of opportunities. There are simply not enough good developers around to create all the new software that users need. Furthermore, a significant number of the developmental personnel in any given organization must often be dedicated to the maintenance or preservation of geriatric software. Given the indirect as well as the direct contribution of software to the economic base of most developed countries, and considering the ways in which software can amplify the powers of the individual, it is unacceptable to allow this situation to continue.

How can we change this dismal picture? Since the underlying problem springs from the inherent complexity of software, our suggestion is to first study how complex systems in other disciplines are organized. Indeed, if we open our eyes to the world about us, we will observe successful systems of significant complexity. Some of these systems are the works of humanity, such as the

Space Shuttle, the England/France tunnel, and large business organizations such as IBM or NTT. Many even more complex systems appear in nature, such as the human circulatory system or the structure of a plant.

1.2 The Structure of Complex Systems

Examples of Complex Systems

The Structure of a Personal Computer. A personal computer is a device of moderate complexity. Most of them are composed of the same major elements: a central processing unit (CPU), a monitor, a keyboard, and some sort of secondary storage device, usually either a floppy disk or a hard disk drive. We may take any one of these parts and further decompose it. For example, a CPU typically encompasses primary memory, an arithmetic/logic unit (ALU), and a bus to which peripheral devices are attached. Each of these parts may in turn be further decomposed: an ALU may be divided into registers and random control logic, which themselves are constructed from even more primitive elements, such as NAND gates, inverters, and so on.

Here we see the hierarchic nature of a complex system. A personal computer functions properly only because of the collaborative activity of each of its major parts. Together, these separate parts logically form a whole. Indeed, we can reason about how a computer works only because we can decompose it into parts that we can study separately. Thus, we may study the operation of a monitor independently of the operation of the hard disk drive. Similarly, we may study the ALU without regard for the primary memory subsystem.

Not only are complex systems hierarchic, but the levels of this hierarchy represent different levels of abstraction, each built upon the other, and each understandable by itself. We choose a given level of abstraction to suit our particular needs. For instance, if we were trying to track down a timing problem in the primary memory, we might properly look at the gate-level architecture of the computer, but this level of abstraction would be inappropriate if we were trying to find the source of a problem in a spreadsheet application.

The Structure of Plants and Animals. In botany, scientists seek to understand the similarities and differences among plants through a study of their morphology, that is, their form and structure. Plants are complex multicellular organisms, and from the cooperative activity of various plant organ systems arise such complex behaviors as photosynthesis and transpiration.

Plants consist of three major structures (roots, stems, and leaves), and each of these has its own structure. For example, roots encompass branch roots, root hairs, the root apex, and the root cap. Similarly, a cross-section of a leaf reveals its epidermis, mesophyll, and vascular tissue. Each of these structures is further composed of a collection of cells, and inside each cell we find yet another level of complexity, encompassing such elements as chloroplasts, mitochondria, a nucleus, and so on. As with the structure of a computer, the parts of a plant form a hierarchy, and each level of this hierarchy embodies its own complexity.

All parts at the same level of abstraction interact in well-defined ways. For example, at the highest level of abstraction, roots are responsible for absorbing water and minerals from the soil. Roots interact with stems, which transport these raw materials up to the leaves. The leaves in turn use the water and minerals provided by the stems to produce food through photosynthesis.

There are always clear boundaries between the outside and the inside of a given level. For this reason, we can say that the parts of a leaf work together to provide the functionality of the leaf as a whole, with little or no direct interaction with the elementary parts of the roots. In simpler terms, there is a clear separation of concerns among the parts at different levels of abstraction.

In a computer, we find NAND gates used in the design of the CPU as well as in the hard disk drive. Likewise, a considerable amount of commonality cuts across all parts of the structural hierarchy of a plant. This is nature's way of achieving an economy of expression. For example, cells serve as the basic building blocks in all structures of a plant; ultimately, the roots, stems, and leaves of a plant are all composed of cells. Yet, although each of these primitive elements is indeed a cell, there are many different kinds of cells. For example, there are cells with and without chloroplasts, cells with walls that are impervious to water and cells with walls that are permeable, and even living cells and dead cells.

In studying the morphology of a plant, we do not find individual parts that are each responsible for only one small step in a single larger process, such as photosynthesis. In fact, there are no centralized parts that directly coordinate the activities of lower level ones. Instead, we find separate parts that act as independent agents, each of which exhibits some fairly complex behavior, and each of which contributes to many higher level functions. Only through the mutual cooperation of meaningful collections of these agents do we see the higher level functionality of a plant.

Turning briefly to the field of zoology, we note that multicellular animals exhibit a hierarchical structure similar to that of plants: collections of cells form tissues, tissues work together as organs, clusters of organs define systems (such as the digestive system), and so on. We cannot help but notice nature's awesome economy of expression: the fundamental building block of all animal matter is the cell, just as the cell is the elementary structure of all plant life. Granted, there are differences between these two. For example, plant cells are enclosed by rigid cellulose walls, but animal cells are not. Notwithstanding these differences, however, both of these structures are undeniably cells. This is an example of commonality that crosses domains.

A number of mechanisms above the cellular level are also shared by plant and animal life. For example, both use some sort of vascular system to transport nutrients within the organism, and both exhibit differentiation by sex among members of the same species.

The Structure of Matter. The study of fields as diverse as astronomy and nuclear physics provides us with many other examples of incredibly complex systems. Spanning these two disciplines, we find yet another structural hierarchy. Astronomers study galaxies that are arranged in clusters, and stars, planets, and various debris are the constituents of galaxies. Likewise, nuclear physicists are concerned with a structural hierarchy, but one on an entirely different scale. Atoms are made up of electrons, protons, and neutrons; electrons appear to be elementary particles, but protons, neutrons, and other particles are formed from more basic components called quarks.

Again we find that a great commonality in the form of shared mechanisms unifies this vast hierarchy. Specifically, there appear to be only four distinct kinds of forces at work in the universe: gravity, electromagnetic interaction, the strong force, and the weak force. Many laws of physics involving these elementary forces, such as the laws of conservation of energy and of momentum, apply to galaxies as well as quarks.

The Structure of Social Institutions. As a final example of complex systems, we turn to the structure of social institutions. Groups of people join together in organizations to accomplish tasks that cannot be done by individuals. Some organizations are transitory, and some endure beyond many lifetimes. As organizations grow larger, we see a distinct hierarchy emerge. Multinational corporations contain companies, which in turn are made up of divisions, which in turn contain branches, which in turn encompass local offices, and so on. If the organization endures, the boundaries among these parts may change, and over time, a new, more stable hierarchy may emerge.

The relationships among the various parts of a large organization are just like those found among the components of a computer, or a plant, or even a galaxy. Thus, the interaction among employees within an individual office is greater than that between employees of different offices. A mail clerk usually does not interact with the chief executive officer of a company but interacts frequently with other people in the mail room. Here too, these different levels are unified by common mechanisms. The clerk and the executive are both paid by the same financial organization, and both share common facilities, such as the company's telephone system, to accomplish their tasks.

The Five Attributes of a Complex System

Drawing from this line of study, we conclude that there are five attributes common to all complex systems. Building upon the work of Simon and Ando, Courtois suggests the following:

1. *"Frequently, complexity takes the form of a hierarchy, whereby a complex system is composed of interrelated subsystems that have in turn their own subsystems, and so on, until some lowest level of elementary components is reached"* [6].

Simon points out that "the fact that many complex systems have a nearly decomposable, hierarchic structure is a major facilitating factor enabling us to understand, describe, and even 'see' such systems and their parts" [7]. Indeed, it is likely that we can understand only those systems that have a hierarchic structure.

Regarding the nature of the primitive components of a complex system, our experience suggests that

> 2. *The choice of what components in a system are primitive is relatively arbitrary and is largely up to the discretion of the observer of the system.*

What is primitive for one observer may be at a much higher level of abstraction for another.

Simon calls hierarchic systems *decomposable*, because they can be divided into identifiable parts; he calls them *nearly decomposable*, because their parts are not completely independent. This leads us to another attribute common to all complex systems:

> 3. *"Intracomponent linkages are generally stronger than intercomponent linkages. This fact has the effect of separating the high-frequency dynamics of the components – involving the internal structure of the components – from the low-frequency dynamics – involving interaction among components" [8].*

This difference between intra- and intercomponent interactions provides a separation of concerns among the various parts of a system, so that it is possible to study each part in relative isolation.

As we have discussed, many complex systems are implemented with an economy of expression. Simon thus notes that

> 4. *"Hierarchic systems are usually composed of only a few different kinds of subsystems in various combinations and arrangements" [9].*

Sometimes, as with plant and animal cells, we find subsystems that are common across different domains.

Earlier, we noted that complex systems tend to evolve over time. As Simon suggests, "complex systems will evolve from simple systems much more rapidly if there are stable intermediate forms than if there are not" [10]. In more dramatic terms, Gall states that

> 5. *"A complex system that works is invariably found to have evolved from a simple system that worked. . . . A complex system designed from scratch never works and cannot be patched up to make it work. You have to start over, beginning with a working simple system" [11].*

As systems evolve, objects that were once considered complex become the primitive objects upon which more complex systems are built.

Organized and Disorganized Complexity

The Canonical Form of a Complex System. The discovery of common abstractions and mechanisms greatly facilitates our understanding of complex systems. For example, with just a few minutes of orientation, an experienced pilot can step into a multi-engine jet aircraft he or she has never flown before, and safely fly the vehicle. Having recognized the properties common to all such aircraft, such as the functioning of the rudder, ailerons, and throttle, the pilot primarily needs to learn what properties are unique to that particular aircraft. If the pilot already knows how to fly a given aircraft, it is far easier to know how to fly a similar one.

This example suggests that we have been using the term *hierarchy* in a rather loose fashion. Most interesting systems do not embody a single hierarchy; instead, we find that many different hierarchies are usually present within the same complex system. For example, an aircraft may be studied by decomposing it into its propulsion system, flight-control system, and so on. This decomposition represents a structural, or "part of" hierarchy. Alternately, we can cut across the system in an entirely orthogonal way. For example, a turbofan engine is a specific kind of jet engine, and a Pratt and Whitney TF30 is a specific kind of turbofan engine. Stated another way, a jet engine represents a generalization of the properties common to every kind of jet engine; a turbofan engine is simply a specialized kind of jet engine, with properties that distinguish it, for example, from ramjet engines.

This second hierarchy represents a "kind of" hierarchy. In our experience, we have found it essential to view a system from both perspectives, seeing its "kind of" hierarchy as well as its "part of" hierarchy. For reasons that will become clear in the next chapter, we call these hierarchies the *class structure* and the *object structure*, respectively.

If we combine the concept of the class and object structure together with the five attributes of a complex system, we find that virtually all complex systems take on the same (canonical) form, as we show in Figure 1-1. Here we see the two orthogonal hierarchies of the system: its class structure and its object structure. Each hierarchy is highly layered, with the more abstract classes and objects built upon more primitive ones. What class or object is chosen as primitive is relative to the problem at hand. Especially among the parts of the object structure, there are well-defined relationships among objects at the same level. Looking inside any given level reveals yet another level of complexity. Notice also that the class structure and the object structure are not completely independent; rather, each object in the object structure represents a specific instance of some class. As the figure suggests, there are usually many more objects than classes of objects within a complex system. Thus, by showing the "part of" as well as the "kind of" hierarchy, we explicitly expose the redundancy of the system under consideration. If we did not reveal a system's class structure, we would have to duplicate our knowledge about the properties of each individual part. With the inclusion of the class structure, we capture these common properties in one place.

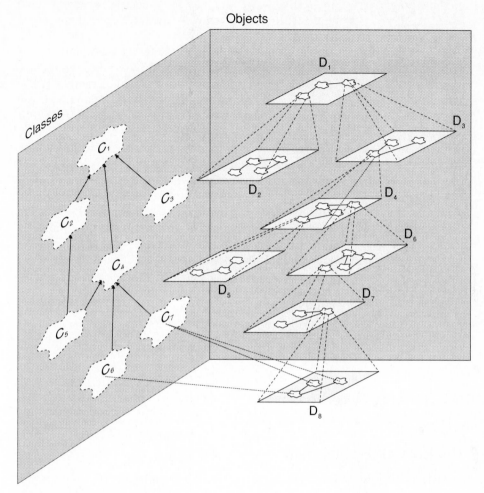

Figure 1-1
The Canonical Form of a Complex System

Our experience is that the most successful complex software systems are those whose designs explicitly encompass a well-engineered class and object structure and whose structure embodies the five attributes of complex systems described in the previous section. Lest the importance of this observation be missed, let us be even more direct: we very rarely encounter software systems that are delivered on time, within budget, and that meet their requirements, unless they are designed with these factors in mind.

The Limitations of the Human Capacity for Dealing with Complexity. If we know what the design of complex software systems should be like, then why do we still have serious problems in successfully developing them? As we discuss in the next chapter, this concept of the organized complexity of software (whose guiding principles we collectively call the *object model)* is relatively new. However, there is yet another factor that dominates: the fundamental limitations of the human capacity for dealing with complexity.

As we first begin to analyze a complex software system, we find many parts that must interact in a multitude of intricate ways, with little perceptible commonality among either the parts or their interactions: this is an example of disorganized complexity. As we work to bring organization to this complexity through the process of design, we must think about many things at once. For example, in an air traffic control system, we must deal with the state of many different aircraft at once, involving such properties as their location, speed, and heading. Especially in the case of discrete systems, we must cope with a fairly large, intricate, and sometimes nondeterministic *state space*. Unfortunately, it is absolutely impossible for a single person to keep track of all of these details at once. Experiments by psychologists, such as those of Miller, suggest that the maximum number of chunks of information that an individual can simultaneously comprehend is on the order of seven, plus or minus two [12]. This channel capacity seems to be related to the capacity of short-term memory. Simon additionally notes that processing speed is a limiting factor: it takes the mind about five seconds to accept a new chunk of information [13].

We are faced with a fundamental dilemma. The complexity of the software systems we are asked to develop is increasing, yet there are basic limits upon our ability to cope with this complexity. How then do we resolve this predicament?

1.3 Bringing Order to Chaos

The Role of Decomposition

As Dijkstra suggests, "The technique of mastering complexity has been known since ancient times: divide et impera (divide and rule)" [14]. When designing a complex software system, it is essential to decompose it into smaller and smaller parts, each of which we may then refine independently. In this manner, we satisfy the very real constraint that exists upon the channel capacity of human cognition: to understand any given level of a system, we need only comprehend a few parts (rather than all parts) at once. Indeed, as Parnas observes, intelligent decomposition directly addresses the inherent complexity of software by forcing a division of a system's state space [15].

Algorithmic Decomposition. Most of us have been formally trained in the dogma of top-down structured design, and so we approach decomposition as a simple matter of algorithmic decomposition, wherein each module in the system denotes a major step in some overall process. Figure 1-2 is an example of one of the products of structured design, a structure chart that shows the relationships among various functional elements of the solution. This particular structure

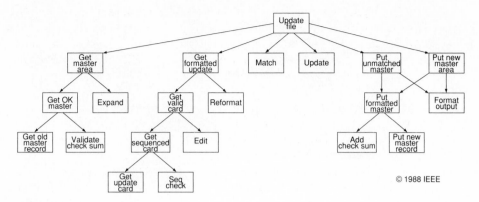

© 1988 IEEE

Figure 1-2
Algorithmic Decomposition

chart illustrates part of the design of a program that updates the content of a master file. It was automatically generated from a data flow diagram by an expert system tool that embodies the rules of structured design [16].

Object-Oriented Decomposition. We suggest that there is an alternate decomposition possible for the same problem. In Figure 1-3, we have decomposed the system according to the key abstractions in the problem domain. Rather than decomposing the problem into steps such as *Get formatted update* and *Add check sum* , we have identified objects such as *Master File* and *Check Sum*, which derive directly from the vocabulary of the problem domain.

Although both designs solve the same problem, they do so in quite different ways. In this second decomposition, we view the world as a set of autonomous agents that collaborate to perform some higher level behavior. *Get formatted update* thus does not exist as an independent algorithm; rather, it exists as an operation upon the object *File of Updates*. Calling this operation creates another object, *Update to Card*. In this manner, each object in our solution embodies its own unique behavior, and each one models some object in the real world. From this perspective, an object is simply a tangible entity which exhibits some well-defined behavior. Objects do things, and we ask them to perform what they do by sending them messages. Because our decomposition is based upon objects and not algorithms, we call this an *object-oriented* decomposition.

Algorithmic versus Object-Oriented Decomposition. Which is the right way to decompose a complex system – by algorithms or by objects? Actually, this is a trick question, because the right answer is that both views are important: the algorithmic view highlights the ordering of events, and the object-oriented view emphasizes the agents that either cause action or are the subjects upon which

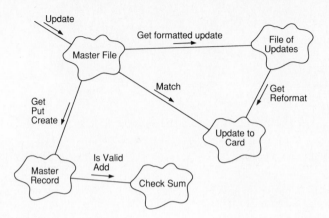

Figure 1-3
Object-Oriented Decomposition

these operations act.[*] However, the fact remains that we cannot construct a complex system in both ways simultaneously, for they are completely orthogonal views. We must start decomposing a system either by algorithms or by objects, and then use the resulting structure as the framework for expressing the other perspective.

Our experience leads us to apply the object-oriented view first because this approach is better at helping us organize the inherent complexity of software systems, just as it helped us to describe the organized complexity of complex systems as diverse as computers, plants, galaxies, and large social institutions. As we will discuss further in Chapters 2 and 7, object-oriented decomposition has a number of highly significant advantages over algorithmic decomposition. Object-oriented decomposition yields smaller systems through the reuse of common mechanisms, thus providing an important economy of expression. Object-oriented systems are also more resilient to change and thus better able to evolve over time, because their design is based upon stable intermediate forms. Indeed, object-oriented decomposition greatly reduces the risk of building complex software systems, because they are designed to evolve incrementally from smaller systems in which we already have confidence. Furthermore, object-oriented decomposition directly addresses the inherent complexity of software by helping us make intelligent decisions regarding the separation of concerns in a large state space.

---

[*] Langdon suggests that this question has been asked since ancient times. As he states, "C. H. Waddington has noted that the duality of views can be traced back to the ancient Greeks. A passive view was proposed by Democritus, who asserted that the world was composed of matter called atoms. Democritus' view places things at the center of focus. On the other hand, the classical spokesman for the active view is Heraclitus, who emphasized the notion of process" [17].

Chapters 8 through 12 demonstrate these benefits through several complete applications, drawn from a diverse set of problem domains. The sidebar in this chapter further compares and contrasts the object-oriented view with more traditional approaches to design.

The Role of Abstraction

Earlier, we referred to Miller's experiments, from which he concluded that an individual can comprehend only about seven, plus or minus two, chunks of information at one time. This number appears to be independent of information content. As Miller himself observes, "The span of absolute judgment and the span of immediate memory impose severe limitations on the amount of information that we are able to receive, process and remember. By organizing the stimulus input simultaneously into several dimensions and successively into a sequence of chunks, we manage to break . . . this informational bottleneck" [18]. He goes on to call this process *recoding*; in more contemporary terms, we call it chunking or *abstraction.*

As Wulf describes it, "We (humans) have developed an exceptionally powerful technique for dealing with complexity. We abstract from it. Unable to master the entirety of a complex object, we chose to ignore its inessential details, dealing instead with the generalized, idealized model of the object" [19]. For example, when studying how photosynthesis works in a plant, we can focus upon the chemical reactions in certain cells in a leaf, and ignore all other parts, such as the roots and stems. We are still constrained by the number of things that we can comprehend at one time, but through abstraction, we use chunks of information with increasingly greater semantic content. This is especially true if we take an object-oriented view of the world, because objects, as abstractions of entities in the real world, represent a particularly dense and cohesive clustering of information.

Chapter 2 examines the meaning of abstraction in much greater detail.

The Role of Hierarchy

Another way to increase the semantic content of individual chunks of information is by explicitly recognizing both the class and object hierarchies within a complex software system. The object structure is important because it illustrates how different objects collaborate with one another through patterns of interaction that we call *mechanisms*. The class structure is equally important, because it highlights the redundancy within a system. Thus, rather than study each individual photosynthesizing cell within a specific plant leaf, it is enough to study one such cell, because we expect that all others will exhibit similar behavior. Although we treat each instance of a particular kind of object as distinct, we may assume that it shares the same behavior as all other instances of that same kind of object. By classifying objects into groups of related abstractions (for example, kinds of plant cells versus animal cells), we come to explicitly

Categories of Design Methods

We find it useful to distinguish between the terms *method* and *methodology*. A method is a disciplined process for generating a set of models that describe various aspects of a software system under development, using some well-defined notation. A methodology is a collection of methods applied across the software development life cycle and unified by some general, philosophical approach. Methods are important for several reasons. Foremost, they instill a discipline into the development of complex software systems. They define the products that serve as common vehicles for communication among the members of a development team. Additionally, methods define the milestones needed by management to measure progress and to manage risk.

Methods have evolved in response to the growing complexity of software systems. In the early days of computing, one simply did not write large programs, because the capabilities of our machines were greatly limited. The dominant constraints in building systems were then largely due to hardware: machines had small amounts of main memory, programs had to contend with considerable latency within secondary storage devices such as magnetic drums, and processors had cycle times measured in the hundreds of microseconds. In the 1960s and 1970s the economics of computing began to change dramatically as hardware costs plummeted and computer capabilities rose. As a result, it was more desirable and now finally economical to automate more and more applications of increasing complexity. High-order programming languages entered the scene as important tools. Such languages improved the productivity of the individual developer and of the development team as a whole, thus ironically pressuring us to create software systems of even greater complexity.

Many design methods were proposed during the 1960s and 1970s to address this growing complexity. The most influential of them was top-down structured design, also known as *composite design*. This method was directly influenced by the topology of traditional high-order programming languages, such as FORTRAN and COBOL. In these languages, the fundamental unit of decomposition is the subprogram, and the resulting program takes the shape of a tree in which subprograms perform their work by calling other subprograms. This is exactly the approach taken by top-down structured design: one applies algorithmic decomposition to break a large problem down into smaller steps.

Since the 1960s and 1970s, computers of vastly greater capabilities have evolved. The value of structured design has not changed, but as Stein observes, "Structured programming appears to fall apart when applications exceed 100,000 lines or so of code" [20]. More recently, dozens of design methods have been proposed, many of them invented to deal with the perceived shortcomings of top-down structured design. The more interesting and successful design methods are cataloged by Peters [21] and Yau and Tsai [22], and in a comprehensive survey by Teledyne-Brown Engineering [23]. Perhaps not surprisingly, many of these methods are largely variations upon a similar theme. Indeed, as Sommerville suggests, most methods can be categorized as one of three kinds [24]:

- Top-down structured design
- Data-driven design
- Object-oriented design

Top-down structured design is exemplified by the work of Yourdon and Constantine [25], Myers [26], and Page-Jones [27]. The foundations of this method derive from the work of Wirth [28, 29] and Dahl, Dijkstra, and Hoare [30]; an important variation on structured design is found in the design method of Mills, Linger, and Hevner [31]. Each of these variations applies algorithmic decomposition. More software has probably been written using these design methods than with any other. Nevertheless, structured design does not address the issues of data abstraction and information hiding, nor does it provide an adequate means of dealing with concurrency. Structured design does not scale up well for extremely complex systems, and this method is largely inappropriate for use with object-based and object-oriented programming languages.

Data-driven design is best exemplified by the early work of Jackson [32, 33] and the methods of Warnier and Orr [34]. In this method, the structure of a software system is derived by mapping system inputs to outputs. As with structured design, data-driven design has been successfully applied to a number of complex domains, particularly information management systems, which involve direct relationships between the inputs and outputs of the system, but require little concern for time-critical events.

Object-oriented design is the method we introduce in this book. Its underlying concept is that one should model software systems as collections of cooperating objects, treating individual objects as instances of a class within a hierarchy of classes. Object-oriented design directly reflects the topology of more recent high-order programming languages such as Smalltalk, Object Pascal, C++, the Common Lisp Object System (CLOS), and Ada.

distinguish the common and distinct properties of different objects, which further helps us to master their inherent complexity [35].

Identifying the hierarchies within a complex software system is not often easy, because it requires the discovery of patterns among many objects, each of which may embody some tremendously complicated behavior. Once we have exposed these hierarchies, however, the structure of a complex system, and in turn our understanding of it, becomes vastly simplified. Chapter 3 considers in detail the nature of class and object hierarchies, and Chapter 4 describes techniques that facilitate our identification of these patterns.

1.4 On Designing Complex Systems

Engineering as a Science and an Art

The practice of every engineering discipline – be it civil, mechanical, chemical, electrical, or software engineering – involves elements of both science and art. As Petroski eloquently states, "The conception of a design for a new structure can involve as much a leap of the imagination and as much a synthesis of experience and knowledge as any artist is required to bring to his canvas or paper. And once that design is articulated by the engineer as artist, it must be analyzed by the engineer as scientist in as rigorous an application of the scientific method as any scientist must make" [36].

The role of the engineer as artist is particularly challenging when the task is to design an entirely new system. Frankly, this is the most common circumstance in software engineering. Especially in the case of reactive systems and systems for command and control, we are frequently asked to write software for an entirely unique set of requirements, often to be executed on a configuration of target processors constructed specifically for this system. In other cases, such as the creation of scientific tools, tools for research in artificial intelligence, or even information management systems, we may have a well-defined, stable target environment, but our requirements may stress the software technology in one or more dimensions. For example, we may be asked to craft systems that are faster, have greater capacity, or have radically improved functionality. In all these situations, we try to use proven abstractions and mechanisms (the "stable intermediate forms," in Simon's words) as a foundation upon which to build new complex systems. In the presence of a large library of reusable software components, the software engineer must assemble these parts in innovative ways to satisfy the stated and implicit requirements, just as the painter or the musician must push the limits of his or her medium. Unfortunately, since such rich libraries rarely exist for the software engineer, he or she must usually proceed with a relatively primitive set of facilities.

The Meaning of Design

In every engineering discipline, design encompasses the disciplined approach we use to invent a solution for some problem, thus providing a path from requirements to implementation. In the context of software engineering, Mostow suggests that the purpose of design is to construct a system that

- "Satisfies a given (perhaps informal) functional specification
- Conforms to limitations of the target medium
- Meets implicit or explicit requirements on performance and resource usage
- Satisfies implicit or explicit design criteria on the form of the artifact
- Satisfies restrictions on the design process itself, such as its length or cost, or the tools available for doing the design" [37]

Design involves balancing a set of competing requirements. The products of design are models that enable us to reason about our structures, make trade-offs when requirements conflict, and in general, provide a blueprint for implementation.

The Importance of Model Building. The building of models has a broad acceptance among all engineering disciplines, largely because model building appeals to the principles of decomposition, abstraction, and hierarchy [38]. Each model within a design describes a specific aspect of the system under consideration. As much as possible, we build new models upon old models in which we already have confidence. Models give us the opportunity to fail under controlled conditions. We evaluate each model under both expected and unusual situations, and then alter them when they fail to behave as we expect or desire.

We have found that in order to express all the subtleties of a complex system, we must use more than one kind of model. For example, when designing a single-board computer, an electrical engineer must take into consideration the gate-level view of the system as well as the physical layout of integrated circuits on the board. This gate-level view forms a logical picture of the design of the system, which helps the engineer to reason about the cooperative behavior of the gates. The board layout represents the physical packaging of these gates, constrained by the board size, available power, and the kinds of integrated circuits that exist. From this view, the engineer can independently reason about factors such as heat dissipation and manufacturability. The board designer must also consider dynamic as well as static aspects of the system under construction. Thus, the electrical engineer uses diagrams showing the static connections among individual gates, as well as timing diagrams that show the behavior of these gates over time. The engineer can then employ tools such as oscilloscopes and digital analyzers to validate the correctness of both the static and dynamic views.

The Elements of Software Design Methods. Clearly, there is no magic, no "silver bullet" [39], that can unfailingly lead the software engineer down the path from requirements to the implementation of a complex software system. In fact, the design of complex software systems does not lend itself at all to cookbook approaches. Rather, as noted earlier in the fifth attribute of complex systems, the design of such systems involves an incremental and iterative process.

Still, sound design methods do inject some much-needed discipline in the development process. The software engineering community has evolved dozens of different design methods, which we can loosely classify into three categories (see sidebar). Despite their differences, all of these methods have elements in common. Specifically, each method includes the following:

- Notation   The language for expressing each model
- Process   The guidelines for the orderly construction of
                    the models
- Tools   The artifacts that eliminate the tedium of
                    model building and enforce rules about the
                    models themselves, so that errors and
                    inconsistencies can be exposed

A sound design method is based upon a solid theoretical foundation, yet offers degrees of freedom for artistic innovation.

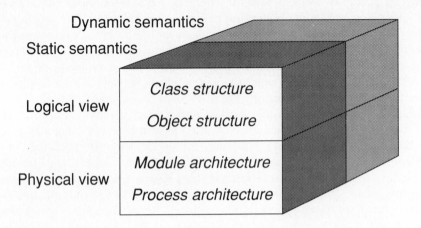

Figure 1-4
The Models of Object-Oriented Design

The Models of Object-Oriented Design. Is there a "best" design method? No, there is no absolute answer to this question, which is actually just a veiled way of asking the earlier question: What is the best way to decompose a complex system? To reiterate, we have found great value in building models that are focused upon the "things" we find in the problem space, forming what we refer to as an *object-oriented decomposition.*

Object-oriented design is the method that leads us to an object-oriented decomposition. By applying object-oriented design, we create software that is resilient to change and written with economy of expression. We achieve a greater level of confidence in the correctness of our software through an intelligent separation of its state space. Ultimately, we reduce the risks of developing complex software systems.

Because model building is so important to the construction of complex systems, object-oriented design offers a rich set of models, which we summarize in Figure 1-4. The models of object-oriented design reflect the importance of explicitly capturing both the class and object hierarchies of the system under design. These models also cover the spectrum of the important design decisions that we must consider in developing a complex system, and so encourage us to craft implementations that embody the five attributes of well-formed complex systems.

Chapter 5 presents each of these four models in detail. Chapter 6 explains the process of object-oriented design, which provides an orderly set of steps for the creation and evolution of these models. Chapter 7 examines the pragmatics of managing a project using object-oriented design.

In this chapter, we have made a case for using object-oriented design to master the complexity associated with developing software systems. Additionally, we have suggested a number of fundamental benefits to be derived from applying this method. Before we present the notation and process of object-oriented design, however, we must study the principles upon which object-oriented design is founded, namely, abstraction, encapsulation, modularity, hierarchy, typing, concurrency, and persistence.

Summary

- Software is inherently complex; the complexity of software systems often exceeds the human intellectual capacity.
- The task of the software development team is to engineer the illusion of simplicity.
- Complexity often takes the form of a hierarchy; it is useful to model both the "kind of" and the "part of" hierarchies of a complex system.
- Complex systems generally evolve from stable intermediate forms.
- There are fundamental limiting factors of human cognition; we can address these constraints through the use of decomposition, abstraction, and hierarchy.
- Complex systems can be viewed either by focusing upon things or processes; there are compelling reasons for applying object-oriented decomposition, in which we view the world as a meaningful collection of objects that collaborate to achieve some higher level behavior.
- Object-oriented design is the method that leads us to an object-oriented decomposition; object-oriented design defines a notation and process for constructing complex software systems, and offers a rich set of logical and physical models with which we may reason about different aspects of the system under consideration.

Further Readings

The challenges associated with developing complex software systems are articulately described in the classic works by Brooks [H 1975] and Brooks [H 1987]. Glass [H 1982], the Defense Science Board [H 1987], and the Joint Service Task Force [H 1982] provide further information on contemporary software practices.

Simon [A 1982] is the seminal reference on the structure of complex systems; Courtois [A 1985] applies these ideas to the domain of software. Peter [I 1986] and Petroski [I 1985] examine complexity in the context of social and physical systems, respectively. Flood and Carson [A 1988] offer a formal study of complexity through the theory of systems science. The report by Miller [A 1956] provides empirical evidence for the fundamental limiting factors of human cognition.

There are a number of excellent references on the subject of software engineering. Ross, Goodenough, and Irvine [H 1980], and Zelkowitz [H 1978] are two of the classic papers summarizing the essential elements of software engineering. Extended works on the subject include Jensen and Tonies [H 1979], Sommerville [H 1985], Vick and Ramamoorthy [H 1984], Wegner [H 1980], and Pressman [H 1987]. Other papers relevant to software engineering may be found in Yourdon [H 1979] and Freeman and Wasserman [H 1983].

Gleick [I 1987] offers a very readable introduction to the science of chaos.

The Object Model

Object-oriented design is built upon a sound engineering foundation, whose elements we collectively call the *object model*. The object model encompasses the principles of abstraction, encapsulation, modularity, hierarchy, typing, concurrency, and persistence. By themselves, none of these principles are new. What is important about the object model is that these elements are brought together in a synergistic way.

Let there be no doubt that object-oriented design is fundamentally different than traditional structured design approaches: it requires a different way of thinking about decomposition, and it produces software architectures that are largely outside the realm of the structured design culture. These differences arise from the fact that structured design methods build upon structured programming, whereas object-oriented design builds upon object-oriented programming. Unfortunately, object-oriented programming means different things to different people. As Rentsch correctly predicted, "My guess is that object-oriented programming will be in the 1980s what structured programming was in the 1970s. Everyone will be in favor of it. Every manufacturer will promote his products as supporting it. Every manager will pay lip service to it. Every programmer will practice it (differently). And no one will know just what it is" [1].

In this chapter, we will show clearly what object-oriented design is and what it is not, and how it differs from other design methods through its use of the seven elements of the object model.

2.1 The Evolution of the Object Model

Trends in Software Engineering

The Generations of Programming Languages. As we look back upon the relatively brief yet colorful history of software engineering, we cannot help but notice two sweeping trends:

- The shift in focus from programming-in-the-small to programming-in-the-large
- The evolution of high-order programming languages

Most new industrial-strength software systems are larger and more complex than their predecessors were even just a few years ago. This growth in complexity has prompted a significant amount of useful applied research in software engineering, particularly with regard to decomposition, abstraction, and hierarchy. The development of more expressive programming languages has complemented these advances. The trend has been a move away from languages that tell the computer what to do (imperative languages) toward languages that describe the key abstractions in the problem domain (declarative languages).

Wegner has classified some of the more popular high-order programming languages in generations arranged according to the language features they first introduced:

- First-Generation Languages (1954–1958)

FORTRAN I	Mathematical expressions
ALGOL 58	Mathematical expressions
Flowmatic	Mathematical expressions
IPL V	Mathematical expressions

- Second-Generation Languages (1959–1961)

FORTRAN II	Subroutines, separate compilation
ALGOL 60	Block structure, data types
COBOL	Data description, file handling
Lisp	List processing, pointers

- Third-Generation Languages (1962–1970)

PL/1	FORTRAN + ALGOL + COBOL
ALGOL 68	Rigorous successor to ALGOL 60
Pascal	Simple successor to ALGOL 60
Simula	Classes, data abstraction

- The Generation Gap (1970–1980)

    Many different languages were invented, but few endured [2]

In successive generations, the kind of abstraction mechanism each language supported changed. First-generation languages were used primarily for scientific and engineering applications, and the vocabulary of this problem domain was almost entirely mathematics. Languages such as FORTRAN I were thus developed to allow the programmer to write mathematical formulas, thereby freeing the programmer from some of the intricacies of assembly or machine language. This first generation of high-order programming languages therefore represented a step closer to the problem space, and a step further away from the underlying machine. Among second-generation languages, the emphasis was upon algorithmic abstractions. By this time, machines were becoming more and more powerful, and the economics of the computer industry meant that more kinds of problems could be automated, especially for business applications. Now, the focus was largely upon telling the machine what to do: read these personnel records first, sort them next, and then print this report. Again, this new generation of high-order programming languages moved us a step closer to the problem space, and further away from the underlying machine. By the late 1960s, especially with the advent of transistors and then integrated circuit technology, the cost of computer hardware had dropped dramatically, yet processing capacity had grown almost exponentially. Larger problems could now be solved, but these demanded the manipulation of more kinds of data. Thus, languages such as ALGOL 60 and, later, Pascal evolved with support for data abstraction. Now a programmer could describe the meaning of related kinds of data (their type) and let the programming language enforce these design decisions. This generation of high-order programming languages again moved our software a step closer to the problem domain, and further away from the underlying machine.

The 1970s provided us with a frenzy of activity in programming language research, resulting in the creation of literally a couple of thousand different programming languages and their dialects. To a large extent, the drive to write larger and larger programs highlighted the inadequacies of earlier languages; thus, many new language mechanisms were developed to address these limitations. Few of these languages survived (have you seen a recent textbook on the languages Fred, Chaos, or Tranquil?); however, many of the concepts that they introduced found their way into successors of earlier languages. Thus, today we have Ada (a successor to ALGOL 68 and Pascal, with contributions from Simula, Alphard, and CLU), CLOS (which evolved from Lisp, LOOPS, and

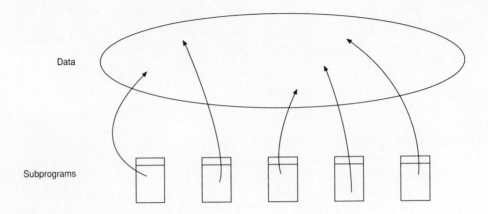

Data

Subprograms

Figure 2-1
The Topology of First- and Early Second-Generation Programming Languages

Flavors), and C++ (derived from a marriage of C and Simula). What is of the greatest interest to us is the class of languages we call *object-based* and *object-oriented*. Object-based and object-oriented programming languages best support the object-oriented decomposition of software.

The Topology of First- and Early Second-Generation Programming Languages. To show precisely what we mean, let's look at each generation of programming languages in a slightly different way. In Figure 2-1, we see the topology of most first- and early second-generation programming languages. This topology shows the basic physical building blocks of the language, and how those parts can be connected. In this figure, we see that for languages such as FORTRAN and COBOL, the basic physical building block of all applications is the subprogram (or the paragraph, for those who speak COBOL). Applications written in these languages exhibit a relatively flat physical structure, consisting only of global data and subprograms. The arrows in this figure indicate dependencies of the subprograms on various data. During design, one can logically separate different kinds of data from one another, but there is little in these languages that can enforce these design decisions. An error in one part of a program can have a devastating ripple effect across the rest of the system, because the global data structures are exposed for all subprograms to see. When modifications are made to a large system, it is difficult to maintain the integrity of the original design. Often, entropy sets in: after even a short period of maintenance, a program written in one of these languages usually contains a tremendous amount of cross-coupling among subprograms, implied meanings of data, and twisted flows of control, thus endangering the reliability of the entire system and certainly reducing the overall clarity of the solution.

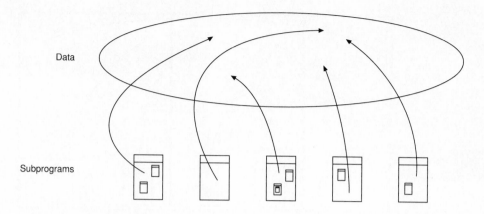

Data

Subprograms

Figure 2-2
The Topology of Late Second- and Early Third-Generation Programming Languages

The Topology of Late Second- and Early Third-Generation Programming Languages. By the mid-1960s, programs were finally being recognized as important intermediate points between the problem and the computer [3]. As Shaw points out, "The first software abstraction, now called the 'procedural' abstraction, grew directly out of this pragmatic view of software. . . . Subprograms were invented prior to 1950, but were not fully appreciated as abstractions at the time. . . . Instead, they were originally seen as labor-saving devices. . . . Very quickly though, subprograms were appreciated as a way to abstract program functions" [4]. The realization that subprograms could serve as an abstraction mechanism had three important consequences. First, languages were invented that supported a variety of parameter-passing mechanisms. Second, the foundations of structured programming were laid, manifesting themselves in language support for the nesting of subprograms and the development of theories regarding control structures and the scope and visibility of declarations. Third, structured design methods emerged, offering guidance to designers trying to build large systems using subprograms as basic physical building blocks. Thus, it is not surprising, as Figure 2-2 shows, that the topology of late second- and early third-generation languages is largely a variation on the theme of earlier generations. This topology addresses some of the inadequacies of earlier languages, namely, the need to have greater control over algorithmic abstractions, but it still fails to address the problems of programming-in-the-large and data design.

The Topology of Late Third-Generation Programming Languages. Starting with FORTRAN II, and appearing in most late third-generation program languages, another important structuring mechanism evolved to address the growing issues of programming-in-the-large. Larger programming projects meant larger

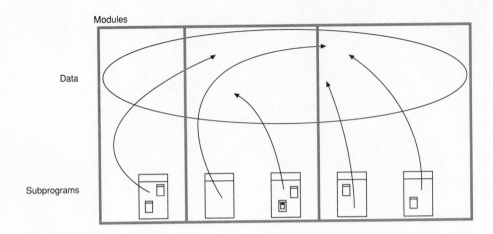

Figure 2-3
The Topology of Late Third-Generation Programming Languages

development teams, and thus the need to develop different parts of the same program independently. The answer to this need was the separately compiled module, which in its early conception was little more than an arbitrary container for data and subprograms, as Figure 2-3 shows. Modules were rarely recognized as an important abstraction mechanism; in practice they were used simply to group logically related subprograms. Most languages of this generation, while supporting some sort of modular structure, had few rules that required semantic consistency among module interfaces. A developer writing a subprogram for one module might assume that it would be called with three different parameters: a floating-point number, an array of ten elements, and an integer representing a Boolean flag. In another module, a call to this subprogram might incorrectly use actual parameters that violated these assumptions: an integer, an array of five elements, and a negative number. Unfortunately, because most of these languages had dismal support for data abstraction and strong typing, such errors could be detected only during execution of the program.

The Topology of Object-Based and Object-Oriented Programming Languages.
The importance of data abstraction to mastering complexity is clearly stated by Shankar: "The nature of abstractions that may be achieved through the use of procedures is well suited to the description of abstract operations, but is not particularly well suited to the description of abstract objects. This is a serious drawback, for in many applications, the complexity of the data objects to be manipulated contributes substantially to the overall complexity of the problem" [5]. This realization had two important consequences. First, data-driven design methods emerged, which provided a disciplined approach to the problems of doing data abstraction in algorithmically oriented languages. Second, theories

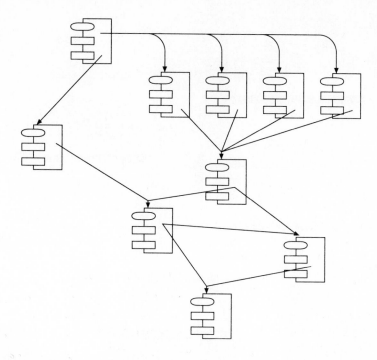

Figure 2-4
The Topology of Small- to Moderate-Sized Applications Using Object-Based and Object-Oriented Programming Languages

regarding the concept of a type appeared, which eventually found their realization in languages such as Pascal.

The natural conclusion of these ideas first appeared in the language Simula and was improved upon during the period of the language generation gap, resulting in the relatively recent development of several languages such as Smalltalk, Object Pascal, C++, CLOS, and Ada. For reasons that we will explain shortly, these languages are called *object-based* or *object-oriented*. Figure 2-4 illustrates the topology of these languages for small- to moderate-sized applications. The physical building block in these languages is the *module,* which represents a logical collection of classes and objects instead of subprograms, as in earlier languages. To state it another way, "If procedures and functions are verbs and pieces of data are nouns, a procedure-oriented program is organized around verbs while an object-oriented program is organized around nouns" [6]. For this reason, the physical structure of a small- to moderate-sized object-oriented application appears as a graph, not as a tree, which is typical of algorithmically oriented languages. Additionally, there is little or no global data. Instead, data and operations are united in such a way that the fundamental logical building blocks of our systems are no longer algorithms, but classes and objects.

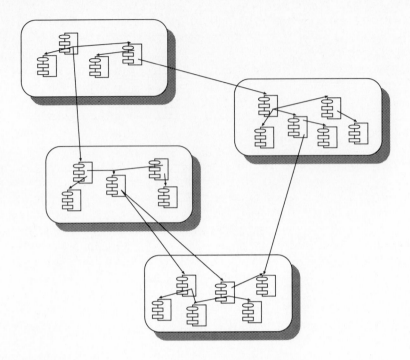

Figure 2-5
The Topology of Large Applications Using Object-Based and Object-Oriented
Programming Languages

By now we have progressed beyond programming-in-the-large and must
cope with programming-in-the-colossal. For very large systems, we find that
classes, objects, and modules provide an essential yet insufficient means of
decomposition. Fortunately, the object model scales up. In large systems, we
find clusters of abstractions built in layers on top of one another. At any given
level of abstraction, we find meaningful collections of objects that cooperate to
achieve some higher level behavior. If we look inside any given cluster to view
its implementation, we unveil yet another set of cooperative abstractions. This is
exactly the organization of complexity described in Chapter 1; its topology is
shown in Figure 2-5.

Foundations of the Object Model

Structured design methods evolved to guide developers who were trying to
build complex systems using algorithms as their fundamental building blocks.
Similarly, object-oriented design methods have evolved to help developers
exploit the expressive power of object-based and object-oriented programming
languages, using the class and object as basic building blocks.

Actually, the object model has been influenced by a number of factors, not just object-oriented programming. Indeed, as the sidebar further discusses, the object model has proven to be a unifying concept in computer science, applicable not only to programming languages, but to the design of user interfaces, databases, knowledge bases, and even computer architectures. The reason for this widespread appeal is simply that an object orientation helps us to cope with the complexity inherent in many different kinds of systems.

Object-oriented design thus represents an evolutionary development, not a revolutionary one; it does not break with advances from the past, but builds upon proven ones. Unfortunately, most programmers today are formally and informally trained only in the principles of structured design. Certainly, many good engineers have developed and deployed countless useful software systems using these techniques. However, there are limits to the amount of complexity we can handle using only algorithmic decomposition; thus we must turn to object-oriented decomposition. Furthermore, if we try to use languages such as C++ and Ada as if they were only traditional, algorithmically oriented languages, we not only miss the power available to us, but we usually end up worse off than if we had used an older language such as C or Pascal. Give a power drill to a carpenter who knows nothing about electricity, and he would use it as a hammer. He will end up bending quite a few nails and smashing several fingers, for a power drill makes a lousy hammer.

OOP, OOD, and OOA

Because the object model derives from so many disparate sources, it has unfortunately been accompanied by a muddle of terminology. A Smalltalk programmer uses *methods*, a C++ programmer uses *virtual member functions*, and a CLOS programmer uses *generic functions*. An Object Pascal programmer talks of a *type coercion*; an Ada programmer calls the same thing a *type conversion*. To minimize the confusion, let's define what is object-oriented and what is not. The glossary provides a summary of all the terms described here, plus many others.

Bhaskar has observed that the phrase *object-oriented* "has been bandied about with carefree abandon with much the same reverence accorded 'motherhood,' 'apple pie,' and 'structured programming' "[7]. What we can agree upon is that the concept of an object is central to anything object-oriented. In the previous chapter, we informally defined an object as a tangible entity that exhibits some well-defined behavior. Stefik and Bobrow define objects as "entities that combine the properties of procedures and data since they perform computations and save local state" [8]. Defining *objects* as *entities* begs the question somewhat, but the basic concept here is that objects serve to unify the ideas of algorithmic and data abstraction. Jones further clarifies this term by noting that "in the object model, emphasis is placed on crisply characterizing the components of the physical or abstract system to be modeled by a programmed system. . . . Objects have a certain 'integrity' which should not – in fact, cannot – be violated. An object can only change state, behave, be manipulated, or stand in relation to other objects in ways appropriate to that

Foundations of the Object Model

As Yonezawa and Tokoro point out, "The term 'object' emerged almost independently in various fields in computer science, almost simultaneously in the early 1970s, to refer to notions that were different in their appearance, yet mutually related. All of these notions were invented to manage the complexity of software systems in such a way that objects represented components of a modularly decomposed system or modular units of knowledge representation" [9]. Levy adds that the following events have contributed to the evolution of object-oriented concepts:

- "Advances in computer architecture, including capability systems and hardware support for operating systems concepts
- Advances in programming languages, as demonstrated in Simula, Smalltalk, CLU, and Ada
- Advances in programming methodology, including modularization and information hiding" [10]

We would add to this list three more contributions to the foundation of the object model:

- Advances in database models
- Research in artificial intelligence
- Advances in philosophy and cognitive science

The concept of an object had its beginnings in hardware over twenty years ago, starting with the invention of descriptor-based architectures and, later, capability-based architectures [11]. These architectures represented a break from the classical von Neumann architectures, and came about through attempts to close the gap between the high-level abstractions of programming languages and the low-level abstractions of the machine itself [12]. According to its proponents, the advantages of such architectures are many: better error detection, improved execution efficiency, fewer instruction types, simpler compilation, and reduced storage requirements. Computers that have an object-oriented architecture include the Burroughs 5000, the Plessey 250, and the Cambridge CAP [13]; SWARD [14]; the Intel 432 [15], Caltech's COM [16], and the IBM System/38 [17]; the Rational R1000, and the BiiN 40 and 60.

Closely related to developments in object-oriented architectures are object-oriented operating systems. Dijkstra's work with the THE multiprogramming system first introduced the concept of building systems as layered state machines [18]. Other pioneering object-oriented operating systems include the Plessey/System 250 (for the Plessey 250 multiprocessor), Hydra (for CMU's C.mmp), CALTSS (for the CDC 6400), CAP (for the Cambridge CAP computer), UCLA Secure Unix (for the PDP 11/45 and 11/70), StarOS (for CMU's Cm*), Medusa (also for CMU's Cm*), and iMAX (for the Intel 432) [19].

Perhaps the most important contribution to the object model derives from the class of programming languages we call object-based and object-oriented. The fundamental ideas of classes and objects first appeared in the language Simula 67. The Flex system, followed by various dialects of Smalltalk, such as Smalltalk-72, -74, and -76, and finally the current version, Smalltalk-80, took Simula's object-oriented paradigm to its natural conclusion by making everything in the language an instance of a class. In the 1970s languages such as Alphard, CLU, Euclid, Gypsy, Mesa, and Modula were developed, which supported the then emerging ideas of data abstraction. More recently, language research has led to the grafting of Simula and Smalltalk concepts onto traditional high-order programming languages. The unification of object-oriented concepts with C has lead to the languages C++ and Objective C. Adding object-oriented programming mechanisms to Pascal has led to the languages Object Pascal, Eiffel, and Ada. Additionally, there are many dialects of Lisp that incorporate the object-oriented features of Simula and Smalltalk, including Flavors, LOOPS, and more recently, the Common Lisp Object System (CLOS). The appendix discusses these and other programming language developments in greater detail.

The first person to formally identify the importance of composing systems in layers of abstraction was Dijkstra. Parnas later introduced the idea of information hiding [20], and in the 1970s a number of researchers, most notably Liskov and Zilles [21], Guttag [22], and Shaw [23], pioneered the development of abstract data type mechanisms. Hoare contributed to these developments with his proposal for a theory of types and subclasses [24].

Although database technology has evolved somewhat independently of software engineering, it has also contributed to the object model [25], primarily through the ideas of the entity-relationship (ER) approach to data modeling [26]. In the ER model, first proposed by Chen [27], the world is modeled in terms of its entities, the attributes of these entities, and the relationships among these entities.

In the field of artificial intelligence, developments in knowledge representation have contributed to an understanding of object-oriented abstractions. In 1975, Minsky first proposed a theory of frames to represent real-world objects as perceived by image and natural language recognition systems [28]. Since then, frames have been used as the architectural foundation for a variety of intelligent systems.

Lastly, philosophy and cognitive science have contributed to the advancement of the object model. The idea that the world could be viewed either in terms of objects or processes was a Greek innovation, and in the seventeenth century, we find Descartes observing that humans naturally apply an object-oriented view of the world [29]. In the twentieth century, Rand expanded upon these themes in her philosophy of objectivist epistemology [30]. More recently, Minsky has proposed a model of human intelligence in which he considers the mind to be organized as a society of otherwise mindless agents [31]. Minsky argues that only through the cooperative behavior of these agents do we find what we call *intelligence*.

object. Stated differently, there exist invariant properties that characterize an object and its behavior. An elevator, for example, is characterized by invariant properties including [that] it only travels up and down inside its shaft. . . . Any elevator simulation must incorporate these invariants, for they are integral to the notion of an elevator" [32].

Object-Oriented Programming. What then, is object-oriented programming (or *OOP,* as it is sometimes written)? We define it as follows:

> *Object-oriented programming is a method of implementation in which programs are organized as cooperative collections of objects, each of which represents an instance of some class, and whose classes are all members of a hierarchy of classes united via inheritance relationships.*

There are three important parts to this definition: object-oriented programming (1) uses *objects*, not algorithms, as its fundamental logical building blocks (the "part of" hierarchy we introduced in Chapter 1); (2) each object is an *instance* of some *class*; and (3) classes are related to one another via *inheritance* relationships (the "kind of" hierarchy we spoke of in Chapter 1). A program may appear to be object-oriented, but if any of these elements is missing, it is not an object-oriented program. Specifically, programming without inheritance is distinctly not object-oriented; we call it *programming with abstract data types*.

By this definition, some languages are object-oriented, and some are not. Stroustrup suggests that "if the term 'object-oriented language' means anything, it must mean a language that has mechanisms that support the object-oriented style of programming well. . . . A language supports a programming style well if it provides facilities that make it convenient to use that style. A language does not support a technique if it takes exceptional effort or skill to write such programs; in that case, the language merely enables programmers to use the techniques" [33]. From a theoretical perspective, one can fake object-oriented programming in non-object-oriented programming languages like Pascal and even COBOL or assembly language, but it is horribly ungainly to do so. Cardelli and Wegner thus say "that a language is object-oriented if and only if it satisfies the following requirements:

- It supports objects that are data abstractions with an interface of named operations and a hidden local state
- Objects have an associated type [class]
- Types [classes] may inherit attributes from supertypes [superclasses]" [34]

For a language to support inheritance means that it is possible to express "kind of" relationships among types, such as a red rose is a kind of flower, and a flower is a kind of plant. If a language does not provide direct support for inheritance, then it is not object-oriented. Cardelli and Wegner distinguish such languages by calling them *object-based* rather than *object-oriented*. Under this definition, Smalltalk, Object Pascal, C++, and CLOS are all object-oriented, and Ada is object-based. However, since objects and classes are elements of both kinds of languages, it is possible and highly desirable for us to use object-oriented design methods for both object-based and object-oriented programming languages.

Object-Oriented Design. The emphasis in programming methods is primarily on the proper and effective use of particular language mechanisms. By contrast, design methods emphasize the proper and effective structuring of a complex system. What then is object-oriented design? We suggest that

> *Object-oriented design is a method of design encompassing the process of object-oriented decomposition and a notation for depicting both logical and physical as well as static and dynamic models of the system under design.*

There are two important parts to this definition: object-oriented design (1) leads to an object-oriented decomposition and (2) uses different notations to express different models of the logical (class and object structure) and physical (module and process architecture) design of a system.

The support for object-oriented decomposition is what makes object-oriented design quite different from structured design: the former uses class and object abstractions to logically structure systems, and the latter uses algorithmic abstractions. We will use the term *object-oriented design* to refer to any method that leads to an object-oriented decomposition. We will occasionally use the acronym *OOD* to designate the particular method of object-oriented design described in this book.

Object-Oriented Analysis. The object model has influenced even earlier phases of the software development life cycle. Traditional structured analysis techniques, best typified by the work of DeMarco [35], Yourdon [36], and Gane and Sarson [37], with real-time extensions by Ward and Mellor [38] and by Hatley and Pirbhai [39], focus upon the flow of data within a system. Object-oriented analysis (or *OOA*, as it is sometimes called) emphasizes the building of real-world models, using an object-oriented view of the world:

> *Object-oriented analysis is a method of analysis that examines requirements from the perspective of the classes and objects found in the vocabulary of the problem domain.*

How are OOA, OOD, and OOP related? Basically, the products of object-oriented analysis can serve as the models from which we may start an object-oriented design; the products of object-oriented design can then be used as blueprints for completely implementing a system using object-oriented programming methods.

2.2 Elements of the Object Model

Kinds of Programming Paradigms

Jenkins and Glasgow observe that "most programmers work in one language and use only one programming style. They program in a paradigm enforced by the language they use. Frequently, they have not been exposed to alternate ways of thinking about a problem, and hence have difficulty in seeing the advantage of choosing a style more appropriate to the problem at hand" [40]. Bobrow and Stefik define a programming style as "a way of organizing programs on the basis of some conceptual model of programming and an appropriate language to make programs written in the style clear" [41]. They further suggest that there are five main kinds of programming styles, here listed with the kinds of abstractions they employ:

- Procedure-oriented   Algorithms
- Object-oriented   Classes and objects
- Logic-oriented   Goals, often expressed in a predicate calculus
- Rule-oriented   If-then rules
- Constraint-oriented   Invariant relationships

There is no single programming style that is best for all kinds of applications. For example, rule-oriented programming would be best for the design of a knowledge base. The object-oriented style, from our observations, is best suited to the broadest set of applications, namely, industrial-strength software in which complexity is the dominant issue.

Each of these styles of programming is based upon its own conceptual framework. Each requires a different mindset, a different way of thinking about the problem. For all things object-oriented, the conceptual framework is the *object model*. There are four major elements of this model:

- Abstraction
- Encapsulation
- Modularity
- Hierarchy

By *major*, we mean that a model without any one of these elements is not object-oriented.

There are three minor elements of the object model:

- Typing
- Concurrency
- Persistence

By *minor*, we mean that each of these elements is a useful, but not essential, part of the object model.

Without this conceptual framework, you may be programming in a language such as Smalltalk, Object Pascal, C++, CLOS, or Ada, but your design is going to smell like a FORTRAN, Pascal, or C application. You will have missed out on or otherwise abused the expressive power of the object-based or

Abstraction focuses upon the essential characteristics of some object, relative to the perspective of the viewer.

object-oriented language you are using for implementation. More importantly, you are not likely to have mastered the complexity of the problem at hand.

Abstraction

The Meaning of Abstraction. Abstraction is one of the fundamental ways that we as humans cope with complexity. Hoare suggests that "abstraction arises from a recognition of similarities between certain objects, situations, or processes in the real world, and the decision to concentrate upon these similarities and to ignore for the time being the differences" [42]. Shaw defines an abstraction as "a simplified description, or specification, of a system that emphasizes some of the system's details or properties while suppressing others. A good abstraction is one that emphasizes details that are significant to the reader or user and suppresses details that are, at least for the moment, immaterial or diversionary" [43]. Berzins, Gray, and Naumann recommend that "a concept qualifies as an abstraction only if it can be described, understood, and analyzed independently of the mechanism that will eventually be used to realize it" [44]. Combining these different viewpoints, we define an abstraction as follows:

An abstraction denotes the essential characteristics of an object that distinguish it from all other kinds of objects and thus provide crisply defined conceptual boundaries, relative to the perspective of the viewer.

An abstraction focuses on the outside view of an object, and so serves to separate an object's essential behavior from its implementation. Abelson and Sussman call this behavior/implementation division an *abstraction barrier* [45] achieved by applying the principle of least commitment, through which the interface of an object provides its essential behavior, and nothing more [46]. We like to use an additional principle that we call the principle of least astonishment, through which an abstraction captures the entire behavior of some object, no more and no less.

Deciding upon the right set of abstractions for a given domain is the central problem in object-oriented design. Because this topic is so important, the whole of Chapter 4 is devoted to it.

Seidewitz and Stark suggest that "there is a spectrum of abstraction, from objects which closely model problem domain entities to objects which really have no reason for existence" [47]. From the most to the least useful, these kinds of abstractions include the following:

• Entity abstraction	An object that represents a useful model of a problem-domain entity
• Action abstraction	An object that provides a generalized set of operations, all of which perform the same kind of function
• Virtual machine abstraction	An object that groups together operations that are all used by some superior level of control, or operations that all use some junior-level set of operations
• Coincidental abstraction	An object that packages a set of operations that have no relation to each other

We strive to build entity abstractions, because they directly parallel the vocabulary of a given problem domain.

A *client* is any object that uses the resources of another object. We characterize the behavior of an object by considering the operations that its clients may perform upon it, as well as the operations that it may perform upon other objects. This view forces us to concentrate upon the outside view of an object. We call the entire set of operations that a client may perform upon an object its *protocol*. A protocol denotes the ways in which an object may act and react, and thus constitutes the entire static and dynamic outside view of the abstraction.

As an aside, the terms *operation, method,* and *member function* evolved from three different programming cultures (Ada, Smalltalk, and C++, respectively). They all mean virtually the same thing, and so we will use them interchangeably.

All abstractions have static as well as dynamic properties. For example, a file object takes up a certain amount of space on a particular memory device; it has a name, and it has contents. These are all static properties. The value of each of these properties is dynamic, relative to the lifetime of the object: a file object may grow or shrink in size, its name may change, its contents may change. In a procedure-oriented style of programming, the activity that changes the dynamic value of objects is the central part of all programs: things happen when subprograms are called and statements are executed. In a rule-oriented style of programming, things happen when new events cause rules to fire, which in turn may trigger other rules, and so on. In an object-oriented style of programming, things happen whenever we operate upon an object (in Smalltalk terminology, when we *send a message* to an object). Thus, invoking an operation upon an object elicits some reaction from the object. What operations we can meaningfully perform upon an object and how that object reacts constitute the entire behavior of the object.

Examples of Abstraction. Let's illustrate these concepts with some examples. Our purpose here is to show how we can concretely express abstractions, not so much how we find the right abstractions for the given problem. We defer a complete treatment of this latter topic to Chapter 4.

On a hydroponics farm, plants are grown in a nutrient solution, without sand, gravel, or other soils. Maintaining the proper greenhouse environment is a delicate job, and depends upon the kind of plant being grown and its age. One must control diverse factors such as temperature, humidity, light, pH, and nutrient concentrations. On a large farm, it is not unusual to have an automated system that constantly monitors and adjusts these elements. Simply stated, the purpose of an automated gardener is to efficiently carry out, with minimal human intervention, growing plans for the healthy production of multiple crops.

One of the key abstractions in this problem is that of a sensor. Actually, there are several different kinds of sensors. Anything that affects production must be measured, and so we must have sensors for air and water temperature, humidity, light, pH, and nutrient concentrations, among other things. Viewed from the outside, an air temperature sensor is simply an object that knows how to measure the temperature at some specific location. What is a temperature? It is some numeric value, within a limited range of values and with a certain precision, that represents degrees in the scale of Fahrenheit, Centigrade, or Kelvin, whichever is most appropriate for our problem. What then is a location? It is some identifiable place on the farm at which we desire to measure the temperature; presumably, there are only a few such locations. What is important for an air temperature sensor is not so much where it is located, but the fact that it has a unique location and identity from all other air temperature sensors. Now we are ready to ask What operations can a client perform upon an air temperature sensor? Our design decision is that a client can calibrate it, as well as ask what the current temperature is.

Let's use Ada to capture these design decisions. For those readers who are not familiar with Ada, or for that matter any of the other object-based and object-oriented languages we use in this book, the appendix provides a brief overview of each language, with examples. In Ada, we might write the following package specification that captures our abstraction of an air temperature sensor:

```
package Temperature_Sensors is

    type Temperature is delta 0.01 range -10.0 .. 150.0;
    — temperature in degrees Fahrenheit

    type Location is range 0 .. 63;
    — a number denoting the location of a sensor

    type Air_Temperature_Sensor is limited private;
    — the air temperature sensor class

    procedure Initialize (The_Sensor   : in Air_Temperature_Sensor;
                          Its_Location : in Location);
    procedure Calibrate (The_Sensor        : in out Air_Temperature_Sensor;
                         Actual_Temperature : in     Temperature);

    function Current_Temperature (The_Sensor : in Air_Temperature_Sensor)
      return Temperature;

private
    ...
end Temperature_Sensors;
```

This package exports three types, Temperature, Location, and Air_Temperature_Sensor. The type Temperature is a fixed point type representing temperature in degrees Fahrenheit. The type Location denotes the places where air temperature sensors may be deployed throughout the farm. Lastly, the type Air_Temperature_Sensor captures our abstraction of a sensor itself; its representation is hidden in the private part and body of the package.

Because each type represents a class and not an individual object, we must first create an *instance* so that we have something upon which to operate. For example, we might write:

```
with Temperature_Sensors;
use Temperature_Sensors;
    ...
    Greenhouse_1_Temperature_Sensor : Air_Temperature_Sensor;
    Greenhouse_2_Temperature_Sensor : Air_Temperature_Sensor;
    The_Temperature : Temperature;
begin
    Initialize(Greenhouse_1_Temperature_Sensor, Its_Location => 1);
    Initialize(Greenhouse_2_Temperature_Sensor, Its_Location => 2);
    The_Temperature := Current_Temperature(Greenhouse_1_Temperature_Sensor);
    ...
end;
```

The abstraction we have described thus far is passive; some other object must operate upon an air temperature sensor to determine its value. There is another possible abstraction that may be more or less appropriate depending upon the broader system-design decisions we might make. Rather than the air temperature sensor being passive, we might make it active, so that it is not acted upon but rather acts upon other objects whenever the temperature changes a certain number of degrees. This abstraction is almost the same as our first one, except that we must turn our interface inside out. Thus, we might write the following:

```
package Temperature_Sensors is

    type Temperature is delta 0.01 range -10.0 .. 150.0;
    -- temperature in degrees Fahrenheit

    type Location is range 0 .. 63;
    -- a number denoting the location of a sensor

    generic
        with procedure Temperature_Has_Changed (The_Location    : in Location;
                                                 New_Temperature : in Temperature);
        with procedure Temperature_Alarm (The_Location    : in Location;
                                           New_Temperature : in Temperature);
    package Air_Temperature_Sensors is

        type Air_Temperature_Sensor is limited private;
        -- the air temperature sensor class

        procedure Initialize (The_Sensor       : in Air_Temperature_Sensor;
                              Its_Location      : in Location;
                              Lower_Alarm_Limit : in Temperature;
                              Upper_Alarm_Limit : in Temperature);
        procedure Calibrate (The_Sensor        : in out Air_Temperature_Sensor;
                             Actual_Temperature : in     Temperature);

    private
        ...
    end Air_Temperature_Sensors;

end Temperature_Sensors;
```

This package is a bit more complicated than the first, but it captures our new abstraction quite well. The only operations we may perform upon an air temperature sensor object are `Initialize` and `Calibrate`. During its lifetime, each air temperature sensor may itself invoke the operations `Temperature_Has_Changed` or `Temperature_Alarm` to notify some other object that an interesting event has occurred. This package thus shows how in Ada we can describe our design decisions regarding what operations we can perform upon an object, as well as the operations an object can perform upon others.

    Let's consider a different abstraction, this time using C++. For each crop, there must be a growing plan that describes how temperature, light, nutrients, and other factors should change over time to maximize the harvest. A growing plan is a legitimate entity abstraction, because it forms part of the vocabulary of the problem domain. Each crop has its own growing plan, but the growing plans for all crops take the same form. Basically, a growing plan is a table of times versus actions. For example, on day 15 in the lifetime of a certain crop, our growing plan might be to maintain an air temperature of 78°F for 16 hours, turn on the lights for 14 of these hours, and then drop the air temperature to 65°F for the rest of the day. We might also want to add certain extra nutrients in the middle of the day, yet maintain a slightly acidic pH.

From the perspective of the outside of each growing-plan object, we must be able to establish the details of a plan, modify a plan, and execute a plan. For example, there might be an object that sits at the boundary of the human/machine interface and translates human input into plans. This is the object that establishes the details of a growing plan, and so it must be able to change the state of a growing-plan object. There must also be an object that carries out the growing plan, and it must be able to read the details of a plan for a particular time.

As this example points out, no object stands alone; every object cooperates with other objects to achieve some behavior. Our design decisions about how these objects collaborate define the boundaries of each abstraction and thus the protocol of each object.

Using C++, we might capture our design decisions for a growing plan as follows:

```
typedef int    day;
typedef int    hour;
typedef float temperature;
typedef float ph;
typedef float concentration;
enum  boolean {OFF, ON};

class GrowingPlan {
    ...
public:
    GrowingPlan ();
    GrowingPlan (const GrowingPlan&);
    virtual ~GrowingPlan ();

    virtual void clearThePlan ();
    virtual void establish (day          theDay,
                            hour         theHour,
                            temperature  theTemperature,
                            boolean      lightsOn,
                            ph           thePh,
                            concentration theNutrientConcentration);

    virtual temperature   desiredTemperature (day theDay, hour theHour) const;
    virtual boolean       lightStatus        (day theDay, hour theHour) const;
    virtual ph            desiredPh          (day theDay, hour theHour) const;
    virtual concentration desiredNutrients   (day theDay, hour theHour) const;

};
```

Notice our use of the typedefs. Our style is always to explicitly declare types so that they are expressed in the vocabulary of our problem domain, unless there is some compelling reason to do otherwise. In the interface of the class `GrowingPlan`, we have intentionally left out the private members (designated by the ellipses), because at this point in our design we wish to focus only upon the behavior of the class, not its representation. In C++, members are private unless explicitly asserted otherwise. In the public part, we have exported *constructor* and *destructor member functions* (which provide for the birth and death of an object, respectively), two *modifiers* (the member functions `clearThePlan` and `establish`), and four *selectors*, one to query each of the interesting aspects of a growing plan at a given day and hour of the day. Our style is also to declare each member function as `virtual` unless there is a compelling reason to do otherwise, so that any subclasses of this class can redefine the operation as necessary.

As in our Ada example, the class `GrowingPlan` represents only our abstraction, not an object upon which a client may operate. Therefore at some place in our program, we must create instances of this class.

Encapsulation

The Meaning of Encapsulation. The abstraction of an object should precede the decisions about its implementation. Once an implementation is selected, it should be treated as a secret of the abstraction and hidden from most clients. As Ingalls wisely suggests, "No part of a complex system should depend on the internal details of any other part" [48]. Whereas abstraction "helps people to think about what they are doing," encapsulation "allows program changes to be reliably made with limited effort" [49].

Abstraction and encapsulation are complementary concepts: abstraction focuses upon the outside view of an object and *encapsulation* – also known as *information hiding* – prevents clients from seeing its inside view, where the behavior of the abstraction is implemented. In this manner, encapsulation provides explicit barriers among different abstractions. For example, consider again the structure of a plant: to understand how photosynthesis works at a high level of abstraction, we can ignore details such as the roots or the mitochondria in plant cells. Similarly, in designing a database application, it is standard practice to write programs so that they don't care about the physical representation of data, but depend only upon a schema that denotes the data's logical view [50]. In both of these cases, objects at higher levels of abstraction are shielded from lower level implementation details.

Liskov goes as far as to suggest that "for abstraction to work, implementations must be encapsulated" [51]. In practice, this means that each class must have two parts: an interface and an implementation. The *interface* of a class captures only its outside view, encompassing our abstraction of the behavior common to all instances of the class. The *implementation* of a class comprises the representation of the abstraction as well as the mechanisms that achieve the desired behavior. This explicit division of interface/implementation represents a

Encapsulation hides the details of the implementation of an object.

clear separation of concerns: the interface of a class is the one place where we assert all of the assumptions that a client may make about any instances of the class; the implementation encapsulates details about which no client may make assumptions. Britton and Parnas call these details the "secrets" of an abstraction [52].

To summarize, we define *encapsulation* as follows:

> *Encapsulation is the process of hiding all of the details of an object that do not contribute to its essential characteristics.*

In practice, one hides the representation of an object, as well as the implementation of its methods.

Examples of Encapsulation. To illustrate the use of encapsulation, let's return to the problem of the hydroponics gardening system. Another key abstraction in this problem domain is that of a heater, used to maintain a fixed temperature in each greenhouse. A heater is at a fairly low level of abstraction, and thus we might decide that there are only three meaningful operations that we can perform upon this object: turn it off, turn it on, and find out if it is running. As is common with our style, we also include metaoperations, namely, constructor and destructor operations that initialize and free instances of this class, respectively. Because our system might have multiple heaters, we use the initialize method to associate each software object with a physical heater. Given these design decisions, we might write the interface of the class `Heater` in Smalltalk as follows:

```
Heater methodsFor: 'initialize-release'

    initialize: theLocation
    release
```

```
Heater methodsFor: 'modifiers'

    turnOff
    turnOn
```

```
Heater methodsFor: 'selectors'

    isOn
```

Together with suitable documentation that describes the meaning of each of these operations, this interface represents all that a client needs to know about instances of the class `Heater`.

Turning to the inside view of this class, we have an entirely different perspective. One reasonable implementation decision might be to use an electromechanical relay that controls the power going to each physical heater, with the relays in turn commanded by messages sent along serial ports from the computer. Sending a character with all bits set to one might turn on the heater, and sending a character with all bits set to zero might turn off the heater. We can thus complete the implementation of the class `Heater` as follows:

```
Object subclass: #Heater
    instanceVariableNames: 'thePort isOn'
    classVariableNames: ''
    poolDictionaries: ''
    category: 'Hydroponics Gardening System'
```

```
initialize: theLocation
    "Initialize the heater device driver by opening an RS232 port
    associated with the given location. theLocation is expected to
    be of the class Location."

    thePort ← RS232Port open: theLocation.
    isOn ← false
```

```
release
    "Release the RS232 port associated with this heater."

    thePort release.
    thePort ← nil
```

```
isOn
    "Return true if the heater is on, false otherwise."

    ↑isOn
```

turnOff

>"Turn off the heater by writing a character with all bits reset
>to the RS232 port."
>
>| aString |
>aString ← String new: 1.
>aString at: 1 put: (Character value: 0).
>thePort sendBuffer: aString.
>isOn ← false.
>aString release

turnOn

>"Turn on the heater by writing a character with all bits set
>to the RS232 port."
>
>| aString |
>aString ← String new: 1.
>aString at: 1 put: (Character value: 255).
>thePort sendBuffer: aString.
>isOn ← true.
>aString release

The two instance variables (`thePort` and `isOpen`) form the representation of this class which, according to the rules of Smalltalk, are encapsulated. If a developer writes code outside of this class that references these variables, Smalltalk refuses to accept the code by responding with an error message.

Suppose that for whatever reason the hardware architecture of our system changed, and its designers decided to use memory-mapped I/O instead of serial communication lines. We would not need to change the interface of this class; we would only need to modify its implementation. Because of Smalltalk's obsolescence rules, we would have to recompile this class and the closure of its clients, but because the functional behavior of this abstraction would not change, we would not have to modify any code that used this class unless a particular client depended upon the time or space characteristics of the original implementation (which would be highly undesirable and so very unlikely, in any case).

Intelligent encapsulation localizes design decisions that are likely to change. As a system evolves, its developers might discover that in actual use, certain operations take longer than acceptable or that some objects consume more space than is available. In such situations, the representation of an object is often changed so that more efficient algorithms can be applied or so that one can optimize for space by calculating rather then storing certain data. This ability to change the representation of an abstraction without disturbing any of its clients is the essential benefit of encapsulation.

Ideally, attempts to access the underlying representation of an object should be detected at the time a client's code is compiled. How a particular language should address this matter is debated with great religious fervor in the object-oriented programming language community. As we have seen, Smalltalk prevents a client from directly accessing the instance variables of another class; violations are detected at the time of compilation. On the other hand, Object

Pascal does not encapsulate the representation of a class, so there is nothing in the language that prevents clients from referencing the fields of another object. CLOS takes an intermediate position, giving the developer explicit control over encapsulation. Each *slot* may have one of the slot options `:reader`, `:writer`, or `:accessor,` which grant a client read access, write access, or read/write access, respectively. If none of these options are used, then the slot is fully encapsulated. C++ offers even more flexible control over the visibility of member objects and member functions. Specifically, members may be placed in the public, private, or protected parts of a class. Members declared in the public parts are visible to all clients; members declared in the private parts are fully encapsulated; and members declared in the protected parts are visible only to the class itself and its subclasses. C++ also supports the notion of *friends*: cooperative classes that are permitted to see each other's private parts.

Hiding is a relative concept: what is hidden at one level of abstraction may represent the outside view at another level of abstraction. The underlying representation of an object can be revealed, but in most cases only if the creator of the abstraction explicitly exposes the implementation, and then only if the client is willing to accept the resulting additional complexity. Thus, encapsulation cannot stop a developer from doing stupid things: as Stroustrup points out, "Hiding is for the prevention of accidents, not the prevention of fraud" [53]. Of course, nothing in any of the programming languages we use in this book prevents a human from literally seeing the implementation of a class, although an operating system might deny access to a particular file that contains the implementation of a class. In practice, there are times when one must study the implementation of a class to really understand its meaning, especially if the external documentation is lacking.

Modularity

The Meaning of Modularity. As Myers observes, "The act of partitioning a program into individual components can reduce its complexity to some degree. . . . Although partitioning a program is helpful for this reason, a more powerful justification for partitioning a program is that it creates a number of well-defined, documented boundaries within the program. These boundaries, or interfaces, are invaluable in the comprehension of the program" [54]. In some languages, such as Smalltalk, there is no concept of a module, and so the class forms the only physical unit of decomposition. In many others, including Object Pascal, C++, CLOS, and Ada, the module is a separate language construct, and therefore warrants a separate set of design decisions. In these languages, classes and objects form the logical structure of a system; we place these abstractions in *modules* to produce the system's physical architecture. Especially for larger applications, in which we may have many hundreds of classes, the use of modules is essential to help manage complexity.

Liskov states that "modularization consists of dividing a program into modules which can be compiled separately, but which have connections with other modules. We will use the definition of Parnas: 'The connections between

Modularity packages abstractions into discrete units.

modules are the assumptions which the modules make about each other' " [55]. Most languages that support the module as a separate concept also distinguish between the interface of a module and its implementation. Thus, it is fair to say that modularity and encapsulation go hand in hand. As with encapsulation, particular languages support modularity in diverse ways. For example, modules in C++ are nothing more than separately compiled files. The traditional practice in the C/C++ community is to place module interfaces in files named with a *.h* suffix; these are called *header files*. Module implementations are placed in files named with a *.c* suffix. Dependencies among files can then be asserted using the #include macro. This approach is entirely one of convention; it is neither required nor enforced by the language itself. Object Pascal is a little more formal about the matter. In this language, the syntax for *units* (its name for modules) distinguishes between module interface and implementation. Dependencies among units may be asserted only in a module's interface. Ada goes one step further. A `package` (its name for modules) has two parts, the package specification and the package body. Unlike Object Pascal, Ada allows connections among modules to be asserted separately in the specification and body of a package. Thus, it is possible for a package body to depend upon modules that are otherwise not visible to the package's specification.

Deciding upon the right set of modules for a given problem is almost as hard a problem as deciding upon the right set of abstractions. Zelkowitz is absolutely right when he states that "because the solution may not be known when the design stage starts, decomposition into smaller modules may be quite difficult. For older applications (such as compiler writing), this process may become standard, but for new ones (such as defense systems or spacecraft control), it may be quite difficult" [56].

Modules serve as the physical containers in which we declare the classes and objects of our logical design. This is no different than the situation faced by the electrical engineer designing a board-level computer. NAND, NOR, and NOT gates might be used to construct the necessary logic, but these gates must be physically packaged in standard integrated circuits, such as a 7400, 7402, or 7404. Lacking any such standard software parts, the software engineer has considerably more degrees of freedom – as if the electrical engineer had a silicon foundry at his or her disposal.

For tiny problems, the developer might decide to declare every class and object in the same package. For anything but the most trivial software, a better solution is to group logically related classes and objects in the same module, and expose only those elements that other modules absolutely must see. This kind of modularization is a good thing, but it can be taken to extremes. For example, consider an application that runs on a distributed set of processors and uses a message passing mechanism to coordinate the activities of different programs. In a large system, like that described in Chapter 12, it is common to have several hundred or even a few thousand kinds of messages. A naive strategy might be to define each message class in its own module. As it turns out, this is a singularly poor design decision. Not only does it create a documentation nightmare, but it makes it terribly difficult for any users to find the classes they need. Furthermore, when decisions change, hundreds of modules must be modified or recompiled. This example shows how information hiding can backfire [57]. Arbitrary modularization is sometimes worse than no modularization at all.

In traditional structured design, modularization is primarily concerned with the meaningful grouping of subprograms, using the criteria of coupling and cohesion. In object-oriented design, the problem is subtly different: the task is to decide where to physically package the classes and objects from the design's logical structure, which are distinctly different from subprograms.

Our experience indicates that there are several useful technical as well as nontechnical guidelines that can help us achieve an intelligent modularization of classes and objects. As Britton and Parnas have observed, "The overall goal of the decomposition into modules is the reduction of software cost by allowing modules to be designed and revised independently. . . . Each module's structure should be simple enough that it can be understood fully; it should be possible to change the implementation of other modules without knowledge of the implementation of other modules and without affecting the behavior of other modules; [and] the ease of making a change in the design should bear a reasonable relationship to the likelihood of the change being needed" [58]. There is a pragmatic edge to these guidelines. In practice, the cost of recompiling the body of a module is relatively small: only that unit need be recompiled and the application relinked. However, the cost of recompiling the *interface* of a module is relatively high. Especially with strongly typed languages, one must recompile the module interface, its body, all other modules that depend upon this interface, the modules that depend upon these modules, and so on. Thus, for very large programs (assuming that our development environment does not support incremental compilation), a change in a single module interface might result in many hours of recompilation. Obviously, a manager cannot often afford to allow this. For this reason, a module's interface should be as narrow as possible, yet still satisfy the needs of all using modules. Our style is to hide as much as we can in the implementation of a module. Incrementally shifting declarations from a module implementation to its interface is far less painful and destabilizing than ripping out extraneous interface code.

The developer must therefore balance two competing technical concerns: the desire to encapsulate abstractions, and the need to make certain abstractions visible to other modules. Parnas, Clements, and Weiss offer the following guidance: "System details that are likely to change independently should be the secrets of separate modules; the only assumptions that should appear between modules are those that are considered unlikely to change. Every data structure is private to one module; it may be directly accessed by one or more programs within the module but not by programs outside the module. Any other program that requires information stored in a module's data structures must obtain it by calling module programs" [59]. In other words, strive to build modules that are cohesive (by grouping logically related abstractions) and loosely coupled (by minimizing the dependencies among modules). From this perspective, we may define modularity as follows:

> *Modularity is the property of a system that has been decomposed into a set of cohesive and loosely coupled modules.*

Thus, the principles of abstraction, encapsulation, and modularity are synergistic. An object provides a crisp boundary around a single abstraction, and both encapsulation and modularity provide barriers around this abstraction.

Two additional technical issues can affect modularization decisions. First, since modules usually serve as the elementary and indivisible units of software that can be reused across applications, a developer might chose to package classes and objects into modules in a way that makes their reuse convenient. Second, many compilers generate object code in segments, one for each module. Therefore, there may be practical limits on the size of individual modules. With regard to the dynamics of subprogram calls, the placement of declarations within modules can greatly affect the locality of reference and thus the paging behavior of a virtual memory system. Poor locality happens when subprogram calls occur across segments and lead to cache misses and page thrashing that ultimately slow down the whole system.

Several competing nontechnical needs may also affect modularization decisions. Typically, work assignments in a development team are given on a module-by-module basis, and so the boundaries of modules may be established to minimize the interfaces among different parts of the development organization. Senior designers are usually given responsibility for module interfaces, and more junior developers complete their implementation. On a larger scale, the same situation applies with subcontractor relationships. Abstractions may be packaged so as to quickly stabilize the module interfaces as agreed upon among the various companies. Changing such interfaces usually involves much wailing and gnashing of teeth – not to mention a vast amount of paperwork – and so this factor often leads to conservatively designed interfaces. Speaking of paperwork, modules also usually serve as the unit of documentation and configuration management. Having ten modules where one would do means ten times the paperwork, and so, unfortunately, sometimes the documentation requirements drive the module design decisions (usually in the most negative way). Security may also be an issue: most code may be considered unclassified, but other code that might be classified secret or higher is best placed in separate modules.

Juggling these different guidelines is difficult, but don't lose sight of the most important point: finding the right classes and objects and then organizing them into separate modules are *entirely independent* design decisions. The identification of classes and objects is part of the logical design of the system, but the identification of modules is part of the system's physical design. One cannot make all the logical design decisions before making all the physical ones, or vice versa; rather, these design decisions happen iteratively.

Examples of Modularity. Let's look at modularity in the hydroponics gardening system. Suppose that instead of building some special-purpose hardware, we decide to use a commercially available workstation for the user interface. At this workstation, an operator could create new growing plans, modify old ones, and follow the progress of currently active ones. Because Object Pascal is available on a variety of platforms, we might choose to use it to implement this part of the system.

One of the key abstractions here is that of a growing plan. We might therefore create a module called `UGrowingPlans`, whose purpose is to collect all of the classes associated with individual growing plans. In Object Pascal, we might write the framework of this unit as follows:

```
unit UGrowingPlans; interface
   ...
implementation
   {$I UGrowingPlans.incl.p}
end.
```

The ellipses mark the location of the declarations that must be exposed to other units. The implementations of these classes, objects, and free subprograms then appear in the implementation of this module, the unit we named `UGrowingPlans.incl.p`.

We might also define a module called `UGardeningDialogs`, whose purpose is to collect all of the code associated with dialog boxes. This unit most likely depends upon the classes declared in the interface of `UGrowingPlans`, and so we might write its framework as follows:

```
unit UGardeningDialogs; interface

uses
    MemTypes, QuickDraw, OSIntf, ToolIntf, PackIntf, CursorCtl,
    UMAUtil, UViewCoords, UFailure, UMemory, UMenuSetup,
    UObject, UList, UAssociation, UMacApp,
    UGrowingPlans;
    ...
implementation
    {$I UGardeningDialogs.incl.p}
end.
```

This unit implementation requires a number of lower level interfaces, and so its interface must import several other units in addition to `UGrowingPlans`.

Our design might include many other units, such as `UGardeningCommands`, `UGardeningViews`, `UGardeningDocuments`, and `UGardeningApplication`, each of which imports the interface of lower level units. Ultimately, we must define some main program from which we can invoke this application from the operating system. In object-oriented design, defining this main program is often the least important decision, whereas in traditional structured design, the main program serves as the root, the keystone that holds everything else together. We suggest that the object-oriented view is more natural, for as Meyer observes, "Practical software systems are more appropriately described as offering a number of services. Defining these systems by single functions is usually possible, but yields rather artificial answers. . . . Real systems have no top" [60].

Hierarchy

The Meaning of Hierarchy. Abstraction is a good thing, but in all except the most trivial applications, we may find many more different abstractions than we can comprehend at one time. Encapsulation helps manage this complexity by hiding the inside view of our abstractions. Modularity helps also, by giving us a way to cluster logically related abstractions. Still, this is not enough. A set of abstractions often forms a hierarchy, and by identifying these hierarchies in our design, we greatly simplify our understanding of the problem.

We define hierarchy as follows:

Hierarchy is a ranking or ordering of abstractions.

The two most important hierarchies in a complex system are its class structure (the "kind of" hierarchy) and its object structure (the "part of" hierarchy).

Examples of Hierarchy: Single Inheritance. Inheritance is the most important "kind of" hierarchy, and as we noted earlier, it is an essential element of object-oriented systems. Basically, inheritance defines a relationship among classes, wherein one class shares the structure or behavior defined in one or more classes (called *single inheritance* and *multiple inheritance*, respectively).

Abstractions form a hierarchy.

Inheritance thus represents a hierarchy of abstractions, in which a subclass inherits from one or more superclasses. Typically, a subclass augments or redefines the existing structure and behavior of its superclasses.

Consider the different kinds of growing plans we might use in the hydroponics gardening system. An earlier section described our abstraction of a very generalized growing plan. Different crops, however, might demand specialized growing plans. For example, the growing plan for all fruits might be different from the plan for all vegetables, or for all floral crops. A standard fruit-growing plan is therefore a kind of growing plan that encapsulates specialized behavior, such as the knowledge of when to harvest the fruit. We can assert this "kind of" relationship among abstractions in C++ as follows:

```
class StandardFruitGrowingPlan : public GrowingPlan {

public:
    StandardFruitGrowingPlan ();
    StandardFruitGrowingPlan (const StandardFruitGrowingPlan&);
    virtual ~StandardFruitGrowingPlan ();

    virtual int daysUntilHarvest (day currentDay) const;

private:
    day timeToHarvest;

};
```

This class declaration means that the class `StandardFruitGrowingPlan` is just like its superclass, `GrowingPlan`, except that objects of this specialized class have an additional member object (`timeToHarvest`), a different constructor and destructor, and a new virtual member function (`daysUntilHarvest`). Using this class, we could declare even more specialized subclasses, such as the class `StandardAppleGrowingPlan`.

As we evolve our inheritance hierarchy, the structure and behavior that are the same for different classes will tend to migrate to common superclasses. This is why we often speak of inheritance as being a *generalization/specialization* hierarchy; in some circles, inheritance is called the *is a* hierarchy. Superclasses represent generalized abstractions, and subclasses represent specializations in which fields and methods from the superclass are added, modified, or even hidden. In this manner, inheritance lets us state our abstractions with an economy of expression. Indeed, neglecting the "kind of" hierarchies that exist can lead to bloated, inelegant designs. As Cox points out, "Without inheritance, every class would be a free-standing unit, each developed from the ground up. Different classes would bear no relationship with one another, since the developer of each provides methods in whatever manner he chooses. Any consistency across classes is the result of discipline on the part of the programmers. Inheritance makes it possible to define new software in the same way we introduce any concept to a newcomer, by comparing it with something that is already familiar" [61].

There is a healthy tension among the principles of abstraction, encapsulation, and hierarchy. As Danforth and Tomlinson point out, "Data abstraction attempts to provide an opaque barrier behind which methods and state are hidden; inheritance requires opening this interface to some extent and may allow state as well as methods to be accessed without abstraction" [62]. For a given class, there are usually two kinds of clients: objects that invoke operations upon instances of the class, and subclasses that inherit from the class. Liskov therefore notes that, with inheritance, encapsulation can be violated in one of three ways: "The subclass might access an instance variable of its superclass, call a private operation of its superclass, or refer directly to superclasses of its superclass" [63]. Different programming languages trade off support for encapsulation and inheritance in different ways, but among the languages used in this book, C++ offers the greatest flexibility. Specifically, the interface of a class may have three parts: *private* parts, which declare members that are visible only to the class itself, *protected* parts, which declare members that are visible only to the class and its subclasses, and *public* parts, which are visible to all clients.

Examples of Hierarchy: Multiple Inheritance. The previous example illustrated the use of single inheritance: the subclass `StandardFruitGrowingPlan` had exactly one superclass, the class `GrowingPlan`. For some abstractions, it is useful to provide inheritance from multiple superclasses. For example, suppose that we choose to define a class representing a kind of plant. In CLOS, we might declare this class as follows:

```
(defclass plant ()
    ((name                 :initarg  :name
                           :reader   plant-name)
     (date-planted         :initarg  :date-planted
                           :reader   date-planted)
     (germination-time     :initarg  :germination-time
                           :reader   germination-time)
     (actual-germination :initform nil
                           :accessor actual-germination))
    (:documentation "The base class of all plants.")))
```

According to this class definition, each instance of the class `plant` will have four slots (`name`, `date-planted`, `germination-time`, and `actual-germination`). Methods for initializing each slot are provided (the :initarg and :initform slot options), as well as methods for reading the first three slots (the :reader slot option), and reading and writing the fourth slot (the :accessor slot option).

Our analysis of the problem domain might suggest that flowering plants and fruits and vegetables have specialized properties. For example, given a flowering plant, its expected time to flower and time to seed might be important to us. Similarly, the time to harvest might be an important part of our abstraction of all fruits and vegetables. One way we could capture our design decisions would be to make two new classes, a `flowering-plant` class and a `fruit/vegetable-plant` class, both subclasses of the class plant. However, what if we need to model a plant that both flowered and produced fruit? For example, florists commonly use blossoms from apple, cherry, and plum trees. For this model, we would need to invent a third class, a `flowering/fruit/vegetable-plant`, that duplicated information from the `flowering-plant` and `fruit/ vegetable-plant` classes.

A better way to express our abstractions and thereby avoid this redundancy is to use multiple inheritance. First, we would invent classes that independently capture the properties unique to flowering plants and fruits and vegetables:

```
(defclass flowering-plant-mixin ()
    ((time-to-flower :initarg :time-to-flower
                        :reader  time-to-flower)
     (time-to-seed   :initarg :time-to-seed
                        :reader  time-to-seed))
    (:documentation "A mixin class for flowering plants."))

(defclass fruit/vegetable-plant-mixin ()
    ((time-to-harvest :initarg :time-to-harvest
                        :reader  time-to-harvest))
    (:documentation "A mixin class for fruits and vegetables."))
```

Notice that these two classes have no superclass; they stand alone. These are called *mixin* classes, because they are meant to be mixed together with other classes to produce new subclasses. For example, we can define a `flowering-plant` class as follows:

```
(defclass flowering-plant (plant flowering-plant-mixin)
    ()
    (:documentation "A flowering plant class."))
```

Similarly, a `fruit/vegetable-plant` class can be declared as follows:

```
(defclass fruit/vegetable-plant (plant fruit/vegetable-plant-mixin)
    ()
    (:documentation "A fruit or vegetable plant."))
```

In both cases, we form the subclass by inheriting from two superclasses. Instances of the subclass `flowering-plant` thus include the slot `germination-time` (inherited from the class `plant`) as well as the slot `time-to-flower` (inherited from the class `flowering-plant-mixin`). Now, suppose we want to declare a class for a plant that has both flowers and fruit. We might write the following:

```
(defclass flowering/fruit/vegetable-plant (plant
                              flowering-plant-mixin
                              fruit/vegetable-plant-mixin)
    ()
    (:documentation "A flowering fruit or vegetable plant."))
```

Examples of Hierarchy: Aggregation. Whereas these "kind of" hierarchies denote generalization/specialization relationships, "part of" hierarchies describe aggregation relationships. For example, a flowering plant object is built up of six subobjects (the four slots defined in the class `plant`, and the two slots defined in the class `flowering-plant-mixin`). When dealing with hierarchies such as these, we often speak of *levels of abstraction*, a concept first described by Dijkstra [64]. In terms of its "kind of" hierarchy, a high-level abstraction is generalized, and a low-level abstraction is specialized. Therefore, we say that a plant class is at a higher level of abstraction then a flowering-plant class. In terms of its "part of" hierarchy, a class is at a higher level of abstraction than any of the classes that make up its implementation. Thus, the class `StandardFruitGrowingPlan` is at a higher level of abstraction than the type `day`, upon which it builds.

Typing

The Meaning of Typing. The concept of a *type* derives primarily from the theories of abstract data types. As Deutsch suggests, "A type is a precise characterization of structural or behavioral properties which a collection of entities all share" [65]. For our purposes, we will use the terms *type* and *class* interchangeably.* Although the concepts of a type and a class are similar, we include typing as a separate element of the object model because the concept of a type places a very different emphasis upon the meaning of abstraction. Specifically, we state the following:

> *Typing is the enforcement of the class of an object, such that objects of different types may not be interchanged, or at the most, they may be interchanged only in very restricted ways.*

Typing lets us express our abstractions so that the programming language in which we implement them can be made to enforce design decisions. Wegner observes that this kind of enforcement is essential for programming-in-the-large [67]. We consider it a minor element, however, because a given programming language may be strongly typed, weakly typed, or even untyped, yet still be called object-based or object-oriented.

---

* A type and a class are not exactly the same thing; some languages actually distinguish these two concepts. For example, early versions of the language Trellis/Owl permitted an object to have both a class and a type. Even in Smalltalk, objects of the classes `SmallInteger`, `LargeNegativeInteger`, and `LargePositiveInteger` are all of the same type, `Integer`, although not of the same class [66]. For most mortals, however, separating the concepts of type and class is utterly confusing and adds very little value. It is sufficient to say that a class implements a type.

Strong typing prevents mixing abstractions.

Examples of Typing: Strong and Weak Typing. Returning to the user interface segment of the hydroponics gardening system, suppose that we have the following (incomplete) classes written in Object Pascal:

```
TShape = object (TObject)

    fPosition : Point;

    procedure TShape.Draw (Area : Rect);

    function TShape.IsVisible : Boolean;

end;

TText = object (TShape)

    fValue : Str255;

    procedure TText.Draw (Area : Rect); override;

end;

TGreenhouse = object (TShape)

    fHydroponics_Tanks : array[1 .. 10] of THydroponicsTank;

    procedure TGreenhouse.Initialize;
```

```
procedure TGreenhouse.Draw (Area : Rect); override;

end;
```

In Object Pascal, all fields and methods declared in the interface of a class are public. The implementation of such classes is therefore visible, which is why we say that Object Pascal does not allow us to fully encapsulate our abstractions.

The class `TShape` inherits from the base class `TObject` and serves as the superclass of any object that can be drawn on a workstation screen. `TText` and `TGreenhouse` are both subclasses of this class, and represent more specialized objects that can be drawn. `TShape` thus declares the common method `Draw`, so that all drawable objects have this behavior; the subclasses `TText` and `TGreenhouse` specialize this method to draw text and an iconic representation of a greenhouse, respectively.

Since Object Pascal is a strongly typed language, we must explicitly assert the type of each variable, subprogram parameter, and class field when we declare it. For example, suppose that we have the following declarations:

```
AnObject    : TObject;
AShape      : TShape;
ATextString : TText;
AGreenhouse : TGreenhouse;
```

We might then create new objects with the following statements:

```
new (AnObject);
new (AShape);
new (ATextString);
new (AGreenhouse);
```

Variables such as `ATextString` are not objects. To be precise, `ATextString` is simply a name we use to designate an object of the class `TText`: when we say "the object `ATextString`," we really mean the instance of `TText` denoted by the variable `ATextString`. We will explain this subtlety again in the next chapter.

Because Object Pascal is strongly typed, statements that invoke methods are checked for type correctness at the time of compilation. For example, the following statements are legal:

```
AShape.Draw(SomeArea);      {Draw is defined for the class TShape}
ATextString.Draw(SomeArea); {Draw is defined for the class TText}
```

However, the following statements are not legal and would be rejected at compilation time:

```
AnObject.Draw(SomeArea); {Illegal}
ATextString.Initialize;  {Illegal}
```

Neither of these two statements is legal because the methods `Draw` and `Initialize` are not defined for the class of the corresponding variable, nor for any superclasses of its class. On the other hand, the following statement is legal:

```
if AGreenhouse.IsVisible then
    ...
```

Although `IsVisible` is not defined in the class `TGreenhouse`, it is defined in the class `TShape`, from which the class `TGreenhouse` inherits its structure and behavior.

Consider this same example in Smalltalk, an untyped language. Variables are untyped, as in the following local declaration:

```
|anObject aShape ATextString aGreenhouse|
```

A statement such as

```
anObject draw: SomeArea.
```

would be accepted at compilation time, but its exact meaning could not be known until execution time. If the variable `anObject` happened to denote an object of the class `Shape` (whose class had knowledge of the method `draw`), then execution would proceed normally. On the other hand, if `anObject` denoted an instance of the predefined Smalltalk class `Bag` (which has no knowledge of the method `draw`), then evaluating this statement would ultimately lead to a "message not understood" error at runtime.

A strongly typed language is one in which all expressions are guaranteed to be type-consistent. The meaning of type consistency is best illustrated by the following example, using the previously declared Object Pascal variables. The following assignment statements are legal:

```
AnObject := AnObject;
AShape := ATextString;
```

The first statement is legal because the class of the variable on the left side of the statement (`TObject`) is the same as the class of the expression on the right side. The second statement is also legal because the class of the variable on the left side (`TShape`) is a superclass of the variable on the right side (`TText`).

Consider the following statements:

```
AGreenhouse := AShape;      {Illegal}
ATextString := AGreenhouse; {Illegal}
```

Neither of these statements is legal because the class of the variable on the left side of the assignment statement is a subclass of the class of the expression on the right.

In some situations, it is necessary to convert a value from one type to another. For example, given the predefined class `TList` from a class library for Object Pascal, we have the operation `Each`, which allows us to visit every element in the list:

```
procedure TList.Each (procedure DoToItem (Item : TObject));
```

If we know that our list object will always contain objects of the class TGreenhouse, then we may explicitly coerce the value of one type to another, as in the following legal assignment statement:

```
procedure DoToItem (Item : TObject);
begin
    ...
    AGreenhouse := TGreenhouse(Item);
    ...
end;
```

This assignment statement is type-consistent, although it is not completely type-safe. For example, if the list happened to contain an object of the class TText at runtime, then the coercion would fail with an execution error.

As Tesler points out, there are a number of important benefits to be derived from using strongly typed languages:

- "Without type checking, a program in most languages can 'crash' in mysterious ways at runtime.

- In most systems, the edit-compile-debug cycle is so tedious that early error detection is indispensable.

- Type declarations help to document programs.

- Most compilers can generate more efficient object code if types are declared" [68].

Untyped languages offer greater flexibility, but even with untyped languages, as Borning and Ingalls observe, "In almost all cases, the programmer in fact knows what sorts of objects are expected as the arguments of a message, and what sort of object will be returned" [69]. In practice, the safety offered by strongly typed languages usually more then compensates for the flexibility lost by not using an untyped language, especially for programming-in-the-large.

Examples of Typing: Static and Dynamic Binding. The concepts of strong typing and static typing are entirely different. Strong typing refers to type consistency, whereas static typing – also known as *static binding* or *early binding* – refers to the time when names are bound to types. Static binding means that the types of all variables and expressions are fixed at the time of compilation; *dynamic binding* (also called *late binding*) means that the types of all variables and expressions are not known until runtime. Because strong typing and binding are independent concepts, a language may be both strongly and statically typed (Ada), strongly typed yet support dynamic binding (Object Pascal and C++), or untyped yet support dynamic binding (Smalltalk). CLOS fits somewhere between C++ and Smalltalk, in that an implementation may either enforce or ignore any type declarations asserted by a programmer.

Let's again illustrate these concepts with an example from Object Pascal. Earlier, we used the class TList, which is found in a class library for Object Pascal, and represents a singly linked list. Its (highly elided) declaration follows:

```
TList = object (TObject)
    ...
    procedure TList.InsertFirst (Item : TObject);
    procedure TList.Each (procedure DoToItem (Item : TObject));
    ...
end;
```

Here we see two methods: the first for adding items to the list (a *modifier*), and the second for visiting every item in the list (an *iterator*). Because Object Pascal supports dynamic binding, we may have either homogeneous lists, in which all elements are of the same class, or heterogeneous lists whose elements are all of different classes, as long as each item is an instance of the class TObject or any of its subclasses.

Assume that we have an object of the class TList named AList, representing a heterogeneous list of objects that are all of the class TShape or its subclasses. We can thus write statements such as the following:

```
AList.InsertFirst (AShape) ;
AList.InsertFirst (ATextString) ;
AList.InsertFirst (AGreenhouse) ;
```

All of these statements are type-consistent because the type of each actual parameter is of the same class (or subclass) as the corresponding formal parameter (TObject).

Suppose now that we want to draw each object in the list. We might write the following procedure and statement:

```
procedure Draw_Item (Item : TObject);
begin
    TShape (Item) .Draw (SomeArea) ;
end;
...
AList.Each (Draw_Item) ;
```

The call to the operation Each invokes the list iterator, which in turn calls the procedure Draw_Item for each object in the list. Notice that in the procedure Draw_Item, we have to coerce the variable Item to the class TShape so that we can invoke the operation Draw, which we defined for the class TShape and its subclasses. At the time of compilation, however, we cannot know the exact subclass of the object designated by the formal parameter Item: it might be of the class TText or TGreenhouse, for instance. This is an example of dynamic binding.

Fortunately, because we can control what goes into the list, it is safe for us to coerce the formal parameter Item to an object of the class TShape. Because the method Draw is defined in the class TShape, it is type-consistent to invoke this method. Thus, the effect of invoking the iterator Each is to walk down the list and invoke the `Draw` method of each object we find along the way. Because each object may be of a different class, each object may respond differently to the invocation of the `Draw` method. Ultimately, this means that we cannot know until runtime what `Draw` method is actually called. This feature is called *polymorphism*; it represents a concept in type theory in which a single name (such as a variable declaration) may denote objects of many different classes that are related by some common superclass. Any object denoted by this name is therefore able to respond to some common set of operations [70]. The opposite of polymorphism is *monomorphism*, which is found in all languages that are both strongly typed and statically bound, such as Ada.

Polymorphism exists when the features of inheritance and dynamic binding interact. It is perhaps the most powerful feature of object-oriented programming languages next to their support for abstraction, and it is what distinguishes object-oriented programming from more traditional programming with abstract data types. As we will see in the following chapters, polymorphism is also an important concept in object-oriented design.

Concurrency

The Meaning of Concurrency. For certain kinds of problems, an automated system may have to handle many different events simultaneously. Other problems may involve so much computation that they exceed the capacity of any single processor. In each of these cases, it is natural to consider using a distributed set of computers for the target implementation or to use processors capable of multitasking. A single process – also known as a *thread of control* – is the root from which independent dynamic action occurs within a system. Every program has at least one thread of control, but a system involving concurrency may have many such threads: some that are transitory, and others that last the entire lifetime of the system's execution. Systems executing across multiple CPUs allow for truly concurrent threads of control, whereas systems running on a single CPU can only achieve the illusion of concurrent threads of control, usually by means of some time-slicing algorithm.

Lim and Johnson point out that "designing features for concurrency in OOP languages is not much different from [doing so in] other kinds of languages – concurrency is orthogonal to OOP at the lowest levels of abstraction. OOP or not, all the traditional problems in concurrent programming still remain" [71]. Indeed, building a large piece of software is hard enough; designing one that encompasses multiple threads of control is much harder because one must worry about such issues as deadlock, livelock, starvation, mutual exclusion, and race conditions. Fortunately, as Lim and Johnson also point out, "At the highest levels of abstraction, OOP can alleviate the concurrency problem for the majority of programmers by hiding the concurrency inside reusable abstractions" [72]. Black et al. therefore suggest that "an object model is appropriate for a

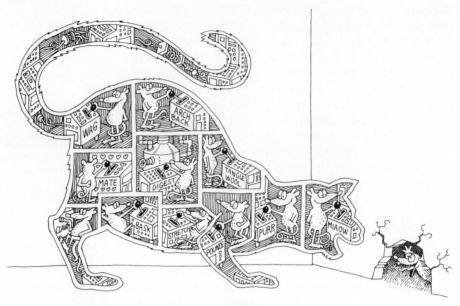

Concurrency allows different objects to act at the same time.

distributed system because it implicitly defines (1) the units of distribution and movement and (2) the entities that communicate" [73].

Whereas object-oriented programming focuses upon data abstraction, encapsulation, and inheritance, concurrency focuses upon process abstraction and synchronization [74]. The object is a concept that unifies these two different viewpoints: each object (drawn from an abstraction of the real world) may represent a separate thread of control (a process abstraction). Such objects are called *active*. In a system based on an object-oriented design, we can conceptualize the world as consisting of a set of cooperative objects, some of which are active and thus serve as centers of independent activity. Given this conception, we define concurrency as follows:

> *Concurrency is the property that distinguishes an active object from one that is not active.*

Examples of Concurrency. Our discussion of abstraction introduced an Ada package specification for a sequential class representing air temperature sensors. Our variation of this package captured the design of an active sensor class, whose behavior was to periodically determine the current temperature and then send a message to another object whenever the temperature changed a certain number of degrees. Ada's mechanism for expressing a concurrent process is the task, and therefore, we might complete this representation of the type

`Air_Temperature_Sensor` as follows (ignoring the need for the calibration operation):

```
task type Air_Temperature_Sensor is
    entry Initialize (Its_Location      : in Location;
                      Lower_Alarm_Limit : in Temperature;
                      Upper_Alarm_Limit : in Temperature);
end Air_Temperature_Sensor;
```

For every instance of this task type, we generate a new process. From an object-oriented perspective, there is exactly one operation that we can perform upon objects of this type. Specifically, we can initialize it, by telling the object its location and its upper and lower temperature limits, outside of which other objects are notified (via the generic formal subprogram parameter, `Temperature_Alarm`).

Suppose that each physical sensor uses memory-mapped I/O. To read the value of a particular sensor, we need only reference some location in memory. In Ada, we might express these design decisions by hiding the following declarations in the body of the package `Air_Temperature_Sensors`:

```
type Word is range -(2**15 -1) .. (2**15 - 1);
for Word'Size use 16;

Sensor_Memory_Map : array (Location) of Word;
for Sensor_Memory_Map use at 16#377FF0#;

Time_Interval : constant Duration := 2.0;
```

These declarations are hidden because they are part of the secrets of this abstraction, such as the fact that the memory map starts at hexidecimal location 377FF0 and that each raw sensor value is a 16-bit number. The constant `Time_Interval` represents how often we want to read the physical sensor (in this case, once every two seconds).

The basic idea of the sensor task is to read the memory map every `Time_Interval` seconds and then report to other objects any changes or alarm conditions. Ignoring the issues of calibration and termination, we might implement the body of this task type as follows:

```
task body Air_Temperature_Sensor is
    Current_Location     : Location;
    Sensor_Value         : Word;
    Current_Temperature  : Temperature;
    Previous_Temperature : Temperature := Temperature'Last;
    Lower_Limit          : Temperature;
    Upper_Limit          : Temperature;
    Next_Time            : Calendar.Time := Calendar.Clock;
begin
    accept Initialize (Its_Location      : in Location;
                       Lower_Alarm_Limit : in Temperature;
                       Upper_Alarm_Limit : in Temperature) do
        Current_Location := Its_Location;
```

```
        Lower_Limit := Lower_Alarm_Limit;
        Upper_Limit := Upper_Alarm_Limit;
    end Initialize;
    loop
        delay (Next_Time - Calendar.Clock);
        Sensor_Value:= Sensor_Memory_Map(Current_Location);
        Current_Temperature := Temperature(Float(Sensor_Value) * Temperature'Delta);
        if (Current_Temperature /= Previous_Temperature) then
            if (Current_Temperature < Lower_Limit)  or
               (Current_Temperature > Upper_Limit) then
                Temperature_Alarm(Current_Location, Current_Temperature);
            else
                Previous_Temperature := Current_Temperature;
                Temperature_Has_Changed(Current_Location, Current_Temperature);
            end if;
        end if;
        Next_Time := Next_Time + Time_Interval;
    end loop;
end;
```

For clarity, this implementation has several more local variables than one would probably use in production code.

Once the active object is initialized, its process loops every two seconds, during which time the physical sensor value is read. If this value is different than the previous reading, the algorithm continues. If this new reading also exceeds the upper or lower temperatures established upon initialization, then the procedure `Temperature_Alarm` is called. Otherwise, the procedure `Temperature_Has_Changed` is called, to notify some other object of the change.

One of the realities about concurrency is that once you introduce it into a system, you must consider how active objects synchronize their activities with one another as well as with objects that are purely sequential. For example, if two active objects try to send messages to a third object, we must be certain to use some means of mutual exclusion, so that the state of the object being acted upon is not corrupted when both active objects try to update its state simultaneously. This is the point where the ideas of abstraction, encapsulation, and concurrency interact. In the presence of concurrency, it is not enough simply to define the methods of an object; we must also make certain that the semantics of these methods are preserved in the presence of multiple threads of control.

There are a number of experimental concurrent object-oriented programming languages, such as Actors, Orient 84/K, and ABCL/1, that provide mechanisms for active objects and synchronization. The appendix provides references to these and other languages. Among the languages used in this book, only Smalltalk and Ada directly support multitasking (Smalltalk has the class Process and Ada incorporates the concept of a task type). Concurrent objects in C++ are possible through the use of the Unix system call *fork*. Object Pascal and CLOS are typically used for sequential applications only; they do not have primitives for concurrency.

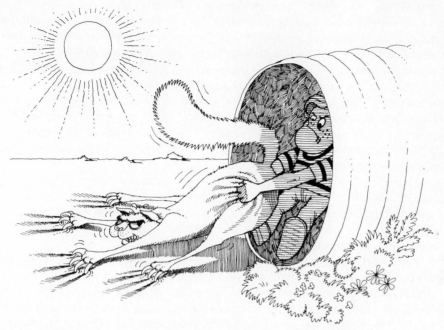

Persistence saves the state and class of an object across time or space.

Persistence

An object in software takes up some amount of space and exists for a particular amount of time. Atkinson et al. suggest that there is a continuum of object existence, ranging from transitory objects that arise within the evaluation of an expression, to objects in a database that outlive the execution of a single program. This spectrum of object persistence encompasses the following:

- "Transient results in expression evaluation
- Local variables in procedure activations
- Own variables [as in ALGOL 60], global variables, and heap items whose extent is different from their scope
- Data that exists between executions of a program
- Data that exists between various versions of a program
- Data that outlives the program" [75]

Traditional programming languages usually address only the first three kinds of object persistence; persistence of the last three kinds is typically the domain of database technology. This leads to a clash of cultures that sometimes results in very strange designs: programmers end up crafting *ad hoc* schemes for storing objects whose state must be preserved between program executions, and database designers misapply their technology to cope with transient objects [76].

Unifying the concepts of concurrency and objects gives rise to concurrent object-oriented programming languages. In a similar fashion, introducing the concept of persistence to the object model gives rise to object-oriented databases. In practice, such databases build upon proven technology, such as sequential, indexed, hierarchical, network, or relational database models, but then offer to the programmer the abstraction of an object-oriented interface, through which database queries and other operations are completed in terms of objects whose lifetime transcends the lifetime of an individual program. This unification vastly simplifies the development of certain kinds of applications. In particular, it allows us to apply the same design methods to the database and nondatabase segments of an application.

There are only a handful of object-oriented databases, such as TAXIS, SDM, DAPLEX, and GEM [77]. None of the five languages we use in the applications support persistence directly, so we have no examples to offer here. As we will see in Chapters 9 and 10, however, it is possible to achieve the illusion of persistence in these languages.

Persistence deals with more than just the lifetime of data. In object-oriented databases, not only does the *state* of an object persist, but its *class* must also transcend any individual program so that every program interprets this saved state in the same way. This clearly makes it challenging to maintain the integrity of a database as it grows, particularly if we must change the class of an object.

Our discussion thus far pertains to persistence in time. In most systems, an object, once created, consumes the same physical memory until it ceases to exist. However, for systems that execute upon a distributed set of processors, we must sometimes be concerned with persistence across space. In such systems, it is useful to think of objects that can move from machine to machine, and that may even have different representations on different machines. We examine this kind of persistence further in the application in Chapter 12.

To summarize, we define persistence as follows:

> *Persistence is the property of an object through which its existence transcends time (i.e. the object continues to exist after its creator ceases to exist) and/or space (i.e. the object's location moves from the address space in which it was created).*

2.3 Applying the Object Model

Benefits of the Object Model

As we have shown, the object model is fundamentally different than the models embraced by the more traditional methods of structured analysis, structured design, and structured programming. This does not mean that the object model abandons all of the sound principles and experiences of these older methods. Rather, it introduces several novel elements that build upon these earlier models. Thus, the object model offers a number of significant benefits that other models simply do not provide. Most importantly, the use of the object model leads us to construct systems that embody the five attributes of well-structured complex systems. In our experience, there are five other practical benefits to be derived from the application of the object model.

First, the use of the object model helps us to exploit the expressive power of all object-based and object-oriented programming languages. As Stroustrup points out, "It is not always clear how best to take advantage of a language such as C++. Significant improvements in productivity and code quality have consistently been achieved using C++ as 'a better C' with a bit of data abstraction thrown in where it is clearly useful. However, further and noticeably larger improvements have been achieved by taking advantage of class hierarchies in the design process. This is often called object-oriented design and this is where the greatest benefits of using C++ have been found" [78]. Our experience has been that, without the application of the elements of the object model, the more powerful features of languages such as Smalltalk, Object Pascal, C++, CLOS, and Ada are either ignored or greatly misused.

Next, the use of the object model encourages the reuse not only of software but of entire designs [79]. We have found that object-oriented systems are often smaller than equivalent non-object-oriented implementations. Not only does this mean less code to write and maintain, but greater reuse of software also translates into cost and schedule benefits.

Third, the use of the object model produces systems that are built upon stable intermediate forms, and thus are more resilient to change. This also means that such systems can be allowed to evolve over time, rather than be abandoned or completely redesigned in response to the first major change in requirements.

Chapter 7 explains further how the object model reduces the risk of developing complex systems, primarily because integration is spread out across the life cycle rather than occurring as one big bang event. The object model's guidance in designing an intelligent separation of concerns also reduces development risk and increases our confidence in the correctness of our design.

Finally, the object model appeals to the workings of human cognition, for as Robson suggests, "Many people who have no idea how a computer works find the idea of object-oriented systems quite natural" [80].

Applications of the Object Model

The object model has proven applicable to a wide variety of problem domains. Figure 2-6 lists many of the domains for which systems exist that may properly be called object-oriented. The Bibliography provides an extensive list of references to these and other applications.

Object-oriented design may be the only method we have today that can be employed to attack the complexity inherent in very large systems. In all fairness, however, the use of object-oriented design may be ill-advised for some domains, not for any technical reasons, but for nontechnical ones, such as the absence of a suitably trained staff or good development environment.

Air traffic control	Investment strategies
Animation	Mathematical analysis
Avionics	Medical electronics
Banking and insurance software	Music composition
Business data processing	Office automation
Chemical process control	Operating systems
Command and control systems	Petroleum engineering
Computer aided design	Reusable software components
Computer aided education	Robotics
Computer integrated manufacturing	Software development environments
Databases	Space station software
Document preparation	Spacecraft and aircraft simulation
Expert systems	Telecommunications
Film and stage storyboarding	Telemetry systems
Hypermedia	User interface design
Image recognition	VLSI design

Figure 2-6
Applications of the Object Model

Open Issues

To effectively apply the elements of the object model, we must next address several open issues:

- What exactly are classes and objects?
- How does one properly identify the classes and objects that are relevant to a particular application?
- What is a suitable notation for expressing the design of an object-oriented system?
- What process can lead us to a well-structured object-oriented system?
- What are the management implications of using object-oriented design?

These issues are the themes of the next five chapters.

Summary

- The maturation of software engineering has led to the development of object-oriented analysis, design, and programming methods, all of which address the issues of programming-in-the-large.
- There are several different programming paradigms: procedure-oriented, object-oriented, logic-oriented, rule-oriented, and constraint-oriented.

- The object model provides the conceptual framework for object-oriented methods; the object model encompasses the principles of abstraction, encapsulation, modularity, hierarchy, typing, concurrency, and persistence.

- An abstraction denotes the essential characteristics of an object that distinguish it from all other kinds of objects and thus provide crisply defined conceptual boundaries, relative to the perspective of the viewer.

- Encapsulation is the process of hiding all of the details of an object that do not contribute to its essential characteristics.

- Modularity is the property of a system that has been decomposed into a set of cohesive and loosely coupled modules.

- Hierarchy is a ranking or ordering of abstractions.

- Typing is the enforcement of the class of an object, such that objects of different types may not be interchanged, or at the most, they may be interchanged only in very restricted ways.

- Concurrency is the property that distinguishes an active object from one that is not active.

- Persistence is the property of an object through which its existence transcends time and/or space.

- The application of the object model leads to systems that embody the five attributes of well-structured complex systems.

Further Readings

The concept of the object model was first introduced by Jones [F 1979] and Williams [F 1986]. Kay's Ph.D. thesis [F 1969] established the direction for much of the work in object-oriented programming that followed.

Shaw [J 1984] provides an excellent summary regarding abstraction mechanisms in high-order programming languages. The theoretical foundation of abstraction may be found in the work of Liskov and Guttag [H 1986], Guttag [J 1980], and Hilfinger [J 1982]. Parnas [F 1979] provides the seminal work on information hiding. The meaning and importance of hierarchy are discussed in the work edited by Pattee [J 1973].

There is a wealth of literature regarding object-oriented programming. Cardelli and Wegner [J 1985] and Wegner [J 1987] provide an excellent survey of object-based and object-oriented programming languages. The tutorial papers of Stefik and Bobrow [G 1986], Stroustrup [G 1988], and Nygaard [G 1986] are good starting points on the important issues of object-oriented programming. The books by Cox [G 1986], Meyer [F 1988], Schmucker [G 1986], and Kim and Lochovsky [F 1989] offer extended coverage of these topics.

Object-oriented design methods were first formalized by Booch [F 1981, 1982, 1986, 1987, 1989]. Variations of this method include HOOD [F 1987], as used in the European Space Station project, and GOOD, as introduced by Seidewitz and Stark [F 1988]. Similar object-oriented design methods have been proposed by Wirfs-Brock and Wilkerson [F 1989] (emphasizing a responsibility-driven approach), Constantine

[F 1989], and Wasserman [F 1989]. Related works include Ross [F 1987] on the topic of entity modeling, and Abelson and Sussman [H 1985] on the general topic of programming.

Object-oriented analysis methods were introduced by Shlaer and Mellor [B 1988] and Bailin [B 1988], with later contributions by Coad and Yourdon [B 1990].

An excellent collection of papers dealing with all topics of object-oriented computing may be found in Peterson [G 1987] and Schriver and Wegner [G 1987]. The proceedings of several yearly conferences on object-oriented computing are also excellent sources of material. Three of the more interesting forums include the USENIX C++ conferences, OOPSLA (Object-Oriented Programming Systems, Languages, and Applications), and ECOOP (European Conference on Object-Oriented Programming).

Classes and Objects

Both the engineer and the artist must be intimately familiar with the materials of their trade. When we use object-oriented methods to design complex software systems, the basic building blocks are classes and objects. Since we have thus far provided only informal definitions of these two elements, in this chapter we turn to a detailed study of the nature of classes and objects, including an examination of guidelines for crafting quality abstractions and mechanisms.

3.1 The Nature of an Object

What Is and What Isn't an Object

The ability to recognize physical objects is a skill that humans learn at a very early age. A brightly colored ball will attract an infant's attention, but typically, if you hide the ball, the child will not try to look for it; when the object leaves her field of vision, as far as she can determine, it ceases to exist. It is not until near the age of one that a child normally develops what is called the *object concept*, a skill that is of critical importance to future cognitive development. Show a ball to a one-year-old and then hide it, and she will usually search for it even though it is not visible. Through the object concept, a child comes to realize that objects have a permanence and identity apart from any operations upon them [1].

Earlier, we informally defined an object as a tangible entity that exhibits some well-defined behavior. From the perspective of human cognition, an object is any of the following:

- A tangible and/or visible thing
- Something that may be apprehended intellectually
- Something toward which thought or action is directed

Thus, we add to our informal definition the idea that an object models some part of reality and is therefore something that exists in time and space. Indeed, in software, the term *object* was first formally applied in the Simula language, and objects typically existed in Simula programs to simulate some aspect of reality [2].

Real-world objects are not the only kinds of objects that are of interest to us in software design. Other important kinds of objects are inventions of the design process whose collaborations with other such objects serve as the mechanisms that provide some higher level behavior [3]. This leads us to the more refined definition of Smith and Tockey, who suggest that "an object represents an individual, identifiable item, unit, or entity, either real or abstract, with a well-defined role in the problem domain" [4]. In even more general terms, we define an object as anything with a crisply defined boundary [5].

Consider for a moment a manufacturing plant that processes composite materials for making such diverse items as bicycle frames and airplane wings. Manufacturing plants are often divided into separate shops: mechanical, chemical, electrical, and so forth. Shops are further divided into cells, and in each cell we have some collection of machines, such as die stamps, presses, and lathes. Along a manufacturing line, we might find vats containing raw materials, which are used in a chemical process to produce blocks of composite materials, which in turn are formed and shaped to produce end items, such as bicycle frames and airplane wings. Each of the tangible things we have mentioned thus far is an object. A lathe has a crisply defined boundary that separates it from the block of composite material it operates upon; a bicycle frame has a crisply defined boundary that distinguishes it from a cell of machines.

Some objects may have crisp conceptual boundaries, yet represent intangible events or processes. For example, a chemical process in a manufacturing plant may be treated as an object, because it has a well-defined conceptual boundary, interacts with certain other objects in a set of operations that unfolds over time, and exhibits a well-defined behavior. Similarly, consider a CAD/CAM system for modeling solids. Where two solids such as a sphere and a cube intersect, they may form an irregular line of intersection. Although it does not exist apart from the sphere and the cube, this line is still an object with crisply defined conceptual boundaries.

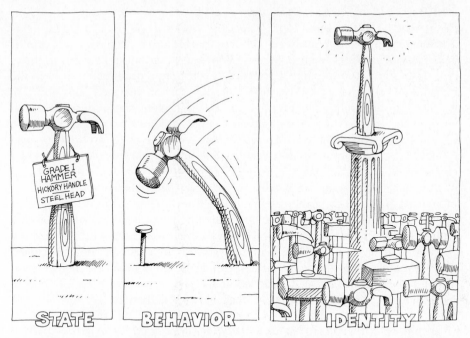

An object has state, exhibits some well-defined behavior, and has a unique identity.

Some objects may be tangible, yet have fuzzy physical boundaries. Objects such as rivers, fog, and crowds of people fit this definition. Just as the person holding a hammer tends to see everything in the world as a nail, so the developer with an object-oriented mindset begins to think that everything in the world is an object. This perspective is a little naive, because there are some things that are distinctly not objects. For example, attributes such as time, beauty, or color are not objects, nor are emotions such as love and anger. On the other hand, these things are all potentially properties of other objects. For example, we might say that a man (an object) loves his wife (another object), or that a particular cat (yet another object) has gray fur.

Thus, it is useful to say that an object is something that has crisply defined boundaries, but this is not enough to guide us in distinguishing one object from another, nor does it allow us to judge the quality of our abstractions. Our experience therefore suggests the following definition:

An object has state, behavior, and identity; the structure and behavior of similar objects are defined in their common class; the terms instance and object are interchangeable.

The following sections examine the terms of this formal definition.

State

The Meaning of State. Consider a vending machine that dispenses soft drinks. The usual behavior of such objects is such that when one puts coins in a slot and pushes a button to make a selection, eventually a drink emerges from the machine. What happens if a user first makes a selection and then puts money in the slot? Most vending machines just sit and do nothing, because the user has violated the basic assumptions of their operation. Similarly, suppose that the user ignores the warning light that says "Correct change only," and puts in extra money. Most machines are user-hostile; they will happily swallow the excess coins.

In each of these circumstances, we see how the behavior of an object is influenced by its history: the order in which one operates upon the object is important. The reason for this time-dependent behavior is the existence of state within the object. For example, one essential state associated with the vending machine is the amount of money currently entered by a user but not yet applied to a selection. Other important properties include the amount of change available and the quantity of soft drinks on hand.

From this example, we may form the following definition:

The state of an object encompasses all of the (usually static) properties of the object plus the current (usually dynamic) values of each of these properties.

For example, another property of a vending machine is that it can accept coins. This is a static property, meaning that it is an essential characteristic of a vending machine. On the other hand, the actual quantity of coins accepted at any given moment represents the dynamic value of this property, and is affected by the order of operations upon the machine. This quantity increases as a user inserts coins, and then decreases when a salesperson services the machine. Our definition says that values are "usually dynamic" because in some cases values are static. For example, the serial number of a vending machine is a static property with a static value.

A property is an inherent or distinctive characteristic, trait, quality, or feature that contributes to making an object uniquely that object. For example, one essential property of an elevator is that it is constrained to travel up and down and not horizontally. Properties are usually static, because attributes such as these are unchanging and fundamental to the nature of the object. We say "usually" static, because in some circumstances the properties of an object may change. For example, consider an autonomous robot that can learn about its environment. It may first recognize an object that appears to be a fixed barrier, only to learn later that this object is in fact a door that can be opened. In this case, the object created by the robot as it builds its conceptual model of the world gains new properties as new knowledge is acquired.

All properties have some value. This value might be a simple quantity, or it might denote another object. For example, part of the state of an elevator might have the value three, denoting the current floor on which the elevator is located. In the case of the vending machine, the state of the vending machine encompasses many other objects, such as a collection of soft drinks. These individual drinks are in fact distinct objects; their properties are different from those of the machine (they can be consumed, whereas a vending machine cannot), and they can be operated upon in distinctly different ways. Thus, we distinguish between objects and simple values: simple quantities such as the number three are "atemporal, unchangeable, and non-instantiated," whereas objects "exist in time, are changeable, have state, are instantiated, and can be created, destroyed, and shared" [6].

The fact that every object has state implies that every object takes up some amount of space, be it in the physical world or in computer memory.

Examples of State. Consider the structure of a personnel record. In C++ we might write the following declaration:

```
struct PersonnelRecord
{
    char   *name[100];
    int    socialSecurityNumber;
    char   *department[10];
    float  salary;
};
```

Each component of this structure denotes a particular property of the abstraction. This declaration denotes a class, not an object, because it does not represent a specific instance. To declare objects of this class, we must write

```
PersonnelRecord deb, dave, karen, jim, tom, denise;
```

Here, we have six distinct objects, each of which takes up some amount of space in memory. None of these objects shares its space with any other object, although each of them has the same properties; thus their states have a common representation.

It is good engineering practice to encapsulate the state of an object rather than expose it as in the preceding declaration. For example, we might rewrite that class declaration as follows:

```
class PersonnelRecord {
public:
    char   *employeeName () const;
    int    employeeSocialSecurityNumber () const;
    char   *employeeDepartment () const;
protected:
    void   setEmployeeName (char *name);
    void   setEmployeeSocialSecurityNumber (int number);
    void   setEmployeeDepartment (char *department);
    void   setEmployeeSalary (float salary);
    float  employeeSalary () const;
private:
    char   *name[100];
    int    socialSecurityNumber;
```

```
char *department[10];
float salary;
};
```

This declaration appears slightly more complicated, but it is vastly superior for a number of reasons. Specifically, we have written this class so that its representation is hidden from all other clients. If we change the structure of this class, we may have to recompile some code, but semantically, no client will be affected by this change (in other words, existing code will not break). Also, we have captured our design decisions about the problem space by explicitly stating the operations that we may perform upon objects of this class. In particular, we grant all clients the right to retrieve the name, social security number, and department of an employee, but only special clients have permission to set the values of these properties. Furthermore, only special clients may retrieve the salary of an employee, whereas normal clients may not. Another reason why this declaration is better than the previous one has to do with reuse. As we will see in a later section, inheritance makes it possible for us to reuse this abstraction, and then specialize it in interesting ways.

As a result of this practice, we may say that all objects within a system encapsulate some state, and that all of the state within a system is encapsulated by objects.

Behavior

The Meaning of Behavior. No object exists in isolation. Rather, objects are acted upon, and themselves act upon other objects. Thus, we may say that

Behavior is how an object acts and reacts, in terms of its state changes and message passing.

In other words, "The behavior of an object is completely defined by its actions" [7].

An operation is some action that one object performs upon another in order to elicit a reaction. For example, a client might invoke the operations Add and Pop to grow and shrink a queue object, respectively. A client might also invoke the operation Length_Of, which returns a value denoting the size of the queue object, but does not alter the state of the queue itself. In languages such as Smalltalk, we speak of one object passing a message to another. Generally, a message is simply an operation that one object performs upon another, although the mechanism used is somewhat different. For our purposes, the terms *operation* and *message* are interchangeable.

In object-based and object-oriented programming languages, operations that clients may perform upon an object are typically declared as *methods*, which are part of the declaration of the class of the object. C++ uses the term *member function* to denote the same concept, so we will use the terms *method* and *member function* interchangeably.

Examples of Behavior. Consider the declaration of a queue class in Ada:

```
generic
    type Item is private;
package Simple_Queue is

    type Queue is limited private;

    procedure Copy   (From_The_Queue : in      Queue;
                      To_The_Queue   : in out Queue);
    procedure Clear (The_Queue       : in out Queue);
    procedure Add   (The_Item        : in      Item;
                      To_The_Queue   : in out Queue);
    procedure Pop   (The_Queue       : in out Queue);

    function Is_Equal   (Left         : in Queue;
                         Right        : in Queue) return Boolean;
    function Length_Of (The_Queue : in Queue) return Natural;
    function Is_Empty  (The_Queue : in Queue) return Boolean;
    function Front_Of  (The_Queue : in Queue) return Item;

    generic
        with procedure Process (The_Item : in  Item;
                                Continue : out Boolean);
    procedure Iterate (Over_The_Queue : in Queue);

    Overflow  : exception;
    Underflow : exception;

private
    ...
end Simple_Queue;
```

The type `Queue` represents a class, not an object. Because this is a generic package, we have a parameterized class. In order to declare queue objects whose elements are all integer values, we would first instantiate the generic package:

```
package Integer_Queue is new Simple_Queue (Item => Integer);
```

Next, we may declare four queue objects as follows:

```
A, B, C, D : Integer_Queue.Queue;
use Integer_Queue;
```

Continuing, we may operate upon these objects as in the following code fragment:

```
Add(1, To_The_Queue => A);
Add(3, To_The_Queue => A);
Add(5, To_The_Queue => A);
Copy(From_The_Queue => A, To_The_Queue => B);
Pop(B);
Pop(B);
```

After execution of these statements, the queue denoted by A would contain three items (with 1 at its front), and the queue denoted by B would contain only one item (with 3 at its front). Each of these objects embodies some state, and this state affects the behavior of each object.

The Meaning of Operations. In practice, we have found that a client typically performs five kinds of operations upon an object. The three most common kinds of operations follow:

- Modifier   An operation that alters the state of an object;
                      a writer or accessor operation

- Selector   An operation that accesses the state of an
                      object, but does not alter the state; a reader
                      operation

- Iterator   An operation that permits all parts of an object
                      to be accessed in some well-defined order[*]

Because these operations are so logically dissimilar, we have found it useful to apply a coding style that highlights their differences. For example, in declaring the package `Simple_Queue`, we first declare all modifiers as procedures (the operations `Copy`, `Clear`, `Add`, and `Pop`), then declare all selectors as functions (the operations `Is_Equal`, `Length_Of`, `Is_Empty`, and `Front_Of`), and then declare any iterators as generic procedures (the operation `Iterate`).

In languages such as Smalltalk, C++, and CLOS, it is possible to declare two other kinds of operations:

- Constructor   An operation that creates an object and/or
                      initializes its state

- Destructor   An operation that frees the state of an object
                      and/or destroys the object itself

In C++, constructors and destructors are declared as part of the definition of a class, whereas in Smalltalk and CLOS, such operations are typically part of the protocol of a metaclass (that is, the class of a class).

In Smalltalk, operations may only be declared as methods, since the language does not allow us to declare procedures or functions separate from any class. In contrast, languages such as Object Pascal, C++, CLOS, and Ada allow the developer to write operations as free subprograms. *Free subprograms* are procedures or functions that serve as nonprimitive operations upon an object or objects of the same or different classes. Free subprograms are typically grouped according to the classes upon which they are built; therefore, we call such collections of free subprograms *class utilities*. For example, given the preceding

---

[*] Lippman suggests a slightly different categorization: manager functions, implementor functions, helping functions, and access functions [8].

declaration of the package `Integer_Queue`, we might write the following procedure declaration in a separate package of class utilities:

```
procedure Pop_Until_Item_Found (The_Queue : in out Integer_Queue.Queue;
                                The_Item  : in       Integer);

Item_Not_Found : exception;
```

The purpose of this operation is to pop the queue repeatedly until the given item is found at the head of the queue. If the queue is emptied before the item is found, then the exception is raised. This operation is not primitive; it can be built from lower level operations that are already a part of the `Simple_Queue` class.

Thus, we may say that all methods are operations, but not all operations are methods: some operations may be expressed as free subprograms. In practice, we are inclined to declare most operations as methods, although as we will discuss in a later section, there are sometimes compelling reasons to do otherwise, such as when a particular operation affects two or more objects of different classes, and there is no particular benefit in declaring that operation in one class over the other.

Collectively, all of the methods and free subprograms associated with a particular object comprise the *protocol* of that object. The protocol of an object thus defines the envelope of that object's allowable behavior, and comprises the entire static and dynamic outside view of the object. For example, it is meaningful to pop a queue, but popping is simply not part of the nature of a vending machine.

Objects as Machines. The existence of state within an object means that the order in which operations are invoked is important. This gives rise to the idea that each object is like a tiny, independent machine [9]. Indeed, for some objects, this time ordering of operations is so pervasive that we can best formally characterize the behavior of the object in terms of an equivalent finite state machine.

Objects may be either active or passive. An *active object* is simply one that encompasses its own thread of control, whereas a *passive object* does not. Active objects are generally autonomous, meaning that they can exhibit some behavior without being operated upon by another object. Passive objects, on the other hand, can only undergo a state change when explicitly acted upon. In this manner, the active objects in our system serve as the roots of control. If our system involves multiple threads of control, then we will usually have multiple active objects. Sequential systems have exactly one active object at a time (that is, exactly one thread of control).

Identity

The Meaning of Identity. Khoshafian and Copeland offer the following definition:

> *"Identity is that property of an object which distinguishes it from all other objects"* [10].

They go on to note that "most programming and database languages use variable names to distinguish temporary objects, mixing addressability and identity. Most database systems use identifier keys to distinguish persistent objects, mixing data value and identity" [11]. The failure to recognize the difference between the name of an object and the object itself is the source of many kinds of errors in object-oriented programming.

Examples of Identity. Consider the following declaration in Object Pascal:

```
TPaletteItem = object(TObject)

    kId       : Integer;
    kFrame    : Rect;

    procedure TPaletteItem.Initialize (ID : Integer; Frame : Rect);
    procedure TPaletteItem.Free; override;
    procedure TPaletteItem.Draw (Area : Rect);
    procedure TPaletteItem.Highlight (FromHL, ToHL : HLState);

    function TPaletteItem.IsMouseHit (TheMouse : Point) : Boolean;

end;
```

`TPaletteItem` is a class and must therefore be included in the type declarations within a program or block.

To declare instances of this class, we might write the following:

```
Item_1, Item_2, Item_3 : TPaletteItem;
```

This declaration must be located among part of the variable declarations within a program or block.

As Figure 3-1a shows, the elaboration of this declaration sets aside three locations in memory (called *object reference variables* in Object Pascal terminology) whose names are `Item_1`, `Item_2`, and `Item_3`, respectively, but whose initial values are undefined. In other words, these names do not currently designate any object. To create an object, we must explicitly use the Object Pascal procedure `new`:

```
new(Item_1); new(Item_2);
```

Upon execution, each of these statements creates one object, and then gives the object reference variable some value that designates this object. These statements do not initialize the state of the objects, so we must do so explicitly:

```
SetRect(ARect, 1, 1, 32, 32);
Item_1.Initialize(1001, ARect);
SetRect(ARect, 1, 33, 32, 64);
Item_2.Initialize(1002, ARect);
```

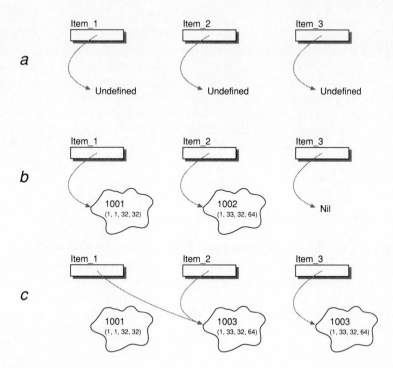

Figure 3-1
The Meaning of Object Identity

Figure 3-1b illustrates the result of executing these statements.

Because one object is distinguished from all others, the identity of each object is preserved even when the state of that object is completely changed. This is like the Zen question about a river: Is a river still the same river from one day to the next, even though the same water never flows through it? For example, we might next execute the statements:

```
Item_2.kId := 1003;
new(Item_3);
SetRect(ARect, 1, 33, 32, 64);
Item_3.Initialize(1003, ARect);
```

The object designated by Item_2 still exists, although its state has changed. We have also created another object, designated by Item_3, that may be distinguished from the object designated by Item_2, although these two objects have the same values for their state. Notice that we say "the object designated by Item_2," rather than "the object Item_2." The first phrase is more precise, although we will sometimes uses these phrases interchangeably.

What happens if we now execute the following statement?

```
Item_1 := Item_2;
```

A very bad thing happens, indeed, as illustrated by Figure 3-1c. First, the object originally designated by `Item_1` is no longer accessible; it is garbage that can never be referenced again. Also, `Item_1` and `Item_2` now designate the same object. This is a situation we call *structural sharing*, meaning that a given object can be named in more than one way (in other words, it has an alias). Structural sharing is often dangerous because it allows us to alter the state of an object via one name without notice to clients who use the second name. For example, executing the statement

```
Item_1.kId := 1004;
```

alters the state of the object designated by `Item_2` as well.

The Meaning of Object Assignment and Equality. Structural sharing takes place when the identity of an object is duplicated by assignment to a second name. In most interesting object-oriented applications, using aliases simply cannot be avoided. It is very important, therefore, to recognize when structural sharing occurs, so that the desired semantics are achieved. All the programming languages we use in this book permit structural sharing, using the following assignment operators:

- Smalltalk   ←
- Object Pascal   :=
- C++   =
- CLOS   let
- Ada   :=

To copy an object without introducing structural sharing, Smalltalk provides the methods `shallowCopy` (which copies the object, but shares its state) and `deepCopy` (which copies the object as well as its state). Object Pascal supplies similar facilities through the predefined methods `Clone` and `ShallowClone`. In C++, it is common practice to overload the assignment operator, in order to provide copy semantics upon assignment rather than structural sharing. In both CLOS and Ada, one must explicitly write operations that provide copy semantics for each class.

Closely related to the issue of assignment is that of equality. Although it seems like a simple concept, equality can mean one of two things. First, equality can mean that two names designate the same object. Second, equality can mean that the objects are different but their state is identical. For example, in Figure 3-1c, both kinds of equality evaluate to true between `Item_1` and `Item_2`. However, only the second kind of equality evaluates to true between `Item_2` and `Item_3`.

Just as they use different assignment operators, different languages may treat equality differently. For testing whether or not two names designate the same object, we have the following operators:

- Smalltalk   `==`
- Object Pascal   `=`
- C++   `==`
- CLOS   `eql`
- Ada   `=`

Smalltalk and C++ permit these operators to be redefined. For testing whether or not the states of two objects are equal, we have the following operators:

- Smalltalk   `=`
- Object Pascal   *user defined*
- C++   *user defined*
- CLOS   `equalp`
- Ada   *user defined*

The Lifetime of an Object. The lifetime of an object extends from the time it is first created (and thus consumes space) until that space is reclaimed. To explicitly create an object, we must use the following methods:

- Smalltalk   `new`
- Object Pascal   `new`
- C++   `new`
- CLOS   `make-instance`
- Ada   `new`

In C++, whenever an object is created, the constructor defined in that object's class is automatically invoked. Smalltalk, C++, and CLOS permit their respective creation methods to be overridden.

In C++ and Ada, the method `new` creates an object on the program's free store (also called the *heap*). In these two languages, it is also possible to create a transitory object on the program's stack frame simply by declaring a variable of a given class and elaborating its declaration.

An object exists even if all references to it are lost as long as it continues to consume space. In Smalltalk and CLOS, objects are destroyed automatically during garbage collection when all references to them have been lost. In C++ and Ada, an object created on the program's stack frame is automatically destroyed when control passes beyond the scope of the variable designating that object. To explicitly destroy an object, we may use the following methods:

- Smalltalk   `release`
- Object Pascal   `free`
- C++   `delete`
- Ada   `delete`

In C++, whenever an object is destroyed, the destructor defined in that object's class is automatically invoked. In C++ and Ada, the method `delete` is applicable only to objects that were created explicitly on the free store. Also, both Smalltalk and C++ permit their respective destruction methods to be overridden.

3.2 Relationships Among Objects

Kinds of Relationships

An object by itself is intensely uninteresting. Objects contribute to the behavior of a system by collaborating with one another. As Ingalls suggests, "Instead of a bit-grinding processor raping and plundering data structures, we have a universe of well-behaved objects that courteously ask each other to carry out their various desires" [12]. For example, consider the object structure of an airplane, which has been defined as "a collection of parts having an inherent tendency to fall to earth, and requiring constant effort and supervision to stave off that outcome" [13]. Only the collaborative efforts of all the component objects of an airplane enable it to fly.

The relationship between any two objects encompasses the assumptions that each makes about the other, including what operations can be performed and what behavior results. We have found that two kinds of object hierarchies are of particular interest in object-oriented design, namely:

- Using relationships
- Containing relationships

Seidewitz and Stark call these *seniority* and *parent/child* relationships, respectively [14].

Using Relationships

The Meaning of Using Relationships Among Objects. Figure 3-2 illustrates using relationships among several objects. In this figure, a line between two object icons represents the existence of a using relationship between the two and means that messages may pass along this path. As the magnified part of the figure shows, if the object An Escalator Controller uses An Escalator, then the first object may send messages to the second (as shown by the

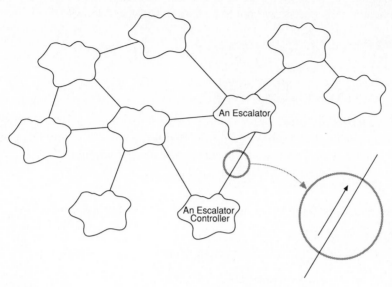

Figure 3-2
Using Relationships Among Objects

directed line). Message passing between two objects is usually unidirectional, although bidirectional communication is also possible.

Given a collection of objects involved in using relationships, each object may play one of three roles:

- Actor

  An object that can operate upon other objects but that is never operated upon by other objects; in some contexts, the terms *active object* and *actor* are interchangeable

- Server

  An object that never operates upon other objects; it is only operated upon by other objects

- Agent

  An object that can both operate upon other objects and be operated upon by other objects; an agent is usually created to do some work on behalf of an actor or another agent

Examples of Using Relationships Among Objects. In a simple chemical process, we might have two valves that control the flow of two different liquids into a single crucible and another valve that drains the crucible. Certain chemical reactions also require a temperature ramp, which slowly raises the temperature of a substance, holds it at that temperature for a fixed period, and then lets it cool to ambient temperature. One of the key abstractions in such problems is thus a heater, whose class we might declare in CLOS as follows:

```
(defclass heater () ())

(defmethod turn_on ((h heater)) ... )
(defmethod turn_off ((h heater)) ... )
(defmethod current_temperature ((h heater)) ... )
```

Here we define the class `heater` and include three methods. We have shown the implementation of each method in elided form, since it is not important to our discussion here. To create an instance of this class, we might write

```
(setq a_heater (make-instance 'heater))
```

We might next capture our abstraction of a crucible class as follows:

```
(defclass crucible ()
    ((temperature :initform 0 :accessor set_point)))

(defmethod set_temperature ((c crucible) (f float) (s integer))
    (turn_on a_heater)
    ...
    (turn_off a_heater))
```

We have partly elided the implementation of the method `set_temperature`. The desired behavior of this method is to bring the crucible `c` to the temperature `f` for `s` seconds. Notice that to achieve this behavior, the implementation of this method includes sending the messages `turn_on` and `turn_off` to the heater object.

To create an instance of this crucible class we might write

```
(setq a_crucible (make-instance 'crucible))
```

Next, we might declare a class representing valves and create three instances:

```
(defclass valve () ())

(setq v_1 (make-instance 'valve))
(setq v_2 (make-instance 'valve))
(setq v_3 (make-instance 'valve))
```

We will assume the existence of all the methods necessary to open and close valves. Continuing, we might next declare a class representing a process controller, which coordinates the actions of the valves and the crucible, and then create one instance:

```
(defclass process_controller () ())

(defmethod start_process ((c process_controller)) ... )

(setq a_process_controller (make-instance 'process_controller))
```

Now, consider what happens when we invoke the following method:

(start_process a_process_controller)

The object named `a_process_controller` first sends messages to the objects named `valve_1` and `valve_2` (to open and then close the valves) and then sends the message `set_temperature` to the object named `a_crucible`. The object named `a_crucible` in turn sends the messages `turn_on` and `turn_off` to the object named `a_heater`. Finally, the object `a_process_controller` sends a message to the object `valve_3` to drain the crucible.

In this example, the objects `a_heater`, `valve_1`, `valve_2`, and `valve_3` act as servers: they are operated upon, but they do not operate upon any other object. The objects `a_crucible` and `a_process_controller` are both agents, because they both act and react.

The Meaning of Synchronization. Whenever one object passes a message to another with which it has a using relationship, the two objects must be synchronized in some manner. For objects in a completely sequential application, this synchronization is usually accomplished by subprogram calls. However, objects involved with multiple threads of control require more sophisticated synchronization in order to deal with the problems of mutual exclusion that can occur in concurrent systems. This leads us to yet another way to classify kinds of objects:

- Sequential object   A passive object whose semantics are guaranteed only in the presence of a single thread of control

- Blocking object   A passive object whose semantics are guaranteed in the presence of multiple threads of control

- Concurrent object   An active object whose semantics are guaranteed in the presence of multiple threads of control

All the examples shown thus far in this chapter are sequential objects.

Containing Relationships

The Meaning of Containing Relationships Among Objects. We may decide that a particular escalator is made up of other objects such as a motor and a motion sensor. In other words, the motor and motion sensor are encapsulated as part of the escalator's state. We illustrate this concept in Figure 3-3.

There are trade-offs between containing and using relationships. Containing rather than using an object is sometimes better because containing reduces the number of objects that must be visible at the level of the enclosing object. On the other hand, using is sometimes better than containing because containing

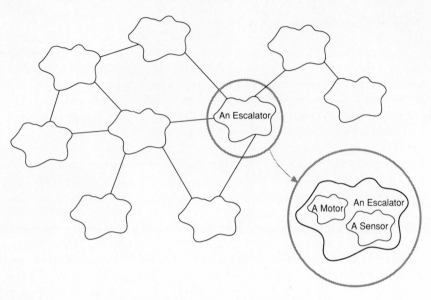

Figure 3-3
Containing Relationships Among Objects

leads to undesirable tighter coupling among objects. Intelligent engineering decisions require careful weighing of these two factors.

Examples of Containing Relationships Among Objects. If we are building an abstraction of an apartment, we might decide that all apartment objects should encompass a kitchen, a bathroom, a bedroom, and a family room. We might write this in Smalltalk as follows:

```
Object subclass: #Apartment
        instanceVariableNames: 'aKitchen aBathroom aBedroom aFamilyRoom '
        classVariableNames: ''
        poolDictionaries: ''
        category: 'Simulation'
```

Whenever we create an object of the class `Apartment`, we would also like to create its component objects. Assuming that we have classes representing kitchens, bathrooms, bedrooms, and family rooms, we might define the following method for the class `Apartment`:

initialize

```
"Initialize the apartment by creating its rooms."
aKitchen ← Kitchen new.
aBathroom ← Bathroom new.
aBedroom ← Bedroom new.
aFamilyRoom ← FamilyRoom new.
```

Now we can execute the following statement to create and initialize a local apartment object:

```
| anApartment |
anApartment ← Apartment new initialize.
```

and consequently create its four subobjects as a side effect of initialization. Because Smalltalk encapsulates its state, these subobjects are not visible to clients outside of the apartment object. Objects such as `anApartment` are known as *compound*, *composite*, or *aggregate objects*.

3.3 The Nature of a Class

What Is and What Isn't a Class

The concepts of a class and an object are tightly interwoven, for we cannot talk about an object without regard for its class. However, there are important differences between these two terms. Whereas an object is a concrete entity that exists in time and space, a class represents only an abstraction, the "essence" of an object, as it were. Thus, we may speak of the class Mammal, which represents the characteristics common to all mammals. To identify a particular mammal in this class, we must speak of "this mammal" or "that mammal."

In everyday terms, we may define a class as "a group, set, or kind marked by common attributes or a common attribute; a group division, distinction, or rating based on quality, degree of competence, or condition" [15].[*] In the context of object-oriented design, we define a class as follows:

A class is a set of objects that share a common structure and a common behavior.

A single object is simply an instance of a class.

What isn't a class? An object is not a class, although, curiously, as we will describe later, a class may be an object. Objects that share no common structure and behavior cannot be grouped in a class because, by definition, they are unrelated, except by their general nature as objects.

The Outside and Inside Views of a Class

Meyer [16] and Snyder [17] have both suggested that programming is largely a matter of "contracting": the various functions of a larger problem are decomposed into smaller problems by subcontracting them to different elements of the design. Nowhere is this idea more evident than in the design of classes.

---

[*] By permission. From *Webster's Third New International Dictionary* © 1986 by Merriam-Webster Inc., publisher of the Merriam-Webster ® dictionaries.

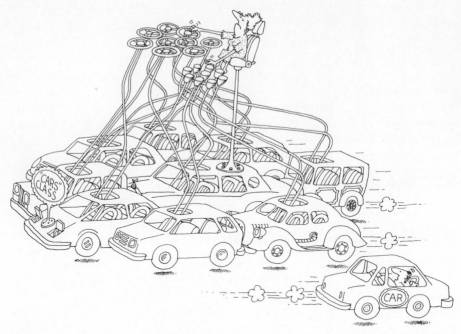

A class represents a set of objects that share a common structure and a common behavior.

Whereas an individual object is a concrete entity that performs some role in the overall system, the class captures the structure and behavior common to all related objects. Thus, a class serves as a sort of binding contract between an abstraction and all of its clients. By capturing these design decisions in the interface of a class, a strongly typed programming language can detect violations of this contract during compilation.

This view of programming as contracting leads us to distinguish between the outside view and the inside view of a class. The *interface* of a class provides its outside view and therefore emphasizes the abstraction while hiding its structure and the secrets of its behavior. This interface primarily consists of the declarations of all the operations applicable to instances of this class, but it may also include the declaration of other classes, constants, variables, and exceptions as needed to complete the abstraction. By contrast, the *implementation* of a class is its inside view, which encompasses the secrets of its behavior. The implementation of a class primarily consists of the implementation of all of the operations defined in the interface of the class.

We can further divide the interface of a class into three parts:

• Public	A declaration that forms part of the interface of a class and is visible to all clients that are visible to it

- Protected   A declaration that forms part of the interface of
                           a class but is not visible to any other classes
                           except its subclasses

- Private   A declaration that forms part of the interface of
                           a class but is not visible to any other classes

Of the languages we use in this book, C++ does the best job in allowing a developer to make explicit distinctions among these different parts of a class's interface. If necessary, one may use structures in C++ to define a completely unencapsulated class. Ada permits declarations to be public or private, but not protected. In Smalltalk, Object Pascal, and CLOS, these distinctions must be enforced by programming convention.

The state of an object must have some representation, which is typically expressed as constant and variable declarations placed in the private part of a class's interface. In this manner, the representation common to the objects of a class is encapsulated, and changes to this representation do not functionally affect any clients. In fact, in Smalltalk, such declarations may only be private. Languages such as C++, CLOS, and Ada permit declarations to be public as well as private, but in Object Pascal the structure of a class is always public.

The careful reader may wonder why the representation of an object is part of the interface of a class (albeit a private part), not of its implementation. The reason is one of practicality; to do otherwise requires either object-oriented hardware or very sophisticated compiler technology. Specifically, when a compiler processes an object declaration such as the following (in C++):

```
Shape aShape;
```

it must know how much memory to allocate to the object. If we defined the representation of an object in the implementation of a class, we would have to complete the class's implementation before we could use any clients, thus defeating the very purpose of separating the outside and inside views of a class.

The constants and variables that form the representation of a class are known by various terms, depending upon the particular language. Smalltalk uses the term *instance variable*, Object Pascal uses the term *field*, C++ uses the term *member object*, and CLOS uses the term *slot*. We will use these terms interchangeably to denote parts of the representation of the state of an object.

3.4 Relationships Among Classes

Kinds of Relationships

Consider for a moment the similarities and differences among the following classes of objects: flowers, daisies, red roses, yellow roses, and petals. We can make the following observations:

- A daisy is a kind of flower.
- A rose is a (different) kind of flower.
- Red roses and yellow roses are both kinds of roses.
- A petal is a part of both kinds of flowers

From this simple example we conclude that classes, like objects, do not exist in isolation. Rather, for a particular problem domain, the key abstractions are usually related in a variety of interesting ways, forming the class structure of our design [18].

We assert relationships between two classes for one of two reasons. First, a class relationship might indicate some sort of sharing. For example, daisies and roses are both kinds of flowers, meaning that both have brightly colored petals, both emit a fragrance, and so on. Second, a class relationship might indicate some kind of semantic connection. Thus, we say that red roses and yellow roses are more alike than are daisies and roses, and daisies and roses are more closely related than are petals and flowers.

There are three basic kinds of class relationships [19]. The first of these is generalization, denoting a "kind of" relationship. For instance, a rose is a kind of flower, meaning that a rose is a specialized subclass of the more general class, flower. The second is aggregation, which denotes a "part of" relationship. Thus, a petal is not a kind of a flower; it is a part of a flower. The third is association. Briefly, association denotes some semantic connection among otherwise unrelated classes. As an example, roses and candles are largely independent classes, but they both represent things that we might use to decorate a dinner table.

Several common approaches have evolved in programming languages to express generalization, aggregation, and association. Specifically, most object-based and object-oriented languages support some combination of the following relationships among classes:

- Inheritance relationships
- Using relationships
- Instantiation relationships
- Metaclass relationships

An alternate approach to inheritance involves a language mechanism called *delegation*, in which objects are viewed as prototypes (also called *exemplars*) that delegate their behavior to related objects, thus eliminating the need for classes [20].

Inheritance is perhaps the most powerful of these relationships and may be used to express both generalization and association. In our experience, inheritance is a necessary yet insufficient means of expressing all of the rich relationships that may exist among the key abstractions in a given problem domain. We also need using relationships, which support aggregation. Furthermore, we need instantiation relationships, which, like inheritance, support both generalization and association, although in an entirely different way. Metaclass relationships are quite different and are not explicitly supported by every object-based or object-oriented programming language. Basically, a metaclass is the class of a class; thus it allows us to treat classes as objects.

Inheritance Relationships

Examples of Inheritance Relationships Among Classes. After space probes are launched, they report back to ground stations with information regarding the status of important subsystems (such as electrical power and propulsion systems) and different sensors (such as radiation sensors, mass spectrometers, cameras, micrometeorite collision detectors, and so on). Collectively, this relayed information is called *telemetry data*. Telemetry data commonly is transmitted as a bit stream consisting of a header, which includes a time stamp and some key identifying the kind of information that follows, plus several frames of processed data from the various subsystems and sensors. Because this appears to be a straightforward aggregation of different kinds of data, we might be tempted to define a record type for each kind of telemetry data. For example, in C++, we might write

```
struct Time {
    int elapsedDays;
    int seconds;
};

struct ElectricalData {
    Time       timeStamp;
    int        id;
    float      fuelCell1Voltage, fuelCell2Voltage;
    float      fuelCell1Amperes, fuelCell2Amperes;
    float      currentPower;
};
```

There are a number of problems with these declarations. First, the representation of `ElectricalData` is completely unencapsulated. Thus, there is nothing to prevent a client from changing the value of important data such as the `id` or `currentPower` (which is directly proportional to the current voltage and amperes drawn from both fuel cells). Furthermore, the representation of this structure is exposed, so if we were to change the representation (for example, by adding new elements or changing the bit alignment of existing ones), every client would be affected. We would certainly have to recompile every reference to this structure. More importantly, such changes might violate the assumptions that clients had made about this exposed representation and cause the logic in our program to break down. In addition, this structure is largely devoid of meaning. A number of operations could apply to instances of this structure as a whole (such as sending the data, or calculating a check sum to detect errors during transmission), but there is no way to associate these operations with this structure. Lastly, suppose our analysis of the system's requirements reveals the

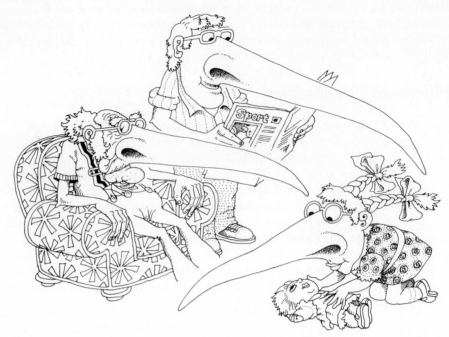

A subclass may inherit the structure and behavior of its superclass.

need for several hundred different kinds of telemetry data, including other electrical data that encompassed the preceding information and also included voltage readings from various test points throughout the system. We would find
that declaring these additional structures would create a considerable amount of
redundancy, both in terms of replicated structures and common functions.

A better way to capture our design decisions would be to declare one class
for each kind of telemetry data. In this manner, we could hide the representation of each class and associate the data with the operations that applied to it.
Still, this approach does not address the problem of redundancy.

A far better solution, therefore, is to capture our design decisions by building a hierarchy of classes, in which specialized classes inherit the structure and
behavior defined by more generalized classes. For example:

```
class TelemetryData {
public:
    TelemetryData ();
    TelemetryData (const TelemetryData&);
    virtual ~TelemetryData ();
    virtual void send ();
    Time currentTime () const;
protected:
    int id;
private:
    Time timeStamp;
};
```

This declares a class with constructors and a destructor, as well as the functions send and currentTime, which are visible to all clients. The member object id is slightly more encapsulated, and because it is declared as protected, it is visible only to classes that further inherit from this class. The member object time is declared as private; thus it is entirely encapsulated and visible only to the body of the class TelemetryData. However, because we have declared the function currentTime as public, it is possible for a client to access the timeStamp, but not change it.

Now, let's rewrite our declaration of the class ElectricalData:

```
class ElectricalData : public TelemetryData {
public:
    ElectricalData (float v1, float v2, float a1, float a2);
    ElectricalData (const ElectricalData&);
    virtual ~ElectricalData ();
    virtual void send ();
    virtual float currentPower () const;
protected:
    float fuelCell1Voltage, fuelCell2Voltage, fuelCell1Amperes, fuelCell2Amperes;
};
```

This class inherits the structure and behavior of the class TelemetryData, but adds to its structure (with the four new member objects) and redefines its behavior (namely, the meaning of the function send). Why don't we have currentPower as a member object, as we did in the earlier declaration of the ElectricalData structure? The reason is that such a declaration is unnecessary; we can just as easily calculate this value on demand with the function currentPower.

The Meaning of Single Inheritance Relationships Among Classes. Simply stated, inheritance is a relationship among classes wherein one class shares the structure or behavior defined in one (*single inheritance*) or more (*multiple inheritance*) other classes. We call the class from which another class inherits its *superclass*. Hence, TelemetryData is a superclass of ElectricalData. Similarly, we call a class that inherits from one or more classes a *subclass*; ElectricalData is a subclass of TelemetryData. Inheritance therefore defines a "kind of" hierarchy among classes, in which a subclass inherits from one or more superclasses. Thus, ElectricalData is a specialized kind of the more generalized class TelemetryData. As we have seen, a subclass typically augments or redefines the existing structure and behavior of its superclasses. The ability of a language to support this kind of inheritance distinguishes object-oriented from object-based programming languages.

Figure 3-4 illustrates the single inheritance relationships among the superclass TelemetryData and its various subclasses. Each relationship-arrow denotes a "kind of" or "is a" relationship. Thus, CameraData is a kind of SensorData, which in turn is a kind of TelemetryData. This is identical to the hierarchy one finds in a semantic net, a tool often used by researchers in cognitive science and artificial intelligence to organize knowledge about the world

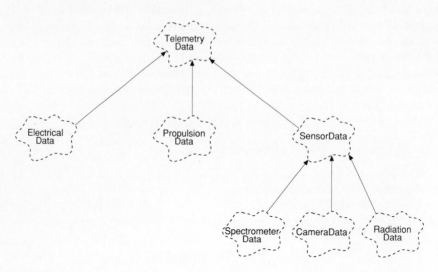

Figure 3-4
Single Inheritance Relationships Among Classes

[21]. Indeed, as we discuss further in Chapter 4, designing a suitable inheritance hierarchy among abstractions is largely a matter of intelligent classification.

We expect that some of the classes in Figure 3-4 will have instances, and some will not. For example, we expect to have instances of each of the most specialized classes, such as `ElectricalData` and `SpectrometerData`. However, we are not likely to have any instances of the intermediate, more generalized classes, such as `SensorData` or even `TelemetryData`. Classes with no instances are called *abstract classes*. An abstract class is written with the expectation that its subclasses will add to its structure and behavior, usually by completing the implementation of its (typically) incomplete methods. In fact, in Smalltalk, a developer may force a subclass to redefine the method introduced in an abstract class by using the method `subclassResponsibility` to implement a body for the abstract class's method. If the subclass fails to redefine it, then invoking the method results in an execution error. C++ similarly allows the developer to assert that an abstract class's method cannot be invoked directly, by initializing its declaration to zero. Such a method is called a *pure virtual function*, and the language prohibits the creation of instances whose class exports such functions.

The most generalized class in a class structure is called the *base class*. Most applications have many such base classes, which represent the most generalized categories of abstractions within the given domain. Some languages include a topmost base class, which serves as the ultimate superclass of all classes. In Smalltalk this class is called `Object`, and in Object Pascal it is named `TObject`. CLOS implicitly defines `standard-class` as the most general superclass of all defclass classes; t is the implicit superclass of standard-class, as well as of most ordinary types. C++ has an anonymous ultimate base class.

A given class typically has two kinds of clients [22]:

- Instances
- Subclasses

It is often useful to define different interfaces for these two kinds of clients [23]. This is precisely the motivation for the public, protected, and private parts of a class definition in C++: a designer can choose what members are visible to instances, to subclasses, and to both clients. In Smalltalk, the developer has less control over visibility: instance variables are visible to subclasses but not to instances, and all methods are visible to both instances and subclasses (one can mark a method as private, but this hiding is not enforced by the language). In Object Pascal, fields and methods are all public, and in CLOS, slots are visible to all subclasses, but their visibility to instances may be controlled by the use of the slot options :reader, :writer, and :accessor.

Inheritance means that subclasses inherit the structure of their superclass. Thus, in our earlier example, the instances of the class ElectricalData include the member objects of the superclass (id and timeStamp), as well as those of the more specialized class (fuelCell1Voltage, fuelCell2Voltage, fuelCell1Amperes, and fuelCell2Amperes). Smalltalk, Object Pascal, C++, and CLOS all permit a subclass to augment the structure of its superclass. In each case, however, the introduction of a new member object whose name duplicates that of an existing member object is treated as an error. Also, none of these languages allows a subclass to reduce the structure of its subclass.

There is a very real tension between inheritance and encapsulation. To a large degree, the use of inheritance exposes some of the secrets of an inherited class. Practically, this means that to understand the meaning of a particular class, you must often study all of its superclasses, sometimes including their inside views.

Subclasses also inherit the behavior of their superclasses. Thus, instances of the class ElectricalData may be acted upon with the operations currentTime (inherited from the superclass), currentPower (defined in the superclass), and send (redefined from the superclass). Most object-oriented programming languages permit methods from a superclass to be inherited as well as excluded and also permit methods to be added and redefined in a subclass. In Smalltalk, Object Pascal, and CLOS, any superclass method may be redefined in a subclass (in CLOS, such operations are called *generic functions*). In Object Pascal, one asserts that an inherited method is to be redefined by using the keyword *override* in the declaration of the subclass. In C++, the developer has a bit more control. Member functions that are declared as *virtual* (such as the function send in our earlier example) may be redefined in a subclass; members declared otherwise may not be redefined (such as the function currentTime).

The Meaning of Single Polymorphism. For the class `TelemetryData`, we might implement the member function `send` as follows:

```
void TelemetryData :: send () {
    // transmit the id
    // transmit the timeStamp
};
```

Notice that we explicitly name the class with which this function is associated. Although the body of this member function is incomplete (we have just commented on the desired action), this example reflects the fact that we may separate the interface and the implementation of a method (in CLOS, if one declares a method in the absence of a generic function, the generic function is implicitly declared). Turning to the implementation of `send` for the class `ElectricalData`, we might write

```
void ElectricalData :: send () {
    TelemetryData::send();
    // transmit the fuelCell1Voltage and the fuelCell2Voltage
    // transmit the fuelCell1Amperes and the fuelCell2Amperes
    // transmit the currentPower
};
```

In the implementation of this member function, the desired behavior is first to invoke the corresponding function defined in the superclass and then to augment this behavior by sending the data associated with this specialized class.

Suppose that we have instances of each of these two classes (although this would not be typical for the class `TelemetryData`):

```
TelemetryData telemetry;
ElectricalData electrical (5.0, -5.0, 3.0, 7.0);
```

Suppose also that the objects designated by the variables named `telemetry` and `electrical` have been created. Now, if we have the following function:

```
void sendTelemetryData (TelemetryData &D) {
    D.send();
};
```

What happens when we invoke the following two statements?

```
sendTelemetryData(telemetry);
sendTelemetryData(electrical);
```

In the first case, we transmit a bit stream consisting of just an `id` and a `timeStamp`, and in the second case, we transmit a bit stream consisting of an `id`, a `timeStamp`, and five other floating-point values. How is this so? Ultimately, the body of the function `sendTelemetryData` simply executes the single statement `D.send()`, which does not explicitly distinguish the class of `D`.

The answer is due to polymorphism. Basically, *polymorphism* is a concept in type theory in which a name (such as the parameter `D`) may denote objects of many different classes that are related by some common superclass. Thus, any object denoted by this name is able to respond to some common set of operations in different ways.

As Cardelli and Wegner note, "Conventional typed languages, such as Pascal, are based on the idea that functions and procedures, and hence operands, have a unique type. Such languages are said to be monomorphic, in the sense that every value and variable can be interpreted to be of one and only one type. Monomorphic programming languages may be contrasted with polymorphic languages in which some values and variables may have more than one type" [24]. The concept of polymorphism was first described by Strachey [25], who spoke of *ad hoc* polymorphism, by which symbols such as "+" could be defined to mean different things. Today, in modern programming languages, we call this concept *overloading*. For example, in C++ and Ada, one may declare procedures and functions with the same names, as long as their invocations can be distinguished by their parameter profiles, consisting of the number and types of their arguments and the types of their returned values. Strachey also spoke of *parametric polymorphism*, which today we simply call *polymorphism*.

Without polymorphism, the developer ends up writing code consisting of large case or switch statements. For example, in Pascal, we could not create a hierarchy of classes for the various kinds of telemetry data; rather, we would have to define a single, large, variant record encompassing the properties associated with all the kinds of data. To distinguish one variant from another, we would have to examine the tag associated with the record. Thus an equivalent procedure to `sendTelemetryData` might be written in Pascal as follows:

```
const
    Electrical   = 1;
    Propulsion   = 2;
    Spectrometer = 3;
...
procedure Send_Telemetry_Data (TheData : Data);
begin
    case TheData.Kind of
        Electrical: SendElectricalData(TheData);
        Propulsion: SendPropulsionData(TheData);
        ...
    end
end;
```

To add another kind of telemetry data, we would have to modify the variant record and add to any case statement that operated upon instances of this record. This is particularly error-prone, and, furthermore, adds instability to the design.

With inheritance, there is no need for a monolithic type, since we may separate different kinds of abstractions. As Kaplan and Johnson note, "Polymorphism is most useful when there are may classes with the same protocols" [26]. With polymorphism, large case statements are unnecessary, because each object implicitly knows its own type.

Inheritance without polymorphism is possible, but it is certainly not very useful. This is the situation in Ada, in which one can declare derived types, but because the language is monomorphic, the actual operation being called is always known at the time of compilation.

Polymorphism and late binding go hand in hand. With polymorphism, the binding of a method to a name is not determined until execution. In C++, the developer may control whether a member function uses early or late binding. Specifically, if the method is declared as virtual, then late binding is employed, and the function is considered to be polymorphic. If this virtual declaration is omitted, then the method uses early binding and thus can be resolved at the time of compilation. How an implementation selects a particular method for execution is described in the sidebar.

Inheritance and Typing. Consider again the redefinition of the member function send:

```
void ElectricalData :: send () {
    TelemetryData::send();
    // transmit the fuelCell1Voltage and the fuelCell2Voltage
    // transmit the fuelCell1Amperes and the fuelCell2Amperes
    // transmit the currentPower
};
```

Most object-oriented programming languages permit the implementation of a subclass's method to invoke a method defined by some superclass. As this example shows, it is common for the implementation of a redefined method to invoke the method of the same name defined by a parent class. In Smalltalk and Object Pascal, one may refer to any method of an immediate ancestor class by using the keywords super and inherited, respectively. In these languages, one may also refer to the object for which a method was invoked by the special parameter named self. In C++, one can invoke the method of any ancestor (as long as it is visible) by prefixing the method name with the name of the class, as in the example; an object may reference itself using the implicitly declared pointer named this. In CLOS, one may use the function call-next-method to achieve a similar effect.

In our experience, a developer usually needs to invoke a superclass method either before or after doing some other action. In this manner, subclass methods play the role of augmenting the behavior defined in the superclass. In CLOS, these different method roles are made explicit by declaring a method with the qualifiers :before, :after, and :around. A method without a qualifier is considered a *primary* method and does the central work of the desired behavior. *Before* methods and *after* methods augment the behavior of a primary method; they are called before and after the primary method, respectively [34]. *Around* methods form a wrapper around a primary method, which may be invoked at some place inside the around method by the call-next-method function.

Invoking a Method

In traditional programming languages, invoking a subprogram is a completely static activity. In Pascal for example, for a statement that calls the subprogram P, the compiler can generate code that creates a new stack frame, places the proper arguments on the stack, and then changes the flow of control to begin executing the code associated with P. However, in languages that support some form of polymorphism, namely, Smalltalk, Object Pascal, C++, and CLOS, invoking an operation is dynamic because the class of the object being operated upon may not be known until runtime. Matters are even more complicated when we add inheritance to the situation. Inheritance without polymorphism is largely the same as a simple subprogram call, but inheritance with polymorphism requires a much more sophisticated technique.

Consider the class hierarchy shown in Figure 3-5, which shows the base class Shape along with three subclasses named Circle, Triangle, and Rectangle. Rectangle also has a subclass, named Solid Rectangle. In the class Shape, suppose that we define the instance variable theCenter (representing the *X* and *Y* center of the shape in some coordinate system), along with the following operations:

- Set Center   Set the (*X*, *Y*) center.
- Draw   Draw the shape.
- Center   Return the current (*X*, *Y*) center.

The operations Set Center and Center are common to all subclasses, and therefore need not be redefined. However, the operation Draw must be redefined by each of the subclasses, since they alone know how to draw themselves. Thus, since the class Shape is an abstract class, Draw has an empty implementation (it is a pure virtual function, in C++ terminology).

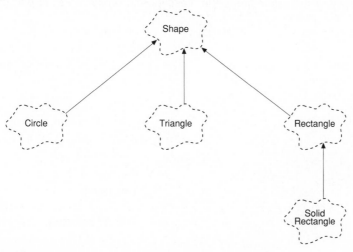

Figure 3-5
Shape Class Diagram

The class `Circle` must include the instance variable `theRadius` and appropriate operations to set and retrieve its value. Here, the operation `Draw` draws a circle of the given radius, centered at (*X, Y*). Similarly, the class `Rectangle` must include the instance variables `theHeight` and `theWidth`, along with appropriate operations to set and retrieve their values. Here, the operation `Draw` draws a rectangle with the given height and width, again centered around (*X, Y*). The subclass `Solid Rectangle` inherits all characteristics of the class `Rectangle`, but redefines the behavior of the operation `Draw`. The semantics of `Draw` for the class `Solid  Rectangle` are to first call `Draw` as defined in its superclass (`Rectangle`) and then color in the shape.

Figure 3-6 illustrates a use of these classes that requires polymorphism. Here, we find a heterogeneous list of shapes, meaning that the list may contain objects of any of the `Shape` subclasses. Suppose now that we have some client object that wishes to draw all of the shapes found in this list. Our approach is to iterate through the list and invoke the operation `Draw` upon each object we encounter. In this situation, the compiler cannot statically generate code to invoke the proper `Draw` operation, because the class of the object being operated upon is not known until runtime.

Because Smalltalk is a typeless language, method dispatch is completely dynamic. When the client sends the message `Draw` to a shape found in the list, here is what happens:

- The shape object looks up the message in its class's message dictionary.
- If the message is found, the code for that locally defined method is invoked.
- If the message is not found, we look for the message in each superclass.

This process continues up the superclass hierarchy until the message is found, or until we reach the topmost base class, `Object`, without finding the message. In the latter case, Smalltalk ultimately passes the message `doesNotUnderstand`, to signal an error.

The key to this algorithm is the message dictionary, which is part of each

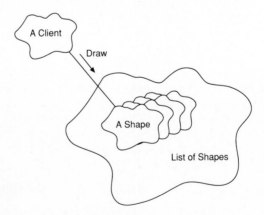

Figure 3-6
Shape Object Diagram

class's representation and is therefore hidden from the client. This dictionary is created when the class is created, and contains all the methods to which instances of this class may respond. Searching for the message is time-consuming; method lookup in Smalltalk takes about 1.5 times as long as a simple subprogram call. All production-quality Smalltalk implementations optimize method dispatch by supplying a cached message dictionary, so that commonly passed messages may be invoked quickly. Caching typically improves performance by 20–30% [27].

The operation `Draw` defined in the subclass `Solid Rectangle` poses a special case. We said that `Draw's` implementation first calls `Draw` as defined in the superclass `Rectangle`. In Smalltalk, we specify a superclass method by using the keyword `super`. Then, when we pass the message `Draw` to `super`, Smalltalk uses the same method dispatch algorithm as above, except that the search begins in the superclass of the object instead of its class.

Studies by Deutsch suggest that polymorphism is not needed about 85% of the time, so message passing can be reduced to simple procedure calls [28]. Duff notes that in such cases, the developer often makes implicit assumptions that permit an early binding of the object's class [29]. Unfortunately, typeless languages have no convenient means for communicating these implicit assumptions to the compiler.

Strongly typed languages such as Object Pascal and C++ do let the developer assert such information. Because we want to avoid method dispatch wherever possible but must still allow for the occurrence of polymorphism, invoking a method in these languages proceeds a little differently than in Smalltalk.

In C++, the developer can decide if a particular operation is to be bound late by declaring it to be virtual; all other methods are considered to be bound early, and thus the compiler can statically resolve the method call to a simple subprogram call. In our example, we might have declared `Draw` as a virtual member function, and the methods `Set Center` and `Center` as nonvirtual, since they need not be redefined. The developer can also declare nonvirtual methods as inline, which avoids the subprogram call and thus achieves the affect of a macro expansion. Of course, inline expansion is not free; it trades off space for time.

To handle virtual member functions, most C++ implementations use the concept of a v-table, which is defined for each object when the object is created (and thus when the class of the object is fixed). This table typically consists of a list of pointers to virtual functions. For example, if we create an object of the class `Rectangle`, then the v-table will have an entry for the virtual function `Draw`, pointing to the closest implementation of `Draw`. If the class `Shape` had the virtual function `Rotate`, which was not redefined in the class `Rectangle`, then the v-table entry for `Rotate` would point to the implementation of `Rotate` in the class `Shape`. In this manner, runtime searching is eliminated: referring to a virtual member function of an object is just an indirect reference through the appropriate pointer, which immediately invokes the correct code without searching [30].

The operation `Draw` for the class `Solid Rectangle` introduces a special case in C++. To make the implementation of this method refer to the method `Draw` in the superclass, C++ requires the use of the scope operator. Thus, one would write:

```
Rectangle::Draw();
```

Studies by Stroustrup suggest that a virtual function call is just about as efficient as a normal function call [31]. In the presence of single inheritance, a virtual function call requires only about three or four additional memory references than a normal function call; multiple inheritance adds only about five or six memory references.

Method dispatch in CLOS is much more complicated, because of the notions of `:before`, `:after`, and `:around` methods. An operation is defined as a generic function, and each generic function may be associated with many methods. The existence of multiple polymorphism further complicates matters.

Method dispatch in CLOS normally uses the following algorithm:

- Determine the types of the arguments.
- Calculate the set of applicable methods.
- Sort the methods from most specific to most general, according to the object's class precedence list.
- Call all `:before` methods.
- Call the most specific primary method.
- Call all `:after` methods.
- Return the value of the primary method [32].

The amazing thing about CLOS is that with metaobject programming, one may redefine the very algorithm used for generic dispatch. In practice, however, one typically uses the predefined process. As Winston and Horn wisely point out, "The CLOS algorithm is complicated, however, and even wizard-level CLOS programmers try to get by without thinking about it, just as physicists try to get by with Newtonian mechanics rather than dealing with quantum mechanics" [33].

In Figure 3-4, all of the subclasses are also subtypes of their parent class. Thus, instances of `ElectricalData` are considered to be subtypes as well as subclasses of `TelemetryData`. The fact that typing parallels inheritance relationships is common to most strongly typed object-oriented programming languages, including Object Pascal and C++. Because Smalltalk and CLOS are typeless, or at most weakly typed, this issue is less of a concern in those languages.

The parallel between typing and inheritance is to be expected when we view the generalization/specialization hierarchies created through inheritance as the means of capturing the semantic connection among abstractions. Again, consider the declarations in C++:

```
TelemetryData telemetry;
ElectricalData electrical (5.0, -5.0, 3.0, 7.0);
```

The following assignment statement is legal:

```
telemetry = electrical; //electrical is a subtype of telemetry
```

but the following one is not:

```
electrical = telemetry; //illegal: telemetry is not a subtype of electrical
```

To summarize, an assignment of object X to object Y is possible if the type of X is the same as the type of Y, or a subtype of Y.

Most strongly typed languages do permit conversion of the value of an object from one type to another, but usually only if there is some superclass/subclass relationship between the two. For example, in C++ one can explicitly write conversion operators for a class using what are called *type casts*. In Object Pascal, the same mechanism is called a *type coercion*. Typically, one uses type conversion to convert an instance of a more specific class for assignment to a more general class. Such conversions are type-safe, meaning that they are checked for semantic correctness at compilation time. We can sometimes convert a variable of a more general class to one of a more specific class. However, such operations are not type-safe, because they can fail during execution time if the object being coerced is incompatible with the new type. Such conversions are actually not uncommon, since the developer often knows the real types of certain objects. For example, in the absence of parameterized types, it is common practice to build classes such as sets and bags that represent collections of objects. Because we want to permit collections of instances of arbitrary classes, we typically define these collection classes to operate upon instances of some base class, such as TObject in Object Pascal. Thus, iteration operations defined for such a class would only know how to return objects of this base class. However, within a particular application, a developer might only place objects of some specific subclass of TObject in the collection. To invoke a class-specific operation upon objects visited during iteration, the developer must explicitly coerce each object visited to the expected type. Again, this operation would fail at execution time if an object of some unexpected type appeared in the collection.

A strongly typed language permits an implementation to better optimize method *dispatch* (lookup), often reducing the message to a simple subprogram call. However, there is occasionally a dark side to making the type hierarchy of a system parallel the inheritance hierarchy. Specifically, changing the structure or behavior of some superclass can affect the correctness of its subclasses. As Micallef states, "If subtyping rules are based on inheritance, then reimplementing a class such that its position in the inheritance graph is changed can make clients of that class type-incorrect, even if the external interface of the class remains the same" [35]. This leads us to question the very purpose of inheritance. As we noted earlier in this chapter, inheritance may be used to indicate sharing or to suggest some semantic connection. As stated another way by Snyder, "One can view inheritance as a private decision of the designer to 'reuse' code because it is useful to do so; it should be possible to easily change such a decision. Alternatively, one can view inheritance as making a public declaration that objects of the child class obey the semantics of the parent class, so that the child class is merely specializing or refining the parent class" [36]. In Smalltalk, Object Pascal, and CLOS, these two views are united. However, in C++ the developer has greater control over the implications of inheritance. Specifically, if we assert that the superclass of a given subclass is public (as in our example of the class ElectricalData), then we mean that the subclass is also a subtype of the superclass, since both share the same interface (and therefore the same structure and behavior). Alternately, in the declaration of a class, one may assert that a superclass is private, meaning that the structure and behavior of the superclass is shared but the subclass is not a subtype of the superclass. Practically, this means that for private superclasses, the public and protected members of the superclass become private members of the subclass. Thus, no subtype relationship is formed, because the two classes no longer present the same interface to other clients.

By way of an example, consider the following class declaration:

```
class InternalElectricalData : private ElectricalData {
public:
    InternalElectricalData (float v1, float v2, float a1, float a2);
    InternalElectricalData (const InternalElectricalData&);
    virtual ~InternalElectricalData ();
    ElectricalData::currentPower;
};
```

With this declaration, methods such as send are not visible to any clients of this class, because the superclass ElectricalData is declared to be private. Because InternalElectricalData is not a subtype of ElectricalData, this also means that we cannot assign instances of InternalElectricalData to objects of the superclass, as we can for classes using public superclasses. Lastly, note that we have made the member function currentPower visible by explicitly naming the function. Without this explicit naming, it would be treated as private. As you would expect, the rules of C++ prohibit one from making a member in a subclass more visible than it is in its superclass. Thus, the member object id, declared as a protected member in the class TelemetryData, could not be made public by explicit naming as done for currentPower.

In Ada, the moral equivalent of this distinction can be achieved by using derived types versus subtypes. Specifically, a subtype of a type defines no new type, but only a constrained subtype, while a derived type defines a new, incompatible type, which shares the same representation as its parent type. As the next section shows, there is great tension between applying inheritance for reuse and applying using relationships.

The Meaning of Multiple Inheritance Relationships Among Classes. Thus far, we have talked about single inheritance, in which each subclass has exactly one superclass. However, as Vlissides and Linton point out, although single inheritance is very useful, "it often forces the programmer to derive from one of two equally attractive classes. This limits the applicability of predefined classes, often making it necessary to duplicate code. For example, there is no way to derive a graphic that is both a circle and a picture; one must derive from one or the other and reimplement the functionality of the class that was excluded" [37]. Multiple inheritance is supported by C++ and CLOS and, to a limited degree, by Smalltalk. The need for multiple inheritance in object-oriented programming languages is still a topic of great debate. In our experience, we find multiple

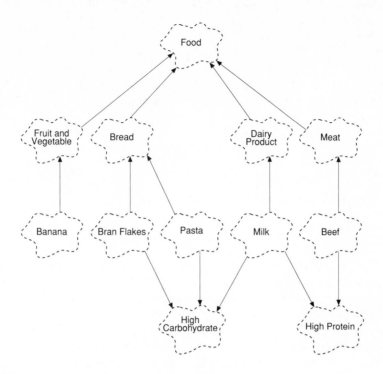

Figure 3-7
Multiple Inheritance Relationships Among Classes

inheritance to be like a parachute: you don't always need it, but when you do, you're really happy to have it on hand.

Consider for a moment how one might classify different foods, such as bananas, bran flakes, pasta, milk, and beef. One approach would be to place each into one of the four basic food groups: fruits and vegetables, breads, dairy products, and meats. Inheritance is an appropriate relationship to capture these design decisions, because it represents a "kind of" hierarchy: milk is a kind of dairy product, which in turn is a kind of food.

However, there are many other equally satisfactory ways to classify foods. For example, we might classify a particular food as being a substantial source of protein or carbohydrates. Single inheritance is not expressive enough to capture this lattice of relationships; thus we must turn to multiple inheritance.

Figure 3-7 illustrates such a class structure. Here we see that foods such as bran flakes are kinds of breads, as well as substantial sources of carbohydrate. Similarly, beef is a kind of meat as well as a kind of high-protein source. The classification of milk involves a more complicated set of relationships: it is a kind of dairy product, as well as a source of carbohydrates and protein.

To capture these design decisions using CLOS, we might declare the base class Food and the four abstract classes that represent the basic food groups:

```
(defclass food () (...))
(defclass fruit-and-vegetable (food) (...))
(defclass bread (food) (...))
(defclass dairy-product (food) (...))
(defclass meat (food) (...))
```

We have elided the declaration of each class's slots. Next, we declare the classes that represent high nutrient levels. These classes have no explicit superclass:

```
(defclass high-carbohydrate () (...))
(defclass high-protein () (...))
```

Continuing, we declare the classes that represent specific kinds of foods:

```
(defclass banana (fruit-and-vegetable) (...))
(defclass bran-flakes (bread high-carbohydrate) (...))
(defclass pasta (bread high-carbohydrate) (...))
(defclass milk (dairy-product high-carbohydrate high-protein) (...))
(defclass beef (meat high-protein) (...))
```

Each of these classes has more than one superclass.

Designing a suitable class structure involving inheritance, especially multiple inheritance, is a difficult task. As we explain in the next chapter, this is often an incremental and iterative process. Two problems present themselves when we have multiple inheritance: how do we deal with name collisions from different superclasses, and how do we handle repeated inheritance.

Name collisions are possible when two or more different superclasses use the same name for some element of their interfaces, such as instance variables and methods. For example, suppose that the classes high-carbohydrate and high-protein both had slots named percentage, representing the concentration of the respective nutrient. Since the class milk inherits from both of these classes, what does it mean to inherit two slots with the same name? There are basically three approaches to resolving this clash. First, the language semantics might regard a name clash as illegal, and reject the compilation of the class. This is the approach taken by Smalltalk and Eiffel. In Eiffel, however, it is possible to rename items so that there is no ambiguity. Second, the language semantics might regard the same name introduced by different classes as referring to the same slot, which is the approach taken by CLOS. Third, the language semantics might permit the clash, but require that all references to the name fully qualify the source of its declaration. This is the approach taken by C++.

The second problem is repeated inheritance, which Meyer describes as follows: "One of the delicate problems raised by the presence of multiple inheritance is what happens when a class is an ancestor of another in more than one way. If you allow multiple inheritance into a language, then sooner or later someone is going to write a class D with two parents B and C, each of which has a class A as a parent – or some other situation in which D inherits twice (or more) from A. This situation is called repeated inheritance and must be dealt with properly" [38]. As an example, suppose that we define the following class:

```
(defclass breakfast-cereal (bran-flakes milk) (...))
```

This class introduces repeated inheritance of the class `high-carbohydrate`, which is a superclass of both `bran-flakes` and `milk`.

There are three approaches to dealing with the problem of repeated inheritance. First, we can treat occurrences of repeated inheritance as illegal. This is the approach taken by Smalltalk and Eiffel (with Eiffel permitting renaming to disambiguate the duplicate references). Second, we can permit duplication of superclasses, but require the use of fully qualified names to refer to members of a specific copy. This is one of the approaches taken by C++. Third, we can treat multiple references to the same class as denoting the same class. This is the approach taken by C++ when the repeated superclass is introduced as a virtual base class. A virtual base class exists when a subclass names another class as its superclass and marks that superclass as virtual, to indicate that it is a shared class. Similarly, in CLOS repeated classes are shared, using a mechanism called the *class precedence list.* This list, calculated whenever a new class is introduced, includes the class itself and all of its superclasses, without duplication, and is based upon the following rules:

- A class always has precedence over its superclass.
- Each class sets the precedence order of its direct superclasses [39].

In this approach, the inheritance graph is flattened, duplicates are removed, and the resulting hierarchy is resolved using single inheritance [40]. This is akin to the computation of a topological sort of classes. If a total ordering of classes can be calculated, then the class that introduces the repeated inheritance is accepted. Note that this total ordering may be unique, or there may be several possible orderings. If no ordering can be found (for example, when there are cycles in the class dependencies), the class is rejected. In our example, the class `breakfast-cereal` would be accepted, because there is a unique ordering of superclasses; the superclass hierarchy includes exactly one (shared) appearance of the class `high-carbohydrate`.

The existence of multiple inheritance gives rise to a style of classes called *mixins.* Mixins derive from the programming culture surrounding the language Flavors: one would combine ("mix in") little classes to build classes with more sophisticated behavior. As Hendler observes, "A mixin is syntactically identical to a regular class, but its intent is different. The purpose of such a class is solely to . . . [add] functions to other flavors [classes] – one never creates an instance of a mixin" [41]. In Figure 3-7, the classes `high-carbohydrate` and `high-protein` are mixins. Neither of these classes can stand alone; rather, they are used to augment the meaning of some other class. In CLOS, it is common practice to build a mixin using only before and after methods to augment the behavior of existing primary methods. Thus, we may simply define a mixin as a class that embodies a single, focused behavior and is used to augment the behavior of some other class via inheritance. The behavior of a mixin is usually completely orthogonal to the behavior of the classes with which it is combined. A class that is constructed primarily by inheriting from mixins and does not add its own structure or behavior is called an *aggregate class.*

The Meaning of Multiple Polymorphism. Suppose that we define the following generic function:

```
(defgeneric display (food))
```

The purpose of this generic function is to draw a picture of the food in the current window. We expect that each subclass will provide methods for this generic function. In this manner, polymorphism comes into play, so that whenever we invoke this method for a particular object, the right picture gets drawn, because the object itself knows its class. This is an example of single polymorphism, meaning that the method is specialized (is polymorphic) on exactly one parameter.

Suppose now that we need a slightly different behavior, depending upon the exact display device we use. In one case, we would want the method display to draw a picture; in another, we would want it to print a textual representation. We could declare two different, but very similar, generic functions. However, this is not entirely satisfying, because of the redundancy.

In CLOS, however, we can write methods called *multi-methods* that are specialized on more than one parameter. For example, we might define the following generic function:

```
(defgeneric display (food display-device))
```

To invoke this function, we must supply an instance of some subclass of food, and some instance of a subclass of display-device. Upon invocation of this function, CLOS selects a suitable primary method that matches the classes of the actual parameters. If no such method is found, CLOS signals an appropriate runtime error. This is an example of multiple polymorphism.

Using Relationships

An Example of a Using Relationship Among Classes. Often, inheritance is not adequate to capture the complex relationships among different abstractions. For example, consider the relationships between a library and books. A library is not a kind of a book; rather, a library uses books. In Object Pascal, we might write the following:

```
TLibrary = object (TObject)
    ...
    procedure TLibrary.Initialize;
    procedure TLibrary.Checkout (ABook : TBook);
    procedure TLibrary.Checkin  (ABook : TBook);
    ...
end;
```

We have elided the fields of this class, as well as the rest of its methods.

In order to compile this class, we must first compile the class TBook, because it is used in the interface of TLibrary. For the class TLibrary to use the class TBook simply means that TLibrary is visible to TBook and that the interface or implementation of TLibrary can reference the interface (but not the implementation) of TBook. For example, in the implementation of the method Checkout, we might send a message to the object ABook, telling it that it has been checked out and to update its state accordingly. Thus, we see that using relationships among classes are related to, but slightly different from, using relationships among objects. To generalize, an instance of TLibrary (and its subclasses) can send messages to instances of TBook (and its subclasses).

The Meaning of Using Relationships Among Classes. There are two different flavors of using relationships: a class's interface can use another class (as in the preceding example), or a class's implementation can use another class. In the first case, the used class must also be visible to any clients. For example, any code that checks out a book from a library must be visible to both the class TLibrary (in order to invoke the method Checkout) as well as TBook (in order to declare objects of the class). In the second case, the used class is hidden as part of the secret of the using class. For example, in the implementation of the class TLibrary, we might use the class TList, so that we can declare objects that hold collections of books. The class TList need not be visible to the interface of TLibrary, but only to its implementation.

Along the lines of these using relationships, we may also express the cardinality of the relationship. For example, we can assert that every library may contain n books, but that every book is owned by exactly one library. This is an example of a *1:n* relationship. Alternately, we might decide that for every library, there is exactly one collection, and that every collection is part of exactly one library. This is an example of a *1:1* relationship. Other cardinalities are possible, such as *m:n* relationships.

Figure 3-8 illustrates these two kinds of using relationships among classes. Notice how we distinguish between a class used in the interface versus one used in the implementation of another class, and how we express the cardinality of these relationships.

As noted in the previous chapter, the encapsulation of abstractions is a good thing. However, it does sometimes get in the way, especially with regard to using relationships among classes. For example, suppose we created the class TSortedBookList, which needed access to the underlying representation of TBook in order to implement an efficient sorting method. Normally, most object-oriented programming languages do not let us relax the rules of information hiding. However, in C++, this is exactly the reason for the concept of a friend class. A friend is needed to declare a method involving two or more objects of different classes, whose implementation for any one class must reference the private parts of the corresponding classes that are also friends. In short, declaring a method or entire class to be a friend means that it is possible to access members that would otherwise be private. As in life, friends must be chosen

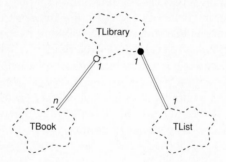

Figure 3-8
Using Relationships Among Classes

wisely, because they imply a certain trust between two classes, namely, that underlying assumptions will not be violated, even though the inside view of the class is laid bare.

Multiple inheritance is often confused with using relationships. For example, we might define a class named `telephone`, by inheriting from other classes representing phone pads, microphones, and speakers. Alternately, we might define the class `telephone` by using these classes. Both approaches might achieve the same effect, but in entirely different ways. In our experience, using multiple inheritance to indicate aggregation (the idea that an object contains other objects) is a bad idea. A telephone is not a kind of a microphone; rather, a telephone uses a microphone. Conceptually, it is far better to apply using relationships in this case. Our rule of thumb is that if an abstraction is greater than the sum of its component parts, then using relationships are more appropriate. If an abstraction is a kind of some other abstraction, or if it is exactly equal to the sum of its components, then inheritance is a better approach.

Instantiation Relationships

Examples of Instantiation Relationships Among Classes. With a strongly typed language, we like to use every opportunity to apply types to capture and then enforce our design decisions. For example, suppose that we are crafting an abstraction of an grocery store, in which we have ten checkout lanes. In Object Pascal and Ada, we might define a domain-specific integer type whose values are constrained to the range 1 to 10, representing a specific lane. At a slightly higher level of abstraction, we might create a set class, to represent collections of employees who are free to be assigned to a particular checkout lane. However, our understanding of the problem tells us that such collections will contain only employees, not other objects, such as customers or, even worse, vegetables. Ideally, we would like to define our set class so that we can precisely state the class of object allowed in the set and then let the typing rules of our language prohibit us from doing otherwise.

A set is an example of a *container class*, which is a class whose instances are collections of other objects. Container classes may denote *homogeneous* collections, meaning that all objects in the collection are of the same class, or they may represent *heterogeneous* collections, in which the objects may be of different classes although they must all share some common superclass. The most common kinds of container classes include stacks, lists, strings, queues, dequeues, rings, maps, sets, bags, trees, and graphs [42].

In Ada, we may define a set class as follows:

```
generic
    type Item is private;
package Simple_Set is

    type Set is limited private;

    procedure Copy          (From_The_Set : in     Set;
                             To_The_Set   : in out Set);
    procedure Clear         (The_Set      : in out Set);
    procedure Add           (The_Item     : in     Item;
                             To_The_Set   : in out Set);
    procedure Remove        (The_Item     : in     Item;
                             From_The_Set : in out Set);
    procedure Union         (Of_The_Set   : in Set;
                             And_The_Set  : in Set;
                             To_The_Set   : in out Set);
    procedure Intersection  (Of_The_Set   : in     Set;
                             And_The_Set  : in     Set;
                             To_The_Set   : in out Set);
    procedure Difference    (Of_The_Set   : in     Set;
                             And_The_Set  : in     Set;
                             To_The_Set   : in out Set);

    function Is_Equal           (Left      : in Set;
                                 Right     : in Set) return Boolean;
    function Extent_Of          (The_Set   : in Set) return Natural;
    function Is_Empty           (The_Set   : in Set) return Boolean;
    function Is_A_Member        (The_Item  : in Item;
                                 Of_The_Set : in Set) return Boolean;
    function Is_A_Subset        (Left      : in Set;
                                 Right     : in Set) return Boolean;
    function Is_A_Proper_Subset (Left      : in Set;
                                 Right     : in Set) return Boolean;

    Overflow            : exception;
    Item_Is_In_Set      : exception;
    Item_Is_Not_In_Set  : exception;

private
    ...
end Simple_Set;
```

Notice again our style of writing class interfaces, which explicitly separates the modifier and selector methods.

Given this class, plus the definition of a class named `Employee`, we may now instantiate this class by asserting that items are all instances of the class `Employee`:

```
package Employee_Set is new Simple_Set (Item => Employee);
```

Assuming that we have a set object named `Available_Employees`, and employee objects named `Mike`, `Paul`, `Dave`, `Bob`, and `Brett`, we can now write expressions as follows:

```
Add(Bob, To_The_Set => Available_Employees);
Add(Paul, To_The_Set => Available_Employees);
Add(Brett, To_The_Set => Available_Employees);
Remove(Mike, From_The_Set => Available_Employees);
if Is_A_Member(Dave, Of_The_Set => Available_Employees then ...
```

Ada's strong typing rules will reject any statements that try to add, remove, or test for objects that are not employees.

The Meaning of Instantiation Relationships Among Classes. There are basically four ways to build container classes. First, we can use macros. This is the style one must currently use with C++, but as Stroustrup observes, this "approach does not work well except on a small scale" [43] because maintaining such macros is clumsy; furthermore, each instantiation results in a new copy of the code. Second, we can take the approach used by Smalltalk and reply upon inheritance and late binding [44]. With this approach, we may build only heterogeneous container classes, because there is no way to assert the specific class of the container's elements; every item is treated as if it were an instance of the base class `Object`. Third, we may take an approach commonly used in Object Pascal. Here, we build generalized container classes, as in Smalltalk, but then use explicit type-checking code to enforce the convention that the contents are all of the same class, which is asserted when the container object is created. Fourth, we may take the approach first introduced by CLU and provide a mechanism for parameterizing classes [45]. A *parameterized class* (also known as a *generic class*) is one that serves as a template for other classes – a template that may be parameterized by other classes, objects, and/or operations. A parameterized class must be instantiated (that is, its parameters must be filled in) before objects can be created. Ada and Eiffel both support generic class mechanisms, and C++ is expected to support them in the near future.

Figure 3-9 illustrates the application of class instantiation relationships. Note that to instantiate the class `Simple_Set`, we must also use the class `Employee`. Indeed, instantiation relationships almost always require some using relationships, which make visible the actual classes used to fill in the template.

Meyer has pointed out that inheritance is a more powerful mechanism than genericity and that much of the benefit of genericity can be achieved through

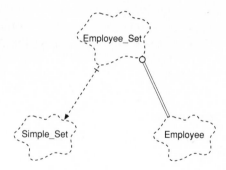

Figure 3-9
Instantiation Relationships Among Classes

inheritance, but not vice versa [46]. In practice, we find it helpful to use a language that supports both inheritance and parameterized classes.

Parameterized classes may be used for much more than building container classes. As Stroustrup points out, "Type parameterization will allow arithmetic functions to be parameterized over their basic number type so that programmers can (finally) get a uniform way of dealing with integers, single-precision floating-point numbers, double-precision floating point-numbers, etc." [47]. From a design perspective, parameterized classes are also useful in capturing certain design decisions about the interface of a class. Whereas a class definition can name the operations that one may perform upon instances of that class, the generic part of a template can be used to declare the operations that instances of that class are allowed to perform upon other objects. For example, we might declare an ordered list class, that represents collections of objects that are sorted according to some criteria. We can parameterize this list class with a method that is called to determine the relative order of a particular object in the collection. This is an example of an operation that list objects can invoke upon other objects. By parameterizing the class in this manner, we make it more loosely coupled and therefore more reusable, because now it does not depend upon a specific class; it can be instantiated with any class that is able to provide this ordering function.

Metaclass Relationships

The Meaning of Metaclass Relationships Among Classes. The three kinds of class relationships discussed thus far – inheritance, using, and instantiation – together cover all the important kinds of class relationships that most developers will ever need. However, if we take the idea of the object model just one step further, we discover yet another possible kind of relationship. We have said that every object is an instance of some class. What if we treat a class itself as an object that can be manipulated? To do so, we must ask, what is the class of a class? The answer is simply, a metaclass. To state it another way, a *metaclass* is a class whose instances are themselves classes.

Robson motivates the need for metaclasses by noting that "in a system under development, a class provides an interface for the programmer to interface with the definition of objects. For this use of classes, it is extremely useful for them to be objects, so that they can be manipulated in the same way as all other descriptions" [48]. Metaclasses are directly supported by Smalltalk and CLOS, although, as we will see, the metaclass facilities of CLOS are much more powerful.

In Smalltalk, the primary purpose of a metaclass is to provide operations for initializing class variables and for creating the metaclass' single instance [49]. By convention, a Smalltalk metaclass typically contains examples that show the use of the metaclass's class.

Examples of Metaclass Relationships Among Classes. Suppose that we have a class called `Timer`, whose instances encapsulate the knowledge of the current time, based upon the seconds that have elapsed since the system was activated. We want our abstraction to permit any number of objects of this class, but we want each object to share the same value of time. This means that we must have some sort of shared state, and this state must be initialized before any object is created. Typically, the state of an object is held in instance variables, although we may also use class variables. A class variable is just like an instance variable, except that it is shared by all instances of the class. We may declare the class `Timer` and its instance method in Smalltalk as follows:

```
Object subclass: #Timer
    instanceVariableNames: ''
    classVariableNames: 'ElapsedSeconds TimerProcess'
    poolDictionaries: ''
    category: 'Simulation'

Timer methodsFor: 'accessing'
```

elapsedSeconds

```
    "Return an integer value representing the number of seconds that have
     elapsed since the system was activated."

    ↑ElapsedSeconds
```

`ElapsedSeconds` and `TimerProcess` are declared as class variables, meaning that they are shared by all instances of the class `Timer`. To initialize these class variables, we may declare the `Timer` metaclass, as follows:

```
Timer class
    instanceVariableNames: ''
```

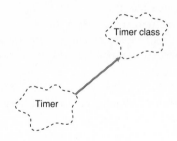

Figure 3-10
Metaclass Relationships Among Classes

Timer class methodsFor: 'initialize-release'

initialize

"Reset elapsedSeconds, then start the process to update elapsedSeconds
every second."

ElapsedSeconds ← 0.
TimerProcess ← [[(Delay forSeconds: 1) wait.
                    self elapsedSeconds: self elapsedSeconds + 1.
                    true]
            whileTrue] newProcess.
        TimerProcess resume

release

"Stop the process to update elapsedSeconds every second."

TimerProcess terminate

The method `initialize` is called a *class method*. Upon its invocation, a new process (called `TimerProcess`) is created, which repeatedly waits for one second, then increments the class variable `elapsedSeconds`.

In Smalltalk, every class has exactly one metaclass (`Timer`'s metaclass is called `Timer class`), although our design typically needs to show only those for which there is domain-specific behavior. To use the classes in our example, we first initialize the class `Timer` by evaluating the following statement:

Timer initialize.

Because `Timer` is itself a class, `initialize` is defined in the object's class, namely, the metaclass `Timer class`. Figure 3-10 illustrates this metaclass relationship.

What is the class of `Timer`'s metaclass? In Smalltalk, every metaclass (including `Metaclass class`) is an instance of `Metaclass`. `Metaclass` is a subclass of `ClassDescription`, which is a subclass of `Behavior`, which in turn is a subclass of the base class, `Object`.

Although C++ does not explicitly support metaclasses, it does have provisions for class variables and class methods. Specifically, one may declare a member object or a member function as *static*, meaning that the member is shared by all instances of the class.

As we have said, support for metaclasses in CLOS is more powerful than in Smalltalk. Through the use of metaclasses, one may redefine the very semantics of elements such as class precedence, generic functions, and methods. The primary benefit of this facility is that it permits experimentation with alternate object-oriented programming paradigms and facilitates the construction of software development tools, such as browsers.

In CLOS, the predefined class named `standard-class` is the metaclass of all untyped classes defined via `defclass`. This metaclass defines the method `make-instance`, which implements the semantics of how instances are created. `Standard-class` also defines the algorithm for computing the class precedence list. CLOS allows the behavior of both of these methods to be redefined.

Methods and generic functions may also be treated as objects in CLOS. Because they are somewhat different than the usual kinds of objects, class objects, method objects, and generic function objects are collectively called *metaobjects*. Each method is an instance of the predefined class `standard-method`, and each generic function is treated as an instance of the class `standard-generic-function`. Because the behavior of these predefined classes may be redefined, it is possible to change the meanings of methods and generic functions.

3.5 The Interplay of Classes and Objects

Relationships Between Classes and Objects

Classes and objects are separate yet intimately related concepts. Specifically, every object is the instance of some class, and every class has zero or more instances. For practically all applications, classes are static; therefore, their existence, semantics, and relationships are fixed prior to the execution of a program. Similarly, the class of most objects is static, meaning that once an object is created, its class is fixed. In sharp contrast, however, objects are typically created and destroyed at a furious rate during the lifetime of an application.

For example, consider the classes and objects in the implementation of an air traffic control system. Some of the more important abstractions include planes, flight plans, runways, and air spaces. By their very definition, the meanings of these classes of objects are relatively static. They must be static, for otherwise one could not build an application that embodied knowledge of such commonsense facts as that planes can take off, fly, and then land, and that two planes should not occupy the same space at the same time. Conversely, the instances of these classes are dynamic. At a fairly slow rate, new runways are built, and old ones are deactivated. Faster yet, new flight plans are filed, and old ones are filed away. With great frequency, new planes enter a particular air space, and old ones leave.

The Role of Classes and Objects in Design

During analysis and the early stages of design, the developer has two primary tasks:

- Identify the classes and objects that form the vocabulary of the problem domain.

- Invent the structures whereby sets of objects work together to provide the behaviors that satisfy the requirements of the problem.

Collectively, we call such classes and objects the *key abstractions* of the problem, and we call these cooperative structures the *mechanisms* of the implementation.

During this phase of development, the focus of the developer must be upon the outside view of these key abstractions and mechanisms. This view represents the logical framework of the system, and therefore encompasses the class structure and object structure of the system. In the later stages of design and then moving into implementation, the task of the developer changes: the focus is on the inside view of these key abstractions and mechanisms, involving their physical representation. We may express these design decisions as part of the system's module architecture and process architecture.

3.6 On Building Quality Classes and Objects

Measuring the Quality of an Abstraction

Ingalls suggests that "a system should be built with a minimum set of unchangeable parts; those parts should be as general as possible; and all parts of the system should be held in a uniform framework" [50]. With object-oriented design, these parts are the classes and objects that make up the key abstractions of the system, and the framework is provided by its mechanisms.

In our experience, the design of classes and objects is an incremental, iterative process. Frankly, except for the most trivial abstractions, we have never been able to define a class exactly right the first time. As Chapters 4 and 7 will explain, it takes time to smooth the conceptual jagged edges of our initial abstractions. Of course, there is a cost to refining these abstractions, in terms of recompilation, understandability, and the integrity of the fabric of our system design. Therefore, we want to come as close as we can to being right the first time.

How can one know if a given class or object is well designed? We suggest that there are five meaningful metrics:

- Coupling
- Cohesion
- Sufficiency
- Completeness
- Primitiveness

Coupling is a notion borrowed from structured design, but with a liberal interpretation, it also applies to object-oriented design. Stevens, Myers, and Constantine define coupling as "the measure of the strength of association established by a connection from one module to another. Strong coupling complicates a system since a module is harder to understand, change, or correct by itself if it is highly interrelated with other modules. Complexity can be reduced by designing systems with the weakest possible coupling between modules" [51]. A counterexample to good coupling is given by Page-Jones, in his description of a modular stereo system in which the power supply is located in one of the speaker cabinets [52].

Coupling with regard to modules is still applicable to object-oriented design, but coupling with regard to classes and objects is equally important. However, there is tension between the concepts of coupling and inheritance. On the one hand, weakly coupled classes are desirable; on the other hand, inheritance – which tightly couples superclasses and their subclasses – helps us to exploit the commonality among abstractions.

The idea of cohesion also comes from structured design. Simply stated, cohesion measures the degree of connectivity among the elements of a single module (and for object-oriented design, a single class or object). The least desirable form of cohesion is coincidental cohesion, in which entirely unrelated abstractions are thrown into the same class or module. For example, consider a class comprising the abstractions of dogs and spacecraft, whose behaviors are quite unrelated. The most desirable form of cohesion is functional cohesion, in which the elements of a class or module all work together to provide some well-bounded behavior. Thus, the class `Dog` is functionally cohesive if its semantics embrace the behavior of a dog, the whole dog, and nothing but the dog.

Closely related to the ideas of coupling and cohesion are the criteria that a class or module should be sufficient, complete, and primitive. By *sufficient*, we mean that the class or module captures enough characteristics of the abstraction to permit meaningful and efficient interaction. To do otherwise renders the component useless. For example, if we are designing the class `Set`, it is wise to include an operation that removes an item from the set, but our wisdom is futile if we neglect an operation that adds an item. In practice, violations of this characteristic are detected very early; such shortcomings rise up almost every time we build a client that must use this abstraction. By *complete*, we mean that the interface of the class or module captures all of the meaningful characteristics of the abstraction. Whereas sufficiency implies a minimal interface, a complete interface is one that covers all aspects of the abstraction. A complete class or module is thus one whose interface is general enough to be commonly usable to any client. Completeness is a subjective matter, and it can be overdone. Providing all meaningful operations for a particular abstraction overwhelms the user and is generally unnecessary, since many high-level operations can be composed from low-level ones. For this reason, we also suggest that classes and modules be primitive. *Primitive* operations are those that can be efficiently implemented only if given access to the underlying representation of the abstraction. Thus, adding an item to a set is primitive, because to implement this operation Add, the underlying representation must be visible. On the other hand, an operation adding four items to a set is not primitive, since this operation can be implemented just as efficiently upon the more primitive Add operation, without having access to the underlying representation. Of course, efficiency is also a subjective measure. An operation is indisputably primitive if we can implement it only through access to the underlying representation. An operation that could be implemented on top of existing primitive operations, but at the cost of significantly more computational resources, is also a candidate for inclusion as a primitive operation.

Heuristics for Choosing Operations

Trade-offs of Functional Semantics. Crafting the interface of a class or module is plain hard work. Typically, we makes a first attempt at the design of a class, and then, as we and others create clients, we find it necessary to augment, modify, and further refine this interface. Eventually, we may discover patterns of operations or patterns of abstractions that lead us to invent new classes or to reorganize the relationships among existing ones.

Within a given class, it is our style to keep all operations primitive, so that each exhibits a small, well-defined behavior. We call such methods *fine-grained*. We also tend to separate methods that do not communicate with one another. In this manner, it is far easier to construct subclasses that can meaningfully redefine the behavior of their superclasses. The decision to contract out a behavior to one versus many methods may be made for two competing reasons: lumping a particular behavior in one method leads to a simpler interface but larger, more complicated methods; spreading a behavior across methods leads to a more complicated interface, but simpler methods. As Meyer observes, "A good designer knows how to find the appropriate balance between too much contracting, which produces fragmentation, and too little, which yields unmanageably large modules" [53].

It is common in object-oriented design to design the methods of a class as a whole, because all these methods cooperate to form the entire protocol of the abstraction. Thus, given some desired behavior, we must decide in which class to place it. Halbert and O'Brien offer the following criteria to be considered when making such a decision:

- "Reusability   Would this behavior be more useful in
                                more than one context?

- Complexity   How difficult is it to implement the
                                behavior?

- Applicability   How relevant is the behavior to the
                                type in which it might be placed?

- Implementation knowledge   Does the behavior's implementation
                                depend upon the internal details of a
                                type?" [54]

We usually choose to declare the meaningful operations we may perform upon an object as methods in the definition of that object's class (or superclass). However, in languages such as Object Pascal, C++, CLOS, and Ada, we may also declare such operations as free subprograms, which we then group in class utilities. In C++ terminology, a *free subprogram* is a nonmember function. Because free subprograms cannot be redefined as methods can, they are less general. However, utilities are helpful in keeping a class primitive and in reducing the coupling among classes, especially if these higher level operations involve objects of many different classes.

Trade-offs of Time and Space Semantics. Once we have established the existence of a particular operation and defined its functional semantics, we must decide upon its time and space semantics. This means that we must specify our design decisions about the amount of time it takes to complete an operation and the amount of storage it needs. Such decisions are often expressed in terms of best, average, and worst cases, with the worst case specifying an upper limit on what is acceptable.

Closely related to the issue of time and space complexity is that of synchronization. In most of the languages we use, synchronization among objects is simply not an issue, because our programs contain exactly one thread of control, meaning that all objects are sequential. We speak of message passing in such situations as simple, because its semantics are most akin to simple subprogram calls. However, in languages that support concurrency, such as Ada, we must concern ourselves with more sophisticated forms of message passing, so as to avoid the problems created if two threads of control act upon the same object in unrestrained ways. Objects whose semantics are preserved in the presence of multiple threads of control are either blocking or concurrent objects, depending upon whether the object itself is active.

We have found it useful to express concurrency semantics for each individual operation as well as for the object as a whole, since different operations may require different kinds of synchronization. Message passing may thus take one of the following forms:

- Synchronous   An operation commences only when the
                            sender has initiated the action and the receiver

is ready to accept the message; the sender and receiver will wait indefinitely until both parties are ready to proceed.

- Balking

The same as synchronous, except that the sender will abandon the operation if the receiver is not immediately ready.

- Timeout

The same as synchronous, except that the sender will only wait for a specified amount of time for the receiver to be ready.

- Asynchronous

A sender may initiate an action regardless of whether the receiver is expecting the message.

The form can be selected on an operation-by-operation basis, but only after the functional semantics of the operation have been decided upon.

Heuristics for Choosing Relationships

Metrics for Choosing Relationships. Choosing the relationships among classes and among objects is linked to the selection of operations. If we decide that object X sends message M to object Y, then either directly or indirectly, X's class must be visible to Y's class, otherwise, we could not name the operation M in the body of X's class; and X must be visible to Y, otherwise Y cannot be known to X. By visibility, we mean the ability of one abstraction to see another and thus reference resources in its outside view. Abstractions are visible to one another only where their scopes overlap. Coupling is thus a measure of the degree of visibility.

One useful guideline in choosing the relationships among objects is called the Law of Demeter, which states that "the methods of a class should not depend in any way on the structure of any class, except the immediate (top-level) structure of their own class. Further, each method should send messages to objects belonging to a very limited set of classes only" [55]. The basic effect of applying this law is the creation of loosely coupled classes, whose implementation secrets are encapsulated. Such classes are fairly unencumbered, meaning that to understand the meaning of one class, you need not understand the details of many other classes.

In looking at the class structure of an entire system, we may find that its inheritance hierarchy is either wide and shallow, narrow and deep, or balanced. Class structures that are wide and shallow usually represent forests of free-standing classes that can be mixed and matched [56]. Class structures that are narrow and deep represent trees of classes that are related by a common ancestor [57]. There are advantages and disadvantages to each approach. Forests of classes are more loosely coupled, but they may not exploit all the commonality that exists. Trees of classes exploit this commonality, so that individual classes are smaller than in forests. However, to understand a particular class, it is usually necessary to understand the meaning of all the classes it inherits from or uses. The proper shape of a class structure is highly problem-dependent.

One must make similar trade-offs between inheritance and using relationships. For example, should the class `Car` inherit or use the classes named `Engine` and `Wheel`? In this case, we suggest that a using relationship is more appropriate than an inheritance relationship. Meyer states that between the classes `A` and `B`, "inheritance is appropriate if every instance of `B` may also be viewed as an instance of `A`. The client [using] relationship is appropriate when every instance of `B` simply possesses one or more attributes of `A`" [58]. From another perspective, if the behavior of an object is more than the sum of its individual parts, then creating a using relationship rather than an inheritance relationship between the appropriate classes is probably superior.

The Role of Mechanisms and Visibility. Deciding upon the relationship among objects is mainly a matter of designing the mechanisms whereby these objects interact. The question the developer must ask is simply Where does certain knowledge go? For example, in a manufacturing plant, materials (called *lots*) enter manufacturing cells to be processed. As they enter certain cells, we must notify the room's manager to take appropriate action. We now have a design choice: is the entry of a lot into a room an operation upon the room, an operation upon the lot, or an operation upon both? If we decide that it is an operation upon the room, then the room must be visible to the lot. If we decide that it is an operation upon the lot, then the lot must be visible to the room, because the lot must know what room it is in. Lastly, if we consider this to be an operation upon both the room and the lot, then we must arrange for mutual visibility. We must also decide on some visibility relationship between the room and the manager (and not the lot and the manager); either the manager must know the room it manages, or the room must know of its manager.

During the design process, it is occasionally useful to state explicitly how one object is visible to another. There are basically three such ways that object `X` may be made visible to object `Y`:

- Same lexical scope   `Y` is within the scope of `X`; thus, `X` can explicitly name `Y`.

- Parameter   `Y` is passed as a parameter to some operation applicable to `X`.

- Field   `Y` is a field of `X`.

A variation upon each of these is the idea of shared visibility. For example, `Y` might be a field of `X`, but `Y` might also be visible to other objects in different ways. In Smalltalk, this kind of visibility usually represents a dependency between two objects. Shared visibility involves structural sharing, meaning that one object does not have exclusive access to another: the shared object's state may be altered via more than one path. Such visibility relationships are often unavoidable, and it is therefore useful to indicate this fact explicitly during the design process.

Heuristics for Choosing Implementations

Only after we complete the design of the outside view of a given class or object do we turn to its inside view. This perspective involves two different design decisions: a choice of representation for a class or object and the placement of the class or object in a module.

Choosing the Representation of a Class or Object. The representation of a class or object should almost always be one of the encapsulated secrets of the abstraction. This makes it possible to change the representation (for example, to alter the time and space semantics) without violating any of the functional assumptions that clients may have made. As Wirth wisely states, "The choice of representation is often a fairly difficult one, and it is not uniquely determined by the facilities available. It must always be taken in light of the operations that are to be performed upon the data" [59]. For example, given a class whose objects denote a set of flight plan information, do we optimize the representation for fast searching or for fast insertion and deletion? We cannot optimize for both, so we must choose based upon the expected use of these objects. Sometimes it is not easy to choose, and we end up with families of classes, whose interfaces are virtually identical but whose implementations are radically different, in order to provide different time and space behavior.

One of the more difficult trade-offs when selecting the implementation of a class is between computing the value of an object's state versus storing it as a field. For example, suppose we have the class `Cone`, which includes the method `Volume`. Invoking this method returns the volume of the object. As part of the representation of this class, we are likely to use fields for the height of the cone and the radius of its base. Should we have an additional field in which we store the volume of the object, or should the method `Volume` just calculate it every time [60]? If we want this method to be fast, we should store the volume as a field. If space efficiency is more important to us, we should calculate the value. Which representation is better depends entirely upon the particular problem. In any case, we should be able to choose an implementation independently of the class's outside view; indeed, we should even be able to change this representation without its clients caring.

Choosing the Placement of a Class or Object in a Module. Similar issues apply to the declaration of classes and objects within modules. For Smalltalk, this is a not an issue, because there is no concept of a module within the language. It is a different matter for Object Pascal, C++, CLOS, and Ada, which support the notion of the module as a separate language construct. The competing requirements of visibility and information hiding usually guide our design decisions about where to declare classes and objects. Generally, we seek to build functionally cohesive, loosely coupled modules. Many nontechnical factors influence these decisions, such as matters of reuse, security, and documentation. Like the design of classes and objects, module design is not to be taken lightly. As Parnas, Clements, and Weiss note with regard to information hiding, "Applying this principle is not always easy. It attempts to minimize the expected cost of software over its period of use and requires that the designer estimate the likelihood of changes. Such estimates are based on past experience and usually require knowledge of the application area as well as an understanding of hardware and software technology" [61].

Summary

- An object has state, behavior, and identity.
- The structure and behavior of similar objects are defined in their common class.
- The state of an object encompasses all of the (usually static) properties of the object plus the current (usually dynamic) values of each of these properties.
- Behavior is how an object acts and reacts in terms of its state changes and message passing.
- Identity is that property of an object which distinguishes it from all other objects.
- The two kinds of object hierarchies include using and containing relationships.
- A class is a set of objects that share a common structure and a common behavior.
- The four kinds of class hierarchies include inheritance, using, instantiation, and metaclass relationships.
- Key abstractions are the classes and objects that form the vocabulary of the problem domain.
- A mechanism is a structure whereby a set of objects work together to provide a behavior that satisfies some requirement of the problem.
- The quality of an abstraction may be measured by its coupling, cohesion, sufficiency, completeness, and primitiveness.

Further Readings

MacLennan [G 1982] discusses the distinction between values and objects. The work by Meyer [J 1987] proposes the idea of programming as contracting.

Much has been written on the topic of class hierarchies, with particular emphasis upon approaches to inheritance. The papers by Albano [G 1983], Brachman [J 1983], Hailpern and Nguyen [G 1987], and Wegner and Zdonik [J 1988] provide an excellent theoretical foundation for all the important concepts and issues. Cook and Palsberg [J 1989] provide a formal treatment of inheritance using denotational semantics. Wirth [J 1987] proposes a related approach for record type extensions, as used in the language Oberon. Ingalls [G 1986] provides a useful discussion on the topic of multiple polymorphism. Practical guidance on the effective use of inheritance is offered by Meyer [G 1988] and Halberd and O'Brien [G 1988]. LaLonde and Pugh [J 1985] examine the problems of teaching the effective use of specialization and generalization.

Meyer [G 1986] examines the relationships between genericity and inheritance, as viewed by the language Eiffel. Stroustrup [G 1988] proposes a mechanism for parameterized types in C++.

An alternative to class-based hierarchies is provided by delegation, using exemplars. This approach is examined in detail by Stein [G 1987].

Classification

Classification is the means whereby we order knowledge. In object-oriented design, recognizing the sameness among things allows us to expose the commonality within key abstractions and mechanisms, and eventually leads us to simpler designs. Unfortunately, there is no golden path to classification. To the reader accustomed to finding cookbook answers, we unequivocally state that there are no simple recipes for identifying classes and objects. There is no such thing as the "perfect" class structure, nor the "right" set of objects. As in any engineering discipline, our design choices are a compromise shaped by many competing factors.

At a conference on software engineering, several developers were asked what rules they applied to identify classes and objects. Stroustrup, the designer of C++, responded "It's a Holy Grail. There is no panacea." Gabriel, one of the designers of CLOS, stated, "That's a fundamental question for which there is no easy answer. I try things" [1]. Fortunately, there does exist a vast legacy of experience with classification in other disciplines. From more classical approaches, the techniques of object-oriented analysis, domain analysis, and various hybrid methods have emerged, each of which offers several useful rules of thumb for identifying the classes and objects relevant to a particular problem. These heuristics are the focus of this chapter.

Classification is the means whereby we order knowledge.

4.1 The Importance of Proper Classification

Classification and Object-Oriented Design

The identification of classes and objects is the hardest part of object-oriented design. Our experience shows that identification involves both discovery and invention. Through discovery, we come to recognize the key abstractions and mechanisms that form the vocabulary of our problem domain. Through invention, we devise generalized abstractions as well as new mechanisms that regulate how objects should collaborate. Ultimately, discovery and invention are both problems of classification, and classification is fundamentally a problem of finding sameness. When we classify, we seek to group things that have a common structure or exhibit a common behavior.

Intelligent classification is actually a part of all good science. As Michalski and Stepp observe, "An omnipresent problem in science is to construct meaningful classifications of observed objects or situations. Such classifications facilitate human comprehension of the observations and the subsequent development of a scientific theory" [2]. Not surprisingly, then, classification is relevant to every aspect of object-oriented design. Classification helps us to identify generalization, specialization, and aggregation hierarchies among classes. By recognizing the common patterns of interaction among objects, we come to invent the mechanisms that serve as the soul of our implementation. Classification also guides us in making decisions about modularization. We may choose to place certain classes and objects together in the same module or in different modules, depending upon the sameness we find among these declarations; coupling and cohesion are simply measures of this sameness. Classification also plays a role in allocating processes to processors. We place certain processes together in the same processor or different processors, depending upon how these processes are related functionally.

The Difficulty of Classification

Examples of Classification. In the previous chapter, we defined an object as something that has a crisply defined boundary. However, the boundaries that distinguish one object from another are often quite fuzzy. For example, look at your leg. Where does your knee begin, and where does it end? In recognizing human speech, how do we know that certain sounds connect to form a word, and are not instead a part of any surrounding words? Consider also the design of a word processing system. Do characters constitute a class, or are whole words a better choice? How do we treat arbitrary, noncontiguous selections of text? Also, what about sentences, paragraphs, or even whole documents: are these classes of objects relevant to our problem?

The fact that intelligent classification is difficult is hardly new information. Since there are parallels to the same problems in object-oriented design, consider for a moment the problems of classification in two other scientific disciplines: biology and chemistry.

Until the eighteenth century, the prevailing scientific thought was that all living organisms could be arranged from the most simple to the most complex, with the measure of complexity being highly subjective (not surprisingly, humans were usually placed at the top of this list). In the mid-1700s, however, the Swedish botanist Carolus Linnaeus suggested a more detailed taxonomy for categorizing organisms, according to what he called *genus* and *species*. A century later, Darwin proposed the theory that natural selection was the mechanism of evolution, whereby present-day species evolved from older ones. Darwin's theory depended upon an intelligent classification of species. As Darwin himself states, naturalists "try to arrange the species, genera, and families in each class, on what is called the natural system. But what is meant by this system? Some authors look at it merely as a scheme for arranging together those living objects which are most alike, and for separating those which are most unlike" [3]. In contemporary biology, classification denotes "the establishment of a hierarchical system of categories on the basis of presumed natural relationships among organisms" [4]. The most general category in a biological taxonomy is the kingdom, followed in order of increasing specialization, by phylum, subphylum, class, order, family, genus, and, finally, species. Historically, a particular organism is placed in a specific category according to its body structure, internal structural characteristics, and evolutionary relationships. More recently, classification has been achieved by grouping organisms that share a common generic heritage: organisms that have similar DNA are grouped together.

To a computer scientist, biology may seem to be a stodgily mature discipline, with well-defined criteria for classifying organisms. This is simply not the case. As the biologist May reports, "At the purely factual level, we do not know to within an order of magnitude how many species of plants and animals we share the globe with: fewer than 2 million are currently classified, and estimates of the total number range from under 5 million to more than 50 million" [5]. Furthermore, different criteria for classifying the same organisms yield different results. Martin suggests that "it all depends on what you want classification to do. If you want it to reflect precisely the genetic relatedness among species, that will give you one answer. But if you want it instead to say something about levels of adaptation, then you will get another" [6]. The moral here is that even in scientifically rigorous disciplines, classification is highly dependent upon the reason for the classification.

Similar lessons may be learned from chemistry [7]. In ancient times, all substances were thought to be some combination of earth, air, fire, and water. By today's standards (unless you are an alchemist), these do not represent very good classifications. In the mid-1600s, the chemist Robert Boyle proposed that elements were the primitive abstractions of chemistry, from which more complex compounds could be made. It wasn't until over a century later, in 1789, that the chemist Lavoisier published the first list of elements, containing some twenty-three items, some of which were later discovered not to be elements at all. The discovery of new elements continued and the list grew, but finally, in 1869, the chemist Mendeleyev proposed the periodic law that gave a precise criteria for organizing all known elements, and could predict the properties of those yet undiscovered. The periodic law was not the final story in the classification of the elements. In the early 1900s, elements with similar chemical properties but different atomic weights were discovered, leading to the idea of isotopes of elements. The lesson here is simple: as Descartes states, "The discovery of an order is no easy task. . . . yet once the order has been discovered there is no difficulty at all in knowing it" [8].

The Incremental and Iterative Nature of Classification. We have not said all this to defend lengthy software development schedules, although to the manager or end user, it does sometimes seem that software engineers need centuries to complete their work. Rather, we have told these stories to point out that intelligent classification is intellectually hard work, and that it best comes about through an incremental and iterative process. This incremental and iterative nature is evident in the development of such diverse software technologies as graphical user interfaces, database standards, and even fourth-generation languages. As Shaw has observed in software engineering, "The development of individual abstractions often follows a common pattern. First, problems are solved *ad hoc*. As experience accumulates, some solutions turn out to work better than others, and a sort of folklore is passed informally from person to person. Eventually, the useful solutions are understood more systematically, and they are codified and analyzed. This enables the development of models that

Different observers will classify the same object in different ways.

support automatic implementation and theories that allow the generalization of the solution. This in turn enables a more sophisticated level of practice and allows us to tackle harder problems – which we often approach *ad hoc*, starting the cycle over again" [9].

The incremental and iterative nature of classification directly impacts the construction of class and object hierarchies in the design of a complex software system. In practice, it is common to assert a certain class structure early in a design and then revise this structure over time. Only at later stages in the design, once clients have been built that use this structure, can we meaningfully evaluate the quality of our classification. On the basis of this experience, we may decide to create new subclasses from existing ones (derivation). We may split a large class into several smaller ones (factorization), or create one larger class by uniting smaller ones (composition). Occasionally, we may even discover previously unrecognized commonality, and proceed to devise a new class (abstraction) [10].

Why then, is classification so hard? We suggest that there are two important reasons. First, there is no such thing as a "perfect" classification, although certainly some classifications are better than others. As Coombs, Raiffa, and Thrall state, "There are potentially at least as many ways of dividing up the world into object systems as there are scientists to undertake the task" [11]. Any classification is relative to the perspective of the observer doing the classification. Flood and Carson give the example that the United Kingdom "could be seen as an economy by economists, a society by sociologists, a threatened chunk of nature by conservationists, a tourist attraction by some Americans, a military threat by rulers of the Soviet Union, and the green, green grass of home to the more romantic of us Britons" [12]. Second, intelligent classification requires a tremendous amount of creative insight. Birtwistle, Dahl, Myhrhaug, and Nygard observe that "sometimes the answer is evident, sometimes it is a matter of taste, and at other times, the selection of suitable components is a crucial point in the analysis" [13]. This fact recalls the riddle, "Why is a laser beam like a goldfish? . . . because neither one can whistle" [14]. Only a creative mind can find sameness among such otherwise unrelated things.

4.2 Identifying Classes and Objects

Classical and Modern Approaches

The problem of classification has been the concern of countless philosophers, linguists, cognitive scientists, and mathematicians, even since before the time of Plato. It is reasonable to study their experiences and apply what we learn to object-oriented design. Historically, there have only been three general approaches to classification:

- Classical categorization
- Conceptual clustering
- Prototype theory [15]

Classical Categorization. In the classical approach to categorization, "All the entities that have a given property or collection of properties in common form a category. Such properties are necessary and sufficient to define the category" [16]. For example, married people constitute a category: one is either married or not, and the value of this property is sufficient to decide to which group a particular person belongs. On the other hand, tall people do not form a category, unless we can agree to some absolute criteria for what distinguishes the property of tall from not tall.

Classical categorization comes to us first from Plato, and then from Aristotle through his classification of plants and animals, in which he uses a technique much akin to the contemporary children's game of Twenty Questions (Is it an animal, mineral, or vegetable? Does it have fur or feathers? Can it fly?) [17]. Later philosophers, most notably Aquinas, Descartes, and Locke, adopted this approach. As Aquinas stated, "We can name a thing according to the knowledge we have of its nature from its properties and effects" [18].

The classical approach to categorization is also reflected in modern theories of child development. Piaget observed that around the age of one, a child typically develops the concept of object permanence; shortly thereafter, the child acquires skills in classifying these objects, first using basic categories such as

A Problem of Classification

Figure 4-1 contains ten items, labeled *A* to *J*, each of which represents a train. Each train includes an engine (on the right) and from two to four cars, each shaped differently and holding different loads. Before reading further, spend the next few minutes by arranging these trains into any number of groups you deem meaningful. For example, you might create three groups: one for trains whose engines have all black wheels, one for trains whose engines have all white wheels, and one for trains whose engines have black and white wheels.

This problem comes from the work by Stepp and Michalski on conceptual clustering [19]. As in real life, there is no "right" answer. In their experiments, subjects came up with some ninety-three different classifications. The most popular classification was by the length of the train, forming three groups (trains with two, three, and four cars). The second most popular classification was by engine wheel color, as we suggested. Of these ninety-three classifications, some forty of them were totally unique.

Our use of this example confirms Stepp and Michalski's study. Most of our subjects have used the two most popular classifications, although we have encountered some rather creative groupings. For example, one subject arranged these trains into two groups: one group represented trains labeled by letters containing straight lines *(A, E, F, H, and I)* and the other group representing trains labeled by letters containing curved lines. This is truly an example of nonlinear thinking: creative, albeit bizarre.

Once you have completed this task, let's change the requirements (again, as in real life). Suppose that circles represent toxic chemicals, rectangles represent lumber, and all other shapes of loads represent passengers. Try classifying the trains again, and see how this new knowledge changes your classification.

Among our subjects, the clustering of trains changed significantly. Most subjects classified trains according to whether or not they carried toxic loads. We conclude from this simple experiment that more knowledge about a domain, up to a point, makes it easier to achieve an intelligent classification.

dogs, cats, and toys [20]. Later, the child discovers more general categories (such as animals) and more specific ones (such as collies and beagles) [21].

To summarize, the classical approach uses related properties as the criteria for sameness among objects. Specifically, one can divide objects into disjoint sets depending upon the presence or absence of a particular property. Minsky suggests that "the most useful sets of properties are those whose members do not interact too much. This explains the universal popularity of that particular combination of properties: size, color, shape, and substance. Because these attributes scarcely interact at all with one another, you can put them together in any combination whatsoever, to make an object that is either large or small, red or green, wooden or glass, and having the shape of a sphere or a cube" [22]. In a general sense, properties may denote more than just measurable characteristics; they may also encompass observable behaviors. For example, the fact that a bird can fly but a fish cannot is one property that distinguishes an eagle from a salmon.

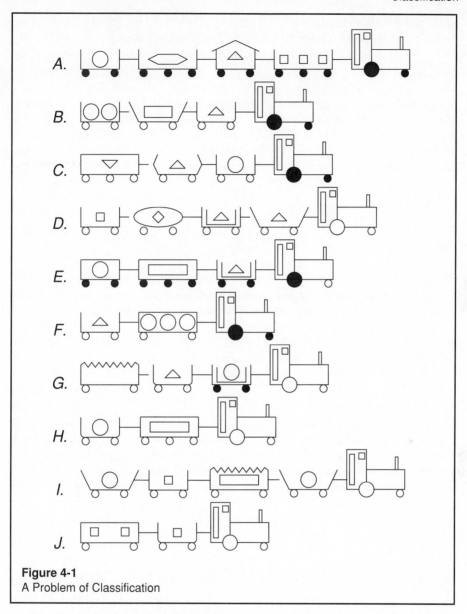

Figure 4-1
A Problem of Classification

The particular properties that should be considered in a given situation are highly domain-specific. For instance, the color of a car may be important for the purposes of inventory control in an automobile manufacturing plant, but it is not at all relevant to the software that controls the traffic lights within a metropolitan area. This is in fact why we say that there are no absolute measures of perfection, although a given class structure may be better suited to one application than another. As James suggests, "No one scheme of classification, more than any other, represents the real structure or order of nature. Nature indifferently submits to any and all divisions which we wish to make among existing things. Some classifications may be more significant than others, but only by reference to our interests, not because they represent reality more accurately or adequately" [23].

Conceptual Clustering. *Conceptual clustering* is a more modern variation of the classical approach, and largely derives from attempts to explain how knowledge is represented. As Stepp and Michalski state, "In this approach, classes (clusters of entities) are generated by first formulating conceptual descriptions of these classes and then classifying the entities according to the descriptions" [24]. For example, we may state a concept such as "a love song." This is a concept more than a property, for the "love songness" of any song is not something that may be measured empirically. However, if we decide that a certain song is more of a love song than not, we place it in this category. Thus, conceptual clustering represents more of a probabilistic clustering of objects.

Prototype Theory. Classical categorization and conceptual clustering are sufficiently expressive to account for most of the classifications we ever need in the design of complex software systems. However, there are still some situations in which these approaches are inadequate. This leads us to the more recent approach to classification, called *prototype theory*, which derives primarily from the work of Rosch and her colleagues in the field of cognitive psychology [25].

There are some abstractions that have neither clearly bounded properties nor concepts. As Lakoff explains the problem, "Wittgenstein pointed out that a category like game does not fit the classical mold, since there are no common properties shared by all games. . . . Though there is no single collection of properties that all games share, the category of games is united by what Wittgenstein calls family resemblances. . . . Wittgenstein also observed that there was no fixed boundary to the category game. The category could be extended and new kinds of games introduced, provided that they resembled previous games in appropriate ways" [26]. This is why the approach is called prototype theory: a class of objects is represented by a prototypical object, and an object is considered to be a member of this class if and only if it resembles this prototype in significant ways.

Classification and Object-Oriented Design Revisited. To the developer in the trenches fighting changing requirements amidst limited resources and tight schedules, our discussion may seem to be far removed from the battlefields of reality. Actually, these approaches to classification have direct application to object-oriented design. In our experience, we identify classes and objects first according to the properties relevant to our particular domain. Such abstractions are usually available for the picking, because they are directly part of the vocabulary of our problem space [27]. If this approach fails to yield a satisfactory class structure, then we next consider clustering objects by concepts. If either of these two fails to capture our understanding of the problem domain, then we consider classification by association, through which clusters of objects are defined according to how closely each resembles some prototypical object.

More directly, these three approaches to classification provide the theoretical foundation of object-oriented analysis, domain analysis, and various other methods, which we may apply to identify classes and objects in the design of a complex software system.

Object-Oriented Analysis

The boundaries between analysis and design are somewhat fuzzy, although the focus of each is quite distinct. In object-oriented analysis, we seek to model the world by identifying the classes and objects that form the vocabulary of the problem domain, and in object-oriented design, we invent the abstractions and mechanisms that provide the behavior that this model requires. As such, object-oriented analysis is the ideal front end to object-oriented design.

Shlaer and Mellor suggest that candidate classes and objects usually derive from one of the following sources [28]:

- Tangible things   Cars, telemetry data, pressure sensors
- Roles   Mother, teacher, politician
- Events   Landing, interrupt, request
- Interactions   Loan, meeting, intersection

From the perspective of data modeling, Ross offers a similar list [29]:

- People   Humans who carry out some function
- Places   Areas set aside for people or things
- Things   Physical objects, or groups of objects, that are tangible
- Organizations Formally organized collections of people, resources, facilities, and capabilities having a defined mission, whose existence is largely independent of individuals
- Concepts   Principles or ideas not tangible *per se;* used to organize or keep track of business activities and/or communications
- Events   Things that happen, usually to something else at a given date and time, or as steps in an ordered sequence

Coad and Yourdon suggest yet another set of sources of potential objects [30]:

- Structure   "Kind of" and "part of" relationships

- Other systems   External systems with which the application
                         interacts
- Devices   Devices with which the application interacts
- Events remembered   An historical event that must be recorded
- Roles played   The different roles users play in interacting
                         with the application
- Locations   Physical locations, offices, and sites important
                         to the application
- Organizational units   Groups to which users belong

At a higher level of abstraction, Coad introduces the idea of subject areas, which are basically logical groups of classes that relate to some higher level system function.

Domain Analysis

Closely related to the methods of object-oriented analysis are those of domain analysis. Whereas object-oriented analysis typically focuses upon one specific problem at a time, domain analysis seeks to identify the classes and objects that are common to all applications within a given domain, such as missile avionics systems, compilers, or accounting software. If you are in the midst of a design and stuck for ideas as to the key abstractions that exist, domain analysis can help by pointing you to the key abstractions that have proven useful in other related systems. Domain analysis works well because, except for special situations, there are very few truly unique kinds of software systems.

The idea of domain analysis was first suggested by Neighbors. We define domain analysis as "an attempt to identify the objects, operations, and relationships [that] domain experts perceive to be important about the domain" [31]. Moore and Bailin suggest the following steps in domain analysis:

- "Construct a strawman generic model of the domain by consulting with domain experts.
- Examine existing systems within the domain and represent this understanding in a common format.
- Identify similarities and differences between the systems by consulting with domain experts.
- Refine the generic model to accommodate existing systems" [32].

Domain analysis may be applied across similar applications (vertical domain analysis), as well as to related parts of the same application (horizontal domain analysis). For example, when starting to design a new patient-monitoring system, it is reasonable to survey the architecture of existing systems to understand what key abstractions and mechanisms were previously employed and to evaluate which were useful and which were not. Similarly, an accounting system must provide many different kinds of reports. By treating these reports as a single domain, a domain analysis can lead the developer to an understanding of the key abstractions and mechanisms that serve all the different kinds of reports. The resulting classes and objects reflect a set of key abstractions and mechanisms generalized to the immediate report-generation problem; therefore, the resulting design is likely to be simpler than if each report had been analyzed and designed separately.

Who exactly is a domain expert? Often, a domain expert is simply a user, such as a train engineer or dispatcher in a railway system. A domain expert need not be a software engineer; more commonly, he or she is simply a person who is intimately familiar with all the elements of a particular problem. A domain expert speaks the vocabulary of the problem domain.

Some managers may be concerned with the idea of direct communication between developers and end users (for some, even more frightening is the prospect of letting an end user see a developer!). For highly complex systems, domain analysis may involve a formal process, using the resources of multiple domain experts and developers over a period of many months. In practice, such a formal analysis is rarely necessary. Often, all it takes to clear up a design problem is a brief meeting between a domain expert and a developer. It is truly amazing to see what a little bit of domain knowledge can do to assist a developer in making intelligent design decisions. Indeed, we find it highly useful to have many such meetings throughout the design of a system. Domain analysis is rarely a monolithic activity; it is better focused if we consciously choose to analyze a little, then design a little.

Alternate Approaches

Object-oriented analysis and domain analysis are the techniques we prefer to use with object-oriented design. Two alternate approaches have been suggested, however, that merit discussion.

Informal English Description. The first alternative is a radically simple technique, first proposed by Abbott, who suggests writing an English description of the problem (or a part of a problem) and then underlining the nouns and verbs [33]. The nouns represent candidate objects, and the verbs represent candidate operations upon them. This technique lends itself to automation, and such a system has been built at the Tokyo Institute of Technology and at Fujitsu [34].

Abbott's approach is useful because it is simple and because it forces the developer to work in the vocabulary of the problem space. However, it is by no means a rigorous approach, and it definitely does not scale well to anything beyond fairly trivial problems. Human language is a terribly imprecise vehicle of expression, so the quality of the resulting list of objects and operations depends upon the writing skill of its author. Furthermore, any noun can be verbed, and any verb can be nouned; therefore, it is easy to skew the candidate list to emphasize either objects or operations.

Structured Analysis. The second alternative to identifying classes and objects uses the products of structured analysis as a front end to object-oriented design. This technique is appealing simply because a large number of analysts are skilled in structured analysis, and many CASE tools exist that support the automation of these methods.

We start with an essential model of the system, as described by data flow diagrams and the other products of structured analysis. These diagrams provide us with a reasonably formal model of the problem. From this model, we may proceed to identify the meaningful classes and objects in our problem domain in three different ways.

McMenamin and Palmer suggest starting with an analysis of the data dictionary and proceeding to analyze the model's context diagram. As they state, "With your list of essential data elements, think about what they tell you or what they describe. If they were adjectives in a sentence, for instance, what nouns would they modify? The answers to this question make up the list of candidate objects" [35]. These candidate objects typically derive from the surrounding environment, from the essential inputs and outputs, and from the products, services, and other resources managed by the system.

The next two techniques involve analyzing individual data flow diagrams. Given a particular data flow diagram (using the terminology of Ward/Mellor [36]), candidate objects may be derived from the following:

- External entities
- Data stores
- Control stores
- Control transformations

Candidate classes derive from two sources:

- Data flows
- Control flows

This leaves us with data transformations, which we assign either as operations upon existing objects or as the behavior of an object we invent to serve as the agent responsible for this transformation.

Seidewitz and Stark suggest another technique, which they call *abstraction analysis*. Abstraction analysis focuses upon the identification of central entities, which are similar in nature to central transforms in structured design. As they state, "In structured analysis, input and output data are examined and followed inwards until they reach the highest level of abstraction. The processes between the inputs and the outputs form the central transform. In abstraction analysis a designer does the same, but also examines the central transform to determine which processes and states represent the best abstract model of what the system does" [37]. After identifying the central entity in a particular data flow diagram, abstraction analysis proceeds to identify all the supporting entities by following the afferent and efferent data flows from the central entity, and grouping the processes and states encountered along the way. In practice, Seidewitz and Stark have found abstraction analysis a difficult technique to apply successfully, and as an alternative recommend object-oriented analysis methods [38].

We must emphasize that structured design, as normally coupled with structured analysis, is entirely orthogonal to the principles of object-oriented design. Our experience indicates that structured analysis can be a suitable front end to object-oriented design, but only if the developer resists the urge to fall back into the abyss of the structured design mindset. Another very real danger is that fact that many analysts tend to write data flow diagrams that reflect a design rather than an essential model of the problem. It is tremendously difficult to build an object-oriented system from a model that is so obviously biased towards algorithmic decomposition. This is why we prefer object-oriented analysis and domain analysis as front ends to object-oriented design: there is simply less danger of polluting the design with preconceived algorithmic notions.

If you must use structured analysis as a front end, for whatever honorable reasons, we suggest that you stop writing data flow diagrams as soon as they start to smell of a design instead of an essential model. Also, it is a healthy practice to walk away from the products of structured analysis once the design is fully underway. Remember that the products of development, including data flow diagrams, are not ends in themselves; they should be viewed simply as tools along the way that aid the developer's intellectual comprehension of the problem and its implementation. One typically writes a data flow diagram and then invents the mechanisms that implement the desired behavior. Practically speaking, the very act of design changes the developer's understanding of the problem, making the original model somewhat obsolete. Keeping the original model up to date with the design is terribly labor intensive, is not amenable to automation, and, frankly, doesn't add a lot of value. Thus, only the products of structured analysis that are at a sufficiently high level of abstraction should be retained. They capture an essential model of the problem, and so lend themselves to any number of different designs.

4.3 Key Abstractions and Mechanisms

Identifying Key Abstractions

Finding Key Abstractions. A *key abstraction* is a class or object that forms part of the vocabulary of the problem domain. The primary value of identifying such abstractions is that they give boundaries to our problem; they highlight the things that are in the system and therefore relevant to our design, and suppress the things that are outside the system and therefore superfluous. The identification of key abstractions is highly domain-specific. As Goldberg states, the "appropriate choice of objects depends, of course, on the purposes to which the application will be put and the granularity of information to be manipulated" [39].

The identification of key abstractions involves two processes: discovery and invention. Through discovery, we come to recognize the abstractions used by domain experts; if the domain expert talks about it, then the abstraction is usually important [40]. Through invention, we create new classes and objects that are not necessarily part of the problem domain, but are useful artifacts in the design or implementation. For example, a customer using an automated teller speaks in terms of accounts, deposits, and withdrawals; these words are part of the vocabulary of the problem domain. A developer of such a system uses these same abstractions, but must also introduce new ones, such as databases, screen managers, and so on. These key abstractions are artifacts of the particular design, not of the problem domain.

Perhaps the most powerful way to identify key abstractions is to look at the problem or design and see if there are any abstractions that are similar to the classes and objects that already exist. Since this is a problem of classification, we can use any of the classical or modern techniques described earlier in this chapter. This approach emphasizes the reuse of abstractions and is intrinsic to the process of object-oriented design.

Refining Key Abstractions. Once we identify a certain key abstraction as a candidate, we must evaluate it according the the metrics described in the previous chapter. As Stroustrup suggests, "Often this means that the programmer must focus on the questions: how are objects of this class created? can objects of this class be copied and/or destroyed? what operations can be done on such objects? If there are no good answers to such questions, the concept probably wasn't 'clean' in the first place, and it might be a good idea to think a bit more about the problem and the proposed solution instead of immediately starting to 'code around' the problems" [41].

Given a new abstraction, we must place it in the context of the existing class and object hierarchies we have designed. Practically speaking, this is neither a top-down nor a bottom-up activity. As Halbert and O'Brien observe, "You do not always design types in a type hierarchy by starting with a supertype and then creating the subtypes. Frequently, you create several seemingly disparate types, realize they are related, and then factor out their common characteristics into one or more supertypes. . . . several passes up and down are usually required to produce a complete and correct program design" [42]. Again, this is not a recommendation to hack, but an observation, based upon experience, that object-oriented design is both incremental and iterative.

Placing classes and objects at the right levels of abstraction is difficult. Sometimes we may find a general subclass, and so may choose to move it up in the class structure, thus increasing the degree of sharing. This is called *class promotion* [43]. Similarly, we may find a class to be too general, thus making inheritance by a subclass difficult because of the large semantic gap. This is called a *grainsize conflict* [44]. In either case, we strive to identify cohesive and loosely coupled abstractions, so as to mitigate these two situations.

Classes and objects should be at the right level of abstraction: neither too high nor too low.

Naming things properly – so that they reflect their semantics – is often treated lightly by most developers, yet is important in capturing the essence of the abstractions we are describing. Software should be written as carefully as English prose, with consideration given to the reader as well as to the computer. Consider for a moment all the names we may need just to identify a single object: we have the name of the object itself, the name of its class, and the name of the module in which that class is declared. Multiply this by thousands of objects and possibly hundreds of classes, and you have a very real naming problem.

We offer the following suggestions:

- Objects should be named with proper noun phrases, such as `TheSensor` or `AShape`.
- Classes should be named with common noun phrases, such as `Sensors` or `Shapes`.
- Modifier operations should be named with active verb phrases, such as `Draw` or `Move`.
- Selector operations should imply a query or be named with verbs of the form "to be," such as `ExtentOf` or `IsOpen`.

Identifying Mechanisms

Finding Mechanisms. As in the process of Jackson System Development (JSD) [45], in object-oriented design we first identify key abstractions to form a model of reality; only then do we add behavior to these abstractions to derive the observable behaviors of the system [46]. As noted in the previous chapter, we use the term *mechanism* to describe any structure whereby objects work together to provide some behavior that satisfies a requirement of the problem. Whereas the design of a class embodies the knowledge of how individual objects behave, a mechanism represents a design decision about how collections of objects cooperate.

For example, consider a system requirement for an automobile: pushing the accelerator should cause the engine to run faster, and releasing the accelerator should cause the engine to run slower. How this actually comes about is absolutely immaterial to the driver. Any mechanism may be employed as long as it delivers the required behavior, and thus which mechanism is selected is largely a matter of design choice. More specifically, any of the following designs might be considered:

- A mechanical linkage from the accelerator to the carburetor (the most common mechanism).
- An electronic linkage from a pressure sensor below the accelerator to a computer that controls the carburetor (a drive-by-wire mechanism).
- No linkage exists; the gas tank is placed on the roof of the car, and gravity causes fuel to flow to the engine. Its rate of flow is regulated by a clip around the fuel line; pushing on the accelerator pedal eases tension on the clip, causing the fuel to flow faster (a low-cost mechanism).

Which mechanism a developer chooses from a set of alternatives is most often a result of other factors, such as cost, reliability, manufacturability, and safety.

Just as it is rude for a client to violate the interface of another object, so it is socially unacceptable for objects to step outside the boundaries of the rules of behavior dictated by a particular mechanism. Indeed, it would be surprising for a driver if stepping on an accelerator turned on the car's lights instead of causing the engine to run faster.

Whereas key abstractions reflect the vocabulary of the problem domain, mechanisms are the soul of the design. During the design process, the developer must consider not only the design of individual classes, but also how instances of these classes work together. Once a developer decides upon a particular mechanism, the work is distributed among many objects by defining suitable methods in the appropriate classes.

Mechanisms represent strategic design decisions. Similarly, the design of a class structure represents a strategic decision; in contrast, however, the interface of an individual class is more of a tactical design decision. These strategic

Mechanisms are the means whereby objects collaborate to provide some higher level behavior.

decisions must be made explicitly; otherwise we will end up with a mob of relatively uncooperative objects, all pushing and shoving to do their work with little regard for other objects. The most elegant, lean, and fast programs embody carefully engineered mechanisms.

Examples of Mechanisms. Consider the drawing mechanism commonly used in graphical user interfaces. Several objects must collaborate to present an image to a user: a window, a view, the model being viewed, and some client that knows when (but not how) to display this model. The client first tells the window to draw itself. Since it may encompass several subviews, the window next tells each of its subviews to draw themselves. Each subview in turn tells its model to draw itself, ultimately resulting in an image shown to the user. In this mechanism, the model is entirely decoupled from the window and view in which it is presented: views can send messages to models, but models cannot send messages to views. Smalltalk uses a variation of this mechanism called the *model-view-controller (MVC)* paradigm [47].

Mechanisms thus represent another level of design reuse, higher than the reuse of individual classes. For example, the MVC paradigm is the foundation of the Smalltalk user interface. The MVC paradigm builds on another mechanism, the dependency mechanism, which is embodied in the behavior of the Smalltalk base class `Object`, and thus pervades the entire Smalltalk class library.

Examples of mechanisms may be found in a multitude of systems. For example, the structure of an operating system may be described at the highest level of abstraction according to the mechanism used to dispatch programs. A particular design might be monolithic (such as MS-DOS), or it may employ a kernel (such as Unix) or a process hierarchy (as in the THE operating system) [48]. In artificial intelligence, a variety of mechanisms have been explored for the design of reasoning systems. One of the most widely used paradigms is the blackboard mechanism, in which individual knowledge sources independently update a blackboard. There is no central control in such a mechanism, but any change to the blackboard may trigger an agent to explore some new problem-solving path [49].

This completes our study of classification and of the concepts that serve as the foundation of object-oriented design. The next three chapters focus on the method itself, including its notation, process, and practical application.

Summary

- The identification of classes and objects is the fundamental issue in object-oriented design; identification involves both discovery and invention.
- Classification is fundamentally a problem of clustering.
- Classification is an incremental and iterative process, made difficult because a given set of objects may be classified in many equally proper ways.
- The three approaches to classification include classical categorization (classification by properties), conceptual clustering (classification by concepts), and prototype theory (classification by association with a prototype).
- Object-oriented analysis suggests that candidate classes and objects derive from tangible things, roles, events, and interactions.
- Domain analysis seeks to identify the classes and objects that are common to similar applications within a given domain or related parts of the same application.
- Key abstractions reflect the vocabulary of the problem domain and may either be discovered from the problem domain, or invented as part of the design.
- Mechanisms are the soul of the design, and represent strategic design decisions regarding the collaborative activity of many different kinds of objects.

Further Readings

The problem of classification is timeless. In his work titled *Statesman*, Plato introduces the classical approach to categorization, through which objects with similar properties are grouped. In *Categories*, Aristotle picks up this theme and analyzes the differences between classes and objects. Several centuries later, Aquinas, in *Summa Theologica*, and then Descartes, in *Rules for the Direction of the Mind*, ponder the philosophy of classification.

Classification is also an essential human skill. Theories regarding its acquisition during early childhood development were pioneered by Piaget, and are summarized by Maier [A 1969]. Lefrancois [A 1977] offers a very readable introduction to these ideas and provides an excellent discourse on children's acquisition of the object concept.

Many cognitive scientists have explored the problems of classification in great detail. Newell and Simon [A 1972] provide an unmatched source of material regarding human classification skills. More general information may be found in Simon [A 1982], Hofstadter [I 1979], Siegler and Richards [A 1982], and Stillings, Feinstein, Garfield, Rissland, Rosenbaum, Weisler, and Baker-Ward [A 1987]. Lakoff [A 1987], a linguist, offers insights into the ways different human languages have evolved to cope with the problems of classification and what this reveals about the mind. Minksy [A 1986] approaches this subject from the opposite direction, starting with a theory regarding the structure of the mind.

Cognitive scientists use the term conceptual clustering to describe an approach to knowledge representation through classification. Conceptual clustering is described in detail by Michalski and Stepp [A 1983, 1986], Peckham and Maryanski [J 1988], and Sowa [A 1984].

Domain analysis is a means of finding key abstractions and mechanisms by examining the vocabulary of the problem domain. Iscoe [B 1988] has made several important contributions to this subject. Additional information may be found in Iscoe, Browne, and Weth [B 1989], Moore and Bailin [B 1988], and Arango [B 1989].

The discovery of classes and objects may proceed from any number of different models that capture the requirements of the problem domain. Abbott [F 1983] proposes that this search start from a textual description of the problem. Ward [B 1989] and Seidewitz and Stark [F 1986] suggest starting from the products of structured analysis, namely, data flow diagrams. Veryard [B 1984] examines the same problem from the perspective of data modeling.

Mathematicians have attempted to devise empirical approaches to classification, leading to what is called measurement theory. Stevens [A 1946] and Coombs, Raiffa, and Thrall [A 1954] provide the seminal work on this topic.

The Classification Society of North America publishes a journal twice a year, containing a variety of papers on the problems of classification.

The Method

Which innovation leads to a successful design and which to a failure is not completely predictable. Each opportunity to design something new, either bridge or airplane or skyscraper, presents the engineer with choices that may appear countless. The engineer may decide to copy as many seemingly good features as he can from existing designs that have successfully withstood the forces of man and nature, but he may also decide to improve upon those aspects of prior designs that appear to be wanting.

HENRY PETROSKI
To Engineer is Human

The Notation

Designing is not the act of drawing a diagram; a diagram simply captures a design. If you follow the work of any engineer – software, civil, mechanical, chemical, architectural, or whatever – you will soon realize that the one and only place that a design is conceived is in the mind of the designer. As this design unfolds over time, it is often captured on such high-tech media as white boards, napkins, and scraps of paper [1].

Still, having a well-defined and expressive notation is important. First, standard notation makes it possible for one person to formulate a design and then communicate it to others. Draw an electrical circuit, and the symbol for a transistor will be understood by virtually every electrical engineer in the world. Similarly, if an architect in New York drafts the plans for a house, a builder in San Francisco will have little trouble understanding where to place doors, windows, and electrical outlets. Second, as Whitehead states in his seminal work on mathematics, "By relieving the brain of all unnecessary work, a good notation sets it free to concentrate on more advanced problems" [2]. Third, an expressive notation makes it possible to eliminate much of the tedium of checking the consistency and correctness of these designs by using automated tools. As a report by the Defense Science Board states, "Software development is and always will be a labor-intensive technology. . . . Although our machines can do the dog-work and can help us keep track of our edifices, concept development is the quintessentially human activity. . . . The part of

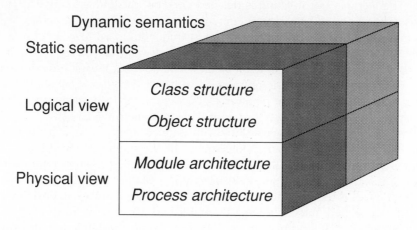

Figure 5-1
The Models of Object-Oriented Design

software development that will not go away is the crafting of conceptual structures; the part that can go away is the labor of expressing them" [3].

5.1 Elements of the Notation

The Need for Multiple Views

It is impossible to capture all the subtle details of a complex software system in just one kind of diagram. As Kleyn and Gingrich observe, "One must understand both the structure and the function of the objects involved. One must understand the taxonomic structure of the class objects, the inheritance mechanisms used, the individual behaviors of objects, and the dynamic behavior of the system as a whole. The problem is somewhat analogous to that of viewing a sports event such as tennis or a football game. Many different camera angles are required to provide an understanding of the action taking place. Each camera reveals particular aspects of the action that could not be conveyed by one camera alone" [4].

Figure 5-1 indicates the different models (first introduced in Chapter 1) we have found to be important in object-oriented design. Collectively, these different models are highly expressive: they allow a developer to capture all of the interesting design decisions one must make, and they are complete enough to serve as blueprints for implementation in almost any object-based or object-oriented programming language. This notation scales up as well: we have found these models to be applicable for systems as small as a few hundred lines of code, as well as for ones of more than several million lines of code.

The fact that our notation is detailed does not mean that every aspect of it must be used at all times. As Weinberg notes, "In other design fields, such as architecture, the rough sketch is the most frequently used graphic device, and precise detailed drawings are rarely used at all until the creative part of the design work is finished" [5]. Remember, a notation is a means of documenting the design of a system; it is not an end in itself. Therefore, one should apply only those elements of the notation that are necessary to convey the intended meaning, and nothing more. Just as it is dangerous to overspecify a set of requirements, so it is dangerous to overdesign a solution to a problem. For example, on a blueprint, an architect may show the general location of a light switch in a room, but its exact location will not be established until the construction manager and owner do an electrical walkthrough, after the house has been framed. If the designers and implementors of a software-intensive system are highly skilled and have already established a close working relationship, then rough sketches suffice. If, on the other hand, the implementors are not quite so skilled, or if the designers and implementors are separated geographically, in time, or by contract, then more detail will be required in the design process. The notation we present in this chapter covers each of these situations.

Different programming languages sometimes use different terms to express the same concept. The notation we present in this chapter is largely language-independent, as any good design notation should be. Of course, some elements of the notation may have no parallel in a given language and should be avoided if that language is to be used for implementation. For example, free subprograms cannot be declared in Smalltalk, and therefore class utilities should not be used in a design that will be implemented in Smalltalk. There is nothing wrong with tailoring this notation in language-specific ways. For example, the qualification associated with an operation might be tailored for CLOS to identify primary methods, as well as :before, :after, and :around methods. Similarly, an object-oriented design tool for C++ might ignore the template for a class and use C++ as the program description language (PDL) directly.

This is a fairly short chapter, because its purpose is simply to describe the syntax and semantics of the notation for object-oriented design. We will provide a few examples of this notation using the problem of the hydroponics gardening system that we introduced in Chapter 2. This chapter does not explain how we derived the figures; that is the topic of Chapters 6 and 7. Chapters 8 through 12 demonstrate the practical application of this notation through a series of extended applications.

Logical Versus Physical Models

In practice, we have found it essential to separate independent kinds of design decisions. Among other things, a developer must consider the following fundamental issues in object-oriented design:

- What classes exist and how are those classes related?
- What mechanisms are used to regulate how objects collaborate?

- Where should each class and object be declared?
- To what processor should a process be allocated, and for a given processor, how should its multiple processes be scheduled?

Answers to these four questions can be expressed in each of the following diagrams, respectively:

- Class diagrams
- Object diagrams
- Module diagrams
- Process diagrams

These four diagrams form the basic notation of object-oriented design.

The first two diagrams are part of the logical view of a system, because they serve to describe the existence and meaning of the key abstractions that form the design. The remaining two diagrams are part of the physical structure of the system, because they are used to describe the concrete software and hardware components of an implementation.

Static Versus Dynamic Semantics

The four diagrams we have described thus far are largely static. However, events happen dynamically in all software-intensive systems: objects are created and destroyed, objects send messages to one another in an orderly fashion, and in some systems, messages get sent simultaneously. Frankly, describing a dynamic event in a static medium such as a picture is a difficult problem, but it confronts virtually every scientific discipline. In object-oriented design, we express the dynamic semantics of a design through two additional diagrams:

- State transition diagrams
- Timing diagrams

Each class may have a state transition diagram associated with it that indicates how the time ordering of external events can affect the state of each instance of the class. A single object diagram represents a snapshot in time of an otherwise transitory event or configuration of objects; thus, we may use a timing diagram in conjunction with each object diagram to show the time ordering of messages as they are sent and evaluated. In some circumstances, structured English or a reasonably expressive PDL are appropriate substitutes for timing diagrams. Additionally, either timing diagrams or a PDL can be used to document the dynamic semantics of how processes are scheduled in a process diagram.

The Role of Tools

Given automated support for any notation, one of the things that tools can do is to help bad designers create ghastly designs much more quickly than they ever could in the past. Great designs come from great designers, not from great tools. Tools simply empower the individual, freeing him or her to concentrate upon the truly creative aspects of designing. Thus, there are some things that tools can do well and some things that tools cannot do at all. For example, when we show a message being passed from one object to another in an object diagram, a tool can ensure that the message is in fact part of the object's protocol; this is an example of consistency checking. When we use a certain icon to show connectivity among classes or to state invariants, such as "every object in an object diagram is an instance of some class," we expect that a tool can enforce these conventions. Similarly, a tool can tell us if certain classes or methods of a given class are never used; this is an example of completeness checking. Finally, a sophisticated tool might tell us how long it takes to complete a certain operation or if the potential for deadlock exists among a collection of active objects; this is an example of analysis. On the other hand, a tool cannot tell us that we ought to invent a new class so as to simplify our class structure. We might consider trying to use some expert system technology to build such a tool, but this requires (1) an expert both in object-oriented design and the problem domain and (2) the ability to articulate rules about the heuristics for classification, as well as a great deal of commonsense knowledge. We don't expect such tools to emerge in the near future, although we can always hope; in the meantime, we have real systems to create.

5.2 Class Diagrams

Classes, Class Relationships, and Class Utilities

A *class diagram* is used to show the existence of classes and their relationships in the logical design of a system. A single class diagram represents all or part of the class structure of a system. For a small system, a single class diagram will usually suffice, but the design of most systems requires a set of such diagrams to document its class structure.

The three most important elements of a class structure are classes, class relationships, and class utilities (for languages that support the declaration of free subprograms).

Classes. Figure 5-2 shows the icon we use to represent a class in a class diagram. For mostly historical reasons, its shape is that of an amorphous blob; some call it a *cloud*. This icon represents an abstraction with some crisply defined boundaries. The dashed lines that form the outline of this icon indicate that clients generally operate only upon instances of a class, not the class itself. The name of the class is required, and is placed inside the blob. If the name is

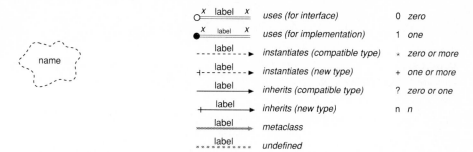

Figure 5-2
Icon for a Class

Figure 5-3
Icons for Class Relationships and Cardinality

particularly long, it can either be elided, or the icon magnified. Every class name must be unique to the enclosing class category.

Class Relationships. Chapter 3 described the variety of relationships that are meaningful among classes, including inheritance, using, instantiation, and metaclass relationships. We support early conceptualization of a class hierarchy by including an "undefined" relationship. The icons for each kind of class relationship are summarized in Figure 5-3. Each relationship may include a label (which may be omitted) to document the name or role of the relationship. If a label is used, the symbol • may be applied to indicate the direction from which the label is to be read.

A using relationship is indicated by a double line with a circle placed at one end to designate the class that uses the resources of another. For example, if we use a double line to indicate a relationship between classes A and B and then place an unfilled circle near class A, we are asserting that A's interface uses the resources of class B. If we use a filled circle instead, we are asserting that A's implementation uses the resources of class B. During early stages of design, it is usually sufficient to show just the interface relationships. Only as implementation decisions are made does a developer consider showing the implementation relationships as well.

In some circumstances, especially in modeling the classes that form part of a database, there is great value in showing the cardinality among classes that use one another. Figure 5-3 also shows the icons we use to express cardinality which are derived from the symbols used to write regular expressions for Unix's *grep* tool. For example, between the classes A and B, if we place the symbol 1 near A and the symbol + near B, this means that for every instance of A, we may have one or more instances of B, and that for every instance of B, there is exactly one instance of A. If needed, we can also form more complicated cardinality assertions by using the relational operators =, <>, >, <, <=, and >=.

A class relationship wherein class A instantiates class B is indicated by a single dashed line, with the arrow pointing to the class being instantiated (such

Figure 5-4
Icon for a Class Utility

as B). This kind of relationship is meaningful only for languages that support some sort of parameterized class or generic mechanism.

An inheritance relationship appears the same as an instantiation relationship, except that a single solid line is used. In practice, inheritance relationships are the most common, followed by using relationships. By convention, we generally don't show the inheritance of one class from a topmost base class, such as TObject in Object Pascal, unless there is some compelling reason to do so. Classes that stand alone are usually considered to have been direct ancestors of this base class. If instances of the subclass are not type compatible with instances of the superclass (or, in Ada terms, if we have a *derived type*), then we place a perpendicular line across the relationship line, opposite the arrow.

The icon for a metaclass relationship uses a single gray line. In some languages, such as Smalltalk, every class has a metaclass, but we generally choose to document only those metaclasses that add their own domain-specific behavior.

An undefined relationship, denoted by a dashed gray line without an arrowhead, is used by the designer to assert that some sort of class relationship exists, but that a decision about the precise kind of relationship has been deferred.

Class Utilities. The icon for a class utility is shown in Figure 5-4. It is similar to the icon for a single class, but is distinguished by a shadow. The class utility icon represents either a single free subprogram or a collection of such free subprograms. If the language of implementation does not permit this construct, it can be omitted. The name of the class utility is required, and is placed inside the blob. As with classes, if the name is particularly long, it can either be elided, or the icon magnified. Every class utility name must be unique to the enclosing class category. One may express class relationships involving class utilities, but in general, only the using and instantiation relationships are ever applied.

Example of a Class Diagram. Figure 5-5 provides an example of this notation, drawn from the problem of the hydroponics gardening system. This is just one of the several class diagrams that constitute the class structure of the gardening system. It shows the classes Heater and Cooler inheriting from the more general class Actuator. The class EnvironmentalController uses the classes Heater, Cooler, and Lights in its implementation. For every heater and cooler object, there is exactly one instance of the class EnvironmentalController,

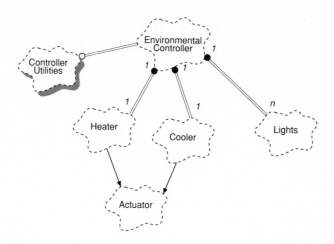

Figure 5-5
Hydroponics Gardening System Class Diagram

and for every environmental controller object, there is exactly one heater and one cooler. In contrast, there may be many (*n*) objects of the class `Lights` associated with each environmental controller, but only one controller for every light object. This diagram also shows the existence of a collection of free subprograms called `ControllerUtilities`, which use the resources of the class `EnvironmentalController`.

Class Categories and Class Category Visibility

Class Categories. A typical class diagram may contain anywhere from one to several dozen classes. However, the class structure of a large system may contain as many as several hundred or a few thousand classes. Trying to put all these classes in one class diagram becomes unwieldy. To deal with this problem, we need some means of organizing classes into meaningful chunks, which leads us to the idea of a class category.

In few object-oriented programming languages, classes may be nested inside other classes. This rarely constitutes a major design decision; it is usually done for convenience of implementation or to restrict visibility of the nested class. A more important design issue is the identification of categories of classes (also known as *subject areas*), each of which represents a logical collection of classes or other class categories. Most object-based and object-oriented programming languages do not directly support such a construct, but for programming-in-the-large, it is an absolutely essential design concept. In practice, a large system has one top-level class diagram, consisting of the class categories at the highest level of abstraction. Such a diagram allows a developer to understand the general logical architecture of a system, because it shows the

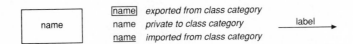

Figure 5-6
Icons for Class Categories and Visibility

highest level organization of the key abstractions that form the vocabulary of the problem domain. Each class category denotes another class diagram; thus, if we pick any one of the class categories from this topmost diagram and zoom into its implementation, we may find either a simple class diagram consisting of classes, class relationships, and class utilities, or (for very large problems) another class diagram containing other class categories, which in turn represent other object diagrams.

The icon for a class category appears in Figure 5-6: a rectangle with the name of the category inside the icon. The naming rules for class categories are the same as for classes and class utilities. As we have said, a class category explodes to another class diagram. Any class diagram may contain both class categories and individual classes.

Class Category Visibility. Since a class category represents an encapsulated name space, some of the entities it encloses may be visible outside the class category, some may be private to the class category, and others may have been imported from other visible class categories. To designate the visibility of a named entity contained in a class category, we may use the icons in Figure 5-6. An unadorned name represents an entity that is private to the class category; it may not be referenced by anything outside of that category. A name framed by a rectangle represents an entity that is contained in the class category but is exported and therefore visible in all other class categories that import it. For example, suppose that class A is exported from class category X. If the class category X is visible to the class category Y, then class A is visible to all the entities contained in class category Y. In other words, A is imported to Y. Although A is declared in class category X, it will also appear in the class diagram for Y, with its name underlined.

Relationships among class categories are represented by the directed line shown in Figure 5-6. To show that the class category Y imports classes declared in X (that is, X is visible to Y), we would draw a directed line from Y to X. Each class category visibility may include a label (which may be omitted) to document the name or role of the relationship.

A problem arises when trying to show the use of base classes and other common container classes. Classes that are part of a predefined class library, such as MacApp, typically must be made visible to every other part of the system. It is good style to place all such classes in their own class category, but now we must make this category visible to every other class category. A class

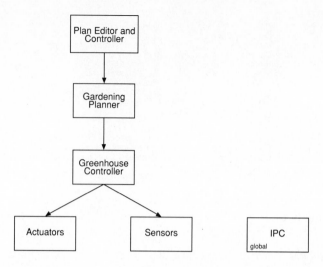

Figure 5-7
Hydroponics Gardening System Top-Level Class Diagram

diagram can thus become very cluttered. To deal with this problem, we permit a developer to mark a class category as global to a given class diagram by placing the word *global* in the lower left corner of the class category icon. This means that all entities exported by this class category are imported by every other class category in the same object diagram.

Example of Class Categories. Figure 5-7 shows an example of a class diagram that uses class categories; it is the top-level class diagram of the hydroponics gardening system. This is a typical layered system: abstractions that are close to the boundaries of the physical system (namely, actuators and sensors) are at the lowest levels, and abstractions that are closest to the user are at the top. The class category labeled IPC (for interprocess control) is global, indicating that its resources are visible to all other class categories in this diagram. If we zoom in to any of the six class categories shown here, we will find another, more detailed, class diagram such as that in Figure 5-5.

Class Diagram Templates

The icons described thus far provide the developer with a notation to describe the class structure of a system at a fairly abstract level. Browsing through such object diagrams lets the reviewer comprehend a large system with relative ease. However, graphics alone are not enough; we must have some substance behind the pictures. In particular, we must provide a means of documenting the meaning of each class: its superclasses, its fields, and its operations.

```
Name:                         identifier
Documentation:                text
Visibility:                   exported | private | imported
Cardinality:                  0 | 1 | n
Hierarchy:
    Superclasses:             list of class names
    Metaclass:                class name
Generic parameters:           list of parameters
Interface | Implementation
(Public/Protected/Private):
    Uses:                     list of class names
    Fields:                   list of field declarations
    Operations:               list of operation declarations
Finite state machine:         state transition diagram
Concurrency:                  sequential | blocking | active
Space complexity:             text
Persistence:                  static | dynamic
```

Figure 5-8
Template for a Class

Class Templates. For each class in a class diagram, we also have a class template in the format shown in Figure 5-8 (this is not to be confused with a C++ template for a parameterized class; unfortunately, there are only so many descriptive names to go around). A class template captures all the important aspects of a class described in Chapter 3. This template is fairly detailed, but in practice we do not expect a developer to fill it in completely, unless, of course, it is important to show this level of detail. In fact, early in the design process, such templates will be completed only very sparsely; as the design progresses, further detail will be added when it is known. If the underlying implementation language is expressive enough, it is actually reasonable to forgo these templates and express the design in the given language directly.

The first two elements of this template are self-explanatory. The third element, visibility, indicates whether the class is exported, private, or imported relative to its enclosing class category. Next, the cardinality of the class captures how many instances we will allow; typically, the values of this element are 0, 1, or n. The role this class plays in the class hierarchy is expressed by the next two elements. Depending upon the implementation language, the class may have zero, one, or more superclasses and a metaclass as well. In any case, the classes mentioned here are derived from the relationships shown in the class diagram; they are shown in the template only for completeness and understandability. If the language permits it, the next element provides any parameters to this class (for example, generic parameters for Ada, or macros and parameterized classes for C++).

The next three fields are repeated up to four times: three times for the interface and once for the implementation of the class. If the implementation language permits it, the interface of the class can be divided into public, protected, and private parts. Thus, C++ might use all three of these interface parts, Ada would use only the public and private parts, and Object Pascal would use only the public parts. In any case, this is the most important section of the class template, because it is here that we capture the outside view of the class. As explained in Chapter 3, this outside view includes any instance variables and class variables (documented in the *fields* element) as well as all operations. For each field, we may document its name, if it is a constant or a variable, its class, any domain constraints (for example, field L is an integer whose value is constrained to be in the range from 1 to 100), and how the field is initialized. Again, we don't have to document all of these things, just those parts of the design that are important to us. The template is complete enough, however, to express all of the interesting aspects of a field. Continuing, the *operations* element actually denotes a list of operations, and each operation has its own template, which we will describe shortly. The *uses* element is similar to the superclass and metaclass, in that we place it here only for completeness and understandability. All using relationships are actually established graphically in the object diagram.

In practice, a developer will fill in only the public, protected, and private parts of the template during the early stages of design. Then, as implementation decisions are made, the fields and operations that form the representation of the class are filled in.

The class template contains four other fields that document the dynamic semantics and time and space behavior of instances of this class. The element named *finite state machine* represents a state transition diagram; we will discuss the notation for state transition diagrams in detail shortly. The element named *concurrency* documents if instances of this class are sequential, blocking, or active. Naturally, these semantics must be compatible with the concurrency semantics associated with each operation. For example, if a class is marked as sequential, none of its operations can have guarded, concurrent, or multiple semantics. The next element, space complexity, documents the space consumed by instances of this class. Size may be expressed in actual memory units or in more relative terms (typically in terms of what is called *big O* notation [6]). The last element documents the persistence of objects of this class. A *persistent* object is one whose state and class may persist beyond the lifetime of the program that created it, and a *transitory* object is one whose lifetime does not extend beyond its enclosing program.

Class properties such as superclasses, metaclasses, and used classes are asserted in the object diagram, but they are also displayed in the class template. Similarly, some of the elements of the template may be displayed in the graphic representation of a class. Specifically, we have found it useful to show the cardinality, concurrency, and persistence of the class along with the class icon (as we did for the class category icon, we place such adornments in the lower left of the icon). In this manner, someone who is reading an object diagram can easily ascertain the important aspects of the design, such as which classes are abstract and which are active (and thus embody their own thread of control). Again, let us emphasize that the developer does not have to include all of these details, but only those that are necessary to convey the essential aspects of a class's design.

Class Utility Templates. The template for a class utility appears in Figure 5-9. Since a class utility represents a collection of free subprograms (and, more

Name:	identifier
Documentation:	text
Category:	text
Qualification:	text
Formal Parameters:	list of parameter declarations
Result:	class name
Preconditions:	PDL	object diagram
Action:	PDL	object diagram
Postconditions:	PDL	object diagram
Exceptions:	list of exception declarations
Concurrency:	sequential	guarded	concurrent	multiple
Time complexity:	text
Space complexity:	text

Name:	identifier
Documentation:	text
Visibility:	exported	private	imported
Generic parameters:	list of parameters
Interface	Implementation:	
Uses:	list of class names
Fields:	list of field declarations
Operations:	list of operation declarations

Figure 5-9
Template for a Class Utility

Figure 5-10
Template for an Operation

rarely, global constants and variables), its template is a small subset of that for classes. In particular, we have only an interface and implementation part. The fields and operations documented in the interface form the outside view of this class utility; those that are part of the implementation are not visible outside the utility.

Operation Templates. Both class and class utility templates may include lists of operations. For less rigorous designs, it is sufficient simply to state the name of the operation, its parameters, and its meaning (using free-form text). If we need a more detailed design documentation, we may use a template for each operation, as illustrated in Figure 5-10.

The first two elements of this template are self-explanatory. The next element, category, provides a way to group logically related operations, much as one can do in Smalltalk browsers. For example, we might group all state-changing operations into a category labeled *modifiers* and all state-preserving operations into a category labeled *selectors*. In any case, the category of an operation is just a notational convenience and is particularly useful whenever a class has more than just a handful of operations. The next element, qualification, is most often used when the implementation language is CLOS. Here we may document if this operation represents a primary method, or if it is a :before, :after, or :around method (or whatever options are defined for the class's method combination type). We complete the static view of the operation by listing its formal parameters and result (for functions only).

The dynamic semantics of each operation are documented in the next four fields. Here we may document the meaning of the operation either very informally by using free-form text in the *action* field or more formally by asserting preconditions, postconditions, and exceptional conditions as well. The semantics of an operation may sometimes point to another object diagram that shows the relationships among the objects participating in the operation and the dynamic semantics of the operation (shown in a timing diagram or with PDL). In any case, the designer certainly does not have to document each operation in gruesome detail (which may amount to more work than just implementing the

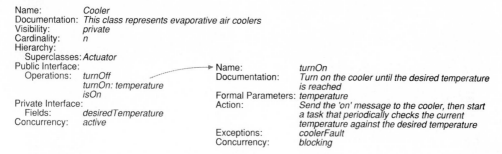

Figure 5-11
Hydroponics Gardening System Class Diagram Templates

operation itself); rather, an appropriate level of detail for each operation should be chosen, given the needs of the eventual reviewer.

The last three elements of this template document the concurrency semantics and the time and space complexity of each operation. As explained in Chapter 3, an operation may be sequential, meaning that its semantics are guaranteed only in the presence of a single thread of control. Alternately, the semantics of an operation may be guaranteed when called by multiple processes, but with different approaches to synchronization: guarded, concurrent, or multiple.

Example of Class Diagram Templates. Figure 5-11 shows the class diagram templates for the class `Cooler` and its operation `turnOn`.

5.3 State Transition Diagrams

States and State Transitions

Just looking at a class diagram does not tell us how instances of individual classes behave dynamically. As we have discussed, the dynamic behavior associated with certain classes is best documented through the use of *state transition diagrams*. These diagrams show the state space of a class, the events that cause a transition from one state to another, and the actions that result from a state change. State transition diagrams are thus intimately related to other parts of the notation: a class template may include a state transition diagram, and the actions described in a particular state transition diagram may point to other object diagrams.

States. The circle in Figure 5-12 represents a single state. This icon is quite simple, and shows only the name of the state. The state name is required, and (like other names) if it is particularly long, it can be elided, or the icon can be

Figure 5-12
Icons for State Transition Diagrams

magnified. Every state name must be unique to the given state transition diagram.

Typically, state transition diagrams associated with a class have neither a start state nor a stop state: when the object is created, it enters a state depending upon the surrounding context, and when the object is destroyed, all associated state becomes moot. When it is important to show explicit start and stop states, there are two variations to this icon. Specifically, a start state is denoted by drawing the state icon with an unfilled double line, and a stop state is denoted by drawing the state icon with a filled double line.

State Transitions. The only relationship that is meaningful among states is a state transition. It is possible to have a state transition between two different states, as well as from one state back to itself. As Figure 5-12 shows, a state transition is drawn as a directed line from the initial state to the new state. Each such line must be labeled with the name of at least one event that causes the state transition and may be labeled with the resulting action. Event and action names need not be unique within a single state transition diagram, because the same event can cause a transition to many different states, and the same action may result from several different transitions.

State Transition Diagram Templates

State Transition Templates. Just as for classes, class utilities, and operations, there is a template for every state transition, as shown in Figure 5-12. Since we associate every state transition with an action, this kind of finite state machine is called a *Mealy model*, as opposed to a *Moore model*, in which actions are associated with states.

The action associated with a particular transition may be expressed through the use of PDL or it may point to another object diagram. This is the same approach we used to document the semantics of operations.

Example of a State Transition Diagram. Figure 5-13 provides an example of a state transition diagram for the class `EnvironmentalController` from the hydroponics gardening system.

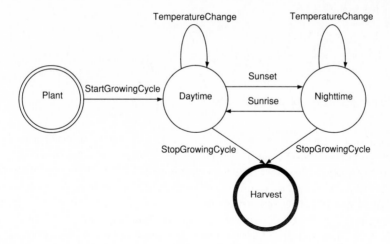

Figure 5-13
Hydroponics Gardening System State Transition Diagram

5.4 Object Diagrams

Objects and Object Relationships

An *object diagram* is used to show the existence of objects and their relation-ships in the logical design of a system. A single object diagram represents all or part of the object structure of a system; typically, the design of a system requires a set of object diagrams. The purpose of each object diagram is to illustrate the semantics of key mechanisms in the logical design. Classes are largely static in the design of a system, whereas objects are much more transitory, in that many of them may be created and destroyed during the execution of a single pro-gram. Therefore, we use object diagrams to capture the dynamic semantics of operations and finite state machines. A single object diagram may thus represent a time-lapse snapshot in time of an otherwise transitory event. In this sense, object diagrams are prototypical: each one represents the interactions that may occur among a collection of objects, no matter what specifically named in-stances participate in the mechanism.

There are important relationships between class diagrams and object dia-grams, paralleling the interplay of classes and objects. Specifically, each object in an object diagram denotes some (specific or arbitrary) instance of a class. Additionally, the operations used in an object diagram must be consistent with the operations defined in the associated classes. For example, if we show object R sending the message M to object S, then the operation M must be defined for S's class. Of course, consistency works in both directions. If, during the

Figure 5-14
Icons for Objects and Object Relationships

incremental evolution of our design, we decide to delete operation N defined for a certain class, this change may make some object diagrams obsolete.

We need both class and object diagrams to document the logical design of a system, because these diagrams show entirely different design decisions. Class diagrams document the key abstractions in our system, and object diagrams highlight the important mechanisms that manipulate these abstractions.

The two most important elements of an object diagram are objects and object relationships.

Objects. Figure 5-14 shows the icon we use to represent an object in an object diagram. This icon is similar to the one we use for a class, except that we use solid lines to show that this is an instance, not a class. The name of the object is required but may be elided, or the icon may be magnified, if the name is particularly long. Object names need not be unique; in fact, many objects within a program have no name that is explicitly known at the source level of a program. For this reason, object names need not be precise but can denote some indefinite instance that is representative of the abstraction, such as `aCooler` or `aTemperatureSensor`. Or course, specific instances may be named if the problem warrants it. For example, we might refer to the object `Greenhouse7` or `HotWaterValveforZone3`.

Properties of an object may appear in the lower left corner of the object icon, just as the icons for classes may include adornments such as cardinality and concurrency semantics. The most important properties to include are the concurrency and persistence semantics of each object, which derive from the semantics of the object's class. Thus, by glancing at a single object diagram, a reader can quickly determine where the threads of control are rooted as well as which objects are static and which are not.

Object Relationships. A relationship between two objects simply means that the objects can send messages to one another. Since messages are typically bidirectional, we use lines without arrowheads to designate these relationships, as Figure 5-14 shows. We use a solid line for object relationships that we can model in software inside the system, and grey lines for ones that are outside the system (such as for documenting the feedback loops in heating and cooling systems). In the early stages of design, it is sufficient to document the associations among classes in this fairly sparse way: we show that two objects can pass messages to one another, but we defer specifying what these messages are.

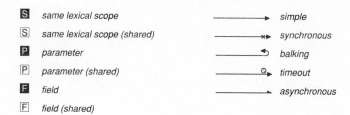

Figure 5-15
Symbols for Object Visibility and Message Synchronization

Object Visibility and Synchronization

We may want to add detail to our object diagrams in two ways.

Object Visibility. First, we may document how two objects see one another. This particular adornment is not always necessary and should be included only when there is compelling reason to do so. Recall that Chapter 3 described six ways in which an object might be visible to another object; Figure 5-15 shows the icons we use to represent these different forms of visibility. For example, if object R is a shared field of object S, then we illustrate this kind of visibility by placing the icon for a shared field along the R and S relationship, near the object R.

Our understanding of the visibility among objects may be aided by the spatial arrangement of objects within an object diagram. For example, we typically place actor objects at the top of such diagrams, and server objects at the bottom. Similarly, to show aggregation, we may nest one object icon inside another.

Message Synchronization. It is equally important to show how related objects interact, which leads us to the second kind of adornment. Specifically, our notation allows us to show the messages passed from object S to object R, by drawing a directed line along the object relationship, labeled with the name of the message. This line points to the object being operated upon, although data may then flow either with or against the direction of the line (with it as a parameter to the operation, against it as the result of a function call or parameter).

For purely sequential systems, drawing a simple directed line is sufficient to express the interaction between two objects. However, things are a bit more complicated in the presence of multiple threads of control. For example, if the two objects are active, then a message from S to R may be delayed (because R is not ready to respond to the message), or it may fail (because S cannot wait for a response). We may also have messages that interrupt an otherwise busy object. In all, there are five different kinds of message synchronization, which were described in Chapter 3: simple, synchronous, balking, timeout, and asynchronous. Figure 5-15 shows these icons, which are adapted from the work

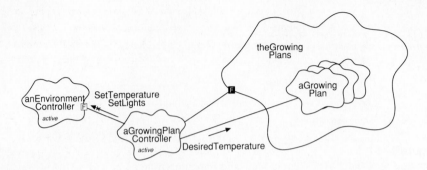

Figure 5-16
Hydroponics Gardening System Object Diagram

by Buhr [7]. Each of these icons may also be labeled with a list of message names.

Example of an Object Diagram. Figure 5-16 provides an example of the icons used in an object diagram. As this figure shows, the object named `aGrowingPlanController` sends two messages to the object named `anEnvironmentController`: `SetTemperature` and `SetLights`. Message passing is synchronous between the two active objects. We also show that `anEnvironmentController` is a field of `aGrowingPlan`, but it is shared, meaning that there are aliases to the object denoted by this field. The collection `theGrowingPlans` is also a field of `aGrowingPlanController`, but this is an unshared field, meaning that the identity of this object is not known anywhere else. The object named `theGrowingPlans` represents a collection consisting of individual growing-plan objects, and to show that they are nested, we place them inside the icon for `theGrowingPlans`. We may use the same technique to show nested classes, class utilities, and modules. In the design we show here, the object `aGrowingPlanController` may send the message `DesiredTemperature` (a selector) to individual growing plans. Here, the message passing semantics are simple, because growing-plan objects are sequential.

Object Diagram Templates

Objects and messages in an object diagram both have templates that can provide more detailed information.

Object Templates. Figure 5-17 provides the template for an object. This template documents the class of the object, which by implication tells us the operations that clients may perform upon the object in the object diagram. The template also lets us state the persistence of the object, an object property that must be compatible with the persistence qualities stated in the definition of the class. Specifically, if the corresponding class template states that all instances are

Object
Name: *identifier*
Documentation: *text*
Class: *class name*
Persistence: *persistent | static | dynamic*

Message
Operation: *operation name*
Documentation: *text*
Frequency: *aperiodic | periodic*
Synchronization: *simple | synchronous | balking |*
                 timeout | asynchronous

Figure 5-17
Template for Objects and Messages

transitory, then the object's persistence can only be static (the object exists during the entire execution of a program) or dynamic (the object is created and destroyed dynamically during the execution of a program). If the class template indicates that instances may be persistent, then the object may be dynamic, static, or persistent (it exists after the program in which it was created terminates).

Message Templates. Figure 5-17 also provides the template for a message. This template serves to point us back to a specific operation defined for the class of the object, which in turn provides the detailed semantics of the operation. We may also assert timing information here, such as whether or not this message is sent periodically, and if so, how often. This detail is most useful to include when designing time-critical applications. Including it here makes it possible to construct analysis tools that determine the end-to-end time it takes to complete operations or to evaluate mechanisms.

5.5 Timing Diagrams

Time-Ordered Events

By themselves, object diagrams are static: they show a cooperative collection of objects that pass messages to one another, but they don't show the flow of control, nor do they show the ordering of events. The state transition diagrams associated with some classes don't help either, since they only show how state changes take place within a single object, not among a set of collaborating objects. To document the semantics of most mechanisms, additional information is vital. Thus we include in our notation three possible ways to document the dynamics of message passing in an object diagram.

The first approach is very simple. We label each message in an object diagram with a number indicating the relative order in which it is invoked. Thus, message 1 will be passed first, then message 2, and so on. This works well for a strictly orderly flow of control, but it is inadequate if we want to express a conditional flow of control (i.e., if condition C is true, then message M is passed, otherwise, message N is passed). This leads us to the second approach, in which we include PDL with every object diagram to describe the order of

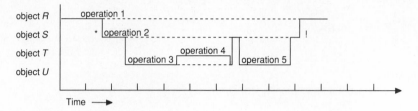

Figure 5-18
Icon for a Timing Diagram

events. For most designs, PDL is the approach of choice, because it is expressive, understandable, and amenable to automated support.

Icons for Timing Diagrams

A third approach that we have found useful has its roots in the timing diagrams used by hardware engineers. Figure 5-18 illustrates how we have adapted this technique to object-oriented design. Here we see that a *timing diagram* is a graph that places time along the horizontal axis and objects along the vertical axis. Time may be expressed in either absolute or relative units and extends in increasing values to the right. As for the objects, we include only those whose mutual interaction we wish to show to document a mechanism. As we move from left to right along the time axis, an operation may be invoked. For example, we may start with operation 1 for object R. As time passes, the implementation of this operation invokes operation 2 for object S, which in turn eventually passes message 3 to object T, and so on. The dashed lines in the diagram indicate a dynamic nesting of messages. For example, when operation 3 completes, control passes back to operation 2, which is then free to do other things.

Timing diagrams may be marked to show object creation (the *) and destruction (the !). Timing diagrams can also be used to document hard-real-time constraints, such as deadlines. For example, we may mark the amount of time budgeted for a given operation (from the operation template). If there are multiple active objects and therefore multiple threads of control represented in a single diagram, it may be necessary to use one PDL fragment or timing diagram for each thread, usually by stacking timing diagrams on top of one another and aligning each time axis.

Typically, a given object diagram may include more than one timing diagram. For example, we may use one primary timing diagram to show the typical dynamic behavior of the mechanism, another to show the impact of asynchronous external events, and yet another to show the flow of control in the face of an exceptional condition. Again, one does not have to use timing diagrams for every object diagram, but they are quite useful when we must document time-critical activities.

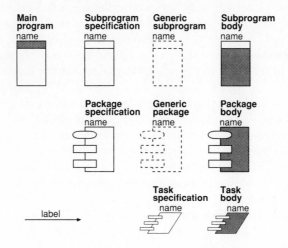

Figure 5-19
Icons for Modules and Module Visibility

5.6 Module Diagrams

Modules and Module Visibility

Class diagrams and object diagrams are used to document the logical design of a system. We now turn to the notation for the physical design of a system, consisting of the software and hardware modules that concretely implement the logical design.

A *module diagram* is used to show the allocation of classes and objects to modules in the physical design of a system; a single module diagram represents all or part of the module architecture of a system. (Other writers have called these *Boochgrams* or *Gradygrams*, but we prefer the more benign name, *module diagrams*.) As noted in Chapter 2, some object-based and object-oriented programming languages support the concept of a module as separate from a class or object. This construct may be as simple as separately compiled files, as in C++, or as sophisticated as the idea of packages in Ada. In either case, the task of the designer is to decide how to allocate classes, class utilities, objects, and other declarations to physical modules. Languages that do not support modules clearly do not require this notation.

The two most important elements of a module architecture are modules and module visibility.

Modules. Figure 5-19 shows the icons we use to represent different kinds of modules in a module diagram. The icons are general enough to be used with all of the object-based and object-oriented programming languages used in this book, but a given language may not support all of these kinds of modules. In particular, Ada supports every one of these modules, but languages such as Object Pascal and C++ only support separately compiled files, which are the equivalent of packages (but with less rigorously enforced semantics). The name of the module is required and is placed at the top of the icon. If the name is long, it can be elided, or the icon can be magnified. Every module name must be unique to the enclosing subsystem. Like the names of classes and utilities, module names may have adornments. Thus, an unadorned name represents a module that is private to its enclosing subsystem. A name framed by a rectangle represents a module that is exported from a subsystem, and an underlined name represents a module that is imported from another subsystem. A nesting of modules may be shown by drawing one icon inside another, as for classes, class utilities, and objects.

Notice in particular the icon we use to represent a main program. Every design must have at least one main program, which represents the root from which the program is activated. Systems that are expected to execute on a distributed collection of computers may have more than one main program.

Module Visibility. The only relationship we may have between two modules is a compilation dependency, represented by the directed line shown in Figure 5-19. For example, to show that module G depends upon module H (perhaps because, in C++ terms, G includes module H), we draw a directed line from G to H, showing that H is now visible to G. We may add a label to this line to further document its meaning. Asserting these relationships makes it possible to determine a legal compilation order for Unix *make* tools and to detect cycles in compilation dependencies.

Example of a Module Diagram. Figure 5-20 provides an example of a simple module diagram, drawn from the physical design of the hydroponics gardening system. Here we find six modules: two of them are imported from some other subsystem, and one is exported from the enclosing subsystem. Notice that we illustrate modules that have two parts (as in the interface and implementation units of Object Pascal) by placing the icon for a package specification on top of the icon for a package body. This particular module diagram represents a fairly typical layered design: only the resources necessary to implement this subsystem are imported, and only a very narrow interface (in this case, one package) is exported.

This physical design maps to the class structure illustrated in Figure 5-5. Specifically, our physical design places the classes for Heater, Cooler, and Lights in the imported package GreenhouseActuators. Similarly, the class EnvironmentalController and its utilities is declared in the local module named EnvironmentalControllers.

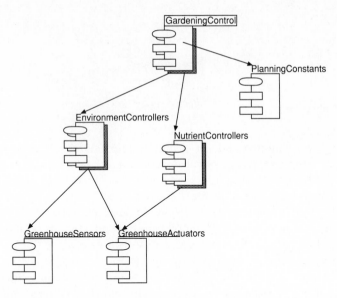

Figure 5-20
Hydroponics Gardening System Module Diagram

Subsystems

As noted in Chapter 2, a large system may be decomposed into many hundreds if not a few thousand modules. Trying to comprehend the physical design of such a system is impossible without further chunking. In practice, developers use informal conventions to collect related modules in directory structures. For similar reasons, we introduce the notion of a subsystem for module diagrams, which parallels the role played by the class category for class diagrams. Subsystems represent clusters of logically related modules and are very helpful for programming-in-the-large.

Unfortunately, most programming languages do not support the concept of a subsystem; creating a subsystem is not the same as nesting packages inside one another. For this reason, we claim that languages even as sophisticated as Ada are too small: the single package is a necessary but insufficient mechanism of decomposition for large systems. Fortunately, most software development environments do permit the designer to work with groups of modules, an abstraction provided by directories in most configuration management and version-control tools. The value of a subsystem is that we can explicitly document decisions about visibility among a logical collection of modules.

In practice, a large system has one top-level module diagram, consisting of the subsystems at the highest level of abstraction. Through this diagram a developer comes to understand the general physical architecture of a system. Each subsystem denotes another module diagram; thus, as with class categories,

Figure 5-21
Icon for a Subsystem

we can pick a subsystem and zoom into its implementation. A given module diagram may contain modules or subsystems, but not both.

The Subsystem Icon. The icon for a subsystem is shown in Figure 5-21. The naming rules and adornments for subsystem names are the same as for all other uses of names. Subsystems have compilation dependencies as do modules; thus the icon for module visibility applies to subsystems as well.

A subsystem module diagram almost, but not exactly, parallels a class diagram at the level of class categories. We say not exactly, because these are two very different views of the same system. Whereas class categories are layered mainly in a "kind of" hierarchy, subsystems are layered in more of a "parts of" hierarchy, in which subsystems build (they do not inherit) upon the resources of lower level subsystems. Since many nontechnical reasons may drive a module decomposition (such as subcontractor relationships, security requirements, and reuse), a module architecture is usually homeomorphic, not exactly isomorphic, to its class structure. For example, we may choose to put all printing resources in one file, so that the linker will collect the associated code in one segment, thereby reducing the amount of thrashing that might occur during execution.

Example of a Subsystem. Figure 5-22 illustrates the preceding point. Here we see the top-level module diagram for the hydroponics gardening system, consisting of four subsystems. Generally speaking, the classes defined in the class categories `Actuators`, `Sensors`, and `IPC` (from Figure 5-7) are declared in the subsystem named `GardeningSystemDevices`. The classes associated with the class category `GreenhouseController` map to the subsystem `GardeningSystemController`, and the classes in the remaining two class categories are spread across the subsystems `GardeningSystemPlanner` and `GardeningSystemPlanDatabase`.

Module Diagram Templates

Module Template Static Semantics. The module icons shown thus far are useful in producing an easily understood representation of the modules that form the physical structure of the system under design. As for all the other icons we have shown, there is substance behind the picture. The template for a module is shown in Figure 5-23. As this template shows, the most important

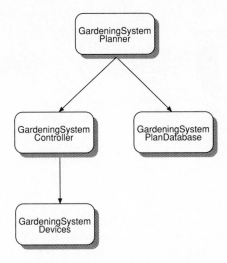

Figure 5-22
Hydroponics Gardening System Top-Level Module Diagram

documentation associated with a module is an accounting of the various declarations it contains. A given module template has a list of declarations, which
may include classes, class utilities, objects, and any other language-specific
declarations. In practice, we find that it is usually sufficient to show only the
allocation of the most important classes and objects to modules and leave the
allocation of all other supporting abstractions to the implementation and evolution of the system. Remember, a design notation intentionally leaves out some
details, and serves only as a blueprint for implementation and understanding.

Depending upon the particular programming language and the software
development environment used, the name of a module may be different than
that of the file in which it is stored. For example, in CLOS, package names are
typically the same as the names of their files, but in Object Pascal, we might
have a unit called `UDialogs`, but catalog it in a file called `UDiag.p`. If it is
important for us to keep track of the location of modules in the file system of
our development environment, the documentation element of each module
template can be used to record the module's file name.

Name: *identifier*
Documentation: *text*
Declarations: *list of declarations*

Figure 5-23
Template for a Module

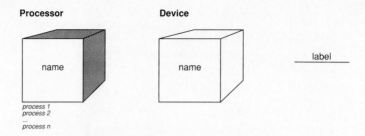

Figure 5-24
Icons for Processors, Devices, and Connections

Module Template Dynamic Semantics. All the diagrams we have studied thus far have both static and dynamic semantics, although module diagrams are typically static. However, in some applications, modules may have dynamic semantics. For example, for an application in which memory is a scare commodity, we may have to swap the code associated with particular modules during execution by using code overlays. We can describe such dynamic semantics through the use of a timing diagram or PDL associated with a module diagram.

5.7 Process Diagrams

Processors and Devices

Process Architecture. As we mentioned in Chapter 2, many large systems require that we design more than just a single, monolithic program; we must sometimes design a system that consists of multiple programs executing upon a distributed collection of computers, which requires design decisions that are quite different than those associated with the identification of classes and objects. For this reason, we choose to use *process diagrams* to visualize and then reason about the problem of allocating processes to processors in the physical design of a system. A single process diagram represents all or part of the process architecture of a system; typically, a design will include only one process diagram, although particularly complex systems may require several. Even for systems that execute on a single processor, process diagrams are useful if our implementation happens to involve devices or active objects, meaning that there may be multiple processes (threads of control) at one time.

The three most important elements of a process architecture are processors, devices, and connections. A *processor* is a piece of hardware capable of executing programs; a *device* has no such computing power.

Processors and Devices. Figure 5-24 shows the icons we use to represent processors and devices. The name of the processor or device is required; naming rules for processors and devices are the same as for modules, except that there may be no adornments to show exports or imports. The icons in the figure are standard, but it is reasonable and in fact desirable for developers and tools to allow alternate icons, as long as each icon can be classified as a processor or a device. For example, we might define icons to represent an embedded micro-computer (a processor), a disk, a terminal, and an A/D converter (all devices), and then use these icons in a process diagram instead of the standard icons. By doing so, we can offer a representation of the physical platform of our imple-mentation that speaks directly to our hardware and systems architects, as well as to the end users of the system, who are probably not experts in software development.

A processor icon typically includes an adornment in its lower left corner, enumerating the programs and processes (active objects) that execute on the processor, and how they are scheduled. We will elaborate upon the possible options for scheduling shortly.

Processor and Device Connections

Connections. Processors and devices must communicate with one another. Using the line shown in Figure 5-24, we may show the connection between a device and a processor, a processor and a processor, or a device and a device. A connection usually represents some direct hardware coupling (such as an RS232 cable, an Ethernet connection, or a fiber optics cable), although it can represent more indirect couplings, such as satellite-to-ground communications. Connections are usually considered to be bidirectional, although if a particular connection is unidirectional, an arrow may be added to show the direction. Each connection may include a label (which may be omitted), to document the name or role of the connection. As for processors and devices, a developer or tool can supply alternate, problem-specific icons to represent connections.

Example of a Process Diagram. Figure 5-25 provides an example of a process diagram for the design of the hydroponics gardening system. Note that the tar-get of our application consists of several computers: one central computer, and one for each greenhouse. Programs running on the greenhouse computers cannot communicate with one another directly; they can communicate only with programs running on the central computer. For simplicity, we have chosen not to show any devices in this diagram.

Process Diagram Templates

The icons shown thus far allow the user to visualize the hardware design of our system. From the perspective of the software designer and systems architect, process diagrams also contain important information in the templates for pro-cessors, devices, and connections.

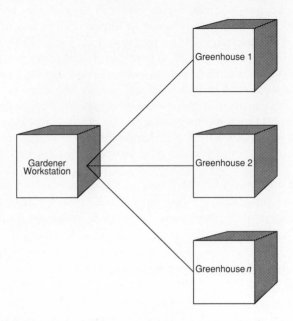

Figure 5-25
Hydroponics Gardening System Process Diagram

Processor and Process Templates. Figure 5-26 shows the templates for processors and individual processes. For each processor, we can document elements such as the characteristics of the computer (its manufacturer and model number, the amount of main memory, etc.). More importantly, we can document what processes we choose to allocate to this processor; a single process represents a main program (from a module diagram) or an active object (designated in an object or class diagram). We use a process template to document an individual thread of control; a process template also includes its relative priority (which may or may not be static), if there is one. If our implementation is simple, we may have only one process, namely, the main program itself; more complicated systems may have dozens of processes at one time. Not all of them may be active simultaneously, but by using processor templates to collect information about all potential processes, we can reason about their worst-case scheduling. In particular, we can reason about load balancing, that is, the even distribution of processes to processors, so that at no point in time do we ever exceed the computational power of a given processor (and thus cause a process to be delayed or missed altogether).

Process Scheduling. We must have some way to decide how to schedule the execution of processes within a processor. There are basically five general

Processor
Name: *identifier*
Documentation: *text*
Characteristics: *text*
Processes: *list of processes*
Scheduling: *preemptive | nonpreemptive |*
                 cyclic | executive | manual

Process
Name: *identifier*
Documentation:*text*
Priority: *integer*

Device and Connection
Name: *identifier*
Documentation:*text*
Characteristics: *text*

Figure 5-26
Templates for Processors, Processes, Devices, and Connections

approaches to scheduling, and we may document which of these is used in the processor template:

- Preemptive

    Higher priority processes that are ready to execute may preempt lower priority ones that are currently executing; typically, processes with equal priority are given a time slice in which to execute, so that computational resources are fairly distributed.

- Nonpreemptive

    The current process continues to execute until it relinquishes control.

- Cyclic

    Control passes from one process to another, and each process is given a fixed amount of processing time, usually called a frame; processes may be allocated time in frames or subframes.

- Executive

    Some algorithm controls process scheduling.

- Manual

    Processes are scheduled by a user outside of the system.

To further explain the scheduling used by a specific processor, it is sometimes useful to include a timing diagram or a fragment of PDL, particularly if executive scheduling is used. PDL and timing diagrams are also useful when we have to document the dynamic behavior of programs and objects that may migrate from processor to processor.

Device and Connection Templates. Figure 5-26 also provides the template for devices and connections. From a software perspective, devices and connections are of minimal importance. However, from the perspective of the users of the system, these templates help in documenting our design assumptions.

5.8 Applying the Notation

The Products of Object-Oriented Design

This chapter has described the essential products of object-oriented design. Typically, a design includes sets of class diagrams, object diagrams, module diagrams, and process diagrams. The top of our design, that is, the highest-level view of the design, may be found in three places: the topmost class diagram (showing the major abstractions in the logical design of the system), the topmost module diagram (showing the key elements of the physical software design), and the main process diagram (showing the key elements of the physical hardware design). The key mechanisms used in our implementation are found in various object diagrams.

End-to-end connectivity exists among these diagrams, permitting us to trace requirements from implementation back to specification. Starting with a process diagram, a processor may designate a main program, which is defined in some module diagram. This module diagram may encompass the definition of a collection of classes and objects, whose definitions we will find in the appropriate class or object diagrams. Finally, the definitions of individual classes point to our requirements, because these classes in general directly reflect the vocabulary of the problem space.

The notation described in this chapter can be used manually, although for larger applications, it cries out for automated tool support. Tools can provide consistency checking, completeness checking, and analysis, and they can help a designer browse through the products of a design in relatively unconstrained ways. While looking at a module diagram, a developer might want to study a particular mechanism; a tool helps to locate an object allocated to a particular module. While looking at this object in an object diagram, the developer might then want to view the class of a particular object and perhaps also see its place in the inheritance lattice. Last, if this were an active object, the developer might use a tool to find the processor to which this thread of control is allocated. Using tools in this manner frees developers from the tedium of keeping all the details of the design consistent, allowing them to focus upon the creative aspects of the design process.

Scaling Up and Scaling Down

We have found this notation and its variants applicable both to small systems consisting of just a few hundred lines of code and to very large systems consisting of several million lines of code. As we will see in the next two chapters, this notation is particularly applicable to an incremental, iterative approach to design. One does not create a diagram and then walk away from it, treating it as some sacred, immutable artifact. Rather, these diagrams evolve during the design process as new design decisions are made and more detail is established.

We have also found this notation to be largely language-independent. It is most applicable to any of a wide spectrum of object-based and object-oriented programming languages, and is especially applicable to the five languages we use in this book.

At this point, we have established the syntax and semantics of our notation for the method of object-oriented design. The next two chapters examine the process of object-oriented design. This discussion is followed by five applications that demonstrate the practical application of object-oriented design to a variety of different kinds of problems.

Summary

- Designing is not the act of drawing a diagram; a diagram simply captures a design.
- In the design of a complex system, it is important to view the design from multiple perspectives: its logical and physical structure, and its static and dynamic semantics.
- The notation for object-oriented design includes four basic diagrams (class diagrams, object diagrams, module diagrams, and process diagrams) and two supplementary diagrams (state transition diagrams and timing diagrams).
- A class diagram is used to show the existence of classes and their relationships in the logical design of a system; a class diagram represents all or part of the class structure of a system.
- An object diagram is used to show the existence of objects and their relationships in the logical design of a system; an object diagram represents all or part of the object structure of a system and primarily illustrates the semantics of key mechanisms in the logical design. A single object diagram represents a snapshot in time of an otherwise transitory event or configuration of objects.
- A module diagram is used to show the allocation of classes and objects to modules in the physical design of a system; a module diagram represents all or part of the module architecture of a system.
- A process diagram is used to show the allocation of processes to processors in the physical design of a system; a process diagram represents all or part of the process architecture of a system.
- A state transition diagram is used to show the state space of an instance of a given class, the events that cause a transition from one state to another, and the actions that result from a state change.
- A timing diagram is used to show the dynamic interactions among various objects in an object diagram.

Further Readings

A tremendous amount has been written on the topic of notations for software analysis and design. Critics may say this represents a vast wasteland of diagrams, but some genuinely useful approaches have evolved. The book by Martin and McClure [H 1988] is a general reference to many of the more popular notations.

An early form of the notation described in this chapter was first documented by Booch [F 1981]. This notation later evolved to incorporate the expressive power of semantic nets (Stillings et al. [A 1987] and Barr and Feigenbaum [J 1981]), entity-relationship diagrams (Chen [E 1976]), entity models (Ross [F 1987]), and Petri nets (Peterson [J 1977], Sahraoui [F 1987], and Bruon and Balsamo [F 1986]). The icons representing objects and packages were inspired by the work at Intel on the iAPX 432 [D 1981]. The notation for object diagrams derives from Seidewitz [F 1985]. The notation for expressing concurrency semantics is adapted from the work of Buhr [F 1988, 1989]. The use of state transition diagrams derives from Harel [F 1987, 1988].

Other useful approaches to documenting object-oriented designs include those of Fischer [C 1987], Kelly [F 1986], Grosch [F 1983], Cunningham and Beck [F 1986], Kleyn and Gringrich [K 1988], and Schwan and Matthews [K 1986].

The Process

The amateur software engineer is always in search of some sort of magic, some earthshaking technological innovation whose application will immediately make the process of software development easy. It is the mark of the professional software engineer to know that no such panacea exists. Amateurs often want cookbook steps to follow; professionals know that rigid approaches to design only lead to largely useless design products that resemble a progression of lies, behind which developers shield themselves because no one is willing to admit that poor design decisions should be changed early, rather than late. Finally, when the amateur software engineer focuses upon creating the documentation for the design, he or she worries more about how it looks to the customer than about the substance it contains. The professional acknowledges that documentation is important, but does not let the required products drive the creative process of design itself.

The process of object-oriented design is the antithesis of cookbook approaches. As we will see in this chapter, object-oriented design is more of an incremental, iterative process, in which the products of design gently unfold over time.

6.1 Design as an Incremental, Iterative Process

Round-Trip Gestalt Design

Is design a top-down or a bottom-up process? This issue is debated with religious fervor in the software engineering community. There is relatively much more experience with design in the hardware community, so we posed this question to a computer architect and VLSI designer. His answer was quite revealing [1]. Assume that we are faced with the problem of staffing an organization to design and implement a fairly complex piece of computer hardware. We might use horizontal staffing, in which we have a waterfall progression of products, with systems architects feeding logic designers feeding circuit designers. This is an example of top-down design, and requires designers who are "tall skinny men," as Druke calls them, because of the narrow yet deep skills that each must possess. Alternately, we might use vertical staffing, in which we have good all-around designers who take slices of the entire project, from architectural conception through circuit design. The skills that these designers must have leads Druke to call them "short fat men." Unfortunately, given its inherent complexity, software development often demands that we employ "tall fat people."

Our experience indicates that design is neither strictly top-down, nor strictly bottom-up. Instead, as Druke suggests, well-structured complex systems are best created through the use of "round-trip gestalt design." This style of design emphasizes the incremental and iterative development of a system through the refinement of different yet consistent logical and physical views of the system as a whole. We suggest that round-trip gestalt design is the foundation of the process of object-oriented design.

To those formally schooled in structured design methods, object-oriented design may seem to be a terribly unconstrained and fuzzy process. We do not deny it. However, we must also point out that one cannot dictate creativity by the mere definition of a few steps to follow or products to create. Certainly, the more we know about the problem to be solved, the easier it is to solve it. For example, if you have built one house by hand from the ground up, building the second one will generally be easier, because you know better what you must do first, then second, and so on. It is the same for software development; indeed, this is often the reason for the radically high rates of productivity that have been reported by some software factories [2]. In such organizations, the problem being solved is usually well defined (payroll processing, for example) and one for which many implementations may already have been crafted. In these domains, the process is almost entirely codified. The designers of a new system in such problem domains already understand what the important abstractions are; they already know what mechanisms ought to be employed, and they generally know the range of behavior that is expected of such a system. This suggests that it is possible to reuse not only software components, but entire designs and requirements. Creativity is still important in such a design process, but here the problem is sufficiently constrained as to already address most of the important design issues. Productivity is therefore artificially high, relative to entirely unique kinds of applications.

The experiments by Curtis and his colleagues reinforce these observations. Curtis studied the work of professional software developers by videotaping them in action and then analyzing the different activities they undertook (analysis, design, implementation, etc.) and when. From these studies, he concluded that "software design appears to be a collection of interleaved, iterative, loosely-ordered processes under opportunistic control. . . . Top-down balanced development appears to be a special case occurring when a relevant design schema is available or the problem is small. . . . Good designers work at multiple levels of abstraction and detail simultaneously" [3].

As noted in Chapter 1, most software systems are highly unique, and therefore their developers have only a restricted basis of experience from which to draw. In such circumstances, the best we can do during the design process is to take a stab at the design, step back and analyze it, then return to the products of the design and make improvements based upon our new understanding. We repeat this process until we are confident about the correctness and completeness of the overall design. As Heinlein suggests, "When faced with a problem you do not understand, do any part of it you do understand, then look at it again" [4]. This is just another way of describing round-trip gestalt design.

The Activities and Products of Object-Oriented Design

Round-trip gestalt design represents the process of object-oriented design; the multiple models of object-oriented design presented in the previous chapter form the products of object-oriented design. There is great synergy in uniting these two concepts. Specifically, our rich notation lets us model our problem in a number of different ways, and thereby allows us to focus upon relatively independent parts of the problem at different times. The fact that we employ an evolutionary process means that we can work with whatever model makes the most sense at any given time for our particular problem. For example, we might first express our design of the class structure of a system in a set of class diagrams. Next, we might invent some mechanisms that use these abstractions, which we document in a series of object diagrams. Designing the details of these mechanisms leads us back to the class structure, through which we establish the protocol of each class and perhaps rearrange the inheritance lattice to exploit the commonality that we have discovered. Eventually, at the end of the design process, we end up with a set of diagrams that provide different views of the system, yet are all coherent and consistent, having incrementally evolved from earlier stable – albeit not as detailed – models of the system under design.

This incremental, iterative approach inherent in object-oriented design makes it orthogonal to traditional waterfall life-cycle approaches to software development. Actually, to be very critical, our experience is that a rigid waterfall life cycle is a fundamentally poor process, and generally violates many of the principles of sound engineering practice. This is not to say that the design process should be entirely unstructured. Rather, we suggest that it allow an evolutionary development. Such a view is consistent with Boehm's spiral model of software development, which "creates a risk-driven approach to the software process, rather than a strictly specification-driven or prototype-driven process" [5].

Object-oriented design is not a process that starts with a requirements specification, ends with a blueprint for implementation, and requires a miracle somewhere in between. In our experience, the process of object-oriented design generally tracks the following order of events:

- Identify the classes and objects at a given level of abstraction.
- Identify the semantics of these classes and objects.
- Identify the relationships among these classes and objects.
- Implement these classes and objects.

This is an incremental process: the identification of new classes and objects usually causes us to refine and improve upon the semantics of and relationships among existing classes and objects. It is also an iterative process: implementing classes and objects often leads us to the discovery or invention of new classes and objects whose presence simplifies and generalizes our design.

How do we start the object-oriented design process, and when do we stop? In simple terms, we start by discovering the classes and objects that form the vocabulary of our problem domain. Our final goals are to "identify all problem-domain entities that will play a role in the application, to specify the interaction between entities, to associate with each entity the function performed by or on the entity, and to analyze these functions to a level at which they are properly understood" [6]. We may thus stop the process of object-oriented design whenever we find that there are no new key abstractions or mechanisms, or when the classes and objects we have already discovered may be implemented by composing them from existing reusable software components. In either case, there is little reason to further design new things; the task is now to implement the models we have already invented.

The remainder of this chapter examines the activities of each of these four major steps and the products that result. In the next chapter, we look at the practical implications of this process, primarily from the perspective of managers who must direct projects using object-oriented design, since this process involves different milestones and a fundamentally different approach to resource allocation and risk management than those of traditional processes. The remaining five chapters of the book put the process of object-oriented design into practice, with examples using a wide range of object-based and object-oriented programming languages.

6.2 Identifying Classes and Objects

Activities

The first step involves two activities: the discovery of the key abstractions in the problem space (the significant classes and objects) and the invention of the important mechanisms that provide the behavior required of objects that work together to achieve some function. How do we find such abstractions and mechanisms? The answer is through domain analysis, using the techniques described in Chapter 4. Essentially, the developer must act as an abstractionist. By studying the problem's requirements and/or by engaging in discussions with domain experts, the developer must learn the vocabulary of the problem domain. The tangible things in the problem domain, the roles they play, and the events that may occur form the candidate classes and objects of our design, at its highest level of abstraction.

We emphasize that these are just candidate classes and objects, because at this point in our design, we are only beginning to define the boundaries of the abstractions that are important to us. We expect these boundaries to change subtly over time as we discover commonalties among these classes and objects and as we improve upon the design of the mechanisms we have invented. Although their outside views may change in only minor ways, we find that the classes and objects we identify at this early stage of design usually carry through the entire design process. This is actually to be expected, because it is a consequence of the principles of the object model that the products of object-oriented design directly reflect our model of reality.

Consider for a moment the design of the hydroponics gardening system. A cursory reading of its requirements would reveal tangible things such as growing plans and crops as well as environmental attributes such as air temperature and nutrient concentration. All these abstractions are essential to the problem and are therefore part of the candidate classes and objects in the design of our solution.

Products

The products of this step may range from very informal to very formal. At one end of the spectrum, it may be sufficient to simply list the names of significant classes and objects, using meaningful names that imply their semantics. We call this simply a "list of things," which, by its very nature, is open-ended [7]. Some of the things on this list may turn out to be classes, some objects, and others simply attributes of objects. At the other end of the spectrum, we may formally specify the meaning of these abstractions and mechanisms by filling out the appropriate class and object templates.

In most cases, this step takes a small amount of time relative to the other three steps. Often, a single chief designer will draft a list of candidate classes and objects and then review this list with peers as a kind of sanity check. The primary value of such a list is that it defines a common vocabulary of discourse among the developers. It may also be appropriate for a designer to draft some class diagrams or object diagrams to show how the various classes and objects work together. If the physical decomposition of the system is important (as it may be when subcontractor relationships are involved), then drafts of module diagrams may also be created at this time. Finally, if there is a hardware element to the system, it is also useful to draft the necessary process diagrams.

6.3 Identifying the Semantics of Classes and Objects

Activities

The second step involves one basic activity, that of establishing the meanings of the classes and objects identified from the previous step. Here, the developer acts as a detached outsider, viewing each class from the perspective of its interface so as to identify the things we can do to each instance of a class and the things that each object can do to another object.

This step is much harder than the first and takes much longer. This is the phase in which there may be fierce debates, wailing and gnashing of teeth, and general name-calling during design reviews. Finding classes and objects is the easy part; deciding upon the protocol of each object is hard. For this reason, the process of object-oriented design becomes iterative at this point. Concocting the protocol for a given object may require decisions that change the meaning of another object. In general, the existence of our key abstractions does not change; we only shift their boundaries.

One useful technique to guide these activities involves writing a script for each object, which defines its life cycle from creation to destruction, including its characteristic behaviors.

For example, in designing the hydroponics gardening system, we might first create a class whose instances represent growing plans. We might make the design decision that such objects embody the knowledge of the specific details of the growing plan for a particular crop, including how to carry out this plan. Later, we may decide that the protocol of this class is too complicated, and so we create another class, a growing-plan manager, which alone knows how to implement the plans saved as part of the state of growing-plan objects. This evolutionary design decision thus creates at least one new class and also changes the outside view of the original class.

Products

The products of this step reflect the incremental nature of object-oriented design. To document our design decisions regarding the meaning of each class and object, we generally refine the templates we drafted in the previous step. This means that we must document all of the static and dynamic semantics of each key abstraction and mechanism as best we can at this point in time. We might also draft new object diagrams to document any mechanisms we might have invented in this step of the process. Lastly, we might decide to prototype parts of the design, in order to analyze our current design and evaluate alternate approaches to subproblems that management considers areas of high risk.

6.4 Identifying the Relationships Among Classes and Objects

Activities

The third step is largely an extension of the activities of the previous one. Here, we establish exactly how things interact within the system. With regard to the key abstractions, this means that we must assert the using, inheritance, and other kinds of relationships among classes. For the objects in our implementation, this means that we must establish the static and dynamic semantics of each mechanism.

There are two related activities here that cause us to refine the earlier products of our design. First, we must discover patterns: patterns among classes, which cause us to reorganize and simplify the system's class structure, and patterns among cooperative collections of objects, which lead us to generalize the mechanisms already embodied in the design. This part of the design process calls upon all of the creative skills of the designer; successes here are what distinguish good designs from great ones. Second, we must make visibility decisions: how do classes see one another, how do objects see one another, and, equally important, what classes and objects should not see one another. These decisions help us to make intelligent packaging decisions in the design of the module architecture of our system.

The discovery of patterns and the making of visibility decisions also may cause us to refine the protocols of various classes from earlier steps, so that we end up with common abstractions and mechanisms defined in just one place.

One technique we have found useful to guide these activities is the use of CRC cards, as defined by Beck and Cunningham [8]. A CRC card (for class, responsibility, collaboration) is simply a 3 x 5 index card, one for each class of objects, upon which one writes the class name, its responsibilities (its behaviors), and the classes with which it collaborates. A designer can then spatially organize these cards and refine their contents according to execution scripts of the life cycles of objects, as introduced in the previous step.

Consider again the design of the hydroponics gardening system. If we step back from the design products that we have invented thus far, we might realize that the mechanism used to store the information about individual growing plans could be applied to storing information about user preferences in the growing-plan editor of the user interface. This is a pattern of key abstractions and mechanisms that can only be discovered by a leap of insight from a designer (human or automated) who takes a gestalt view of the system. Its implementation means that one, not two, mechanisms are needed to support common behavior required in two very different parts of the system.

We must emphasize that at this point in the design, our focus is still entirely upon the outside view of the key abstractions and mechanisms that exist. It is generally premature during these first three steps to consider the representation of the classes and objects in our system, simply because we do not yet know enough about how each abstraction and mechanism will be used.

Products

The products of this step include the completion of most of the logical models of the design. Here we refine the class diagrams from the previous steps, taking into account the patterns we have discovered and the visibility decisions we have made. We also complete the details of the object diagrams that document the essential mechanisms in our solution. In practice, our approach to creating such diagrams is quite straightforward. Using the notation from the previous chapter, we first draw the objects that we know cooperate in certain ways. Next, we select pairs of objects and ask if there is a relationship between them. If the answer is yes, then we ask the next two questions: how do these objects relate and what messages does each send to the other? This usually causes us to refine the protocol of the corresponding classes, and this very refinement may cause us to discover yet new patterns. This is why we say that object-oriented design is an iterative process.

At this point, we may begin to create the essential module diagrams for our solution (or refine earlier ones) to take into account any visibility decisions we may have made. We strive to build classes, objects, and modules that are cohesive and loosely coupled. Thus, at this point, our products are complete enough for us to evaluate our design on the basis of these and the other metrics discussed in Chapter 3. Depending upon the outcome of this analysis, we may need to alter our design as necessary to improve the quality of our key abstractions and mechanisms.

In this step, we also continue to develop prototypes. We may create new prototypes, to again test alternative design approaches for elements of the system that we consider to be of high risk. We may also refine older prototypes, so as to create prototypes of increasing functionality that eventually evolve into the final implementation of the delivered system. Working in this manner, we always have an executable representation of our design.

6.5 Implementing Classes and Objects

Activities

The fourth step is not necessarily the last step. This step involves two activities: making design decisions concerning the representation of the classes and objects we have invented, and allocating classes and objects to modules, and programs to processors. This is the point in the design process where we first take an inside view of each class and module, to decide how its behavior should be implemented.

Unless our key abstractions and mechanisms are all trivial, it is at this point that we often must return to the first step and apply this process again to the inside view of existing classes and modules. In this way, we repeat the design process, but this time we focus on a lower level of abstraction. Does this mean that object-oriented design is a top-down process? Still, the answer is "not exactly." In practice, we design the higher level key abstractions and mechanisms first, involving those classes and objects that are directly part of the vocabulary of the problem domain. However, at any level of design, we must often leap to lower level key abstractions and mechanisms, because they serve as more primitive classes and objects upon which we compose all higher level classes and objects. This again illustrates that object-oriented design involves a round-trip gestalt design process.

Products

By this step in the design process, we will have established the concrete interface of each class and object important to us at a given level of abstraction. Our products therefore include the refinement of the class structure of the system, and in particular the completion of the implementation part of each important class template. The same kind of completeness comes about for module diagrams and, if the system architecture demands it, process diagrams.

Summary

- The process of object-oriented design is neither top-down nor bottom up; rather, the process of object-oriented design is best described as round-trip gestalt design, which emphasizes the incremental and iterative development of a system, through the refinement of different yet consistent logical and physical views of the system as a whole.

- The process of object-oriented design starts with the discovery of the classes and objects that form the vocabulary of our problem domain; it stops whenever we find that there are no new primitive abstractions and mechanisms or when the classes and objects we have already discovered may be implemented by composing them from existing reusable software components.

- The first step in the process of object-oriented design involves the identification of the classes and objects at a given level of abstraction; here, the important activities are the discovery of key abstractions and the invention of important mechanisms.

- The second step involves the identification of the semantics of these classes and objects; the important activity here is for the developer to act as a detached outsider, viewing each class from the perspective of its interface.
- The third step involves the identification of the relationships among these classes and objects; here, we establish how things interact within the system, with regard to the static as well as the dynamic semantics of the key abstractions and important mechanisms.
- The fourth step involves the implementation of these classes and objects; the important activities here involve choosing a representation for each class and object, and allocating classes and objects to modules, and programs to processes; this step is not necessarily the last step, for its completion usually requires that we repeat the entire process, this time at a lower level of abstraction.

Further Readings

There are several variations on the theme of the process of object-oriented design. Comparisons of some of the more popular approaches may be found in Boehm-Davis and Ross [H 1984], Kelly [F 1986], and Mannino [F 1987]. Comparisons of a number of other design methods, including object-oriented design, may be found in the comprehensive study by Webster [F 1988].

An early form of the process described in this chapter was first documented by Booch [F 1982]. Berard later elaborated upon this work in [F 1986]. Some related approaches include GOOD (General Object-Oriented Design) by Seidewitz and Stark [F 1985, 1986, 1987], SOOD (Structured Object-Oriented Design) by Lockheed [C 1988], MOOD (Multiple view Object-Oriented Design) by Kerth [F 1988], and HOOD (Hierarchical Object-Oriented Design) by CISI Ingenierie and Matra, for the European Space Station [F 1987]. Wasserman, Pircher, and Muller [F 1988], Mills [H 1986], and Constantine [F 1989] have reported on the marriage of object-oriented design and structured design in methods called, not surprisingly, object-oriented structured design (OOSD).

A number of other methodologists have proposed similar object-oriented design processes, for which the bibliography provides an extensive set of references. Some of the more important contributions come from Alabios [F 1988], Boyd [F 1987], Buhr [F 1984], Cherry [F 1987, 1990], Felsinger [F 1987], Firesmith [F 1986], Hines and Unger [G 1986], Jacobson [F 1985], Jamsa [F 1984], Kadie [F 1986], Masiero and Germano [F 1988], Nielsen [F 1988], Nies [F 1986], Rajlich and Silva [F 1987], and Shumate [F 1987]. The basic steps of object-oriented design described in this chapter are also similar to those proposed by Bailin [B 1988], Barry, Thomas, Altoft, and Wilson [C 1987], Chen [E 1976], Coad [B 1989], Date [E 1986], Goldberg and Kay [G 1977], Gouda, Han, Jensen, Johnson, and Kain [F 1977], Henderson [J 1986], Jackson [H 1983], Keene [G 1989], Mascot [H 1987], Pinson and Weiner [G 1988], Smith and Smith [E 1980], and Yourdon [H 1989].

Pragmatics

Software design today remains a very labor-intensive business; to a large extent, it is best characterized as a cottage industry [1]. A recent report by Kishida, Teramoto, Torri, and Urano notes that, even in Japan, the software industry "still relies mainly on the informal paper-and-pencil approach in the upstream development phases" [2].

Compounding matters is the fact that designing is not an exact science. For example, consider the design of a complex database using entity-relationship modeling, one of the foundations of object-oriented design. As Hawryszkiewycz observes, "Although this sounds fairly straightforward, it does involve a certain amount of personal perception of the importance of various objects in the enterprise. The result is that the design process is not deterministic: different designers can produce different enterprise models of the same enterprise" [3].

Therefore, we may reasonably conclude that no matter how sophisticated the design method, no matter how well-founded its theoretical basis, we cannot ignore the practical aspects of designing systems for the real world. This means that we must consider sound management practices with regard to such issues as resource allocation, milestones, configuration management, and version control. To the technologist, these are intensely dull topics; to the professional software engineer, these are realities that must be faced if one wants to be successful in building complex software systems. Thus, this

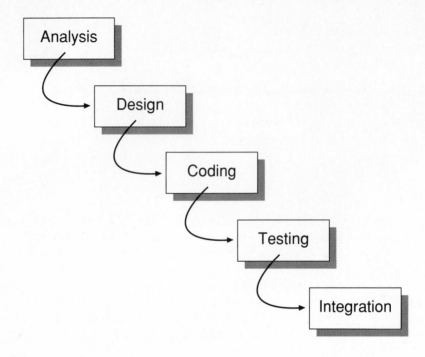

Figure 7-1
The Traditional Waterfall Software Development Life Cycle

chapter examines the pragmatics of object-oriented design, considering the role of this method in the software development life cycle and its impact upon management practices.

7.1 Object-Oriented Design in the Life Cycle

The Software Development Life Cycle

Figure 7-1 illustrates the phases of the traditional waterfall software development life cycle, which is part of the very fabric of all too many companies: it is sometimes treated as a sacred, immutable process in which work blindly flows down from one phase to another. Often, the organizational structure of such companies directly parallels the phases of this life cycle. Notwithstanding the inertia of tradition, the problems of a rigidly applied waterfall life cycle are well known. As Boehm points out:

- "The waterfall model does not adequately address the concerns of developing program families and organizing software to accommodate change.
- The waterfall model assumes a relatively uniform progression of elaboration steps.
- The waterfall model does not accommodate the sort of evolutionary development made possible by rapid prototyping capabilities and fourth-generation languages.
- The waterfall model does not address the possible future modes of software development associated with automatic programming capabilities, program transformation capabilities, and 'knowledge-based software assistant' capabilities" [4].

Boehm's third point is particularly relevant in light of object-oriented design because, as we have mentioned many times, object-oriented design embodies an incremental, iterative process. Quite the opposite, the fundamentalist view of the waterfall life cycle is that products from an early phase are written in granite, which then serve as the costly-to-change input of a later phase. As Hatley and Pirbhai suggest, "This view obscures the true nature of systems development: it has always been an iterative process in which any given step can feed back and modify decisions made in a preceding one" [5]. This reality is a primary motivation for Boehm's spiral model of software development.

Just because object-oriented design involves an incremental, iterative process does not mean that one must abandon all the good management practices learned from the experience of the waterfall life cycle. Analysis is still important, and the need for a well-articulated design does not disappear. However, to the manager and developer with experience only in the waterfall life cycle, the life cycle of object-oriented design seems frightening and foreign, because some of the traditional management techniques simply don't make sense anymore. For example, rather than exhibiting a distinct integration phase, object-oriented design sees integration as an activity that occurs incrementally.

Figure 7-2 shows the software development life cycle for object-oriented design. Here we see that design is not a distinct, monolithic phase; rather, it is just a step along the way in the incremental, iterative development of a system, whose steps may feed back to each other. In a later section, we examine the ways in which object-oriented design affects staffing, milestones and products, release management, quality assurance, and tool support. For the moment, let's study the phases of this object-oriented software development life cycle.

Analysis

The Activities of Analysis. Analysis is the phase that first brings together the users and the developers of a system, uniting them with a common vocabulary drawn from the problem domain. As Mellor et al. state, "The purpose of analysis is to provide a description of a problem. The description must be complete,

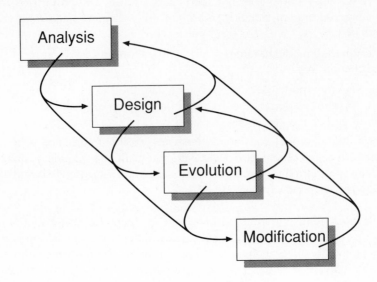

Figure 7-2
Object-Oriented Design in the Software Development Life Cycle

consistent, readable, and reviewable by diverse interested parties, [and] testable against reality" [6]. The products of analysis are often used to articulate the functions of a system. By *function*, we do not mean an algorithmic abstraction. Rather, in the context of requirements analysis, a function denotes a single, outwardly visible and testable behavior. For example, a function of an information management system might be to allow various kinds of database queries.

The boundaries between analysis and design may at times seem fuzzy. For example, identifying the key abstractions from the problem domain may be viewed either as a part of analysis or a part of design. Nonetheless, the purposes of analysis and design are quite different. In analysis, we seek to model the world by identifying the classes and objects that form the vocabulary of the problem domain; in object-oriented design, we invent the abstractions and mechanisms that provide the behavior that this model requires. Stated in another way, analysis tells us about the desired behavior of the system we must build, whereas design generates the blueprints for the implementation of that system.

It is absolutely critical to separate the activities of analysis and design. There is nothing worse than finding a requirements document that includes items that are not really requirements, but mandates that you design the system in a certain way. On the other hand, it is equally dangerous to try to "completely" analyze a system before even thinking about moving forward with design – such an attempt marks the beginning of analysis paralysis.

Analysis Methods. There are many different kinds of analysis methods, some of which are suitable as front ends to object-oriented design. The most popular analysis method today is structured analysis, as typified by the work of Yourdon [7], DeMarco [8], and Gane and Sarson [9], with real-time extensions by Ward and Mellor [10] and Hatley and Pirbhai [11]. It appears that the products of any variety of structured analysis methods can be used as a front end to the process of object-oriented design [12]. Indeed, as we noted in Chapter 4, abstraction analysis offers a mapping between the data flow diagrams of structured analysis and the classes and objects of object-oriented design.

Structured analysis is an attractive front end to object-oriented design primarily because it is well known, many people are trained in its techniques, and many tools support its notation. However, structured analysis is not the optimal front end to object-oriented design. It is hard to know when a particular data flow diagram ceases to represent an essential model of the problem and instead articulates a design decision. Furthermore, structured analysis can sometimes perpetuate an algorithm-oriented view of the problem, which makes the job of object-oriented design much more difficult.

The current trend in analysis methods is toward object-oriented analysis, as typified by the work of Shlaer and Mellor [13] and Coad and Yourdon [14]. As Smith and Tockey define it, object-oriented analysis includes "the process of identifying and modeling the essential object classes and the logical relationships and interactions among them" [15]. This process is quite close to the process of object-oriented design. Practically speaking, this means that the products of object-oriented analysis may be used almost directly at the start of the object-oriented design process. The object-oriented designer refines these products by inventing new abstractions and mechanisms that use these classes and objects in clever ways.

Other analysis methods have been found to be appropriate as front ends to object-oriented design, including SADT [16], SREM [17] and entity-relationship modeling [18]. No matter which analysis method is employed, the important factor is that the products of analysis provide us with a complete enough model of the problem from which we may begin to design a solution.

Design

Starting the Design Process. When does one start to design? Realistically, design can commence as soon as we have some (possibly incomplete) formal or informal model of the problem to be solved. If we start designing too early, we may not know enough about the problem to make intelligent design trade-offs. If we start designing too late, we risk wasting resources in doing too detailed an analysis, which can overwhelm the designer with a torrent of extraneous and unnecessary details. For these reasons, we suggest the strategy of "analyze a little, design a little." In this manner, each attempt at design can help to focus the process of analysis by directing it to aspects of the system that are important in crafting a solution.

In the real world, analysts and designers may not be closely coupled. This is usually true when the software development effort is subcontracted, but it should not prevent designers from applying the idea of "analyze a little, design a little." Try out a design based upon your current understanding of the requirements, step back from the design to study its merits and shortcomings, and then improve upon it. This process refines a designer's understanding of the requirements, and this improved understanding feeds back into the analysis process. Now, we do not mean to advocate design by trial and error, the style of development used by hackers. Rather, we suggest that design should proceed by using a series of consciously selected prototypes, each of which models some important aspect of the design of the system, and all of which grow collectively in functionality over time.

Stopping the Design Process. When does one stop designing? This is also a difficult question, for it is possible to overdesign a solution. An architect would rarely think about marking the exact location of heating ducts or light switches on a general house plan. These are decisions to be made in the field as part of the implementation or, when there are unusual requirements, in lower level designs established by the electrical or heating contractor. So it should be with the design of software systems. Design only the key abstractions and important mechanisms, so that you have a blueprint that is sufficient for implementation, and defer to a later phase those aspects of the solution that have little or no bearing upon the observable behavior of the system.

Break a large problem into subproblems, so that specialists in that particular problem domain can carry on the design process. Within a large system, we might identify aspects that are clearly network problems, or database problems, or user interface problems. The rule of thumb we use is that one can stop designing when key abstractions are simple enough to require no further decomposition, but can be composed from existing reusable software components.

Evolution

The Activities of Evolution. The evolution of a system in the object-oriented software development life cycle combines the traditional aspects of coding, testing, and integration. The result is that with object-oriented design, we never encounter a "big-bang" event of system integration. Instead, the development process results in the incremental production of a series of prototypes, which eventually evolve into the final implementation. We must again strongly state our position on prototyping: one must always have an honorable purpose in mind when setting out to prototype some aspect of a system: never use a prototype as an excuse to hack, rather than design.

Page-Jones suggests a number of advantages to this kind of incremental development:

- "Important feedback to the users is provided when it's most needed, most useful, and most meaningful.
- Users can use several skeleton system versions to allow them to make a smooth transition from their old system to their new system.
- The project is less likely to be axed if it falls behind schedule.
- Major system interfaces are tested first and most often.
- Testing resources are distributed more evenly.
- Implementors can see early results from a working system, so their morale is improved.
- If time is short, coding and testing can begin before the design is finished" [19].

We would add to this list the fact that building evolutionary prototypes encourages the activity of trying and then evaluating alternate designs, so that one can make intelligent design trade-offs. This practice is quite common in other engineering disciplines; unfortunately, it is not so common in the computer sciences.

System development is largely a matter of trying to satisfy a number of competing constraints, including functionality, time, and space. One is always limited by the largest constraint. For example, if the weight of a computer is a critical factor (as it is in spacecraft design), then the weight of individual memory chips must be considered. The amount of memory permitted by the weight allowance limits the size of the program that may be loaded. Relax any given constraint, and other design alternatives become possible; tighten any constraint, and certain designs become useless. By evolving the implementation of a software system, we can determine which constraints are really important and which are not. For this reason, designing for functionality first and performance second is a viable approach, because early in the design, we typically do not know enough to understand where the performance bottlenecks will arise in the system. By analyzing the behavior of prototypes, through histogramming or other such techniques, a developer can better understand how to tune a system over time.

Kinds of Evolutionary Changes. In practice, we find that the following kinds of changes to a design are to be expected during the evolution of a system:

- Adding a new class
- Changing the implementation of a class
- Changing the representation of a class
- Reorganizing the class structure
- Changing the interface of a class

Each kind of change comes about for different reasons, and each has a different cost.

A developer will add new classes when new key abstractions are discovered or new mechanisms are invented. The cost of making such changes is usually inconsequential in terms of computing resources and management overhead.

Changing the implementation of a class is also generally not costly. In object-oriented design, we usually create the interface of a class first and then stub out its implementation. Once the interface stabilizes to a reasonable extent, we can choose a representation for that class and complete the implementation of its methods. The implementation of a particular method may be changed again, usually to fix a bug or improve its performance. We might also change the implementation of a method to take advantage of new methods defined in an existing or newly added superclass. In any case, changing the implementation of a method is not costly, especially if one has previously encapsulated the class's implementation.

In a similar vein, one might alter the representation of a class. Usually, this is done to make instances of the class more space efficient or to create more time-efficient methods. If the representation of the class is encapsulated, as is possible in Smalltalk, C++, CLOS, and Ada, then a change in representation will not logically disrupt how clients interact with instances of that class (unless, of course, this new representation does not provide the behavior expected of the class). On the other hand, if the representation of the class is not encapsulated, as is also possible in Object Pascal, C++, and Ada, then a change in representation is much more dangerous, because clients may have been written that depend upon a particular representation. This is especially true in the case of subclasses: changing the representation of a superclass affects the representation of all of its subclasses. In any case, changing the representation of a class incurs a cost: one must recompile its interface, its implementation, all of its clients (namely, its subclasses and instances), all of its client's clients, and so on.

Reorganizing the class structure of a system is common, although less so than the other kinds of changes we have mentioned. As Stefik and Bobrow observe, "Programmers often create new classes and reorganize their classes as they understand the opportunities for factoring parts of their programs" [20]. The reorganization of a class structure usually takes the form of changing inheritance relationships, adding new abstract classes, and shifting the implementation of common methods to classes higher in the class structure. In practice, reorganizing the class structure of a system usually happens frequently at first, and then stabilizes over time as its developers better understand how all the key abstractions work together. Reorganizing the class structure is to be encouraged in early stages of design because it can result in great economy of expression, meaning that we have smaller implementations and fewer classes to comprehend and maintain. However, reorganization of the class structure does not come without a cost. Typically, changing the location of a class high in the hierarchy makes all the classes below it obsolete and requires their recompilation (and thus the recompilation of the classes that depend on them, and so on).

An equally important kind of change that occurs during the evolution of a system is a change to the interface of a class. A developer usually changes the interface of a class either to add some new behavior or to add an operation that was always part of the abstraction but was initially not exported and is now needed by some client. In practice, using the heuristics for building quality classes that we discussed in Chapter 3 (specifically, the concepts of building primitive, sufficient, and complete interfaces) reduces the likelihood of such changes. However, our experience is that such changes are inevitable. We have never written a nontrivial class whose interface was exactly right the first time.

We rarely remove an existing method; this is typically done only to better encapsulate an abstraction. More commonly, we add a new method or override a method defined in some superclass. In all three cases, the change is costly, because it logically affects all clients, making them obsolete and forcing their recompilation. Fortunately, these latter kinds of changes – adding and overriding methods – are upwardly compatible. In fact, we find in practice that well over three-quarters of all interface changes made during the evolution of a system are upwardly compatible. This makes it possible to apply sophisticated compiler technology, such as incremental compilation, to reduce the impact of these changes. Incremental compilation allows us to recompile single declarations and statements one at a time, instead of entire modules, meaning that the recompilation of most clients can be optimized away.

Why is recompilation cost even an issue? For small systems, it is not an issue, because recompiling an entire program might take only a few minutes. However, for large systems, it is an entirely different matter. Recompiling a million-line program might take as much as a day of computer time. Can you imagine making a change to the software for a shipboard computer system and then telling the captain that she cannot put to sea because you are still recompiling? In the extreme, recompilation costs may be so high as to inhibit developers from making changes that are reasonable improvements. Recompilation is a particularly important issue with object-oriented programming languages, because inheritance introduces compilation dependencies [21]. For strongly typed object-oriented programming languages, recompilation costs may be even higher; in such languages, one trades off compilation time for safety.

The key to maintaining sanity during the evolution of a system under development is twofold: focus on building stable interfaces and encapsulate design decisions that are likely to change.

Modification

Lehman and Belady have made a number of cogent observations regarding the maturation of a deployed software system:

- "A program that is used in a real-world environment necessarily must change or become less and less useful in that environment (the law of continuing change).

- As an evolving program changes, its structure becomes more complex unless active efforts are made to avoid this phenomenon (the law of increasing complexity)" [22].

Thus, we distinguish the preservation of a software system from its maintenance. During maintenance, developers will be asked to add new functionality, or modify some existing behavior. These maintainers are often a different group of people than the original developers.

Our observation is that modification involves activities that are little different than those required during the evolution of a system. Especially if we have done a good job in the original object-oriented design, adding new functionality or modifying some existing behavior will come naturally. In practice, we have certainly found this to be the case, even for the very largest of systems.

7.2 Managing a Project

Staffing

Resource Allocation. We have found that the application of object-oriented design leads to shorter development schedules and higher quality software that is more likely to meet its real requirements. One of the more surprising aspects of managing projects using object-oriented design is that there is usually a reduction in the total amount of resources needed and a shift in the timing of their deployment. Figure 7-3 illustrates this phenomenon.

In this chart, the vertical axis represents human resources in terms of engineering months of effort. The thick horizontal line normalizes to the level of resources typically used in the traditional waterfall life cycle. With object-oriented design, resources must be allocated differently. Resources spent for analysis do not change much, but more resources are required during design, mainly because more work than usual is accomplished. This increase doesn't necessarily translate into more people; it more often represents a few good people working for a longer time. During coding, far fewer resources are required with object-oriented design, mainly because the work remaining is highly bounded. Testing also requires fewer resources, primarily because adding new functionality to a class is achieved mainly by modifying a class that is known to behave correctly in the first place. Finally, integration requires vastly fewer resources than traditional design approaches do, because integration happens incrementally throughout the development life cycle. The net sum of all the human resources required for object-oriented design is usually equal to or less than that required for traditional approaches, and the resulting product tends to be of far better quality.

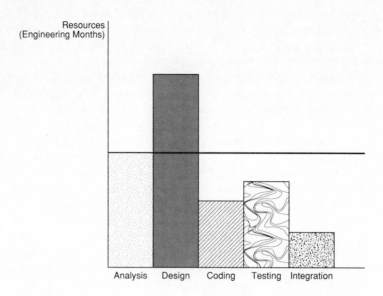

Figure 7-3
Resource Allocation with Object-Oriented Design

Development Team Skills. We have also seen a shift in roles among the members of the software development team. With object-oriented design, four kinds of developers are needed:

- System architects
- Class designers
- Class implementors
- Application programmers

The system architects are the visionaries. They are the most senior developers, and are best qualified to make strategic design decisions. The next-most senior developers are given the role of class designers, who are responsible for creating the class structure of a system and inventing its mechanisms. Generally, each class designer will be responsible for creating and maintaining the interface of some major class category or subsystem. Less senior people are assigned the role of class implementors. These people don't have as broad a working knowledge regarding the architectural implications of class design, but they do know how to properly select the representation of classes and how to implement them. Class implementors usually work under the supervision of a class designer. Application programmers are the more junior designers, but they are still experts in the particular problem domain. These developers take the products of the class implementors and put them together using the mechanisms invented by the class designers to satisfy some required function of the system.

This breakdown of skills addresses the staffing problem faced by many software development organizations, which usually have only a handful of really good designers and many more less experienced ones. The advantage of the approach to staffing that is encouraged by object-oriented design is that it gives a career path to the more junior people: that is, junior developers work under more senior developers in a mentor/apprentice relationship. As they gain experience in using well-designed classes, over time they learn to design their own quality classes.

As we mentioned earlier, object-oriented design makes it possible to use smaller development teams. It is not unusual for a team of roughly 30–40 developers to produce more than a million lines of production-quality code in a single year. We agree with Boehm, who observes that "the best results occur with fewer and better people" [23]. Unfortunately, trying to staff a project with fewer people than traditional folklore suggests are needed may produce resistance. Such an approach jeopardizes the attempts of some managers to build empires. Other managers like to hide behind the large numbers of employees, because more people represents more power. Furthermore, if a project fails, there are more subordinates upon whom to heap the blame.

Just because a project applies the most sophisticated design method or the latest fancy tool doesn't mean a manager has the right to abdicate responsibility for hiring designers who can think or to let a project run on autopilot [24]. Management is an active process, not a passive one.

Milestones and Products

Milestones. Perhaps the primary reason that the process of object-oriented design seems so alien to managers new to the method is that they wonder how, with an incremental and iterative approach to design, you know you are making progress. Progress can be measured by reaching certain milestones laid out over time, which are little different than those for traditional methods. What is different, however, is what constitutes the successful completion of a milestone.

It is best to carry out a few formal and many more informal design reviews during the development process. In the earliest design reviews, the developers, domain experts, and users should review the draft of the class structure of the design and its basic mechanisms, as described by a series of object diagrams. As these key abstractions and mechanisms mature, later design reviews can cover the products of the logical and physical design of the system in more detail. These later design reviews also typically include demonstrations and reviews of working prototypes.

In this manner, the users, managers, and developers of a system all get a perspective on the progress being made. The client can best measure progress by seeing the executable prototypes and by reviewing the products of the design. Managers may review the same materials, but they can also perceive the health of the project in other ways, as we will see shortly.

Perhaps the most dreadful way a manager can measure progress is by measuring the lines of code produced. The number of line feeds in a fragment of source code has absolutely no correlation to its completeness or complexity. Contributing to the shortcomings of this Neanderthal approach is the ease of playing games with the numbers, resulting in productivity figures that may differ from one another by as much as two orders of magnitude. For example, what exactly is a line of code? Does one count physical lines, or semicolons? What about counting multiple statements that appear on one line or statements that cross line boundaries? Similarly, how does one measure the labor involved? Are all personnel counted, or just the programmers? Is the workday measured as an eight-hour day, or is the time a programmer spends working in the wee hours of the morning also counted? Traditional complexity measures, better suited to early generation programming languages, also have minimal correlation with completeness and complexity, and are therefore largely useless when applied to object-based and object-oriented programming languages.

A far better way to measure productivity derives from the practice of continuous integration. In this evolutionary approach, there is no big-bang integration event; thus one can measure progress by counting the classes in the logical design, or the modules in the physical design, that are completed and working. Another way of measuring progress is by measuring the stability of key interfaces (that is, how often they change). At first, the interfaces of all key abstractions will change daily if not hourly. Over time, the most important interfaces will stabilize first, the next most important interfaces will stabilize second, and so on. Towards the end of the development life cycle, only a few insignificant interfaces will need to be changed, since most of the emphasis is on getting the already designed classes and modules working together. Occasionally, a few changes may be needed in a critical interface, but such changes are usually upwardly compatible. Even so, such changes are made only after careful thought about their impact. These changes can then be incrementally introduced into the production system as part of the usual release cycle, which we will discuss shortly.

One must often reconcile the incremental and iterative process of object-oriented design with the more rigid milestones imposed by some external agency, especially with government-sponsored projects. The problem is made easier by a customer who is sympathetic to the realities of software development, and object-oriented design in particular, and will allow liberal interpretations of documentation requirements. For example, rather than documenting inputs, processing, and outputs, we instead document interfaces and behaviors.

Products. The development of a software system involves more than the writing of the raw source code. Other products of design offer other ways to give the manager and user insight into the progress of the project, and, what is equally important, they leave behind a legacy of design decisions for the eventual maintainers of the system. The products of object-oriented design include sets of class diagrams, object diagrams, module diagrams, and process diagrams, as described in Chapter 5. Together, these diagrams offer traceability back to the system's software requirements. Process diagrams denote programs, which are the root modules found in the module diagrams. Each module represents the implementation of some combination of classes and objects, which are in turn found in the class diagrams and object diagrams, respectively. Finally, object diagrams denote mechanisms specified by the requirements, and class diagrams represent the key abstractions that form the vocabulary of the problem domain.

Because these products must have a context, they should be grouped together in meaningful ways into design documents. The design of each major software segment of a system should be expressed in its own design document. In practice, we have found the following document structure to be helpful in capturing the logical design of a system using object-oriented methods:

- Required functions
- Class and object diagrams
- Class and object templates
- Results of executable prototypes

Later in the development process, this design document would be augmented to capture all relevant physical design decisions. Thus, its structure would appear as follows:

- Required functions
- Class and object diagrams
- Class and object templates
- Module and process diagrams
- Module and process templates
- Results of executable prototypes

Much of what each such a design document contains can be derived from the implementation by the use of semiautomatic tools.

Release Management

Davis et al. suggest that "when using incremental development, software is deliberately built to satisfy fewer requirements initially, but is constructed in such a way as to facilitate the incorporation of new requirements and thus achieve higher adaptability" [25]. From the perspective of the ultimate user of the system, we would therefore expect to see a stream of executable prototypes emerge from the software development organization, each with increasing functionality, eventually evolving into the final production system. From the perspective of those inside the organization, many more prototypes are actually constructed, but some are then frozen and baselined in order to stabilize important system interfaces and thus produce a release for the customer.

For larger projects, an organization commonly produces an internal release of a system every few weeks and then releases a running system to its customers for review every few months, according to the needs of the project. In the steady state, a release consists of a set of compatible subsystems (and their modules) along with their associated logical and physical design documentation. Building a release is possible whenever the major subsystems of a project are stable enough and work together well enough to provide some new level of functionality.

Consider this stream of releases from the perspective of an individual developer, who might be responsible for implementing the modules of a particular subsystem. He or she would always have a working version of that subsystem, that is, a version under development. In order to proceed with development, at least the interfaces of all the imported subsystems must be available. As this working version becomes stable, it is released to a test and integration team, who are responsible for collecting a set of compatible subsystems for the entire system. Eventually, this collection of subsystems would be frozen and baselined, and made part of an internal release. This internal release becomes the current operational prototype, visible to all developers who need to further refine their particular part of its implementation. In the meantime, the individual developer can work on a newer version of his or her subsystem. Thus, development can proceed in parallel, with stability possible because of well-defined and well-guarded subsystem interfaces.

Practically speaking, this means that at any given point in the evolution of a system, multiple versions of a particular module may exist: there might be a version for the current prototype under development, one for the current internal release, and one for the latest customer release. This intensifies the need for reasonably powerful configuration management and version control tools. For smaller projects, individual modules are the most effective unit for configuration management. For larger projects, which may involve many tens of thousands of modules, we have found it best to use the class category or subsystem as the unit of configuration management.

Source code is not the only product that should be placed under configuration management. The same concepts apply to the other products of object-oriented design, namely class diagrams, object diagrams, module diagrams, and process diagrams.

Quality Assurance

The use of object-oriented design doesn't give one the license to abandon the established practices of quality assurance. Specifically, peer reviews (walkthroughs) of designs are still very important in object-oriented design. The value that object-oriented design brings is that its notation highlights most of the important elements of a design so that reviews can concentrate on more critical topics than source code formatting and local style conventions. In early walkthroughs, reviews should focus on the static and dynamic semantics of the system's key abstractions and mechanisms, as embodied in class and object diagrams, respectively. Later design reviews should focus upon the physical design of the system, as embodied in module and process diagrams.

Closely related to the topic of walkthroughs is that of testing. Again, the use of object-oriented design doesn't change any basic testing practices; what does change is the granularity of the units tested. Unit testing, in which individual classes and modules are tested, is best done by class implementors and application programmers. Since most classes and modules do not stand alone, the developer must usually create a test scaffolding with which to exercise that unit. In practice, we find it best to retain most old tests and test results rather than throw them away, so that as a particular class or module evolves, these tests can be used as regression tests. In this manner, changes to a class or module can be tested to assure that the new unit at least provides the same behavior as in its previous version.

Integration testing is done in two parts. First, before a subsystem is released, a class designer tests the functionality of the entire subsystem. The lessons about using test scaffoldings for individual classes and modules apply here also, although at this stage, one is usually testing whole mechanisms at a time. Second, the test and integration team, which is responsible for assembling compatible subsystems into a complete system, runs system-level tests. They too might use test scaffoldings to automatically run regression tests upon each new release of the system.

To summarize, the responsibility of the test and integration team is to establish policies and standards for testing. Unit testing is then done by individual class implementors, subsystem testing is accomplished by class designers, and system testing is provided by the test and integration team. This approach builds confidence in the lower level abstractions of the system first, in terms of its key abstractions and mechanisms

Tool Support

With early generation languages, it was enough for a development team to have a minimal tool set: an editor, a compiler, a linker, and a loader were often all that were needed (and often all that existed). If the team were particularly lucky, they might even get a source-level debugger. Complex systems change the picture entirely: trying to build a large software system with a minimal tool set is equivalent to building a multistory building with stone hand tools.

Object-oriented design changes the picture as well. Traditional software development tools embody knowledge only about source code, but since object-oriented design highlights key abstractions and mechanisms, we need tools that can focus on richer semantics. We have identified at least six different kinds of tools that are very useful in object-oriented design.

Kinds of Tools. The first tool is a graphics-based system supporting the object-oriented design notation presented in Chapter 5. Such a tool can be used very early in the development process to enforce the notational conventions of object-oriented analysis and design, maintain control over the design products, and coordinate the design activities of a team of developers. This tool can be used throughout the life cycle, as the design evolves into a production implementation. Such a tool is also useful in systems maintenance. Specifically, we have found it possible to reverse-engineer much of the design of an object-oriented system, thus producing at least the class structure and module architecture of the design. This feature is quite important: with traditional CASE tools, developers may generate marvelous pictures, only to find that these pictures are out of date once the implementation is created, because programmers fiddle with the implementation without updating the design. Reverse engineering makes it less likely that design documentation will ever get out of step with the actual implementation.

The next tool we have found important for object-oriented design is a browser that knows about the class structure and module architecture of a system. Class hierarchies can become so complex that it is difficult even to find all of the abstractions that are part of the design or are candidates for reuse [26]. While examining a program fragment, a developer may want to see the definition of the class of some object. Upon finding this class, he or she might wish to visit some of its superclasses. While viewing a particular superclass, the developer might want to browse through all uses of that class, before installing a change to its interface. This kind of browsing is extremely clumsy if one has to worry about files, which are an artifact of the physical, not the logical, design decisions. For this reason, browsers are an important tool for object-oriented design. For example, Smalltalk allows one to browse all the classes of a system in the ways we have described. Similar facilities exist for all of the languages we use in this book, although to different degrees of sophistication.

Another tool we have found to be important, if not absolutely essential, is an incremental compiler. As we pointed out earlier, the kind of evolutionary development that goes on in object-oriented design cries out for an incremental compiler that can compile single declarations and statements. Meyrowitz notes that "Unix as it stands, with its orientation towards the batch compilation of large program files into libraries that are later linked with other code fragments, does not provide the support that is necessary for object-oriented programming. It is unacceptable to require a ten minute compile and link cycle simply to change the implementation of a method and to require a one hour compile and link cycle simply to add a field to a high-level superclass! Incrementally compiled methods and incrementally compiled. . . . field definitions are a must for quick debugging" [27]. Incremental compilers exist for most of the languages described in this book, although most implementations consist of traditional, batch-oriented compilers.

Next, we have found that nontrivial projects need debuggers that know about class and object semantics. When debugging a program, we often need to examine the instance variables and class variables associated with an object. Traditional debuggers for non-object-oriented programming languages do not embody knowledge about classes and objects. Thus, trying to use a standard C debugger for C++ programs, while possible, doesn't permit the developer to find the really important information needed to debug an object-oriented program. The situation is especially critical for object-oriented programming languages that support multiple threads of control. At any given moment during the execution of such a program, there may be several active processes. These circumstances require a debugger that permits the developer to exert control over all the individual threads of control, usually on an object-by-object basis.

Especially for larger projects, one must have configuration management and version control tools. As mentioned earlier, for smaller projects, single modules serve as the best unit of control; for larger projects, the subsystem is the best unit of configuration management.

The last tool we have found important with object-oriented design is a class librarian. Most of the languages we use in this book have predefined class libraries. As a project matures, this library grows as domain-specific reusable software components are added over time. It does not take long for such a library to grow to enormous proportions, which makes it difficult for a developer to find a class or module that meets his or her needs. One reason that a library can become so large is that a given class commonly has multiple implementations, each of which has different time and space semantics. If the perceived cost (usually inflated) of finding a certain component is higher then the perceived cost (usually underestimated) of creating that component from scratch, then all hope of reuse is lost. For this reason, it is important to have at least some minimal librarian tool that allows developers to locate classes and modules according to different criteria and add useful classes and modules to the library as they are developed.

Organizational Implications. This need for powerful tools creates a demand for two specific positions within the development organization: a librarian and a toolsmith. The duties of the librarian are to maintain the class library for a project. Without active effort, such a library can become a vast wasteland of junk classes that no developer would ever want to walk through. Also, it is often necessary to be proactive to encourage reuse, and a librarian can facilitate this process by scavenging the products of current design efforts. The duties of a toolsmith are to create domain-specific tools and tailor existing ones for the needs of a project. For example, a project might need common test scaffolding to test certain aspects of a user interface, or it might need a customized class browser. A toolsmith is in the best position to craft these tools, usually from components already in the class library. Such tools can also be used for later developmental efforts.

A manager already faced with scarce human resources may lament that powerful tools, as well as designated librarians and toolsmiths, are an unaffordable luxury. We do not deny this reality for some resource-constrained projects. However, in many other projects, we have found that these activities go on anyway, usually in an *ad hoc* fashion. We advocate explicit investments in tools and people to make these *ad hoc* activities more focused and efficient, which adds real value to the overall development effort.

7.3 The Benefits and Risks of Object-Oriented Design

The Benefits of Object-Oriented Design

The early adopters of new technologies such as object-oriented design usually embrace them for one of two reasons. First, they seek a competitive advantage (such as reduced time to market, greater product flexibility, or schedule predictability) through new techniques that may offer a tremendous payoff. Second, they may have complex problems that don't seem to have any other solution. If these early adopters produce enough success stories, then other, more risk-aversive organizations will follow their paths.

Object-oriented design is not a new technology, but it is not exactly a mature technology either, mainly because far fewer people are experienced in the method than in, for example, structured design. We certainly expect this situation to reverse itself eventually. In the interim, we have already found many success stories among early adopters. Frankly, we realize that people must see for themselves that the object model really does address the problems of developing complex software systems. For the moment, you will have to take it on faith that there are indeed considerable benefits to be gained from the use of object-oriented design.

In Chapter 2, we suggested that the use of the object model leads us to construct systems that embody the attributes of well-structured complex systems. The object model forms the conceptual framework for object-oriented design, and thus these benefits are true of the method also. In that chapter, we also noted the following benefits of applying the object model (and thus object-oriented design):

- Exploits the expressive power of all object-based and object-oriented programming languages
- Encourages the reuse of software components
- Leads to systems that are more resilient to change
- Reduces development risk
- Appeals to the working of human cognition

A number of case studies reinforce these findings; in particular, they point out that the object-oriented approach can reduce development time and the size of the resulting source code [28].

There is not yet enough experience with object-oriented programming to understand how object-oriented design affects formal software economics models, such as CoCoMo or Price-S.

The Risks of Object-Oriented Design

On the darker side of object-oriented design, we find that two areas of risk must be considered:

- Performance
- Start-up costs

Performance Risks. There is definitely a performance cost for sending a message from one object to another in an object-oriented programming language. As we pointed out in Chapter 3, for method invocations that cannot be resolved statically, an implementation must do a dynamic lookup in order to find the method defined for the class of the receiving object. Studies indicate that a method invocation may take from 1.75 to 2.5 times as long as a simple subprogram call [29, 30]. On the positive side, let's focus on the operative phrase, "cannot be resolved statically." Experience indicates that dynamic lookup is really needed in only about twenty percent of most method invocations. Thus, with a strongly typed language, a compiler can often determine which invocations can be statically resolved and then generate code for a subprogram call rather than a method lookup.

Another source of performance overhead comes not so much from the nature of object-based and object-oriented programming language but from the way they are used in conjunction with object-oriented design. As we have stated many times, object-oriented design leads to the creation of systems whose components are built in layers of abstraction. One implication of this layering is that individual methods are generally very small, since they build on lower level methods. Another implication of this layering is that sometimes methods must be written to gain protected access to the otherwise encapsulated fields of an object. This plethora of methods means that we end up with a glut of method invocations. Invoking a method at a high level of abstraction usually results in a cascade of method invocations; high-level methods usually invoke lower level ones, and so on. For applications in which time is a limited resource, so many method invocations may be unacceptable. On the positive side again, such layering is essential for the understandability of a system; it may be impossible ever to get a complex system working without starting with a layered design. Our recommendation is to design for functionality first, and then instrument the running system to determine where the timing bottlenecks actually exist. These bottlenecks can often be removed by declaring the appropriate methods as inline (thus trading off space for time), unencapsulating certain fields, or – in extreme cases – turning the object into a simple record, rather than an instance of a class.

A related performance risk derives from the encumbrance of classes: a class deep in an inheritance lattice may have many superclasses, whose code must be included when linking in the most specific class. For small object-oriented applications, this may practically mean that deep class hierarchies are to be avoided, because they require an excessive amount of object code. This problem can be mitigated somewhat by using a compiler and linker that eliminate all dead code.

Yet another source of performance overhead with object-based and object-oriented programming languages derives from the paging behavior of running applications. Most compilers allocate object code in segments, with the code for each compilation unit (usually a single file) placed in one or more segments. This model presumes a high locality of reference: subprograms within one segment call subprograms in the same segment. However, in object-oriented systems, there is rarely such locality of reference. For large systems, classes are usually declared in separate files, and since the methods of one class usually build upon those of other classes, a single method invocation may involve code from many different segments. This violates the assumptions that most computers make about the runtime behavior of programs, particularly for computers with pipelined CPUs and virtual memory systems. Again on the positive side, this is why we separate logical and physical design decisions. If a running system thrashes during execution owing to excessive segment swapping, then fixing the problem is largely a matter of changing the physical allocation of classes to modules. This is a design decision in the physical model of the system, which has no effect upon its logical design.

One remaining performance risk with object-oriented systems comes from the dynamic allocation and destruction of objects. Allocating an object on a heap is a dynamic action as opposed to statically allocating an object either globally or on a stack frame, and heap allocation usually costs more computing resources. For many kinds of systems, this property does not cause any real problems, but for time-critical applications, one cannot afford the cycles needed to complete a heap allocation. There is a simple solution for this problem: we recommend that the dynamic creation of such objects be completed as part of the elaboration of the program, and not during any time-critical algorithms.

One other positive note: certain properties of object-oriented systems often overshadow all these sources of performance overhead. For example, Russo and Kaplan report that the execution time of a C++ program is often faster than that of its functionally equivalent C program [31]. They attribute this difference to the use of virtual functions, which eliminate the need for some kinds of explicit type checking and control structures. Indeed, in our experience, the code sizes of object-oriented systems are commonly smaller than their functionally equivalent non-object-oriented implementations.

Start-up Costs. For some projects, the start-up costs associated with object-oriented design may prove to be a very real barrier to adopting the method. Using any such new technology requires the capitalization of software development tools. Also, if a development organization is using a particular object-based or object-oriented programming language for the first time, they usually have no established base of domain-specific software to reuse. In short, they must start from scratch or at least figure out how to interface their object-oriented applications with existing non-object-oriented ones. Finally, using object-oriented design for the first time will surely fail without the appropriate training. An object-based and object-oriented programming language is not "just another programming language" that can be learned in a three-day course or by reading a book. It takes time to develop the proper mindset for object-oriented design, and this new way of thinking must be embraced by both developers and their managers alike.

The Transition to Object-Oriented Design

This change of mindset is an important point. As Kempf reports, "Learning object-oriented programming may well be a more difficult task than learning 'just' another programming language. This may be the case because a different style of programming is involved rather than a different syntax within the same framework. That means that not a new language but a new way of thinking about programming is involved" [32].

How do we develop this object-oriented mindset? We recommend the following:

- Provide formal training to both developers and managers in the elements of the object model.
- Use object-oriented design in a low-risk project first, and allow the team to make mistakes; use these team members to seed other projects and act as mentors for the object-oriented approach.
- Expose the developers and managers to examples of well-structured object-oriented systems.

Good candidate projects include software development tools or domain-specific class libraries, which can then be used as resources in later projects.

In our experience, it takes only a few weeks for a professional developer to master the syntax and semantics of a new programming language. It may take several more weeks for the same developer to begin to appreciate the importance and power of classes and objects. Finally, it may take as many as six months of experience for that developer to mature into a competent class designer. This is not necessarily a bad thing, for in any discipline, it takes time to master the art.

We have found that learning by example is often an efficient and effective approach. Once an organization has accumulated a critical mass of applications written in an object-oriented style, introducing new developers and managers to object-oriented design is far easier. Developers start as application programmers, using the well-structured abstractions that already exist. Over time, developers who have studied and used these components under the supervision of a more experienced person gain sufficient experience to develop a meaningful conceptual framework of the object model and become effective class designers.

Let's now turn to a series of applications that illustrate the practical application of object-oriented design, implemented using a variety of languages and covering a number of different problem domains.

Summary

- The software development life cycle using object-oriented design emphasizes the incremental, iterative development of a system.
- Structured analysis is an attractive front end to object-oriented design; object-oriented analysis provides an even more effective precursor.
- Design can start whenever there is a (possibly incomplete) formal or informal model of the problem to be solved; it stops when composition rather than further decomposition dominates.
- In object-oriented design, there is never a big-bang event of system integration.
- Several kinds of changes to a design are to be expected during the evolution of a system using object-oriented design; each kind of change involves a different cost.
- The use of object-oriented design impacts the management practices of staffing, milestones and products, release management, quality assurance, and tool support.
- There are many benefits to the application of object-oriented design and some risks as well; experience indicates that the benefits far outweigh the risks.
- The transition in an organization to the use of the object model requires a change in mindset; learning an object-based or object-oriented programming language is more than learning "just another programming language."

Further Readings

The use of structured analysis methods as a front end to object-oriented design is described by Alabios [F 1988] and Stark [F 1986]. Using object-oriented analysis methods as a front end to object-oriented design is described by Bailin and Moore [B 1987], Cernosek, Monterio, and Pribyl [B 1987], Dahl [B 1987], Mellor, Hecht, Tryon, and Hywari [B 1988], Smith and Tockey [F 1988], and Stoecklin, Adams, and Smith [B 1987].

The work by Aron [H 1974] offers a comprehensive look at the challenges of managing the individual programmer as well as teams of programmers. For a refreshingly realistic study of what really goes on during the development of complex systems, when pragmatics chases theory out the window, see the works by Glass [G 1982], Lammers [H 1986], and Humphrey [H 1989]. Additionally, DeMarco and Lister [H 1987] and Yourdon [H 1989] offer a number of very useful recommendations to the manager of complex software systems under development.

Suggestions on how to accomplish the transition of individuals and organizations to using the object model are described by Goldberg [C 1978], Goldberg and Kay [G 1977], and Kempf [G 1987].

Vonk [H 1990] rovides a comprehensive study of prototyping.

Applications

To build a theory, one needs to know a lot about the basic phenomena of the subject matter. We simply do not know enough about these, in the theory of computation, to teach the subject very abstractly. Instead, we ought to teach more about the particular examples we now understand thoroughly, and hope that from this we will be able to guess and prove more general principles.

MARVIN MINSKY
Form and Content in Computer Science

CHAPTER 8

Smalltalk
Home Heating System

Theory is a wonderful thing, but from the perspective of the practicing engineer, the most elegant theory ever devised is entirely useless if it does not
help us build systems for the real world. The last seven chapters have been
but a prelude to this section of the book, in which we now apply object-oriented
design to the pragmatic construction of software systems. In this and the remaining four chapters, we start with a set of system requirements and then
use the notation and process of object-oriented design to lead us to an implementation. We have chosen a set of applications from widely varying domains,
encompassing process control, scientific tools, information management systems, artificial intelligence, and command and control, each of which involves
its own unique set of problems. Since object-oriented design is appropriate for
use with a spectrum of object-based and object-oriented programming languages, we express our solutions in a different language for each application.
In this chapter, we use Smalltalk; subsequent chapters use Object Pascal,
C++, the Common Lisp Object System (CLOS), and Ada. Because our focus is
on design rather than programming, we do not present the complete implementation of any problem, but we supply enough details to show the mapping
from design to implementation and to highlight particularly interesting aspects
of designing with the given language.

Home Heating System Requirements

The following requirements for the home heating system were originally proposed by White [1] and then extended by Kerth [2].

Figure 8-1 provides a block diagram of the home heating system. The basic function of the system is to regulate the flow of heat to individual rooms of a home in an attempt to maintain a working temperature *tw*, established for each room. The working temperature for each room is calculated by the system as a function of a single desired temperature *td*, (set by the user through a manual input device) and whether or not the room is occupied. If the room is occupied, the working temperature is set to the desired temperature. If the room is vacant, the working temperature is set to (*td* – 5) degrees Fahrenheit. Additionally, the system maintains a weekly living pattern and attempts to raise room temperatures thirty minutes before occupancy is anticipated for a given room. The weekly living pattern is updated when variations to the established pattern occur two weeks in a row.

Each room of the home is equipped with a sensor that continuously measures temperature. Each room of the home is also equipped with an infrared sensor that continuously determines whether or not the room is occupied.

The user interface permits the user to control and monitor the furnace. The following input devices exist:

- Heat switch

  The heat switch controls the functioning of the furnace; it can be turned on and off by the user.

- Desired-temperature input device

  The desired-temperature input device (one per room) continuously provides the value of the desired temperature set by the user.

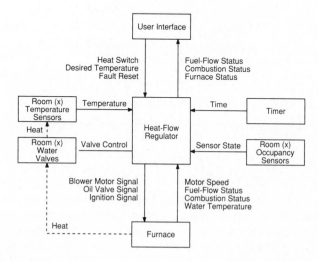

Figure 8-1
Home Heating System Block Diagram

- Fault reset switch/indicator

This is a combined switch and indicator; the user can reset a fault by setting the fault reset switch/indicator to on.

The following display devices are provided:

- Furnace status indicator

The furnace status indicator displays the running/not running state of the furnace.

- Fault reset switch/indicator

This is a combined switch and indicator; the fault reset switch/indicator is automatically turned off by the heat-flow regulator upon the detection of either a fuel-flow or combustion-state fault.

The timer provides a continuously incrementing count, one increment for every second of elapsed time.

Heat is provided to each room of the home by circulating hot water, which is heated by the furnace. Each room is equipped with a water valve that controls the flow of hot water into the room. The valve can be commanded to be either fully open or fully closed.

The furnace consists of a boiler, an oil valve, an ignitor, a blower, and a water-temperature sensor. The furnace heats water in the boiler, and the water can then be circulated to one or more rooms of the home. The furnace is alternately activated and deactivated by the heat-flow regulator as needed to maintain the required temperature for each room. The furnace activation procedure is as follows:

- The system activates the blower motor.
- The system monitors the blower motor speed; when it reaches a predetermined RPM value the system opens the oil valve and ignites the oil.
- When the water temperature reaches a predetermined value, the system opens the appropriate room water valves.
- The furnace status indicator is turned on.

The furnace deactivation procedure is as follows:

- The system closes the oil valve and then, after five seconds, stops the blower motor.
- The system turns the furnace indicator off.
- The system closes all the room water valves.

A fuel-flow status sensor and an optical combustion sensor signal the system if abnormalities occur, in which case the system deactivates the furnace, turns the fault reset switch/indicator off, and closes all the room water valves.

The heat-flow regulator interacts with other components of the home heating system to determine the heating needs for each room and to control the flow of heat necessary to satisfy those requirements. The heat-flow regulator maintains a working temperature, *tw*, and a weekly living pattern for each room without regard to the running/not running state of the furnace. The heat-flow regulator determines that a given room needs heat whenever the room temperature is equal to or less than ($tw - 2$) degrees Fahrenheit and determines that a given room does not need heat whenever the room temperature is equal to or greater than ($tw + 2$) degrees Fahrenheit. If the furnace is not running, the heat switch and the fault reset switch/indicator are both on, and at least one room needs heat, the heat-flow regulator activates the furnace and then routes heat to the appropriate rooms. If the furnace is running, the heat-flow regulator deactivates the furnace whenever either the heat switch or the fault reset switch/indicator is off and no rooms need heat. The minimum time for furnace restart after prior operation is five minutes.

8.1 Analysis

Defining the Boundaries of the Problem

The sidebar provides the requirements for a home heating system. As we read these requirements, we must ask ourselves questions such as, "Is it necessary to model the heat transfer across room walls?" "Are there any unusual safety requirements involving high temperatures?" "Can we do anything with respect to the failure of a water valve or a temperature sensor?" To the degree that our experience allows, we try to relate any new problem to similar ones we have already solved. For example, we might notice that the home heating system is in some ways similar to the hydroponics gardening system presented in Chapter 5, yet is quite different from the command and control system introduced in Chapter 7. Ultimately, we can properly conclude that the home heating system is a problem of process control, not a database problem or a scientific processing problem, although it does contain some elements of both.

Coping with Imperfect Requirements. A complete reading of the sidebar leads us to realize that the stated requirements for the home heating system are incomplete, over-specified, and self-contradictory. But then, these are real requirements, not fabricated ones, and the world is not a perfect place. Even if we did know all the relevant requirements, few useful instruments are at our disposal to precisely articulate them. This is not meant to condemn any particular requirements method; it is just an acknowledgement of the state of the practice, coupled with the fact that we must still build systems in spite of these shortcomings.

With respect to completeness, the given requirements have quite a few gaps. For example, the capacity of the heating system is not mentioned: does it control the temperature of 10 rooms or 10,000 rooms? Does the target environment consist of a single processor or multiple processors? If we have just a single processor, are there any particular processing-speed or memory-size constraints that affect us? For simplicity, we will assume that the system architects working on this problem have given the software developers a single processor as the implementation target. We will also assume that our processor has sufficient capacity for whatever number of rooms the system must manage. Of course, we want to design our software so that the solution can easily accommodate any number of rooms with minimal changes.

The requirements are silent with regard to how the system should respond to concurrent events, such as when occupants of two different rooms simultaneously change the desired room temperature. The home heating system is not a hard-real-time problem (HRT), although the requirements speak of time-critical events on the order of single seconds, not milli- or microseconds. Still, this forces us to consider alternative designs, each with different time and space characteristics. If we want our system to use polling to achieve the illusion of parallelism on a single processor, we must live with the latency of user-visible responses to external events. If we choose instead to build this as an event-driven system, we must require a target processor that can detect and respond to hardware interrupts. Fortunately, we do not need to choose the desired behavior immediately; indeed, it is best that we defer any decision until we have sufficient information about the problem to weigh each alternative intelligently.

Concerning over-specification, the given requirements imply a particular design for the heat-flow regulator. Specifically, the requirements state that the heat-flow regulator is responsible for maintaining the weekly living pattern of each room. Certainly, keeping track of the weekly living pattern is an important system function. However, is it a requirement that the heat-flow regulator be the responsible agent, or is this a design alternative? It is not unusual for requirements to imply a design, but in general, this is not a good thing, for it tends to limit the freedom of the software engineer, leading him or her to neglect better designs that would otherwise radically simplify the solution or improve its chances for an orderly evolution. In this case, we will take a liberal interpretation of the given requirements, and assume that the fundamental requirement is for the system to maintain the weekly living pattern. We will assume that we may choose a mechanism other than the heat-flow regulator to be responsible for managing this knowledge.

It is also not unusual for requirements to be self-contradictory; in fact, the more complex the problem, the more likely it is that some requirements will collide. The requirements stated in the sidebar are no exception. For example, consider the requirements surrounding the fault reset switch/indicator. At one point, the requirements state that "the fault reset switch/indicator is automatically turned off by the heat-flow regulator upon the detection of either a fuel-flow or combustion-state fault." In another place, the requirements state that certain sensors "signal the system if abnormalities occur, in which case the system deactivates the furnace, turns the fault reset switch/indicator off, and closes all room water valves." Thus, in the first case, the requirements imply that turning off the fault reset switch/indicator is an immediate consequence of either a fuel-flow or combustion-state fault. In the second case, they require that the furnace be deactivated before the fault reset switch/indicator is turned off. Which we choose as the actual requirement affects the externally observed behavior of the system. Assuming that the furnace need not be deactivated before turning off the fault reset switch/indicator means that the operator will be notified of a fault immediately upon its detection, but deactivation of the furnace will be slightly delayed. Assuming the converse means a noticeable delay before the operator is made aware of the abnormality, although the furnace will be deactivated immediately. This is a clear clash of requirements, and it is best to clear it up through a discussion with the system's users, perhaps by demonstrating a prototype for each alternative and letting the users decide what their real needs are. For the purposes of this problem, mainly in order to provide fail-safe behavior, we assume that the system deactivates the furnace immediately upon detecting a fault and before any other activity.

Understanding the Vocabulary of the Problem Space. Since both designers and users probably have incomplete knowledge of the total desired behavior of the home heating system, it is best to proceed incrementally. Our approach will be to design and implement a free-standing simulation of the system in Smalltalk, which we can use to demonstrate a concrete interpretation of system functionality to the specifiers of the system. Once we agree upon the behavior of the system – and perhaps in the process negotiate a change in the requirements – we will then modify our system to interface with physical devices such as the actual temperature sensors and water valves, using the unchanged, original design as a foundation.

At this point, it is useful to capture the most important things we already know about the boundaries of our problem. Using structured analysis, we might first sketch a context diagram and its corresponding high-level data flow diagrams. We apply structured analysis in Chapter 10, but for our current problem, this is an unnecessary excess because the stated requirements are reasonably well-defined, and the entities involved are relatively static. Furthermore, we are all experts to some degree in this problem domain: our homes and offices typically have some sort of heating system.

Although we label this step as *analysis*, it is really just an early part of the process of round-trip gestalt design. As shown in Chapter 7, our object-oriented design notation is a reasonable vehicle for documenting what we do know about the key abstractions in the problem domain.

In Figure 8-2, we have drafted an object diagram representing the topmost structure of the system. Here we assert the existence of many of the objects named in our earlier discussion of the system's requirements: the rooms, the heat-flow regulator, the furnace, and the operator interface. The requirements speak of a single user interface, but we note that there are really two kinds of users involved: room occupants and home heating system operators. For reasons that we make clear in the next section, we place only the operator interface at the top level of the system.

Notice that this diagram shows only one external relationship among the given objects. Specifically, it shows that the furnace generates heat, which is released into certain rooms, thus raising their temperature. This is the feedback loop in the system, which is outside the domain that we can properly model in software. Similarly, we do not need to worry about the heating or cooling of rooms from other sources, such as fireplaces or open windows.

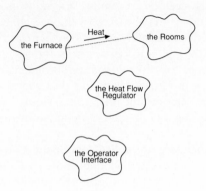

Figure 8-2
Draft Home Heating System Object Diagram

We have explicitly chosen not to show any other relationships among the objects at this level. To do so during this phase of analysis would be premature, since assertions of internal relationships generally denote design decisions. We do expect, however, that when we proceed with design, our draft object diagrams are likely to change in subtle ways and become more detailed because design decisions solidify the boundaries of each object and because our invention of common mechanisms will ultimately unify our implementation.

Earlier, we interpreted the home heating system requirements to mean that the maintenance of a living pattern was a fundamental system function, but not one that had to be provided specifically by the heat-flow regulator. To capture this analysis decision, we have drafted a room object diagram in Figure 8-3. Here we see that each room logically encompasses a water valve, actual- and desired-temperature sensors, a room-occupancy sensor, and a living pattern. We have chosen to place the knowledge of the living pattern within each room rather than to centralize it in the heat-flow regulator for three reasons. First, to make it part of the heat-flow regulator would mean that adding new rooms would involve changing this centralized data store, thus hindering system evolution. Second, placing the knowledge of the living pattern within each room achieves a greater cohesion of abstractions, since a living pattern is unique to each room. Finally, this decision gives us a looser coupling between the heat-flow regulator and individual rooms. The heat-flow regulator needs only to know whether or not a particular room requires heat, since a room itself is in the best position to decide if it needs heat, according to its present occupancy, expected occupancy (as indicated by its living pattern), and current differences between its actual and desired temperature. As in the previous figure, we do not show relationships among the objects of a room, because we still lack sufficient information about the nature of each object to make intelligent decisions regarding its behavior.

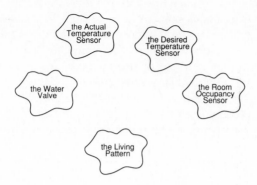

Figure 8-3
Draft Room Object Diagram

Applying Domain Analysis

Now that we have established a rough conceptual model that bounds the elements of the entire home heating system, let's apply the techniques of domain analysis from Chapter 4.

Tangible Things. Starting with the tangible things described in the requirements, we find the following key abstractions:

Home heating system	Timer	Home
Room	Living pattern	Current-temperature sensor
Room-occupancy sensor	Water valve	Desired-temperature sensor
Operator interface	Heat switch	Fault reset switch/indicator
Furnace-status indicator	Furnace	Boiler-temperature sensor
Oil valve	Blower	Ignitor
Heat-flow regulator		

Temperature is one other key abstraction that we find. Temperature is not exactly a tangible thing, but it is a property that can be measured and whose effects can be felt. Furthermore, temperature is certainly an essential part of the vocabulary of the problem domain. By stating that our system deals with temperatures in degrees Fahrenheit and remembering that the system circulates heated water to warm the rooms of a home, we can make some intelligent assumptions regarding the range of temperatures our system is expected to handle. Thus, we need not be concerned with temperatures below the freezing point of water, nor far above the temperature of steam under high pressure.

There is one tangible set of objects mentioned in the requirements that falls outside of the system, namely, users. We consider users to be outside of the system because they are simply the agents that trigger many of the events external to the home heating system; they have no software analog. However, a study of the role of users as key abstractions does lead us to realize that there are actually two kinds of users of interest to us: room occupants and operators. It is useful to divide users into these two categories, because their roles are fundamentally different: one set of users (room occupants) manipulates the desired temperature in individual rooms, and another set (operators) is allowed to reset faults and turn the heat switch on or off. The difference in these roles led us earlier to identify the operator interface as one of the topmost abstractions, rather than combining it with the interface as seen by room occupants.

Events. Let's consider next the external events to which the home heating system must respond. A reading of the requirements suggests that the following events are relevant:

- A room occupant changes the desired temperature.
- A room occupant enters or leaves a room.
- The actual temperature of a room changes.
- A fuel-flow or combustion-state abnormality occurs.
- An operator turns the heat switch on or off.
- The home heating system is powered on or off.
- An operator turns the fault reset switch/indicator on.

All these events are asynchronous; only one periodic event is defined in the requirements:

- Time passes, indicated at one-second intervals.

Although they are not externally generated events, the requirements state that our system has the ability to monitor changes in the speed of the blower motor and the temperature of the boiler water.

Listing these external and internal events helps us define the boundaries of our system by relating these events to the behavior of key abstractions. For example, we may properly decide that the timer is directly responsible for detecting the passage of time, and that other elements, such as the living pattern, only respond to messages from the timer. The identification of external events also helps us define what our system cannot do. For example, we know that the home heating system has no means to detect a water valve failure, and therefore can do nothing in response to such an anomaly.

The identification of external events also allows us to validate the completeness of our list of key abstractions: we should be able to identify at least one key abstraction that can either detect or react to each event. For example, notice that our original list of key abstractions did not contain any primitive object that could meaningfully detect a fuel-flow or combustion-state abnormality. Thus, we are led to assert the existence of two more key abstractions, namely, a fuel-flow fault sensor and a combustion-fault sensor.

Documenting the Key Abstractions. It is certainly useful to enumerate the key abstractions that we find in the problem domain, but for all except the most trivial systems, this is usually insufficient. As we described in Chapter 7, there is great value in expressing our system requirements in an object-oriented manner. Thus, for each of the key abstractions we have identified, we might document our understanding of its imports, exports, and behavior. For example, we might describe our abstraction of the timer as follows:

- Imports   The passage of time, registered at one second
                   intervals as an event from outside the system.

- Exports   A (natural) magnitude, indicating the number
                   of seconds since the home heating system has
                   been powered on.

- Behavior   The magnitude exported by the timer is
                   incremented upon each time event,
                   independent of the activated/deactivated state
                   of the furnace.

Documenting the assumptions we make concerning each key abstraction is also useful. Thus, for the timer we might write:

- Assumptions   The range of magnitude exported by the timer
                   is sufficiently large so that the count never
                   overflows; a 32-bit representation, for
                   example, would permit the timer to operate
                   without overflow for over 130 years.

The alert reader might suggest that documenting all the key abstractions of the home heating system in this manner would be the equivalent to rewriting the original requirements by allocating them to specific key abstractions. Of course, rewriting all the requirements of a large system would be very costly, time-consuming, and unnecessary. In practice, we find it sufficient to document only the most important abstractions in this way. Furthermore, we never do this all at once, since our identification of key abstractions for large systems happens incrementally. We first discover the most important abstractions in the vocabulary of the domain expert; later, we invent generalizations as well as subcomponents of these abstractions. Thus the process of domain analysis leads us to uncover contradictions in the requirements, define vague terminology, unify differing terminology that has the same meaning, and make intelligent decisions regarding the semantics of each key abstraction.

Building a Prototype

Our analysis of the home heating system has provided us with a basic understanding of the key abstractions in the problem domain and the essential functions of the system. We are thus prepared to begin designing a solution that satisfies the stated requirements. It is important at this stage in the software development life cycle to identify reusable software components that we can use to build our system, so that we can compose as much of the home heating system as practical from existing components rather than creating entirely new ones.

Reusing Existing Components. Actively looking for reusable software components that are relevant to a new system is a very important activity in any development. This process is facilitated by rich class libraries that are typically available for object-based and object-oriented programming languages. For example, in the standard class library for Smalltalk-80, we find components such as `StandardSystemView`, which we can use to simulate the operator and room-occupant interfaces. Smalltalk classes that simulate gauges are available commercially [3], and include components such as `CircleMeterView` and `BarGaugeWithScaleView` that we can apply to simulate analog devices, such as the desired- and actual-temperature sensors, respectively.

We cannot apply these classes directly, because they are domain-independent. Instead, we must tailor them so that they express the vocabulary of the home heating system. For this reason, it is suitable for us to prototype the specialization of these classes. The conservative developer might claim that we are jumping into implementation far too early. Certainly, prototyping should never be an excuse for hacking, and one should always have honorable purposes in mind before starting a prototype. The fundamental value of prototyping parts of the home heating system user interface before we go any further into our design is that the very act of prototyping will help us decide if we even need to design certain elements of the system. If we can find a component that is relevant to our problem, that component becomes a primitive abstraction with which we can compose the system; thus we are left with a smaller problem to solve. Prototyping the user interface has one other very important benefit: a prototype gives us the opportunity to further explore the implications of the required behavior of the home heating system user interface, particularly with respect to its concurrency semantics.

Design of the Class Toggle Switch. A review of the key abstractions in the problem domain leads us to invent a generalization of the heat switch and the fault reset switch/indicator. In both cases, what we need is a simulation of a simple toggle switch. For example, we might visualize the heat switch as an object with two views, one labeled *heat on* and the other labeled *heat off*, with only one of these two views highlighted at a time. A user should be able to use a mouse to click on either of the views to simulate flipping the switch. Changing the state of the switch from on to off or from off to on reverses the highlighting of both views and passes an appropriate message to some other agent that can mean-ingfully react to the change in state. Clicking on an already highlighted view does nothing.

If we scavenge through Smalltalk-80's class library, we will find the class `BooleanView`, which is close to what we need. `BooleanView` is a so-called pluggable view: it provides the functionality of a single view that toggles be-tween highlighted and not highlighted, and so hides all the mundane details of displaying, highlighting, and responding to mouse action. Thus, a toggle switch may be composed of two instances of the class `BooleanView`, with one part always reflecting the negated state of the other.

`BooleanView` can be tailored by associating it with a domain-specific model and label. For example, we can create a new instance of the class `BooleanView` by evaluating the following statement:

```
aBooleanView ← BooleanView
            on:     aModel
            aspect: #state
            label:  'a label'
            change: #state:
            value:  true.
```

This is the common style among object-oriented programming languages that support metaclasses: to create and initialize an instance of a class, we invoke a method defined in that class's metaclass.

The class `BooleanView` provides an example of the model-view-controller (MVC) mechanism discussed in Chapter 4. The effect of the above method is to create a new view as well as a corresponding controller. The selector `on:` ex-pects an argument representing the model to be notified whenever there is a mouse click in the view. This gives us a clear separation of concerns among the model, the object that views the model, and the controller that modifies the model.

The objects that make up the model-view-controller mechanism do not have global visibility among themselves. The controller and the view are mutu-ally dependent in that each can send messages to the other. Furthermore, both the controller and the view can send messages to the model: one side effect of the above method is to establish a reference to the model in a field of both the controller and the view. However, the model cannot send messages directly to either the controller or the view. Rather, the model-to-view relationship is main-tained indirectly by the Smalltalk dependency mechanism introduced in Chapter 3 (in this mechanism, each object maintains a list of dependent objects). Thus, another side effect of the above method is that the newly created view is added to the list of the dependents of the given model. Each view has exactly one model, but each model may be visible in multiple views.

Whenever there is a mouse click on a `BooleanView` object, the message `state:` is sent by the view's controller to the model, with a Boolean argument indicating the new switch state. To create a proper model for use with the view, we must therefore implement the method `state:` in the model to do whatever domain-specific actions we require. This is why `BooleanView` is called a *pluggable view*: we need only to "plug in" appropriate objects and methods to tailor the predefined view to our immediate needs. Pluggable views are thus largely equivalent to the more static generic mechanisms found in languages such as CLU and Ada.

A toggle switch requires the use of two instances of the class `BooleanView`. Since this represents an aggregation of objects, it is best that we design the class `ToggleSwitch` to *use* the class `BooleanView`, rather than *inherit* from it. Another compelling reason for applying a using rather than an inheriting class relationship is that the behavior of a toggle switch is more than the behavior of two instances of `BooleanView`: when one view reacts to a mouse click, the state of other must be negated as well. Therefore we make the following design decisions: the superclass of the class `ToggleSwitch` is the base class `Object`, and the class `ToggleSwitch` uses the class `BooleanView`.

We would like to define the class `ToggleSwitch` so that it, too, is pluggable. Specifically, it should have no knowledge of what labels to display nor what actions to take upon a state change. For this reason, we must parameterize the class `ToggleSwitch` with four selectors: an *on* label, an *off* label, an *on* action, and an *off* action. This decision leads us to select the following three instance variables for our representation of the class `ToggleSwitch`:

- `state`   The current on/off state of the toggle switch
- `trueAction`   The block to be performed when the toggle switch state changes from off to on
- `falseAction`   The block to be performed when the toggle switch state changes from on to off

We will also include the following two instance variables. Their presence makes the code for initializing an instance of the class `ToggleSwitch` much clearer, and, as we will see in a later section, they are needed to facilitate the proper placement of the object's two views in its enclosing view:

- `trueView`   The instance of the `BooleanView` representing the *on* view of the toggle switch
- `falseView`   The instance of the `BooleanView` representing the *off* view of the toggle switch

Given these implementation decisions, we can now write a method for the class `ToggleSwitch` to initialize its instance variables:

```
initialize: initialValue
trueLabel: firstLabel
falseLabel: secondLabel
trueAction: firstAction
falseAction: secondAction
```

```
"Initialize a toggle switch. initialValue is expected to be of the class
 Boolean. firstLabel and secondLabel are expected to be of the class
 String. firstAction and secondAction are expected to be of the class
 Block."

state ← initialValue.
trueAction ← firstAction.
falseAction ← secondAction.
trueView ← BooleanView
          on: self
          aspect: #state
          label: firstLabel asText
          change: #state:
          value: true.
falseView ← BooleanView
          on: self
          aspect: #state
          label: secondLabel asText
          change: #state:
          value: false
```

Notice that our comments document the expected class of each selector. Since Smalltalk supports dynamic binding of objects to names, the language cannot enforce our assumptions regarding the proper objects to use when applying this method. Thus, an unsuspecting programmer could invoke the above method using an inappropriate object. Smalltalk would happily perform the method, and the programmer would not realize the mistake until the first time there was a mouse click in the offending view. Dynamic binding is essential in some cases, but it does require the programmer to be more careful.

Why did we define this `initialize` method in the class `ToggleSwitch` rather than defining a method in its metaclass, as we saw done for `BooleanView`? Defining a metaclass method is appropriate if we want to both create and initialize an instance of a class, or if we must initialize some class variables. By defining an `initialize` method in the class itself, a client can create an object (using the methods `new` or `new:` inherited from the class `Behavior`), initialize the object and then later reinitialize that same object. This approach thus offers slightly more flexibility, because it leaves us with a more primitive interface: for the same `ToggleSwitch` object, a client can reinitialize it with new labels and actions, whereas if we established the initial state of the instance variables only at object-creation time, we would have to supply additional methods to reset this state.

The method `state:` is essential to the proper functioning of this class. Because we have used the same model to create both instances of the class `BooleanView`, events detected by either controller will funnel to the same model. Thus, as defined by the pluggable view `BooleanView`, the message `state:` is sent either by the `trueView` or the `falseView` controller, depending upon which one detects the mouse click. The action of the method `state:` must therefore be to set the instance variable `state` to its new value, notify both views that a change of state has occurred, and then perform the `trueAction` or the `falseAction` as appropriate. We may capture these semantics in the method as follows:

state: aBoolean

> "Set the state of the toggle switch. aBoolean is expected to be of the class Boolean."

```
state = aBoolean
    ifFalse:
        [state ← aBoolean.
        self changed: #state.
        state
            ifTrue:
                [trueAction value]
            ifFalse:
                [falseAction value]]
```

The only nonobvious part of this method lies in sending the message `changed:`. You may recall from Chapter 3 that in the Smalltalk dependency mechanism, the `changed:` method is used to send the message `update:` to all dependents of an object, indicating that the parent object has changed its state in some manner. Since the objects denoted by the `trueView` and `falseView` fields are both listed as dependents of a toggle switch, the message `update:` with the argument `#state` is sent to both. In this manner, both views are ultimately notified of a change in state, even though only one of them detected a mouse click. The following statements achieve the same effect as the single invocation of the `changed:` method:

```
trueView update: #state.
falseView update: #state.
```

We prefer to use the `changed:` method because it is a more general mechanism, and thus we would rarely ever need to modify the `state:` method even if we chose a radically different view architecture for the toggle switch.

The action of the method `update:` for the class `BooleanView` is to ask the model its current state and then highlight the view accordingly. Since instance variables in Smalltalk are not directly visible outside of an object (in other words, they are encapsulated), we must supply a selector to return the value of the current state. The method `state` as defined for the class `ToggleSwitch` is therefore quite simple:

state

> "Return the state of the toggle switch."
> ↑state

Figure 8-4 illustrates the essential behavior of an instance of the class `ToggleSwitch`. In this object diagram we see the relationships among a toggle switch, its corresponding views, and whichever of their controllers detects a

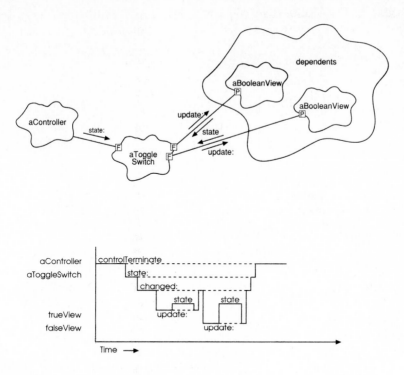

Figure 8-4
Toggle Switch Object Diagram

mouse click. The toggle switch object is visible to the controller object as one of its fields. The two views of the toggle switch object are visible in two ways: through the fields `trueView` and `falseView`, and as components in the collection of the switch's dependents. As dependents, they are therefore accessible as parameters through iteration across this collection.

The relevant flow of control is expressed by the timing diagram. Action starts when a mouse click is detected by either controller. The message `controlTerminate` is sent to the controller, signaling release of the mouse button; `controlTerminate` in turn sends the message `state:` to its model, which then passes the message `update:` to both views via the model's `changed:` method. This `update:` method in each view passes the message `state` back to the model to query the model's current state.

For the purpose of completeness in our abstraction of the toggle switch, we include the methods `trueView` and `falseView`, which serve as selectors that return the value of the instance variables `trueView` and `falseView`, respectively: For example, we may write:

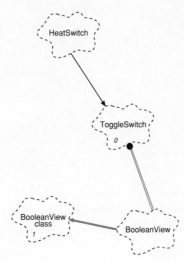

Figure 8-5
Toggle Switch Class Diagram

trueView

> "Return the true view of the toggle switch."

↑trueView

In a later section, we examine how to use these two selectors to place the object's two views in its enclosing view.

Design of the Class HeatSwitch. We may now specialize the class Toggle-Switch to form the class HeatSwitch. Since a heat switch is just a kind of a toggle switch, it is appropriate to apply an inheritance relationship between these two classes, as shown in Figure 8-5. Here we see that the class HeatSwitch inherits from the class ToggleSwitch, which in turn uses for its implementation the class BooleanView (whose metaclass is BooleanView class). For simplicity, we have not shown the classes upon which the class BooleanView is built (namely, SwitchView and View), since the class BooleanView is sufficiently primitive for our purposes.

Notice also that we have stated the cardinality of certain classes. In our design, the class ToggleSwitch is an abstract class; thus it may have no instances and is marked with a cardinality of zero. The figure also shows that in Smalltalk, a metaclass may have only one instance, namely, the class itself. Finally, we have not marked the cardinality of the classes HeatSwitch and BooleanView, which means that an arbitrary number of instances is allowed.

Since the class HeatSwitch inherits from the class ToggleSwitch, most of its behavior is already defined. All we need to do for the class HeatSwitch is provide a suitable initialization method that provides meaningful labels for its two views. Thus, we may write:

initializeOnAction: firstAction offAction: secondAction

> "Initialize the heat switch."
>
> self
>   initialize: false
>   trueLabel: 'heat on'
>   falseLabel: 'heat off'
>   trueAction: firstAction
>   falseAction: secondAction

Notice that it is not appropriate for us simply to redefine the `ToggleSwitch` initialize method, because it uses a different number of parameters.

Design of the Class DesiredTemperatureSensor. In a similar fashion, we may tailor other domain-independent classes. For example, we may simulate a desired-temperature sensor as a view that displays a dial, using the commercially available class `CircleMeterView`. A dial is a more sophisticated view than that provided by the class `BooleanView`: a user may drag a dial needle to a new position representing some analog value. Assuming that the class `DesiredTemperatureSensor` has an instance variable named `value` representing the current desired temperature and an instance variable named `theView` representing the dial's view, we may use the predefined class `CircleMeter-View` and write the following methods for the class `DesiredTemperature-Sensor`:

initialize

> "Initialize the desired-temperature sensor."
>
> | analogGauge |
>
> super initialize.
> analogGauge ← CircleMeterView
>   on: self
>   aspect: #value
>   change: #value:
>   range: (50 to: 90 by: 5).
> theView ← View new.
> theView
>   addSubView: analogGauge
>   in: (0 @ 0 extent: 1 @ 1)
>   borderWidth: 0.
> value ← 65.0.

value: aValue

> "Set the value of the desired-temperature sensor."

```
value = aValue
    ifFalse:
        [value ← aValue.
         self changed: #value.
         self changed: #desiredTemperature]
```

These methods follow the same pattern as for the class `ToggleSwitch`. The class `CircleMeterView` is a pluggable view; thus, among other things, we must supply a message to be passed whenever there is a mouse action completed in the view. This is the purpose of the method `value:`, whose action is to set the instance variable named `value` to the new desired temperature, and then send the `changed:` method to notify its subviews.

Notice also that in this method, we send the symbol `#desired-Temperature` to all the object's dependents. The careful reader may observe that this is redundant; we also send the symbol `#value`. This is indeed true, but we have included both symbols to indicate two different kinds of events, one internal and one external. In both the classes `ToggleSwitch` and `Desired-TemperatureSensor`, we must signal the internal view (an instance of the classes `BooleanView` and `CircleMeterView`, respectively) that a change in state has occurred via the symbol `#value`. Additionally, we must signal some other external objects that can react to the change in state, using the more meaningfully named symbol `#desiredTemperature`. This is similar to our implementation of the class `ToggleSwitch`, where we used the `changed:` method to notify the internal view and performed the blocks `trueAction` or `falseAction` as appropriate as a means of externally reacting to the event.

During the development of our prototype, we had to repair one minor error in the class `CircleMeterView`. Specifically, a reversed sign in a method caused the analog dial to run backwards. This is yet another example of why reusable software components tend to become more stable and robust over time. The discovery of bugs during prototyping should be viewed as a positive event, not a discouraging one, since it is in our best interest to identify errors and other areas of risk early, before we make design decisions that would be costly to reverse.

Prototyping the User Interface. Figure 8-6 provides a screen dump of a Smalltalk session showing prototypes of the operator interface and room-occupant interface using the classes `ToggleSwitch` and `DesiredTemperatureSensor`, plus two other similar classes, namely the class `Indicator` and the class `CurrentTemperatureSensor`. Each window was built with subviews from these domain-specific classes, enclosed in a single instance of the class `StandardSystemView`. The operator interface consists of two instances of the class `ToggleSwitch` and one instance of the class `Indicator`. The room-occupant interface consists of one instance of the class `DesiredTemperature-Sensor`, one instance of the class `Indicator`, and one instance of the class `CurrentTemperatureSensor` (which was in turn built using the class `BarGaugeWithScaleView`).

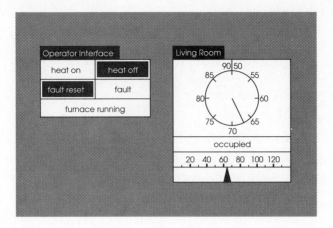

Figure 8-6
User Interface Prototype

Completing this prototype also leads us to another important conclusion: problems of mutual exclusion exist in the user interface. Specifically, we know from our requirements that an internal event may cause the fault reset switch/indicator to be set, and that an operator may reset its state. Without some sort of mutual exclusion, it is possible that these events might interact so as to corrupt the state of the fault reset switch/indicator. For example, the process handling the internal event might change the state of the switch, but then be interrupted by the operator process before its view was made consistent with this state. Indeed, whenever there are two or more active threads of control, as in this situation, we must be on guard to protect the state of any and all shared objects. Thus, our earlier suspicions are confirmed: during design, we must keep in mind the effects of concurrent events in the home heating system.

Let's return to our prototype and modify it so that it exhibits these concurrency semantics. The most common approach to dealing with this simple form of mutual exclusion is to use a *semaphore*. A semaphore surrounds a critical region of code and thus allows only one thread of control at a time to execute that code. Fortunately, Smalltalk-80's class library has the class `Semaphore`, which already offers this abstraction. Therefore, incrementally modifying our existing code is quite easy.

For example, in the class `ToggleSwitch`, we must add an instance variable, which we will call `theSemaphore`. In the initialize method for instances of `ToggleSwitch`, we must add the following statement:

```
theSemaphore ← Semaphore forMutualExclusion.
```

Evaluation of this statement creates and initializes a new semaphore object as part of the state of the toggle switch object. Because we now have a potentially active object as a subobject of a toggle switch, we must gracefully free the semaphore object whenever we free the state of the toggle switch. Thus, we must include the following method:

release

```
"Release the switch."

theSemaphore terminateProcess.
trueAction ← nil.
falseAction ← nil.
super release
```

The only other method we must modify is `state:`. All we must do to the existing code is to wrap it in a critical section. Thus, `state:` now appears as follows:

state: aBoolean

```
"Set the state of the toggle switch. aBoolean is expected to be of the
 class Boolean."

theSemaphore critical:
    [state = aBoolean
        ifFalse:
            [state ← aBoolean.
             self changed: #state.
             state
                 ifTrue:
                     [trueAction value]
                 ifFalse:
                     [falseAction value]]]
```

The addition of this code guarantees that only one process at a time can enter the critical region.

8.2 Design

Object Structure

The process of completing a domain analysis of the home heating system and then building a prototype of its user interface has given us a reasonably good understanding of the key abstractions in the problem domain. Thus, we have completed the first step of object-oriented design, which lies on the boundary of analysis and design – the identification of the topmost classes and objects. We next need to make design decisions regarding the semantics of each of these abstractions, as well as their relationships. We must also invent some mechanisms that exploit the commonality among these abstractions to simplify our overall design. These decisions form the logical model of the system, which we can capture in a set of class and object diagrams. Since we have chosen

Figure 8-7
Top Level Object Diagram

Smalltalk as our implementation language, we need not construct a module diagram. Recall that in Smalltalk, the class serves as the basic unit of modular decomposition, and that for other than categorizing classes (which are more a part of the Smalltalk environment than the language), there is no standard mechanism for packaging classes and objects in different ways.

Top-Level Object Structure. Figure 8-7 illustrates the top-level object structure of the home heating system. From this highest level of abstraction, we see that there is exactly one object, the home heating system itself. As this diagram indicates, we have made the design decision that this one object encompasses multiple threads of control and is statically allocated; its class template, although not shown, indicates that this object is of the class `HomeHeatingSystem`. If we think about the ways in which we can manipulate this object from the outside, we can reasonably assert that we can perform only two meaningful operations, namely:

- `powerDown`
- `powerUp`

These two operations thus form the essential protocol of the interface for the class `HomeHeatingSystem`.

Decomposing the Top Level. There is a structural hierarchy within this topmost object: an object of the class `HomeHeatingSystem` is really composed of a cooperating collection of other objects, including a furnace, a heat switch, water valves, and other objects. In this kind of structural hierarchy, lower-level objects are hidden in the implementation of the enclosing object. It would be a bad design decision to make directly visible instances of all the the key abstractions we listed earlier: to do so would increase complexity, since many of these objects are at quite different levels of abstractions. A far better approach is to review the list of key abstractions and select only those that represent the largest conceptual chunks, that is, the elements at the highest level of abstraction.

The furnace, the heat-flow regulator, the operator interface, and the home appear to be the largest independent conceptual chunks, and therefore we will include only these as direct components of the enclosing home heating system object. We still choose to make the operator interface and not the room-occupant interface visible at this level, since the latter interface is conceptually a part of each room. Notice also that this is a subtly different design than we indicated in our draft object diagram in Figure 8-2. In that figure, we made all rooms directly visible at the highest level of the system. Here, we have decided to use a more general abstraction, namely, that of the home, to represent a set of rooms. A major factor in making this decision was our realization that there is at least one operation that must be performed across all the rooms in a home: under certain failure conditions, the water valves in all rooms must be closed.

Defining the Semantics and Relationships of the Top-Level Objects. Next we must define the semantics of these objects and their relationships. As discussed in Chapter 6, the common approach to drawing an object diagram is first to write down all the objects at the same level of abstraction, then decide upon the relationships within each pair of objects, and then establish the message protocol among objects along the lines of these relationships.

Assume that the furnace and the operator interface are visible to one another. When the furnace becomes activated, it could pass a message to the operator interface, telling it to highlight the furnace-status indicator. As it turns out, this is not a good decision, because the requirements state that after furnace activation and before the indicator is highlighted, the appropriate room water valves are opened. This would require the furnace either to keep track of the rooms needing heat, or to ask for that information from the heat-flow regulator. In either case, this leaves us with a very bad separation of concerns: the furnace and the heat-flow regulator encapsulate very different collections of state; thus, making the furnace and operator interfaces visible to one another blurs this state space and leaves us with more tightly coupled object interfaces. Assume instead that we make the furnace and the home visible to one another. This too turns out to be a very bad decision: if a particular room needs heat, the requirements cause us to keep track of that information regardless of whether or not the furnace is activated. Again, this leaves us with a very poor separation of concerns: the basic functionality of a furnace is to produce heat, not to decide how and when that heat is to be provided to particular rooms. Finally, assume direct visibility between the home and the operator interface. This too is a bad design decision, for there is absolutely no meaningful information that they have to share with one another. For these reasons, we are led to decide that the furnace, operator interface, and home should not be directly visible to one another.

Instead, we decide that these objects should only be visible to the heat-flow regulator, and vice versa. Indeed, this approach matches the physical architecture of the home heating system as illustrated in Figure 8-1. In retrospect, this does not come as much of a surprise, because we intend our design to map closely to our understanding of the real world.

Now, let's consider the operations that the heat-flow regulator can meaningfully perform upon each of the objects to which it has visibility. Thinking about this problem from the perspective of the interface of each object, we derive the following operations:

- On the furnace   `activate`
                          `deactivate`
- On the operator interface `reportFault`
                          `reportFurnaceStatus`
- On the home   `closeAllWaterValves`
                          `closeWaterValve`
                          `openWaterValve`

These operations thus form the basic interface of the furnace, operator interface, and home classes.

Looking at this same problem from the opposite direction, we consider what operations the furnace, home, and operator interface can perform upon the heat-flow regulator:

- By the furnace   `respondToFurnaceFault`
                          `respondToFurnaceNotRunning`
                          `respondToFurnaceRunning`
- By the operator interface `respondToFaultResetSwitch`
                          `respondToHeatSwitchOff`
                          `respondToHeatSwitchOn`
- By the home   `needsHeat`
                          `noLongerNeedsHeat`

Notice how this protocol leaves us with a clear separation of concerns. The knowledge that the furnace encapsulates is simply how to activate, deactivate, and report faults. The operator interface is spatially cohesive: it encapsulates the entire functionality of the operator interface. Similarly, the home is at the same high level of abstraction. The heat-flow regulator does not need to be concerned with details such as the actual temperature in each room, or its current occupancy. The rooms of a home are in the best position to decide if they need heat or not, because all of the relevant state needed to make such a decision is encapsulated in each room. Similarly, the heat-flow regulator is in the best position to decide whether or not a water valve should be opened in a particular room, because it encapsulates all the relevant state needed to make this decision intelligently.

Why did we make the home visible at this level of abstraction, and not the rooms directly? The answer is that the abstraction of the home adds two important elements. First, the use of the home object gives us a means of logically and physically grouping all the rooms of a home. Second, there is the requirement to close the water valves in all rooms in reaction to a furnace fault. By including a home object, we have a meaningful place to put this operation, which appears as an iterator on the home that can visit every room of the home

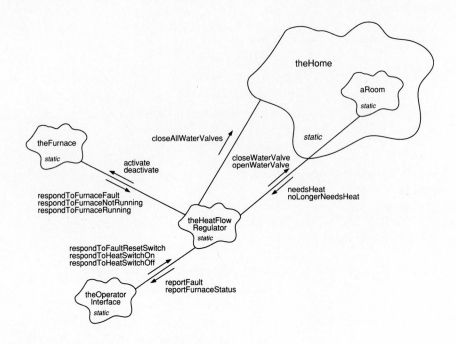

Figure 8-8
Home Heating System Object Diagram

in some undefined order. Thus, the home is at the highest level of abstraction in our design, yet through the home, we can access individual rooms.

We have captured these design decisions in the object diagram in Figure 8-8. Notice here that we have marked each object as statically allocated: we know enough about the problem by now to realize that indeed there is no dynamic creation and destruction of any fundamental object. This is fairly typical of process-control problems. Basic elements such as furnaces and homes don't come and go during the execution of the home heating system; rather, they logically come into existence when the system is powered on and logically disappear when the system is powered off.

At this point, we do not have a complete enough logical design to make any decisions about how these objects can see one another (that is, their relationship kind) nor the nature of their concurrency semantics (specifically, the parallelism that might naturally occur within this system and how messages are synchronized). Therefore, we choose to defer these decisions.

Class Structure

Thus far, we have created abstractions that are reasonably cohesive as well as loosely coupled with one another. We have defined the boundary of each

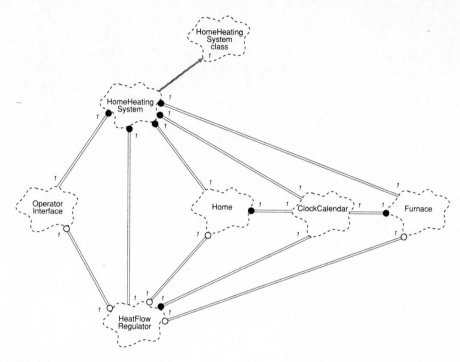

Figure 8-9
Top-Level Class Diagram

object so as to maximize the separation of state spaces and therefore achieve a clear separation of concerns. Certainly, we are not done with our design: we have only invented the interfaces of the most important objects. What remains is the detailed design of each of these objects and a discovery of the commonality among them, followed by a choice of representation. However, it is useful to note that our design process has already established some important boundaries for the class of each of the fundamental objects. Thus, we are now in a position to design the home heating system's class structure, which, as we explained in Chapter 1, defines the soul of the system. Our intent here is not to specify completely the interface of each class in the class structure, because this is something that best evolves incrementally. Naturally we do not want to produce a sloppy design that requires massive reorganization of the class hierarchy as we add more functionality to the system, so we do our best to capture only the most important design decisions first, deferring the smaller decisions that have less impact on the overall system design.

Top-Level Class Structure. Figure 8-9 captures our view of the highest-level class structure. Here we find using relationships rather than inheritance relationships. A home heating system is composed of elements such as a furnace and heat-flow regulator, but it is not a kind of a furnace nor a heat-flow regulator, nor is it equal to the sum of the functionality of its component parts. Thus, we show that the class `HomeHeatingSystem` uses as part of its implementation the classes `OperatorInterface`, `HeatFlowRegulator`, `Home`, and `Furnace`. It also uses the class `ClockCalendar`, which we will describe in more detail shortly. Notice that none of these classes have visibility to the `HomeHeatingSystem`; this is as we would expect, because the class `HomeHeatingSystem` is at a higher level of abstraction than all the others. Figure 8-9 also shows the cardinality of these using relationships: there is exactly one operator interface, heat-flow regulator, home, clock calendar, and furnace. Similarly, each operator interface, heat-flow regulator, home, clock calendar, and furnace belongs to the same home heating system.

As Figure 8-8 indicated, objects of the class `HeatFlowRegulator` must pass messages to objects of the classes `OperatorInterface`, `Home`, and `Furnace`, and objects of the classes `OperatorInterface`, `Home`, and `Furnace` must pass messages to the `HeatFlowRegulator` instance. Therefore, the class `HeatFlowRegulator` must be mutually visible to the classes `OperatorInterface`, `Home`, and `Furnace`. Figure 8-9 captures this design decision clearly; it shows that in each pair of these classes, one uses the other and vice versa.

For example, the implementation of the class `Furnace` must see the interface of the `HeatFlowRegulator` in order to pass messages such as `respondTo-FurnaceFault`, which is defined in the class `HeatFlowRegulator`. This is an example of a using relationship for implementation. Why then does Figure 8-9 show that there is a using relationship for the interface? The reason is that objects of these classes must be initialized with specific instances of their mutually visible classes. For example, in the implementation of the class `Furnace`, we will find statements such as:

> theHeatFlowRegulator respondToFurnaceNotRunning.

With this statement, the furnace sends `respondToFurnaceNotRunning` to the object denoted by the variable `theHeatFlowRegulator`. Thus, it is necessary that the implementation of the class `Furnace` use the interface of the class `HeatFlowRegulator`: this is logically how this message is visible. However, we must ask the question, what is the value of the variable `theHeatFlowRegulator`? The answer is that this variable is an instance variable declared in the class `Furnace`, and therefore must at some point be properly initialized to a specific object of the class `HeatFlowRegulator`. Thus, we might find the following `initialize` method for the class `Furnace`:

initialize: aHeatFlowRegulator
   "Initialize the furnace. aHeatFlowRegulator is expected to be of the class HeatFlowRegulator."

Here we see that the class `HeatFlowRegulator` must logically be visible to the interface as well as the implementation of the class `Furnace`.

Because the interface of the class `Furnace` directly depends upon the interface of the class `HeatFlowRegulator` and vice versa, it would seem that we have a cyclic compilation dependency. As it turns out, this is not a problem in Smalltalk, for two reasons. First, there is no concept of traditional compilation order in Smalltalk; new code is incorporated incrementally rather than compiled in a batch form. Second, and most important, Smalltalk applies dynamic binding of objects to names. Thus, the fact that the interface of the class `Furnace` logically depends upon the class `HeatFlowRegulator` does not mean much in Smalltalk, since the class of a particular parameter need not be known until execution time. Therefore, this apparent cycle is not a concern here, although we could not get away with it in a more strongly typed language. Why then do we bother showing this detail of interface versus implementation visibility? The reason is that this is indeed a relevant design decision, albeit one that cannot be enforced by Smalltalk.

Defining the Semantics and Relationships of the Top-Level Classes. Given the design decisions expressed in the class structure of Figure 8-9, we can now reasonably establish the interfaces of some of these higher level classes. For example, we may write the class template for the class `HomeHeatingSystem` as follows:

Name:	HomeHeatingSystem
Cardinality:	1
Hierarchy:	
Superclasses:	Object
Metaclass:	HomeHeatingSystem class
Public Interface:	
Operations:	powerDown
	powerUp
Implementation:	
Uses:	ClockCalendar
	Furnace
	HeatFlowRegulator
	Home
	OperatorInterface
Fields:	theFurnace
	theHeatFlowRegulator
	theHome
	theOperatorInterface
Concurrency:	active

In Smalltalk, every class has an implicit metaclass. However, when designing, it is only necessary for us to document our decisions surrounding the interesting metaclasses, namely, those that have some problem-specific methods. For example, we may define a method in the metaclass `HomeHeatingSystem class` to create and initialize objects of the class `HomeHeatingSystem`. Thus, we might write the class template of this metaclass as follows:

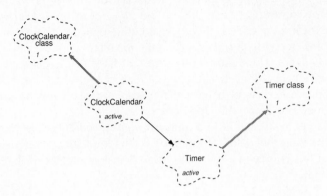

Figure 8-10
Timer Class Diagram

Name: HomeHeatingSystem class
Cardinality: 1
Public Interface:
       Operations: create

In Figure 8-9, we introduced the class ClockCalendar, although this class did not appear in our earlier list of key abstractions. The requirements include a timer that can detect clock ticks occurring at the rate of one per second. However, our requirements also speak of events on the order of minutes (for example, the waiting time to restart the furnace) and even days (the period of time relevant to each living pattern). Thus, we can say that the vocabulary of the problem domain does not involve time in seconds only, but in seconds, minutes, hours, and days. It is necessary to include the class Timer in our design, but it is also reasonable to include a more abstract class, one that deals with this higher abstraction of time. We have therefore invented the class ClockCalendar, which is just like a timer but deals with events in terms of time on the order that is meaningful to our specific problem.

Figure 8-10 documents our design decisions regarding the class structure of the classes ClockCalendar and Timer. Note that the class ClockCalendar inherits from the class Timer, and that both have relevant metaclasses. The metaclasses exist to provide initialization methods; for example, creation of a clock/calendar object initializes the week, hour, minute, and second to their current values, so that the living pattern of each room can be synchronized with the local real time. We want time to be consistent across the system, and therefore we choose to record elapsed seconds in a class variable, so that any instances of Timer and its subclasses share the same value of time. For this reason, we must have metaclass methods in place to initialize this class variable properly.

The suspicious reader may wonder why we choose to separate the classes ClockCalendar and Timer rather than unify them in one class. By separating these two classes, we divide their behavior in a way that makes it more likely

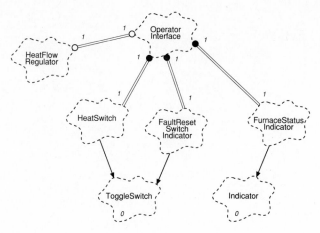

Figure 8-11
Operator Interface Class Diagram

that we could reuse one of them. The class Timer is relatively simple; it knows only how to detect one-second events. The class ClockCalendar, on the other hand, has domain-specific knowledge of how to respond to higher level time events.

The class diagram in Figure 8-10 indicates that instances of the class Timer (and therefore instances of the class ClockCalendar) embody an active thread of control. This is to be expected in a time-critical application such as the home heating system, since the internal state of the system changes with the passage of time. Thus, we must invent some process that tracks these time events, and it is most suitable to do this in the primitive class Timer. For the moment, we will defer deciding how this process works until we focus on the problem of selecting a suitable process architecture for the entire system.

Figure 8-11 captures our design decisions regarding the class structure of the class OperatorInterface. Referring to our earlier prototype, we recall that the operator interface includes a single heat switch, one fault reset switch/indicator, and one furnace-status indicator. Thus, the class OperatorInterface must use these classes for the purposes of its implementation. As with the class HomeHeatingSystem, a using rather than an inheriting relationship is best, because the operator interface is more than the sum of its parts. Here we can apply a using relationship for purposes of implementation, not interface, because HeatSwitch, FaultResetSwitchIndicator, and FurnaceStatusIndicator objects are entirely encapsulated in the implementation of an OperatorInterface object, and need not be seen as part of its interface.

The class HeatSwitch inherits its behavior from the class ToggleSwitch. Figure 8-11 illustrates our decision to have the class FaultResetSwitchIndicator inherit from this same abstract class. Here we assert that a

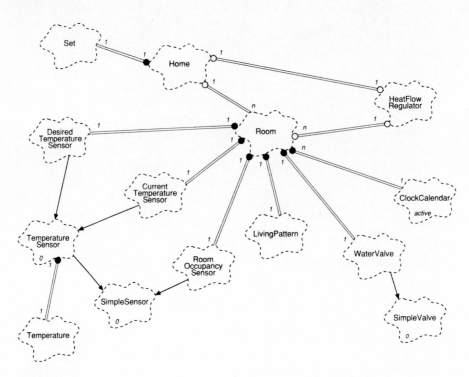

Figure 8-12
Home Class Diagram

`FaultResetSwitchIndicator` object is more like a toggle switch than an indicator. Would the use of multiple inheritance have been appropriate here? Specifically, should the class `FaultResetSwitchIndicator` inherit from both the classes `ToggleSwitch` and `Indicator`? The answer is no, because the switch/indicator object is not really the composite of the behavior of a toggle switch and an indicator; it is just like a toggle switch, except that the user can toggle the switch to only one state, and a programmatic process can toggle it only to the other. This kind of behavior is a specialization of the class `ToggleSwitch`.

Figure 8-12 expresses the class structure of the class `Home`. Logically, a home is a set of rooms. Should we therefore design the class `Home` as a subclass of the predefined class `Set`? The answer is a resounding no. A home indeed has the structure of a set, but it does not have the behavior of a set (such as adding and removing elements, taking the union and intersection of elements, etc). As we decided earlier, there is only one essential operation upon the home, namely the method `closeAllWaterValves`, and two meaningful operations upon a room, specifically, `openWaterValve` and `closeWaterValve`. These are distinctly not set operations.

The purist may object to this approach: a home is like a set, and therefore should be treated as a subclass of a set. Designers are always faced with such issues. Certainly, making the home a subclass of the predefined class `Set` leads to a more rapidly built implementation. Indeed, we often use inheritance in this vigorous manner if we need to build a prototype in a hurry. However, if we are writing production code that others must maintain and evolve, then we lean toward constructing safe abstractions. It does require more effort on the part of the designer, but the payoff is distributed across the useful life of the software.

In choosing a representation for the class `Home`, we therefore conclude that the class `Home` uses the predefined class `Set` in its implementation (to represent a collection of rooms) and the domain-specific class `Room` in its interface. The reason we use the class `Room` in the interface of the class `Home` is that the heat-flow regulator must have visibility to the home as well as to individual rooms in that home. The cardinality of this using relationship shows that a home may contain *n* rooms but that each room belongs to exactly one home.

The rest of this class diagram is relatively straightforward. This class structure reflects the structural hierarchy of a room as we described it in Figure 8-3. Thus, the class `Room` uses the classes `DesiredTemperatureSensor`, `CurrentTemperatureSensor`, `LivingPattern`, `WaterValve`, and `Room-OccupancySensor`. The cardinality of these using relationships indicates our earlier design decision that each room consists of exactly one instance of each of these classes; similarly, each of these instances belongs to exactly one room. We also see that every room object shares the same heat-flow regulator object and that each heat-flow regulator may send messages to different rooms.

Notice in Figure 8-12 that we have invented several new classes. In studying the classes involved in the structural hierarchy of a room, we realize that we can generalize our design by factoring out common class behavior. This recategorization of class functionality led us to invent the abstract class `Temperature-Sensor`, which captures the state common to both desired- and current-temperature sensors, namely some value in degrees Fahrenheit. The class `SimpleSensor` is also an abstract class, but it is even more generalized: it represents a single value that is set by some external device, but the details of how that value is set and what its domain is, are left up to its subclasses. Similarly, the class `Temperature` exists to capture our understanding of the domain of degrees Fahrenheit: its range of values, and its precision. Thus, the abstract class `TemperatureSensor` inherits from the class `SimpleSensor`, but it adds domain-specific knowledge by asserting that the sensor value is of the class `Temperature`.

It is important to realize that this design decision is not enforceable by Smalltalk. In fact, many relevant design decisions expressed in this figure cannot be captured and enforced by Smalltalk. Specifically, the assertion that a temperature sensor is in fact a simple sensor, except that its value is constrained to a certain range of numbers representing Fahrenheit degrees, is an example of a domain constraint upon a class. Therefore, we might reasonably say that the range of degrees that our system should handle is from 0 to 300 degrees Fahrenheit, measured in tenths of a degree. Because Smalltalk uses only late binding of objects to names, it has no convenient static mechanism that lets us directly reflect this design decision. In strongly typed languages, such as Object Pascal and even Ada, we can both express and enforce this design decision at the time of compilation.

The cardinality of each class is a second example of a design decision that cannot easily be enforced by Smalltalk. Figure 8-12 documents our decision that `TemperatureSensor`, `SimpleSensor`, and `SimpleValve` are all abstract classes. However, there is no direct mechanism in Smalltalk that lets us limit the number of instances of a particular class. We could override the `new` method in each class's metaclass to keep count of the number of instances, but this approach is of questionable taste, because it adds complexity to the application without adding a tremendous amount of real value. If we are using Smalltalk, a code review or perhaps even the application of an analysis tool would be sufficient to enforce this design decision. Our current problem is small enough that we can resort to these more manual processes, but for really large problems, having the language itself enforce such design decisions is highly desirable.

A third and final example of the unenforceability of certain design decisions in Smalltalk involves the using visibility among classes. In a Smalltalk environment all classes are globally visible. In Figure 8-12, we show that only the class `Room` uses the class `LivingPattern` as part of its implementation. This is an important design decision, because it documents how we expect to limit visibility among the myriad of classes that are potentially visible and thus allows us to focus on just a few things when we are trying to reason about the behavior of a large system. Unfortunately, there is nothing we can write in Smalltalk to express this restriction of visibility.

If our implementation language cannot enforce certain elements of our design, then why should we even document these design decisions? The reason is that doing so helps us to reason about the semantics of the design and, what is even more important, to leave a legacy of our rationale for those who must maintain and evolve this code after us. Looking at an assembly language program, we cannot easily reconstruct the requirement documents that led to this code. Does this mean that we should only write requirements that can be directly observed in the code? Certainly not, and for the same reason, we should not avoid capturing certain design decisions just because our particular programming language cannot enforce them directly.

Figure 8-13 shows the class structure of the furnace. This structure is quite similar to that shown in Figure 8-12. Here we see that a furnace is composed of a single boiler-temperature sensor, oil-fault sensor, combustion-fault sensor, blower, oil valve, and ignitor. The class `Furnace` must use the corresponding classes of its components.

The class `OilValve` generalizes to the class `SimpleValve`, which as you may recall from Figure 8-12, is also the superclass of the class `WaterValve`. Water valves and oil valves control the flow of two very different substances, but from the software perspective of this problem, both are simply valves that can be opened and closed.

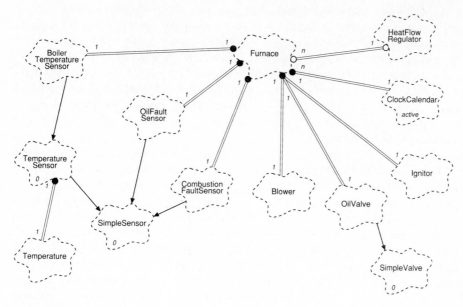

Figure 8-13
Furnace Class Diagram

At this point, we have completed our design of the soul of the system: we know what the key abstractions are and how they relate to one another, and we understand their boundaries. Next, we must choose each major functional piece of the system, complete the design of its interface, and then choose a suitable representation. However, in order to do this detailed design properly, we must establish a process architecture for the system, in light of the lessons we learned from the earlier prototype.

Process Architecture

As we saw in Chapter 2, problems such as the home heating system naturally decompose into relatively independent subproblems. The activity we have focused on thus far is that of designing a reasonable class structure that captures our understanding of the key abstractions in the system. Now that we have this static framework, we can begin to consider the flow of control within the home heating system.

Identifying the Threads of Control. Where are the threads of control within this system? We have already identified one active process, namely, that of the timer (and transitively so, the clock/calendar). If we look at the boundaries of the entire system, we see that a number of asynchronous events motivate the system's behavior, and they appear to be potentially concurrent. For example, occupants of two different rooms might change their desired room temperature simultaneously, while at the same time a room occupant leaves another room, and the temperature in a fourth room drops suddenly because someone opened a window. This observation suggests that the sensors at the fringe of the system should also represent active threads of control. Most of the time, these processes are inactive, waiting for some external stimulus. However, as we have seen, each and all of them can potentially become active at the same time. Let's trace the flow of control of two of these events, and in so doing design a process architecture that both protects the state of shared objects and maximizes the potential for real parallelism.

Instances of the class `ClockCalendar` detect the passage of time, and several other objects in the system must react to these events. Our review of the requirements, mapped back to our static class structure, leads us to suggest that there are only two classes of objects that must respond to time events, namely furnaces and living patterns. The furnace needs to know about time because of two requirements: during deactivation, the blower must be stopped five seconds after the oil valve is closed, and during activation, the furnace cannot be restarted within five minutes after being deactivated. This behavior is best encapsulated by the furnace, and therefore the furnace must keep track of time events. Similarly, the living pattern of each room must respond to the passage of time. The living pattern must maintain information regarding the expected occupancy of a room, measured at thirty-minute intervals. At each half hour, the living pattern might report a change in anticipated occupancy.

The immediate problem is this: how do we notify the furnace and the living pattern of each room that time has passed? The obvious answer is that we could have the clock/calendar object pass a message to each of these objects. But how does the clock/calendar know what objects to send these messages to? Our solution is to use the existing Smalltalk dependency mechanism again. The advantage of using this mechanism is that the class `ClockCalendar` becomes decoupled from the classes `Furnace` and `LivingPattern`. Specifically, the class `ClockCalendar` need not be directly visible to either of these classes. This structure greatly improves the chances of reusing all of these classes, and simplifies our understanding of the class `ClockCalendar` by reducing the number of abstractions we must understand.

Figure 8-14 provides an object diagram that captures this design decision. The furnace and living patterns first register themselves as dependents with an instance of the class `ClockCalendar` (which is globally visible to the furnace and living patterns). As time passes, the clock/calendar sends itself the `changed:` message, and then passes the `update:` message to each of its dependents; notice that the clock/calendar is largely indifferent to the number of dependents it has. An arbitrary number of living patterns can register themselves with the clock/calendar; thus, we need never alter the class `ClockCalendar` to accommodate a change in the number of rooms supported by a particular home heating system.

Notice in this figure that the clock/calendar has visibility to its dependents as parameters (via an iterator defined across the collection of dependents), but

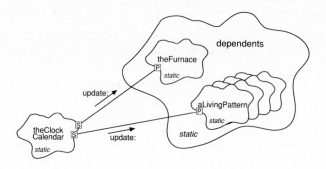

Figure 8-14
Clock/Calendar Object Diagram

that the dependents have global visibility to the clock/calendar. The clock/calendar object must be visible to objects such as the furnace, because the furnace has to register itself with the clock/calendar. The furnace can see the clock/calendar because, as we expressed in Figure 8-13, it uses the class `ClockCalendar`; the corresponding objects are therefore in the same lexical scope.

Because we want all dependents to share the same perception of time, we must design the class `Timer` and its metaclass so that all essential state is kept in class variables, not instance variables. We decide to model the timer as an active process that updates a single value representing a monotonically increasing number of elapsed seconds. Thus, we might write the following class template for the metaclass `Timer class` as follows:

Name:	Timer class
Cardinality:	1
Public Interface:	
Operations:	elapsedSeconds
	elapsedSeconds:
	initialize
	release
Implementation:	
Uses:	Semaphore
Fields:	ElapsedSeconds
	TheSemaphore
	TimerProcess
Concurrency:	active

We may now implement the `initialize` and `release` methods for the metaclass as follows:

initialize

"Reset elapsedSeconds, then start the process to update elapsedSeconds every second."

```
TheSemaphore ← Semaphore forMutualExclusion.
ElapsedSeconds ← 0.
TimerProcess ← [[(Delay forSeconds: 1) wait.
                      self elapsedSeconds: self elapsedSeconds + 1.
                      true] whileTrue] newProcess.
TimerProcess resume
```

release

"Stop the process to update elapsedSeconds every second."

```
TheSemaphore terminateProcess.
TimerProcess terminate
```

In the `initialize` method, we create a new semaphore and timer process. This process, once resumed, wakes up every second and increments the class variable `ElapsedSeconds`.

The method `elapsedSeconds:` is invoked by the timer process, and its action is to notify all dependents of the passage of time. Thus, we may write:

elapsedSeconds: anInteger

"Set the number of seconds that have elapsed since the object was initialized. anInteger is expected to be of the class Integer."

```
TheSemaphore critical:
    [ElapsedSeconds ← anInteger.
     self changed: #elapsedSeconds]
```

Earlier, we invented the class `ClockCalendar` as a domain-specific subclass of the class `Timer`. The class `ClockCalendar` adds behavior to the class `Timer`; specifically the clock/calendar abstraction knows about the passage of time in terms of the day of the week, minutes, and seconds. To implement the class `ClockCalendar` as inheriting from the class `Timer`, we must add the class variables `DayOfWeek`, `Hour`, `Minute`, and `Second`. We can then initialize these class variables with an appropriate `initialize` method for the metaclass `ClockCalendar class`:

initializeDayOfWeek: aDay hour: anHour minute: aMinute

"Initialize the clock/calendar. aDay is expected to be of the class Integer (range 1 to 7), anHour is expected to be of the class Integer (range 0 to 23), and aMinute is expected to be of the class Integer (range 0 to 59)."

```
DayOfWeek ← aDay.
Hour ← anHour.
Minute ← aMinute.
Seconds ← 0.
super initialize
```

Referring back to our requirements, we may conclude that there are two domain-specific time events, namely a five-second event (for turning off the blower) and a thirty-minute event (for the activity of each living pattern). As explained in a later section, we choose to handle the delay of five minutes for furnace restart in a slightly different fashion, since the restart time is dependent upon when the furnace was last deactivated. Given these observations, we may properly decide to override the elapsedSeconds: method so that it notifies its dependents of these two events. Thus, we might write the elaspsedSeconds: method for the metaclass ClockCalendar class as follows:

elapsedSeconds: anInteger

```
"Set the number of seconds that have elapsed since the object was
 initialized, and update the day of the week, hour, and minute.
 anInteger is expected to be of the class Integer."

TheSemaphore critical:
    [ElapsedSeconds ← anInteger.
     self changed: #elapsedSeconds.
     (Seconds rem: 5) = 0
         ifTrue:
             [self changed: #fiveSecondEvent].
     Seconds ← Seconds + 1.
     Seconds = 60
         ifTrue:
             [Seconds ← 0.
              (Minute rem: 30) = 0
                  ifTrue:
                      [self changed: #thirtyMinuteEvent].
              Minute ← Minute + 1.
              Minute = 60
                  ifTrue:
                      [Minute ← 0.
                       Hour ← Hour + 1.
                       Hour = 24
                           ifTrue:
                               [Hour ← 0.
                                DayOfWeek ← DayOfWeek + 1.
                                DayOfWeek = 8
                                    ifTrue:
                                        [DayOfWeek ← 1]]]]]]
```

Our decision to make the timer an active process leads us to make the class LivingPattern a blocking class, because it is possible that objects of the class LivingPattern can be sent messages simultaneously by separate processes, such as the timer process and the room process. Since objects of this class can be manipulated by more than one thread of control, we must somehow guarantee their semantics in the presence of multiple threads of control. By giving it blocking semantics (through the use of an internal semaphore, as we did in the class ToggleSwitch), we achieve this effect. The furnace must likewise offer similar concurrency semantics.

The manner in which we made these concurrency decisions for the classes Furnace and LivingPattern is a good example of how process architecture decisions often proceed. We can usually identify the natural parallelism in the problem by tracing events from outside the system. Identifying the objects that can detect these events leads us to design decisions regarding the concurrency semantics of objects that react to these events.

Dealing with Asynchronous Events. As we have pointed out, asynchronous events may be detected simultaneously by the desired-temperature sensors, current-temperature sensors, and room-occupancy sensors; thus, we consider each of their corresponding classes to be active. Earlier, we showed how the class DesiredTemperatureSensor used the Smalltalk dependency mechanism to notify its dependents that a room occupant changed the desired temperature of a room. Actually, we can use this technique for all of the sensors. For example, a room might register itself with each of its sensors, so that each sensor can send an appropriate update: message back to the room. Just as with the class ClockCalendar, this leaves us with more loosely coupled classes than if we were to choose a different mechanism.

By implication, we realize that the state machine embodied by the class Room must have blocking semantics. The class Room itself is active, because it is composed of subobjects that are themselves active. A similar rationale applies to the class OperatorInterface and the class Furnace. We may treat the classes ToggleSwitch, BoilerTemperatureSensor, OilFaultSensor, and Combustion-FaultSensor as active because they react to asynchronous and potentially simultaneous events. Therefore, the OperatorInterface and Furnace classes must themselves be active.

We may now update our class and object diagrams to incorporate these decisions regarding the process architecture of the home heating system. For example, Figure 8-15 shows the home heating system object diagram marked with the concurrency semantics of each fundamental object. Here we see that there are potentially three threads of control: in the furnace, the operator interface, and the individual rooms. The heat-flow regulator does not encapsulate any active processes but only requires blocking semantics. Furthermore, the home can be sequential, because our design tells us that only one process at a time will ever alter its immediate state (although the state of its individual rooms may be affected by multiple processes). Notice also how the figure indicates that each of the messages passed among these objects may potentially block.

The reader with a sequential mindset may question at this point the relevance of producing any process architecture. As explained in Chapter 2, problems such as the home heating system naturally embody multiple threads of control. In such systems, the order of events is nondeterministic: we cannot tell what will happen first, what will happen second, and so on. In other words, we lose our ability to predict the flow of control, which we have in purely sequential problems. It is therefore essential to design a sound process architecture that avoids all potential of corrupting the state of objects shared by multiple concurrent processes. Fortunately, as we saw in Chapters 3 and 4, there is a very natural mapping of object-oriented constructs to a process architecture; namely, we can treat individual objects as a focus of control. Also, because objects encapsu-

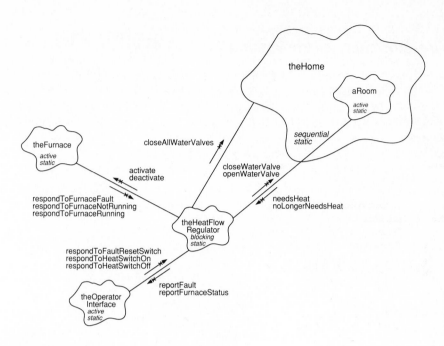

Figure 8-15
Revised Home Heating System Object Diagram

late their state, we can easily preserve the semantics of their state in the presence of multiple threads of control.

One important thing we must do with all the models we build for a given design is to question their behavior under different conditions. We have partially done this by tracing the flow of external events through the home heating system. Another interesting question to ask of our process architecture is simply, What is the program doing when there are no external events? In this situation, as is typical of reactive systems, all the interesting processes are either suspended or blocked. In fact, in our design, when there are no external events, the timer process is suspended, waiting at a delay statement. It wakes up every second, but otherwise, spends most of its time just passively waiting for time to pass.

At this point, we have a stable and predictable design representing the system's class structure and process architecture. We have also modeled, through the use of several object diagrams, the interesting dynamic behavior of the system. We are now ready to evolve the parts of this design into a complete implementation. Along the way, we will construct executable systems, each with an increasing degree of functionality, so that we can progressively evaluate our design and implementation decisions and provide immediate feedback to the users of the system.

8.3 Evolution

Operator Interface Implementation

Based upon the design decisions expressed in the class diagram in Figure 8-11 and the object diagram in Figure 8-15, we can next complete the interface of the class `OperatorInterface` and then choose a suitable representation. We may summarize what we already know about this class in the following class template:

Name:	OperatorInterface
Cardinality:	1
Hierarchy:	
Superclasses:	Object
Public Interface:	
Uses:	HeatFlowRegulator
Operations:	heatStatus
	initialize:
	release
	reportFault
	reportFurnaceStatus:
Implementation:	
Uses:	FaultResetSwitchIndicator
	FurnaceStatusIndicator
	HeatSwitch
Fields:	theFaultResetSwitchIndicator
	theFurnaceStatusIndicator
	theHeatFlowRegulator
	theHeatSwitch
	theView
Concurrency:	active

Figure 8-16 shows the structural hierarchy of the operator interface. Here we see that an operator interface object contains two switches and one indicator. These switches and indicator are all visible as fields of the operator interface. Furthermore, the heat-flow regulator is visible to both the heat switch and the fault reset switch/indicator as well as the operator interface itself.

Let's consider the possible flow of control among these objects. For example, the heat-flow regulator can pass the message `reportFault` to the operator interface. In response to this message, the operator interface object must pass the message `state:` to its fault reset switch/indicator. Because of the concurrency semantics we described earlier, these operations may block temporarily.

The heat switch may also send the message `respondToHeatSwitchOn` to the heat-flow regulator. Recall that we designed our implementation of the class `ToggleSwitch` to be initialized with two blocks: one to be performed when its state toggled from on to off, and another to be performed when its state toggled from off to on. Thus, the initialization of the operator interface should include constructing suitable blocks, which would then be given to the heat switch. A similar block is need for the fault reset switch/indicator. For simplicity in the

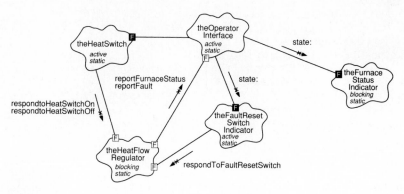

Figure 8-16
Operator Interface Object Diagram

figure, we have not shown the messages that the operator interface passes to its fields upon initialization, but for completeness, we may show its `initialize` method as:

`initialize: aHeatFlowRegulator`

```
"Create the operator interface for the given heat flow regulator.
 aHeatFlowRegulator is expected to be of the class HeatFlowRegulator."

theHeatFlowRegulator ← aHeatFlowRegulator.
theHeatSwitch ← HeatSwitch new.
theHeatSwitch
    initializeOnAction:
        [theHeatFlowRegulator respondToHeatSwitchOn]
    offAction:
        [theHeatFlowRegulator respondToHeatSwitchOff].
theFaultResetSwitchIndicator ← FaultResetSwitchIndicator new.
theFaultResetSwitchIndicator
    initializeOnAction:
        [theHeatFlowRegulator respondToFaultResetSwitchIndicatorOn].
theFurnaceStatusIndicator ← FurnaceStatusIndicator new.
theFurnaceStatusIndicator initialize.
theView ← RestrictedSystemView
            model: nil
            label: 'Operator Interface'
            minimumSize: 150 @ 75.
theView borderWidth: 1.
theView
    addSubView: theHeatSwitch trueView
    in: (0 @ 0 extent: 1 / 2 @ (1 / 3))
    borderWidth: 1.
theView
    addSubView: theHeatSwitch falseView
    in: (1 / 2 @ 0 extent: 1 / 2 @ (1 / 3))
    borderWidth: 1.
```

```
theView
    addSubView: theFaultResetSwitchIndicator trueView
    in: (0 @ (1 / 3) extent: 1 / 2 @ (1 / 3))
    borderWidth: 1.
theView
    addSubView: theFaultResetSwitchIndicator falseView
    in: (1 / 2 @ (1 / 3) extent: 1 / 2 @ (1 / 3))
    borderWidth: 1.
theView
    addSubView: theFurnaceStatusIndicator indicatorView
    in: (0 @ (2 / 3) extent: 1 @ (1 / 3))
    borderWidth: 1.
theView controller openDisplayCentered: 100 @ 125
```

Notice that the argument to the method must be an instance of the class `HeatFlowRegulator`. This value is saved as part of the state of the operator interface object and is also used to construct the blocks passed to the heat switch and the fault reset switch/indicator as part of their initialization. Specifically, whenever the heat switch is toggled from off to on, the heat switch object performs the following block:

```
[theHeatFlowRegulator respondToHeatSwitchOn]
```

The bulk of the remaining code exists to create the window that surrounds the visible simulation of the operator interface. `theView`, a field of the operator interface, is initialized with an instance of the class `RestrictedSystemView`. For simplicity, we did not mention this class in the class template for the class `OperatorInterface`, nor the class diagram in Figure 8-11, although this view class is used in the implementation of the class `OperatorInterface`. `RestrictedSystemView` is a subclass of the predefined `StandardSystemView`, except that it does not allow a user to rename the window.

Subviews are then added to the object denoted by `theView`. This is why we needed the selectors `trueView` and `falseView` defined in the class `ToggleSwitch`, so that we could directly access the switch's two views. The final action of this method is to start up the view's controller, which causes the window to be scheduled for display on the screen.

Room Implementation

Turning to the class `Room`, we may express its design in the following class template:

```
Name:                    Room
Cardinality:             n
Hierarchy:
      Superclasses:      Object
Public Interface:
      Uses:              HeatFlowRegulator
```

Operations:	closeWaterValve
	initialize: location: heatFlowRegulator:
	name
	openWaterValve
	release
Implementation:	
Uses:	ClockCalendar
	CurrentTemperatureSensor
	DesiredTemperatureSensor
	LivingPattern
	WaterValve
Fields:	currentState
	name
	theCurrentTemperatureSensor
	theDesiredTemperatureSensor
	theHeatFlowRegulator
	theLivingPattern
	theRoomOccupancySensor
	theSemaphore
	theView
	theWaterValve
Operations:	expectAndHeating: current: desired: occupied: expected:
	expectAndNoHeating: current: desired: occupied: expected:
	occupiedAndHeating: current: desired: occupied: expected:
	occupiedAndNoHeating: current: desired: occupied: expected:
	setInitialState
	startHeating
	stopHeating
	unoccupiedAndHeating: current: desired: occupied: expected:
	unoccupiedAndNoHeating: current: desired: occupied: expected:
	update:
Concurrency:	active

The interface includes the operations described in the object diagram in Figure 8-15, plus a handful of other operations needed for initialization, release, and display. The implementation of the class Room includes the using relationships and the fields that we discussed previously, but notice that it also includes a number of private operations. These operations are the key to the behavior of all room objects.

The object diagram in Figure 8-17 indicates the important objects that interact with a room. Here we see that the room has direct visibility to the clock/calendar, because they are within the same lexical scope. For simplicity, we do not show any operations along this relationship; during initialization, the room merely registers its living pattern as a dependent of the clock/calendar and thereafter does not send messages to the clock/calendar.

Certain objects are known only to the room through its fields: specifically, the desired-temperature sensor, the current-temperature sensor, the room-occupancy sensor, the living pattern, and the water valve. Conversely, these objects have visibility to the room through the Smalltalk dependency mechanism. Specifically, one of the actions of initializing the room and each of its fields is to make the room a dependent of each sensor and the living pattern.

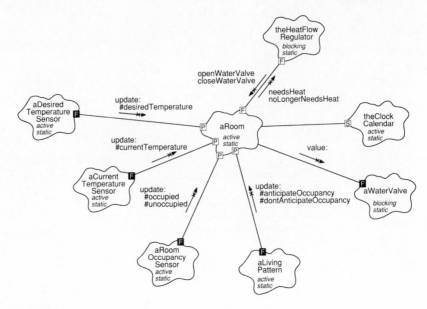

Figure 8-17
Room Object Diagram

Given this arrangement of objects, let's next consider the flow of control between a room and the heat-flow regulator. When the heat-flow regulator sends a message to open or close the room's water valve, the room responds by passing the message `value:` with an appropriate argument to its water valve, which is visible as a field of the room. All of these methods may block because of the concurrency semantics described earlier.

How does the room know when to send the messages `needsHeat` and `noLongerNeedsHeat` to the heat-flow regulator? The room is in the best position to initiate these messages, because it encapsulates all the state necessary to cause an intelligent action. In effect, the room encapsulates a state machine: the events that trigger this state machine come only from the components of a room, specifically, the desired-temperature sensor, the current-temperature sensor, the room-occupancy sensor, and the living pattern. This is why Figure 8-17 shows each of these objects sending an `update:` message with a specific symbol as a parameter. These symbols represent external events that each object can detect and to which the room itself must react. Because we have a reactive system, the order in which these events occur is important; thus, we must use a state machine in the implementation of the room to achieve this time-ordered behavior.

Recall from the requirements that a room can be unoccupied, unoccupied but expecting occupancy, or occupied. Additionally, in each case, the water

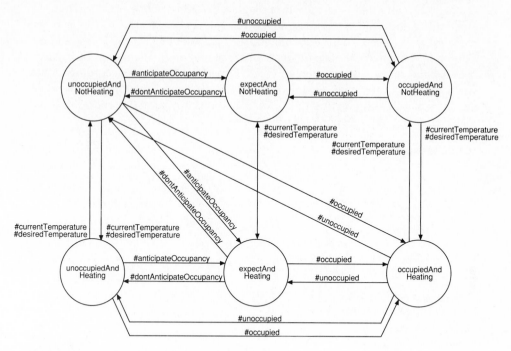

Figure 8-18
Room State Transition Diagram

valve of the room can be open (the room is being heated) or closed (the room is not being heated). Thus, a room may be in one of six relevant states:

- Unoccupied and not being heated
- Unoccupied and being heated
- Expecting occupancy and not being heated
- Expecting occupancy and being heated
- Occupied and not being heated
- Occupied and being heated

When we first create a room, we must determine its initial state. When the home heating system is turned on, some rooms may be occupied and others not, or some may already need to be heated. This is why we include the private method `setInitialState`, which is invoked upon initialization of the room and is responsible for determining the initial room state.

Figure 8-18 shows the state-transition diagram for the class `Room`. Notice that we have not indicated any start states (because the initial state must be determined dynamically) nor any stop states (because the state machine runs for the lifetime of the home heating system).

Transforming this state-transition diagram into Smalltalk code is quite easy. Since all of the objects that can signal relevant events to the room have the room object as one of their dependents, we can use the `update:` method in the class `Room` to signal the room object. One possible implementation of `update:` uses a large set of `if` statements, which dispatch a message according to the value of the current state. Each event requires a state change as well as some action, which is achieved by the private methods we named earlier. Thus, we might write the implementation of this method as follows:

```
update: aMessage

    "Update the state of the room. Possible states are #occupiedAndHeating,
    #occupiedAndNoHeating, #expectAndHeating, #expectAndNoHeating,
    #unoccupiedAndHeating, #unoccupiedAndNoHeating. Possible events are
    #occupied, #unoccupied, #currentTemperature, #desiredTemperature,
    #anticipateOccupancy, and #dontAnticipateOccupancy. Messages may be sent
    to request heat or to stop heat."

    | current desired occupied expected |

    theSemaphore critical:
        [aMessage = #value
            ifFalse:
                [current ← theCurrentTemperatureSensor value.
                    desired ← theDesiredTemperatureSensor value.
                    occupied ← theRoomOccupancySensor value.
                    expected ← theLivingPattern occupancyExpected.
                    currentState = #occupiedAndHeating ifTrue:
                [self
                    occupiedAndHeating: aMessage
                    current: current
                    desired: desired
                    occupied: occupied
                    expected: expected] ifFalse:
            [currentState = #occupiedAndNoHeating ifTrue:
                [self
                    occupiedAndNoHeating: aMessage
                    current: current
                    desired: desired
                    occupied: occupied
                    expected: expected] ifFalse:
            [currentState = #expectAndHeating ifTrue:
                [self
                    expectAndHeating: aMessage
                    current: current
                    desired: desired
                    occupied: occupied
                    expected: expected] ifFalse:
            [currentState = #expectAndNoHeating ifTrue:
                [self
                    expectAndNoHeating: aMessage
                    current: current
                    desired: desired
                    occupied: occupied
```

```
                            expected: expected] ifFalse:
                [currentState = #unoccupiedAndHeating ifTrue:
                    [self
                        unoccupiedAndHeating: aMessage
                        current: current
                        desired: desired
                        occupied: occupied
                        expected: expected] ifFalse:
                [currentState = #unoccupiedAndNoHeating ifTrue:
                    [self
                        unoccupiedAndNoHeating: aMessage
                        current: current
                        desired: desired
                        occupied: occupied
                        expected: expected]]]]]]]]
```

An alternative implementation uses the primitive operation `perform` to dispatch an operation based upon the value `currentState`. The down side of this approach is that it requires each private method to decode the array of arguments supplied by `perform`.

Each of the private methods has a similar selector profile: a symbol representing the event, the current states, the desired temperature, the occupancy status of the room, and whether or not occupancy is expected. Given only this collection of properties, we can write private methods that properly act upon the event, according to the state transition diagram in Figure 8-18.

Consider the private method `occupiedAndNoHeating:`. Three different events might cause a change from the state `occupiedAndNotHeating`, as shown in Figure 8-18:

- The room becomes unoccupied
- The desired temperature changes
- The current temperature changes

If a room becomes unoccupied, then we must move to the state `expectAndNotHeating` or `unoccupiedAndNotHeating`, depending upon whether or not occupancy is expected, which the room's living pattern knows. If the current or desired temperatures change so that the current temperature is more than two degrees below the desired temperature, then we must request heat for the room. We can express these requirements in the following private method:

```
occupiedAndNoHeating: aMessage
current: current
desired: desired
occupied: occupied
expected: expected

    "Respond to a state change. desired and occupied are expected to be of the
    class Temperature, occupied and expected are expected to be of the class
    Boolean."
```

```
aMessage = #unoccupied
    ifTrue:
        [expected
            ifTrue:
                [currentState ← #expectAndNoHeating]
            ifFalse:
                [currentState ← #unoccupiedAndNoHeating]].
aMessage = #currentTemperature | (aMessage = #desiredTemperature)
    ifTrue:
        [current <= (desired - 2)
            ifTrue:
                [currentState ← #occupiedAndHeating.
                 self startHeating]]
```

When there is a change to the state #occupiedAndHeating, this method sends itself a message requesting heat. We may write the private method start-Heating as follows:

startHeating

    "Request heat for this room."

    theHeatFlowRegulator needsHeat: self

Any state transition that moves from a not heating to a heating state ultimately invokes the method startHeating, and any state transition that moves from a heating to a not heating state invokes the method stopHeating.

Furnace Implementation

The implementation of the class Furnace is similar to that of the class Room, in that both embody a state machine triggered through the Smalltalk dependency mechanism by active objects. The furnace's class template appears as follows:

Name:	Furnace
Cardinality:	1
Hierarchy:	
Superclasses:	Object
Public Interface:	
Uses:	HeatFlowRegulator
Operations:	activate
	deactivate
	initialize:
	release
Implementation:	
Uses:	BoilerTemperatureSensor
	ClockCalendar
	CombustionFaultSensor
	Blower
	OilValve
	Ignitor
	OilFaultSensor

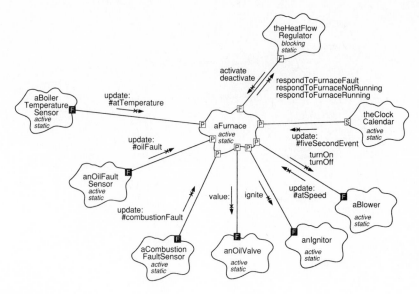

Figure 8-19
Furnace Object Diagram

Fields:	currentState
	itsSemaphore
	theBoilerTemperatureSensor
	theCombustionFaultSensor
	theHeatFlowRegulator
	theBlower
	theOilValve
	theIgnitor
	theOilFaultSensor
	theView
	timeDelay
Operations:	postFault
	postNotRunning
	postRunning
	update:
Concurrency:	active

This interface matches the operations described in the object diagram in Figure 8-15. We do not have as many private methods because the furnace's state machine is much simpler.

The object diagram for the furnace appears in Figure 8-19. As with the class Room, a furnace has multiple nonshared fields. In turn, each of these objects has visibility to the furnace through the Smalltalk dependency mechanism.

The flow of control in the furnace is similar to that in the room. The various sensors, the blower, and the clock/calendar can post update: messages to the furnace with suitable arguments indicating the nature of the events. The

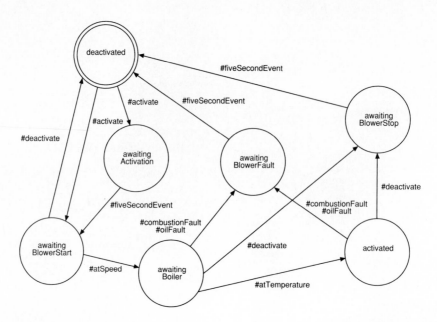

Figure 8-20
Furnace State Transition Diagram

message passing semantics involve potential blocking, which is necessary in order to sequentialize concurrent events.

The requirements for the home heating system include detailed instructions on the process of furnace activation and deactivation. Indeed, these operations constitute the primary behavior embodied by the furnace. Figure 8-20 shows the state machine that captures these requirements. Beginning with the initial state (deactivated), invoking the `activate` method causes the `#activate` event, which changes the state of the furnace to either `awaitingActivation` or `awaitingBlowerStart`. Which state is chosen depends upon how long ago the furnace was deactivated. If the furnace has been deactivated for more than five minutes, we move to the state `awaitingBlowerStart`. Otherwise, we move to the state `awaitingActivation`, in which we check every five seconds to see if sufficient time has passed to start the activation process.

When moving to the state `awaitingBlowerStart`, the action is to turn on the blower. The furnace process waits at this state until signaled by the blower (representing another active thread of control) that it is at speed. Notice that this represents a gap in the requirements: the furnace will wait indefinitely at this state if the blower never comes to speed.

Once the blower is at speed, the furnace state machine opens the oil valve and ignites the oil. The state machine again suspends at this state until either (1) a fault is reported (which changes the furnace state to `awaitingBlowerFault`), (2) the furnace is deactivated (which changes the furnace state to `awaiting-`

BlowerStop), or (3) the water comes up to a suitable temperature (which brings the furnace to the `activated` state).

Normal deactivation of the furnace follows state transitions from `activated` to `awaitingBlowerFault`, to `deactivated`. Upon reaching the deactivated state, one of the final actions of the state machine is to record the time of shutdown. This time is kept in the field `timeDelay`, so that upon reactivation, the state machine process can properly decide to delay activation for up to five minutes.

Heat-Flow Regulator Implementation

The only remaining abstraction to implement is that of the heat-flow regulator. The heat-flow regulator forms the heart of the home heating system, as it is responsible for activating and deactivating the furnace and regulating the flow of heated water to rooms. However, because we have carefully separated the state space of the system and distributed behavior into independent objects, the work of the heat flow regulator is relatively straightforward.

The interface part of the class template for the class `HeatFlowRegulator` is based upon the design decisions we have already made:

```
Name:                    HeatFlowRegulator
Cardinality:             1
Hierarchy:
        Superclasses:    Object
Public Interface:
        Uses:            Furnace
                         Home
                         OperatorInterface
                         Room
        Operations:      initialize: furnace: operator:
                         needsHeat:
                         noLongerNeedsHeat:
                         release
                         respondToFaultResetSwitch
                         respondToFurnaceFault
                         respondToFurnaceNotRunning
                         respondToFurnaceRunning
                         respondToHeatSwitchOff
                         respondToHeatSwitchOn
```

Objects of this class need an instance variable for a semaphore because the class exhibits blocking semantics. The heat-flow regulator also encapsulates a state machine, so we also need a field to hold the current state of this machine. Additionally, objects of this class must have fields containing a reference to the home, the furnace, and the operator interface, because each one expects to have messages passed to it by the heat-flow regulator.

Our requirements state that we must keep track of the rooms requesting heat even if the furnace is not yet activated, which is reasonable, because once the furnace is activated, all rooms that requested heat before that time should be given heat. Therefore, the heat-flow regulator must maintain a collection of

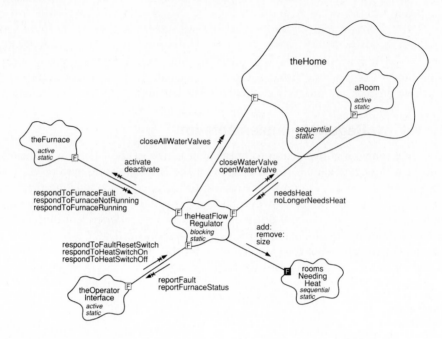

Figure 8-21
Heat-Flow Regulator Object Diagram

rooms that have requested heat. Notice that this list is dynamic: it grows as rooms send the message `needsHeat`, and it shrinks as the water valves in the room are opened, indicating that rooms are being heated. Because under certain conditions we must turn off the furnace (specifically, whenever there is no longer a room needing heat), we must keep track of how many rooms are currently being heated. We do this by including a field that maintains a count of open water valves.

Figure 8-21 shows the object diagram for the heat-flow regulator. This diagram is virtually identical to the top-level object diagram in Figure 8-15, except that we have added more detail. This is to be expected, because the heat-flow regulator turns out to be the center of control in the system. What is different about Figure 8-21, however, is that it includes the `roomsNeedingHeat` object, which is an artifact of our choice of representation for the class.

At this point, our design includes enough implementation decisions to properly establish how these objects are visible to one another, as Figure 8-21 indicates. Thus, the home, the furnace, and the operator interface are all visible as shared fields of the heat-flow regulator. Conversely, the heat-flow regulator is visible to the home, the furnace, and the operator interface as a shared field of those objects.

Notice the messages that the heat flow regulator may pass to the object denoted by the field `roomsNeedingHeat`. Specifically, the heat-flow regulator may add rooms to and remove rooms from the list, as well as invoke the selector `size` to determine the number of rooms in the collection.

A suitable representation for the class of `roomsNeedingHeat` is the class `Set`. Sequential semantics for the collection of rooms are sufficient for our purposes here; we know that because the heat-flow regulator has blocking semantics, there is no potential for multiple processes to interact with the encapsulated field `roomsNeedingHeat`.

We choose to implement the state machine for the heat-flow regulator in the method `update:`. There is nothing magical about implementing the state machine in this particular method: the code for the state machine must reside in some method, and so, for the sake of uniformity with the room and furnace classes, we use the same method for the heat-flow regulator. Using algorithmic decomposition, we can identify each private method that denotes the actions taken by the state machine when presented with a new event. For example, the implementation of the method `activating:` appears as follows:

```
activating: aMessage room: aRoom

    "Respond to a message while in the activating state. Possible events are
    #needsHeat, #noLongerNeedsHeat, #heatSwitchOff, #furnaceFault, and
    #running."

aMessage = #needsHeat
    ifTrue:
        [(roomsNeedingHeat includes: aRoom)
            ifFalse:
                [roomsNeedingHeat add: aRoom].
        ↑nil].
aMessage = #noLongerNeedsHeat
    ifTrue:
        [roomsNeedingHeat remove: aRoom ifAbsent: [].
        roomsNeedingHeat size = 0
            ifTrue:
                [currentState ← #deactivatingNormal.
                [theFurnace deactivate] fork].
        ↑nil].
aMessage = #heatSwitchOff
    ifTrue:
        [currentState ← #deactivatingNormal.
        [theFurnace deactivate] fork.
        ↑nil].
aMessage = #furnaceFault
    ifTrue:
        [currentState ← #deactivatingFault.
        [theFurnace deactivate] fork.
        ↑nil].
aMessage = #running
    ifTrue:
        [currentState ← #running.
        roomsNeedingHeat do: [:x |
            x openWaterValve.
            totalValvesOpen ← (totalValvesOpen + 1)].
```

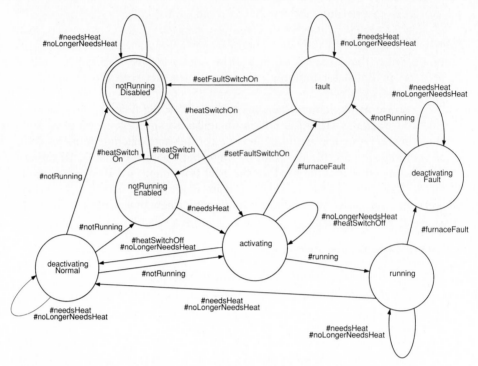

Figure 8-22
Heat Flow Regulator State Transition Diagram

```
roomsNeedingHeat ← Set new.
[theOperatorInterface reportFurnaceStatus: true] fork.
↑nil]
```

Figure 8-22 shows the complete state transition diagram for the class `HeatFlowRegulator`. Notice how the code for the `activating` method maps to this diagram. As the code and diagram indicate, while in the `activating` state, the heat-flow regulator may receive messages denoting the events `#needsHeat` and `#noLongerNeedsHeat`. In both cases, the action of the method is to add rooms to or remove rooms from the list of rooms. If the list shrinks to a zero size, then we move to the state `deactivatingNormal`. Otherwise, we remain in the same state waiting for a signal from the furnace that it is now running (the `#running` event), which causes a transition to the state `running`.

While in the `activating` state, it is also possible to receive a message signalling the event `#heatSwitchOff`, in which case we must deactivate the furnace and move to the `deactivatingNormal` state. Finally, if a furnace fault is reported (the `#furnaceFault` event), then we must deactivate the furnace and move to the state `deactivatingFault`.

There is one subtle detail in all the private methods of the heat-flow regulator. Notice that the `activating: room:` method can send the message deactivate to the furnace. Instead of passing this message directly, we fork a process that does this on behalf of the heat-flow regulator. This is a good example of an *agent*, that is, an object that does some work on behalf of another. We take this approach because we cannot let the heat-flow regulator block while the furnace is deactivating. There may be #needsHeat and #noLongerNeedsHeat events that the method must process, and if the heat-flow regulator blocks, then the rooms sending messages to the heat-flow regulator will also block. In fact, if we do not fork the process, we may end up with a deadlock. The heat-flow regulator sends a deactivate message to the furnace, and in so doing must block until the furnace reports that it is deactivated. The furnace finishes deactivation, and then sends the respondTo-FurnaceNotRunning message back to the heat-flow regulator. This produces a cycle of dependent processes, and thus creates a deadlock: the heat-flow regulator is waiting for the furnace, and the furnace is waiting for the heat-flow regulator. Introducing this forked process eliminates this kind of deadlock.

Why don't we just modify the deactivate method so that the heat-flow regulator still blocks, but the furnace doesn't send the respondTo-FurnaceNotRunning message? If the heat flow-regulator blocks, then any rooms requesting heat or no longer requesting heat block. Thus, the forked process eliminates deadlock but also maximizes the degree of actual parallelism.

By what magic did we realize that deadlock was even an issue? The object diagram in Figure 8-21 clearly points out the existence of a possible cyclic dependency among concurrent objects. Specifically, look at the direction of the messages being passed between the heat-flow regulator and the furnace: they go in both directions. The question the designer must ask in such situations is simply, Is there any chance that such messages will be passed in both directions at the same time? If the answer is yes, then a potential exists for a race condition, or, at the very worst, deadlock. Introducing an agent process breaks the cycle of dependencies.

8.4 Modification

From Simulation to Reality

We have come to the end of our design for the home heating system. The products of the design process include a set of class diagrams and object diagrams, along with their corresponding templates, state transition diagrams, and timing diagrams. Figure 8-23 shows a screen dump of a Smalltalk session running the completed home heating system simulation, which consists of some twenty-nine domain-specific classes for a total of about one hundred methods. Not surprisingly, this interface appears similar to that of the original user interface prototype. This is a result of implementing the system incrementally from

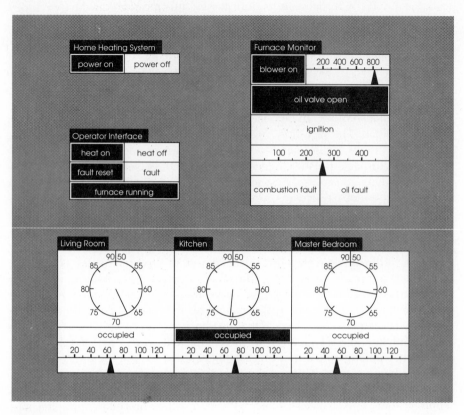

Figure 8-23
Home Heating System Simulation

proven, stable prototypes, rather than analyzing, designing, then implementing in discrete, fully independent steps.

Since our design already reflects our model of reality, moving to a production system with real sensors, furnaces, and toggle switches involves altering only the implementation of parts of our design. In fact, none of the class interfaces of our simulation need change. Rather, because we have carefully encapsulated all representation decisions, we need only modify the implementation of certain classes that lie at the fringe of the system.

Consider how we might modify the class `DesiredTemperatureSensor` to represent a physical device. Assuming that our underlying hardware supports interrupt handling, we need to modify the use of the `value:` method so that it is invoked by the interrupt handler that reacts to a room occupant changing the desired temperature of a room. If our underlying hardware does not support interrupt handling, then we would have to devise a process that polled the desired temperature sensors and then passed the `value:` method. In either case, we would not have to alter the interface of the `DesiredTemperatureSensor` class. Thus, any classes that depend upon this class need not be altered: the fabric of our design remains intact.

A similar approach applies to actuators such as water valves. To modify the class WaterValve to manipulate a physical valve, we need to modify the implementation of the method value: so that it sends the appropriate signal to the physical device. Again, neither the interface nor the logical semantics of this class change, and therefore no other part of the design is affected.

Changing the Requirements

Moving from a simulation to a production system illustrates that we have created a portable design: code is not often portable, but designs usually are. But what happens if we now make some fundamental changes to the requirements? Another hallmark of a good design is that it is resilient to such changes.

Let's consider a simple change in requirements first. Suppose that a certain customer wants to have a home heating system that allows each room to have a different set-back temperature, where a set-back temperature is the temperature maintained in a room when it is unoccupied. The current requirements indicate a set-back temperature that is constant across all rooms. What must we change in our design?

Only the implementation of the class Room needs to be altered. First, we must create a new class, SetBack, to model the sensor in each room through which the room occupant can establish the set-back temperature. The current set-back temperature thus becomes part of each room's state. The room state machine must next be altered to react to events that represent changes in the set-back temperature. Additionally, the decision that is made in the state machine about when a room needs or no longer needs heat must then use this set-back temperature rather than the current constant value. In any case, the interface to the class Room remains unchanged: a room still signals the heat-flow regulator when it needs or no longer needs heat in the same way as in the simulation. Thus, the same abstractions and the same mechanisms still apply in our design; we have only added some new behavior in an incremental way.

Now let's consider a fundamental change in the requirements. Suppose another customer wanted to install the home heating system in a large building that requires two furnaces. How does our design change?

This change is simple to implement. Logically, we just need another instance of the class Furnace. How do we know when to activate or deactivate this second furnace? The answer is that the heat-flow regulator object already has the necessary state at its disposal to make an intelligent decision. For example, when the number of rooms needing heat reaches some amount calculated to tax the capacity of just one furnace, then the heat-flow regulator could cause the activation of the second furnace. This second furnace would be deactivated by the heat-flow regulator when the number of rooms needing heat drops below some calculated level. As with all the other changes we have made, no class interfaces need change, which leaves us with a very stable design.

Further Readings

The problems of process synchronization, deadlock, livelock, and race conditions are discussed in detail in Hansen [H 1977], Ben-Ari [H 1982], and Holt et al. [H 1978]. Mellichamp [H 1983], Glass [H 1983], and Foster [H 1981] offer general references on the issues of developing real-time applications. Concurrency as viewed by the interplay of hardware and software may be found in Lorin [H 1972].

Chapter 2 provides further references regarding the role of concurrency in the object model. The appendix provides a summary of the Smalltalk programming language, with examples.

Object Pascal
Geometrical Optics Construction Kit

Whereas Smalltalk is a "pure" language, in which everything is viewed as an object, Object Pascal is a minimalist object-oriented programming language, in that it adds to Pascal only the most basic support for classes, single inheritance, dynamic binding, and polymorphism. Unlike Smalltalk, Object Pascal is strongly typed.

In this chapter, we apply Object Pascal to a scientific application, namely, the problem of ray tracing as found in geometrical optics, the branch of physics concerned with the phenomena of the reflection and refraction of light. In the previous chapter, the heart of the problem turned out to involve the issues of process synchronization and intelligent distribution of behavior among several autonomous, relatively static objects. In the current problem, two very different issues dominate: the desire for an intuitive and friendly user interface and the need for computational-intensive processing involving dynamic objects.

Geometrical Optics Construction Kit Requirements

The basic function of this tool is to calculate a ray trace for various kinds of thin lenses arranged in series along an optical bench. A user may interactively manipulate parameters such as the focal length and placement of lenses and receive immediate feedback as to the trace of all principle rays and the size, position, and orientation of the resulting images.

A thin lens is one whose thickness can be neglected [1]. Two kinds of thin lenses are of interest to us: converging lenses, which are thicker in the center than at the edges, and diverging lenses, which are thicker at the edges than in the center. Given a converging lens with a real object positioned at infinity on one side of the lens, parallel rays of light from the object will approach the lens and then focus at a point on the opposite side. This point represents the second focal point of the lens, which we label f'. Given a real object positioned on one side of a converging lens at the focal point, which we label f, representing the first focal point, parallel rays of light will emerge from the opposite side. In a thin lens, f and f' are equal in value, and we call that value the *focal length* of the lens.

If the real object is neither at infinity nor at the focal point, the lens will form an image. Letting d represent the distance from the real object to the center of the lens and d' represent the distance from the center of the lens to the image, we can state the following equation representing the relationship of d, d' and f:

$$\frac{1}{d} + \frac{1}{d'} = \frac{1}{f}$$

The magnification, m, of a thin lens is given by the following equation:

$$m = -\frac{d'}{d}$$

The focal length of a converging lens is positive; the focal length of a diverging lens is negative. Thus, given a diverging lens with a real object positioned at infinity on one side of the lens, parallel rays of light from the object will approach the lens and then diverge. If we trace these divergent rays back through the lens, they will appear to focus at the second focal point, which is positioned on the same side as the real object.

The geometrical optics construction kit must be able to model both converging and diverging lenses. There are three basic kinds of converging lenses:

- Converging meniscus
- Plano-convex
- Double convex

There are also three basic kinds of diverging lenses:

- Diverging meniscus
- Plano-concave
- Double concave

Given a real object and a single lens, this tool must determine the size, position, and orientation of the image that is formed, which may be real or virtual. For example, given a real object just beyond the focal length of a converging lens, a real image will form on the opposite side of the lens. Given the same scenario with a diverging lens, no real image will form, since the rays diverge. However, an image will appear to form on the same side as the real object: we call this the *virtual image*. When calculating the ray trace, the tool must distinguish between real and virtual images.

It is possible to extend the concept of image formation to a series of lenses. We assume that all the lenses are arranged so that their centers fall along a line called the *optical axis*. Thus, the image formed by one lens serves as the object for the next lens in the series along the axis, and so on.

The point at which a real or virtual image is formed is determined by the intersection of only three rays, called the *principal rays*, which we describe as follows:

1. "A ray parallel to the axis, after refraction by the lens, passes through the second focal point of a converging lens or appears to come from the second focal point of a diverging lens.

2. A ray through the center of the lens is not appreciably deviated, since the two lens surfaces through which the central ray passes are very nearly parallel and close together if the lens is thin.

3. A ray through (or proceeding toward) the first focal point emerges parallel to the axis" [2].

Figure 9-1 illustrates these concepts. Here we see an optical bench, with measurements given in units of an arbitrary dimension. At the far left, there is one real object, followed by three lenses positioned at 50, 215, and 400 units from the real object, respectively. The first and second lenses in the series are converging lenses (whose focal lengths are 30 and 50), and the third is a diverging lens (with a focal length of −150). The real images are displayed in dark gray, and the virtual image is displayed in light gray.

Real lenses suffer from various chromatic and monochromatic aberrations, such as spherical aberration, in which the principle rays fail to converge to a point. This tool does not need to model such phenomena.

The user interface for the geometrical optics construction kit must follow the Apple user interface guidelines for the Macintosh [3]. Each optics experiment must be displayed in its own resizable and repositionable window. Since a particular experiment may involve many lenses, each window must map to a view of an arbitrary, user-definable size. A user must be able to toggle the display of the

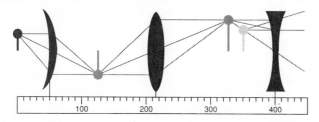

Figure 9-1
An Optics Experiment

optical bench, grid lines (for precise alignment of lenses), and page breaks. The user must also be able to toggle the constraint of mouse movement to a grid of five-unit intervals.

The user must be able to select each of the six different thin lenses from a palette. A selected lens may be positioned, by mouse action, along the optical bench. A dialog must be provided that allows the user to set the focal length of a selected lens. The user must be able to select, drag, cut, copy, clear, and paste single lenses as well as sets of lenses. After any user action that changes image size, position, or orientation, the tool must redisplay the new ray trace. The real object (of which there is exactly one, displayed at position zero along the optical bench) must appear in black. Real images must appear in dark gray, and virtual images must appear in light gray.

A user must be able to display up to four experiments at one time. The usual file operations apply: a user must be able to create new experiments, open old experiments, save experiments, save copies of experiments, and revert to previously saved experiments. A user must also be able to print an experiment.

Undo and redo functions must be provided for all user operations that affect image position, size, and orientation.

9.1 Analysis

Defining the Boundaries of the Problem

The sidebar provides the detailed requirements for the geometrical optics construction kit. We encounter several obviously tangible objects, such as lenses and optical benches, along with objects such as images (both real and virtual), which, while not always visibly tangible, do indeed exist in our mind as abstractions with crisply defined boundaries. What about rays of light? Using the wave model of light in physics, we might argue that light is not an object. For the domain of geometrical optics, however, treating light as an object (as vectors of particles) is an appropriate view of the world because it is effective in modeling the phenomenon of refraction.

Is a focal point an object? A focal point is defined as some point in space at a fixed distance from the center of a thin lens. Our analysis determines that a focal point is not a good candidate for an object: there are no meaningful operations related to focal points. It is better to model the focal length as a property of a lens and the focal point as a consequence of this property. This is similar to the problem of modeling physical objects such as baseballs and cars, whose colors and shapes are not independent objects, but exist as properties of the objects.

An optics experiment itself is also an object, because this term denotes something with a crisply defined boundary. An optics experiment encompasses a collection of lenses, an optical bench, a set of images (both real and virtual), and a set of rays.

Some of the requirements in the sidebar repeat the mathematical foundations of geometrical optics; the remaining requirements address the semantics of the user interface. The latter requirements describe the ways in which a user can interact with the tool to manipulate an optics experiment. Several requirements describe user-visible processes, such as cutting, clearing, copying, pasting, dragging, and selecting. Rather than viewing them as algorithmic abstractions, we may instead invent objects that serve as the agents responsible for carrying out the processes. Thus, rather than having a cutting process, we have instead a cut command object that embodies the knowledge of how to remove lenses from an optical bench. Encapsulating this kind of behavior in an object makes possible some fairly sophisticated user interaction. For example, a cut command object is in the best position to know how to undo a cutting operation and how to save a cut lens so that it can later be pasted back into the same application or even a different one.

What makes our task challenging is that we must build a tool with which a user can manipulate optics experiments in largely unconstrained ways. We do not want to build a user-hostile interface that forces the user to set up and modify optics experiments in steps whose order is rigidly defined by the tool, not the user: this is characteristic of modal, batch-oriented applications. Instead, our requirements lead us to create a "what you see is what you get" (WYSIWYG) editor for optics experiments, which makes explicitly visible the key abstractions that exist in the mind of the user, namely, lenses, images, rays, and optical benches. Thus, with little training in the use of the geometrical optics construction kit, a user can manipulate the tool's abstraction of lenses just as if they were physical objects. The fundamental advantage of such a tool is that it is in many ways more flexible than manipulating real lenses. For example, our requirements permit the user to easily change the focal length of a selected lens; in the physical world, this would require either finding or making a new lens with the desired properties.

It is very important that we take the time necessary to design an intuitive and friendly user interface. In applications such as this, it is often the look and feel of the user interface that makes the difference between a wildly popular application and a quickly discarded one.

Living with a Large Class Library

User interface design is an application-independent technology for which a number of very useful libraries of reusable software components have been developed. Commercially, there exist products such as MIT's X Window System [4], Open Look [5], Microsoft's Windows [6], and IBM's Presentation Manager [7]. Each of these windowing systems is different: some are network-based, and others are kernel-based; some treat individual pixels as the most primitive graphical element, and others manipulate higher-level abstractions, such as rectangles, ovals, and arcs. In any case, all of these products have a common objective: they exist to simplify the task of implementing that part of an application that forms the human-machine interface. We should point out that none of these products sprang up overnight. Rather, the most useful windowing systems evolved over time, from proven, smaller systems. It has taken years of failures and successes for sufficient consensus to emerge in the industry on a meaningful set of abstractions for the problem of building user interfaces. We see many different windowing models because there is no single right answer to the problem of user interface design.

Like Smalltalk, Object Pascal has a rich class library, in the form of Apple's MacApp [8]. Apple characterizes MacApp as "an object-oriented application framework" [9]. MacApp is thus much more than a windowing system; it provides classes for windows, views, dialogs, and controls, and also includes classes representing commands, documents, and whole applications. In simple terms, MacApp consists of a set of classes and free subprograms that embody much of the common behavior necessary to build an application that follows the Macintosh User Interface Guidelines [10]. Indeed, MacApp makes it difficult – although not impossible – to build applications that violate these guidelines.

MacApp comprises a large amount of code. Its Object Pascal implementation has in excess of 40,000 lines of code, spread across about a dozen object-oriented libraries (containing the various classes and global declarations) and several non-object-oriented libraries (containing various free subprograms that support utilities such as menu handling and memory management). In addition to these libraries, there are over sixty units just for Object Pascal that provide programmatic access to the Macintosh Toolbox routines and other common utilities.

Figure 9-2 is a class diagram for MacApp that shows only the inheritance relationships among all of its classes. Note that the base class in MacApp is named `TObject`, and from this class there are defined subclasses of increasing specialization. By convention, all MacApp classes are named `T<something>` to distinguish them from simple Pascal types.

The novice to MacApp is often intimidated by this abundance of classes. What do these classes represent? How do they work together? How can they be tailored to meet domain-specific needs? Which classes are really important, and which can be ignored? These are the questions that we must answer before we can use MacApp to construct any non-trivial application. Fortunately, it is not necessary to comprehend the entire subtlety of a library as large as MacApp, just as it is not necessary to understand how a microprocessor works in order to program a computer in a high-order language. In both cases, however, the raw power of the underlying implementation can be exposed if necessary, but only if the developer is willing to absorb the additional complexity.

The truly hard part of living with any large, integrated class library is learning what mechanisms it embodies. The more one knows about its mechanisms, the easier it is to discover innovative ways to use existing components rather than fabricate new ones from scratch. In practice, we observe that developers generally start by using the most obvious classes in a library. As they grow to trust certain abstractions, they move incrementally to the use of more sophisticated classes. Eventually, developers may discover a pattern in their own tailoring of a predefined class, and so add it to the library as a primitive abstraction. Similarly, a team of developers may realize that certain domain-specific classes keep showing up across systems; these too get introduced into the class library.

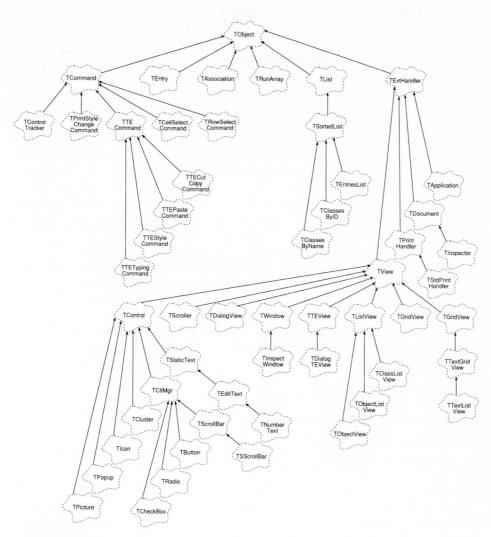

Figure 9-2
MacApp Class Diagram

This is precisely how class libraries grow over time: not overnight, but from smaller, stable intermediate forms.

Analysis of MacApp's Key Mechanisms

Our purpose here is not to offer an exhaustive tutorial on MacApp. However, we must develop a conceptual framework for MacApp, so that we can use its classes as the foundation for the design of the geometrical optics construction kit.

The classes shown in Figure 9-2 capture much of the behavior common to applications that conform to the Macintosh User Interface Guidelines. MacApp's classes provide standard features such as scroll bars, undoable and redoable commands, clusters of buttons, panning of views within a window, and menu management. MacApp also provides much of the common code needed to print views, edit text, and file documents. For example, using MacApp, a developer need only provide the names of all the items in a given menu, their keyboard equivalents (if any), the state of each menu item (for example, enabled or disabled), and the action to be performed when a user selects a given item. MacApp does all the rest, even for hierarchical menus, including handling, tracking the mouse, aborting a menu selection, and invoking the proper action upon menu selection. The primary focus of the developer is to add domain-dependent behavior by creating new subclasses that override existing methods or add new methods and fields, rather than worrying about all the nasty details of low level calls to the Macintosh Toolbox.

Most of the classes shown in Figure 9-2 are abstract classes. In other words, a developer will rarely create an instance of any of the predefined MacApp classes directly, but will instead create instances only of subclasses. In all the important cases (for example, for the class `TApplication`), MacApp gives a runtime error message if certain methods are not overridden.

In order to use MacApp to create a nontrivial application, we must understand how the following mechanisms work:

- Drawing in a view
- Tracking and responding to a mouse action
- Responding to a menu command
- Responding to an event
- Saving and restoring the state of an application in a document

These mechanisms form the core concepts of MacApp. Many other mechanisms are equally relevant, such as for printing, cutting, copying, clearing, pasting, interacting with a user via dialogs, failure recovery, and memory management, but these are best discussed in the context of a complete application.

Drawing in a View. In Figure 9-3, we see a fairly typical Macintosh window, which decomposes into six view objects: the window itself, a palette, two scrollbars, a scroller, and a view of some model. This structural hierarchy is a classical example of a superview/subview relationship. Specifically, the view of the model is a subview of the scroller, which in turn is a subview of the window. Similarly, the palette, the horizontal scrollbar, and the vertical scrollbar are direct subviews of the window.

The class structure of these objects forms an entirely different hierarchy. For example, the window is an instance of a subclass of the class `TWindow`, which itself is a subclass of the class `TView`. Ultimately, `TView` is the superclass of all six objects.

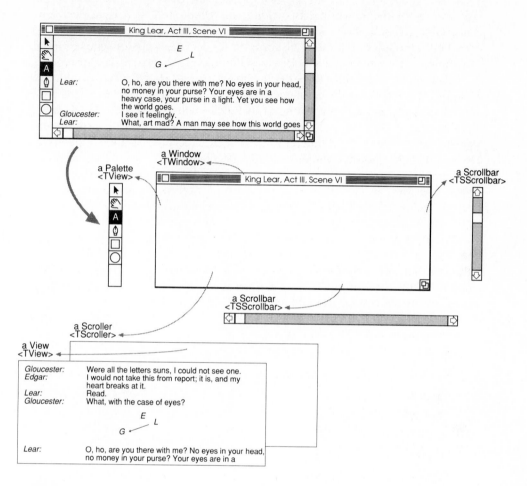

Figure 9-3
Structural Hierarchy of a Window

MacApp places no constraints upon how views are structurally nested. The key to this feature is the fact that the class `TView` includes the following two fields:

- `fSuperView`   The enclosing view of this view object
- `fSubViews`   A list of all views contained in this view object

Since every displayable view object is ultimately a descendent of the class TView, all such objects inherit these two fields.

By convention, the field of each class is named `f<something>` in MacApp. Unlike Smalltalk, Object Pascal is a strongly typed language; every field must therefore be declared to be an instance of a specific class or simple Pascal type. The classes of the preceding two fields are `TView` and `TList`, respectively. Since Object Pascal allows simple polymorphism, the actual object designated by a field can either be a direct instance of the declared class or type or (more commonly) an instance of a subclass or subtype of the declared class or type.

Also unlike Smalltalk, all fields in Object Pascal are unencapsulated. For example, if we have an object named `aWindow`, any client that has visibility to that object can refer directly to one of its fields, such as `aWindow.fDocument`. Furthermore, unlike C++, all methods are public in Object Pascal. Using unencapsulated abstractions is inherently less secure because it allows clients to depend directly upon the underlying implementation of some object; if an object's implementation changes or if we change the meaning of certain of its fields, then we can no longer trust the semantics of any of its clients. For this reason, our style avoids direct references by a client to the fields of an object, although in some cases the convenience outweighs the risk.

The declaration of a class's methods follows its fields. `TView` in particular has a broad, complicated interface: there are ninety-two methods defined for this class, not to mention those inherited from its superclass, `TEvtHandler`. We need not show `TView`'s entire interface, but it is useful to point out that each of these operations may be grouped into one of the following categories:

- Creation/destruction methods
- Coordinate conversion methods
- Subview management methods
- Open/close/activate methods
- Choice handling methods
- Size methods
- Location methods
- Focusing methods
- Drawing methods
- Validation/invalidation methods
- Mouse handling methods
- Cursor handling methods
- Miscellaneous methods
- Clipboard handling methods
- Printing methods
- Resource methods
- Inspecting methods

Most nontrivial subclasses of `TView` add their own unique fields and methods and override the following seven methods:

- DoHighlightSelection
- Draw
- DoSetUpMenus
- Fields
- DoMouseCommand
- DoMenuCommand
- DoSetCursor

Given `TStageDirectionsView` as a subclass of `TView`, consider the following code fragment:

```
var
    StageDirectionsView : TStageDirectionsView;
begin
    new(StageDirectionsView);
    StageDirectionsView.IView(aDocument, anEnclosingView, gZeroVPt, (100, 100),
                      SizeFillPages, SizeFillPages);
    ...
end;
```

Here we first create a new object of the class `TStageDirectionsView` and then initialize it with the given document and superview. The third and fourth parameters of the method `IView` indicate the view's location and initial size relative to its superview. The last two parameters indicate that the view has a variable size, rounded up to the nearest page size.

Views do not stand by themselves; they are ultimately encapsulated inside some window. Windows of arbitrary complexity can be created, but MacApp provides free subprograms for creating the two most common kinds of windows, namely, a window with a single scrollable view, and a window with a scrollable view and a palette, like the one in Figure 9-3. For example, assuming that we already have an object of the class `TStageDirectionsView` and another object of the class `TPaletteView`, we may create a palette window as follows:

```
var
    aWindow : TWindow;
begin
    aWindow := NewPaletteWindow(kWindowResource, kWantHScrollBar, kWantVScrollBar,
                      aDocument, StageDirectionsView, PaletteView,
                      kPaletteWidth, kLeftPalette);
    ...
end;
```

The first parameter indicates the resource ID of the window, referring to a template found in the application's resource file that describes the initial size of the window and its appearance. The next two parameters specify that we want a window containing a view that can scroll both horizontally and vertically. The fourth, fifth, and sixth parameters denote the document, scrollable view, and palette, respectively. The seventh parameter provides the width of the palette, and the last parameter indicates that this palette will appear on the left side of the window.

One side effect of this method is that it creates an anonymous object of the class `TScroller` as a superview of the given scrollable view and as a subview of the window. This is consistent with what we have shown in Figure 9-3. Since the scrollable view is generally larger than what can be displayed on a single screen, this view is enclosed by the `TScroller` object, which is itself an immediate subview of the window object. The class `TScroller` embodies knowledge of scrollbars, so that when the user clicks on the arrow or direction region of a scrollbar or drags the scrollbar's thumb, the `TScroller` object acts upon the scrollable view to properly reposition it in the visible part of the window.

Windows and views are not created in isolation, but by some other object. Most often, windows and their views are created by document objects, which encapsulate the state of the application's underlying model and are thus in the best position to know when to create a window and its views. Thus, we have a clear separation of concerns: documents know when to create windows, but only windows know how they themselves are created.

When and how are objects such as windows and views destroyed in an application? Unlike Smalltalk, Object Pascal does not have any automatic garbage-collection facilities. Instead, a programmer must carefully reclaim the space of all objects that are no longer needed. MacApp does most of the hard work, by knowing when to discard certain objects; for example, when a document is closed or a window is removed from the screen. However, a developer must empower each class that encapsulates state with the knowledge of how to reclaim that state. The hook MacApp uses to do this is the method `Free`, defined in the base class `TObject` and thus made available in all classes. For example, suppose we declared the class `TStageDirectionsView` to have a field named `fDirections` of some subclass of the class `TList`. We would implement the method `Free` as follows:

```
procedure TStageDirections.Free; override;
begin
    fDirections.FreeList;
    inherited Free;
end;
```

Here we first free the space associated with the field `fDirections`, and then call the corresponding method in the object's superclass chain. This style of programming is quite typical of applications written in object-oriented programming languages: the body of the method is concise because it adds only class-specific behavior to the superclass.

Documents generally know best when to create windows, but only windows hold the secrets of how they themselves are created. In a similar fashion, windows embody the knowledge of how to draw themselves, but not when to be drawn. Instead, an application object decides when to redraw a window; for example, when a new document is opened, or when a user clicks on a partially obscured window to activate it. Ultimately, a call is made by an application object to the window method `Update`, which in turn invokes the window `DrawContents`. The effect of `DrawContents` is to call the method `Draw` for the window itself, and then call the method `DrawContents` for each of its subviews. In this manner, drawing proceeds from the top of the superview/subview relationships down, and eventually recurses to cover all subviews that are part of a given window.

The method `Draw` must be redefined for each domain-specific view; for example, `TStageDirectionsView` and `TPaletteView`. The class `TView` defines this method with a null implementation, although certain subclasses have a default implementation for `Draw` and so are rarely redefined (for example, `TSScrollbar`, which displays the standard Macintosh scollbar). Typically, each domain-specific view class contains a field that denotes the objects to be displayed in the view, representing its model. This collection of objects is usually heterogeneous, meaning that they may all be of different classes. For example, in Figure 9-3, the view includes text as well as lines (and rectangles and circles, according to the palette). It is in this situation that polymorphism becomes so useful: we may declare an object of class `TList` as a collection of objects, each of which may be of a different class, but all of which share a common class ancestry to some subclass of `TObject`; for example, we might call this class `TDrawableObject`. Because of the requirements of Object Pascal's typing semantics, we must declare the method `Draw` in this common subclass, but then we must redefine this method in each of `TDrawableObject`'s subclasses to supply class-specific behavior. Thus, to draw the contents of the view whose state consists of a collection of these objects, we simply iterate through the list and invoke the method `Draw` for each object that we find there. If we need to modify our application so that the view can display instances of new classes, we need never modify that view's drawing implementation; instead, we need only create new subclasses of the class `TDrawableObject`.

The object diagram in Figure 9-4 illustrates MacApp's drawing mechanism. The key objects involved in this mechanism are a window, its subviews, and the model displayed by each subview. For our purposes, we consider `fSubViews` to be a private field, because the collection object that this field denotes may not be shared with any other object beyond the window itself (although limitations of Object Pascal make this field public). However, the contents of this collection, namely the window's subviews, are shared objects, because they may be referenced by objects other than the parent view. In particular, each individual subview is typically visible as a field of the enclosing document. Similarly, a subview's model is visible as a field of the subview, and this is also typically a shared field, since the model may be visible in more than one view.

The object diagram in Figure 9-4 captures the static relationships among the objects involved in MacApp's drawing mechanisms. However, recall that an object diagram only represents a snapshot in time of an otherwise transitory event or configuration of objects. Objects such as windows and views are created and destroyed during the lifetime of a program, and thus object diagrams can only capture the most interesting patterns of interactions among a given set

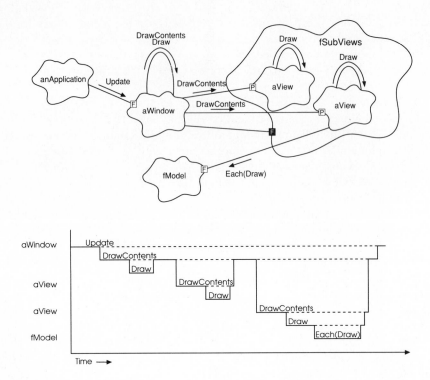

Figure 9-4
MacApp Drawing Mechanism

of objects at a single point in time. For this reason, we use the timing diagram in Figure 9-4 to capture the dynamic aspects of MacApp's drawing mechanism. To draw the contents of a window, some client invokes the window's method `Update`, which in turn invokes the method `DrawContents`. `DrawContents` first invokes the method `Draw` for the window itself, and then `DrawContents` for each of the subviews found in the collection `fSubViews`. `DrawContents` for each subview invokes the method `Draw` for that subview and then invokes `DrawContents` for each of its subviews, and so on, until there are no other subviews left to visit.

It is in the implementation of each view's `Draw` method that we find the domain-specific behavior. For example, if a view has the field `fModel` denoting a heterogeneous list of drawable objects, a typical implementation of the view's `Draw` method is to iterate through all the objects defined in this collection, passing to them the message `Draw`. The individual objects that appear in the view must be defined to embody the knowledge of how to draw themselves (for instance, by making calls to various QuickDraw routines), but they need not know when they are to be drawn.

Without changing the fundamental aspects of this mechanism, we can greatly improve its performance. As we hinted earlier, a model is typically larger than can be displayed in a single window. The view that directly encloses such a model may therefore extend to several physical pages, although the constraints upon the screen size limit us to showing only part of this view in a window. This is the motivation for the class `TScroller`. Specifically, a `TScroller` object is responsible for mapping a part of the image in a scrollable view to a (usually) smaller window. Thus, when we draw a large view, we do not need to draw every object in the view, since many of these objects will fall outside the visible part of the view. The need for optimization becomes more apparent when we realize that the time complexity of drawing an object is at least an order of magnitude greater than that of not drawing that object at all. For this reason, MacApp passes the parameter `Area` to the method `Draw`. When the `Draw` method for a given view is invoked, MacApp first determines the rectangular coordinates of the area that must be redrawn. For example, if a window that was partially obscured by another becomes activated or if a client scrolls a view, MacApp can determine the minimal area of the view that has been invalidated and therefore must be redrawn. The value of this area is passed to the method `Draw` for the view, so that in the implementation of each view's `Draw` method, drawing an object that is outside the invalidated region may be avoided by first checking to see if that object's image overlaps with the value of the area parameter. If it does, then the object is drawn; otherwise, nothing happens.

A domain-specific client can use the same mechanism. For example, suppose we have an application in which a user may apply tools selected from a palette to add, delete, and reposition objects within a view. Whenever an object is modified in a view's model, the area enclosing the affected object may be made known to the view by using one of the view's invalidation methods (such as the method `InvalidRect` defined in the class `TView`). The effect of this method is to accumulate areas of the view that are obsolete and therefore must be redrawn; the area parameter passed to the view's `Draw` method is simply the union of all these invalidated areas.

Tracking and Responding to a Mouse Action. Applications such as the geometrical optics construction kit allow a considerable amount of user interaction through both the keyboard and mouse actions, such as clicking, dragging, and sketching. Earlier, we noted that the class `TView` is a subclass of the class `TEvtHandler`, which embodies the knowledge of how to respond to keystrokes, menu commands, and mouse hits. Returning to Figure 9-3, suppose a user clicked the mouse somewhere inside the scrollable view, in order to select a paragraph for deletion. The mechanism whereby the application responds to this mouse action is illustrated in the object diagram in Figure 9-5.

Here we see that a mouse down event is first detected by an application object, using the main event loop mechanism that we will describe in more.detail shortly. A mouse down event may happen at one of several locations on the screen, namely:

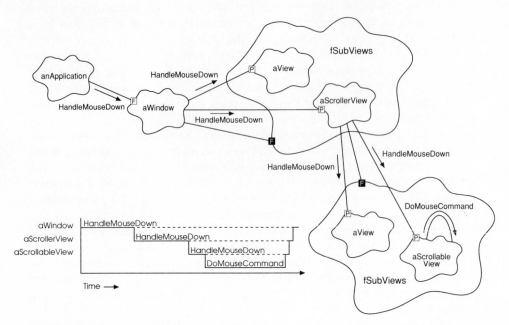

Figure 9-5
MacApp Mouse Action Mechanism

- On the menu bar
- Outside an application window
- In the growbox of an application window
- In the goaway box of an application window
- In the zoom box of an application window
- In the contents of an application window

We will describe the mechanism that MacApp uses to respond to mouse down events in the menu bar later. MacApp automatically handles mouse down events at the next four locations, although the default response can be overridden. To handle a mouse down event in an application window, the user must provide some domain-specific processing.

MacApp's drawing mechanism gives every subview contained in a window the opportunity to draw itself, starting at the top of the superview/subview chain and moving down until all views have been visited. MacApp's mouse action mechanism works very differently: MacApp searches for the bottom-most view in the superview/subview chain that intersects with the location of the mouse action and by default, only that view is given an opportunity to respond to the mouse action. As Figure 9-5 indicates, once an application object detects a mouse down event in the contents of an application window, the application invokes the method `HandleMouseDown` for the corresponding window object. If that window is not the front window (the timing diagram does not show this for reasons of simplicity), `HandleMouseDown` first selects the window to make it active. To locate the lowermost subview enclosing the point of the mouse hit, `HandleMouseDown` next traverses the superview/subview chain using the iterator `LastSubViewThat`, defined in the class `TView`. Because views may have subviews, as in the window/scroller/scrollable view hierarchy shown in Figure 9-5, `HandleMouseDown` is called for each nested view. When `HandleMouseDown` reaches a subview that intersects with the location of the mouse action, and if that subview is at the bottom of the superview/subview chain, then the method `DoMouseCommand` is invoked for that view alone. Searching the superview/subview chain ceases once we encounter a view that meets these criteria.

Domain-specific behavior must be supplied for the method `DoMouseCommand`, much as for the method `Draw` in MacApp's drawing mechanism. In the class `TView`, the implementation of the method `DoMouseCommand` is essentially empty. How we override this method depends upon the requirements of the particular problem domain. For example, if the view is a palette, then the typical action of `DoMouseCommand` is to deselect the last selected tool and then highlight the tool that appears under the mouse cursor. If the view is a scrollable view containing text and graphics, as in Figure 9-3, then the mouse action typically represents the selection or deselection of certain objects, the start of the user dragging all selected objects, or the start of the user applying the currently selected palette tool.

MacApp's typical style is to have `DoMouseCommand` create command objects as agents that do the real work. For example, instead of actually dragging the currently selected objects, `DoMouseCommand` might create a `DraggerCommand` object as an instance of a domain-specific subclass of the class `TCommand`. The value of creating command agents rather than doing the work directly in the view is three-fold. First, it provides greater separation of concerns, allowing views to focus on drawing and detecting events, and command objects to focus on doing, redoing, and undoing actions. Second, we achieve a greater degree of reuse and thus end up writing less code: the behavior embodied by command objects is often needed by both the menu command mechanism and the mouse action mechanism. Third, this approach is more resilient to change. For example, if we wanted to change the visual feedback provided while dragging selected objects, we would not have to alter every view class, but would probably only have to modify certain command methods.

Responding to a Menu Command. When an application detects a mouse down event in the menu bar, MacApp responds through its menu command mechanism. This mechanism cannot use the same superview/subview relationships as the mouse action mechanism, primarily because objects other than views and windows must be given the opportunity to respond to certain menu commands. In particular, views and windows know nothing about opening and closing documents, but documents and applications do; thus they must participate in the menu command mechanism.

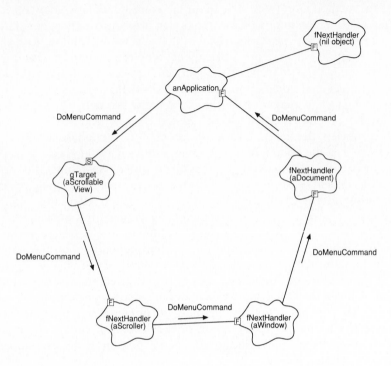

Figure 9-6
MacApp Menu Command Mechanism

The menu command mechanism uses an abstraction called the *command chain*, as we show in the object diagram in Figure 9-6. The command chain is formed using the field fNextHandler, defined in the class TEvtHandler. Thus, every subclass of TEvtHandler, including views, documents, and applications, has this field. The command chain is built by MacApp whenever such an object is initialized. Specifically, every subview is made to point to its superview, every window is made to point to its enclosing document, and every document is made to point to its application object. This command chain is thus much more complex than the superview/subview list. Not only does this chain encompass objects other than view and window objects, but every application object may be referenced by multiple documents, every document may be referenced by multiple windows, and every window may be referenced by multiple views.

The purpose of the command chain is to collect the objects that can respond to a menu command, ordered according to which is in the best position to take action. Specific subviews are given the first chance, followed by their superviews, then their containing window, their document, and finally their application object. Notice that this chain does not start with an application object but with a much lower level object. The head of this chain is designated by the global variable gTarget (by convention, MacApp names all global variables g<something>). Whenever a window is activated, gTarget is typically set to the subview that is most interested in a menu command. For a window that encompasses multiple subviews, a client designates this particular subview when the window is created. The free subprogram `NewPaletteWindow`, for example, designates the scrollable view as the one most interested in menu commands. This convention implies that some subviews might not normally be given the opportunity to participate in the command chain. For example, a palette view is never likely to be part of a command chain, since there is little it could do to respond to any menu command.

When a mouse down event is detected in the menu bar, the application's method `HandleMouseDown` first calls the Macintosh Toolbox routine `Menu-Select` to determine which menu and item were selected. Among other things, this free subprogram tracks the mouse, highlights all enabled menu items, pulls down the menu, and finally returns when the mouse button is released. Assuming that the user did not abandon the menu command by releasing the mouse outside of a menu item, the application object next invokes its method `MenuEvent` to determine which menu and which item were selected and to encode this menu/item pair into a single number, called a *command number*. As Figure 9-6 indicates, the application then invokes the method `DoMenu-Command` for the object designated by the global variable `gTarget`. If this object is unable to respond to the command, the same message is passed to the next object in the chain. This process continues either until an object is found that can react to the menu command, or until `fNextHandler` is nil (which is MacApp's default value for this field in all application objects).

A developer must tailor `DoMenuCommand` to supply domain-specific behavior. Typically, the implementation of this method takes the form of a large case statement, such as the following:

```
begin
    DoMenuCommand := gNoChanges;
    case ACmdNumber is
        cSelectAll:   ...
        cCut:         ...
        cCopy:        ...
        cPaste:       ...
        cClear:       ...
        kDrawingSize: ...
        otherwise     DoMenuCommand := inherited DoMenuCommand(ACmdNumber);
    end;
end;
```

MacApp style names all command constants c<something>, and other kinds of constants as k<something>. Our convention is to name all problem-specific constants k<something> also.

`DoMouseCommand` must test for whatever commands can reasonably be handled by all objects of the given class. For example, a scrollable view might be able to respond to selection, cutting, copying, pasting, clearing, and drawing size commands. A document, on the other hand, might only respond to printing, saving, and reverting commands. If the designated object cannot handle the command, as the preceding code indicates, the approach is simply to call the corresponding method in the superclass. If the superclass cannot respond to this command, it tries its superclass, and so on. Assuming we find no intermediate superclass that can respond to the menu command, control eventually reaches the DoMenuCommand method defined in the class TEvtHandler, whose default implementation is to invoke the method DoMenuCommand for the next object in the command chain. Traversal thus stops when we reach an object whose field fNextHandler is nil (which is typically the value set in the application object). It is rare for traversal to reach the end of the chain, because this means we have a menu command to which no object can react.

With this mechanism, a designer can concentrate upon the desired domain-specific behavior for each class and rely upon default behavior for all common commands such as printing, opening, closing, and saving documents. As with the mouse action mechanism, the common style is for DoMenuCommand to create command objects as agents that do the real work, although an alternative is to do the work in place. We do not usually create command objects for simple actions such as selection; we use them for complex actions such as cutting, copying, pasting, and clearing. Especially if we want to be able to undo and redo an action, it is best to create a command object, and, if we want to use an action in other places, or if the action is particularly complicated, we should also create a command object.

The Macintosh User Interface Guidelines permit menu items to have keyboard equivalents. For example, the command key combination Command-X typically denotes the menu item Cut in the Edit menu. Responding to command key events reuses the menu command mechanism. Specifically, when an application detects a command key combination, the method DoCommandKey is invoked along the command chain. In the default implementation, DoCommandKey does nothing but pass control to the next object in the command chain so that control eventually reaches the application object, which in turn looks up the command number equivalent to the menu/item pair and then invokes the method DoMenuCommand, starting at gTarget and using this command number. The response to a keyboard command for other than a command key combination also uses the command chain. In this case, the method DoKeyCommand is invoked by the application, starting with the object designated by gTarget.

Responding to an Event. In all, there are eight external events to which a MacApp application can respond:

- Mouse up
- Mouse down
- Window activate
- Update window
- Key down
- Disk

- System
- Alien

Many of these events are handled automatically by MacApp. Specifically, it detects and responds to window activation events, window update events, disk insertion and disk ejection events, MultiFinder events, and network events. Mouse up events are generally ignored in applications, except for when the user drags the mouse, double- or triple-clicks the mouse, or releases the mouse button over certain control objects.

MacApp detects all of these events as part of its main event loop mechanism. This mechanism serves as the canonical structure of most modeless applications, that is, those in which we place few constraints upon the order in which a user may interact with the system. In this mechanism, the main thread of control for the application consists of a loop, during which we first either poll or wait for an event. Once an event is detected, we invoke some appropriate operation to handle it. The loop terminates only when the user quits the application.

In MacApp, instances of the class `TApplication` act as agents responsible for carrying out the main event loop mechanism. Therefore, rather than structuring the root of our application as if it were the top of an algorithmic decomposition, we use the main program primarily to declare an instance of a `TApplication` subclass and then invoke its `Run` method (which ultimately drives the action of the main loop). The advantage of using an application object rather than applying an algorithmic abstraction at the root of the application is that this gives us a consistent conceptual model, since everything else in our application consists of sets of collaborating objects.

As explained in Chapter 3, it is good design style to create classes that export primitive operations. For this reason, the method `Run` does not encompass the code for the main loop mechanism directly; rather, it splits its work across several methods. This makes it far easier for a designer to tailor the default behavior of an application object. Briefly, the effect of the method `Run` is to invoke the method `MainEventLoop`. In each pass through the loop, `MainEventLoop` first invokes the application method `PollEvent`, which looks for new events. If an event is found, then `MainEventLoop` invokes the method `GetEvent` to retrieve all the information about the event and then invokes the method `HandleEvent`. `HandleEvent` in turn invokes the application method named `DispatchEvent`, which dispatches a method (such as `HandleMouseDown`) appropriate to the specific kind of event.

Applications in which human/machine interactions dominate frequently involve relatively long periods of time during which the application has nothing to do. The user often spends many seconds thinking about what to do next, during which time valuable computing cycles are wasted. To allow the application to do useful work during these otherwise idle periods, the main event loop mechanism also employs what it calls an *idle chain*. The idle chain is a simple list of objects, each of which is an instance of some subclass of `TEvtHandler`. The head of this list is indicated by the global variable `gHeadCohandler`, and objects are linked via the field fNextHandler, as defined in the class TEvt-Handler. This is the same field used to form the command chain, but since the command chain and the idle chain are orthogonal concepts, a given object (typically) never appears in both chains at the same time.

When there are no events pending, the main event loop mechanism traverses the idle chain, invoking the DoIdle method of each object it encounters, so that object can do whatever domain-specific processing it desires. Every object in the chain also has the field fIdleFreq (defined in the class TEvtHandler), which indicates how often its DoIdle method is to be called. For example, if an application called for a view with some simple flashing elements, then we would probably want an appropriate DoIdle method to be called only every few clock ticks, not every idle cycle.

Saving and Restoring the State of an Application in a Document. The user of the geometrical optics construction kit must be allowed to create optics experiments, manipulate them, and save them for later use. However, MacApp does not embody anything as sophisticated as an object-oriented database, and so does not directly support object persistence. Instead, we must use some other mechanism to provide the illusion of persistence.

MacApp uses the class TDocument to save the state of an application. Logically, a document serves as a heterogeneous repository of anything the application needs to save between executions. For example, a document for the geometrical optics construction kit might represent a single optics experiment consisting of the state of all the lenses arranged along an optical bench. A document might also preserve the state of the application's printer characteristics, user preferences, or the location and size of all currently activated windows.

TDocument is a subclass of the class TEvtHandler, but adds several new fields, such as fTitle (its name), fWindowList (a list of windows belonging to the document), and fChangeCount (the number of changes in the document's state since it was last saved). Typically, a designer never uses this class directly but instead defines a subclass that, among other things, includes a field for each important subview and a field that designates the document's persistent state. We keep this state with the document rather than with the view that displays it simply because views are transitory, whereas documents exist for the meaningful lifetime of the model. Furthermore, since the same model is often shared by more than one view, placing the model with its document provides a stable reference point for each of the more transitory views.

A MacApp program can only have one application object, although each application object may use several, possibly different, document objects. A document object is typically created whenever the application is launched or whenever a user selects the New or Open menu items in the standard File menu. Ultimately, each of these actions results in the invocation of the application method DoMakeDocument. A domain-specific implementation of this function must be provided in a subclass of the class TApplication, and its imple-

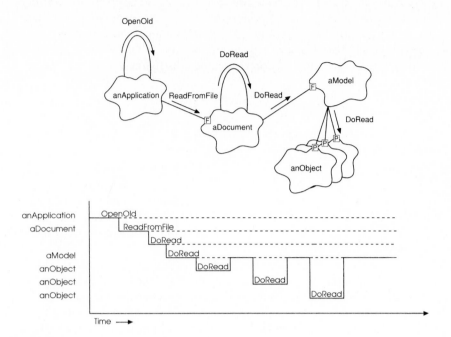

Figure 9-7
MacApp Document Mechanism

mentation is usually quite simple: a document object is created, initialized, and then returned as the function value.

Figure 9-7 illustrates MacApp's document mechanism, whereby the persistent state of the document is recovered. This mechanism starts after the corresponding document object has been created in DoMakeDocument. When the user opens an existing document, either by selecting the Open menu item in the File menu or by opening the document from the Macintosh Finder, a call is made to the application method OpenOld. This method invokes the method ReadFromFile defined in the document class. If the physical file named by the document can be opened, then ReadFromFile invokes the document method DoRead, which we must implement for each TDocument subclass.

Consider the subclass TStageDirectionsDocument, containing the field fDirections to represent the document's persistent state. We must first define some DoRead method for this collection, which we can use as follows:

```
procedure TStageDirectionsDocument.DoRead (ARefNum : Integer;
                                           RsrcExists,
                                           ForPrinting : Boolean); override;
begin
    inherited DoRead(ARefNum, RsrcExists, ForPrinting);
    fDirections.DoRead(ARefNum);
end;
```

We call the inherited `DoRead` method first to give MacApp the opportunity to read in its state (such as printer preferences). Since a document's state typically includes a collection of heterogeneous objects, saving a document must encode the class of each object before registering its state. Then, when `fDirection`'s `DoRead` method is called, its action may appear as follows:

```
<read a value indicating the number of objects that follow>
for Index := 1 to Count do
    begin
        <read a value indicating the class of the object that follows>
        <clone a copy of an object of this class>
        AnObject.DoRead(ARefNum);
    end;
```

This approach is similar to the drawing mechanism, in which the real work is ultimately done by the lowest-level objects. As we will see later, the paradigm of cloning objects from prototypes is a useful one and can be used to create other objects, such as the tools defined by a palette.

At this point, we have only touched upon the more important classes in MacApp. For example, we have not yet studied the class `TTEView` along with its subclasses and mechanisms, which together provide the characteristics of a simple text editor supporting multiple fonts, sizes, and styles. Neither have we studied the mechanisms embodied in `TGridView`, nor the classes that support debugging and error recovery. Finally, we have not presented the classes associated with dialogs. As it turns out, the distinctions between a dialog and a simple window are intentionally blurred by MacApp. Indeed, the simple mechanisms presented so far are fundamental parts of all these other classes. This is not surprising, for as we noted in Chapter 1, systems that exhibit complex behavior are often constructed using only a few relatively simple mechanisms. This is certainly true of MacApp.

On a practical note, we must point out that there are limits to the use of MacApp. In particular, the realities of MacApp's memory management approach limit the number of objects one can create in an application to something on the order of a few thousand, depending upon the complexity of each object. Whereas MacApp is perfectly suited to applications such as the geometrical optics construction kit, different approaches must be used for applications such as computer-aided design (CAD) tools or solids modeling programs, which may include tens of thousands of objects. This does not mean that we must forgo the object model, nor abandon the use of MacApp entirely; it does mean that we must sometimes rely upon hybrid designs. Specifically, instead of treating each conceptual object as a concrete instance of a `TObject` subclass, we may instead have to use simple Pascal types to form the application's model, although we might still be able to use MacApp classes to form the user interface.

9.2 Design

Module Architecture

Decomposing Macintosh Applications. In Smalltalk, the class is the only enforceable unit of decomposition. Although Smalltalk's system browser provides a way to assign classes to different categories, this concept is only marginally useful because it does not restrict the visibility of any class within a group. Consequently, all classes declared within a Smalltalk environment are globally visible. This is not a problem for small systems, but as we scale up to larger and larger applications, we soon reach a point where the lack of a module structure makes our design totally incomprehensible. Without a means of collecting abstractions into increasingly larger chunks, we soon reach the limits of the human ability to comprehend many things at once.

Fortunately, Object Pascal provides a structure for decomposing large systems into separate modules, allowing us to hide certain classes and objects from one another and generally reduce dependencies among abstractions. This is particularly important in a strongly typed language. If we do not reduce dependencies among abstractions, we soon find ourselves constantly recompiling almost everything whenever we make even the smallest of changes. In large systems that evolve over time, this can have a profound effect on schedules, and can actually inhibit change. Using modules to group abstractions and enforce visibility decisions ultimately increases our confidence in the stability and correctness of our system.

In Object Pascal, the syntactic structure for a module is called a *unit*. A unit has two separate parts: an interface and an implementation. A unit interface may contain only constants, types, variables, and function and procedure specifications, and any methods or free subprograms declared in the interface of a unit must be completed in the implementation of that unit. Thus, an interface provides the outside view of an abstraction, and its implementation hides the inside view.

Declarations may be placed in the implementation of a unit, but these are visible only in the implementation of that unit and are therefore hidden from the outside. In particular, we can declare a class in the implementation of a unit so that it cannot be referenced by any other unit. Conversely, any declarations placed in the interface of a unit are visible in the implementation of that unit, as well as in all other units that use that unit. Figure 9-8 illustrates these points. If the implementation of unit C requires the declarations of D, then C must use D. Unlike Ada, Object Pascal only permits dependencies to be asserted in the interface of a unit, even if the used unit is needed only in the implementation. Suppose that a method declared in the interface of unit B needs to name a class or type declared in the interface of unit C. B must use C, but does not need to use unit D. If the interface of unit A needs to see a declaration from the interface

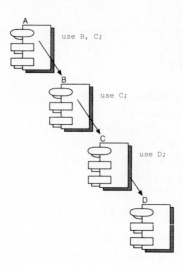

Figure 9-8
Object Pascal Module Architecture

of unit B, then A must also use B. However, since the interface of B depends upon C, unit A must also use unit C.

MacApp enforces a second module structure needed for the Macintosh. Specifically, every application has two parts, a *data fork* and a *resource fork*. Documents associated with an application typically use the data fork to store their state; applications typically use only the resource fork to store their code as well as other resources such as menus, fonts, icons, pictures, and window templates. The advantage of these resources is that they allow us to change the outward appearance of an application without recompiling its source code. For example, suppose we originally wrote a program under the assumption that it would be used only by people who could read English, and that now we wanted to port this application for release in France and Japan. If we had hard-coded the names of menu items or the text in dialog boxes, we would have to modify our source code and recompile everything. This not only leaves us with a configuration management and version control problem, but also reduces our confidence in the correctness of each new version, since we might inadvertently introduce some changes in one version and not the others. If we place these resources in a resource file instead, we only need to modify the application's resources to change its outward appearance, without affecting the source code.

How does the presence of these module structures affect our design? We could just ignore them, and declare everything in one unit. This is not a good idea, because it doesn't address the visibility problems we encounter with Smalltalk. We could go to the other extreme, and place every class in a different unit. This too would be suboptimal; in large systems, we would end up with hundreds if not thousands of such units, making it very difficult even to locate the classes in which we are interested. Furthermore, placing them all in separate

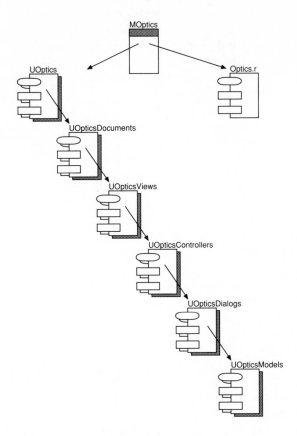

Figure 9-9
Geometrical Optics Construction Kit Module Diagram

units actually increases the complexity of the system, because it requires us to cope with a very tangled web of unit dependencies.

The proper answer is somewhere in the middle of these two extremes, and the techniques presented in Chapter 4 can help lead us to a well-engineered module decomposition. In practice, we have found it best to create modules organized around meaningful collections of classes and objects. By *meaningful,* we mean that each abstraction within such a group is more tightly coupled with other abstractions in the group than with abstractions outside of the group.

Decomposing the Geometrical Optics Construction Kit. Figure 9-9 illustrates our design of the module architecture for the geometrical optics construction kit. Our application is divided into one main program (MOptics), one resource file (Optics.r), and six units. Because we expect each of these units to be large, we can use a compiler directive to force their code to be placed in separate memory segments. Segment allocation is clearly a separate issue than selecting a class and object structure, and doing it as part of the design of the module architecture allows us to reason properly about alternate segmentation approaches without affecting any other part of our design.

The distinct layering of modules in this architecture derives from two factors. The first is past experience. Having built several dozen MacApp applications, we have tried many different module architectures; some of them worked well, and some did not, and the module architecture in Figure 9-9 is just an incarnation of our latest canonical decomposition. This is an example of the reuse of a design. In retrospect, what has worked well is the result of sound engineering principles, which leads us to the second factor. When we decompose a system into modules, the key criterion we apply is the separation of concerns: abstractions should be placed in separate modules if they are loosely coupled. Furthermore, if a certain design decision is likely to change, it is best to hide it so as to shield other abstractions from the consequences of any changes.

Thus, at the bottom of the architecture we have the module UOptics-Models, which contains all the classes and objects related to the essential elements of an optics experiment. This one unit encapsulates most of the domain-specific behavior of the application; every other unit is primarily concerned with the user interface. Next up the module hierarchy is the unit UOpticsDialogs, which contains all the facilities needed to present dialogs for user interaction. UOpticsControllers is built on top of both UOpticsDialogs and UOpticsModels, and in this unit we have all the classes and objects related to user commands. The units UOpticsViews, UOpticsDocuments, and UOptics, in that order, come next. We keep these units separate because they embody three entirely different mechanisms.

For simplicity, Figure 9-9 does not include any of MacApp's units; to do so would make the diagram needlessly complicated, and besides, the purpose of the diagram is to illustrate the domain-specific module architecture of the system. Our conceptual model is that all of MacApp's classes and objects are primitive abstractions visible anywhere in our application.

Notice also that we decided to make each lower level unit visible to the interface of the next higher one. Thus, UOpticsDialogs must use UOpticsModels, UOpticsControllers must use both UOpticsDialogs and UOpticsModels, and so on. Ultimately, the main program, MOptics, must use all six lower level units. We could have reduced these dependencies (although only very slightly), since the interface of each high-level unit must see almost every unit below it. We decided not to optimize these dependencies because to do so would actually have reduced the understandability of the implementation (by making its module architecture irregular). Anyway, eliminating the one or two extraneous dependencies would not greatly affect recompilation time. In fact, during the evolution of our implementation, each unit interface remained relatively stable, and most changes, as we expected, occurred in unit implementations, thus minimizing recompilation due to the obsolescence of other units.

Why did we create the module architecture for our application before we designed its class and object structure? In practice, we sometimes find it useful to sketch out a rough module architecture first, because this gives us a framework in which to incrementally develop our domain-specific classes and objects. For small- to moderate-sized systems such as the geometrical optics construction kit, designing with units or packages provides a suitable framework. For larger systems, such as the one described in Chapter 12, we must design with still higher level subsystems. In each case, these modules form the units of configuration management and version control, as well as the boundaries along which we assign work to members of a development team.

The primary motivation for developing a module architecture early is that this approach encourages early and incremental integration. Thus, one of the first things we might do is create all of these units (each initially empty) and then compile, link, and execute the resulting null program. In this manner, we exercise our programming tools early and ensure that they can accommodate such an architecture. Then, as we incrementally design the classes and objects of our application, we can first test them outside of this framework and then eventually add them to a framework that we already know is stable and functional. Each executable version of our application thus grows in functionality over time, in very controlled, predictable ways.

Object Structure

In the design of the home heating system, all domain-specific objects were static. This is typical of a few problem domains, but it is certainly not characteristic of the vast majority of automatable problems we will ever encounter. For example, the design of the geometrical optics construction kit involves only one obviously static object: the application object itself. At any one time, each application object may include a number of documents, each representing a different optics experiment, and each optics experiment may include an arbitrary number of lenses. Additionally, because this is a modeless application, various command objects, view objects, and dialog objects may be created and destroyed during the lifetime of the application. Just as we did in describing MacApp's key mechanisms, we may use object diagrams to represent the key mechanisms among transitory objects that form our design of the geometrical optics construction kit.

From the requirements, we know that an optics experiment consists of a set of lenses arranged along an optical bench. If we trace the principle rays of light from some real object through this series of lenses, the resulting ray trace may converge to generate images (both real and virtual). This describes the state of an optics experiment. To put it in object-oriented terms, the properties of every optics experiment include a collection of lenses, a set of images, a set of rays, and one real object, and the exact values of these properties may vary from time to time as a user interacts with the application to add, delete, and move individual lenses. We may capture this design decision about the structure of an object experiment in the object diagram of Figure 9-10.

As Figure 9-11 indicates, individual optics experiments do not exist in isolation; they interact with the elements of MacApp's key mechanisms, namely, documents, views, and commands. Here we see that a document consists of an

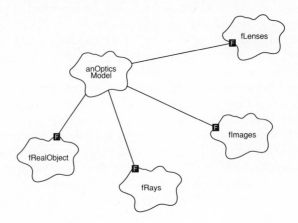

Figure 9-10
Optics Experiment Object Diagram

optics experiment and a view; this is an application of MacApp's document mechanism. Using MacApp's drawing mechanism, the view and the optics experiment work together to keep the visible display of the experiment up to date with the current state of the experiment. Using MacApp's command mechanism, commands may also be created by the view and act as agents that alter the state of an experiment in various ways.

Remember that an object diagram simply shows prototypical patterns of action. Therefore, whether a particular optics experiment contains one or one hundred lenses, or the current command object represents a dragging, sketching, cutting, copying, clearing, or pasting action, the same relationships and interactions apply as shown in the figure.

Class Structure

Identifying the Key Abstractions. As we move farther into the design of the geometrical optics construction kit, we discover that it involves a number of objects that are different yet have common properties. For example, the requirements speak of three kinds of diverging lenses and three kinds of converging lenses. All six of these objects are undeniably lenses, but each has a different shape, and the diverging and converging lenses have different refractive properties. Because we can identify clusters of certain kinds of objects such as these, we must consider the inheritance relationships among the abstractions that exist in our problem domain. If we do not, our design will be the worse for it; we will end up writing more code (because we have not exploited the commonality among abstractions), and our design will not be as extensible nor as maintainable. This is a different situation than in the home heating system; in that problem, inheritance issues were not a dominant concern.

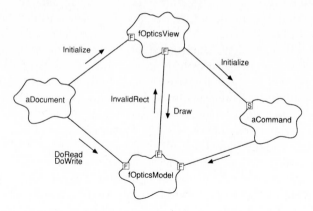

Figure 9-11
Geometrical Construction Kit Object Diagram

A large part of the class structure of an optics experiment is fairly intuitive: there is a class `TLens`, and the classes `TConvergingLens` and `TDivergingLens` both inherit from this base class. Additionally, the following classes are kinds of converging lenses, and therefore inherit from the class `TConvergingLens`:

- `TDoubleConvexLens`
- `TPlanoConvexLens`
- `TConvexMeniscusLens`

The following classes are kinds of diverging lenses, and therefore also inherit from the class `TDivergingLens`:

- `TDoubleConcaveLens`
- `TPlanoConcaveLens`
- `TConcaveMeniscusLens`

Images (both real and virtual) and real objects are also related. Both kinds of objects appear in an optics experiment, except that the one real object is static in a given experiment, and all other images are dynamically conceived. Because in our view of the world these are sufficiently different concepts, we chose to invent two classes, `TRealOrVirtualImage` and `TRealObject`, both of which share common behavior as subclasses of the class `TImage`.

Are the differences between real and virtual images sufficient to warrant inventing two separate classes? According to the requirements, the only difference between these two kinds of objects is that real images must appear in dark gray, and virtual images must appear in light gray. From this line of reasoning, we could make a case for inventing two classes. However, whether an image is real or virtual is simply a matter of which side of a lens that image appears on relative to the location of its original image. Thus, as an alternate approach, we could use state internal to an image (its position relative to the lens) to decide whether to display that shape in dark or light gray. With this approach, one class would suffice. Which design is better? In our opinion, both approaches have merit. However, because we can find no truly compelling reason to create two classes, we will stay with just one class, `TRealOrVirtualImage`.

There is still more commonality to be uncovered. Is there any similarity among lenses and images? The answer is yes: lenses and images both can be displayed in a view, and thus it is likely that there are fields and operations common to these two broad classes of objects. For this reason, we can invent a class `TShape`, which acts as the superclass to both the classes `TLens` and `TImage`.

Our requirements speak of rays of light, and thus we can invent the class `TRays` to capture the behavior common to all rays. Because rays, like lenses and images, can be displayed in a view, we can make `TRays` a subclass of `TShape` also.

As we pointed out in Chapter 3, if an object is composed of other objects, then its class must use the classes of its components. This is the case for the class `TOpticsModel`, which encapsulates the state common to all optics experiments and so uses the classes `TLens`, `TImage`, and `TRays`.

An optical bench also qualifies as an object, because it is a crisply defined abstraction. Although it does not participate in a ray trace, it is a tangible entity, and according to the requirements, it may or may not be visible under user command. For this reason, we invent the class `TOpticalBench` as an adornment to the view that displays an optics experiment.

Figure 9-12 captures most of these class decisions. For simplicity, we have left out the using relationships for the class `TOpticsModel`. Notice also that we have marked several of the classes (such as `TLens`) as abstract classes, since they are generalized classes that require further specialization before any instances may be created.

We must be frank and say that we have made this part of the design look much easier than it actually was. Figure 9-12 represents the class design as it finally appeared, not as it actually evolved. At first, we designed the six kinds of lenses as immediate subclasses of the class `TLens`. As we evolved the design of each class, we realized that there was a pattern. The three converging lenses and the three diverging lenses were sufficiently similar in their representation and behavior that we invented the two intermediate abstract classes, `TConvergingClassLens` and `TDivergingLens`, which we used to collect the common representation and behavior of each kind of lens. This ultimately simplified the design of each of the six most specialized classes. Similarly, we discovered a pattern among lenses, the real object, rays, and images, which led us to invent the class `TShape`. By so doing, we moved the representation and behavior common to all of these subclasses up to a more abstract class, again reducing the overall amount of code we had to write.

This kind of class reorganization is not unusual during the process of development and is simply an example of round-trip gestalt design at work. Of

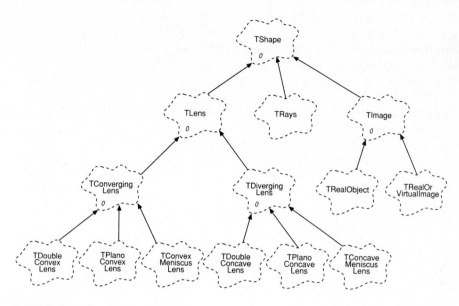

Figure 9-12
Optics Experiment Class Diagram

course, we cannot allow this all the time; if we did, we would be forever making interface changes and spending most of our time recompiling units. Given a large system, each developer would bog down waiting for another's work to become more stable, and eventually, all meaningful progress on the project would cease. In practice, however, what happens is that the class structure of a system tends to be unstable for a while, but then eventually stabilizes as the key architectural decisions are worked out. After that point in development, usually marked by the time at which other developers begin to write code on top of these interfaces and therefore come to demand stability, the only changes one typically makes to a class structure involve inventing new subclasses or adding operations to the interfaces of existing classes. This was exactly our experience with the design of the geometrical optics construction kit. The moral here is to plan for change, because it will happen. To inhibit changing an already spectacularly suboptimal design means that you will be stuck with a suboptimal design for a very long time. Of course, the time may come when the consequences of early bad design decisions make future progress impossible, at which point we have little choice but to correct our design flaws. Such changes are usually much more costly than if we had addressed the problems early on, but still less costly than if we keep hoping that the problem will disappear if we ignore it.

We can now design the interface of each of our classes. We could write a class template for each, but given that Object Pascal is a reasonably expressive language, it is just as good to write these immediately in the implementation language itself. However, we must be careful to avoid making premature repre-sentation decisions. As we have said before, the representation of a class should generally follow the decisions regarding its expected behavior. Thus, we can tune the representation to make it optimal for the expected use of the class; to do otherwise is particularly bad, because clients often come to depend upon a premature representation that is likely to change over time.

Design of the Optics Model. TShape provides the behavior common to all classes that can be drawn in a view. This means that it must embody knowledge about MacApp's drawing mechanism and must know about concepts such as invalidating a view. We might begin the interface to this class as follows:

```
TShape = object (TObject)
    ...
    procedure TShape.IShape (AnOpticsModel : TOpticsModel);
    procedure TShape.Invalidate;

    function TShape.Frame : Rect;

end;
```

The ellipses indicate where we must eventually declare the fields of this class, which we defer because it is an implementation decision.

Note that we have declared the method IShape, which by convention we must call immediately after creating a new object of the class. We typically pro-vide such operations in Object Pascal, because, unlike C++, Object Pascal does not let us declare constructor or destructor operations, and unlike Smalltalk, Object Pascal does not support metaclasses. We have also declared the proce-dure Invalidate to support MacApp's drawing mechanism. This procedure uses the utility function Frame, which returns a rectangle enclosing the object. We exposed this function because we will need it later in support of MacApp's mouse action mechanism.

We have not exported any draw methods because, as we will see, each of the subclasses of TShape requires a slightly different set of parameters from its own Draw method. Since Object Pascal does not support the overloading of method names, we cannot declare these different draw methods in one place.

The class TLens is a bit more complicated because it must embody the behavior common to all lenses. Its interface appears as follows:

```
TLens = object (TShape)
    ...
    procedure TLens.IShape (AnOpticsModel : TOpticsModel); override;
    procedure TLens.SetFocalLength (NewFocalLength : FocalLength);
    procedure TLens.Select;
    procedure TLens.Deselect;
    procedure TLens.Invalidate; override;
    procedure TLens.Highlight (FromHL, ToHL : HLState);
    procedure TLens.DrawLens (DrawPosition : Boolean);
    procedure TLens.Draw (Area : Rect; DrawPosition : Boolean);
    procedure TLens.DoRead (ARefNum : Integer);
```

```
procedure TLens.DoWrite (ARefNum : Integer);

function TLens.DiskSpace : LongInt;
function TLens.Frame : Rect; override;
```

```
end;
```

This class exports the procedure `IShape`, which we override from `TShape`. The procedure `SetFocalLength` exists to do just as its name suggests, but why didn't we just declare some field `fFocalLength` that a client might access directly? To do so would have led to clients that depended upon this specific implementation of this class, not its abstract qualities. Besides, changing the focal length of a lens has a side effect beyond just giving a new value to some field. Specifically, changing the focal length of a lens forces the calculation of a new ray trace. Exposing this method ensures that when a lens is given a new focal length, its enclosing optics model is notified.

The procedures `Select` and `Deselect` are primitive operations upon all lenses and are needed to support MacApp's mouse action mechanism. For example, a user might click the mouse on a lens shown in a view, and ultimately the method `Select` would be called to select that lens.

`Invalidate`, `Highlight`, `DrawLens`, and `Draw` exist to support MacApp's drawing mechanism. We expose `DrawLens` as a primitive operation that always draws a lens (and its position along the optical bench, if the optical bench is visible), as well as the composite operation `Draw`, which calls `DrawLens` only if the frame of the lens falls within the invalidated part of the view.

`DoRead`, `DoWrite`, and `DiskSpace` exist to support MacApp's document mechanism. `DiskSpace` calculates the amount of storage needed to save the state of the object, and `DoRead` and `DoWrite` do the actual work of restoring and saving this state.

The interfaces to the classes `TConvergingLens` and `TDivergingLens` are quite simple. In each, we must override the `IShape` method so that the state of each kind of object is properly established. Thus, we might write

```
TConvergingLens = object(TLens)

    procedure TConvergingLens.IShape (AnOpticsModel : TOpticsModel); override;

end;
```

In a similar manner, the interface of each of the six most specialized lens classes need only override the `IShape` method of its superclass. For example, we might write the interface to the class `TDoubleConvexLens` as follows:

```
TDoubleConvexLens = object(TConvergingLens)

    procedure TDoubleConvexLens.IShape (AnOpticsModel : TOpticsModel); override;

end;
```

It might seem perverse that we have so many small classes like TConverging-Lens and TDoubleConvexLens. Our reasons are worth repeating: there is great value in building simple classes that embody only very specialized behavior. Common behavior then tends to migrate to generalized classes, which means less code has to be written (and therefore maintained), and this leads to improved extensibility and maintainability. Equally important, we strive to invent classes that speak the vocabulary of the problem domain, so that we end up with an application that is inherently understandable. Classes such as TConvergingLens and TDoubleConvexLens are in fact important elements of the problem; by creating these classes, we concretely capture our view of the real world.

Turning to the class TRays, an instance of this class represents all the principle rays that pass through a single lens. Is this class sufficiently primitive? Why don't we instead define a TPrincipleRays class, with subclasses for each of the three principle rays? We could do so, but, at least for the present problem, this would add complexity. As it turns out, the principle rays that pass through a single lens are all intimately related: they all start from the same real object, real image, or virtual image, and they all focus on the same real or virtual image. Furthermore, once we calculate the point at which any two of these rays focus, we can calculate the path of the third ray very easily. If we treated all three rays independently, we would actually end up doing one-third more processing than we really needed. For these reasons, we decided to define the class TRays as encompassing the behavior of all three of the principle rays of a lens.

For the most part, this class requires an interface similar to that for the class TLens: we need operations such as IShape, DrawRays, Draw, and Frame to support MacApp's drawing mechanism. Since the semantics of TRays represent the three principle rays, we must invent a method that sets the state of ray objects so that DrawRays and Draw can do their work properly. According to the requirements, a principle ray is drawn from a real object (or real or virtual image) through a lens. The ray that emanates from the lens can then be drawn back to either a real image (if it focuses on the side opposite the side of the original image) or a virtual image (if it focuses on the same side as the original image). Thus, a single ray may be defined by two contiguous line segments, whose end points are at the original image, somewhere along a line perpendicular to the optical axis, and at the resulting real or virtual image. Therefore, all three principle rays will intersect at the resulting real or virtual image (assuming that they focus at a point other than infinity and assuming we ignore noise due to spherical aberration.

Given only a real object or real or virtual image plus the lens it passes through, it is possible to define a primitive operation for TRays that calculates the point at which its principle rays intersect. The resulting point, together with the original image and the lens, is sufficient state from which we can properly draw all three principle rays. For this reason, we will export the method SetPoint that performs this action, although we can defer how SetPoint works. As we will see shortly, we must revert to structured design methods to further decompose this method, and in so doing, we uncover some additional classes that are relevant to our design.

Given these design decisions, we may write the interface for the class `TRays` as follows:

```
TRays = object (TShape)
   ...
   procedure TRays.IShape (AnOpticsModel : TOpticsModel); override;
   procedure TRays.SetPoint (FromImage : TImage; ThroughLens : TLens);
   procedure TRays.DrawRays;
   procedure TRays.Draw (Area : Rect);

   function TRays.Frame : Rect; override;
   function TRays.ImageAt : Point;

end;
```

As is our style, whenever we define a modifier such as `SetPoint`, we also define a selector such as `ImageAt`, which returns the state associated with the modifier.

The interface of the class `TImage` is very similar to that of `TLens`. The purpose of `TImage` is to capture the behavior common to all real objects and real and virtual images. Thus, we might write the interface of `TImage` as follows:

```
TImage = object (TShape)
   ...
   procedure TImage.IShape (AnOpticsModel : TOpticsModel); override;
   procedure TImage.DrawImage;
   procedure TImage.Draw (Area : Rect);

   function TImage.Frame : Rect; override;

end;
```

`TImage`'s two subclasses mostly redefine these operations. Thus, we might write

```
TRealObject = object (TImage)
   ...
   procedure TRealObject.DrawImage; override;
   procedure TRealObject.Draw (Area : Rect); override;

end;
```

```
TRealOrVirtualImage = object (TImage)
   ...
   procedure TRealImage.SetPosition (TheTop : Point; FromLens : TLens);
   procedure TRealImage.DrawImage; override;
   procedure TRealImage.Draw (Area : Rect); override;

end;
```

The class `TRealOrVirtualImage` exports the method `SetPosition`, whose purpose is to establish the location of the image relative to a given lens. If it is located on the same side of the lens as the real object, we know it is a virtual image; if it is located on the opposite side, we know it is a real image. SetPosition is defined here because it can only be implemented if we have access to the underlying representation of the class.

To complete our design of the key classes involved in optics experiments, we must define the interface of TOpticsModel, which encapsulates all the objects directly related to an experiment. As for the class TLens, we must provide operations that support MacApp's document, drawing, and mouse action mechanisms. Thus, we must include methods such as IOpticsModel, SelectAll, Draw, DoRead, and DiskSpace.

To identify the remaining operations that this class must export, we must think about the behavior we desire for all objects of this class. Since an optics experiment logically includes a collection of lenses, we must include modifiers such as AddLens and RemoveLens, selectors such as NumberOfLenses, and iterators such as EachLens. Should we similarly expose operations that allow a client to manipulate the rays and images that form an experiment? Our answer is a resounding no. A client can do nothing intelligently with these objects, and so we choose to hide the rays and images in the implementation part of an optics experiment.

However, an optics experiment embodies sufficient knowledge and state to accomplish the ray trace, and therefore we choose to export the method TraceRays. This method is at the center of all the domain-specific algorithmic activity within this application. In spite of its importance, we need not worry now about how to implement it; to do so would be defocusing: its implementation would lead us into issues that are at a very low level of abstraction. Fortunately, as we will soon see, its implementation turns out to be quite simple because of the rich interfaces we have already engineered for the class TLens and its subclasses.

Combining all of these design decisions, we can now write the interface of TOpticsModel:

```
TOpticsModel = object(TObject)
    ...
    procedure TOpticsModel.IOpticsModel;
    procedure TOpticsModel.Free; override;
    procedure TOpticsModel.TraceRays;
    procedure TOpticsModel.AddLens (ALens : TLens);
    procedure TOpticsModel.RemoveLens (ALens : TLens);
    procedure TOpticsModel.SelectAll;
    procedure TOpticsModel.DeselectAll;
    procedure TOpticsModel.Highlight (FromHL, ToHL : HLState);
    procedure TOpticsModel.Draw (Area : Rect; DrawPosition : Boolean);
    procedure TOpticsModel.DoRead (ARefNum : Integer);
    procedure TOpticsModel.DoWrite (ARefNum : Integer);
```

```
function TOpticsModel.DiskSpace : LongInt;
function TOpticsModel.CurrentSize : Point;
function TOpticsModel.NumberOfLenses : Integer;
function TOpticsModel.NumberOfSelections : Integer;

procedure TOpticsModel.EachLens (procedure DoToLens (ALens : TLens));
function TOpticsModel.FirstLensThat (function TestLens
                            (ALens : TLens) : Boolean) : TLens;

end;
```

As is our style, and for readability, we have grouped operations as modifiers, selectors, or iterators.

Now that we have defined its interface, let's consider a representation for TOpticsModel. There are a couple of obvious implementations: using a single heterogeneous list of lenses, images, and rays, or using separate lists. We would argue that using a heterogeneous list gives rise to a more complicated and less efficient implementation of certain methods. For example, deleting a lens would require traversal over a list of objects, some of which are guaranteed not to be lenses. Also, calculating a ray trace first involves destroying all old images and rays and then generating new ones, and destroying old images and rays encounters the same problem as deleting lenses from a heterogeneous list. For these reasons, we treat the state of an optics experiment as distinct collections of homogeneous objects. Thus, we may write its fields as follows:

```
fView       : TView;
fLenses     : TLensList;
fImages     : TList;
fRays       : TList;
fRealObject : TRealObject;
```

A model must know the view in which it appears (so that it can invalidate lenses, images, and rays as they change), and so we have included the field fView.

Regardless of the representation, we have to worry about garbage, because the state of an experiment is dynamic; thus we export the method Free. Why did we not export Free in any other class? The answer is that there is a fundamental difference between the state of TOpticsModel objects and objects of any TShape subclass. Objects of the class TOpticsModel encapsulate other objects (such as lenses); thus when we are done with a particular optics model (for example, when we close a document), we must also free its subobjects. On the other hand, the state of objects such as those in the class TLens is quite simple (consisting mainly of scalar values); thus they contain no other objects that need to be freed.

This completes our design of the interfaces for the key classes associated with an optics experiment. According to our module architecture for this system, each of the classes we have described are declared in the interface of the unit UOpticsModels.

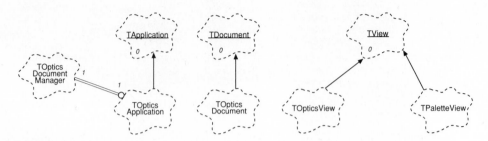

Figure 9-13
Application, Document, and View Class Diagram

Design of the User Interface Classes. The design of the classes comprising the user interface of this application use inheritance quite heavily to specialize existing MacApp classes. Their interfaces include few new operations; instead, they mostly redefine operations defined in their superclass. For the novice to MacApp, knowing what operations to override is often a matter of trial and error, but for the developer who is familiar with MacApp's mechanisms, the task is usually quite straightforward.

Figure 9-13 provides the class structure for the application, document, and view classes of the geometrical optics construction kit. Because the predefined MacApp classes TApplication, TDocument, and TView are essential to this design, we have included them in this diagram; we have underlined their class names to indicate that they are imported from outside our application.

As this diagram shows, we have invented the classes TOpticsApplication and TOpticsDocument, which inherit from the predefined classes TApplication and TDocument, respectively. Similarly, we have created the classes TOpticsView and TPaletteView as subclasses of the class TView. The remaining class in this diagram, TOpticsDocumentManager, is an invention arising from a given requirement. Specifically, our application is required to support up to four documents at one time. Because the processing needed to switch from experiment to experiment is logically self-contained, yet somewhat different than the usual document processing provided by MacApp, we have decided to define a class responsible for providing this behavior. Encapsulating the knowledge of how to manage multiple documents in one class simplifies the subclass TOpticsApplication. The other compelling reason for inventing this class was our expectation that the requirement to process up to four experiments at one time was one that could very likely change. Instances of the class TOpticsDocumentManager must keep track of four different documents. From the outside, we see that this class should know how to add a new document to the application (when the user selects New or Open in the File menu), how to delete a document from the application (when the user selects Close in the File menu), and how to rename a document (when the user selects Save As... in the File menu). Additionally, this class should know how to activate the window associated with a document when the user selects that document's name from an appropriate menu. These four modifiers are primitive operations because we can only implement them if we have access to the underlying implementation of the class; thus, they should be included in the interface of `TOpticsDocumentManager`. With regard to selectors, this class embodies sufficient knowledge to know if any more documents can be opened, or if there are any open documents at all.

We may now write the interface to `TOpticsDocumentManager` as follows:

```
TOpticsDocumentManager = object(TObject)
    ...
    procedure TOpticsDocumentManager.IOpticsDocumentManager;
    procedure TOpticsDocumentManager.DoSetUpMenus;
    procedure TOpticsDocumentManager.AddDocument (ADocument : TOpticsDocument);
    procedure TOpticsDocumentManager.DeleteDocument (ADocument : TOpticsDocument);
    procedure TOpticsDocumentManager.RenameDocument (ADocument : TOpticsDocument);
    procedure TOpticsDocumentManager.FocusOnADocument (ACmdNumber : CmdNumber);

    function TOpticsDocumentManager.CanAddDocument : Boolean;
    function TOpticsDocumentManager.HasOpenDocuments : Boolean;

end;
```

This class also exports the method `IOpticsDocumentManager` to initialize objects, and the method `DoSetUpMenus`, which we need to support MacApp's menu command mechanism.

The class `TOpticsApplication` comes next. For the most part, this class simply redefines certain operations of its base class, `TApplication`, to support domain-specific processing of menus and documents. Because we want this class to use the facilities of the document manager we just designed, we must include a field in `TOpticsApplication` to hold an object of the class `TOpticsDocumentManager`. This field represents a domain-specific state, and therefore we must include appropriate initialization and garbage-collection methods. Thus, we may write the interface to TOpticsApplication as follows:

```
TOpticsApplication = object(TApplication)

    fOpticsDocumentManager : TOpticsDocumentManager;

    procedure TOpticsApplication.IOpticsApplication;
    procedure TOpticsApplication.Free; override;
    procedure TOpticsApplication.DoSetUpMenus; override;
    procedure TOpticsApplication.AddDocument (ANewDocument : TDocument); override;
    procedure TOpticsApplication.DeleteDocument (DocToDelete : TDocument); override;

    function TOpticsApplication.DoMenuCommand
       (ACmdNumber : CmdNumber) : TCommand; override;
    function TOpticsApplication.DoMakeDocument
       (ItsCmdNumber : CmdNumber) : TDocument; override;
    function TOpticsApplication.MakeViewForAlienClipboard : TView; override;

end;
```

`MakeViewForAlienClipboard` exists to support the Macintosh clipboard. When a given application starts, there may be objects in the desk scrap (left over from the clipboard of another application) that the geometrical optics construction kit could process. This method checks for the existence of such objects and creates a clipboard to store any that are found.

The two classes `TOpticsDocumentManager` and `TOpticsApplication` are declared in the unit `UOptics`, in accordance with our earlier module architecture.

The design of the class `TOpticsDocument` is much like that for `TOptics-Application`. Its purpose is primarily to redefine certain methods from its superclass in order to support domain-specific processing of MacApp's menu command and document mechanisms. Thus, we may write its interface as follows:

```
TOpticsDocument = object(TDocument)
    ...
    procedure TOpticsDocument.IOpticsDocument;
    procedure TOpticsDocument.Free; override;
    procedure TOpticsDocument.DoMakeWindows; override;
    procedure TOpticsDocument.DoMakeViews (ForPrinting : Boolean); override;
    procedure TOpticsDocument.DoNeedDiskSpace (var DataForkBytes,
                                      RsrcForkBytes : LongInt); override;
    procedure TOpticsDocument.DoRead (ARefNum : Integer;
                            RsrcExists,
                            ForPrinting : Boolean); override;
    procedure TOpticsDocument.DoWrite (ARefNum : Integer;
                             MakingCopy : Boolean); override;

end;
```

This class is declared in the interface of the unit `UOpticsDocuments`.

Turning to the classes `TOpticsView` and `TPaletteView`, objects of these two classes collaborate to produce a palette window much like that shown in Figure 9-3. Instances of the class `TOpticsView` display the elements of a given optics experiment, whereas instances of the class `TPaletteView` provide a selection of tools that the user may apply to create and modify an optics experiment shown in a corresponding optics view object.

For the most part, the interface of the class `TOpticsView` simply redefines certain operations of its superclass, `TView`, in support of MacApp's drawing and menu command mechanisms. For this reason, we must override the methods `CalcMinSize` (to accommodate variable-sized views), `DoHighlightSelection`, `Draw`, `DoSetUpMenus`, `DoMouseCommand`, `DoMenuCommand`, and `DoSetCursor`.

The requirements state that optics view objects may contain several visual adornments, including grid lines, page breaks, and an optical bench, each of which may or may not be visible according to user preference. These adornments are fundamental to the domain-specific tailoring of this class, and therefore it is reasonable to explicitly export operations that provide this behavior, such as `ToggleDrawOpticalBench` and `ToggleDrawGridlines`. We have decided to export operations that toggle the appropriate Boolean state rather than export two operations that explicitly set a `True` or `False` state for each adorn-ment. This achieves a better mapping to MacApp's menu command mechanism, in which certain menus simply toggle from one state to another. Be aware, however, that these operations do more than just set the state of some Boolean field. As we will see, changing the state of one of these adornments also forces an update of the view. Should we also export selector operations that retrieve the state of these properties? In theory, yes, but because Object Pascal does not encapsulate its fields, and because this state is so primitive, we choose to let a client directly access the appropriate state. This is different than our design decision for the selectors defined in the class `TOpticsDocumentManager`, because in this latter case, we expect that each returned value would have to be calculated rather then accessed directly in a field.

Concerning its representation, each optics view must have visibility to the model that it displays, to conform with MacApp's drawing mechanism. Because we have separated the classes `TOpticsModel` and `TOpticalBench`, we must therefore include two fields, one for each of these objects. An optics view must also have visibility to its palette, so that the view knows which tool the user has selected. Thus, we must include a field to hold a palette object. Finally, we must include a Boolean field for each of the adornments that may be toggled in a view.

Given these design and implementation decisions, we may write the inter-face to `TOpticsView` as follows:

```
TOpticsView = object (TView)

    fOpticsModel      : TOpticsModel;
    fOpticalBench     : TOpticalBench;
    fPaletteView      : TPaletteView;
    fDrawOpticalBench : Boolean;
    fDrawGridLines    : Boolean;
    fDrawPageBreaks   : Boolean;
    fAutoGridEnabled  : Boolean;

    procedure TOpticsView.IOpticsView (ADocument : TDocument;
                                       APalette : TPaletteView;
                                       AModel : TOpticsModel);
    procedure TOpticsView.CalcMinSize (var MinSize : VPoint); override;
    procedure TOpticsView.ToggleDrawOpticalBench;
    procedure TOpticsView.ToggleDrawGridLines;
    procedure TOpticsView.ToggleDrawPageBreaks;
    procedure TOpticsView.ToggleAutoGridEnabled;
    procedure TOpticsView.DoHighlightSelection (FromHL, ToHL : HLState); override;
    procedure TOpticsView.DrawGridLines (Area : Rect);
    procedure TOpticsView.Draw (Area : Rect); override;
    procedure TOpticsView.DoSetUpMenus; override;

    function TOpticsView.DoMouseCommand (var TheMouse : Point;
                                         var Info : EventInfo;
                                         var Hysteresis : Point) : TCommand; override;
    function TOpticsView.DoMenuCommand (ACmdNumber : CmdNumber) : TCommand; override;
```

```
function TOpticsView.DoSetCursor (LocalPoint : Point;
                                  CursorRgn : RgnHandle) : Boolean; override;

end;
```

An object of the class `TPaletteView` presents to the user a palette of tools from which to make a selection. For our application, the relevant tools include a pointer (for selecting lenses) and drawing tools for each of the six kinds of lenses that we must model. `TPaletteView` must encapsulate the knowledge of how to draw these tools as well as how to react to the selection of a new tool by a user. In our design, a palette object doesn't know what to do with a tool, but the view does. Therefore, our design decision is that when a user selects a new tool, a palette object needs only to deselect the old tool and highlight the new one. The display view corresponding to this palette can query the palette for the currently selected tool (which is either a pointer or a lens) when it needs to. To support these decisions, we must provide selectors for the class `TPaletteView`, such as `IsPointer` (returning `True` if the pointer tool is currently selected and `False` otherwise) and `CurrentTool` (which returns an object of a subclass of `TLens`, corresponding to the currently selected lens drawing tool). We may therefore write the interface to this class as follows:

```
TPaletteView = object (TView)
    ...
    procedure TPaletteView.IPaletteView (ADocument : TDocument;
                                         AModel : TOpticsModel);
    procedure TPaletteView.DoHighlightSelection (FromHL, ToHL : HLState);
                                                 override;
    procedure TPaletteView.Draw (Area : Rect); override;

    function TPaletteView.DoMouseCommand (var TheMouse : Point;
                                          var Info : EventInfo;
                                          var Hysteresis : Point) : TCommand;
                                          override;
    function TPaletteView.IsPointer : Boolean;
    function TPaletteView.CurrentTool : TLens;

end;
```

Notice that `CurrentTool` returns an object of the class `TLens`. In reality, however, this function will always return an object of some subclass of `TLens`, such as the class `TPlanoConcaveLens`. Our design of the class structure for the lenses results in all of the interesting behavior common among lenses being defined in the class `TLens`. Therefore, any client that accesses the current tool of a palette can fully manipulate the resulting lens object, even though the exact class of this object cannot be known until execution time. In situations like this, polymorphism and dynamic binding serve us very well. Fortunately, because the resulting objects all share a common class ancestor, `TLens`, we still get the benefits of Object Pascal's compilation-time type checking.

In accordance with our module architecture, the classes `TOpticsView` and `TPaletteView` are declared in the interface of the unit `UOpticsViews`.

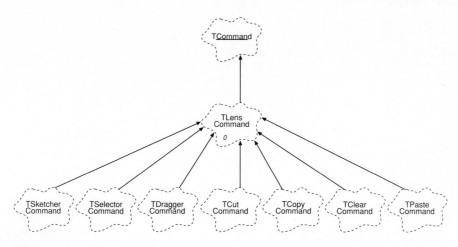

Figure 9-14
Optics Commands Class Diagram

Design of the Experiment Commands. Domain-specific commands are the only other classes essential to our design. According to the requirements, our application must support sketching new lenses along an optical bench, selecting existing lenses, and dragging all selected lenses. Consistent with the Macintosh User Interface Guidelines, our application must also support cutting, copying, clearing, and pasting of lenses within a given optics experiment as well as among experiments. MacApp provides the class TCommand as part of its menu command mechanism, and therefore we can invent subclasses of this class to support all the various domain-specific commands that we need.

Figure 9-14 captures our design decisions regarding these classes. At the bottom of this class hierarchy are seven very specialized classes that are all subclasses of the class TLensCommand, which in turn is a subclass of the MacApp class, TCommand. At first, we made each of the seven specialized classes a direct descendent of TCommand, but we soon discovered a pattern. Each command object needs to have a field that designates the model upon which it acts, and each command needs to share common behavior for constrained mouse tracking. For these reasons, we invented the class TLens-Command and migrated all of this common behavior from the seven specialized classes to this intermediate, abstract class.

We may next write the interface of the class TLensCommand. Because a command acts upon the lenses in an optics experiment, TLensCommand must include a field of the class TOpticsModel. For reasons that will become evident later, we will also include a Boolean field that indicates whether or not the lenses being manipulated by the given command object should display their positions along the optical bench.

Thus, we may write

```
TLensCommand = object(TCommand)

    fOpticsModel  : TOpticsModel;
    fDrawPosition : Boolean;

    procedure TLensCommand.ILensCommand (ASuperView : TView;
                                         AnOpticsModel : TOpticsModel;
                                         DrawPosition : Boolean);
    procedure TLensCommand.TrackConstrain (AnchorPoint,
                                           PreviousPoint : VPoint;
                                           var NextPoint : VPoint); override;

end;
```

The interfaces of all seven specialized classes look very similar. For the most part, we must redefine operations such as `Commit`, `DoIt`, `UndoIt`, and `RedoIt`, which provide the command-specific behavior for each class and are needed to support MacApp's menu command mechanism. How are these methods ever called? Through MacApp's main event loop mechanism, the application method `HandleEvent` first reacts to an event by invoking the method `DispatchEvent`. Once `DispatchEvent` is executed, control returns to `HandleEvent`, which then invokes the application method `PerformCommand` to process any command the event handler may have created (for example, via a domain-specific implementation of `DoMouseCommand`). `PerformCommand` does its most important work by calling the method `DoIt` of the corresponding command object. In a similar fashion, the `UndoIt` and `RedoIt` methods are invoked by the application object as part of its standard menu handling methods.

We can now write the interface of the class `TSketcherCommand` as follows:

```
TSketcherCommand = object(TLensCommand)

    fLens : TLens;

    procedure TSketcherCommand.ILensCommand (ASuperView : TView;
                                             AnOpticsModel : TOpticsModel;
                                             DrawPosition : Boolean); override;
    procedure TSketcherCommand.Free; override;
    procedure TSketcherCommand.Commit; override;
    procedure TSketcherCommand.DoIt; override;
    procedure TSketcherCommand.UndoIt; override;
    procedure TSketcherCommand.RedoIt; override;
    procedure TSketcherCommand.TrackFeedback (AnchorPoint,
                                              NextPoint : VPoint;
                                              TurnItOn,
                                              MouseDidMove : Boolean); override;

    function TSketcherCommand.TrackMouse (ATrackPhase : TrackPhase;
                                          var AnchorPoint, PreviousPoint,
                                          NextPoint : VPoint;
                                          MouseDidMove : Boolean) : TCommand;
                                          override;

end;
```

Because a sketcher object must sketch a particular kind of lens, this class includes the field `fLens` to store this state. As we explain later, a view is responsible for creating a sketch command and then sets this field via the `CurrentTool` method of its corresponding palette object.

Because they are so similar, we will not show the interfaces of the other specialized command classes. All seven classes, as well as the class `TLensCommand`, are declared in the interface of the unit `UOpticsCommands`.

What of the unit `UOpticsDialogs`? Our style is to export a very narrow interface for application-specific dialogs. Dialog windows are commonly constructed from the MacApp classes `TDialogView`; dialog controls are usually instances of classes such as `TPicture`, `TPopup`, `TButton`, `TEditText`, and `TStaticText`. In fact, only a few circumstances require that we invent new dialog subclasses, and virtually all of these classes can be hidden inside the implementation of the dialog unit. Therefore, we can use the unit `UOptics-Dialogs` to export a set of free subprograms that, at a high level of abstraction, exist only to display different dialogs and then return values set by user interaction in the dialog.

What dialogs do we need? This is a different kind of design decision than those we have made so far, for now we must consider the look and feel of the user interface. Our problem requires a window-based system that uses menu selection and mouse action; beyond that, we have little guidance. At this point in our design, we have invented the soul of the application, consisting of its key classes and essential mechanisms. Now we must turn to the design of its user interface, which is best done by devising a consistent, uniform model of interaction for the application as a whole.

9.3 Evolution

User Interface Implementation

The art of user interface design confronts the developer with a myriad of possibilities. For example, should we use a simple command-line interpreter, or perhaps pull-down menus instead (or both)? Must we assume that our output devices are just simple, character-based terminals, or will our displays allow us to devise a kinder, gentler interface using multiple, overlapping windows with graphic views that can be panned and zoomed? And what about commands themselves: should we use cryptic yet concise abbreviations, such as *grep* and *mkfs*, or should we use longer, more meaningful names? Human factors, technical constraints, historical reasons, and the personal preferences of the development team conspire to make crafting a useful, expressive, and self-consistent human/machine interface a very difficult task indeed. Fortunately, standard user interfaces such as Motif [11] and the routines embodied in MacApp have come a long way in helping developers build applications that have a distinctive look and feel.

As we have already seen, we can separate detailed user-interface design decisions from some of the high-level software design decisions. The user interface required by many problems is for the most part often only a cosmetic veneer that surrounds the core of the application, and thus it is possible to devise several different kinds of interfaces for the same system. For applications such as the geometrical optics construction kit and various drawing and painting programs, the user interface is more than a facade; a graceful and expressive user interface is essential to the usefulness of such products. Fortunately, by prototyping a user interface early, before we have completely implemented or even designed all of the mechanisms we need, we can encourage feedback from its eventual users. Timely user feedback helps us to tune the semantics of the interface so that it speaks directly to the vocabulary of the problem domain, and also helps us to purge it of all its idiosyncratic warts, nicks, and scratches.

Our choice of MacApp for our implementation immediately constrains the possibilities of the user interface. These constraints, as well as our requirements, mean that we expect to use windows, pull-down menus, and in fact the whole gamut of mechanisms described in the Macintosh User Interface Guidelines. Thus, our task simplifies to the problem of deciding upon the appearance of the various windows and dialogs in our application, and what menus and commands they use.

Window Design. Figure 9-15 shows a prototypical window that we might use to display an optics experiment, using a palette and a scrollable view. The palette contains a pointer and six sketching tools, one for each kind of lens. A user can click the mouse on the pointer or any one of the tools to select it. We indicate that a particular palette item is selected by reversing its image, as we have done for the pointer in this figure. We have also drawn the scrollable view with most of its adornments, including the optical bench, the one real object, and the horizontal and vertical grid lines.

Menu Design. The Macintosh User Interface Guidelines suggest that all menus should appear in the menu bar, unless there is a compelling reason to do otherwise, and that every application should contain certain standard menus. The first menu we should have is the `Apple` menu, designated by the character . The first item in this menu is used to bring up a dialog box containing the name of the application, its copyright, and, for some applications, help information. Our application uses the following name for this item:

• `About Optics…`

The ellipses indicate to the user that selecting this item will bring up a dialog box. The remaining items in the `Apple` menu are commonly dedicated to desk accessories.

The next standard menu is the `File` menu, whose purpose is to provide simple filing commands such as `Open`, `Close`, and `Save`. It also includes two

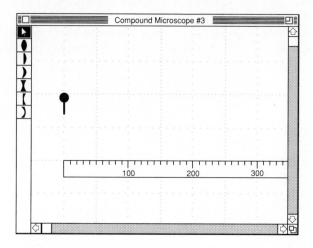

Figure 9-15
Geometrical Optics Construction Kit Window Design

printing commands and a command to quit the application. We include the following items in this menu:

- New
- Open
- Close
- Save
- Save as…
- Save a Copy…
- Revert to Saved
- Page Setup…
- Print…
- Quit

Some of these items, such as New, Open, and Save, have keyboard command-key equivalents (Command-N, Command-O, and Command-S, respectively) defined in the Macintosh User Interface Guidelines. Some menu items may be disabled at certain times. For example, Close should be enabled only when there is at least one open document, and Save should be enabled only when there is an open document that has been recently changed. Because the requirements call for our application to handle up to four open documents at one time, we enable New and Open only when there are less than four documents currently open. To give more positive feedback as to why a user is not allowed to create or open a document, we chose to bring up a dialog that warns a user who attempts to open more than four documents.

The third standard menu, `Edit`, typically includes commands to delete, move, and copy objects. We include the following items in this menu:

- `Undo`
- `Cut`
- `Copy`
- `Paste`
- `Clear`
- `Select All`
- `Show Clipboard`

Most of these items have standard keyboard command-key equivalents. Regarding the clipboard, when a user cuts or copies selected items, they are placed in a special view called the *clipboard*. Items can then be pasted from the clipboard back into an experiment. Since the contents of the clipboard persist after an application quits, the user can cut and paste items among applications, assuming that the applications agree as to the meanings of the items. The `Show Clipboard` command displays the clipboard view, so that the most recently cut or copied objects can be seen.

Now we turn to the nonstandard menus. We invent these menus and their items by asking ourselves what operations a user can perform upon this application as a whole. Not all such operations are well suited as menu items. For example, selecting, dragging, and sketching are best done via mouse actions. Several kinds of nonmouse operations come to mind, however: commands to display the various view adornments, commands to focus on one of the four open documents, and a command to view the properties of a selected lens. We choose to place these commands in one of two menus. The first, called `View`, contains the following items:

- `Drawing Size...`
- `Show Optical Bench`
- `Show Grid Lines`
- `Show Page Breaks`
- `Enable Autogrid`

Selecting the first item in this menu brings up a dialog whereby a user can adjust the size of the view, rounded up to the next largest page size. The remaining four items are toggled commands that reflect the state of a particular adornment. For example, when the optical bench is currently not visible, the second menu item reads as above. When this item is selected, causing the optical bench to be displayed, this item changes to:

- `Hide Optical Bench`

The remaining three menu items behave similarly.

We call the next menu `Experiments`, and it contains the following items:

- `<<...>>`
- `<<...>>`
- `<<...>>`
- `<<...>>`
- `Lens Specifications…`

The first four items represent the names of each of the four open documents. Whenever an existing document is opened, we want its name to appear as an item in this menu. If it is a new document, it is given a name by the application (of the form `Untitled` *n*, where *n* is a monotonically increasing number set by the application). When the application is closed, its name is removed from the menu, and the other names are moved up in the list. We must also remember to rename a document when the user selects the item `Save As…` from the `File` menu. When a user selects an item from the `Experiments` menu designating a particular document, we want the application to bring its corresponding window to the front, so that the user can easily find an experiment amidst all the windows that might clutter a screen.

The last item in this menu, `Lens Specifications…`, is enabled only when there is exactly one lens selected. When a user selects this item, a dialog box appears that shows the kind of the lens, its position along the optical bench, and its focal length. We will allow the user to edit only the focal length of the lens, as specified by our requirements.

As we noted earlier, resources such as menus are best defined in an application's resource file, so that we can change the outward appearance of the application without changing its source code. For example, we may capture our design decisions concerning the contents of the `View` menu by including the following in our resource file:

```
resource 'cmnu' (4) {
    4,
    textMenuProc,
    AllItems & ~(MenuItem2 | MenuItem6),
    enabled,
    "View",
    {/* [1] */ "Drawing Size..", noIcon, "", "", plain, 1001;
     /* [2] */ "-", noIcon, "", "", plain,   nocommand;
     /* [3] */ "Show Optical Bench", noIcon, "", "", plain, 1002;
     /* [4] */ "Show Grid Lines", noIcon, "", "", plain, 1003;
     /* [5] */ "Show Page Breaks", noIcon, "", "", plain, 1004;
```

```
/* [6] */ "-", noIcon, "", "", plain,   nocommand;
/* [7] */ "Enable Autogrid", noIcon, "", "", plain, 1005}
};
```

Dialog Design. Four relevant dialogs correspond to these menus: the About
Optics… dialog; a warning dialog to be used when four documents are already
open and the user tries to create or open another one; the Drawing Size… dialog; and the Lens Specification… dialog. It is not important that we implement
these dialogs now, but because we want them to have a uniform look and feel,
it is important to design them with a consistent style. This is why, in our
module architecture, we placed all dialogs in the unit UOpticsDialogs: being in
the same unit, they can share implementation secrets.

Figure 9-16 shows our prototype of the two most important dialogs. The
Drawing Size… dialog is quite complicated. A user can select the direction in
which pages are numbered (via the two radio buttons) as well as the page size
(by clicking the mouse on the grid, which in turn updates the highlighting and
the height and width static text items). What makes this dialog somewhat hard
to implement, although it is intuitive to the user, is that the grid can change,
depending upon the kind of output device used and the printing direction,
magnification, and paper size selected by the user. The second dialog, used in
the Lens Specification… command, is much simpler; it only allows the user to
edit the focal length item shown in the dialog.

At this point in our design, we can create an interface for these dialogs:

```
unit UOpticsDialogs; interface

uses
    UMacApp, UPrinting, UDialog, ToolUtils, Packages,
    UOpticsModels;

{$S UDial}
procedure InitializeOpticsDialogs;

procedure DisplayAboutOpticsDialog;

procedure DisplayNoMoreDocumentsDialog;

procedure DisplayDrawingSizeDialog (CurrentModelSize : Point;
                                    CurrentResolution : Point;
                                    CurrentPageSize : VPoint;
                                    var CurrentViewSize : VPoint;
                                    var CurrentDirection : VhSelect;
                                    var AcceptChanges : Boolean);
procedure DisplayLensSpecificationDialog(SelectedLens : TLens;
                                         var NewFocalLength : FocalLength;
                                         var AcceptChanges : Boolean);

implementation
    {$I UOpticsDialogs.incl.p}
end.
```

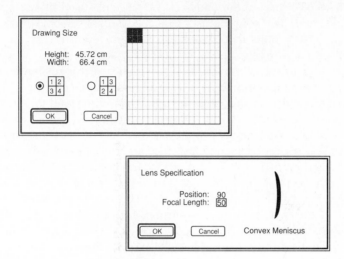

Figure 9-16
Geometrical Optics Construction Kit Dialogs

For completeness, we have provided the entire interface of this unit. Notice the use clause: it is here that we assert dependencies from this unit to other units that are part of MacApp (such as UMacApp, UPrinting, and UDialog) and that are part of our application's code (such as UOpticsModels). Notice also the compiler directive {$S UDial}, which directs that all the compiled code that follows be placed in the segment named UDial. Lastly, the free subprogram InitializeOpticsDialogs exists to initialize certain unit states, such as that of MacApp's dialog unit.

Implementing the User Interface Classes. We are now ready to implement all the unit interfaces we have designed. Because this book focuses on design, not coding, we do not provide a complete implementation of this program here. Besides, the final implementation consists of over 3,000 lines of Object Pascal, and almost 2,000 lines of source in the resource file (but on the other hand, can you imagine designing this application without using a rich class library such as MacApp?). However, there are still some design issues worth discussing. In particular, we need to show further how our design builds on MacApp's mechanisms. We also want to demonstrate how certain representation decisions naturally follow interface decisions. Lastly, we want to show again how, when using object-oriented design techniques, the design of a system evolves incrementally into a complete, executable implementation.

We can start implementing just about any unit body, but we choose to start with the classes that provide the application framework and the user interface so that we can immediately bring up completely executable systems, each with an increasing amount of functionality. Therefore, let us start with the class TOpticsApplication and its agent, TOpticsDocumentManager.

Earlier, we designed the menus and menu items used by the geometrical optics construction kit. From the user's perspective, these commands represent all the nonmouse actions that a user can perform upon the application as a whole. Since our design consists of objects that cooperate to achieve the uniform functionality perceived by the user, each object is responsible only for what it knows about the application's state and internal mechanisms. A corollary of this principle is that certain objects know how to respond to some, but not all, menu commands. A good example of this is found in the class `TOpticsApplication`. Instances of this class are in the best position to control the comings and goings of documents, since an application object is at a higher level of abstraction than a document object. In contrast, an application knows nothing about view adornments, because views are at too low a level of abstraction relative to an application object. Thus, an application object is the best agent in the system to be responsible for handling only certain menu commands such as `New`, `Open`, and `Quit`. Most of the standard commands, such as `Quit`, are handled automatically by MacApp. However, we need slightly deviant behavior for `New` and `Open`, since the application must handle no more than four documents. Our design provides this special document-handling behavior in the class `TOpticsDocumentHandler`, but a document handler object must work in cooperation with an application object. This is why we must override the method `DoMenuCommand` in the class `TOpticsApplication`, which we may implement as follows:

```
function TOpticsApplication.DoMenuCommand (ACmdNumber : CmdNumber) : TCommand;
                                           override;
begin
    DoMenuCommand := GNoChanges;
    case ACmdNumber of
        cAboutApp:
            DisplayAboutOpticsDialog;
        cNew, cOpen:
            if fOpticsDocumentManager.CanAddDocument then
                DoMenuCommand := inherited DoMenuCommand(ACmdNumber)
            else
                DisplayNoMoreDocumentsDialog;
        kDocumentA .. kDocumentD:
            fOpticsDocumentManager.FocusOnADocument(ACmdNumber);
        cSave, cSaveAs, cSaveCopy:
            fOpticsDocumentManager.RenameDocument
                (TOpticsDocument(GetActiveWindowDocument));
        otherwise
            DoMenuCommand := inherited DoMenuCommand(ACmdNumber);
    end;
end;
```

The implementation of this method is quite typical of the object-oriented style: it is short, and does most of its work by building upon lower level methods.

The common form of `DoMenuCommand` is a large case statement, which includes only those items that we can handle locally, named by constants such as `cAboutApp` (defined in MacApp) and `kDocumentA` (defined in our application).

The constants `kDocumentA` through `kDocumentD` represent the command numbers corresponding to the first four menu items of the `Experiments` dialog. The case statement ends with an `otherwise` clause, which invokes the corresponding superclass method to handle the commands that we cannot process locally.

Notice that in this code, much of the interesting work is done by the agent denoted by the field `fOpticsDocumentManager`. The application object and document manager object interact in some very subtle ways. For example, when the command `Open` is invoked and a call to the method `CanAddDocument` returns `True`, control passes to the method `DoMenuCommand` of the application's superclass. The default behavior provided by MacApp is to bring up a dialog with which the user can select a document and then open it. As part of this mechanism, a call is made to the method `AddDocument` defined for the application object. Our design of this class's interface replaces the default `AddDocument` method with our own, which we may implement as follows:

```
procedure TOpticsApplication.AddDocument (ANewDocument : TDocument); override;
begin
    fOpticsDocumentManager.AddDocument(TOpticsDocument(ANewDocument));
    inherited AddDocument(ANewDocument);
end;
```

Here, we first seek the aid of the document manager so that it properly updates the `Experiments` menu and then invoke the default behavior defined by our superclass' method.

Conceptually, a document manager object must keep track of from one to four documents. MacApp already maintains a list of open documents in the global variable `gDocList`, and in general it is foolish to reference an object from more than one place. However, remember that a document manager object sees its documents differently than MacApp does: this is in fact the domain-specific behavior that we desire. Specifically, a document manager object needs to know three things to do its job: the correspondence of a command number to a document, the mapping of a command number to a specific menu item, and the number of open documents.

This information represents the state of a document manager object, and thus we may select a representation for this class:

```
fCmdToDocMap       : array[kDocumentA .. kDocumentD] of TOpticsDocument;
fCmdToMenuItemMap  : array[kDocumentA .. kDocumentD] of Integer;
fNumberOfDocuments : Integer;
```

The first field, `fCmdToDocMap`, represents the mapping from a command number to a document object. This mapping provides greater informational content than does the simple list denoted by the global variable `gDocList`. The second field, `fCmdToMenuItemMap`, provides a mapping from each command number to a menu item. By defining our own local state, in effect we cache exactly the information we need and end up with a time-efficient implementation. This is the same rationale for including the third field, `fNumberOfDocuments`. We could just as easily have obtained this number by looking at the size of the list held in gDocList. However, keeping this local state makes our implementation faster (we avoid a method call to another object) and (we would argue) more understandable. Of course, the trade-off is that we must keep this local state consistent with its corresponding external state.

Bear in mind that the implementation we have chosen for the class TOpticsDocumentManager is but one possible approach. We chose this particular representation because we decided to trade off space for speed. If we realized after building this application that this was an awfully stupid thing to do (perhaps because our application was memory-constrained), we might have little recourse but to change the implementation of this class. Happily, because we designed this class by considering its abstract behavior before its representation, we could choose an alternate representation without violating the expectations of any other client. We would certainly have some recompilation ahead of us, but because we would end up changing only the representation of this class – which is largely hidden – we would not logically affect the semantics of any other object or class that depended upon TOpticsDocumentManager.

In the implementation of AddDocument in the class TOpticsApplication, we called a method of the same name defined in the class TOpticsDocument-Manager. Now that we have chosen a representation, we may implement this method as follows:

```
procedure TOpticsDocumentManager.AddDocument (ADocument : TOpticsDocument);
var
    Index : Integer;
    Menu  : MenuHandle;
    Title : Str255;
begin
    for Index := kDocumentA to kDocumentD do
    if (fCmdToDocMap[Index] = nil) then
        begin
            fCmdToDocMap[Index] := ADocument;
            Menu := GetMenu(kExperimentsMenu);
            HLock(Handle(ADocument.fTitle));
            Title := ADocument.fTitle;
            HUnlock(Handle(ADocument.fTitle));
            SetItem(Menu, fCmdToMenuItemMap[Index], Title);
            ADocument.fCommand := Index;
            leave;
        end;
    fNumberOfDocuments := fNumberOfDocuments + 1;
end;
```

Here we do the necessary work by updating the state of the maps that are local to the document manager object, and by building on lower level operations (such as the Macintosh Toolbox function, GetMenu). Ultimately, we set the name of the proper item in the Experiments menu with a call to the procedure SetItem. Notice that we must maintain the mapping of a document to its command in order to implement the methods DeleteDocument and Rename-Document; when a document is renamed, for example, we must change the name of the menu item corresponding to this document. We do this by storing the command number in a field defined for the document object. How do we know to enable this menu item? Through the document manager's method `DoSetUpMenus`, naturally. Each method therefore ends up being very small, and very focused.

When a user selects a menu item in the menu `Experiments`, the call to the application's method `DoMenuCommand` eventually calls the method `FocusOn-ADocument`, defined in the class `TOpticsDocumentManager`. This method then uses the state in the command number/document map (as set above) to activate the document corresponding to that item:

```
procedure TOpticsDocumentManager.FocusOnADocument (ACmdNumber :CmdNumber);
begin
    fCmdToDocMap[ACmdNumber].fOpticsWindow.Activate(True);
    fCmdToDocMap[ACmdNumber].fOpticsWindow.Select;
end;
```

Thus we have a clear separation of concerns: application objects know some things about documents, but only document managers know about the correspondence of command numbers and documents.

The method `DoMakeDocument` defined in the class `TOpticsApplication` is called when an existing document is created or opened. Our implementation of this method must therefore create and then initialize a document object, which becomes part of the application's state:

```
function TOpticsApplication.DoMakeDocument
    (ItsCmdNumber : CmdNumber) : TDocument; override;
var
    OpticsDocument : TOpticsDocument;
begin
    new(OpticsDocument);
    OpticsDocument.IOpticsDocument;
    DoMakeDocument := OpticsDocument;
end;
```

Here again, we have a concise implementation that builds upon lower level abstractions.

Turning to `TOpticsDocument`, note that this class represents a domain-specific tailoring of the predefined MacApp class, `TDocument`. As such, it participates in MacApp's document mechanism and therefore must know how to read and write optics experiments. Additionally, a document object must be responsible for managing the windows associated with the document. This behavior leads us to a choice of representation for this class. Specifically, we must maintain fields for the window, scrollable view, and palette associated with the document. As noted in our earlier discussion regarding MacApp's document mechanism, we must also maintain an object representing an optics experiment. Thus, we may complete the implementation of this class as follows, declaring it in the class declaration placed in the interface of the unit `UOpticsDocuments`:

```
fOpticsModel  : TOpticsModel;
fOpticsWindow : TWindow;
fOpticsView   : TOpticsView;
fPaletteView  : TPaletteView;
fCommand      : Integer;
```

The field `fCommand` derives from our need in the implementation of the class `TOpticsDocumentManager` to maintain a mapping from a document to a command number.

When a document is created or opened, the default MacApp behavior is first to create the document object via the application's method `DoMake-Document`. Next, and only if this is not a newly created document, the document's persistent state is read from disk, which results in a call to the document's method, `DoRead`. In our typical style, we implement this method by building upon lower level abstractions:

```
procedure TOpticsDocument.DoRead (ARefNum : Integer;
                                  RsrcExists,
                                  ForPrinting : Boolean); override;
begin
    inherited DoRead(ARefNum, RsrcExists, ForPrinting);
    fOpticsModel.DoRead(ARefNum);
end;
```

For both new and old documents, MacApp next invokes the document's methods `DoMakeViews` and `DoMakeWindows`. Again, we implement these methods by building on lower level ones:

```
procedure TOpticsDocument.DoMakeViews (ForPrinting : Boolean); override;
var
    PaletteView : TPaletteView;
    OpticsView  : TOpticsView;
begin
    new(PaletteView);
    PaletteView.IPaletteView(self, fOpticsModel);
    fPaletteView := PaletteView;
    new(OpticsView);
    OpticsView.IOpticsView(self, PaletteView, fOpticsModel);
    fOpticsView := OpticsView;
    fOpticsModel.fView := OpticsView;
end;


procedure TOpticsDocument.DoMakeWindows; override;
var
    aWindow : TWindow;
begin
    aWindow := NewPaletteWindow(kWindowResource, kWantHScrollBar,
                                kWantVScrollBar, self,
                                fOpticsView, fPaletteView,
                                kPaletteImageWidth, kLeftPalette);
    aWindow.AdaptToScreen;
    fOpticsWindow := aWindow;
end;
```

In the method `DoMakeWindows`, we use the free subprogram `NewPalette-Window` as in our earlier example to create a window according to the window design expressed in Figure 9-15.

As we see in the method `DoMakeViews`, the birth of a view object first involves its creation and then its initialization. Initialization of an object primarily exists to establish its first stable state. For example, the initialization of an optics view object proceeds as follows:

```
procedure TOpticsView.IOpticsView (ADocument : TDocument;
                                   APalette : TPaletteView;
                                   AModel : TOpticsModel);
var
    Size         : VPoint;
    OpticalBench  : TOpticalBench;
    APrintHandler : TOpticsPrintHandler;
begin
    SetVPt(Size, 100, 100);
    IView(ADocument, nil, gZeroVPt, Size, SizeFillPages, SizeFillPages);
    fPaletteView := APalette;
    fOpticsModel := AModel;
    new(OpticalBench);
    OpticalBench.IOpticalBench(self);
    fOpticalBench := OpticalBench;
    fDrawOpticalBench := True;
    fDrawGridLines := False;
    fDrawPageBreaks := False;
    fAutoGridEnabled := True;
    new(APrintHandler);
    APrintHandler.IStdPrintHandler(ADocument, self, False, True, True);
    APrintHandler.fShowBreaks := fDrawPageBreaks;
    APrintHandler.fMinimalMargins := True;
    APrintHandler.fPageDirection := H;
end;
```

Initialization usually involves invoking the initialization method defined in a superclass, followed by statements that set the values of various fields. Our style is to set values for all fields, so that no clients of an object are ever taken by surprise. Notice that as part of the initialization of an optics view object, we create a printer handler, which embodies the knowledge of how to print the contents of the view. Because we didn't care for MacApp's default display of page breaks, we created our own print-handler class so that we could override the default behavior (specifically, we wanted to have page numbers displayed in all corners of a page, and MacApp only shows some of these numbers). Why didn't we mention this earlier, when we wrote the interface for most of the units? The reason is that this new class, `TOpticsPrintHandler`, need not be seen by anything other than the implementation of the optics view class. Therefore, we may hide this class from other clients by declaring it in the implementation of the unit `UOpticsViews`.

Optics view objects participate in MacApp's drawing mechanism, and for this reason we had to override the default `Draw` method in our class's interface. An optics object must draw not only the image of the optics experiment, but also the various adornments, such as grid lines and the optical bench. Our implementation of the `Draw` method must take this into account:

```
procedure TOpticsView.Draw (Area : Rect); override;
begin
    inherited Draw(Area);
    if (fDrawGridLines and (not gPrinting)) then
        DrawGridLines(Area);
    if fDrawOpticalBench then
        fOpticalBench.Draw(Area);
    fOpticsModel.Draw(Area, fDrawOpticalBench);
end;
```

We could have written the code that draws the grid lines in place, but by defining the method `DrawGridLines`, we simplify the implementation of `Draw` and thereby make it far more understandable. This is an example of the interplay of object-oriented design and the more traditional structured design methods. In object-oriented design, we start by identifying classes and objects, but we often decompose complex methods into smaller algorithmic abstractions.

Like application and document objects, optics view objects participate in MacApp's menu command mechanisms. Indeed, optics views know best how to respond to commands such as `Cut`, `Copy`, `Show Optical Bench` and `Show Page Breaks`. MacApp makes a call to the method `DoSetUpMenus` for each object involved in the command chain, to give them the opportunity to enable commands that are of interest to them. Thus, we may implement this method for the class `TOpticsView` as follows:

```
procedure TOpticsView.DoSetUpMenus; override;
var Count : Integer;
begin
    inherited DoSetUpMenus;
    Count := fOpticsModel.NumberOfSelections;
    Enable(cCut, (Count > 0));
    Enable(cCopy, (Count > 0));
    CanPaste(kClipType);
    Enable(cClear, (Count > 0));
    Enable(cSelectAll, (Count < fOpticsModel.NumberOfLenses));
    Enable(kDrawingSize, True);
    Enable(kShowOpticalBench, True);
    SetMenuState(kShowOpticalBench, kStringResource, kDrawOpticalBench,
            kDontDrawOpticalBench, fDrawOpticalBench);
    Enable(kShowGridLines, True);
    SetMenuState(kShowGridLines, kStringResource, kDrawGridLines,
            kDontDrawGridLines, fDrawGridLines);
    Enable(kShowPageBreaks, True);
    SetMenuState(kShowPageBreaks, kStringResource, kDrawPageBreaks,
            kDontDrawPageBreaks, fDrawPageBreaks);
    Enable(kEnableAutoGrid, True);
    SetMenuState(kEnableAutoGrid, kStringResource, kUseAutoGrid,
            kDontUseAutoGrid, fAutoGridEnabled);
    Enable(kLensSpecification, (Count = 1));
end;
```

Notice that we enable only those menu items to which optics view objects can react, and the criteria by which we enable a command differs for each item. For example, we enable the `Cut` command only if there is more then one object selected in the optics model. On the other hand, we enable the command `Select All` only if there are some objects in the model that are not yet selected. Items such as `Show Optical Bench` are enabled according to the value of the corresponding field in the optics view objects. A call to the procedure `SetMenuState` reads one of two menu-item names from the resource file, according to the Boolean value it is given as a parameter.

If an object enables a particular menu item, it generally should also process that command whenever the item is selected. This guideline is certainly true for the class `TOpticsView`. In the class `TOpticsApplication`, we implemented the `DoMenuCommand` method by directly calling methods of lower-level abstractions. We will do the same here, but with a twist, since some of the commands that an optics view object can process are trivial. For example, selecting the command `Show Optical Bench` (or `Hide Optical Bench`, depending upon the state of the field `fDrawOpticalBench`) simply toggles the state of the field and changes the corresponding view adornment. This command need not be un-doable, since the user can reverse its action by simply selecting the same menu item again. Therefore, it would be overkill to create a command object to do this work. Alternately, all of the editing commands, including `Cut`, `Copy`, `Paste`, and `Clear`, are undoable. A user who cuts a lens and then realizes that it was the wrong one should be able to undo the command and so put the experiment back to its state before the cut. Because command objects embody the knowledge of how to do, undo, and redo an action, it is best that our application create command objects that act as agents responsible for carrying out these actions.

The implementation of `DoMenuCommand` for the class `TOpticsView` is lengthy, but only because there are so many commands that it can handle. Conceptually, the real work gets done elsewhere:

```
function TOpticsView.DoMenuCommand (ACmdNumber : CmdNumber) : TCommand; override;
var
    Proceed             : Boolean;
    CurrentModelSize    : Point;
    CurrentDirection    : VHSelect;
    CurrentResolution   : Point;
    CurrentPageSize     : VPoint;
    CurrentViewSize     : VPoint;
    AcceptChanges       : Boolean;
    PageStrips          : Point;
    SelectedLens        : TLens;
    NewFocalLength      : FocalLength;
    CutCommand          : TCutCommand;
    CopyCommand         : TCopyCommand;
    PasteCommand        : TPasteCommand;
    ClearCommand        : TClearCommand;
```

```
function CheckLens (Item : TLens) : Boolean;
begin
    CheckLens := Item.fIsSelected;
end;
begin
    DoMenuCommand := gNoChanges;
    case ACmdNumber of
        cSelectAll:
            fOpticsModel.SelectAll;
        cCut:
            begin
                new(CutCommand);
                CutCommand.ILensCommand(self, fOpticsModel, False);
                DoMenuCommand := CutCommand;
            end;
        cCopy:
            begin
                new(CopyCommand);
                CopyCommand.ILensCommand(self, fOpticsModel, False);
                DoMenuCommand := CopyCommand;
            end;
        cPaste:
            begin
                new(PasteCommand);
                PasteCommand.ILensCommand(self, fOpticsModel, False);
                DoMenuCommand := PasteCommand;
            end;
        cClear:
            begin
                new(ClearCommand);
                ClearCommand.ILensCommand(self, fOpticsModel, False);
                DoMenuCommand := ClearCommand;
            end;
        kDrawingSize:
            begin
                CurrentModelSize := fOpticsModel.CurrentSize;
                CurrentDirection :=
                  TStdPrintHandler(fPrintHandler).fPageDirection;
                CurrentResolution := fPrintHandler.fEffectiveDeviceRes;
                CurrentPageSize := fPrintHandler.fViewPerPage;
                CurrentViewSize := fSize;
                DisplayDrawingSizeDialog(CurrentModelSize, CurrentResolution,
                                    CurrentPageSize, CurrentViewSize,
                                    CurrentDirection, AcceptChanges);
                if AcceptChanges then
                    begin
                        if not EqualVPt(CurrentViewSize, fSize) then
                            Resize(CurrentViewSize.H, CurrentViewSize.V, True);
                        if (CurrentDirection <>
                          TStdPrintHandler(fPrintHandler).fPageDirection) then
                            TStdPrintHandler(fPrintHandler).fPageDirection :=
                                CurrentDirection;
                        ForceRedraw;
                    end;
            end;
```

```
        kShowOpticalBench:
            ToggleDrawOpticalBench;
        kShowGridLines:
            ToggleDrawGridLines;
        kShowPageBreaks:
            ToggleDrawPageBreaks;
        kEnableAutoGrid:
            ToggleAutoGridEnabled;
        kLensSpecification:
            begin
                if (fOpticsModel.NumberOfSelections = 1) then
                    begin
                        SelectedLens :=
                            TLens(fOpticsModel.FirstLensThat(CheckLens));
                        DisplayLensSpecificationDialog(SelectedLens,
                                                       NewFocalLength,
                                                       AcceptChanges);
                        if AcceptChanges then
                            begin
                                SelectedLens.SetFocalLength(NewFocalLength);
                                fDocument.fChangeCount := fDocument.fChangeCount + 1;
                            end;
                    end;
            end;
        otherwise
            DoMenuCommand := inherited DoMenuCommand(ACmdNumber);
    end;
end;
```

In this method, we handle the commands `Select All`, `Drawing Size…`, `Show Optical Bench`, `Show Grid Lines`, `Show Page Breaks`, `Enable Autogrid`, and `Lens Specification…` in place. These commands are not undoable, but all of the other commands are undoable. Thus, we see here that processing the various editing commands first involves the creation of a command object of the appropriate class and then its initialization. The newly created command object is passed back as the function result of the `DoMenuCommand` method. According to MacApp's menu command mechanism, the application object method `PerformCommand` eventually receives this command object, whereupon `PerformCommand` invokes the `DoIt` method of the command object.

Notice that our method includes some amount of code for processing the commands `Drawing Size…` and `Lens Specification…`. In both cases, the processing involves retrieving certain state needed by the dialog, invoking the free subprogram corresponding to the appropriate dialog, and then changing the view's state if the user in fact edited the dialog and accepted its new values. This use of dialog resources is quite common.

The method `DoMouseCommand` participates in MacApp's mouse action mechanisms, and from the perspective of its implementation, it looks much the same as the `DoMenuCommand` method. Because we want all mouse actions, namely, selecting, dragging, and sketching, to be undoable, this method must create one of several command objects. How does it know which one to create? The answer is that this depends upon the state of the palette object. If the user has selected a particular lens tool, a mouse action in the optics view represents the start of that lens being sketched. If the user has selected the pointer tool, a mouse action in the optics view represents a group selection (if the mouse is not over any lens) or the start of a dragging action (if there exist selected lenses and the mouse is over a lens). We may express this algorithm as follows:

```
function TOpticsView.DoMouseCommand (var TheMouse : Point;
                                      var Info : EventInfo;
                                      var Hysteresis : Point) : TCommand; override;
var
    SketcherCommand : TSketcherCommand;
    SelectorCommand : TSelectorCommand;
    DraggerCommand  : TDraggerCommand;
    LensUnderMouse : TLens;
procedure CheckLens (Item : TLens);
begin
    if PtInRect(TheMouse, Item.Frame) then
        LensUnderMouse := TItem;
end;
begin
    DoMouseCommand := gNoChanges;
    if fPaletteView.IsPointer then
        begin
            LensUnderMouse := nil;
                fOpticsModel.EachLens(CheckLens);
                if (LensUnderMouse = nil) then
                    begin
                        fOpticsModel.DeselectAll;
                        new(SelectorCommand);
                        SelectorCommand.ILensCommand(self, fOpticsModel,
                                                    fDrawOpticalBench);
                        DoMouseCommand := SelectorCommand;
                    end
                else
                    begin
                        if not Info.TheShiftKey then
                            fOpticsModel.DeselectAll;
                        if (Info.TheShiftKey and LensUnderMouse.fIsSelected) then
                            LensUnderMouse.Deselect
                        else
                            LensUnderMouse.Select;
                        if (fOpticsModel.NumberOfSelections > 0) then
                            begin
                                new(DraggerCommand);
                                DraggerCommand.ILensCommand(self, fOpticsModel,
                                                            fDrawOpticalBench);
                                DraggerCommand.fConstrainsMouse :=
                                    fAutoGridEnabled;
                                DoMouseCommand := DraggerCommand;
                            end;
                    end
        end
    else
```

```
      begin
          fOpticsModel.DeselectAll;
          new(SketcherCommand);
          SketcherCommand.ILensCommand(self, fOpticsModel, fDrawOpticalBench);
          SketcherCommand.fLens := fPaletteView.CurrentTool;
          SketcherCommand.fLens.fOpticsModel := fOpticsModel;
          SketcherCommand.fConstrainsMouse := fAutoGridEnabled;
          DoMouseCommand := SketcherCommand;
      end;
end;
```

Observe how the optics view object cooperates with its palette object. The palette object only knows how to manage the selection of a tool by a user; it does not know what do to with such a selection. The optics view object relies upon the palette to tell it what tool has been selected.

How does a palette view object draw itself? One could use a number of approaches, but the one we have found to be the simplest is to define a picture resource which the palette object draws. To create this picture, one can use any pixel-based painting program, such as MacPaint, and then paste that image into the resource file of the application using a programming tool such as ResEdit. Here again is a case whereby we separate the outwardly observable characteristic of the application from its code. Frankly, we had to edit this picture many times until we were satisfied with its appearance, but we were able to do so without any recompilation of source code, and certainly without affecting the design of our program.

This design decision led us to the following representation for the class:

```
fCurrentTool : 0 .. kKindsOfLenses;
fImage       : PicHandle;
fImageRect   : Rect;
fViewRect    : Rect;
```

The last three fields capture the state of the picture as read from the resource file during initialization of the palette object. Thus, drawing the palette becomes trivial:

```
procedure TPaletteView.Draw (Area : Rect);
begin
    PenNormal;
    DrawPicture(fImage, fImageRect);
    MoveTo((kPaletteImageWidth - 1), 0);
    LineTo((kPaletteImageWidth - 1), kPaletteViewHeight);
end;
```

With a few calls to some QuickDraw routines, we first set the pen characteristics, draw the picture, and then draw a line separating the palette from the scrollable view. The alert reader will observe that we used the constant `kPaletteImageWidth` earlier, in the implementation of the `DoMakeWindows` method defined for the class `TOpticsDocument`. Indeed, this is a classic example of why we declare constants instead of using numeric literals throughout our program: constants help make a program more understandable by making our design decisions explicit, and more maintainable by facilitating the sharing of common static values among abstractions.

The other interesting design consideration in this class involves the function CurrentTool. In our design, CurrentTool is responsible for returning a lens object of the class corresponding to the currently selected palette tool. The optics view object then uses this object in DoMouseCommand, to initialize a sketching command object. Our implementation of CurrentTool could just use a big case statement evaluated on the current item selected, and then create an appropriate lens. But carrying out some class-specific action by explicitly looking at an object-class is somewhat contrary to the object-oriented style: why check the class of an object when the object itself already embodies that knowledge? Instead, our approach is to create a prototype of each possible lens when the application starts, and then just clone copies of whichever lens we need. For this reason, we chose to declare the array PrototypeLenses in the interface of UOpticsModels, which we initialize so that each array item denotes an object of a different lens class. Thus, this array forms a map from tool to lens. This array is best defined in the unit UOpticsModels, but because it must be visible to other units, we must include the following declarations in the unit interface:

```
const
    kKindsOfLenses = 6;
...
var
    PrototypeLenses : array[1 .. kKindsOfLenses] of TLens;

procedure InitializeOpticsModels;
```

The free subprogram InitializeOpticsModels is similar to the procedure InitializeOpticsDialogs defined in the unit UOpticsDialogs. InitializeOpticsModels is called in the main program to create and initialize a prototypical instance of each lens, as in the following code fragment:

```
var
    DoubleConvexLens    : TDoubleConvexLens;
    ...
begin
    new(DoubleConvexLens);
    DoubleConvexLens.IShape(nil);
    PrototypeLenses[kDoubleConvexLensID] := DoubleConvexLens;
    ...
end;
```

Notice again our use of constants such as kDoubleConvexLensID, rather than numeric literals.

Turning now to the implementation of the method CurrentTool, we may write:

```
function TPaletteView.CurrentTool : TLens;
begin
    CurrentTool := TLens(PrototypeLenses[fCurrentTool].Clone);
end;
```

To round out our evolving implementation of the user interface, we turn to the dialogs defined in the unit `UOpticsDialogs`, as shown in Figure 9-16. Although we will not show it here, the implementation of the free subprogram `DisplayDrawingSizeDialog` led us to invent some domain-specific dialog classes that embodied the desired behavior. A second-order effect of this recursive design was that we ended up with some powerful classes that we were able to apply to several other applications. Other dialogs, such as the `Lens Specification...` dialog, also shown in Figure 9-16, proved to be far less complicated. For example, bringing up this latter dialog first involves creating an appropriate window from a template, then setting initial values for each of the dialog controls, and finally turning control over to the user (the method `PoseModally`). When the user dismisses the dialog, control returns to the method, and the function's formal parameters are set accordingly:

```
procedure DisplayLensSpecificationDialog (SelectedLens : TLens;
                                          var NewFocalLength : FocalLength;
                                          var AcceptChanges : Boolean);
var
    Window     : TWindow;
    DialogView : TLensSpecificationDialogView;
    Dismisser  : IDType;
    AString    : Str255;
begin
    Window := NewTemplateWindow(kLensSpecificationResource, nil);
    DialogView := TLensSpecificationDialogView(Window.FindSubView('DLOG'));
    DialogView.fPicture := SelectedLens.fPicture;
    NumToString((SelectedLens.fCenter.H - kOpticalBenchHOffset), AString);
    DialogView.ParamTxt('^0', AString);
    GetIndString(AString, kStringResource, SelectedLens.fName);
    DialogView.ParamTxt('^1', AString);
    if SelectedLens.fConverging then
        begin
            TNumberText(DialogView.FindSubView('focl')).fMinimum := 0;
            TNumberText(DialogView.FindSubView('focl')).fMaximum := MaxInt;
        end
    else
        begin
            TNumberText(DialogView.FindSubView('focl')).fMinimum := -MaxInt;
            TNumberText(DialogView.FindSubView('focl')).fMaximum := 0;
        end;
    TNumberText(DialogView.FindSubView('focl')).
      SetValue(SelectedLens.fFocalLength, kDontRedraw);
    DialogView.SelectEditText('focl', True);
    Dismisser := DialogView.PoseModally;
    if (Dismisser = 'ok  ') then
        NewFocalLength :=
            FocalLength(TNumberText(DialogView.FindSubView('focl')).GetValue);
```

```
    AcceptChanges := (Dismisser = 'ok  ') and
                     (NewFocalLength <> SelectedLens.fFocalLength);
    Window.Close;
end;
```

To have a complete, executable program, we must give it a top. Creating the main program as one of the last implementation activities seems incredibly strange to those wholly under the spell of structured design techniques. However, in object-oriented systems, the root of the system is of little value to us, other than to provide a home for the topmost objects. Thus, for the geometrical optics construction kit, we may finally write the main program, MOptics, as follows:

```
program Optics;

uses
    UMacApp, UPrinting, UDialog, UTEView,
    UOpticsModels, UOpticsDialogs, UOpticsControllers, UOpticsViews,
    UOpticsDocuments, UOptics;

{$S Main}
var
    gOpticsApplication : TOpticsApplication;

begin
    InitUMacApp(10);
    InitPrinting;
    InitializeOpticsModels;
    InitializeOpticsDialogs;
    InitializeOpticsViews;
    new(gOpticsApplication);
    gOpticsApplication.IOpticsApplication;
    gOpticsApplication.Run;
end.
```

At this point we can produce an executable prototype to exercise the most important elements of the user interface. Indeed, we strongly encourage this early integration, so that we can uncover any serious flaws in our interpretation of the requirements or in our choice of mechanisms.

Model Implementation

Once we are satisfied with the user interface, we may complete the design and implementation of the classes contained in the units UOpticsControllers and UOpticsModels. Actually, if we have sufficient development resources, it is possible for the evolution of the user interface and its underlying model to proceed in parallel.

Implementing the TShape Subclasses. Let's select a representation for the class TLens first. We will use an approach similar to the one we used for the class TPaletteView. Thus, we will create a picture resource for each lens (so that we can change it easily), and have the lens draw this picture in its method `Draw`. In addition to the fields required to hold this picture resource, we need additional state. Specifically, we must maintain some easy identification of the lens's class, to use when reading and writing the document state. Since Object Pascal doesn't support object persistence, we have to fake it by encoding each object's class in the document's data file. We also need to remember if the lens is currently selected, and what its current and last positions are. Lastly, we must remember the lens's focal length, whether it is a converging lens or not (which affects the allowable range of values for its focal length), and its scientific name (so that we can display it in the `Lens Specification…` dialog). Given these needs, we may complete the interface of the `TLens` class as follows:

```
fID               : Integer;
fCenter           : Point;
fDraggingCenter   : Point;
fExtentRect       : Rect;
fIsSelected       : Boolean;
fPicture          : PicHandle;
fFocalLength      : Integer;
fConverging       : Boolean;
fName             : Integer;
```

Since `TLens` represents the lowest level of abstraction in our problem, its implementation ends up doing a considerable amount of the real work. For example, reading and writing a document is handled by an application object, but the knowledge of how to read and write an individual lens object is known only by the lens itself. Thus, we may write the lens methods `DoRead` and `DoWrite`, which must complement each other:

```
procedure TLens.DoRead (ARefNum : Integer);
var
    Size            : LongInt;
    TheCenter       : Point;
    TheFocalLength : FocalLength;
begin
    Size := SizeOf(Point);
    FailOSErr(FSRead(ARefNum, Size, @TheCenter));
    fCenter := TheCenter;
    Size := SizeOf(FocalLength);
    FailOSErr(FSRead(ARefNum, Size, @TheFocalLength));
    fFocalLength := TheFocalLength;
end;

procedure TLens.DoWrite (ARefNum : Integer);
var
    TheLensData : LensData;
    Size        : LongInt;
begin
    TheLensData.TheId := fId;
    TheLensData.TheCenter := fCenter;
    TheLensData.TheFocalLength := fFocalLength;
```

```
    Size := SizeOf(LensData);
    FailOSErr(FSWrite(ARefNum, Size, @TheLensData));
end;
```

These methods are not called directly by the application object; they are called by the optics model object to which the lenses belong. For example, the method `DoRead` for `TOpticsModel` appears as follows:

```
procedure TOpticsModel.DoRead (ARefNum : Integer);
var
    Size  : LongInt;
    Count : Integer;
    TheID : Integer;
    ALens : TLens;
    Index : Integer;
begin
    Size := SizeOf(Integer);
    FailOSErr(FSRead(ARefNum, Size, @Count));
    for Index := 1 to Count do
        begin
            Size := SizeOf(Integer);
            FailOSErr(FSRead(ARefNum, Size, @TheId));
            ALens := TLens(PrototypeLenses[TheId].Clone);
            ALens.fOpticsModel := self;
            ALens.DoRead(ARefNum);
            fLenses.Insert(ALens);
        end;
    TraceRays;
end;
```

Notice that this method uses the same `PrototypeLenses` array as we used in the class `TPaletteView`. Observe also that after the model has been read from disk, the very last action is to conduct a ray trace; we will come back to this method shortly.

Implementing the Commands. Once we have completed the implementation of the various lens and optics models methods that are needed for MacApp's drawing mechanism, we can complete the implementation of the command classes. For example, consider the class `TSketcherCommand`, which is responsible for placing a new lens on the optical bench and tracking the mouse while the user drags the lens into position. This class is a subclass of `TLensCommand`, and adds the one field, `fLens`, to the state of its objects.

Recall that a sketcher command object is created in the method `DoMouseCommand` defined in the class `TOpticsView`. Initializing a sketcher command object is straightforward: we first invoke its superclass's method (which initializes the fields defined in the superclass), next initialize the command object with MacApp's defaults, and finally initialize the local field, `fLens`. We may express this as follows:

```
procedure TSketcherCommand.ILensCommand (ASuperView : TView;
                                         AnOpticsModel : TOpticsModel;
                                         DrawPosition : Boolean); override;
begin
    inherited ILensCommand(ASuperView, AnOpticsModel, DrawPosition);
    ICommand(kSketchingCommand, ASuperView.fSuperView.fSuperView.fDocument,
             ASuperView, TScroller(ASuperView.fSuperView));
    fLens := nil;
end;
```

In the class `TCommand`, there is a field called `fChanges`, which is initialized to
`True` by `ICommand`. When an application object performs a command, it increments the change count of the corresponding document (the field `fChange-`
`Count`) only if `fChanges` is `True`. Recall from our earlier discussion on MacApp's
document mechanism that among other things, MacApp checks the
`fChangeCount` field of a document object before it is closed, in order to give the
user the opportunity to save any changes. This is as we would expect. Actions
such as sketching, cutting, pasting, and dragging change the state of a
document object, and we don't want the user to inadvertently lose any such
changes. Here we have yet another example of how a system can exhibit very
complex behavior through some very simple mechanisms.

As we saw in the implementation of the `DoMouseCommand` method defined in
`TOpticsView`, after an optics view object creates a sketcher command object, the
view object initializes the `fLens` field of the sketcher object to the object
denoted by the current tool in the palette. In our implementation of the method
`CurrentTool,fLens` thus denotes a clone of a prototypical lens.

The method `DoIt` is where the real work gets done by objects of the class
`TSketcherCommand`. Basically, we must insert the new lens in the optics model,
mark it as selected, and then cause a new ray trace. We may express this algorithm as follows:

```
procedure TSketcherCommand.DoIt; override;
begin
    fOpticsModel.AddLens(fLens);
    fLens.Select;
    fOpticsModel.TraceRays;
end;
```

`UndoIt` and `RedoIt` are invoked by an application object according to MacApp's
handling of the `Undo` command in the `Edit` menu. The action of `UndoIt` is
simply to reverse the action of `DoIt`, and the action of `RedoIt` is, not
surprisingly, to reverse the action of `UndoIt`. Thus, we may write:

```
procedure TSketcherCommand.UndoIt; override;
begin
    if fView.Focus then
        begin
            fOpticsModel.DeselectAll;
            fOpticsModel.RemoveLens(fLens);
```

```
            fOpticsModel.TraceRays;
        end;
end;


procedure TSketcherCommand.RedoIt; override;
begin
    if fView.Focus then
        begin
            fOpticsModel.DeselectAll;
            DoIt;
        end;
end;
```

MacApp defines a two-part process for executing a command. Before the application method `HandleEvent` executes a new command (via the method `DoIt`), `HandleEvent` first commits the last command (via a call to the command's method `Commit`). It is possible for a command object to be created and then abandoned, and therefore never committed. In any case, before trying to execute a new command, MacApp frees the last command so that old command objects do not accumulate over time. In this manner, a command object can use lazy evaluation; that is, it can defer to the `Commit` method some of its work that would be costly or impossible to undo and redo, such as changing the state of a very large document.

When a sketcher command is executed (via `DoIt`), the object denoted by the field `fLens` is shared by two objects: the sketcher command object itself and the optics model object. If the sketcher command is abandoned, then when we free the command object, we must also free the lens denoted by the field `fLens`. We may thus write:

```
procedure TSketcherCommand.Free; override;
begin
    FreeObject(fLens);
    inherited Free;
end;
```

`FreeObject` is a subprogram defined in MacApp. Its semantics are to first check if the object reference it is given is null, and if it is not, to invoke its `Free` method.

When the sketcher command is committed, the command object must break its association with the lens object, so that when we free the command, we do not also destroy the lens. This is why we used the preceding call to `FreeObject`. Thus, we may complete the `Commit` method as follows:

```
procedure TSketcherCommand.Commit; override;
begin
    fLens := nil;
end;
```

A sketcher command object must do two other very important things: it must properly track the mouse as a user drags a lens into position, and it must provide some visual cues so the user can tell where the object is located along the optical bench. As part of the processing involved in handling a mouse down event, an application object allows the current command the opportunity to track the mouse by calling its own method `TrackMouse`. As the mouse moves, the application object repeatedly calls the `TrackFeedback` method of the object responsible for tracking the mouse (which is usually a command object). Thus, these two methods must work together to provide the user with the illusion that he or she is literally dragging a lens across a screen.

A mouse action has three parts: a mouse down event, a mouse movement, and a mouse up event. Most commands can ignore mouse up events (the exception is for some commands that must draw objects with multiple parts, such as polygons). For the class `TSketcherCommand`, when a mouse down event is detected, `TrackMouse` forces the view to be updated, so that the new lens appears initially. Then, as the mouse moves, `TrackMouse` invalidates the area under the lens. `TrackFeedback` then draws the lens again, but in a different place. Conceptually, you can think of `TrackMouse` as the process that erases a lens, and `TrackFeedback` as the process that draws a new lens. Because MacApp repeats this process rapidly as part of the main event loop mechanism, it appears to the user that the object is begin dragged smoothly across the screen. Flicker usually occurs only when drawing the object takes a long time. In fact, this is why `TrackFeedback` exists. Commonly, when dragging an object, the user does not need to see the whole object, but only a wire outline of its most important parts. In our application, we can have `TrackFeedback` draw the entire lens, because drawing a single picture is not that computationally expensive.

We may now complete the implementation of the `TSketcherCommand` with these two methods:

```
procedure TSketcherCommand.TrackFeedback (AnchorPoint,
                                           NextPoint : VPoint;
                                           TurnItOn,
                                           MouseDidMove : Boolean); override;
var
    APoint : Point;
begin
    if MouseDidMove then
        begin
            PenMode(PatOR);
            APoint := VPtToPt(NextPoint);
            APoint.V := kOpticalAxis;
            APoint.H := Max(APoint.H,
                            (kOpticalBenchHOffset + kMinimumHOffset));
            APoint.H := Min(APoint.H,
                            (fView.fSize.H - kOpticalBenchHOffset
                                           - kMinimumHOffset));
            fLens.fCenter := APoint;
            fLens.DrawLens(fDrawPosition);
        end;
end;
```

```
function TSketcherCommand.TrackMouse (ATrackPhase : TrackPhase;
                                      var AnchorPoint,
                                      PreviousPoint,
                                      NextPoint : VPoint;
                                      MousedidMove : Boolean) : TCommand; override;
begin
    TrackMouse := self;
    if (ATrackPhase = TrackPress) then
        begin
            fView.GetWindow.Update;
            if fView.Focus then;
        end
    else if ((ATrackPhase = TrackMove) and MouseDidMove) then
        begin
            fLens.Invalidate;
            fView.GetWindow.Update;
            if fView.Focus then;
        end;
end;
```

Notice that in the body of `TrackFeedback` we must ensure that the lens does not get dragged outside the range of the optical bench (thus the use of the `Max` and `Min` functions), and that the lens is always placed along the optical axis (a horizontal line, denoted by the constant `kOpticalAxis`).

Because our requirements call for a user to be able to constrain mouse movement to a grid with a granularity of five points (via the `Enable Autogrid` menu command), all commands must implement the `TrackConstrain` method. Thus, assuming that constrained mouse movement is enabled, before methods such as `TrackMouse` and `TrackFeedback` are invoked, MacApp first calls the command's `TrackConstrain` method to give the object the opportunity to constrain the mouse movement to a certain region or by a certain granularity. All commands must share this behavior, which is why we invented the class `TLensCommand` – its `TrackConstrain` implementation serves all command objects:

```
procedure TLensCommand.TrackConstrain (AnchorPoint,
                                       PreviousPoint : VPoint;
                                       var NextPoint : VPoint); override;
begin
    NextPoint.H := (NextPoint.H div kAutoGridSize) * kAutoGridSize;
    NextPoint.V := (NextPoint.V div kAutoGridSize) * kAutoGridSize;
end;
```

Related to command processing is MacApp's clipboard mechanism. The Macintosh User Interface Guidelines expect all applications where possible to support the common editing commands of cutting, copying, clearing, and pasting. The requirements for our current problem also specify this behavior, and this is why we have the specialized command classes `TCutCommand`, `TCopyCommand`, `TClearCommand`, and `TPasteCommand`.

When a cut command object is created (in the optics view's method `DoMenuCommand`), we initialize it with all the lenses currently selected in the view. When we execute this command, its action is to remove the lenses from the optics model, force a new ray trace, and then save these lenses so that they can be pasted back into that or a different view. A copy command does a similar action, except that it copies the lenses but does not remove them from the model. The clear command is a bit different, in that it only removes the selected lenses from the model; it does not copy them. When a paste command is created (which is possible only when there is something to paste), it looks in the same place where the last cut or copy command left its state.

This common storage of cut and copied objects is called the *clipboard*, and each application typically has just one. Basically, a clipboard appears just like any other view, except that a user cannot edit it, but only view it (via the Show Clipboard command). As part of the state of this object, we must maintain a list of objects that were cut or copied and can thus be pasted. This means that a clipboard must be able to process simple objects such as text, or more domain-specific ones such as lenses. The clipboard also allows objects to be cut and pasted across applications. For example, we may want to cut lenses from the geometrical optics construction kit, and paste them into a drawing application; this is in fact how we created most of the figures for this chapter.

Because a clipboard must process objects of domain-specific classes, we must include a suitable TClipboardView class in our application. However, because it is so similar to the view TOpticsView, we show neither its implementation nor its use here.

Applying Algorithmic Decomposition. Assuming we have finished implementing all of the command classes, we are left with the one method with which traditional designers probably would have begun: the method TraceRays, defined in the class TOpticsModel. Why have we left this method for last? It seems to be at the center of all the mathematical processing needed by this application. This is indeed true, but remember our conceptual framework for all object-oriented systems: we view the world as a collection of objects that cooperate with one another to achieve some desired functionality. As such, control – the principle focus of structured design – is not the most important thing to us here.

Only now, when we have all of our key abstractions in place, does it make sense for us to tackle the TraceRays method. If we had viewed this algorithm as a particularly high-risk item, we might earlier, and in parallel with our other development, have employed the services of a physicist to prototype this algorithm. As it turns out, the algorithm used by this method is simple, given the framework of the mechanisms we have already invented.

According to the laws of optical physics, a ray trace starts at some real object and then proceeds from lens to lens, in the order of their increasing distance from the real object. This is why we saved the state of the lenses in an optics model using the list fLenses, which is of the class TLensList. Although we did not show it, TLensList is a subclass of TSortedList, so that when we insert lenses in the optics model, they are placed in order, sorted by position along the optical bench. Thus, in the implementation of TraceRays, we must first destroy all existing images and rays, and then iterate through the list of lenses in the model. Next, we must invalidate the entire view, because we have changed its image completely:

```
procedure TOpticsModel.TraceRays;
var
    Image : TImage;
procedure ProcessLens (Item : TLens);
    ...
begin
    fImages.FreeAll;
    fRays.FreeAll;
    Image := fRealObject;
    EachLens (ProcessLens);
    if (fView <> nil) then
        begin
            fView.GetWindow.ForceRedraw;
            if fView.Focus then;
        end;
end;
```

Because we have decomposed our algorithm into small steps, the local nested procedure ProcessLens has only a small job to do. It must create the principle rays that proceed from the image through the lens, and then create an image object at the point where these rays intersect. If this point is on the same side of the lens as the original image, then we have a virtual image; otherwise, we have a real image. Earlier, we designed the class TRealOrVirtualImage to know the difference, so that real and virtual images would be drawn differently according to their position. Thus, we may complete the nested procedure as follows:

```
procedure ProcessLens (Item : TLens);
var
    Lens               : TLens;
    Rays               : TRays;
    RealOrVirtualImage : TRealOrVirtualImage;
begin
    Lens := Item;
    if (Lens.fFocalLength <> 0) then
        begin
            new(Rays);
            Rays.IShape (self);
            Rays.SetPoint (Image, Lens);
            fRays.InsertFirst (Rays);
            new(RealOrVirtualImage);
            RealOrVirtualImage.IShape (self);
            RealOrVirtualImage.SetPosition (Rays.ImageAt, Lens);
            fImages.InsertFirst (RealOrVirtualImage);
            Image := RealOrVirtualImage;
        end;
end;
```

Let's now turn to the class TRays, for the real action is here. The method SetPoint must determine the point at which the principle rays pass through a lens focus. As it turns out, we only need to process two of the three principle rays, since elementary geometry tells us that two nonparallel lines in the same plane intersect at a point. The easiest ray to follow is the one that passes unchanged from the image through the center of the lens, and the next easiest is the one that starts parallel to the optical axis and refracts toward the focal point.

The hacker would probably already be furiously coding a solution, but let's stop for a moment, and look at this problem from an object-oriented perspective. Are there any new classes or objects of interest to us here? The answer is a resounding yes! We have explained our algorithm in terms of lines, and thus it makes sense to invent a class that reflects this view of the world.

We can best determine the intersection of two lines if we know the equations of the lines, and the equation of each line can be determined by two points. This gives rise to the need for several operations upon line objects, which we may express in the following class declaration:

```
TLine = object (TObject)

    fSlope : Real;
    fDelta : Real;

    procedure TLine.ILine (Point1, Point2 : Point);

    function TLine.Y (X : Real) : Real;
    function TLine.Intersection (ALine : TLine) : Point;

end;
```

The `ILine` and `Intersection` operations do as their names suggest. The function `Y`, given a coordinate along the `X` axis, returns the corresponding value along the `Y` axis according to the equation of the line.

We can place this class and its implementation in the body of the unit `UOpticsModels`, because it need not be seen by another class or object in the system. Now that we have built this class interface, it is fairly easily to complete, using some elementary geometry:

```
procedure TLine.ILine (Point1, Point2 : Point);
begin
    fSlope := (Point1.V - Point2.V) / (Point1.H - Point2.H);
    fDelta := (Point1.V * 1.0) - (Point1.H * fSlope);
end;

function TLine.Y (X : Real) : Real;
begin
    Y := (fSlope * X) + fDelta;
end;

function TLine.Intersection (ALine : TLine) : Point;
var
    X     : Real;
    APoint : Point;
```

```
begin
    if (fSlope = ALine.fSlope) then
        SetPt(APoint, 0, 0)
    else
        begin
            X := (ALine.fDelta - fDelta) / (fSlope - ALine.fSlope);
            APoint.H := trunc(X);
            APoint.V := trunc(Y(X));
        end;
    Intersection := APoint;
end;
```

Completing the method `SetPoint` for the class `TRays` now becomes almost trivial: we create lines for the parts of the two principle rays and then determine their intersection:

```
procedure TRays.SetPoint (FromImage : TImage; ThroughLens : TLens);
var
    FirstLine        : TLine;
    SecondLine       : TLine;
    APoint           : Point;
    SecondFocalPoint : Point;
begin
    fFromImage := FromImage;
    fThroughLens := ThroughLens;
    fLensCenter := fThroughLens.fCenter;
    new(FirstLine);
    FirstLine.ILine(fFromImage.fTop, fThroughLens.fCenter);
    SetPt(APoint,
          fThroughLens.fCenter.H, fFromImage.fTop.V);
    SetPt(SecondFocalPoint,
          (fThroughLens.fCenter.H + fThroughLens.fFocalLength), kOpticalAxis);
    new(SecondLine);
    SecondLine.ILine(APoint, SecondFocalPoint);
    fToPoint := FirstLine.Intersection(SecondLine);
end;
```

Thus, we see a demonstration of the fact that object-oriented design is a recursive process. As with the class `TLine`, when we proceed deeper into our implementation, we often uncover new generalized classes that are further from the vocabulary of the problem domain but are still important elements of the mechanisms we need to satisfy the system's functional requirements. One very important benefit of this recursive process is that we often end up with classes that we can use in other applications; thus our collection of reusable software components grows over time.

Our implementation of the geometrical optics construction kit is now concluded. Figure 9-17 illustrates a screen dump of the executing application.

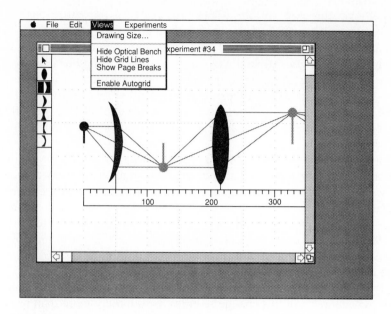

Figure 9-17
Geometrical Optics Construction Kit

9.4 Modification

Adding New Functionality

One mark of a well-structured complex system is that it is resilient to change. In this section, let's consider three improvements to the functionality of the geometrical optics construction kit and see how our design weathers the changes.

The first improvement involves the performance of the TraceRays method. Is there a way we can make this run faster? We could use histogramming tools to point out which routines are soaking up the most time, but simple observation can tell us a great deal. If we watch the running system, we notice that the program seems to spend a considerable amount of its time redrawing the optics view after a ray trace. This is not unusual, because drawing operations are reasonably expensive. However, if we look back at our implementation of the method TraceRays, we see that the code forces the entire view to be redrawn, even if only part of it is affected. Therefore, one obvious improvement is to optimize drawing by invalidating only those areas of the view that are changed.

This means that we must change the implementation of TraceRays only slightly. First, before we free an image or ray, we must tell every object to invalidate itself. Then, in the nested procedure ProcessLens, we invalidate the new image and ray objects just after they are created and initialized. Lastly, we can now remove the call to ForceRedraw, because our other changes are guaranteed to accumulate an area encompassing only the changed parts of the viewMaking these changes causes the view to produce a new ray trace far less abruptly than otherwise. Look at what we have done: using our existing mechanisms in interesting ways, we were able to improve the performance of the system by optimizing only one key algorithm. Furthermore, we were not compulsive about performance issues early in our design, but kept the faith that these issues would be better resolved after we had an existing stable framework from which to work.

Continuing, suppose we convinced the author of the requirements that constraining the application to deal with a maximum of four documents at a time was a pretty arbitrary thing to do. To relax this constraint, we only need to alter the implementation of TOpticsDocumentManager. Specifically, we need to change the representation of the class to use a list of documents rather than an array. We then need to modify a few methods to use this list instead of an array. Finally, we must change the resource that defines the Experiments menu, so that the optics document manager can add and remove menu items.

So here we have a requirements change that simplifies the use of this application. Accommodating this change requires us to modify more than just a single method; however, because we used only one class to encapsulate all behavior necessary to manage multiple documents, and then exposed only the abstract behavior of the class, this change does not affect the semantics of any other class. We do need to recompile some of the higher-level units, but this change does not decrease our level of confidence in the correctness of all other existing classes.

Let's consider one more improvement. Suppose early feedback from users indicates that they would like to have the focal point of a lens displayed, and that this adornment should be toggled much like the menu command Show Grid Lines. This kind of requirements change requires us to change the implementation of more than one class.

Starting at the bottom unit in our design, we must add a new parameter to the methods DrawLens and Draw in the class TLens, indicating whether or not the focal point should be displayed. This parameter is just like the existing parameter DrawPosition. We must make a similar change to the method Draw in the class TOpticalBench. Where should the state of this toggled command live? In the view object, as does the existing field fDrawPageBreaks. In the class TOpticsView, we must modify the Draw method to use this new field. We also need to modify the DoSetUpMenus and DoMenuCommand methods in TOpticsView to process this new command. Lastly, we must add this menu item to our resource file.

The alert reader will realize that we have made three very different kinds of changes to our existing design, and these kinds of changes are typical in object-oriented systems. In the first case, we modified the implementation of a single method. In the second, we modified the implementation of a single class. In the third, we modified the interfaces of a few classes and the implementations of several more. In all of these cases, the changes were upwardly compatible. In other words, we could extend our existing mechanisms and interfaces in simple ways to change the behavior of the system. We did not have to invent any new mechanisms or change the fundamental semantics of any key abstraction. We would argue that our design of the geometrical optics construction kit is therefore a sound one: it can gracefully accommodate a variety of changes in the problem domain.

Changing the Requirements

The skeptical reader may argue otherwise, namely, that we stacked the deck, so to speak, by choosing only those changes that were easy to implement. Let's consider a major requirements change, and see how our design holds up.

Our requirements currently constrain the problem to deal with only a part of the nature of geometrical optics, namely, the physics of refraction. What if we extended our domain to include the physics of reflection? This means that our application would have to handle not only lenses, but also mirrors. To make our problem even more interesting, let's consider flat surfaces as well as spherical ones. We would attack this change from the bottom up. Our reanalysis of the problem indicates that we must now accommodate three new kinds of objects: flat surfaces, concave surfaces, and convex surfaces. The obvious place to put these classes is in the unit `UOpticsModels`; we must also modify the implementation of `TOpticsModel` so that it keeps these mirrors as part of its state. For reasons that will soon become clear, we would design the class `TMirror` to have the same superclass as `TLens`.

What about the method `TraceRays`? The existing class `TRays` doesn't really help, because it only knows about the principle rays that pass through a lens. However, we can still use it as a pattern, and we can certainly build upon the class `TLine`. Thus, our strategy would be to reorganize our class structure; it will now have two classes, `TLensPrincipleRays` and `TMirrorPrincipleRays` that are subclasses of the class `TPrincipleRays`. Because of the clear separation of concerns among these abstractions, their implementation is not particularly hard – just a little tedious.

Moving up in the hierarchy of modules, we would need to make suitable changes to the various command classes. Actually, the logic of the existing command classes is such that command objects care very little about the actual object they manipulate. Thus, the common behavior of lenses and mirrors can migrate to a common subclass, and then we can define all command classes so that they build on this common class. This is an example of the power of polymorphism.

As we move up to higher units of the application, the kinds of changes required are less severe. We must add some new dialogs and new commands (such as `Show Mirror Specification…`), but otherwise, the view, document, and applications classes that we have already defined are fairly independent of changes and extensions in lower-level classes.

In retrospect, the new requirement to process reflective surfaces does indeed force changes throughout our existing implementation. None of these changes, however, rends the fabric of our existing design.

Further Readings

The mathematical foundations of geometrical optics may be found in Sears, Zemansky, and Young [I 1987]. The seminal work by Foley and van Dam [C 1982] discusses the application of the principles of geometrical optics to ray-tracing algorithms for computer graphics.

MacApp, the class library for Object Pascal, is described in *MacApp* [G 1989]. Schmucker [G 1986] presents an introduction to the use of MacApp.

A summary of the Object Pascal programming language, with examples, appears in the appendix. The bibliography offers several references to various windowing systems and object-oriented user interfaces (see section K, "Tools and Environments").

C++
Problem Reporting System

For many business applications, a company will use an off-the-shelf database management system (DBMS) to furnish a generic solution to the problems of concurrent database access, data integrity, security, and backups. But any DBMS must be adapted to the given business enterprise, and organizations have traditionally approached this problem by separating it into two different ones: the design of the data is given over to database experts, and the design of the software for processing transactions against the database is given over to application developers. This technique has certain advantages, but it does involve very real problems. Frankly, there are cultural differences between database designers and programmers, which reflect their different technologies and skills. Database designers tend to see the world in terms of persistent, monolithic tables of information, whereas application developers tend to see the world in terms of its flow of control.

It is impossible to achieve integrity of design in a complex system unless the concerns of these two groups are reconciled. In a system in which data issues dominate, we must be able to make intelligent trade-offs between a database and its applications. A database schema designed without regard for its use is both inefficient and clumsy. Similarly, applications developed in isolation place unreasonable demands upon the database and often result in serious problems of data integrity due to redundancy of data.

Problem Reporting System Requirements

Software with a reputation of being full of errors has a short life, and thus it behooves every software development organization to keep track of error reports. The problem is compounded when an organization is responsible for multiple software products, each of which may have several different versions released to the field at any given time. Errors in a program may be identified through any number of different sources: end users, field-support personnel, the test and integration team, quality-assurance personnel, and developers. Once identified, errors must first be qualified (is it an error in the software, a problem with documentation, or is it simply a misunderstanding by the user?), then assigned to a responsible party, and eventually resolved (fixed, deferred, or rejected as being not reproducible). An analysis of error reports can help software managers properly allocate developmental resources and track the maturity of a product.

Our task is to develop a problem reporting system for a software development company [1]. This system must support multiple software products as well as multiple versions of each product. Because the kinds and versions of products will change over time, the system must be designed to support changing database requirements.

Figure 10-1 provides a simple data flow diagram that illustrates the major transactions in this system. Here we see that error reports may be submitted and then added to a central problem database. What this diagram does not show is that errors may be reported from multiple geographic locations and that they may be submitted either orally, on paper, or electronically. Once in the database, an error report may be assigned to some responsible party or parties. Upon assignment, notification of the new problem is sent to the appropriate person or persons. Typically, an error report from a user is first assigned to response center personnel, who qualify the error. A high percentage of errors can be handled here, because they often turn out to be mistakes by the user rather than software errors. If the error is real, it can be reassigned to a developer (who can in turn reassign it, and so on), who researches the problem and eventually fixes it; the error report is updated along the way. For example, a tester might try to reproduce the error, and adds this information, along with other notes, to the error report. A developer might later modify an internal release of the program to fix the error, and so marks the error as fixed. At any stage, various people may query the database. For example, end users might be allowed to query the database to find out the status of their particular error reports. Managers might generate reports from the database to analyze trends in the use of the product. Also, when the test and integration team generates a new version of the product, they can produce a release note by querying the database for all errors fixed and yet to be fixed for that particular configuration.

For simplicity, we will assume that our problem reporting system uses a line-oriented user interface, although we must allow for more sophisticated interfaces in the future. We will also assume that although error reports may be submitted in many different ways, they all eventually take an electronic form. For various operational reasons, we will use a single, off-the-shelf database management system to store all error reports. However, since many different people may have an interest in a particular error report, we must allow for the illusion of a distributed database.

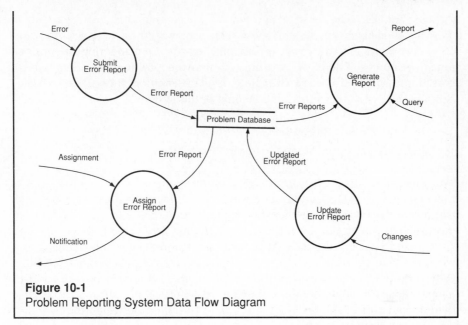

Figure 10-1
Problem Reporting System Data Flow Diagram

In this chapter, we tackle a management information system (MIS) application and show how object-oriented design can address the issues of database and application design in a unified manner. We use C++ as our implementation language, but these techniques can be applied almost as well to non-object-oriented programming languages, such as COBOL.

10.1 Analysis

Defining the Boundaries of the Problem

The sidebar provides the requirements for the design of a problem reporting system, an application that performs very little computational work. Instead, large volumes of data must be stored, retrieved, and moved about. Most of our design work therefore will involve decisions about declarative knowledge (what entities exist and what they mean) rather than procedural knowledge (how things happen). The soul of our design will be found in the central concerns of object-oriented design: the key abstractions that form the vocabulary of the problem domain and the mechanisms that manipulate them.

Applications such as a problem reporting system are by their very nature open-ended. During analysis, we will come to understand the key abstractions that are important to the enterprise at that time: we will identify the kinds of data that must be stored, the reports to be generated, the queries to be processed, and all the other transactions demanded by the business procedures of the company. The operative phrase here is *at that time*, because businesses are not static entities. They must act and react to a changing marketplace, and their information management systems must keep pace with these changes. An obsolete software system can result in lost business or a squandering of precious human resources. Therefore, we must design the problem reporting system expecting that it will change over time. Our observation shows that two elements are likely to change over the lifetime of this system:

- The kinds of data to be stored
- The hardware upon which the application executes

Over time, new kinds of products must be maintained by the company, new customers will be added, and old ones removed. Operational use of this system may reveal the unanticipated need to capture additional information about an error, such as screen dumps in the form of graphic data or perhaps even sound bites in the form of audio data. Also, hardware technology is still changing at a rate faster than software technology, and computers become obsolete within a matter of a few years. However, it is simply neither affordable nor wise to frequently replace a large, complex software system. It is not affordable because the time and cost of developing the software can often outweigh the time and cost of procuring the hardware. It is not wise because introducing a new program every time an old one begins to look jaded adds risk to the business; stability and maturity are valuable features of the software that plays such an important role in the day-to-day activities of an organization.

A corollary to this second factor is the likelihood that the user interface of our application will need to change over time. For many MIS applications, simple line- or screen-oriented interfaces have proven to be adequate. However, falling hardware costs and stunning improvements in graphic user interfaces have made it practical to incorporate more sophisticated technology. Fortunately, unlike the last design problem we studied, the user interface of the problem reporting system is not a fundamental part of the application. The core of this system involves its database; its user interface is largely a skin around this core. It is possible (and highly desirable) to permit a variety of user interfaces for this system. For example, a simple, interactive, line-oriented interface is most likely adequate for users who submit error reports. Hardcopy reports may best be generated in a batch environment, although some managers may wish to use a graphic interface to view trends interactively. For the purposes of our design, we need not dwell upon the nature of the user interface; just about any kind of interface may be employed without altering the fundamental design of the problem reporting system.

On the basis of this discussion, we chose to make two strategic design decisions. First, we chose to use an off-the-shelf DBMS around which to build our application. Designing an *ad hoc* database doesn't make any sense in this situation; the nature of our application would lead us to implement most of the functionality of a commercial DBMS at a vastly greater cost and with much less flexibility in the resulting product. An off-the-shelf DBMS also has the advantage of being reasonably portable. Most popular DBMSs have implementations that run on a spectrum of hardware platforms, from personal computers to mainframes, thus transferring from the developer to the vendor the responsibility of porting the generic DBMS. Second, we chose to have the problem reporting system execute on a distributed network. For simplicity, we will plan for a centralized database that resides on one machine. However, we will allow applications to be targeted to a variety of machines from which they can access this database. This design represents a client/server model; the machine dedicated to the database acts as the server, and it may have many clients. The particular machine on which a client executes (even if it is the local database machine itself) is entirely immaterial to the server. Thus, our application can operate upon a heterogeneous network and allow new hardware technology to be incorporated with minimal impact upon the operation of the system.

The Relational Database Model

Database Models. As described by Date, a database "is a repository for stored data. In general, it is both integrated and shared. By 'integrated' we mean that the database may be thought of as a unification of several otherwise distinct data files, with any redundancy among those files partially or wholly eliminated. . . . By 'shared' we mean that individual pieces of data in the database may be shared among several different users" [2]. With centralized control over a database, "inconsistency can be reduced, standards can be enforced, security restrictions can be applied, and database integrity can be maintained" [3].

Designing an effective database is a difficult task because there are so many competing requirements. The database designer must not only satisfy the functional requirements of the application, but must also address time and space factors. A time-inefficient database that retrieves data long after it is needed is pretty much useless. Similarly, a database that requires a building full of computers and a swarm of people to support it is not very cost-effective.

Database design has many parallels with object-oriented design. In database technology, design is often viewed as an incremental and iterative process involving both logical and physical decisions [4]. As Wiorkowski and Kull point out, "Objects that describe a database in the way that users and developers think about it are called logical objects. Those that refer to the way data are actually stored in the system are called physical objects" [5]. In a process not unlike that of object-oriented design, database designers bounce between logical and physical design throughout the development of the database. Additionally, the ways in which we describe the elements of a database are very similar to the ways in which we describe the key abstractions in an application using object-oriented design. Database designers often use notations such as entity-relationship diagrams to aid them in analyzing their problem. As we will see shortly, class diagrams can be written that map directly to entity-relationship diagrams, but have even greater expressive power.

As Date suggests, every kind of generalized database must address the following question: "What data structures and associated operators should the system support?" [6]. The different answers to this question bring us to three distinctly different database models:

- Hierarchical
- Network
- Relational

Lately, a fourth kind of database model has emerged, namely, *object-oriented databases (OODB)*. OODBs represent a merging of traditional database technology and the object model. OODBs have proven to be particularly useful in domains such as computer-aided engineering (CAE) and computer-aided software engineering (CASE) applications, for which we must manipulate significant amounts of data with a rich semantic content.

The Relational Model. For a variety of technical and nontechnical reasons, the relational database model has proven to be very popular. Because its use is so widespread, because an extensive infrastructure of products and standards support it, and because it satisfies the functional requirements of the problem reporting system, we chose to employ a relational database in our design.

The basic elements of a relational database "are tables in which columns represent things and the attributes that describe them and rows represent specific instances of the things described. . . . The model also provides for operators for generating new tables from old, which is the way users manipulate the database and retrieve information from it" [7].

Consider for a moment a database of parts for an inventory control application. In this enterprise, we have parts, uniquely identified by a part number, along with a descriptive part name. An example follows:

Parts

PNumber	PName
0081735	Resistor, 100 Ω 1/4 watt
0081736	Resistor, 140 Ω 1/4 watt
3891043	Capacitor, 100 pF
9074000	7400 IC quad NAND
9074001	74LS00 IC quad NAND

Here we have a table with two columns, each representing a different attribute. In a relation such as this, the order of rows and columns is insignificant; there may be any number of rows, but no duplicate rows. The heading `PNumber` represents a primary key, meaning that we may use its value to uniquely identify a particular part.

Parts come from suppliers, and so for each supplier we must maintain a unique number, a name, an address, and a telephone number. Thus, we may write the following:

Suppliers

SNumber	SName	SAddress	Telephone
00056	Interstate Supply	2222 Fannin, Amarillo, TX	806-555-0036
03107	Interstate Supply	3320 Scott, Santa Clara, CA	408-555-3600
78829	Universal Products	2171 Parfet Ct, Lakewood, CO	303-555-2405

SNumber is a primary key because its value may be used to uniquely identify a supplier. Notice that each row in this table is unique, although two rows have the same supplier name.

Different suppliers provide various parts at different prices, and so we must also keep a table of prices. For a given part/supplier combination, this table includes the current price:

Prices

PNumber	SNumber	Price
0081735	03107	$0.10
0081735	78829	$0.09
0156999	78829	$367.75
7775098	03107	$10.90
6889655	00056	$0.09
9074001	03107	$1.75

This table has no single primary key. Rather, we must use a combination of PNumber and SNumber to uniquely identify a row in this table. A key formed by combining column values is called a *composite key*. Notice that we do not include part and supplier names because they would be redundant; this information can be found by tracing from PNumber or SNumber back to the part or supplier table. PNumber and SNumber are therefore called *foreign keys*, because their values represent the primary keys of other tables.

We must track inventory with a table for the quantity of all parts currently on hand:

Inventory

PNumber	Quantity
0081735	1000
0097890	2000
0156999	34
7775098	46
6889655	1
9074001	192

We could have included quantity as a column in the parts table. However, we chose not do to so, because in our model of the enterprise, an inventory encompasses only those parts currently stocked in our warehouse, whereas the parts list includes all the possible kinds of parts that can be ordered. These concepts are significantly different, and so we chose to separate their attributes. This is yet another example of the problem of sameness and difference that we first introduced in Chapter 4.

SQL. A user might wish to perform a variety of common transactions upon these tables. For example, we might want to add new suppliers, delete parts, or update quantities in the inventory. We also might want to query these tables in a variety of ways. For instance, we might want a report that lists all the parts we can order from a particular supplier. We might also want a report listing the parts whose inventory is either too low or too high, according to some criteria we give it. Finally, we might want a comprehensive report giving us the cost to restock the inventory to certain levels, using the most inexpensive sources of parts. These kinds of transactions are common to almost every application of a relational DBMS, and so a standard language called SQL (Structured Query Language) has emerged for interacting with relational databases. SQL may be used either interactively or programmatically.

The most important construct in SQL is the select clause, which takes the following form:

```
SELECT <attribute>
FROM   <relation>
WHERE  <condition>
```

For example, to retrieve part numbers for which inventory is less that 100 items, we might write

```
SELECT PART, QUANTITY
FROM   INVENTORY
WHERE  QUANTITY < 100
```

Much more complicated selection is possible. For example, we might want the same report to include the part name instead of the part number:

```
SELECT PNAME, QUANTITY
FROM   INVENTORY, PARTS
WHERE  QUANTITY < 100
AND    INVENTORY.PART = PARTS.PNAME
```

This clause represents a *join*, whereby we combine two or more relations into a single relation. The select clause above doesn't generate a new table, but returns a set of rows. Since a single selection might return some arbitrarily large number of rows, we must have some means of visiting each row at a time. The mechanism SQL uses is the cursor, whose semantics are similar to the iteration operations we spoke of in Chapter 3. For example, one might declare a cursor as follows:

```
DECLARE C CURSOR
    FOR SELECT PNAME, QUANTITY
        FROM   INVENTORY, PARTS
        WHERE  QUANTITY < 100
        AND    INVENTORY.PART = PARTS.PNAME
```

To cause evaluation of this join we write

```
OPEN C
```

Then, to visit each row from the join, we write

```
FETCH C INTO NAME, AMOUNT
```

Finally, when we are done, we close the cursor by executing

```
CLOSE C
```

Instead of using a cursor, we may generate a virtual table that holds the result of the selection. Such a virtual table is called a *view*, and we may operate upon it just as if it were a real table. For example, to create a view containing the part name, supplier name, and cost, we might write:

```
CREATE VIEW V (PNAME, SNAME, COST)
    AS SELECT PARTS.PNAME, SUPPLIERS.SNAME, PRICES.PRICE
        FROM   PARTS, SUPPLIERS, PRICES
        WHERE  PARTS.PNUMBER = PRICES.PNUMBER
        AND    SUPPLIERS.SNUMBER = PRICES.SNUMBER
```

Views are particularly important, because they make it possible for different users to have different views upon the database. Views may be quite different from the underlying relations in the database, and so permit a degree of data independence. Access rights may also be granted to users on a view-by-view basis, thus permitting the writing of secure transactions. Views are a little different from base tables, however, in that views representing joins may not be updated directly.

For our purposes, SQL represents a low level of abstraction. We don't expect end users to be SQL-literate; SQL is not really part of the vocabulary of the problem domain. Instead, we will use SQL within the implementation of our application, exposing it to all sophisticated tool builders, but hiding it from the mere mortals who must interact with the system on a daily basis.

Database Analysis

As Date asks, "Given a body of data to be represented in a database, how do we decide on a suitable logical structure for that data? In other words, how do we decide what relations are needed and what their attributes should be? This is the database design problem" [8]. As it turns out, identifying the key abstractions of a database is much like the process of identifying classes and objects in object-oriented design.

Normalization. The simplest yet most important goal in database design is the concept that each fact should be stored in exactly one place. This eliminates redundancy, simplifies the process of updating the database, facilitates the maintenance of database integrity (that is, self-consistency and correctness), and reduces storage requirements. Achieving this goal is not particularly easy (and, as it turns out, not always important). Nevertheless, it is the most desirable characteristic we seek in our design.

Normalization theory has evolved as a technique for achieving this goal (although it is not the only relevant principle [9]). Normalization is a property of a table; we say that a particular table is in *normal form* if it satisfies certain properties. There are several levels of normal forms, each of which builds upon the other [10]:

• First normal form (1NF)	Each attribute represents an atomic value (nondecomposible attributes)
• Second normal form (2NF)	Table is in 1NF, and each attribute depends entirely upon the key (functionally independent attributes)
• Third normal form (3NF)	Table is in 2NF, and no attribute represents a fact about another attribute (mutually independent attributes)

Tables in 3NF "consist of 'properties of the key, the whole key, and nothing but the key' " [11].

The tables we have shown as examples are all in 3NF. There are higher forms of normalization, mainly relating to multivalued facts, but these are not of great importance to us here.

There are some practical limitations to SQL which mean that normalization is not the only criterion we must use to guide our database design. In particular, SQL defines only a very limited set of data types, namely, characters, fixed-length strings, integers, and fixed- and floating-point numbers. Implementations occasionally extend this set of types; nonetheless, the representation of data such as pictures or long fragments of text is not supported directly. Also, as we pointed out earlier, SQL does not permit updates to views that represent joins.

Domain Analysis of the Problem Reporting System. We are now ready to perform a domain analysis for the problem reporting system. For now, we will just accumulate a list of its key abstractions; later we will assemble them in normalized tables.

Problem reports are initiated by someone; so that we can trace back to their source, we must record the following information about the submitter:

• Submitter name
• Submitter telephone
• Customer ID

Each customer is given a registration ID, representing the license to use a specific release of a specific product. A registration ID can be used to validate the submitter's right to use the product and to receive support. For each registration, we must keep track of the following information:

- Registration date
- Release ID
- Customer ID

The same customer might be registered to use many different products. Furthermore, different submitters from the same customer organization might initiate problem reports. In our analysis, we would like to validate whether or not the submitter is actually associated with the customer to which the registration is given. Operationally, this helps us to determine if pirated copies of the product are being used by other than the licensed organization. For a customer, we maintain the following information keyed to a unique customer ID:

- Company name
- Company address

A release may represent an internal or distributed version of a product, and a particular product might have many releases at one time. Thus, we must keep track of the following information for each release:

- Product ID
- Release date

Along with its unique ID, and we must remember other information about particular products:

- Product name
- Responsible group numbers

The concept of a responsible group is this: every product distributed by a software company is supported by some development or maintenance team (or teams). It is to these teams that errors associated with that product must be made known. Every group has a unique ID, name, and a leader, and so we include the information:

- Group ID
- Group name
- Group leader

Groups are made up of employees of the software company, and so information about each employee is a relevant part of our enterprise:

- Employee ID
- Employee name
- Employee user name

An employee name is a full personal name; the user name represents an electronic mailing address. Each employee is a member of one or more groups; employees include developers, maintainers, field personnel, and marketing personnel. Particularly important customers may be assigned field-support and marketing representatives. Thus, as part of our customer information we include the following:

- Field-support representative
- Marketing representative

A problem is reported by a submitter for a particular release of a product. Along with some ID that uniquely identifies the problem report, we must record the following information:

- Submitter ID
- Date submitted
- Submitter priority
- Release ID
- Problem summary
- Detailed problem description

A detailed problem description may be just about anything: lengthy prose, hardcopy, pictures, and so on. Early in its life, the problem is assigned to a responsible group and then to a specific individual for action. Each assigned individual may update the following information:

- Internal priority
- Current status

The status of a problem report reflects where it is in the maintenance cycle, encompassing

- Not yet processed
- Reviewing
- In progress
- Fixed

- Defer
- Not a problem
- Not reproducible

and the ever-popular state

- No action

A given report may have multiple maintenance reports. A single maintenance report represents an analysis, commentary, test, or the random musings of someone working on the problem. Each maintenance report must include the following:

- Maintenance report description
- Creator
- Date created
- Problem report ID

When a report is closed out, we must attach a summary statement of its final disposition (such as repairs made), plus the ID of the new product release that will contain the fix. This information can be used to generate release notes for new product releases that incorporate the error fixes:

- Maintenance summary
- Fixed in release

Lastly, we include one other piece of information:

- Auditors

indicating a collection of people who must be notified as changes to a problem report occur.

A Schema for the Problem Reporting System. The "list of things" we have assembled covers all the abstractions that are relevant to the problem reporting system, but as it stands, it is disorganized. So that we can define a normalized schema for our database, we must arrange these classes into a meaningful hierarchy.

We start by identifying the most general clusters of information. Our analysis suggests that there are nine such clusters: problem reports, maintenance reports, products, releases, groups, employees, customers, submitters, and registrations. We capture these design decisions in the class diagram shown in Figure 10-2.

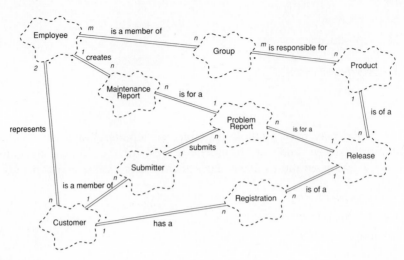

Figure 10-2
Problem Reporting System Class Diagram

It is no accident that this diagram resembles an entity-relationship diagram. Here, we have marked the relationships among these classes with their cardinality, plus a meaningful label that characterizes the relationship (the • indicates from which direction to apply the label). As the figure shows, a group is responsible for one or more products, for which there may be several releases. A submitter (who is a member of a company) may submit problem reports, and any number of such reports may exist for a given release.

Figure 10-3 continues our documentation of the class structure for the problem reporting system, showing the important relationships among products, releases, groups, and employees. Notice that we apply using relationships where there is a clear ownership between two classes. We have also introduced two intermediate abstractions, group leader and group member, to distinguish between significantly different kinds of employees. From this diagram, we may now write a schema for this part of the database:

PRODUCTS
    product ID
    product name

RELEASES
    release ID
    product ID
    release date

GROUPS
    group ID
    group name
    group leader

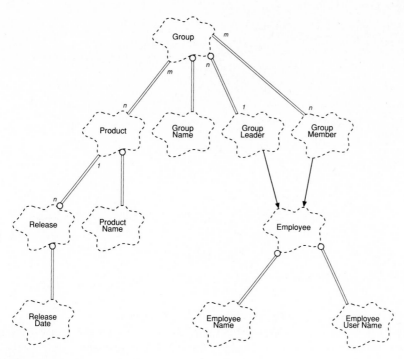

Figure 10-3
Products, Releases, Groups, and Employees

<u>EMPLOYEES</u>
    employee ID
    employee name
    employee user name

These tables are all in 3NF.

We have left the relationships between groups and products and between groups and group members undefined, because there is no compelling reason for one to use the other. A product might have as part of its state a list of responsible groups, and it would be equally possible to define a group to include a list of products for which it is responsible. These kinds of multivalued (*1:n* and *m:n*) relationships are problematic, because, if not handled properly, they introduce redundancy. Our solution is to generate two intermediate tables:

<u>PRODUCT RESPONSIBILITIES</u>
    product ID
    group ID

<u>GROUP ASSIGNMENTS</u>
    group ID
    employee ID

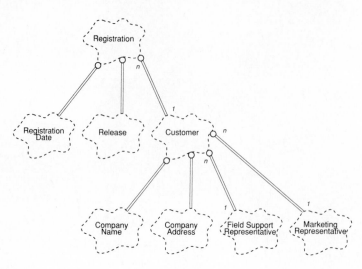

Figure 10-4
Registrations and Customers

The two items in each table constitute a composite key.

We show the class structure for registrations and customers in Figure 10-4, whose structure we may write directly in the following schema:

REGISTRATIONS
        registration ID
        registration date
        release ID
        customer ID

CUSTOMERS
        customer ID
        company name
        company address
        field-support representative
        marketing representative

No intermediate tables are needed; the ownership relationships are clear.

This leaves us with the abstractions of submitters, problem reports, maintenance reports, and change auditors. We illustrate the design of these database elements in Figures 10-5 and 10-6.

From these two diagrams, we may devise the following tables for our database schema:

SUBMITTERS
        submitter ID
        submitter name
        submitter telephone
        customer ID

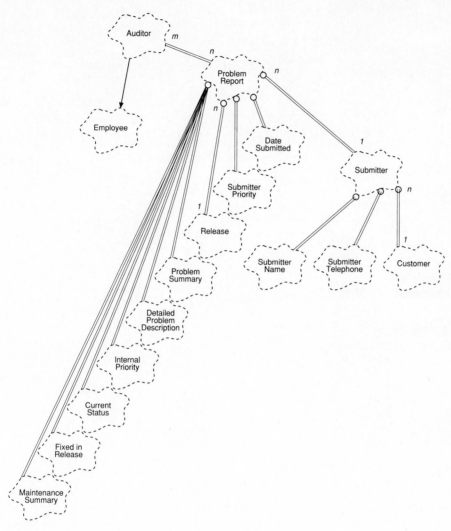

Figure 10-5
Submitters, Problem Reports, and Change Auditors

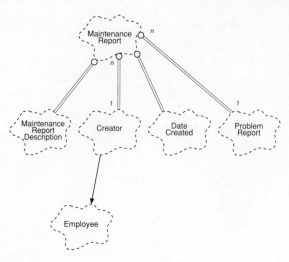

Figure 10-6
Maintenance Reports

PROBLEM REPORTS
        problem report ID
        submitter ID
        date submitted
        submitter priority
        release ID
        problem summary
        detailed problem description
        internal priority
        current status
        fixed in release
        maintenance summary

AUDITORS
        problem report ID
        employee ID

MAINTENANCE REPORTS
        maintenance report ID
        maintenance report description
        creator
        date created
        problem ID

Notice that we have introduced two subclasses of employees. An auditor denotes an employee who must be notified whenever a problem report changes (for example, when a new maintenance report is added), and a creator denotes an employee who can create maintenance reports.

The tables we have shown have been normalized so as to reduce redundancy in the database. At this point, our descriptions are sufficiently complete (except for choices of representation) to enable a database administrator to write the SQL statements necessary to express the database schema. However, what we have produced so far represents a low level of abstraction. In particular, users of the problem reporting system do not care that artifacts such as auditor tables exist. Submitters have a much simpler conceptual model of a problem report, and so to them, tables are an implementation issue. We must therefore continue with our design to build up these higher level abstractions.

10.2 Design

Process Architecture

For a variety of reasons, we earlier made the strategic design decision that the problem reporting system would execute on a distributed network. The immediate implication of this decision is that our application does not consist of a single program as in the last two applications; rather, it consists of a set of programs that collaborate to achieve the desired system functionality.

We can make a reasonable first cut at a process architecture by considering the different roles that users play in interacting with the problem reporting system. In our earlier analysis, we identified seven such roles:

- Submitter (of a problem report)
- Creator (of a maintenance report)
- Auditor
- Group leader
- Group member
- Field representative
- Marketing representative

By applying a use-case analysis to these roles, we can identify the following transactions:

- Submit problem report
- Forward problem report
- Update problem report
- Create maintenance report
- Query database

In reviewing this list, we realize that we have neglected one user role. Any database requires a myriad of maintenance tasks be performed, such as backups, exporting and importing data from foreign sources, tweaking reports, measuring database performance, and so on. Loosely speaking, these activities are performed by a database administrator (DBA) whose responsibility is to ensure the efficient and effective use of the database. Many of these functions are provided by using an off-the-shelf DBMS, and so we need not dwell upon them, other than to recognize that these activities are important operational considerations.

All of the above transactions represent some fundamental, user-visible behavior of the problem reporting system. We may design each one as a separate program, or we could wrap all of them within a simple executive program, from which the user chooses a specific transaction to perform. In either case, we must decide where these transactions execute. At one extreme, we could decide that any program may execute on any computer in the network; but there is always a price for being completely general, so we might consider allocating each transaction to a specific computer. In this application, our decision to use an off-the-shelf, centralized database renders such extremes unnecessary.

The process diagram in Figure 10-7 captures our design decision, which offers a compromise between these two extremes. As this figure shows, we have chosen to place the commercial DBMS on its own computer, which acts as the database server for the entire network. This computer might be as simple as a personal computer or as powerful as a mainframe. By using a commercial DBMS that can port easily to a variety of platforms, we provide a migration path to accommodate changing demands upon the database. This computer is also used for all the various DBA functions. The other computers on this network are generalized, as far as the problem reporting system is concerned. We will allow any transaction to be performed on any other computer, although if we have a heterogeneous network (meaning that many different kinds of computers are involved), some nodes may be unable to perform certain transactions (perhaps because they lack certain display or printing devices).

To enable these transactions to interact with one another independently, regardless of the network upon which they execute, we must design a generalized communications mechanism. Figure 10-7 also captures this design decision. Here we show that transactions executing on one computer communicate with the database by using a remote procedure call (RPC) mechanism. With RPC, it is possible to write a program on computer *A* that calls a subprogram implemented on computer *B*. In a similar fashion, we have decided to use electronic mail as the means of passing problem reports around the network. Electronic mail is an attractive approach because it is typically a standard facility in many heterogeneous networks, and it is a mechanism that is already familiar to users on the network. This approach is a classic example of building new mechanisms in terms of old ones. By leveraging off existing mechanisms such as RPC and electronic mail, we simplify our work (because we have incrementally less work to do) and reduce our risk (because we are building upon proven mechanisms).

Figure 10-7 represents system design decisions that we can use to reason about operational considerations. For example, how does a customer submit a

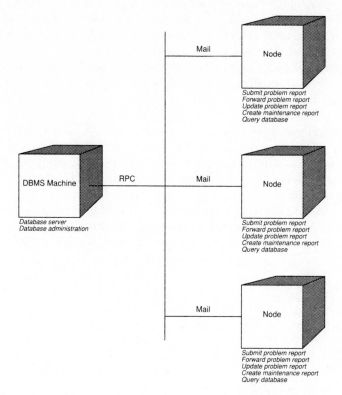

Figure 10-7
Problem Reporting System Process Diagram

problem report? The answer to this question depends upon business policies, not technical issues. In practice, we might permit customers to dial up a specific computer on the network and enter their problem reports directly. Alternately, we might funnel all problem reports through a central response center: customers phone or write in problem reports, and company personnel enter the information into the problem reporting system. Our choice has no serious technical implications, because we have designed a general mechanism that can be adapted to either approach.

Database Schema

We may continue our design by capturing the database schema in C++. Now, we are interested in the classes as viewed from inside the problem reporting system, at a level of abstraction that is close to the relational database and not necessarily in the vocabulary of the problem domain. Thus, the classes we show in this section (written in C++) parallel the database schema (described in SQL).

Our task is made relatively easy because we have decided upon a class structure for these abstractions, as illustrated in Figures 10-2 through 10-6. At this level of abstraction, our classes are largely structural in nature, meaning that instances of these classes serve as simple repositories for the data extracted from or sent to the relational database. These classes have no domain-specific operations defined for them. However, as we will see in subsequent sections, we will use these classes as building blocks to which we add increasingly higher level behavior.

The reason that these classes are at such a low level of abstraction is simply that SQL is a low-level abstraction. As we described earlier, SQL defines only a minimal set of domain-independent data types. Thus, our lowest-level C++ classes simply mirror these SQL types, but add the domain-specific structure of each kind of relation.

If we examine all the different tables in our database schema, we find that only nine elementary types of data are used. So that all clients that use these types may share a common representation, we write the following `typedefs`:

```
typedef int    ID;
typedef char*  Name;
typedef char*  Address;
typedef int    Telephone;
typedef char*  Date;
typedef int    Priority;
typedef char*  Summary;
typedef char*  FileName;
enum     Status {Reviewing,InProgress,Fixed,Defer,
                 NotAProblem,NotReproducible,NoAction};
```

Most of these definitions are self-explanatory. For example, IDs (such as `ProblemReportIDs` and `CustomerIDs`) are simply numbers; similarly, `Names` and `Addresses` are strings of characters. `Status`, as we decided earlier, is an enumeration of seven distinct values. As our design evolves, we can easily change any of these definitions with minimal impact to the rest of our design.

The motivation for the `FileName` definition requires further discussion. As we noted earlier, SQL places severe limitations on the types of attributes in a relation. Although SQL permits variable-length strings and binary data, most implementations restrict the amount of data to some fairly small size, often on the order of 256 bytes or less. This limitation is entirely unsatisfactory for recording lengthy descriptions, and so we must add a level of indirection; we will make the design decision that problem descriptions and maintenance-report descriptions are stored in individual files; the corresponding attribute value is simply its file name, fully qualified so that it can be uniquely found somewhere on the network.

We next assume the existence of an abstract class named `Relation` to serve as the superclass of all relations. This class exports the operations that are common to all relations, and so simplifies the production of specialized classes using C++ classes rather than plain `structs`, as one would typically use in C. For example, we may express the abstractions for products, releases, groups, and employees as follows:

```
class LowLevelProduct : public Relation {
public:
    ID   ProductID;
    Name ProductName;
};

class LowLevelRelease : public Relation {
public:
    ID   ReleaseID;
    ID   ProductID;
    Date ReleaseDate;
};

class LowLevelGroup : public Relation {
public:
    ID   GroupID;
    Name GroupName;
    ID   GroupLeader;
};

class LowLevelEmployee : public Relation {
public:
    ID   EmployeeID;
    Name EmployeeName;
    Name EmployeeUserName;
};
```

For reasons that will become clear shortly, our convention here is to prefix the name of each class with the adjective `LowLevel`.

Product responsibilities and group assignments tie instances of these classes together:

```
class LowLevelProductResponsibility : public Relation {
public:
    ID ProductID;
    ID GroupID;
};

class LowLevelGroupAssignment : public Relation {
public:
    ID GroupID;
    ID EmployeeID;
};
```

Continuing with the problem report class, we may write the following:

```
class LowLevelProblemReport : public Relation {
public:
    ID        ProblemReportID;
    ID        Submitter;
    Date      DateSubmitted;
    Priority  SubmitterPriority;
    ID        ReleaseID;
    Summary   ProblemSummary;
    FileName  DetailedProblemDescription;
    Priority  InternalPriority;
    Status    CurrentStatus;
    ID        FixedInRelease;
    Summary   MaintenanceSummary;
};
```

The remainder of these low-level classes are just as simple, and so we do not show them here.

SQL Mechanism

The classes described so far are indeed low-level; they are conceptually much closer to the implementation than to the problem space. It would be far better if we had a higher level view of a problem report, so that a transaction could manipulate them as if they were whole objects instead of pieces found in many distinct tables. In fact, since virtually every transaction must manipulate a problem report as a whole, it would be best if the abstraction of a table were entirely hidden from the higher level components of the problem reporting system.

Building Abstractions upon SQL. This is exactly what we illustrate in Figure 10-8. Here we see that a DBMS server (which resides on the DBMS machine) manipulates all of the low-level problem reports. On each node, there is a DBMS client that communicates with the server to provide all transactions with whole problem reports. Thus, as transactions create, update, and move about these problem reports, they do so in high-level terms, and the DBMS client/server pair ensures that these high-level operations are properly mapped to the necessary low-level ones. Because this represents a mapping from domain-specific records to lower level SQL statements, we call this an SQL mechanism.

We have already designed the low-level classes that are close to the database. Next, let's make a pass at the design of a class for problem reports that is closer to the problem domain. We start by performing a quick domain analysis over all the kinds of transactions relevant to this enterprise, so as to

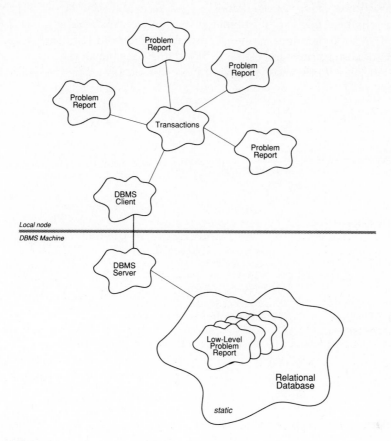

Figure 10-8
SQL Mechanism

identify a list of operations we might wish to perform upon all instances of this class. As it turns out, there are only three general kinds of operations:

- Submitting   Submitting a problem report for the first time
- Reading   Visiting elements of problem reports to produce arbitrary query reports, such as for listing all the problems associated with a particular release
- Updating   Modifying a problem report, for example, by changing its status or adding a maintenance report

We have not included forwarding as an operation upon a problem report, for reasons that will become clear in the next section.

These three groups of operations suggest three different flavors of problem reports: one kind that can be submitted (but only once!), another kind that we can only read about, and another kind that we can both read and write. This division of abstractions can best be reflected in a class hierarchy.

We begin with the most general of these abstractions as the base class for a problem report; thus we may write the read-only version as follows:

```
class ProblemReport {
public:

    ProblemReport ();
    ProblemReport (const ProblemReport&);
    virtual ~ProblemReport ();

    virtual Submitter         SubmitterOfReport () const;
    virtual Date              DateOfReport () const;
    virtual Priority          SubmitterPriorityOfReport () const;
    virtual Release           ReleaseWithProblem () const;
    virtual Summary           SummaryOfProblem () const;
    virtual Description       DescriptionOfProblem () const;
    virtual Priority          InternalPriorityOfReport () const;
    virtual Status            StatusOfReport () const;
    virtual Release           ReleaseWithFix () const;
    virtual Auditors          AuditorsOfReport () const;
    virtual MaintenanceReports MaintenanceReportsForProblem () const;

protected:

    Submitter          TheSubmitter;
    Date               TheDate;
    Priority           TheSubmitterPriority;
    Release            TheProblemRelease;
    Summary            TheSummary;
    Description        TheDescription;
    Priority           TheInternalPriority;
    Status             TheStatus;
    Release            TheFixedRelease;
    Auditors           TheAuditors;
    MaintenanceReports TheMaintenanceReports;

    virtual int SetProblemReportID (ID AnID);
    virtual ID  IdOfProblemReport () const;

private:

    ID ProblemReportID;
};
```

We assume that this class has visibility to the classes and types that it uses, including `Release`, `Status`, `Priority`, and so on.

As is our style in C++, we have provided a constructor and destructor for the class. Also, we have hidden the representation of this class from all clients except its subclasses, which is why we have declared the various member objects as `protected:`. So that any client may read the state of instances of this class, we have exported selector operations. As is also our style in C++, we have declared these member functions as virtual, so that subclasses may redefine their behavior. Unless there is some compelling reason to prohibit a subclass from redefining an operation, we always mark member functions as virtual.

The member object `ProblemReportID` is a special case. We have declared it private, because we want to prohibit all clients from changing its value. We do export the member function `SetProblemReportID`, but its implementation provides a "write-once" behavior. Since no subclass has direct visibility to the member object, no redefinition of `SetProblemReportID` can alter the member object's value. Hence, there is no opportunity to violate the sanctity of this abstraction. This level of protection is crucial because, as we will see in the next section, the ability to uniquely identify a particular problem report is essential in maintaining the integrity of the database.

We may next specialize this base class to add write capabilities. Because this subclass inherits the public selector functions from its superclass, the class `ModifiableProblemReport` denotes objects that may be both read and written:

```
enum Boolean {False, True};

class ModifiableProblemReport : public ProblemReport {
public:

    ModifiableProblemReport ();
    ModifiableProblemReport (const ModifiableProblemReport&);
    virtual ~ModifiableProblemReport ();

    virtual int SetInternalPriority (Priority& APriority);
    virtual int SetStatusOfReport (Status& AStatus);
    virtual int SetReleaseOfFix (Release& ARelease);
    virtual int AddAuditor (Auditor& AnAuditor);
    virtual int RemoveAuditor (Auditor& AnAuditor);
    virtual int AddMaintenanceReport (MaintenanceReport& AMaintenanceReport);
    virtual int Update ();

    virtual Boolean IsUpdated () const;
};
```

C++ does not furnish an exception handling mechanism, so we must provide one by convention. A modifier operation such as `SetReleaseOfFix` returns an `int` value. If the operation completes normally, it returns a zero value; if it fails, it returns an integer suggestive of the nature of the error.

Notice that we export operations to add and remove auditors, since the list of employees to be notified may change during the lifetime of the problem report. Similarly, we export an operation to add new maintenance reports (but not to remove one), because we wish to retain all such reports as the analysis of the problem unfolds.

We may further specialize `ProblemReport` to form the class `Initial-ProblemReport`, which knows how to register itself with the database:

```
class InitialProblemReport : public ProblemReport {
public:

    InitialProblemReport ();
    InitialProblemReport (const InitialProblemReport&);
    virtual ~InitialProblemReport ();

    virtual int SetSubmitter (Submitter& ASubmitter);
    virtual int SetSubmitterPriority (Priority& APriority);
    virtual int SetRelease (Release& ARelease);
    virtual int SetSummary (Summary& ASummary);
    virtual int SetDescription (Description& ADescription);
    virtual int SubmitProblemReport ();
    virtual Boolean IsSubmitted () const;

};
```

Although we do not show them here, we have similarly structured classes at this
level of abstraction for the following key abstractions:

• Auditor	A subclass of Employee
• Auditors	A collection of auditors
• Creator	A subclass of Employee
• Customer	A customer
• Customers	A collection of customers
• Description	A detailed problem description
• Employee	The employee base class
• Employees	A collection of employees
• FieldRepresentative	A subclass of Employee
• Group	A collection of employees
• GroupLeader	A subclass of Employee
• GroupMember	A subclass of Employee
• MaintenanceReport	Information about fixing a problem
• MaintenanceReports	A collection of maintenance reports
• Product	A product
• Products	A collection of products
• Registration	Registration of a product by a customer
• Registrations	A collection of registrations
• Release	A product release
• Releases	A collection of releases
• Submitter	A submitter of a problem report
• Submitters	A collection of submitters

These abstractions are all close to the vocabulary of the problem domain, and so we make their definitions available to the agents that perform transactions instead of exposing them to the low-level SQL-oriented abstractions. Additionally, since transactional agents all perform many of the same composite operations, such as formatting values for display, composing arbitrary queries, and retrieving objects that satisfy these queries from the database, we can exploit this commonality by composing a set of class utilities.

Bridging the Semantic Gap. For a moment, let's return to the abstractions at the level of the relational database, where we assume the existence of a programmatic interface. For example, using an Oracle relational database, we have functions that may be called from a C++ program to create a cursor, process an SQL statement, roll back a transaction, and so on [12]. Because arbitrary SQL statements can be passed through to the database, the full functionality of the relational database is available to programs, including creation of tables and views, selection, insertion, update, and deletion. This feature acts as a trapdoor through which sophisticated tool builders can access the database.

The conceptual distance between this programmatic interface and high-level classes such as `ProblemReport` represents a large semantic gap. For example, an instance of the class `ModifiableProblemReport` is a primitive abstraction to a transactional agent, but from its inside view, it represents a flattening of data from several tables in the database. Updating a modifiable report requires updating several tables, because SQL disallows performing an update upon a join. Thus, the question is, how do we unite these two levels of abstraction?

We will not deny that this is hard work. Indeed, this semantic gap is one of the primary factors that has motivated the development of object-oriented databases. Let's address this problem by looking at two different mappings.

Consider the following: given a product, retrieve the name of the responsible group. For simplicity, we will assume that there is only one responsible group, not multiple groups as our design permits. We start with partial definitions of the class `Product` and the class `Group`:

```
class Group {
public:
    virtual Name NameOfGroup () const;
};

class Product {
public:
    virtual Group GroupResponsibleForProduct () const;
protected:
    Group ResponsibleGroup;
};
```

Given an instance of the class `Product`, we can write the following statement:

```
TheName = TheProduct.GroupResponsibleForProduct().NameOfGroup()
```

Execution of this statement retrieves the name of the group responsible for the product. The key to its operation is deferring the evaluation of member objects. When we create the object `TheProduct`, its constructor need not retrieve a value for all of its member objects. In particular, we might only retrieve the ID for the product's group rather than all the data for the group. Then, when we invoke the operation `GroupResponsibleForProduct`, the following happens (in pseudocode):

```
// if the group object has already been retrieved from the database then
//      return the group object
// else
//      execute an SQL statement which selects this group given its ID
//      create the group object
//      return the group object
```

This algorithm uses lazy evaluation, meaning that we defer accessing the database until we need the information. To do otherwise consumes more space and leads to duplicate instances of the same group.

Next consider the operation `Update`, defined for the class `ModifiableProblemReport`. From the perspective of a transaction client, updating is an atomic action, but from the inside view, we cannot update the object directly, because its data spans multiple tables (one of the limitations of SQL). Thus, in pseudocode, the member function `Update` must do the following work:

```
// lock all of the tables used in the join
// for each table used in the join
//      update the table
// unlock the tables
```

`Update` thus ensures the integrity of the database by treating the update of the joined tables as an atomic action. In practice, the implementation of this operation is slightly more complicated because we must take into account situations wherein we cannot lock the tables we need immediately (perhaps because some other process has already done so). Additionally, we must be prepared to roll back our transaction in the event of errors.

We may apply these two techniques to just about every behavioral mapping. Further analysis of these techniques also suggests that they have a lot in common: both manipulate individual tables as well as columns and rows within a table. This leads us to define the following intermediate classes:

- `Table`
- `Column`
- `Row`

which parallel the generic SQL concepts of the same names. We may then specialize these classes to form the abstractions

- DeferredRecord
- DeferredField

which provide the behavior of deferred access. In this manner, classes such as Group and Product can be built by mixing in these lower level ones (using multiple inheritance).

Our purposes here do not require further description of these intermediate classes, because they don't reveal any additional important design decisions.

Transmission Mechanism

Our study of the requirements reveals that two other important behaviors can be satisfied by a single common mechanism:

- Notifying group leaders and group members of a new problem report
- Notifying auditors (such as field representatives) of progress made in fixing a problem

Earlier, we made the decision to use the existing mail services of the network to send notices about problem reports. This lets us leverage off existing facilities, and so integrates the problem reporting system into the infrastructure already familiar to its users.

Building upon Mail Facilities. The object diagram in Figure 10-9 illustrates the transmission mechanism. Just as in the SQL mechanism, each node has a local DBMS client that communicates with the DBMS server on the database machine. Each node also has a local mail server with a programmatic interface, through which transactions may send messages to a remote mail client, where either a user or a process running in the background (a daemon) reads the mail.

Let's consider the operational implications of this design decision. Returning to an analysis of the requirements, we uncover the following activities that can use this mechanism:

- When a new report is submitted, a mail message is sent to an individual in the response center designated to filter all new reports.
- If the report requires further action (i.e., there really is an error), then the response center notifies the group or groups responsible for the corresponding product.
- Periodically, the leader of the responsible group reviews the new reports, and assigns them for action to a group member or members.
- As these group members study the problem, they may add maintenance reports or decide that another developer or group should handle it; they may thus forward the report.

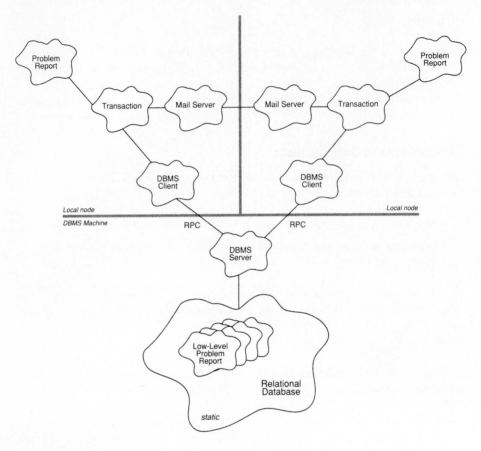

Figure 10-9
Transmission Mechanism

- When the problem is resolved, the final transaction that closed out the report also notifies the customer through the field representative or marketing representative.
- At any point in this cycle, interested parties (the auditors) may express an interest in a report, and ask to be notified when changes occur; any modifying transactions thus generate notification messages to all auditors.

The programmatic interface to an existing electronic mail system might look something like this:

```
// <mailer.h>

typedef char*      UserName;
typedef UserName* UserNames[];

int CreateMailBox (UserName AUser);

int OpenMailBox ();
int CloseMailBox ();


int DisplayHeaders ();
int ReadMessage (int MessageNumber);
int Reply ();
int SendMessage (UserName  ToUser,
                 UserNames CC,
                 char*     Subject,
                 char*     Text);

int NumberOfMessages ();
int NumberOfUnreadMessages ();
```

This interface is decidedly not very object-oriented (the world is not a perfect place!), although we can make it appear to be so. Our approach is to develop a mixin class, which denotes objects that can be mailed. The basic behavior this class provides is the ability to mail instances of itself:

```
// <mailer mixin.h>

#include "mailer.h"

class MailerMixin {
public:

    int Notify (UserName Destination, UserNames CopiesTo);

protected:

    virtual char* SubjectOfMessage () = 0;
    virtual char* TextOfMessage () = 0;

};
```

SubjectOfMessage and TextOfMessage are pure virtual functions, meaning that the class itself provides no implementation, but requires its subclasses to provide an implementation. The member function Notify is just about as simple, as is typical for mixin classes:

```
int MailerMixin::Notify (UserName Destination, UserNames CopiesTo) {
    return SendMessage (Destination, CopiesTo,
                    SubjectOfMessage (), TextOfMessage ());
```

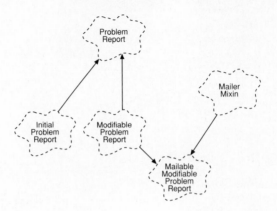

Figure 10-10
Problem Report Class Diagram

Using multiple inheritance, we may mix in this behavior to form a variety of useful classes. For example, we might produce a mailable, modifiable problem report:

```
class MailableModifiableProblemReport : public ModifiableProblemReport,
                               public MailerMixin {
protected:
    virtual char* SubjectOfMessage ();
    virtual char* TextOfMessage ();
}
```

Figure 10-10 illustrates the hierarchy of this class.

Instances of this class combine the behavior of `ModifiableProblemReport` with the ability to notify auditors and other users. To complete the implementation of this class, we merely need to provide a body for the member functions `SubjectOfMessage` and `TextOfMessage`, which in this case might include the problem summary and its unique ID.

Designing Reliable Network Communication. As Figure 10-9 shows, mail servers lie along the interfaces between nodes. We assume that these servers provide the necessary behavior to handle network errors. For example, if a connection to a particular node is lost, we expect a mail server to keep trying, or, at the very least, to send a message back to the originator stating that the mail could not be delivered. Thus, we can be confident that messages will not be lost, and that if errors do occur, they will be handled in predictable ways.

We must provide equally fail-safe behavior between the DBMS server and its clients. Specifically, we must design the client and server classes so that they cooperate if the link between them fails. To ensure reliable communication, we will empower them with the following behavior:

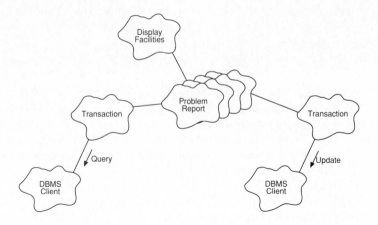

Figure 10-11
Query/Update Mechanism

- A DBMS client keeps a queue of database actions; normally, this queue is emptied as soon as actions arrive, but if the link is down, the client caches the actions until the link is restored.
- The DBMS server provides a positive indication to the client that an action was either committed or rolled back, so that the transaction that caused the action can take appropriate action.

These kinds of design decisions represent a common practice in object-oriented design: as our design proceeds, we examine logical collections of objects, and then decide how they should collaborate. In this manner, we produce key abstractions and mechanisms with a clear separation of concerns.

10.3 Evolution

Common Operations

Applying a Use-Case Analysis. To further identify the common mechanisms needed for the problem reporting system, let's study the behavior of a specific problem report as it passes through a review cycle. The key objects that interact during this phase are shown in Figure 10-11.

Action starts when a developer is notified of a new report. As we decided earlier, this notification comes by electronic mail, which provides a summary and designation of the report. From this information, the developer can initiate a query transaction, which reaches into the database and provides an instance of the class `ProblemReport` (or one of its subclasses). In the general case, a broad query might retrieve multiple instances, as in the case of a request for all problem reports regarding a specific product submitted over a month-long period. The developer might review a particular report on a computer terminal, or perhaps even make a hard copy listing for later review in the comfort of home. Eventually, the developer might create a maintenance report through an update transaction.

But herein lies a potential problem. While developer A is studying his or her copy of the problem report, developer B might add a new maintenance report to the same problem report, thus making A's copy obsolete. In its more general statement, the problem is to ensure that concurrent events happen in a controlled and meaningful order in the distributed network. As it turns out, this problem is endemic to all sorts of distributed systems. For example, when making airline reservations, it is not uncommon for the reservation agent to tell you that seat 35A is available, only to find that another agent in a different city allocated the seat before your agent could do so.

Asking how to resolve this problem is the wrong question; the proper question is What behavior do we want the system to exhibit? Only after answering this question can we say how to create that behavior.

The behavior we desire is this: when developer A tries to modify the problem report in the above scenario, a message will come back (either as part of the transaction, or via mail), stating that the update could not occur because a more recent version of the problem report was already registered. Upon receipt of this message, the developer can then decide what to do: query for the latest version of the problem report and then resubmit the maintenance report, do nothing, or perhaps go talk to developer B. In any case, we leave the control up to the user, not the system.

Selecting Among Alternate Designs. Now we can decide how to implement this behavior. There appear to be three possible design alternatives. First, we might implement a truly distributed database, rather than the abstraction of a distributed database, which we have built on top of a centralized database. With this mechanism, changes to problem reports get broadcast to all copies of the report, no matter where they are on the network. This mechanism has the advantage of almost totally eliminating synchronization among shared problem reports, but it comes at a very high cost: it is computationally expensive and generally slows down the entire network with a great deal of traffic. Hence, we reject this approach.

Second, we might time-stamp each problem report. This idea is computationally simple, and totally correct in theory; unfortunately, it is a total disaster in practice. The reason for its failure is that it is incredibly difficult to get every system in a heterogeneous network to agree upon a common time. Every system clock might be off slightly, and partial network failures wreak havoc by getting clocks wildly out of synch. Even broadcasting the time across the network doesn't help, because it adds to network traffic, and can be assumed to be accurate only as frequently as the broadcast is made. Ergo, we reject this approach also.

The third approach is far simpler. As our classes are now defined, each problem report is distinguished by a unique ID, which is the same for all copies. We can distinguish among copies by adding another member object to the class ProblemReport, which we call VersionNumber. When the problem report is first submitted, this member object is set to zero. Every time the database is accessed and the problem report retrieved or updated, the DBMS server increments the version number. This number can then be used to detect an out-of-synch update.

For example, suppose developer A retrieves the problem report P for the first time. Its version number is now 1. If developers B and then C do the same, their copies are numbered 2 and 3, respectively. Now suppose that B updates the problem report. Upon updating, the version number is incremented again (to 4), and B's copy is updated to that number as well. If either A or C now try to update their copy, the transaction will fail, because a report with a higher number is already in the database.

This is the alternative we choose. Its great advantages are that it is excruciatingly simple, and it works for electronic as well as printed copies of problem reports. To provide this behavior, we produce another mixin class, which we may combine with any problem report for which we need to synchronize updates:

```
class VersionNumberMixin {
public:

    VersionNumberMixin ();
    VersionNumberMixin (const VersionNumberMixin&);
    virtual ~VersionNumberMixin ();

    int VersionNumber () const;

protected:

    int  SetVersionNumber (int ANumber);
    void IncrementVersionNumber ();

private:

    int TheVersionNumber;

};
```

Note that none of these member functions are declared as virtual, since we see no reason to permit subclasses to redefine this fundamental behavior.

The member object TheVersionNumber is initialized to zero by the constructor, and the selector simply returns the value of the otherwise private member object:

```
int VersionNumberMixin::VersionNumber () {
    return TheVersionNumber;
};
```

`IncrementVersionNumber` does just what its name implies:

```
void VersionNumberMixin::IncrementVersionNumber () {
    TheVersionNumber++;
};
```

Finally, `SetVersionNumber` sets the version number only if the given number is larger than the current version number:

```
int VersionNumberMixin::SetVersionNumber (int ANumber) {
    if (ANumber > TheVersionNumber)
        return TheVersionNumber = ANumber;
    else
        return 0;
}
```

Identifying Common User Actions. Earlier, we noted that users of the problem reporting system may take on any of seven different roles. Each one embodies different state, and for this reason we developed a class hierarchy of employees, with subclasses such as creator, auditor, group leader, and so on. This hierarchy of users suggests a similar hierarchy of transaction classes that we may mix in with employees. For example a submitter, an auditor, a field representative, and a marketing representative all should have the ability to query a report (i.e., see a read-only version), but none of them should be allowed to modify the report; these users are all passive. On the other hand, users such as group leaders and group members should be able to query as well as update a report.

Relative to a user, where does an operation such as "update the problem report" belong? This is not an operation upon a user; rather, it is an operation that a particular user can invoke. By granting certain powers to user objects and denying others, we not only better reflect the vocabulary of the problem space, but also furnish a more secure and reliable system.

We may provide such behavior by using mixin classes. These classes add very little state of their own; they are primarily behavioral in nature. For example, we might write the following:

```
class Updater {
public:

    Updater (ModifiableProblemReport& AReport);
    Updater (const Updater&);
    virtual ~Updater ();

    virtual int           CommitTheReport ();
    ModifiableProblemReport ReportToBeUpdated () const;

private:
    ModifiableProblemReport TheReport;
};
```

To represent a user who can update a report, we create an instance of the following class:

```
class EmployeeWithUpdateRights : public Employee, public Updater {
public:
    EmployeeWithUpdateRights (ModifiableProblemReport& AReport);
};
```

We may provide similar classes for operations such as querying and submitting.

Utilities and Application Generators

Identifying Common Utilities. Our personal style of design arises from the concept of building general mechanisms, not immutable policies. For example, we could have implemented an *ad hoc* database or a home-grown interprogram communications protocol to address the needs for data persistence and report notification. Instead of taking this approach, however, we chose to use more general mechanisms upon which a number of different policies could be implemented. In our experience, this strategy pays off handsomely, especially in applications that require an incremental and iterative style of development, because it allows us to build upon proven code and makes it far easier to tune the application as operational use dictates.

As noted early in this chapter, database design is indeed an incremental and iterative activity, as is object-oriented design. The needs of every data-centered system are different, and unless we are duplicating the functionality of a proven, existing system, there is simply no way that we can empirically validate every design decision until the system is finally in operational use. Using healthy doses of analysis, testing, and personal experience, we can get close to being right, but reality suggests that we will still need to tweak the database early in its life, to tune and calibrate it to the use and abuse it is subjected to on a daily basis. As Hawryszkiewycz points out, all sorts of important database problems arise during design and then in actual use, many of which require only a little fiddling to make enormous differences in performance:

- "Too many logical records accessed in an access step
- Too many access steps for an access requirement
- Excessive use of intermediate files and sorting
- Too many physical records accessed in an access step
- Excessive storage use
- Excessive overheads caused by the DBMS or by operating system functions" [13]

By building general mechanisms, we give maintainers the ability to open the hood of the implementation and tune it, yet not alter its basic design.

Thus, in addition to the mechanisms we have already described, we seek to design programmatic interfaces to exploit the commonality of other key abstractions. Given the existing infrastructure, two specific kinds of facilities come to mind: utilities and application generators.

By *utilities*, we mean collections of nonprimitive operations that are generally applicable to a single class or several classes. As explained in Chapter 3, class utilities generally grow over time as developers discover patterns of use for certain abstractions. Rather than scattering redundant code throughout the system, it is best to collect these common algorithms in a place where they can be shared.

We have already identified a few such utilities, but others come to mind. In particular, a domain analysis of the transactions reveals the following candidates for inclusion as utilities:

- Query utilities   The definitions of query expressions that can be used programmatically, thus hiding the SQL implementation.

- Mail utilities   Facilities for common mail operations, such as forwarding a message to a list of users, or formatting message subject lines and bodies in a standard way.

- Logging utilities   Common facilities for recording information about the use of the problem reporting system, such as network problems, starting and stopping the database, and so on.

Let's examine the outside view of one of these modules. Logging utilities might be used to record a variety of kinds of system events. We can distinguish different kinds of events as follows:

- Debug message
- Success message
- Failure message
- Warning message
- Error message
- Note message

Because these are distinct events, each is a candidate for the definition of a unique class. However, because there are similarities among these events (for example, each are just strings), they are best defined as subclasses of a common superclass, `Message`:

```
class Message {
public:
    Message (char* TheString);
    Message (const Message&);
    virtual ~Message();
```

```
    virtual char* Value ();
private:
    char* TheValue;
};
```

Different kinds of messages have a different representation. For example:

- Debug   `89/08/25 09:41:06 ??? Temporary view created`
- Success `89/08/25 09:43:06 +++ Backup completed`
- Failure   `89/08/25 09:41:06 --- Unable to forward message`
- Warning `89/08/25 10:00:76 !!! Space on volume 3 is low`
- Error   `89/08/25 11:41:06 *** Wrong password entered`
- Note   `89/08/25 23:16:57 ... Waiting for database login`

Thus, the common behavior of the class `Message` is to date- and time-stamp each message as it is created. The specialized behavior of each subclass is to add the appropriate prefix.

Next, we might define a simple class named `Log`, whose sole purpose is to take messages and write them to a file.

```
class Log {
public:
    Log ();
    Log (const Log&);
    virtual ~Log ();

    virtual int  Open (char* AFile);
    virtual int  Close ();
    virtual void Put (Message& TheMessage);

private:
    ofstream TheFile;

};
```

We might also include the utility `Filter`, which reads log files and copies only certain kinds of messages to another file for later use:

```
int Filter (File *LogFile,
            File *Destination,
            Boolean IncludeDebugMessages,
            Boolean IncludeSuccessMessages,
            Boolean IncludeFailureMessages,
            Boolean IncludeWarningMessages,
            Boolean IncludeErrorMessages,
            Boolean IncludeNotes);
```

Using pipes, we could apply this utility to build even more interesting tools. Over time, we would expect the tools that prove especially useful to be incorporated into the logging utilities module.

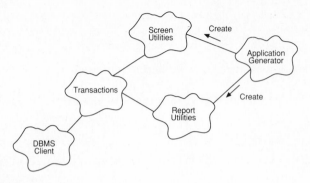

Figure 10-12
Transaction Utilities

The Role of Application Generators. Domains such as the problem reporting system often include many different kinds of screen templates and hardcopy reports that must be generated. For large systems, these parts of the application are not technically difficult to write, just horribly tedious. This is precisely why application generators (or *4GLs*, for *fourth-generation languages*) are so popular for business enterprises.

Figure 10-12 shows our strategy: all transactions that interact with users build upon the resources of both screen utilities and report utilities. These are both programmatic entities that have been created automatically by application generators; given the specification of the desired screen or report, they generate the proper templates. Thus, the design task is not to build hundreds of similar screen and report utilities, but to create one or two generalized application generators that produce these utilities. In practice, if the domain is sufficiently constrained, this approach can greatly reduce the amount of new code that must be written.

Because it is a problem unto itself, we will not describe the design of the application generators. A developer may choose to use off-the-shelf application generators or, if there is compelling reason to do so, to write a domain-specific one using object-oriented techniques.

Module Architecture

As our design has evolved, we have written dozens of classes and utilities, spread over many different files. From our experience, a reasonably complete problem reporting system consists of about 20–30,000 lines of C++. Without C++, and without our fierce dedication to seeking out commonality among key abstractions and mechanisms, we would expect a non-object-oriented version to be about 50% larger.

Since we are developing a system and not just a single program, it is important to establish a stable module architecture early in the life cycle. Figure 10-13 captures these design decisions for the problem reporting system. The system is highly layered, as we would expect it to be. The lowest-level classes and objects are found in the network facilities subsystem, which embodies the transmission mechanism. The SQL mechanism is found in the database facilities subsystem, along with all the classes that provide the high-level view of the abstractions relevant to this enterprise. The various utilities and application generator-produced modules are to be found in the transaction facilities subsystem. Lastly, the roots of the user-visible programs are to be found at the highest level of the system, in the subsystem named `User Applications`.

Not only does this structure help us organize the many physical modules in the system, but it serves to allocate the resources of the development team. Furthermore, it helps us in managing releases of the system over time. The allocation of modules to subsystems was no accident in this regard: we placed them in modules not only according to how logically related they were, but also according to which part of the system we expected to change most often.

10.4 Modification

Adding New Functionality

Once the problem reporting system is made operational, we can expect a period of time during which the database administrator must tweak the system. If this system is replacing an existing one, the DBA might have to write small programs to transfer existing problem reports. Here again, our strategy of building mechanisms helps, because the DBA can build upon the tool-building facilities that we have exposed for this very purpose.

Once the system is in operation, we may also discover that our analysis was lacking. This is not a mark of incompetence on our part; it simply reflects the fact that introducing any new system changes the way people do their work, leading them to new ways of doing business.

Let's consider one such change. A submitter may enter a new report that applies to several releases of several different products. Similarly, two different reports might be filed for the same problem, and it would be best if we did not duplicate our analysis. These operational considerations suggest that we need some mechanism for splitting and grouping error reports.

To implement this behavior, our strategy is to design another mixin class, called `Genealogy`, which provides the state of the parent and children of an object. For example, if problem report P is split into reports X and Y, then P is the parent of X and Y, and they in turn are the children of P. The same technique applies for grouping reports.

With this new state, we can reimplement transactions in subclasses of the class `ProblemReport`. For example, updating a report that has been split simply means that its children get updated as well. Updating one child causes notification of the group responsible for the other children, so that changes can be coordinated. Similarly, changing the status of a problem report that is the result

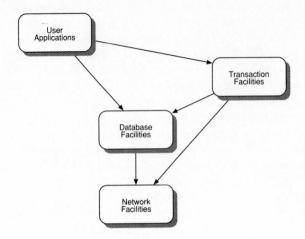

Figure 10-13
Problem Reporting System Module Diagram

of joining several reports causes notification of the auditors of each of the individual reports. This change, although operationally significant, is thus upwardly compatible with our existing design.

Changing the Requirements

Suppose we now want a graphical user interface as a front end to the system, so that clerks and other nonprogrammers can easily interact with it.

As it turns out, his kind of change does not disturb our existing framework. Our design isolates each mechanism, other than those involving an application generator, from a particular user interface. This clear separation of concerns was intentional, because we expected the user interface to change. Unlike the user interface of the geometrical optics construction kit in the previous chapter, the user interface of the problem reporting system is largely window dressing that covers the outside of the design.

Further Readings

A comprehensive treatment of relational databases may be found in Date [E 1981, 1983; 1986]. Additionally, Date [E 1987] offers a description of the SQL standard. Various approaches to data analysis may be found in Veryard [B 1984], Hawryszkiewycz [E 1984], and Ross [F 1987].

Object-oriented databases represent the merging of conventional database technology and the object model. Reports of research in this field may be found in papers by Davis et al. [H 1983], Kim and Lochovsky [E 1989], and Zdonik and Maier [E 1990].

A summary of C++, with examples, appears in the appendix.

Common Lisp Object System Cryptanalysis

Sentient creatures exhibit a vastly complex set of behaviors that spring from the mind through mechanisms that we only poorly understand. For example, think about how you solve the problem of planning a route through a city to run a set of errands. Consider also how, when walking through a dimly lit room, you are able to recognize the boundaries of objects and avoid stumbling. Furthermore, think about how you can focus on one conversation at a party while dozens of people are talking simultaneously. None of these kinds of problems lends itself to a straightforward algorithmic solution. Optimal route planning is known to be an *np-complete* problem. Navigating through dark terrain involves deriving understanding from visual input that is (very literally) fuzzy and incomplete. Identifying a single speaker from dozens of sources requires that the listener distinguish meaningful data from noise and then filter out all unwanted conversation from the remaining cacophony.

Researchers in the field of artificial intelligence have pursued these and similar problems to improve our understanding of human cognitive processes. Activity in this field often involves the construction of intelligent systems that mimic certain aspects of human behavior. Erman, Lark, and Hayes-Roth point

Cryptanalysis Requirements

Cryptography "embraces methods for rendering data unintelligible to unauthorized parties" [1]. Using cryptographic algorithms, messages (plaintext) may be transformed into cryptograms (ciphertext) and back again.

One of the most basic kinds of cryptographic algorithms, employed since the time of the Romans, is called a *substitution cipher*. With this cipher, every letter of the plaintext alphabet is mapped to a different letter. For example, we might shift every letter to its successor: *A* becomes *B*, *B* becomes *C*, *Z* wraps around to become *A*, and so on. Thus, the plaintext

CLOS is an object-oriented programming language

may be enciphered to the cryptogram

DMPT jt bo pckfdu-psjfoufe qsphsbnnjoh mbohvbhf

Most often, the substitution of letters is jumbled. For example, *A* becomes *G*, *B* becomes *J*, and so on. As an example, consider the following cryptogram:

PDG TBCER CQ TCK AL S NGELCH QZBBR SBAJG

Hint: the letter *C* represents the plaintext letter *O*.

It is a vastly simplifying assumption to know that only a substitution cipher was employed to encode a plaintext message; nevertheless, deciphering the resulting cryptogram is not an algorithmically trivial task. Deciphering sometimes requires trial and error, wherein we make assumptions about a particular substitution and then evaluate their implications. For example, we may start with the one- and two-letter words in the cryptogram and hypothesize that they stand for common words such as *I* and *a*, or *it*, *in*, *is*, *of*, *or*, and *on*. By substituting the other occurrences of these ciphered letters, we may find hints for deciphering other words. For instance, if there is a three-letter word that starts with *o*, the word might reasonably be *one*, *our*, or *off*.

We can also use our knowledge of spelling and grammar to attack a substitution cipher. For example, an occurrence of double letters is not likely to represent the sequence *qq*. Similarly, we might try to expand a word ending with the letter *g* to the suffix *ing*. At a higher level of abstraction, we might assume that the sequence of words *it is* is more likely to occur than the sequence *if is*. Also, we might assume that the structure of a sentence typically includes a noun and a verb. Thus, if our analysis has identified a verb but no actor or agent, we might start a search for adjectives and nouns.

Sometimes we may have to backtrack. For example, we might have assumed that a certain two-letter word was *or*, but if the substitution for the letter *r* causes contradictions or blind alleys in other words, then we might have to try the word *of* or *on* instead, and consequently undo other assumptions we had based upon this earlier substitution.

This leads us to the requirement of our problem: devise a system that, given a cryptogram, transforms it back to its original plaintext, assuming that only a simple substitution cipher was employed.

out that "intelligent systems differ from conventional systems by a number of attributes, not all of which are always present:

- They pursue goals which vary over time.
- They incorporate, use, and maintain knowledge.
- They exploit diverse, *ad hoc* subsystems embodying a variety of selected methods.
- They interact intelligently with users and other systems.
- They allocate their own resources and attention" [2].

Any one of these properties is sufficiently demanding to make crafting intelligent systems a very difficult task. When we consider that intelligent systems are being developed for a variety of domains that affect both life and property, such as for medical diagnosis or aircraft routing, the task becomes even more demanding because we must design these systems so that they are never actively dangerous: artificial intelligences rarely embody any kind of commonsense knowledge.

Although the field has at times been oversold by an overly enthusiastic press, the study of artificial intelligence has given us some very sound and practical ideas, among which we count approaches to knowledge representation and the evolution of problem solving architectures for intelligent systems, including rule-based expert systems and the blackboard model. In this chapter, we turn to the design of an intelligent system that solves cryptograms using a blackboard framework in a manner that parallels the way a human would solve the same problem. As we will see, the use of object-oriented design is very well suited to this domain.[*]

11.1 Analysis

Defining the Boundaries of the Problem

As outlined in the sidebar, our problem is one of cryptanalysis, the transformation of ciphertext back to plaintext. In its most general form, deciphering cryptograms is an intractable problem that defies even the most sophisticated of techniques. For example, DES (the data encryption standard, a public-key encryption algorithm that uses multiple applications of substitution and transposition ciphers) appears to be free of any mathematical weaknesses and thus is

---

[*] We will use CLOS to implement our solution, but please realize that CLOS is not limited to AI applications; it is equally appropriate in any of the domains we cover in this book. CLOS is particularly well-suited to an incremental and iterative style of development, which, as we have pointed out, is essential for the construction of all kinds of complex software systems.

safe against all currently known kinds of attack. Happily, our problem is much simpler, because we limit ourselves to single substitution ciphers.

Spend the next few minutes solving the following cryptogram, and as you proceed, record how you did it (no fair reading ahead!):

Q AZWS DSSC KAS DXZNN DASNN

As a hint, we note that the letter *W* represents the plaintext *V*.

Trying an exhaustive search is pretty much senseless. Assuming that the plaintext alphabet encompasses only the 26 uppercase English characters, there are 26! (approximately 4.03×10^{26}) possible combinations. Thus, we must try something other than a brute force attack. An alternate technique is to make an assumption based upon our knowledge of sentence, word, and letter structure, and then follow this assumption to its natural conclusions. Once we can go no further, we choose the next most promising assumption that builds upon the first one, and so on, as long as each succeeding assumption brings us closer to a solution. If we find that we are stuck, or we reach a conclusion that contradicts a previous one, we must backtrack and alter an earlier assumption.

Here is our solution, showing the results at each step:

1. According to the hint, we may directly substitute *V* for *W*.

Q AZ<u>V</u>S DSSC KAS DXZNN DASNN

2. The first word is small, so it is probably either an *A* or an *I*; let's assume that it is an *A*.

<u>A</u> AZ<u>V</u>S DSSC KAS DXZNN DASNN

3. The third word needs a vowel, and it is likely to be the double letters. It is probably neither *II* nor *UU*, and it can't be *AA* because we have already used an *A*. Thus, we might try *EE*.

<u>A</u> AZ<u>VE</u> D<u>EE</u>C KA<u>E</u> DXZNN DA<u>E</u>NN

4. The fourth word is three letters long, and ends in an *E*; it is likely to be the word *THE*.

<u>A</u> <u>H</u>Z<u>VE</u> D<u>EE</u>C <u>THE</u> DX<u>I</u>NN D<u>HE</u>NN

5. The second word needs a vowel, but only an *I*, *O*, or *U* (we've already used *A*). Only the *I* gives us a meaningful word.

<u>A</u> <u>HIVE</u> D<u>EE</u>C <u>THE</u> DX<u>I</u>NN D<u>HE</u>NN

6. There are few four-letter words that have a double *E*, including *DEER*, *BEER*, and *SEEN*. Our knowledge of grammar suggests that the third word should be a verb, and so we select *SEEN*.

<u>A</u> <u>HIVE</u> <u>SEEN</u> <u>THE</u> <u>SXINN</u> <u>SHENN</u>

7. This sentence is not making any sense (hives cannot see), and so we probably made a bad assumption somewhere along the way. The problem seems to lie with the vowel in the second word, and so we might consider reversing our initial assumption.

<u>I</u> <u>HAVE</u> <u>SEEN</u> <u>THE</u> <u>SXINN</u> <u>SHENN</u>

8. Let's attack the last word. The double letters can't be *SS* (we've used an *S*, and besides, *SHESS* doesn't make any sense), but *LL* forms a meaningful word.

<u>I</u> <u>HAVE</u> <u>SEEN</u> <u>THE</u> <u>SXINN</u> <u>SHELL</u>

9. The final word is part of a noun phrase, and so is probably an adjective (*STALL*, for example, is rejected on this account). Searching for words that fit the pattern *S?ALL* yields SMALL.

<u>I</u> <u>HAVE</u> <u>SEEN</u> <u>THE</u> <u>SMALL</u> <u>SHELL</u>

Thus, we have reached a solution.

We may make the following three observations about this problem solving process:

- We applied many different sources of knowledge, such as knowledge about grammar, spelling, and vowels.

- We recorded our assumptions in one central place and applied our sources of knowledge to these assumptions to reason about their consequences.

- We reasoned opportunistically. At times, we reasoned from general to specific rules (if the word is three letters long and ends in *E*, it is probably *THE*) and at other times, we reasoned from the specific to the general (*?EE?* might be *DEER*, *BEER*, or *SEEN*, but since the word must be a verb and not noun, only *SEEN* satisfies our hypothesis).

What we have described is a problem-solving approach known as a *blackboard model*. The blackboard model was first proposed by Newell in 1962, and later incorporated by Reddy and Erman into the Hearsay and Hearsay II projects, both of which dealt with the problems of speech recognition [3]. The blackboard model proved to be useful in this domain, and the framework was soon applied successfully to other domains, including signal interpretation, the modeling of three-dimensional molecular structures, image understanding, and planning [4]. Blackboard frameworks have proven to be particularly distinguished with regard to the representation of declarative knowledge, and are space- and time-efficient when compared with alternate approaches [5].

Architecture of the Blackboard Framework

Englemore and Morgan explain the blackboard model by analogy to the problem of a group of people solving a jigsaw puzzle:

> "Imagine a room with a large blackboard and around it a group of people each holding over-size jigsaw pieces. We start with volunteers who put on the blackboard (assume it's sticky) their most 'promising' pieces. Each member of the group looks at his pieces and sees if any of them fit into the pieces already on the blackboard. Those with the appropriate pieces go up to the blackboard and update the evolving solution. The new updates cause other pieces to fall into place, and other people go to the blackboard to add their pieces. It does not matter whether one person holds more pieces than another. The whole puzzle can be solved in complete silence; that is, there need be no direct communication among the group. Each person is self-activating, knowing when his pieces will contribute to the solution. No *a priori* established order exists for people to go up to the blackboard. The apparent cooperative behavior is mediated by the state of the solution on the blackboard. If one watches the task being performed, the solution is built incrementally (one piece at a time) and opportunistically (as an opportunity for adding a piece arises), as opposed to starting, say, systematically from the left top corner and trying each piece" [6].

As Figure 11-1 indicates, the blackboard framework consists of three elements: a blackboard, multiple knowledge sources, and a controller that mediates among these knowledge sources [7]. Notice how the following description parallels the principles of the object model. According to Nii, "The purpose of the blackboard is to hold computational and solution-state data needed by and produced by the knowledge sources. The blackboard consists of objects from the solution space. The objects on the blackboard are hierarchically organized into levels of analysis. The objects and their properties define the vocabulary of the solution space" [8].

As Englemore and Morgan further explain, "The domain knowledge needed to solve a problem is partitioned into knowledge sources that are kept separate and independent. The objective of each knowledge source is to contribute information that will lead to a solution to the problem. A knowledge source takes a set of current information on the blackboard and updates it as encoded in its

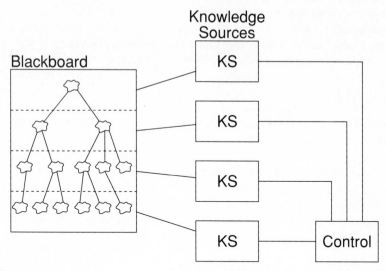

Figure 11-1
A Blackboard Framework

specialized knowledge. The knowledge sources are represented as procedures, sets of rules, or logic assertions" [9].

Knowledge sources, or KSs for short, are domain-specific. In speech recognition systems, knowledge sources might include agents that can reason about phonemes, words, and sentences. In image recognition systems, knowledge sources would include agents that know about simple picture elements, such as edges and regions of similar texture, as well as higher level abstractions representing the objects of interest in each scene, such as houses, roads, fields, cars, and people.

Generally speaking, knowledge sources parallel the hierarchic structure of objects on the blackboard. Furthermore, each knowledge source uses objects at one level as its input and then generates and/or modifies objects at another level as its output. For instance, in a speech recognition system, a knowledge source that embodies knowledge about words might look at a stream of phonemes (at a low level of abstraction) to form a new word (at a higher level of abstraction). Alternately, a knowledge source that embodies knowledge about sentence structure might hypothesize the need for a verb (at a high level of abstraction); by filtering a list of possible words (at a lower level of abstraction), this knowledge source can verify the hypothesis.

These two approaches to reasoning represent forward chaining and backward chaining, respectively. *Forward chaining* involves reasoning from specific assertions to a general assertion, and *backward chaining* starts with a hypothesis, then tries to verify the hypothesis from existing assertions. This is why we say that control in the blackboard model is opportunistic: depending upon the circumstances, a knowledge source might be selected for activation that uses either forward or backward chaining.

Knowledge sources usually embody two elements, namely, preconditions and actions. The preconditions of a knowledge source represent the state of the blackboard in which the knowledge source shows an interest. For example, a precondition for a knowledge source in an image recognition system might be the discovery of a relatively linear region of picture elements (perhaps representing a road). Triggering a precondition causes the knowledge source to focus its attention on this part of the blackboard and then take action by processing its rules or procedural knowledge.

Under these circumstances, polling is unnecessary: when a knowledge source thinks it has something interesting to contribute, it notifies the blackboard controller. Figuratively speaking, it is as if each knowledge source raises its hand to indicate that it has something useful to do; then, from among eager knowledge sources, the controller calls on the one that looks the most promising.

Analysis of Knowledge Sources

Let's return to our specific problem, and consider the knowledge sources that can contribute to a solution. As is typical with most knowledge engineering applications, the best strategy is to sit down with an expert in the domain and record the heuristics that this person applies to solve the problems in the domain. For our present problem, this might involve trying to solve a number of cryptograms and recording our thinking process along the way.

Our analysis suggests that thirteen knowledge sources are relevant; they appear with the knowledge they embody in the following list:

• Common prefixes	Common word beginnings such as re, *anti*, and *un*
• Common suffixes	Common word endings such as *ly, ing, es,* and *ed*
• Consonants	Nonvowel letters
• Direct substitution	Hints given as part of the problem statement
• Double letters	Common double letters, such as *tt, ll,* and *ss*
• Letter frequency	Probability of the appearance of each letter
• Legal strings	Legal and illegal combinations of letters, such as *qu* and *zg*, respectively
• Pattern matching	Words that match a specified pattern of letters
• Sentence structure	Grammar, including the meanings of noun and verb phrases
• Small words	Possible matches for one-, two-, three-, and four-letter words

- Solved   Whether or not the problem is solved, or if no further progress can be made
- Vowels   Nonconsonant letters
- Word structure   The location of vowels and the common structure of nouns, verbs, adjectives, adverbs, articles, conjunctives, etc.

From an object-oriented perspective, each of these knowledge sources represents a candidate class in our design: each instance embodies some state (its knowledge), each exhibits certain class-specific behavior (a suffix knowledge source can react to words suspected of having a common ending), and each is uniquely identifiable (a small-word knowledge source is independent of the pattern-matching knowledge source).

We may also arrange these knowledge sources in a hierarchy. Specifically, some knowledge sources operate upon sentences, others upon letters, still others on contiguous groups of letters, and the lowest-level ones on individual letters. Indeed, this hierarchy reflects the objects that may appear on the blackboard: sentences, words, strings of letters, and letters.

11.2 Design

Design of the Blackboard

We are now ready to design a solution to the cryptanalysis problem using the blackboard framework we have described. This is a classic example of reuse-in-the-large, in that we are able to reuse a proven architecture as the foundation of our design. The structure of the blackboard framework suggests that among the highest-level objects in our system are a blackboard, several knowledge sources, and a controller. For the most part, our remaining task is to identify the domain-specific classes and objects that specialize these general abstractions.

Blackboard Objects. The objects that appear on a blackboard exist in a structural hierarchy that parallels the different levels of abstraction of our knowledge sources. Thus, we have the following three classes:

- `sentence`   A complete cryptogram
- `word`   A single word in the cryptogram
- `cipher-letter`   A single letter of a word

Knowledge sources must also share knowledge about the assumptions each makes, so we include the following class of blackboard objects:

- `assumption`   An assumption made by a knowledge source

Finally, it is important to know what plaintext and ciphertext letters in the alphabet have been used in assumptions made by the knowledge sources, so we include the following class:

- `alphabet`   The plaintext alphabet, the ciphertext
                     alphabet, and the mapping between the two

Is there anything in common among these five classes? We answer with a resounding yes: each one represents objects that may be placed on a blackboard, and that very property distinguishes them from, for example, knowledge sources and controllers. Thus, we invent the following class as the superclass of every object that may appear on a blackboard:

```
(defclass blackboard-object ()
    ())
```

Looking at this class from its outside view, we define two applicable operations:

- `add-object`   Add the object to the blackboard
- `remove-object`   Remove the object from the blackboard

Dependencies and Assumptions. Sentences, words, and cipher-letters also have one thing in common: each is dependent upon certain knowledge sources. A given knowledge source may express an interest in one of these objects; therefore, a sentence, word, or cipher-letter must maintain a reference to each such knowledge source, so that when an assumption about the object changes, the appropriate knowledge sources can be notified that something interesting has happened. This mechanism is similar to the Smalltalk dependency mechanism we used in Chapter 9. Thus, we write

```
(defclass dependent ()
    ((the-references :accessor references)))
```

The one slot defined for this class, `the-references`, denotes the list of knowledge sources upon which an object depends. We also define the following operations for this class:

- `add-dependency`   Add a reference to the knowledge source
- `remove-dependency` Remove a reference to the knowledge source
- `dependency-p`   A selector: is the object dependent upon the
                       knowledge source?
- `each-dependency`   An iterator: visit each dependency

We use the CLOS style of naming predicates (such as `dependency-p`) by using the `-p` suffix.

Dependency is an independent property that can be "mixed in" with other classes; thus, it is well-suited to having its own mixin class. For example, a cipher-letter is a blackboard object as well as a dependent, so we can combine these two classes to achieve the desired behavior. Using mixins in this way increases the reusability and separation of concerns in our design.

Cipher-letters and alphabets also have a property in common: instances of both of these classes may have assumptions made about them. For example, a certain knowledge source might assume that the ciphertext letter *K* represents the plaintext letter *P*. Thus, we include the following mixin class:

```
(defclass assumable-object ()
    ())
```

In our design, assumptions are not made about sentences and words, but only about single letters as in cipher-letters and alphabets. In particular, cipher-letters represent single letters about which assumptions might be made, and alphabets comprise many letters, each of which might have a different assumption made about it. Because cipher-letters and alphabets have such different state regarding assumptions, we define no slots for the class `assumable-object`; instead, we expect its subclasses to provide the necessary state. Thus, `assumable-object` serves only to define common operations, which are then implemented by specific subclasses.

We define the following operations for instances of this class:

- `state-assumption`   Make an assumption
- `retract-assumption`   Retract an assumption
- `plain-assoc`   Given a plaintext letter, return its ciphertext equivalent
- `cipher-assoc`   Given a ciphertext letter, return its plaintext equivalent
- `plain-letter-defined-p`   A selector: is the plaintext letter defined?
- `cipher-letter-defined-p`   A selector: is the ciphertext letter defined?
- `plain-letter-asserted-p`   A selector: is the plaintext letter asserted?
- `cipher-letter-asserted-p`   A selector: is the ciphertext letter asserted?

These operations suggest that we should distinguish between two kinds of ciphertext/plaintext mappings: an assumption, which is a temporary mapping, and an assertion, which is a permanent mapping. During the solution of a cryptogram, knowledge sources will make many assumptions, and as we move closer to a final solution, these mappings eventually become assertions. We can explicitly capture this design decision in our classes. First, we have the following class `assumption`:

```
(defclass assumption (blackboard-object)
   ((the-knowledge-source  :accessor the-knowledge-source
                           :initarg  :the-knowledge-source)
    (the-reason            :accessor the-reason
                           :initarg  :the-reason)
    (the-plain-letter      :accessor the-plain-letter
                           :initarg  :the-plain-letter)
    (the-cipher-letter     :accessor the-cipher-letter
                           :initarg  :the-cipher-letter)
    (the-assumable-objects :accessor the-assumable-objects)))
```

We treat assumptions as blackboard objects because they represent state that is of general interest to all knowledge sources. The various slots represent the following properties:

- `the-knowledge-source`   The knowledge source that made the assumption
- `the-reason`   The reason the knowledge source made the assumption
- `the-plain-letter`   The plaintext letter about which the assumption is being made
- `the-cipher-letter`   The assumed value of the plaintext letter
- `the-assumable-objects`   The blackboard objects to which the assumption applies

The need for each of these slots is largely derived from the very nature of an assumption: a particular knowledge source made an assumption about a plaintext/ciphertext mapping, and did so for a certain reason (usually because some rule was triggered). The need for the last slot, `the-assumable-objects`, is less obvious. We include it because of the problem of backtracking. If we ever have to reverse an assumption, we must notify all blackboard objects for which the assumption was originally made, so that they in turn can alert the knowledge sources they depend upon (via the dependency mechanism) that their meaning has changed.

Next, we have the subclass named `assertion`:

```
(defclass assertion (assumption)
   ())
```

The classes `assumption` and `assertion` share the following operations:

- `state-assumption`   Make an assumption
- `retract-assumption`   Retract an assumption
- `retractable-p`   A selector: is the assumption temporary?

All assumption objects answer `true` to the predicate `retractable-p`, whereas all assertion objects answer `false`. Additionally, once made, an assertion can neither be restated nor retracted.

Design of the Blackboard Objects. Let's complete our design of the `sentence`, `word`, and `cipher-letter` classes, followed by the `alphabet` class. A sentence is quite simple: it is a blackboard object as well as a dependent, and it denotes a list of words that comprise the sentence. Thus, we may write

```
(defclass sentence (blackboard-object dependent)
   ((the-words :accessor the-words)))
```

In addition to the operations `add-object` and `remove-object` defined by its superclass `blackboard-object`, plus the four operations defined in `dependent`, we add the following two sentence-specific operations:

- `sentence-value` Return the current value of the sentence
- `solved-p` Return `true` if there is an assertion for all
  words in the sentence

At the start of the problem, `sentence-value` returns a string representing the original cryptogram. Once `solved-p` evaluates true, the operation `sentence-value` may be used to retrieve the plaintext solution.

Like the sentence class, a word is a kind of blackboard object as well as a kind of dependent. Furthermore, a word denotes a collection of letters. To assist the knowledge sources that manipulate words, we include a reference from a word to its sentence, as well as from a word to the previous and next word in the sentence. Thus, we may write the following:

```
(defclass word (blackboard-object dependent)
   ((the-letters       :accessor the-letters)
    (the-sentence      :accessor the-sentence
                       :initarg  :the-sentence)
    (the-previous-word :accessor the-previous-word)
    (the-next-word     :accessor the-next-word
                       :initarg :the-next-word)))
```

Similar to the sentence operations, we define the following two word operations:

- `word-value` Return the current value of the word
- `solved-p` Return `true` if there is an assertion for every
  letter in the word

We may next define the class `cipher-letter`. An instance of this class is a kind of blackboard object, an assumable object, and a dependent as well. In addition to the inherited behaviors, each cipher-letter object has a value (such as the ciphertext letter *H*) as well as a list of assumptions regarding its corresponding plaintext letter. Thus, we may write the following:

```
(defclass cipher-letter (blackboard-object assumable-object dependent)
    ((the-word               :accessor the-word
                             :initarg  :the-word)
     (the-cipher-letter      :accessor the-cipher-letter
                             :initarg  :the-cipher-letter)
     (the-plain-assumptions :accessor the-plain-assumptions)))
```

The slot named `the-plain-assumptions` may contain many assumption objects in the order of their creation, with the most recent assumption in this list representing the current assumption. The reason we choose to keep a history of all assumptions is to permit knowledge sources to look at earlier assumptions that were rejected, so that they can learn from earlier mistakes.

There is only one new operation for this class:

- `letter-value`   Return the current value of the letter

As we mentioned earlier, we must also provide an implementation for the eight operations defined for its superclass, `assumable-object`.

Consider next the class named `alphabet`. This class represents the entire plaintext and ciphertext alphabet, plus the mappings between the two. This information is important because each knowledge source can use it to determine which mappings have been made and which are yet to be done. For example, if we already have an assertion that the ciphertext letter *C* is really the letter *M*, then an alphabet object records this mapping so that no other knowledge source can apply the plaintext letter *M*. For efficiency, we need to query about the mapping both ways: given a ciphertext letter, return its plaintext mapping, and given a plaintext letter, return its ciphertext mapping. We may define the `alphabet` class as follows:

```
(defclass alphabet (blackboard-object assumable-object)
    ((the-plaintext-map  :accessor the-plaintext-map)
     (the-ciphertext-map :accessor the-ciphertext-map)))
```

Just as for the class `cipher-letter`, we must redefine the `assumable-object` operations to use the state associated with the alphabet.

Now we can define the class `blackboard`. This class uses the five main classes we described earlier; thus we may write it as follows:

```
(defclass blackboard ()
    ((the-assumptions :accessor the-assumptions)
     (the-sentence    :accessor the-sentence)
     (the-words       :accessor the-words)
     (the-letters     :accessor the-letters)
     (the-alphabet    :accessor the-alphabet
                      :initform (make-instance 'alphabet))))
```

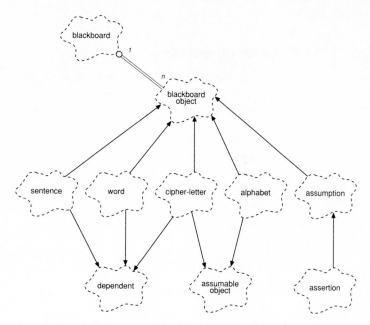

Figure 11-2
Blackboard Class Diagram

We have no :initarg nor :initform option for most of the slots because, initially, a blackboard contains no assumptions, sentences, words, or letters. However, a clean blackboard does include an alphabet (with no mappings), and for this reason we use the :initform option for the last slot.

The blackboard class provides operations such as state-assumption and retract-assumption, which it shares with all instances of the class assumption, and the operations add-object and remove-object, which it shares with all instances of the class blackboard-object. Our design includes five blackboard-specific operations:

- reset   Clean the blackboard
- assert-problem   Place an initial problem on the blackboard
- solved-p   Return true if the sentence is solved
- retrieve-solution   Return the solved plaintext sentence
- connect   Attach the knowledge source to the blackboard

The last operation is needed to create a dependency between a blackboard and its knowledge sources.

We summarize our design of the classes associated with the blackboard class in the class diagram shown in Figure 11-2. This diagram primarily shows inheritance relationships; for simplicity, it omits using relationships, such as that between an assumption and an assumable object.

Design of the Knowledge Sources

In a previous section, we identified thirteen knowledge sources relevant to this problem. Just as we did for the blackboard objects, we may design a class structure encompassing these knowledge sources and thereby elevate all common characteristics to more abstract classes.

Design of Specialized Knowledge Sources. Assume for the moment the existence of an abstract class called `knowledge-source`, whose purpose is much like that of the class `blackboard-object`. Rather than treat each of the thirteen knowledge sources as a direct subclass of this more general class, it is useful to first perform a domain analysis and see if there are any clusters of knowledge sources. Indeed, there are such groups: some knowledge sources operate on whole sentences, others upon whole words, others upon contiguous strings of letters, and still others on individual letters. We may capture our design decisions by writing the following:

```
(defclass sentence-knowledge-source (knowledge-source)
    ())

(defclass word-knowledge-source (knowledge-source)
    ())

(defclass string-knowledge-source (knowledge-source)
    ())

(defclass letter-knowledge-source (knowledge-source)
    (()))
```

For each of these abstract classes, we may provide specific subclasses. For example, the subclasses of the abstract class `sentence-knowledge-source` include

```
(defclass sentence-structure-knowledge-source (sentence-knowledge-source)
    ())

(defclass solved-knowledge-source (sentence-knowledge-source)
    ())
```

Similarly, the subclasses of the intermediate class `word-knowledge-source` include

```
(defclass word-structure-knowledge-source (word-knowledge-source)
    ())

(defclass small-word-knowledge-source (word-knowledge-source)
    ())
```

```
(defclass pattern-matching-knowledge-source (word-knowledge-source
                                              pattern-matcher)
    ())
```

The last class requires some explanation. Earlier, we said that the purpose of this class was to propose words that fit a certain pattern. We can use pattern matching symbols similar to those used by Unix's *grep* tool:

- Any item   ?
- Not item   ~
- Closure item   *
- Start group   {
- Stop group   }

With these symbols, we might give an instance of this class the pattern `?E~{A E I O U}`, thereby asking it to give us from its dictionary all the three-letter words starting with any letter, followed by an *E*, and ending with any letter except a vowel. Since we expect pattern matching to be a generally useful facility for other parts of this system, as well as for other applications, we choose to develop a mixin class rather than encapsulate it in the pattern matching knowledge source. For the same reason, we also choose to make the `pattern-matcher` class a subclass of a more general class named `dictionary`. Thus, a dictionary object serves as a repository of words from which we may access individual words directly, but then a pattern-matcher object acts as a filter by accessing words from a dictionary according to a given pattern. We may capture these design decisions as follows:

```
(defclass dictionary ()
    ())
```

```
(defclass pattern-matcher (dictionary)
    ())
```

We have not completed the design of the slots for these two classes because the details of their implementation do not concern us at this point. We might view a dictionary as a list of words, or as a randomly accessible stream, but no matter which representation we choose, the necessary behavior required by instances of this class remains the same.

Continuing, we may declare the subclasses of the class `string-knowledge-source` as follows:

```
(defclass common-prefix-knowledge-source (string-knowledge-source)
    ())
```

```
(defclass common-suffix-knowledge-source (string-knowledge-source)
    ())
```

```
(defclass double-letter-knowledge-source (string-knowledge-source)
    ())
```

```
(defclass legal-string-knowledge-source (string-knowledge-source)
    ())
```

Lastly, we can write the subclasses of the abstract class `letter-knowledge-source`:

```
(defclass direct-substitution-knowledge-source (letter-knowledge-source)
    ())
```

```
(defclass vowel-knowledge-source (letter-knowledge-source)
    ())
```

```
(defclass consonant-knowledge-source (letter-knowledge-source)
    ())
```

```
(defclass letter-frequency-knowledge-source (letter-knowledge-source)
    ())
```

Generalizing the Knowledge Sources. As it turns out, there are only two primary operations that apply to all these specialized classes:

- `reset`   Restart the knowledge source
- `evaluate-blackboard`   Evaluate the state of the blackboard

The reason for this simple interface is simply that knowledge sources are relatively autonomous entities: we point one to an interesting blackboard object, and then tell it to evaluate its rules according to the current global state of the blackboard. As part of the evaluation of its rules, a given knowledge source might do any one of several things:

- Propose an assumption about the substitution cipher
- Discover a contradiction among previous assumptions, and cause the offending assumption to be retracted
- Propose an assertion about the substitution cipher
- Tell the controller that it has some interesting knowledge to contribute

These are all general actions that are independent of the specific kind of knowledge source. To generalize even further, these actions represent the behavior of an inference engine. Simply stated, an *inference engine* is an object that, given a set of rules, evaluates those rules either to generate new rules (forward-chaining) or to prove some hypothesis (backward-chaining). Thus, we propose the following class:

```
(defclass inference-engine ()
    ((the-rules :accessor the-rules :initarg :the-rules)))
```

The slot defined for this class holds all the rules appropriate to the inference engine. This class has only one primary operation:

- `evaluate-rules`   Evaluate the rules of the inference engine

Thus, the main purpose of each specialized knowledge source is to establish its knowledge-specific rules. The operation `evaluate-blackboard` first invokes `evaluate-rules`, and then selects any of the four actions we discussed earlier.

What exactly is a rule? To illustrate, we might write the following rule for the common suffix knowledge source:

```
'((* I ? ?)
    (* I N G)
    (* I E S)
    (* I E D))
```

This rule means that, given a string of letters matching the pattern *I?? (the antecedent), the candidate suffixes include *ING*, *IES*, and *IED* (the consequents). To summarize, we may define a class that represents a rule as follows:

```
(defclass rule ()
    ((the-antecedent :accessor the-antecedent)
     (the-consequent :accessor the-consequent)))
```

In terms of its class structure, we may thus say that a knowledge source is a kind of inference engine. Similarly, because every knowledge source depends upon some collection of blackboard objects, it is also fair to say that a knowledge source is a dependent. In this manner, we incorporate the dependency mechanisms for knowledge sources just as we did for blackboard objects.

We may capture these design decisions as follows:

```
(defclass knowledge-source (inference-engine dependent)
    ((the-blackboard  :accessor the-blackboard)
     (the-controller  :accessor the-controller)
     (the-assumptions :accessor the-assumptions)))
```

This class includes the slots `the-blackboard` and `the-controller` as a means of referencing the objects with which it operates. The slot named `the-assumptions` exists so that the knowledge source can keep track of all the assumptions it has ever made (and perhaps learn from its mistakes).

Instances of the class `blackboard` serve as a repository of blackboard objects. For a similar reason, we need a `knowledge-sources` class, denoting the entire collection of knowledge sources for a particular problem. Thus, we may write

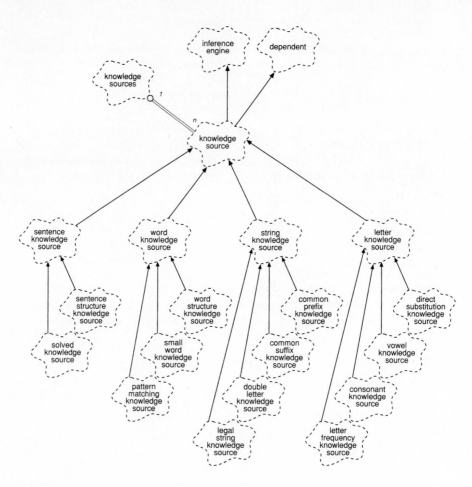

Figure 11-3
Knowledge Sources Class Diagram

```
(defclass knowledge-sources ()
    ((the-knowledge-sources :accessor the-knowledge-sources
                           :initform (make-knowledge-sources)))))
```

We include the `:initform` slot option so that when we create an instance of the class `knowledge-sources`, we also create the thirteen individual knowledge source objects. We may perform three operations upon instances of this class:

- `restart` — Restart the knowledge sources
- `start-knowledge-sources` — Give each knowledge source its initial conditions
- `connect` — Attach the knowledge source to the blackboard or to the controller

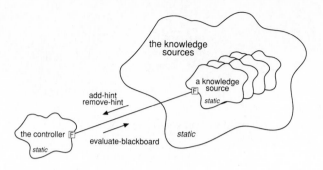

Figure 11-4
Controller Mechanism

Figure 11-3 provides the class structure of the `knowledge-source` classes, according to our design decisions.

Design of the Controller

Figure 11-4 describes how the controller and individual knowledge sources interact. At each stage in the solution of a cryptogram, a particular knowledge source might discover that it has a useful contribution to make, and so gives a hint to the controller. Conversely, it might decide that its earlier hint no longer applies, and so may remove the hint. Once all knowledge sources have been given a chance, the controller selects the most promising hint and activates the appropriate knowledge source by invoking its `evaluate-blackboard` operation.

How does the controller decide which knowledge source to activate? We may devise a few suitable rules:

- An assertion has a higher priority than an assumption.
- The solver knowledge source provides the most useful hints.
- The pattern matcher knowledge source provides higher priority hints than the sentence structure knowledge source.

We could use the dependent mixin class to provide a repository of hints for the controller. However, because these hints are prioritized, it is better to produce a subclass, whose behavior is to order these dependents:

```
(defclass ordered-dependent (dependent)
    ())
```

Instances of this class are just like instances of the `dependent` class, except that the operation `add-dependency` does its work according to some ordering function.

Knowing that the controller uses this class, we may write the following interface:

```
(defclass controller ()
   ((the-hints              :accessor the-hints)
    (the-knowledge-sources :accessor the-knowledge-sources)))
```

The slot named `the-hints` represents an instance of the class `ordered-dependent`.

Seven operations apply to controller objects:

- `reset`   Restart the controller
- `add-hint`   Add a knowledge source hint
- `remove-hint`   Remove a knowledge source hint
- `process-next-hint`   Evaluate the next highest priority hint
- `solved-p`   A selector: return `true` if the problem is solved
- `unable-to-proceed-p` A selector: return `true` if the knowledge sources are stuck
- `connect`   Attach the controller to the knowledge source

11.3 Evolution

Integrating the Blackboard Framework

Now that we have defined the key abstractions for our domain, we may continue by putting them together to form a complete application. Because CLOS is a loosely typed language, it is possible (and desirable) for us to develop the methods of our system incrementally and iteratively. Indeed, our style is to implement and test the system one mechanism at a time.

Integrating the Topmost Objects. Figure 11-5 is an object diagram that captures our design of the topmost object in the system, paralleling the structure of the generic blackboard framework in Figure 11-1.

We may capture these design decisions in the class named `cryptographer`:

```
(defclass cryptographer ()
   ((the-blackboard         :accessor the-blackboard
                            :initform (make-instance 'blackboard))
    (the-knowledge-sources :accessor the-knowledge-source
                            :initform (make-instance 'knowledge-sources))
    (the-controller         :accessor the-controller
                            :initform (make-instance 'controller))))
```

We provide the `:initform` option for each slot, so that whenever we create an instance of this class, its state is properly initialized. Our style is to not use a

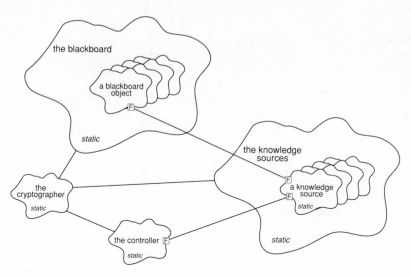

Figure 11-5
Cryptanalysis Object Diagram

`:type` slot option, although we do know the slot's type, because the `:initform` option leaves little chance that we will violate our design decision. Besides, CLOS can only identify type violations at the time of execution.

We define three primary operations for this class:

- `initialize-instance`   Connect the blackboard, knowledge sources, and controller
- `reset`   Restart the application
- `decipher`   Solve the given cryptogram

In typical CLOS style, we choose to define a function that acts as a generator of instances for the class `cryptographer`. We may write this as follows:

```
(defun create-cryptographer ()
    (defvar *cryptographer* (make-instance 'cryptographer)))
```

Invoking this function creates the special variable `*cryptographer*`, which denotes an instance of the class `cryptographer`. The use of the `defvar` macro is appropriate here, because `*cryptographer*` is meant to be global in scope.

The behavior we require during initialization is to create the dependencies between the blackboard and its knowledge sources, and between the knowledge sources and the controller. Although we have referred to the operation `initialize-instance`, we need not call it directly, because `initialize-instance` is a primary method called automatically by `make-instance`. The best

place to create these dependencies, therefore, is in an :after method of
initialize-instance, which we may write as follows:

```
(defmethod initialize-instance :after ((application cryptographer))
    (connect (the-blackboard application) (the-knowledge-sources application))
    (connect (the-knowledge-sources application) (the-controller application)))
```

Notice how we use the various accessor methods to reference the individual
slots of the cryptographer object.

The reset method is equally simple: all it must do is reset the slots of cryptographer object:

```
(defmethod reset ((application cryptographer))
    (reset (the-blackboard application))
    (reset (the-knowledge-sources application))
    (reset (the-controller application))
    t)
```

Notice that we defined the cryptographer method decipher to require a string
as the given cipher. We did so in order to decouple the mechanism of deciphering from the way the user inputs the cryptogram; as is our style, we strive to
build general mechanisms, not specific policies. Thus, the root of our application takes the form of a function that builds upon the decipher method:

```
(defun decode ()
    (reset *cryptographer*)
    (format t "~&Enter the ciphertext => ")
    (let ((plaintext (decipher *cryptographer* (string-upcase (read-line)))))
        (cond
            ((equal "" plaintext)
                (format t "~&Unable to decode the ciphertext")
                ())
            (t
                (format t "~&Plaintext => ~a" plaintext)
                t)))))
```

We use the let form to declare the locally scoped variable plaintext, whose
value is set to the value returned by the decipher method. Notice also that we
force conversion of the input string from the user to uppercase, to simplify the
work of our knowledge sources.

The decipher method is slightly more complicated. Basically, we must first
invoke the method assert-problem to set up the problem on the blackboard.
Next, we must start the knowledge sources by bringing their attention to this
new problem. Finally, we must loop, telling the controller to process the next
hint at each new pass, either until the problem is solved or until all the knowledge sources are unable to proceed. We may capture these design decisions as
follows:

```
(defmethod decipher ((application cryptographer) ciphertext)
    (check-type ciphertext string)
    (let ((controller (the-controller application)))
        (assert-problem (the-blackboard application) ciphertext)
        (start-knowledge-sources (the-knowledge-sources application))
        (loop
            (when (unable-to-proceed-p controller) (return ""))
            (when (solved-p controller (return (retrieve-solution controller)))
            (process-next-hint controller)))))
```

This method has two arguments, named `application` and `ciphertext`. We want to distinguish this method on the first argument, so we qualify it with the class `cryptographer`. This is not a multimethod (meaning that it discriminates upon the class of more than argument), so we don't qualify the second argument, although for security, we do check its type.

Continuing, let's look at one of the blackboard methods and one of the controller methods used in `decipher`, namely, `assert-problem` and `retrieve-solution`.

The `assert-problem` method is particularly interesting, because it must generate an entire set of blackboard objects. For reasons that will become clear, we choose to process the string from right to left. In pseudocode, our algorithm is as follows:

```
;; trim all leading and trailing blanks from the string
;; return from the method if the resulting string is empty
;; create a sentence object
;; add the sentence to the blackboard
;; create a word object (this will be the rightmost word in the sentence)
;; add the word to the sentence
;; add the word to the blackboard
;; for each character in the string, from right to left
;;      if the character is a space
;;          make the current word the next word
;;          create a word object
;;          add the word to the sentence
;;          add the word to the blackboard
;;      else
;;          create a cipher-letter object
;;          add the letter to the word
;;          add the letter to the blackboard
```

We can express this algorithm in CLOS as follows:

```
(defmethod assert-problem ((the-blackboard blackboard) (ciphertext))
    (check-type ciphertext string)
    (let ((the-string     (string-trim '(#\space) ciphertext))
          (current-word    ())
          (next-word       ())
          (current-letter ()))
        (when (string-equal "" the-string) (return-from assert-problem nil))
        (setf (the-sentence the-blackboard) (make-instance 'sentence))
```

```
(setf current-word
  (make-instance 'word
    :the-sentence  (the-sentence the-blackboard)
    :the-next-word next-word))
(push current-word (the-words (the-sentence the-blackboard)))
(push current-word (the-words the-blackboard))
(dotimes (index (length the-string) t)
    (let ((the-character
      (char the-string (- (- (length the-string) 1) index))))
        (if (eq '#\space the-character)
            (and (setf next-word current-word)
                 (setf current-word
                   (make-instance 'word
                     :the-sentence (the-sentence the-blackboard)
                     :the-next-word next-word))
                 (setf (the-previous-word next-word) current-word)
                 (push current-word
                   (the-words (the-sentence the-blackboard)))
                 (push current-word (the-words the-blackboard)))
            (and (setf current-letter
                   (make-instance 'cipher-letter
                     :the-word current-word
                     :the-cipher-letter the-character))
                 (push current-letter (the-letters current-word))
                 (push current-letter (the-letters the-blackboard))))))
t))
```

Like `decipher`, `assert-problem` is not a multimethod, and so we only qualify the first argument.

The controller method `retrieve-solution` is far simpler; we simply return the value of the sentence on the blackboard:

```
(defmethod retrieve-solution ((the-blackboard blackboard))
    (sentence-value (the-sentence the-blackboard)))
```

The method `sentence-value` is only slightly more complicated. We generate a string by concatenating the value of each word in the sentence, with a space in between:

```
(defmethod sentence-value ((the-sentence sentence))
    (let ((the-string ()))
        (dolist (a-word (the-words the-sentence) t)
            (setf the-string
              (concatenate 'string the-string (word-value a-word) " ")))
        (string-right-trim '(#\space) the-string)))
```

In a similar manner, the method `word-value` generates a string by concatenating the value of each letter in the word:

```
(defmethod word-value ((the-word word))
    (let ((the-string ()))
        (dolist (a-letter (the-letters the-word) t)
            (push (letter-value a-letter) the-string))
        (reverse (coerce the-string 'string))))
```

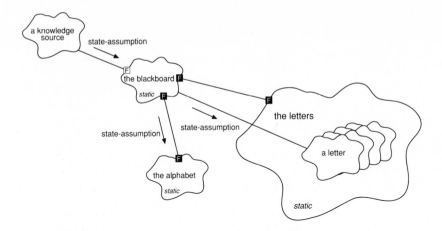

Figure 11-6
Assumption Mechanism

The method `letter-value` is slightly more complicated. If an assumption for this letter exists, then we must return the most recent assumption. Otherwise, we return the initial cipher-letter value:

```
(defmethod letter-value ((the-letter cipher-letter))
    (if (null (the-plain-assumptions the-letter))
        (the-cipher-letter the-letter)
        (the-plain-letter (first (the-plain-assumptions the-letter)))))
```

Implementing the Assumption Mechanism. At this point, we have implemented the mechanisms that allow us to set and retrieve values for blackboard objects. Now, let's turn to a slightly different topic, namely, the mechanism for making assumptions about blackboard objects. This is a particularly interesting issue, because assumptions are dynamic; they are routinely created and destroyed during the process of forming a solution.

Figure 11-6 illustrates the basic flow of control when a knowledge source states an assumption. Once the knowledge source creates an assumption, it notifies the blackboard, which in turn makes the assumption for its alphabet and then for each letter to which the assumption applies. Let's look at the implementation of this mechanism, starting with the most specific blackboard objects first.

Stating an assumption about a cipher-letter is fairly straightforward: we simply push the assumption on the list of assumptions that form part of the state of a cipher letter. Thus, we may write the following:

```
(defmethod state-assumption (the-assumption (the-object cipher-letter))
    (check-type the-assumption assumption)
    (push the-assumption (the-plain-assumptions the-object))
    t)
```

This method discriminates upon the second argument only, and so we qualify it, not the first.

Our design of the `assumption` class includes the means whereby each assumption object keeps track of the objects it affects in the slot named `the-assumable-objects`. Thus, when we make an assumption about a cipher-letter, we must add the letter to this list. Since an assumption may affect an alphabet in the same way, we may generalize this behavior to the class `assumable-object` (of which both `cipher-letter` and `alphabet` are subclasses) in the following `:after` method:

```
(defmethod state-assumption :after (the-assumption (the-object assumable-object))
    (push the-object (the-assumable-objects the-assumption)))
```

This is a good example of how to use `:after` methods: if part of the processing associated with a generic function can be identified as applying to either a more general or more specific set of classes, this processing is a candidate for a `:before`, `:after`, or `:around` method.

What if an assertion has already been made about the letter? If so, then we must not permit a new assumption to be stated. To stop any further action before the state of the letter is changed, we can write the following `:around` method:

```
(defmethod state-assumption :around (the-assumption (the-object cipher-letter))
    (if (plain-letter-asserted-p the-object (the-plain-letter the-assumption))
        nil
        (call-next-method)))
```

We use an `:around` method instead of a `:before` method because an `:around` method allows us to decide if the primary method should even be called (using `call-next-method`). In the code above, if we discover that the letter already has an assertion, we simply return `nil`.

You may recall that the method `plain-letter-asserted-p` is a predicate defined for all assumable objects. For the class `cipher-letter`, we implement it as follows:

```
(defmethod plain-letter-asserted-p ((the-object cipher-letter) the-letter)
    (check-type the-letter character)
    (and (not (null (the-plain-assumptions the-object)))
        (not (retractable-p (first (the-plain-assumptions the-object))))))
```

This method returns `true` only if there are any assumptions, and then only if the last assumption is not an assertion. Thus, we must specialize the method `retractable-p` for the classes `assumption` and `assertion`:

```
(defmethod retractable-p ((the-assumption assumption))
   t)

(defmethod retractable-p ((the-assumption assertion))
   nil)
```

Stating an assumption for an `alphabet` object requires a different `:around` and primary method, because its state is fundamentally different from that of a cipher-letter. For example, the `:around` method tests to see if there is already an assertion about either the ciphertext letter or the plaintext letter of the given assumption:

```
(defmethod state-assumption :around (the-assumption (the-object alphabet))
   (if (or (plain-letter-asserted-p the-object
              (the-plain-letter the-assumption))
           (cipher-letter-asserted-p the-object
              (the-cipher-letter the-assumption)))
       nil
       (call-next-method)))
```

The primary method is also more complicated. First, in pseudocode, we state its algorithm as follows:

```
;; set plain to the assumption's plaintext letter
;; set cipher to the assumption's ciphertext letter
;; create a new plain/cipher association, and add it to plain's assumptions
;; create a new cipher/plain association, and add it to cipher's assumptions
```

We may express this in CLOS as follows:

```
(defmethod state-assumption (the-assumption (the-object alphabet))
   (check-type the-assumption assumption)
   (let ((plain (the-plain-letter the-assumption))
         (cipher (the-cipher-letter the-assumption))
         (plain-map (the-plaintext-map the-object))
         (cipher-map (the-ciphertext-map the-object)))
      (if (plain-letter-defined-p the-object plain)
          (push the-assumption (second (assoc plain plain-map)))
          (setf (the-plaintext-map the-object)
             (acons plain (list (list the-assumption)) plain-map)))
      (if (cipher-letter-defined-p the-object cipher)
          (push the-assumption (second (assoc cipher cipher-map)))
          (setf (the-ciphertext-map the-object)
             (acons cipher (list (list the-assumption)) cipher-map)))
      t))
```

Notice that in this method, we must check to see if either the plaintext or ciphertext letter is already defined. If so, then we simply add a new association; if not, then we must initialize the state of the appropriate plain/cipher or cipher/plain mapping as an association list. Since the fact that an alphabet is represented as two association lists is encapsulated, no client need know about these details; thus all normal access is through methods at a much higher level

of abstraction. For example, we hide this representation from all clients that
must ask if either a plaintext or ciphertext letter is asserted:

```
(defmethod plain-letter-asserted-p ((the-object alphabet) the-letter)
    (check-type the-letter character)
    (let ((the-association (assoc the-letter (the-plaintext-map the-object))))
        (and (not (null the-association))
            (not (retractable-p (first (second the-association)))))))

(defmethod cipher-letter-asserted-p ((the-object alphabet) the-letter)
    (check-type the-letter character)
    (let ((the-association (assoc the-letter (the-ciphertext-map the-object))))
        (and (not (null the-association))
            (not (retractable-p (first (second the-association)))))))
```

Let's generalize this operation even further. Very often, a knowledge source will
need to know if, given an entire set of letters, some or all of them were either
asserted or defined. Thus, we would like to write forms such as this:

```
(some-letters-p 'plain-letter-asserted-p
                (the-letters the-blackboard)
                '(#\A #\E #\I #\O #\U))
```

This form returns `true` if any vowels are defined on the blackboard. We may
implement this form as a macro:

```
(defmacro some-letters-p (text source letters)
    (list `dolist (list `item letters `nil)
        (list `if (list text source `item)
            (list `return `t))))
```

With a slight modification, we may write a macro to check that all letters match
some predicate:

```
(defmacro all-letters-p (text source letters)
    (list `dolist (list `item letters `t)
        (list `if (list `not (list text source `item))
            (list `return `nil))))
```

Now we are ready to implement the `state-assumption` method for the blackboard itself. In pseudocode, we may write

```
;; add the assumption to the blackboard's list of assumptions
;; state the assumption for the blackboard's alphabet
;; for each letter on the blackboard
;;      state the assumption for the letter
```

We may implement this in CLOS as follows:

```
(defmethod state-assumption (the-assumption (the-blackboard blackboard))
    (check-type the-assumption assumption)
    (push the-assumption (the-assumptions the-blackboard))
    (state-assumption the-assumption (the-alphabet the-blackboard)))
```

```
(dolist (item (the-letters the-blackboard) t)
  (if (equal (the-cipher-letter item) (the-cipher-letter the-assumption))
      (state-assumption the-assumption item))))
```

In its most naive implementation, retracting an assumption simply undoes the work of `state-assumption`. For example, to retract an assumption about a cipher-letter, we just pop its list of plaintext assumptions, up to and including the assumption we are retracting. In this manner, the given assumption and all assumptions that built upon it are undone.

A more sophisticated mechanism is possible. For example, suppose that we made an assumption that a certain one-letter word is really just the letter *I* (assuming we need a vowel). We might make a later assumption that a certain double-letter word is *NN* (assuming we need a consonant). If we then find we must retract the first assumption, we probably don't have to retract the second one. This approach requires us to add a new slot to the class `assumption`, so that we can keep track of what assumptions are dependent upon others.

Adding New Knowledge Sources

Now that we have the key abstractions of the blackboard framework in place and mechanisms like those for stating and retracting assumptions are working, our next step is to implement the `inference-engine` class, since all knowledge sources depend upon it. As we mentioned earlier, this class has only one really interesting operation, namely, `evaluate-rules`. We will not show its details here, because this particular method reveals no new important design issues.

Once we are confident that our inference engine works properly, we may incrementally add each knowledge source. We emphasize the use of an incremental process for two reasons:

- For a given knowledge source, it is not clear what rules are really important until we apply them to real problems.
- Debugging the knowledge base is far easier if we implement and test smaller related sets of rules, rather than trying to test them all at once.

Fundamentally, implementing each knowledge source is a problem of knowledge engineering. For a given knowledge source, we must confer with an expert (perhaps ourselves or a cryptologist) to decide what rules are meaningful. As we test each knowledge source, our analysis may reveal that certain rules are useless, others are either too specific or too general, and perhaps some are missing. We may then choose to alter the rules of a given knowledge source or even add new sources of knowledge.

Figure 11-7 illustrates the mechanism that each knowledge source uses to manipulate blackboard objects. Note that each knowledge source maintains a list of blackboard objects in which it is interested (via the slot named `the-references`, which is inherited from the superclass named `dependent`).

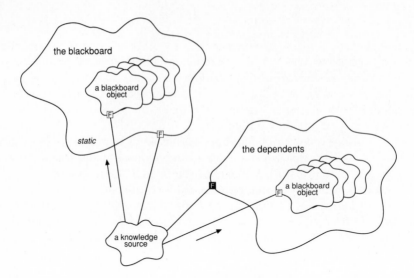

Figure 11-7
Knowledge Source Mechanism

Additionally, each knowledge source is connected to the blackboard and can see the state of all blackboard objects. Once a knowledge source is triggered, according to the controller mechanism described in Figure 11-4, it starts its inference engine to process its collection of dependent objects. The result of this evaluation, as we described earlier, is usually to state or retract assumptions, using the assumption mechanism shown in Figure 11-6.

As we implement each knowledge source, we may discover common rules and/or common behavior. For example, the `word-structure-knowledge-source` and the `sentence-structure-knowledge-source` share a common behavior, because both must know how to evaluate rules regarding the legal ordering of certain constructs. The former knowledge source is interested in the arrangement of letters; the latter knowledge source is interested in the arrangement of words. In either case, the processing is the same; thus it is reasonable for us to alter the knowledge source class structure by developing a new mixin class, called `structure-knowledge-source`, in which we place this common behavior.

This new knowledge source class hierarchy highlights the fact that evaluating a set of rules is dependent upon both the kind of knowledge source as well as the kind of blackboard object. For example, given a specific knowledge source, it might use forward-chaining on one kind of blackboard object, and backward-chaining on another. Furthermore, given a specific blackboard object, how it is evaluated will depend upon which knowledge source is applied. This gives us an opportunity to write our methods even more concisely, by using CLOS's facility for multimethods, which are multiply polymorphic. For example, given the following generic function:

```
(defgeneric evaluate-rules
  (the-knowledge-source the-blackboard-object))
```

we may write multimethods that specialize on the class of the knowledge source as well as the class of the blackboard object. For example, we might write

```
(defmethod evaluate-rules
  ((the-structure-knowledge-source structure-knowledge-source)
   (the-blackboard-object blackboard-object))
  ...)
```

which specializes on the `structure-knowledge-source` but applies to any kind of blackboard object. Alternately, we might write

```
(defmethod evaluate-rules
  ((the-small-word-source small-word-knowledge-source)
   (the-word word))
  ...)
```

in which the classes `small-word-knowledge-source` and `word` are both used when dispatching the generic function to determine the applicable methods defined by the user.

11.4 Modification

Adding New Functionality

In this section, we consider an improvement to the functionality of the crypt-analysis system and observe how our design weathers the change.

In any intelligent system, it is important to know what the final answer is to a problem, but it is often equally important to know how the system arrived at this solution. Thus, we desire our application to be introspective: it should keep track of when knowledge sources were activated, what assumptions were made and why, and so on, so that we can later question it, for example, about why it made an assumption, how it arrived at another assumption, and when a particular knowledge source was activated.

To add this new functionality, we need to do two things. First, we must devise a mechanism for keeping track of the work that the controller and each knowledge source does, and second, we must modify the appropriate methods so that they record this information. Figure 11-8 illustrates this introspection mechanism. Basically, the design calls for the knowledge sources and the controller to register what they did in some central repository.

Let's start by devising the classes needed to support this mechanism. First, we might define the class `action`, which serves to record what a particular knowledge source or controller did:

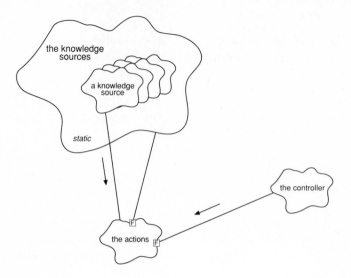

Figure 11-8
Introspection Mechanism

```
(defclass action ()
    ((who   :accessor who   :initform :who)
     (what  :accessor what  :initform :what)
     (why   :accessor why   :initform :why)))
```

For example, if the controller selected a particular knowledge source for activation, it would create an instance of this class, set the who slot to itself, set the what slot to the knowledge source, and set the why slot to some explanation (perhaps including the current priority of the hint).

Now, we need a collection class to hold these actions:

```
(defclass actions ()
    ((the-actions :accessor the-actions)))
```

We must include an instance of this class as part of the state of the class cryptographer.

The first part of our task is done, and the second part is just as easy. Consider for a moment where important events take place in our application. As it turns out, there are five primary places:

- Methods that state an assumption
- Methods that retract an assumption
- Methods that activate a knowledge source
- Methods that cause rules to be evaluated
- Methods that register hints from a knowledge source

CLOS's `:before` and `:after` methods make the task quite easy.

For example, consider the generic function `state-assumption`. This operation is specialized for both cipher-letters and alphabets. However, we may record this event by using a generalized `:after` method:

```
(defmethod state-assumption :after (the-assumption (the-object assumable-object))
    (let ((the-action (make-instance 'action
                          :who  the-object
                          :what the-assumption
                          :why  ()))))
        (push the-action (the-actions *cryptographer*))))
```

Thus, we need not alter the code associated with any primary method; rather, we can add this new behavior entirely by adding new `:before` or `:after` methods.

To complete our work here, we must also implement an object that can answer who, what, when, and why questions from the user. The design of such an object is not terribly difficult, because all the information it needs to know may be found as the state of instances of the class `actions`.

Changing the Requirements

Once we have a stable implementation, many new requirements can be incorporated with minimal change to our design. Let's consider three kinds of new requirements:

- The ability to decipher languages other than English
- The ability to decipher using transposition ciphers as well as single substitution ciphers
- The ability to learn from experience

The first change is fairly easy, because the fact that our application uses English is largely immaterial to our design. Assuming the same character set is used, it is mainly a matter of changing the rules associated with each knowledge source. Actually, changing the character set is not that difficult either, because even the `alphabet` class is not dependent upon what characters it manipulates.

The second change is much harder, but it is still possible in the context of the blackboard framework. Basically, our approach is to add new sources of knowledge that embody information about transposition ciphers. Again, this change does not alter any existing key abstraction or mechanism in our design; rather, it involves the addition of new classes that use existing facilities, such as the `inference-engine` class and the assumption mechanism.

The third change is the hardest of all, mainly because machine learning is on the fringes of our knowledge in artificial intelligence. As one approach, when the controller discovers it can no longer proceed, it might ask the user for a hint. By recording this hint, along with the actions that led up to the system being stuck, the blackboard application can avoid a similar problem in the future. We can incorporate this simplistic learning mechanism without vastly altering any of our existing classes; as with all the other changes, this one can build on existing facilities.

Further Readings

Englemore and Morgan [C 1988] furnish a comprehensive treatment of blackboard systems, including their evolution, theory, design, and application. Among other topics, there are descriptions of two object-oriented blackboard systems, BB1 from Stanford, and BLOB, developed for the British Ministry of Defense. Other useful sources of information regarding blackboard systems may be found in Hayes-Roth [J 1985] and Nii [J 1986].

Detailed discussions concerning forward- and backward-chaining in rule-based systems may be found in Barr and Feigenbaum [J 1981]; Brachman and Levesque [J 1985]; Hayes-Roth, Waterman, and Lenat [J 1983]; and Winston and Horn [G 1989].

Meyer and Matyas [I 1982] cover the strengths and weaknesses of various kinds of ciphers, along with algorithmic approaches to breaking them.

A summary of the Common Lisp Object System, with examples, appears in the appendix.

Ada
Traffic Management System

The economics of software development have progressed to the point where it is now feasible to automate many more kinds of applications than ever before, ranging from embedded microcomputers that control automobile engines to tools that eliminate much of the drudgery associated with producing an animated film and systems that manage the many functions of a manned spacecraft. The distinguishing characteristic of the larger systems is that they are all extremely complex. Building systems so that their implementation is small is certainly an honorable task, but reality tells us that certain large problems demand large implementations. For some massive applications, it is not unusual to find software development organizations that employ several hundred programmers who must collaborate to produce a million or more lines of code against a set of requirements that are guaranteed to change during development. Such projects rarely involve the development of single programs; they more often encompass multiple, cooperative programs that must execute across a distributed target system consisting of many computers connected to one another in a variety of ways. To reduce development risk, such projects usually involve a central organization that is responsible for systems architecture and integration; the remaining work is subcontracted to other companies.

Traffic Management System Requirements

The traffic management system has two primary functions: train routing and train-systems monitoring. Related functions include traffic planning, train-location tracking, traffic monitoring, collision avoidance, failure prediction, and maintenance logging. Figure 12-1 provides a block diagram for the major elements of the traffic management system [1].

The locomotive analysis and reporting system includes several discrete and analog sensors for monitoring elements such as oil temperature, oil pressure, fuel quantity, alternator volts and amperes, throttle setting, engine RPM, water temperature, and drawbar force. Sensor values are presented to the train engineer via the on-board display system and to dispatchers and maintenance personnel elsewhere on the network. Warning or alarm conditions are registered whenever certain sensor values fall outside of normal operating range. A log of sensor values is maintained to support maintenance and fuel management.

The energy management system advises the train engineer in real time as to the most efficient throttle and brake settings. Inputs to this system include track profile and grade, speed limits, schedules, train load, and power available, from which the system can determine fuel-efficient throttle and brake settings that are consistent with the desired schedule and safety concerns. Suggested throttle and brake settings, track profile and grade, and train position and speed are made available for display on the on-board display system.

The on-board display system provides the human/machine interface for the train engineer. Information from the locomotive analysis and reporting system, the energy management system, and the data management unit are made available for display. Soft keys exist to permit the engineer to select different displays.

The data management unit serves as the communications gateway between all on-board systems and the rest of the network, to which all trains, dispatchers, and other users are connected.

Train-location tracking is achieved via two devices on the network: location transponders and the Navstar global positioning system (GPS) system. The locomotive analysis and reporting system can determine the general location of a train via dead reckoning by counting wheel revolutions. This information is augmented by information from location transponders, which are placed every kilometer along a track and at critical track junctions. These transponders relay their identity to passing trains via their data management units, from which a more exact train location may be determined. Trains may also be equipped with GPS receivers, from which train location may be determined to within one meter.

A wayside interface unit is placed wherever there is some controllable device (such as a switch) or a sensor (such as an infrared sensor for detecting overheated wheel bearings). Each wayside interface unit may receive commands from a local ground-terminal controller (for example, to turn a signal on or off). Devices may be overridden by local manual control. Each unit can also report its current setting. A ground-terminal control serves to relay information to and from passing trains and to and from wayside interface units. Ground-terminal controllers are placed along a track, spaced close enough so that every train is always within range of at least one terminal.

Every ground-terminal controller relays its information to a common network control system. Connections between the network-control system and each ground-terminal controller may be made via microwave link, landlines, or fiber optics, depending upon the remoteness of each ground-terminal controller. The network control system monitors the health of the entire network and can automatically route information in alternate ways in the event of equipment failure.

The network control system is ultimately connected to one or more dispatch centers, which comprise the rail-operations control system and other users. At the rail-operations control system, dispatchers can establish train routes and track the progress of individual trains. Individual dispatchers control different territories; each dispatcher's control console may be set up to control one or more territories. Train routes include instructions for automatically switching trains from track to track, setting speed restrictions, setting out or picking up cars, and allowing or denying train clearance to a specific track section. Dispatchers may note the location of track work along train routes for display to train engineers. Trains may be stopped from the rail-operations control system (manually by dispatchers or automatically) when hazardous conditions are detected (such as a runaway train, track failure, or a potential collision condition). Dispatchers can also call up any information available to individual train engineers, as well as send movement authority, wayside device settings, and plan revisions.

Track layouts and wayside equipment may change over time. The numbers of trains and their routes may change daily. The system must be designed to permit incorporation of new sensor, network, and processor technology.

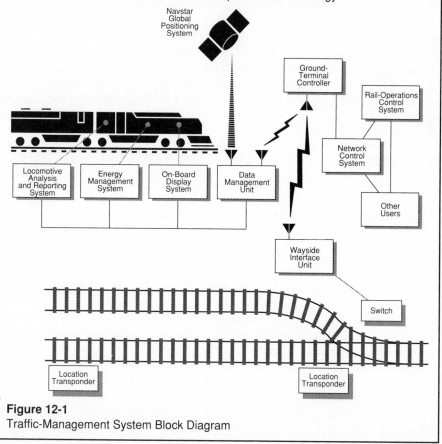

Figure 12-1
Traffic-Management System Block Diagram

Thus, the development team as a whole never assembles as one; it is distributed over space and – because of the personnel turnover common in large projects – over time.

A developer who is content with writing small, stand-alone, single-user, window-based tools finds the problems associated with building massive applications staggering – so much so that it is folly even to try. However, the actuality of the business and scientific world is such that complex software systems must be built. Indeed, in some cases, it is folly not to try. Imagine using a manual system to control air traffic around a major metropolitan center or to manage the life-support system of a manned spacecraft or the accounting activities of a multinational bank. Successfully automating such systems not only addresses the very real problems at hand, but also leads to a number of tangible and intangible benefits, such as lower operational costs, greater safety, and increased functionality. Of course, the operative word here is *successfully*. Building complex systems is plain hard work, and requires the application of the best engineering practices we know, along with the creative insight of a few great designers.

This chapter tackles such a problem, to demonstrate that the notation and process of object-oriented design scale up to programming-in-the-colossal. The language we use is Ada, which is object-based, not object-oriented (because it lacks support for inheritance). We chose Ada because, of the languages we apply in this book, it is the best suited for large applications. Indeed, Ada is the language of choice for many massive applications, including the FAA's Advanced Automation System, the European Space Station, and financial management systems for the U.S. Army and Finland's largest banks.

12.1 Analysis

Defining the Boundaries of the Problem

To most people living in the United States, trains are an artifact of an era long past; in Europe, the situation is entirely the opposite. Unlike the United States, Europe has few national and international highways, and gasoline and automobile prices are comparatively very high. Thus, trains are an essential part of the continent's transportation network; tens of thousands of kilometers of track carry people and goods daily, both within cities and across national borders. In all fairness, trains do still provide an important and economical means of transporting goods within the United States. Additionally, as major metropolitan centers grow more crowded, light rail transport is increasingly viewed as an attractive option to easing congestion and addressing the problems of pollution from internal combustion engines.

Still, railroads are a business and consequently must be profitable. Railroad companies must delicately balance the demands of frugality and safety and the pressures to increase traffic against efficient and predictable train scheduling. These conflicting needs suggest an automated solution to train traffic management, including computerized train routing and monitoring of all elements of the train system.

Such automated and semiautomated train systems exist today in Sweden, Great Britain, West Germany, France, and Japan [2]. A similar system, called the Advanced Train Control System, is under development in Canada and the United States, with participation by Amtrak, Burlington, the Canadian National Railway Company, CP Rail, CSX Transportation, the Norfolk and Western Railway Company, the Southern Railway Company, and Union Pacific [3]. The motivation for each of these systems is largely economic and social: lower operating costs and more efficient utilization of resources are the goals, with improved safety as an integral byproduct.

The sidebar provides the high-level requirements for a train traffic management system. Obviously, this is a highly simplified statement of requirements. In practice, detailed requirements for an application as large as this come about only after the viability of an automated solution is demonstrated, and then only after many hundreds of person/months of analysis involving the participation of numerous domain experts and the eventual users and clients of the system. Ultimately, the requirements for a large system may encompass thousands of pages of documentation, specifying not only the general behavior of the system, but intricate details such as the screen layouts to be used for human/machine interaction.

Even from these highly elided system requirements, we can make two observations about the process of developing the traffic management system:

- The design must be allowed to evolve over time.
- The implementation must rely upon existing standards to the largest extent practical.

Our experience with developing large systems has been that an initial statement of requirements is never complete, sometimes vague, and always self-contradictory. For these reasons, we must consciously concern ourselves with the management of uncertainty during design, and we suggest that the design of such a system be deliberately allowed to evolve over time in an incremental and iterative fashion. As we pointed out in Chapter 7, the very process of design gives both users and developers better insight into what requirements are really important – better than any paper exercise in writing requirements documents in the absence of an existing implementation or prototype. Also, since developing the software for a large system may take several years, software requirements must be allowed to change to take advantage of the rapidly changing hardware technology. It is undeniably futile to craft an elegant software design targeted to a hardware technology that is guaranteed to be obsolete by the time the system is fielded. This is why we suggest that, whatever mechanisms we craft as part of our software design, we should rely upon existing standards for communications, graphics, networking, and sensors. For truly novel systems, it is sometimes necessary to invent new hardware or software technology. However, this adds risk to a large project, which already involves a customarily high risk. Software development clearly remains the technology of highest risk in the successful deployment of any large automated application, and our goal is to limit this risk to a manageable level, not to increase it.

Since the focus of this book is upon design, not analysis, we will not dwell upon a domain analysis for the traffic management system. Besides, analyzing the requirements for a large system is beyond the scope of any single book. However, we do suggest that object-oriented analysis is an ideal method for use in the analysis of large systems such as this one, primarily because it helps unite the users and developers of the system through a common vocabulary drawn from the problem space. We therefore expect the documentation that results from this analysis to crisply define the key abstractions in the problem and their desired behavior.

In the rest of this chapter, we use our object-oriented design notation to express design decisions for the traffic management system. The size of this problem clearly prevents us from providing a complete design or implementation as we have done for earlier applications, but we will illustrate how one can express a high-level software architecture for a large system.

System Requirements Versus Software Requirements

Large projects are usually organized around some small, centrally located team responsible for establishing the overall system architecture, with the actual development work subcontracted out to other companies or different teams within the same company. Even during analysis, system architects usually have in mind some conceptual model that divides the hardware and software elements of the implementation. One may argue that this is design, not analysis, but we counter by saying that one must start constraining the design space at some point. Indeed, it is difficult to ascertain if the block diagram in Figure 12-1 represents system requirements or a system design. Regardless of this issue, the block diagram clearly suggests that the system architecture at this stage of development is principally object-oriented. For example, it shows complex objects such as the energy management system and the rail-operations control system, each of which performs a major function in the system. This is just as we discussed in Chapter 4: in large systems, the objects at the highest levels of abstraction are clustered along the lines of major system functions. How we identify and refine these objects during analysis is little different than how we do so during design.

Once we have a strawman architecture at the level of a block diagram like the one in Figure 12-1, we can articulate system requirements in the context of each block, just as we have done in the sidebar. For more detail, we might use data flow diagrams, object diagrams, or structured prose to illustrate how these various parts interact, including whatever level of detail is necessary to communicate the desired behavior of the system as a whole.

Eventually, we must translate these system requirements into requirements for the hardware and software segments of the system, so that different organizations, each with different skills, can proceed in parallel to attack their particular part of the problem. Making these hardware and software trade-offs is a difficult task, particularly if the hardware and software organizations are loosely coupled, and especially if they are parts of entirely different companies. Sometimes, it is intuitively obvious that certain hardware should be employed. For example, one might use off-the-shelf terminals or workstations for both the on-board display system and for the displays in the rail-operations control centers. Similarly, it may be obvious, for example, that software is the right implementation vehicle for describing train schedules. The decisions about which platform to use for everything else, either a hardware or software implementation, depends as much on the personal preferences of the system architects as on anything else. One might throw special hardware at the problem where performance needs are critical, or use software where flexibility is more important.

For the purposes of our problem, we assume that an initial hardware architecture has been chosen by the system architects. This choice need not be considered irreversible, but at least it gives us a starting point in terms of which to allocate software requirements. Indeed, as we proceed with our design, we need the freedom to trade off hardware and software: we might later decide that additional hardware is needed to satisfy some requirement, or that certain functions can be performed better through software than hardware.

Figure 12-2 illustrates the target hardware for the traffic management system, using our notation for process diagrams. This process architecture parallels the block diagram of the system in Figure 12-1. Specifically, there is one computer on board each train, encompassing the locomotive analysis and reporting system, the energy management system, the on-board display system, and the data management unit. We expect that some of the on-board devices, such as the display, are intelligent, but we assume that these devices are not necessarily programmable. Continuing, each location transponder is connected to a transmitter, through which messages may be sent to passing trains; no computer is associated with a location transponder. On the other hand, each collection of wayside devices (each of which encompasses a wayside interface unit and its switches) is controlled by a computer which may communicate via its transmitter and receiver with a passing train or a ground-terminal controller. Each ground-terminal controller ultimately connects to a local area network, one for each dispatch center (encompassing the rail-operations control system). Because of the need for uninterrupted service, we have chosen to place two computers at each dispatch center: a primary computer and a backup computer that we expect will be brought on-line whenever the primary computer fails. During idle periods, the backup computer can be used to serve the computational needs of other, lower priority users

When operational, the traffic management system may involve hundreds of computers, including one for each train, one for each wayside interface unit, and two at each dispatch center. The process diagram only shows the presence of a few of these computers, since the configurations of similar computers are completely redundant.

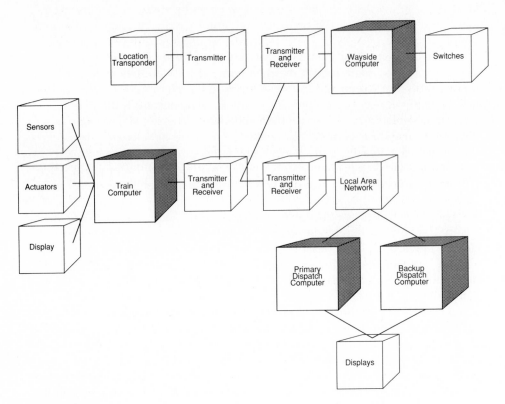

Figure 12-2
Traffic Management System Process Diagram

As we discussed in Chapter 7, the key to maintaining sanity during the development of any complex project is to engineer sound and explicit interfaces among the key parts of the system. This is particularly important when defining hardware and software interfaces. At the start, interfaces can be loosely defined, but they must quickly be formalized so that different parts of the system can be developed, tested, and released in parallel. Well-defined interfaces also make it far easier to make hardware/software trade-offs as opportunities arise, without disrupting already completed parts of the system. Furthermore, we cannot expect all of the developers in a large development organization to be programming athletes. We must therefore leave the specification of these key abstractions and mechanisms to our best system architects.

Key Abstractions and Mechanisms

A study of the requirements for the traffic management system suggests that we really have four different subproblems to solve:

- Networking
- Database
- Human/machine interface
- Real-time analog device control

How did we come to identify these problems as those involving the greatest development risk?

The thread that ties this entire system together is a distributed communications network. Messages pass by radio from transponders to trains, between trains and ground-terminal controllers, between trains and wayside interface units, and between ground-terminal controllers and wayside interface units. Messages must also pass between dispatch centers and individual ground-terminal controllers. The safe operation of this entire system depends upon the timely and reliable transmission and reception of messages.

Additionally, this system must keep track of the current locations and planned routes of many different trains simultaneously. We must keep this information current and self-consistent, even in the presence of concurrent updates and queries from around the network. This is basically a distributed database problem.

The engineering of the human/machine interfaces poses a different set of problems. Specifically, the users of this system are principally train engineers and dispatchers, none of whom are necessarily skilled in using computers. The user interface of an operating system such as Unix might be marginally acceptable to a professional software engineer, but it is largely regarded as user-hostile by end users of applications such as the traffic management system. All forms of user interaction must therefore be carefully engineered to suit this domain-specific group of users.

Lastly, the traffic management system must interact with a variety of sensors and actuators. No matter what the device, the problems of sensing and controlling the environment are similar, and so should be dealt with in a consistent manner by the system.

Each of these four subproblems involves largely independent issues. Our system architects need to identify the key abstractions and mechanisms involved in each, so that we can assign experts in each domain to tackle their particular subproblem in parallel with the others.

If we do a brief domain analysis across these four problems, we find that there are three high-level key abstractions:

- Trains   Include locomotives and cars
- Tracks   Encompass profile, grade, and wayside devices
- Plans   Include schedules, orders, clearances, authority, and crew assignments

Every train has a current location on the tracks, and each train has exactly one active plan. Similarly, the number of trains at each point on the tracks may be zero or one; for each plan, there is exactly one train, involving many points on the tracks.

Continuing, we may devise a key mechanism for each of the four subproblems:

- Message passing mechanism
- Train-plan mechanism
- Display mechanism
- Sensor mechanism

Why do we even worry about these mechanisms so early in the design process? The reason is that these four mechanisms form the soul of our design. They represent approaches to what we have identified as the areas of highest development risk. It is essential that we deploy our best system architects here to experiment with alternative approaches and eventually settle upon a framework from which more junior developers may compose the rest of the system.

12.2 Design

Message Passing Mechanism

By *message*, we don't mean method invocation, as in an object-oriented programming language; we are referring to a concept in the vocabulary of the problem domain at a much higher level of abstraction. For example, typical messages in the traffic management system include signals to activate wayside devices, indications of trains passing specific locations, and orders from dispatchers to train engineers. In general, these kinds of messages are passed at two different levels within the traffic management system:

- Between computers and devices
- Among computers

Our interest is in the second level of message passing. Because our problem involves a geographically distributed communications network, we must consider issues such as noise, equipment failure, and security.

Analysis of the Communications Requirements. We may make a first cut at identifying these messages by examining each pair of communicating computers, as shown in our process diagram (Figure 12-2). For each pair, we must ask two questions: First, what information should be passed from one computer to the other, and at what level of abstraction should this information be? There is no empirical solution for these questions. Rather, we must use an incremental, iterative approach until we are satisfied that the right messages are being passed and that there are no communications bottlenecks in the system (perhaps because of too many messages over one path, or messages being too large or too small).

It is absolutely critical at this level of design to focus upon the substance, not the form, of these messages. Too often, we have seen system architects start off by selecting a bit-level representation for messages. The real problem with prematurely choosing such a low-level representation is that it is guaranteed to change and thus disrupt every client that depends upon a particular representation. Furthermore, at this point in the design process, we cannot know enough about how these messages will be used to make intelligent decisions about time- and space-efficient representations.

By focusing upon the substance of these messages, we mean to urge a focus upon the outside view of each class of messages. In other words, we must decide upon the purpose and semantics of each message, and what operations we can meaningfully perform upon each message.

The class diagram in Figure 12-3 captures our design decisions regarding some of the most important messages in the traffic management system. Note that all messages are ultimately instances of a generalized class named `Message`, which encompasses the behavior common to all messages. Three abstract classes represent the major categories of messages, namely, train status messages, train-plan messages, and wayside device messages. Each of these classes is further specialized, and our final design might include hundreds of such specialized classes. Thus, the existence of the abstract classes becomes even more important; without them, we would end up with hundreds of unrelated – and therefore difficult to maintain – modules representing each specialized class. As our design unfolds, we are likely to discover other important groupings of messages and then invent other specialized intermediate abstract classes.

Translating the Design into Implementation. How might we translate this design into an implementation in Ada, which is an object-based programming language and thus does not directly support inheritance? In practice, we find it common to design as if inheritance were possible and then use a variety of implementation techniques to fake it if the language does not directly support inheritance. In Ada, the common approach is to use a combination of generic packages (representing parameterized classes) and discriminated private types (representing abstract classes). As Figure 12-3 suggests, the class `Message` is actually a parameterized class, which is implemented in Ada as a type exported from a generic package and contains the operations common to all messages, such as sending and receiving. Abstract classes such as `Train_Status_Message` can then be represented as private types, with a discriminant for each subclass. For example, we might draft the outside view of the class `Train_Status_Message` as follows:

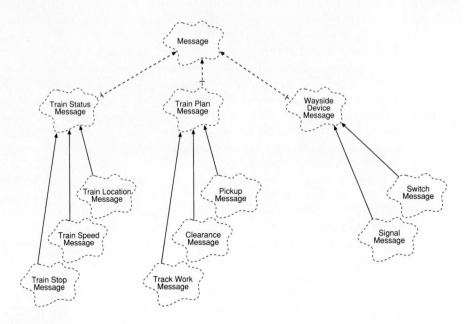

Figure 12-3
Message Class Diagram

```
with System_Classes;
package Train_Status_Messages is

     type Kind is (Train_Location, Train_Speed, Train_Stop);
     type Train_Status_Message (The_Kind : Kind) is private;

     procedure Set_Location (The_Message  : in out Train_Status_Message;
                             The_Location : in      System_Classes.Location);
     procedure Set_Speed    (The_Message  : in out Train_Status_Message;
                             The_Speed    : in      System_Classes.Speed);
     procedure Stop         (The_Message  : in out Train_Status_Message);

     function Location_Of (The_Message : in Train_Status_Message)
        return System_Classes.Location;
     function Speed_Of    (The_Message : in Train_Status_Message)
        return System_Classes.Speed;
     function Is_Stopped   (The_Message : in Train_Status_Message) return Boolean;

private
     ...
end Train_Status_Messages;
```

The package `System_Classes` contains the definitions for common classes such as `Location` and `Speed`.

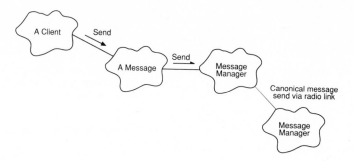

Figure 12-4
Message Passing Mechanism

Each instantiation of the class `Message` introduces a new type, as shown in the class diagram. Because they are structurally related, subclasses of the intermediate classes (such as `Train_Status_Message`) introduce compatible types.

Once we have designed the interface of each of the most important messages, we can write programs that build upon these classes to simulate the creation and reception of streams of messages. We can use these programs as a temporary scaffolding to test different parts of the system during development and before the pieces with which they interface are completed.

The class diagram in Figure 12-3 is unquestionably incomplete. In practice, we find that we can identify the most important messages first, and let all others evolve as we uncover the less common forms of communication. Using an obtect-oriented design allows us to add these messages incrementally without disrupting the existing design of the system, because such changes are generally upwardly compatible.

Once we are satisfied with this class structure, we can begin to design the message passing mechanism itself. Here we have two competing goals: to devise a mechanism that provides for the reliable delivery of messages, and does so at a high enough level of abstraction so that clients need not to worry about how message delivery takes place. Such a message passing mechanism allows its clients to make simplifying assumptions about how messages are sent and received.

Figure 12-4 captures our design of the message passing mechanism. To send a message, a client invokes the operation `Send` (defined in the superclass `Message`) upon the message object. This operation in turn invokes an asynchronous `Send` operation upon some centralized `Message_Manager` object. We choose to make this an asynchronous operation because we don't want to make the client wait for the message to be sent across a radio link, which requires time for encoding, decoding, and perhaps retransmission because of noise. Eventually, this `Message_Manager` converts the value of each specialized message object into some canonical form, probably consisting of a stream of letters and numbers, and then sends this stream to its proper destination over the communications network.

Our design of the `Message_Manager` places it at the application layer in the ISO OSI model for networks [4]. This allows all message-sending clients and message-receiving clients to operate at the highest level of abstraction, namely, in terms of application-specific messages. The purpose of the `Message_Manager` object is to handle all the low-level details of the physical transfer of such messages.

Let's turn to the outside view of the `Message_Manager`. Basically, one of these objects must reside on every computer that can send or receive messages. Its essential semantics are to guarantee the transmission and reception of all kinds of messages. Since certain fatal failures may occur that prevent message passing (such as failure of a radio transmitter), this object must handle a variety of exceptional conditions.

Ada's generic packages are well-suited to expressing these semantics. First, we parameterize a package with a discrete type to represent each of the possible kinds of messages. This generic package encapsulates two inner generic procedures, one for sending and one for receiving messages. The implementation of individual message classes may instantiate either or both of these procedures by supplying them with a message type and an operation for converting the value of the message to or from some canonical form. Thus, the inside view of each message class hides the details of this lower-level message representation. Each message class should build upon some collection of canonical message utilities, so that common conversion routines are shared.

We may declare the `Message_Manager` package as follows:

```
with Network_Classes;
generic
    type Message_Kind is (<>);
package Message_Manager is

    generic
        type Message is private;
        with function String_To_Message (The_String : in String)
          return Message;
    procedure Send (The_Message : in Message;
                    From        : in Network_Classes.Id;
                    To          : in Network_Classes.Id;
                    Retry       : in Network_Classes.Retry_Count;
                    Acknowledge : in Boolean);

    generic
        type Message is private;
        with function Message_To_String (The_Message : in Message) return String;
    procedure Receive (The_Message : out Message;
                       From        : in  Network_Classes.Id;
                       To          : in  Network_Classes.Id);
```

```
function Kind_Of_Message return Message_Kind;

Transmision_Error : exception;
Reception_Error   : exception;

end Message_Manager;
```

The package `Network_Classes` contains the definitions for common classes, such as an `ID` type for uniquely identifying nodes along the communications network. Notice also the declaration of the two exceptions, `Transmission_Error` and `Reception_Error`, which may be raised whenever a message cannot be sent or is received incompletely.

We expect the final implementation of this generic package to be a bit more complex. For example, we might want to overload the sending and receiving operations to include options for synchronous communication or for timeouts. We might also want to add more exceptions, so that the causes of transmission and reception errors can be identified precisely. In any case, our design of this module allows all clients to work at the highest level of abstraction, namely, in terms of domain-specific messages. On the other hand, the implementation of this module hides a number of complex secrets. Specifically, the module must build upon common lower-level abstractions to deal with the physical transfer of messages, which may involve their encryption and decryption and the use of codes to detect and correct errors, so as to ensure reliable communication in the presence of noise or equipment failures.

Train-Plan Mechanism

As we noted earlier, the concept of a train plan is central to the operation of the traffic management system. Each train has exactly one active plan, and each plan is assigned to exactly one train and may involve many different orders and locations on the track.

Our first step is to decide exactly what parts constitute a train plan. To do so, we need to consider all the potential clients of a plan and how we expect each of them to use that plan. For example, some clients might be allowed to create plans, others might be allowed to modify plans, and still others might be allowed only to read plans. In this sense, a train plan acts as a repository for all the pertinent information associated with the route of one particular train and the actions that take place along the way, such as picking up or setting out cars.

Figure 12-5 captures our design decisions regarding the structure of the `Train_Plan` class. As in Chapter 10, we use a class diagram to show the parts that compose a train plan (much as a traditional entity-relationship diagram would do). Thus, we see that each train plan has exactly one crew and may have many general orders and many actions. We expect these actions to be time-ordered, with each action composed of information such as time, a

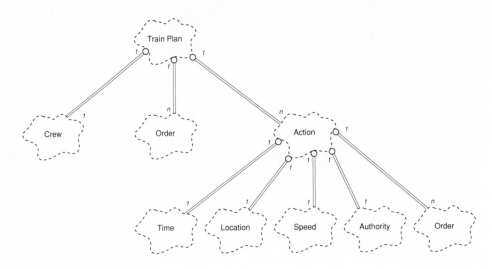

Figure 12-5
Train-Plan Class Diagram

location, speed, authority, and orders. For example, a specific train plan might consist of the following actions:

Time	Location	Speed	Authority	Orders
0800	Pueblo	As posted		Depart yard
0815	Pueblo	As posted	See Yardmaster	Pick up 50 cars
1100	Colorado Springs	40 MPH		Set out 30 cars
1300	Denver	45 MPH		Set out 20 cars
1600	Pueblo	As posted		Return to yard

As we did for the `Message` class and its subclasses, we can design the most important elements of a train plan early in the development process; its details will evolve over time, as we actually apply plans to various kinds of clients.

The fact that we may have a plethora of active and inactive train plans at any one time confronts us with the database problem we spoke of earlier. The class diagram in Figure 12-5 can serve as an outline for the logical schema of this database. The next question we might therefore ask is simply, Where are train plans kept?

In a more perfect world, with no communication noise or delays and infinite computing resources, our solution would be to place all train plans in a single, centralized database. This approach would yield exactly one instance of each train plan. However, the real world is much more perverse, and so this solution is not practical. We must expect communication delays, and we don't have unlimited processor cycles. Thus, having to access a plan located in the dispatch center from a train would not at all satisfy our real-time and near-real-time requirements However, we can create the illusion of a single,

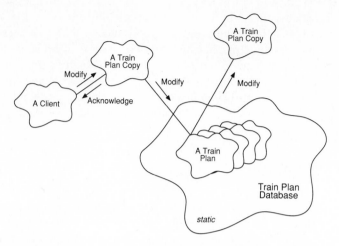

Figure 12-6
Train-Plan Mechanism

centralized database in our software. Basically, our solution is to have a database of train plans located on the computers at the dispatch center, with copies of individual plans distributed as needed at sites around the network. For efficiency, then, each train computer could retain a copy of its current plan. Thus, on-board software could query this plan with negligible delay. If the plan changed, either as a result of dispatcher action or (less likely) by the decision of the train engineer, our software would have to ensure that all copies of that plan were updated in a timely fashion.

The way this works is the function of our train-plan mechanism, shown in Figure 12-6. The primary version of each train plan resides in a centralized database at a dispatch center, with zero or more copies scattered about the network. Whenever some client requests a copy of a particular train plan, the state of this primary version is cloned and transmitted to the client, and the location of the copy in the network is recorded in the database. Now, suppose that a client on a train needed to make a change to a particular plan, perhaps as a result of some action by the train engineer. Ultimately, this client would invoke operations upon its copy of the train plan and so modify its state. These operations would also send messages to the centralized database, to modify the state of the primary version of the plan in the same way. Since we record the location in the network of each copy of a train plan, we can also broadcast messages from the centralized repository that force a corresponding update to the state of all remaining copies. To ensure that changes are made consistently across the network, we could employ a record-locking mechanism, so that train-plan changes would not be committed until all copies and the primary version were updated.

This mechanism applies equally well if some client at the dispatch center initiates the change, perhaps as a result of some dispatcher action. First, the primary version of the plan would be updated, and then changes to all copies would be broadcast throughout the network, using the same mechanism. In either case, how exactly do we broadcast these changes? The answer is that we use the message passing mechanism devised earlier. Specifically, we would need to add to our design some new train-plan messages and then build our train-plan mechanism upon this lower level message passing mechanism.

Using commercial, off-the-shelf database management systems on the dispatch computers allows us to address any requirements for database backup, recovery, audit trails, and security.

Display Mechanism

Using off-the-shelf technology for our database needs helps us to focus upon the domain-specific parts of our problem. We can achieve similar leverage for our display needs by using standard graphics facilities, such as GKS, PHIGS, or X Windows. Using off-the-shelf graphics software effectively raises the level of abstraction in our system, so that developers never need to worry about manipulating the visual representation of displayable objects at the pixel level. Still, it is important to encapsulate our design decisions regarding how various objects are represented visually.

For example, consider displaying the profile and grade of a specific section of track. Our requirements dictate that such a display may appear in two different places: at a dispatch center and on board a train (with the display focusing only upon the track that lies ahead of the train). Assuming that we have some class whose instances represent sections of track, we might take two approaches to representing the state of such objects visually. First, we might have some display-manager object that builds a visual representation by querying the state of the object to be displayed. Alternately, we could eliminate this external object and have each displayable object encapsulate the knowledge of how to display itself. We prefer this second approach, because it is simpler and more in the spirit of the object model.

There is a potential down side to this approach, however. Ultimately, we might have many different kinds of displayable objects, each implemented by different groups of developers. If we let the implementation of each displayable object proceed independently, we are likely to end up with redundant code, different implementation styles, and a generally unmaintainable mess. A far better solution is to do a domain analysis of all the kinds of displayable objects, determine what visual elements they have in common, and devise an intermediate set of class utilities that provide display routines for these common picture elements. These class utilities in turn can build upon lower level, off-the-shelf graphics packages.

Figure 12-7 illustrates this design, showing that the implementation of all displayable objects shares common class utilities. These utilities in turn build upon lower level X Window servers, which are hidden from all of the higher-level classes.

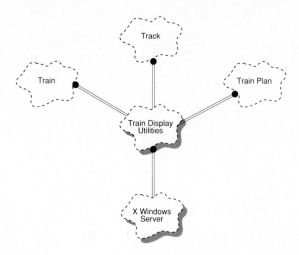

Figure 12-7
Display Mechanism

The principle advantage of this approach is that it limits the impact of any lower level changes resulting from hardware/software tradeoffs. For example, if we find that we need to replace our display hardware with more or less power-ful devices, then we need only reimplement the routines in `Train_Display_Utilities`. Without this collection of routines, low-level changes would require us to modify the implementation of every displayable object.

Sensor Mechanism

As our requirements suggest, the traffic management system includes many dif-ferent kinds of sensors. For example, sensors on each train monitor the oil temperature, fuel quantity, throttle setting, water temperature, drawbar load, and so on. Similarly, active sensors in some of the wayside devices report among other things the current positions of switches and signals. The kinds of values returned by the various sensors are all different, but the processing of different sensor data is all very much the same. For example, assuming that our computers use memory-mapped I/O, each sensor value is ultimately read as a set of bits from a specific place in memory and then converted to some sensor-specific value. Furthermore, most sensors must be sampled periodically. If a value is within a certain range, then nothing special happens other than notify-ing some client of the new value. If this value exceeds certain preset limits, then a different client might be warned. Finally, if this value goes far beyond its lim-its, then we might need to sound some sort of alarm, and notify yet another client to take drastic action (for example, when locomotive oil pressure drops to dangerous levels).

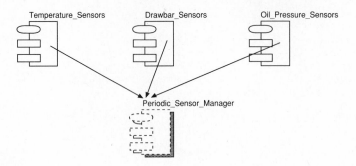

Figure 12-8
Sensor Mechanism

Replicating this behavior for every kind of sensor is not only tedious and error-prone, it also usually results in redundant code. Without exploiting this commonality, different developers will end up inventing multiple solutions to the same problem, leading to the proliferation of slightly different sensor mechanisms and, in turn, a system that is more difficult to maintain. It is highly desirable, therefore, to do a domain analysis of all periodic, nondiscrete sensors, so that we might invent a common sensor mechanism for all kinds of sensors.

Let's take an outside view of this common class by asking what operations we can perform upon its instances. We can think of three: two of them modifiers and one of them a selector. First, we must be able to tell a sensor to start sensing. As we do so, we must also tell it how often to update its sensor value, and define a range of safe and unsafe values. For completeness, we should also include an operation that tells a sensor to stop sensing. Lastly, we might include a selector to force a reading of the sensor's current value.

Might anything go wrong during the lifetime of a sensor? A client might try to start a sensor that is already running (we view stopping an already stopped sensor as not an error). Also, there might be some fatal hardware error associated with the sensor, which we can detect whenever we try to read its value. Fortunately, Ada's exception handling facility provides a means of notifying clients of such error conditions.

The operations that we can perform upon an object are only half of its outside view; we must also consider what operations this object requires of other objects. For this general sensor class, we can envision four operations: three modifiers and one selector. The three modifiers respectively provide the current value of the sensor, a warning to a client of an abnormal value, and an alert to a client of a dangerous value. Lastly, we need a selector to tell the sensor how to convert a raw stream of bits into a value for a specific kind of sensor. This knowledge best comes from outside of the sensor class.

Ada does not support subprogram variables, but it does allow generic units to have subprogram parameters. This solution works quite well for our needs here, because the physical sensors themselves are statically allocated. We may capture these design decisions in Ada as follows:

```
with System_Classes;
generic
    type Value is private;
    with procedure Notify_Client (The_Value : in Value);
    with procedure Warn_Client   (The_Value : in Value);
    with procedure Alert_Client  (The_Value : in Value);
    with function Scale          (The_Raw_Value : in Integer) return Value;
package Periodic_Sensor_Manager is

    type Sensor (Memory_Address : System_Classes.Address) is private;

    procedure Start  (The_Sensor        : in out Sensor;
                      Frequency          : in      Duration;
                      Warning_High_Limit : in      Value;
                      Warning_Low_Limit  : in      Value;
                      Alert_High_Limit   : in      Value;
                      Alert_Low_Limit    : in      Value);
    procedure Stop   (The_Sensor        : in out Sensor);

    function Current_Value_Of (The_Sensor : in Sensor) return Value;

    Sensor_Is_Already_Started : exception;
    Sensor_Failure            : exception;

private
    ...
end Periodic_Sensor_Manager;
```

We assume that the package `System_Classes` contains a suitable declaration for the discrete type `Address`, representing a physical memory location. Using this type, we can declare the type `Sensor` with a discriminate value representing the I/O port in the memory map associated with this sensor.

Because this is a generic unit, we cannot use it directly; we must provide an instantiation for each kind of sensor, as we show in Figure 12-8. We expect that the system architects would provide a number of standard instantiations that other developers could use directly. The mechanism we have invented here works best for periodic, continuous sensors; it is not well matched to discrete sensors (such as switches), nor to sensors that register single events rather than continuous values (such as the event of cars being coupled to a locomotive). If our domain analysis reveals many such sensors, it would be worthwhile to craft a similar mechanism for them.

12.3 Evolution

Module Architecture

For large systems, the package is a necessary but insufficient means of decomposition; thus, for this problem, we must focus upon a subsystem-level decomposition. Two important factors suggest that we should next devise the module architecture of the traffic management system, representing its physical software structure.

The software design for very large systems must often commence before the target hardware is completed. Software design frequently takes far longer than hardware design, and in any case, trade-offs must be made against each along the way. This implies that hardware dependencies in the software must be isolated to the greatest extent possible, so that software design can proceed in the absence of a stable target environment. It also implies that the software must be designed with the idea of replaceable subsystems in mind. In a command and control system such as the traffic management system, we might wish to take advantage of new hardware technology that has matured during the development of the system's software.

We must also have an early and intelligent physical decomposition of the system's software, so that subcontractors working on different parts of the system (perhaps even using different programming languages) can work in parallel. As we explained in Chapter 7, there are often many nontechnical reasons that drive the physical decomposition of a large system. Perhaps the most important of these concerns the assignment of work to independent teams of developers. Subcontractor relationships are usually established early in the life of a complex system, often before there is enough information to make sound technical decisions regarding proper subsystem decomposition.

We recommend that system architects be given the opportunity to experiment with alternative subsystem decompositions, so that we can have a fairly high level of confidence that our global physical design decisions are sound. This may involve prototyping on a large scale (but with all subsystem implementations stubbed out) and simulations of processor loading, message traffic, and external events. These prototypes and simulations can then carry on through the maturation of this system, as vehicles for regression testing.

How do we select a suitable subsystem decomposition? As we suggested in Chapter 4, the highest-level objects are often clustered around functional lines. Again, this is not orthogonal to the object model, because by the term *functional*, we do not mean algorithmic abstractions, embodying simple input/output mappings. We are speaking of system functions that represent outwardly visible and testable behaviors, resulting from the cooperative action of logical collections of objects. Thus, the highest-level abstractions and mechanisms that we first identify are good candidates around which to organize our subsystems. We may assert the existence of such subsystems first, and then evolve their interfaces over time.

The module diagram in Figure 12-9 represents our design decisions regarding the top-level module architecture of the traffic management system. Here we see a highly layered architecture, with each level encompassing the functions of the four subproblems we identified earlier, namely, networking, database, real-time analog device control, and the human/machine interface.

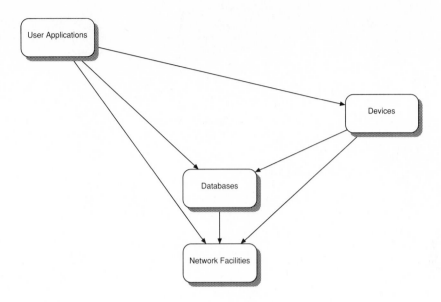

Figure 12-9
Traffic Management System Top Level Module Diagram

Subsystem Specification

If we focus upon the outside view of any of these subsystems, we find that it has all the characteristics of an object. It has a unique, albeit static, identity; it embodies a significant amount of state, and it exhibits very complex behavior. Subsystems serve as the repositories of other classes, class utilities, and objects; thus, they are best characterized by the resources they export. Practically, with the use of Ada, these resources are captured in the form of logical collections of compilation units, most of which are packages.

The module diagram in Figure 12-9 is useful but incomplete, because each subsystem in this diagram is far too large to be developed by a small team of developers. We must zoom inside each of the top-level subsystems, and further decompose them.

Figure 12-10 shows the module diagram for the subsystem `Network Facilities`. Here, we see that one subsystem is private (`Radio Communication`) and one is exported (`Messages`). The private package hides the details of software control of a physical device, while the exported subsystem provides the functionality of the message passing mechanism we designed earlier.

The subsystem named `Databases` builds upon the resources of the `Network Facilities` subsystem and serves to implement the train-plan mechanism we created earlier. As shown in Figure 12-11, the `Databases` subsystem breaks out into several distinct parts. Here we see that the subsystem

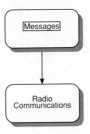

Figure 12-10
Network Facilities Module Diagram

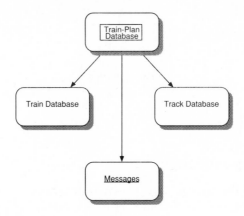

Figure 12-11
Databases Module Diagram

`Train-Plan Database` is exported from `Databases`, meaning that its resources are available to other subsystems that explicitly import it. The `Train-Plan Database` subsystem also builds upon the resources of two private subsystems (`Train Database` and `Track Database`) and one imported subsystem (`Messages`).

Continuing, the `Devices` subsystem also decomposes naturally into several smaller subsystems. As shown in Figure 12-12, we have decided to group the software related to all wayside devices into one subsystem and the software associated with all on-board locomotive actuators and sensors into another. These two subsystems are available to clients of the `Devices` subsystem, and both are built upon the resources of the `Train-Plan Database` and `Messages`. Thus, we have designed the `Devices` subsystem to implement the sensor mechanism we described earlier.

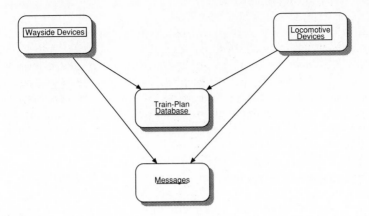

Figure 12-12
Devices Module Diagram

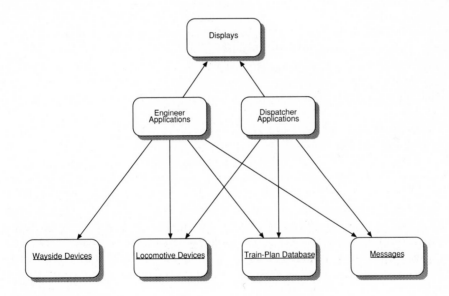

Figure 12-13
User Applications Module Diagram

Finally, as shown in Figure 12-13, we have chosen to decompose the top-level `User Applications` subsystem into several smaller subsystems, including `Engineer Applications` and `Dispatcher Applications`, to reflect the different roles of the two main users of the traffic management system. The subsystem `Engineer Applications` includes resources that provide all the train engineer/machine interaction specified in the requirements, including the functionality of the locomotive analysis and reporting system and the energy management system. We include the subsystem `Dispatcher Applications` to encompass the software that provides the functionality of all dispatcher/machine interactions. Both `Engineer Applications` and `Dispatcher Applications` share common private resources, as exported from the subsystem `Displays`, which embodies the display mechanism we described earlier.

This design leaves us with four top-level subsystems, encompassing ten smaller ones, to which we have allocated all of the key abstractions and mechanisms we invented earlier. Equally important, these lower level subsystems form the units for work assignments and the units for configuration management and version control. Even at this early stage of design, we may now start generating a stream of releases, composed of compatible versions of each subsystem. As suggested in Chapter 7, each subsystem should be owned by one person, yet may be implemented by many more. The subsystem owner directs the detailed design and implementation of the subsystem and manages its interface relative to other subsystems at the same level of abstraction. Thus, the management of a very large development project is made possible by taking a very complex problem and decomposing it into several smaller ones.

The key to making this work is the careful engineering of subsystem interfaces. Once engineered, these interfaces must be rigorously guarded. How do we determine the outside view of each subsystem? The answer is by looking at each subsystem as an object. Thus, we ask the same questions we did in Chapter 4 for much more primitive objects: what state does this object embody, what operations can clients meaningfully perform upon it, and what operations does it require of other objects?

For example, consider the subsystem `Train-Plan Database`. It builds upon three other subsystems (`Messages`, `Train Database`, and `Track Database`) and has several important clients: the subsystems `Wayside Devices`, `Locomotive Devices`, `Engineer Applications`, and `Dispatcher Applications`. The `Train-Plan Database` embodies a relatively straightforward state, specifically, the state of all train plans. Of course, the twist is that this subsystem must support the behavior of the the distributed train-plan mechanisms. Thus, from the outside, clients see a monolithic database, but from the inside, we know that this database is really distributed, and must therefore be constructed on top of the message passing mechanism found in the subsystem `Messages`.

What operations can we perform upon the `Train-Plan Database`? All the usual database operations seem to apply: adding records, deleting records, modifying records, and querying records. We would eventually capture all of these design decisions in the form of Ada packages that make up this subsystem and provide the declarations of all these operations.

At this stage in the design, we would continue the design process for each subsystem. Again, we expect that these interfaces will not be exactly right at first; we must allow them to evolve over time. Happily, as for smaller objects, our experience suggests that most of the changes we will need to make to these interfaces will be upwardly compatible, assuming that we did a good job up front in characterizing the behavior of each subsystem in an object-oriented manner.

12.4 Modification

Adding New Functionality

Old software never dies, it just gets maintained or preserved, especially for systems as large as this one. This is the reason we still find software in production use that was developed over twenty years ago (which is absolutely ancient in software years). As more users apply the traffic management system, and as we adapt this design to new implementations, clients will discover new, unanticipated uses for existing mechanisms, creating pressure to add new functionality to the system.

Let's consider a significant addition to our requirements, namely, payroll processing. Specifically, suppose that our analysis shows that train-company payroll is currently being supported by a piece of hardware that is no longer being manufactured and that we are at great risk of losing our payroll processing capability because a single serious hardware failure would put our accounting system out of action forever. For this reason, we might chose to integrate payroll processing with the traffic management system. At first, it is not difficult to conceive how these two seemingly unrelated problems could coexist; we could simply view them as separate applications, with payroll processing running as a background activity.

Further examination shows that there is actually tremendous value to be gained from integrating payroll processing. You may recall from our earlier discussion that, among other things, train plans contain information about crew assignments. Thus, it is possible for us to track actual versus planned crew assignments, and from this we can calculate hours worked, amount of overtime, and so on. By getting this information directly, our payroll calculations will be more precise and certainly more timely.

What does adding this functionality do to our existing design? Very little. Our approach would be to add one more subsystem inside the `User Applications` subsystem, representing the functionality of payroll processing. At this location in the architecture, such a subsystem would have visibility to all the important mechanisms upon which it could build. This is indeed quite common in well-structured object-oriented systems: a significant addition in the requirements for the system can be dealt with fairly easily by building new applications upon existing mechanisms.

Let's consider an even more radical change. Suppose we wanted to introduce expert system technology into our system by building a dispatcher's assistant that could advise about traffic routing and emergency responses. How would this new requirement affect our design?

Again, the answer is very little. Our solution would be to add a new subsystem between the subsystems `Train-Plan Database` and `Dispatcher Applications`, because the knowledge base embodied by this expert system parallels the contents of the `Train-Plan Database`; furthermore, the subsystem `Dispatcher Applications` is the sole client of this expert system. We would need to invent some new mechanisms to establish the manner in which advice is presented to the ultimate user. For example, we might use a blackboard architecture, as we did in the previous chapter.

Changing the Target Hardware

As we mentioned, hardware technology is still moving at a faster pace than our ability to generate software. For this reason, the target hardware for large systems becomes obsolete far earlier than does its software. For example, after several years of operational use, we might decide it was necessary to replace the displays on each train and at each dispatch center. How might this affect our existing design? If we have kept our subsystem interfaces at a high level of abstraction during the evolution of our system, this hardware change would affect our software in only minimal ways. Since we chose to encapsulate all design decisions regarding specific displays, no other subsystem was ever written to depend upon the specific characteristics of a given workstation; the system encapsulates all such hardware secrets. This means that the behavior of workstations was hidden in the subsystem named `Displays`. Thus, this subsystem acts as an abstraction firewall, which shields all other clients from the intricacies of our particular display technology.

In a similar fashion, a radical change in telecommunications standards would affect our implementation, but only in limited ways. Specifically, our design ensures that only the subsystem named `Messages` knows about network communications. Thus, even a fundamental change in networking would never affect any higher level client; the subsystem `Messages` shields them from the perversity of the real world.

None of the changes we have introduced rends the fabric of our existing design. This is indeed the ultimate mark of a well-designed, object-oriented system.

Further Readings

The requirements for the traffic management system are based upon those for the Advanced Train Control System, as described by Murphy [C 1988].

Message translation and verification occur in virtually all command and control systems. Plinta, Lee, and Rissman [C 1989] provide an excellent discourse on the issues, and offer the design of a mechanism for passing messages in a type-safe way across processors in a distributed system.

A summary of the Ada programming language, with examples, appears in the appendix.

Afterword

For books are only partly from the minds and the guts of their authors. A large part of them comes from somewhere else, and we the authors sit at our typewriters waiting for books to happen.

GUY LEFRANCOIS
Of Children

Object-oriented design is by no means the final word in design methodology; however, it does represent a fusion of some of the best ideas about building complex systems. As we have seen, object-oriented systems have been built for a variety of problem domains, and object-oriented design has been successfully applied in systems involving a few hundred lines of code, as well as in systems consisting of 1 – 10 million lines of code. We do not yet have sufficient experience to state conclusively that this design method is appropriate for even larger systems involving many tens of millions of lines of code, but we are hopeful. As is the sign of any healthy, vibrant discipline, we expect that object-oriented design will continue to evolve as we learn from applying it to real systems of yet unimaginable complexity.

Indeed, the demand for complex software continues to rise at a staggering rate. The ever-growing capabilities of our hardware and an increasing social awareness of the utility of computers create tremendous pressure to automate more and more applications of even greater complexity. The fundamental value of object-oriented design, with its well-defined notation and process, is that it releases the human spirit so that it can focus its creative energies upon the truly demanding parts of the design of a complex system.

Object-Based and Object-Oriented Programming Languages

The use of object-oriented design is not restricted to any one particular language; it is applicable to a wide spectrum of object-based and object-oriented programming languages. As important as design is, however, we cannot ignore the details of coding, for ultimately our software must be expressed in some language. Indeed, as Wulf has suggested, a programming language serves three purposes:

- "It is a design tool
- It is a vehicle for human consumption
- It is a vehicle for instructing a computer" [1]

This appendix is intended for the reader who may not be familiar with some of the five object-based and object-oriented programming languages we use for the applications in this book. It provides a summary description of each of them and introduces the reader to several other important ones.

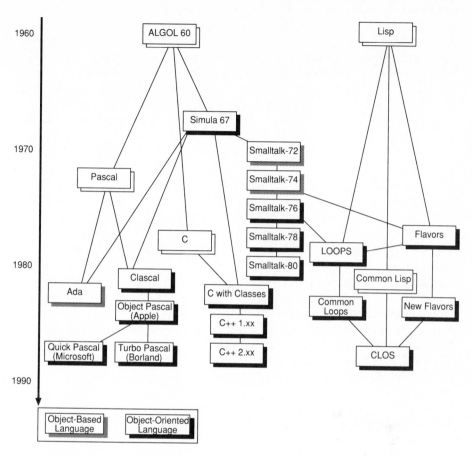

Figure A-1
A Genealogy of Object-Based and Object-Oriented Programming Languages

A.1 Concepts

Currently, there are well over 2,000 different high-order programming languages. We see so many different languages because each was shaped by the particular requirements of its perceived problem domain. Furthermore, the existence of each new language enabled developers to move on to more and more complex problems. With each previously unexplored application, language designers learned new lessons that changed their basic assumptions about what was important in a language and what was not. This evolution of languages was also heavily influenced by progress in the theory of computing, which has led to a formal understanding of the semantics of statements, modules, abstract data types, and processes.

As we discussed in Chapter 2, programming languages may be grouped into one of four generations, according to whether they support mathematic, algorithmic, data, or object-oriented abstractions. The most recent advances in programming languages have been due to the influence of the object model. By our count, there are currently over 100 different object-based and object-oriented programming languages today. As we also discussed in Chapter 2, a language is considered object-based if it directly supports data abstraction and classes; an object-oriented language is one that is object-based, but provides additional support for inheritance as a means of expressing hierarchies of classes.

The common ancestor of almost every contemporary object-based and object-oriented programming language is Simula, developed in the 1960s by Dahl, Myhrhaug, and Nygard [2]. Simula built upon the ideas of ALGOL, but added the concepts of encapsulation and inheritance. Perhaps even more important, Simula – as a language for describing systems and for developing simulations – introduced the discipline of writing programs that mirror the vocabulary of their problem domain.

Figure A-1 is inspired by the work of Schmucker [3] and shows the genealogy of the five most influential and widely used object-based and object-oriented programming languages: Smalltalk, Object Pascal, C++, CLOS, and Ada. Their importance in the construction of complex systems is exactly why we chose them for the applications in this book.

In the next several sections, we examine each of these languages in more detail, relative to the support they offer to the elements of the object model.

A.2 Smalltalk

Background

Smalltalk was created by the members of the Xerox Palo Alto Research Center Learning Research Group as the software element of the Dynabook, a visionary project of Alan Kay. Simula was the primary influence upon the language, although Smalltalk also took some ideas from the language FLEX and the work of Seymore Papert and Wallace Feurzeig. Smalltalk represents both a language and a software development environment. It is a "pure" object-oriented programming language, in that everything is viewed as an object – even integers and classes. Next to Simula, Smalltalk is perhaps the most important object-oriented programming language, because its concepts have influenced not only the design of almost every subsequent object-oriented programming language, but also the look and feel of graphic user interfaces such as the Macintosh user interface and Motif, which are now largely taken for granted.

Smalltalk evolved over almost a decade of work, and was the product of synergistic group activity. Dan Ingalls was the lead architect during most of Smalltalk's development, but there were also seminal contributions by Peter

Abstraction	Instance variables	Yes
	Instance methods	Yes
	Class variables	Yes
	Class methods	Yes
Encapsulation	Of variables	Private
	Of methods	Public
Modularity	Kinds of modules	None
Hierarchy	Inheritance	Single
	Generic units	No
	Metaclasses	Yes
Typing	Strongly typed	No
	Polymorphism	Yes (single)
Concurrency	Multitasking	Yes (defined by classes)
Persistence	Persistent objects	No

Table A-1
Smalltalk

Deutsch, Glenn Krasner, and Kim McCall. In parallel, the elements of the Smalltalk environment were developed by James Althoff, Robert Flegal, Ted Kaehler, Diana Merry, and Steve Putz. Among other important roles that they played, Adele Goldberg and David Robson served as chroniclers of the Smalltalk project.

There are five identifiable releases of Smalltalk, indicated by their year of release: Smalltalk-72, -74, -76, -78, and the most current incarnation, Smalltalk-80. Smalltalk-72 and -74 did not provide support for inheritance, but they did lay much of the conceptual foundation of the language, including the ideas of message passing and polymorphism. Later releases of the language turned classes into first-class citizens, thus completing the view that everything in the environment could be treated as an object. Smalltalk-80 has been ported to a variety of machine architectures, and is now available commercially, primarily on personal computers and workstations.

Overview

Ingalls states that "the purpose of the Smalltalk project is to support children of all ages in the world of information. The challenge is to identify and harness metaphors of sufficient simplicity and power to allow a single person to have access to, and creative control over, information which ranges from number and text through sounds and images" [4]. To this end, Smalltalk is built around two simple concepts: everything is treated as an object, and objects communicate by passing messages.

We summarize the features of Smalltalk in Table A-1, relative to the seven elements of the object model. Although the table does not indicate it, multiple inheritance is possible in Smalltalk by the redefinition of certain primitive methods [5].

Example

Consider the problem in which we have a heterogeneous list of shapes, in which each particular shape object might be a circle, a rectangle, or a solid rectangle (this is similar to the problem we introduced in Chapter 3). Smalltalk has an extensive class library that already contains classes for circles and rectangles, and so our solution in this language would be almost trivial; this demonstrates the importance of reuse. However, for the sake of comparison, let's assume that we only have primitive classes for drawing lines and arcs. Therefore, we might define the class AShape as follows:

```
Object subclass: #AShape
    instanceVariableNames: 'theCenter '
    classVariableNames: ''
    poolDictionaries: ''
    category: 'Appendix'

initialize
    "Initialize the shape"

    theCenter ← Point new

setCenter: aPoint
    "Set the center of the shape"

    theCenter ← aPoint

center
    "Return the center of the shape"

    ↑theCenter

draw
    "Draw the shape"

    self subclassResponsibility
```

We may next define the subclass ACircle as follows:

```
AShape subclass: #ACircle
    instanceVariableNames: 'theRadius '
    classVariableNames: ''
    poolDictionaries: ''
    category: 'Appendix'

setRadius: anInteger
    "Set the radius of the circle"

    theRadius ← anInteger
```

radius
>   "Return the radius of the circle"
>
>   ↑theRadius

draw
>   "Draw the circle"
>
> ```
> | anArc index |
> anArc ← Arc new.
> index ← 1.
> [index <= 4]
>     whileTrue:
>         [anArc
>             center: theCenter
>             radius: theRadius
>             quadrant: index.
>             anArc display.
>             index ← index + 1]
> ```

Continuing, the subclass ARectangle may be defined as follows:

AShape subclass: #ARectangle
>   instanceVariableNames: 'theHeight theWidth '
>   classVariableNames: ''
>   poolDictionaries: ''
>   category: 'Appendix'

setHeight: anInteger
>   "Set the height of the rectangle"
>
>   theHeight ← anInteger

setWidth: anInteger
>   "Set the width of the rectangle"
>
>   theWidth ← anInteger

height
>   "Return the height of the rectangle"
>
>   ↑theHeight

width
>   "Return the width of the rectangle"
>
>   ↑theWidth

draw
>   "Draw the rectangle"
>
> ```
> | aLine upperLeftCorner |
> aLine ← Line new.
> upperLeftCorner ← theCenter x - (theWidth / 2) @ (theCenter y - (theHeight / 2)).
> aLine beginPoint: upperLeftCorner.
> ```

```
aLine endPoint: upperLeftCorner x + theWidth @ upperLeftCorner y.
aLine display.
aLine beginPoint: aLine endPoint.
aLine endPoint: upperLeftCorner x + theWidth @ (upperLeftCorner y + theHeight).
aLine display.
aLine beginPoint: aLine endPoint.
aLine endPoint: upperLeftCorner x @ (upperLeftCorner y + theHeight).
aLine display.
aLine beginPoint: aLine endPoint.
aLine endPoint: upperLeftCorner.
aLine display
```

Lastly, the subclass ASolidRectangle may be defined as:

```
ARectangle subclass: #ASolidRectangle
    instanceVariableNames: ''
    classVariableNames: ''
    poolDictionaries: ''
    category: 'Appendix'
```

draw
```
    "Draw the solid rectangle"

    | upperLeftCorner lowerRightCorner |
    super draw.
    upperLeftCorner ← theCenter x - (theWidth quo: 2) + 1 @
                    (theCenter y - (theHeight quo: 2) + 1).
    lowerRightCorner ← upperLeftCorner x + theWidth - 1 @
                    (upperLeftCorner y + theHeight - 1).
    Display
        fill: (upperLeftCorner corner: lowerRightCorner)
        mask: Form gray
```

References

The primary references for Smalltalk are *Smalltalk-80: The Language*, by Goldberg and Robson [6]; *Smalltalk-80: The Interactive Programming Environment*, by Goldberg [7]; and *Smalltalk-80: Bits of History, Words of Advice*, by Krasner [8].

A.3 Object Pascal

Background

Object Pascal was created by developers from Apple Computer, Incorporated (some of whom were involved in the development of Smalltalk), in conjunction with Niklaus Wirth, the designer of Pascal. Object Pascal's immediate ancestor is Clascal, an object-oriented version of Pascal for the Lisa. Object Pascal was

Abstraction	Instance variables	Yes
	Instance methods	Yes
	Class variables	No
	Class methods	No
Encapsulation	Of variables	Public
	Of methods	Public
Modularity	Kinds of modules	Unit (interface/implementation)
Hierarchy	Inheritance	Single
	Generic units	No
	Metaclasses	No
Typing	Strongly typed	Yes
	Polymorphism	Yes (single)
Concurrency	Multitasking	No
Persistence	Persistent objects	No

Table A-2
Object Pascal

made publicly available in 1986 and is the first object-oriented programming language supported by the Macintosh Programmer's Workshop (MPW), the development environment for Apple's family of Macintosh Computers. The class library for MPW, called MacApp, provides the framework for constructing applications that conform to the Macintosh User Interface Guidelines.

Object Pascal has inspired two other object-oriented versions of Pascal: Quick Pascal, by Microsoft, and Turbo Pascal 5.x, by Borland.

Overview

As Schmucker states, "Object Pascal is a 'bare bones' object-oriented language. It makes no provision for class methods, class variables, multiple inheritance, or metaclasses. These concepts were specifically excluded in an attempt to streamline the learning curve encountered by most novice object-oriented programmers" [9].

We summarize the features of Object Pascal in Table A-2, relative to the seven elements of the object model.

Example

Since Object Pascal supports the separate compilation of unit interfaces and implementations, it is common practice to place the outside view and the inside view of each class in different files. For the shape problem, we might declare the interface of each class as follows:

```
unit UShapes; interface

uses
    UMacApp, UPrinting, UDialog, ToolUtils, Packages, UMacAppUtilities;

type

    TShape = object(TObject)

        fCenter : Point;

        procedure IShape;
        procedure SetCenter (TheCenter : Point);
        procedure Draw;

        function Center : Point;

    end;

    TCircle = object(TShape)

        fRadius : Integer;

        procedure IShape; override;
        procedure SetRadius (TheRadius : Integer);
        procedure Draw; override;

        function Radius : Integer;

    end;

    TRectangle = object(TShape)

        fHeight : Integer;
        fWidth  : Integer;

        procedure IShape; override;
        procedure SetHeight (TheHeight : Integer);
        procedure SetWidth  (TheWidth  : Integer);
        procedure Draw; override;

        function Height : Integer;
        function Width  : Integer;

    end;

    TSolidRectangle = object(TRectangle)

        procedure Draw; override;

    end;

implementation
    {$I UShapes.incl.p}
end.
```

Notice that although all fields are unencapsulated in Object Pascal, it is common style to assume that they are private and accessible only via method calls.

In another file, we may complete the implementation of each of these methods, primarily through the use of the graphics facilities defined by QuickDraw:

```
procedure TShape.IShape;
var
    APoint : Point;
begin
    SetPt(APoint, 0, 0);
    fCenter := APoint;
end;

procedure TShape.SetCenter (TheCenter : Point);
begin
    fCenter := TheCenter;
end;

procedure TShape.Draw;
begin
end;

function TShape.Center : Point;
begin
    Center := fCenter;
end;

procedure TCircle.IShape; override;
begin
    inherited IShape;
    fRadius := 0;
end;

procedure TCircle.SetRadius (TheRadius : Integer);
begin
    fRadius := TheRadius;
end;

procedure TCircle.Draw; override;
var
    ARect : Rect;
begin
    PenNormal;
    SetRect(ARect, fCenter.h, fCenter.v, fCenter.h, fCenter.v);
    InsetRect(ARect, -fRadius, -fRadius);
    FrameOval(ARect);
end;

function TCircle.Radius : Integer;
begin
    Radius := fRadius;
end;
```

```
procedure TRectangle.IShape; override;
begin
    inherited IShape;
    fHeight := 0;
    fWidth := 0;
end;

procedure TRectangle.SetHeight (TheHeight : Integer);
begin
    fHeight := TheHeight;
end;

procedure TRectangle.SetWidth  (TheWidth  : Integer);
begin
    fWidth := TheWidth;
end;

procedure TRectangle.Draw; override;
var
    ARect : Rect;
begin
    PenNormal;
    SetRect(ARect, fCenter.h, fCenter.v, fCenter.h, fCenter.v);
    InsetRect(ARect, -round(fWidth / 2), -round(fHeight / 2));
    FrameRect(ARect);
end;

function TRectangle.Height : Integer;
begin
    Height := fHeight;
end;

function TRectangle.Width  : Integer;
begin
    Width := fWidth;
end;

procedure TSolidRectangle.Draw; override;
var
    ARect : Rect;
begin
    inherited Draw;
    SetRect(ARect, fCenter.h, fCenter.v, fCenter.h, fCenter.v);
    InsetRect(ARect, (1 - round(fWidth / 2)), (1 - round(fHeight / 2)));
    FillRect(ARect, Gray);
end;
```

References

The primary reference for Object Pascal is the *Macintosh Programmer's Workshop Pascal 3.0 Reference* [10].

A.4 C++

Background

C++ was designed by Bjarne Stroustrup of AT&T Bell Laboratories. The immediate ancestor of C++ is a language called *C with Classes*, also developed by Stroustrup in 1980. In turn, C with Classes was heavily influenced by the languages C and Simula. C++ is largely a superset of C. However, in one sense, C++ is simply a "better C," in that it provides type checking, overloaded functions, and many other improvements. Most importantly, however, C++ adds object-oriented programming features to C.

There are two major publicly released versions of C++: version 1.0 and version 2.0. Version 1.0 and its minor releases added basic object-oriented programming features to C, such as single inheritance and polymorphism, plus type checking and overloading. Version 2.0, released in 1989, improved upon the previous versions in a variety of ways (such as the introduction of multiple inheritance), based upon extensive experience with the language by a relatively large user community. Future versions of C++ are expected to include support for generic units and exception handling.

Early translator technology for C++ involved the use of a preprocessor for C, called *cfront*. Because this translator emitted C code as an intermediate representation, it was possible to port C++ to virtually every Unix architecture quite quickly. Now, C++ translators and native compilers are available commercially for almost every kind of instruction-set architecture.

Overview

Stroustrup states that "C++ was primarily designed so that the author and his friends would not have to program in assembler, C, or various modern high-order languages. Its main purpose is to make writing good programs easier and more pleasant for the individual programmer. There never was a C++ paper design; design, documentation, and implementation went on simultaneously" [11]. C++ corrects many of the deficiencies of C, and adds to the language support for classes, type checking, overloading, free store management, constant types, references, inline functions, derived classes, and virtual functions [12].

We summarize the features of C++ in Table A-3, relative to the seven elements of the object model.

Example

Again we reimplement the shape problem. The common style in C++ is to place the outside view of each class in header files. Thus, we may write:

Abstraction	Instance variables	Yes
	Instance methods	Yes
	Class variables	Yes
	Class methods	Yes
Encapsulation	Of variables	Public, protected, private
	Of methods	Public, protected, private
Modularity	Kinds of modules	File (header/body)
Hierarchy	Inheritance	Multiple
	Generic units	No
	Metaclasses	No
Typing	Strongly typed	Yes
	Polymorphism	Yes (single)
Concurrency	Multitasking	Yes (defined by class)
Persistence	Persistent objects	No

Table A-3
C++

```
struct Point {int X; int Y;};

class Shape {
    public:
        Shape ();
        void SetCenter (Point ACenter);
        virtual void Draw () = 0;
        Point Center ();
    private:
        Point TheCenter;
};

class Circle : public Shape {
    public:
        Circle ();
        void SetRadius (int AnInteger);
        virtual void Draw ();
        int Radius ();
    private:
        int TheRadius;
};

class Rectangle : public Shape {
    public:
        Rectangle ();
        void SetHeight (int AnInteger);
        void SetWidth (int AnInteger);
        virtual void Draw ();
        int Height ();
        int Width ();
```

```
   private:
       int TheHeight;
       int TheWidth;
};

class SolidRectangle : public Rectangle {
   public:
       virtual void Draw ();
};
```

The definition of C++ does not include a class library. For our purposes, we assume the existence of a programmatic interface to X Windows, and the global objects `Display`, `Window`, and `GraphicsContext` (which are needed by `Xlib`). Thus, we may complete the methods above in a separate file, as follows:

```
Shape::Shape () {
   TheCenter.X = 0;
   TheCenter.Y = 0;
};

void Shape::SetCenter (Point ACenter) {
   TheCenter = ACenter;
};

Point Shape::Center () {
   return TheCenter;
};

Circle::Circle ()  {
   TheRadius = 0;
};

void Circle::SetRadius (int AnInteger) {
   TheRadius = AnInteger;
};

void Circle::Draw () {
   int X = (Center().X - TheRadius);
   int Y = (Center().Y - TheRadius);
   XDrawArc(Display, Window, GraphicsContext, X, Y,
           (TheRadius * 2), (TheRadius * 2), 0, (360 * 64));
};

int Circle::Radius () {
   return TheRadius;
};

Rectangle::Rectangle () {
   TheHeight = 0;
   TheWidth = 0;
};

void Rectangle::SetHeight (int AnInteger) {
   TheHeight = AnInteger;
};
```

```
void Rectangle::SetWidth (int AnInteger) {
    TheWidth = AnInteger;
};

void Rectangle::Draw () {
    int X = (Center().X - (TheWidth / 2));
    int Y = (Center().Y - (TheHeight / 2));
    XDrawRectangle(Display, Window, GraphicsContext, X, Y, TheWidth, TheHeight);
};

int Rectangle::Height () {
    return TheHeight;
};

int Rectangle::Width () {
    return TheWidth;
};

void SolidRectangle::Draw () {
    Rectangle::Draw();
    int X = (Center().X - (Width() / 2));
    int Y = (Center().Y - (Height() / 2));
    gc OldGraphicsContext = GraphicsContext;
    XSetForeground(Display, GraphicsContext, Grey);
    XDrawFilled(Display, Window, GraphicsContext, X, Y, Width(), Height());
    GraphicsContext = OldGraphicsContext;
};
```

References

The primary reference for C++ is the *UNIX System V AT&T C++ Language System, Release 2.0 Product Reference Manual* [13]. Other important references in this series include the *Selected Readings* [14], *Release Notes* [15], and *Library Manual* [16].

A.5 Common Lisp Object System

Background

There are literally dozens of dialects of Lisp, including MacLisp, Standard Lisp, SpiceLisp, S-1 Lisp, Nil, ZetaLisp, InterLisp, and Scheme. Starting in the early 1980s, a plethora of new dialects of Lisp emerged that supported object-oriented programming, many of which were invented to support ongoing research in knowledge representation. Spurred by the success in standardizing Guy Steele's Common Lisp, a similar effort was undertaken in 1986 to standardize these object-oriented dialects. The idea of such a standardization was put forth at the summer 1986 ACM Lisp and Functional Programming Conference, resulting in

Abstraction	Instance variables	Yes
	Instance methods	Yes
	Class variables	Yes
	Class methods	Yes
Encapsulation	Of variables	:reader, :writer, :accessor
	Of methods	Public
Modularity	Kinds of modules	Package (monolithic)
Hierarchy	Inheritance	Multiple
	Generic units	No
	Metaclasses	Yes
Typing	Strongly typed	Optional
	Polymorphism	Yes (multiple)
Concurrency	Multitasking	Yes
Persistence	Persistent objects	Not directly

Table A-4
CLOS

the formation of a special working group as part of the X3J13 ANSI committee (for the standardization of Common Lisp). Because this new dialect was conceived to be a proper superset of Common Lisp, it was called the Common Lisp Object System, or CLOS for short. Bob Mathis and Guy Steele convened the ANSI committee; Daniel Bobrow chaired the committee, whose members included Sonya Keene, Linda DeMichiel, Patrick Dussud, Richard Gabriel, James Kempf, Gregor Kicazles, and David Moon.

The design of CLOS was heavily influenced by the languages New Flavors and CommonLoops. After about two years of work, the complete specification of CLOS was first published in late 1988.

Overview

Keene reports that there were three design goals for CLOS:

- "CLOS should be a standard language extension that includes the most useful aspects of the existing object-oriented paradigms.
- The CLOS programmer interface should be powerful and flexible enough for developing most application programs.
- CLOS itself should be designed as an extensible protocol, to allow for customization of its behavior and to encourage further research in object-oriented programming" [17].

We summarize the features of CLOS in Table A-4, relative to the seven elements of the object model. Although CLOS does not support persistent objects directly, there are straightforward extensions using the metaobject protocol to add persistency [18].

Example

Again we reimplement the shape problem. We start with the relevant classes:

```
(defclass point ()
    ((x :initarg :x :accessor x :type integer)
     (y :initarg :y :accessor y :type integer)))

(defclass shape ()
    ((center :initarg :center :accessor center :type point)))

(defclass rectangle (shape)
    ((height :initarg :height :accessor height :type integer)
     (width  :initarg :width  :accessor width  :type integer)))

(defclass solid-rectangle (rectangle)
    ())

(defclass circle (shape)
    ((radius :initarg :radius :accessor radius :type integer)))
```

We include some methods applicable to rectangles:

```
(defmethod left ((r rectangle))
    (- (x (center r)) (/ (width r) 2)))

(defmethod right ((r rectangle))
    (+ (x (center r)) (/ (width r) 2)))

(defmethod top ((r rectangle))
    (+ (y (center r)) (/ (height r) 2)))

(defmethod bottom ((r rectangle))
    (- (y (center r)) (/ (height r) 2)))
```

The definition of CLOS does not include a class library. For our purposes, we assume the existence of a programmatic interface to a set of resources similar to Object Pascal's Quickdraw, giving us the facilities for drawing lines, arcs, and filling areas. We also assume the existence of a window class, whose instances represent the visible window in which shapes are drawn. Thus, we may write the drawing methods as follows:

```
(defgeneric draw (shape surface))

(defmethod draw ((s shape) window) ())
```

```
(defmethod draw ((r rectangle) window)
    (draw-line window (left r) (bottom r) (left r) (top r))
    (draw-line window (left r) (bottom r) (right r) (bottom r))
    (draw-line window (right r) (bottom r) (right r) (top r))
    (draw-line window (left r) (top r) (left r) (top r)))

(defmethod draw :after ((sr solid-rectangle) window)
    (fill-area window *gray-shade* (left sr) (bottom sr) (right sr) (top sr)))

(defmethod draw ((c circle) window)
    (draw-arc gw (center c) (radius c) 0 360))
```

References

The primary reference for CLOS is the *Common Lisp Object System Specification* [19].

A.6 Ada

Background

The United States Department of Defense (DoD) is perhaps the largest user of computers in the world. By the mid-1970s, software development for its systems had reached crisis proportions: projects were often late, over budget, and they often failed to meet their stated requirements. It was evident that the problems would only get worse as software development costs continued to rise and the demand for software increased at an exponential rate. To help resolve these problems, which were further compounded by the proliferation of hundreds of different languages, the DoD sponsored the development of a single, common, high-order programming language. In a sense, Ada represents one of the first engineered production-quality languages. A set of requirements was developed starting in 1975 and culminated in the Steelman document, which was released in 1978. An international request for proposal was then issued, inviting companies to design a language based upon these requirements, which drew seventeen responses. This number was reduced to four, then two, and then one by an extensive design and evaluation period involving hundreds of computer scientists across the world.

The winning design was originally called the Green language (so called because of its color code during the competition), and was then renamed Ada, in honor of Ada Augusta, Countess of Lovelace, who was noted for her early observations on the potential power of the computer. The primary author of this language was Jean Ichbiah of France. Other members of the design team included Bernd Krieg-Brueckner, Brian Wichmann, Henry Ledgard, Jean-Claude Heliard, Jean-Loup Gailly, Jean-Raymond Abrial, John Barnes, Mike Woodger, Olivier Roubine, S. A. Schuman, and S. C. Vestal.

Abstraction	Instance variables	Yes
	Instance methods	Yes
	Class variables	No
	Class methods	No
Encapsulation	Of variables	Public, private
	Of methods	Public, private
Modularity	Kinds of modules	Package (specification/body)
Hierarchy	Inheritance	No
	Generic units	Yes
	Metaclasses	No
Typing	Strongly typed	Yes
	Polymorphism	No
Concurrency	Multitasking	Yes (defined by language)
Persistence	Persistent objects	No

Table A-5
Ada

The immediate ancestors of Ada are Pascal and its derivatives, including Euclid, Lis, Mesa, Modula, and Sue. A number of concepts from ALGOL 68, Simula, CLU, and Alphard were also incorporated. The ANSI standard for Ada was finally released in 1983. Translators for Ada were slow in coming, but today, there are translators for almost every major family of instruction-set architectures. Although Ada was originally sponsored by the DoD, it has found an important worldwide role in government and commercial software projects, and is usually the language of choice for massive software projects, such as the United States and European Space Station efforts. Since ANSI standards must be reviewed every five years, a project called Ada 9x has been established to update this standard. The original language definition will probably change in a number of small ways, involving clarifications, the filling of gaps, and the correction of errors. In its current definition, Ada is object-based, not object-oriented. However, a number of proposals would add object-oriented programming extensions to Ada.

Overview

According to its designers, Ada was designed with three concerns in mind:

- Program reliability and maintenance
- Programming as a human activity
- Efficiency [20]

We summarize the features of Ada in Table A-5, relative to the seven elements of the object model.

Example

Again we reimplement the shape problem. The common style in Ada is to place class definitions in a package specification. For this example, we chose to place each class in a separate package:

```
package Points is

    type Point is record
                    X : Natural;
                    Y : Natural;
                end record;

end Points;

with Points;
package Circles is

    type Circle is private;

    procedure Set_Center (The_Circle : in out Circle; The_Center : in Point);
    procedure Set_Radius (The_Circle : in out Circle; The_Radius : in Natural);
    procedure Draw       (The_Circle : in       Circle);

    function Center_Of (The_Circle : in Circle) return Point;
    function Radius_Of (The_Circle : in Circle) return Natural;

private
    type Circle is record
                    Center : Point;
                    Radius : Natural;
                end record;
end Circles;

with Points;
package Rectangles is

    type Rectangle (Is_Solid : Boolean := False) is private;

    procedure Set_Center (The_Rectangle : in out Rectangle;
                          The_Center    : in     Point);
    procedure Set_Height (The_Rectangle : in out Rectangle;
                          The_Height    : in     Natural);
    procedure Set_Width  (The_Rectangle : in out Rectangle;
                          The_Width     : in out Natural);
    procedure Draw       (The_Rectangle : in     Rectangle);

    function Center_Of (The_Rectangle : in Rectangle) return Point;
    function Height_Of (The_Rectangle : in Rectangle) return Natural;
    function Width_Of  (The_Rectangle : in Rectangle) return Natural;
```

```
private
    type Rectangle (Is_Solid : Boolean is record
                                        Center : Point;
                                        Height : Natural;
                                        Width  : Natural;
                               end record;
end Rectangles;
```

We may complete the implementation of each of these packages as follows, assuming the existence of an Ada binding to X Windows and the global variables `Display`, `Window`, and `Graphics_Context`:

```
procedure Set_Center (The_Circle : in out Circle; The_Center : in Point) is
begin
    The_Circle.Center := The_Center;
end Set_Center;

procedure Set_Radius (The_Circle : in out Circle; The_Radius : in Natural) is
begin
    The_Circle.Radius := The_Radius;
end Set_Radius;

procedure Draw (The_Circle : in Circle) is
    X : Integer := The_Circle.Center.X - The_Circle.The_Radius;
    Y : Integer := The_Circle.Center.Y - The_Circle.The_Radius;
begin
    XDrawArc(Display, Window, Graphics_Context, X, Y,
            (The_Circle.The_Radius * 2), (The_Circle.The_Radius * 2),
            0, (360 * 64));
end Draw;

function Center_Of (The_Circle : in Circle) return Point is
begin
    return The_Circle.Center;
end Center_Of;

function Radius_Of (The_Circle : in Circle) return Natural is
begin
    return The_Circle.Radius;
end Radius_Of;

procedure Set_Center (The_Rectangle : in out Rectangle;
                      The_Center    : in     Point) is
begin
    The_Rectangle.Center := The_Center;
end Set_Center;

procedure Set_Height (The_Rectangle : in out Rectangle;
                      The_Height    : in     Natural) is
begin
    The_Rectangle.Height := The_Height;
end Set_Height;
```

```
procedure Set_Width (The_Rectangle : in out Rectangle;
                     The_Width     : in out Natural) is
begin
    The_Rectangle.Width := The_Width;
end Set_Width;

procedure Draw (The_Rectangle : in Rectangle) is
    X : Integer := The_Rectangle.The_Center.X - (The_Rectangle.The_Width / 2);
    Y : Integer := The_Rectangle.The_Center.Y - (The_Rectangle.The_Height / 2);
    Old_Graphics_Context : GC := Graphics_Context;
begin
    XDrawRectangle(Display, Window, Graphics_Context, X, Y,
                   The_Rectangle.The_Width, The_Rectangle.The_Height);
    if The_Rectangle.Is_Solid then
        XSetForeground(Display, Graphics_Context, Grey);
        XDrawFilled(Display, Window, Graphics_Context, X, Y,
                    The_Rectangle.The_Width, The_Rectangle.The_Height);
        Graphics_Context := Old_Graphics_Context;
    end if;
end Draw;

function Center_Of (The_Rectangle : in Rectangle) return Point is
begin
    return The_Rectangle.Center;
end Center_Of;

function Height_Of (The_Rectangle : in Rectangle) return Natural is
begin
    return The_Rectangle.Height;
end Height_Of;

function Width_Of  (The_Rectangle : in Rectangle) return Natural is
begin
    return The_Rectangle.Width;
end Width_Of;
```

References

The primary reference for Ada is the *Reference Manual for the Ada Programming Language* [21]

A.7 Other Object-Oriented Programming Languages

Saunders [22] provides a survey of over eighty different object-oriented programming languages. He suggests that object-oriented programming languages may be grouped into seven categories [23]:

- Actor   Languages supporting delegation
- Concurrent   Object-oriented languages emphasizing
                        concurrency

ABCL/1	Concurrent Smalltalk	Lore	Plasma II
ABE	CSSA	Mace	POOL-T
Acore	CST	MELD	PROCOL
Act/1	Director	Mjolner	Quick Pascal
Act/2	Distributed Smalltalk	ModPascal	Quicktalk
Act/3	Eiffel	Neon	ROSS
Actor	Emerald	New Flavors	SAST
Actors	ExperCommonLisp	NIL	SCOOP
Actra	Extended Smalltalk	O-CPU	SCOOPS
Ada	Felix Pascal	OakLisp	Self
Argus	Flavors	Oberon	Simula
ART	FOOPlog	Object Assembler	SINA
Berkeley Smalltalk	FOOPS	Object Cobol	Smalltalk
Beta	FRL	Object Lisp	Smalltalk AT
Blaze	Galileo	Object Logo	Smalltalk V
Brouhaha	Garp	Object Oberon	Smallworld
C with Classes	GLISP	Object Pascal	SPOOL
C++	Gypsy	Objective-C	SR
C_talk	Hybrid	ObjVLisp	SRL
Cantor	Inheritance	OOPC	STROBE
Clascal	InnovAda	OOPS+	T
Classic Ada	Intermission	OPAL	Trellis/Owl
CLOS	Jasmine	Orbit	Turbo Pascal 5.x
Cluster 86	KL-One	Orient84/K	Uniform
Common Loops	KRL	OTM	UNITS
Common Objects	KRS	PCOL	Vulcan
Common ORBIT	Little Smalltalk	PIE	XLISP
Concurrent Prolog	LOOPS	PL/LL	Zoom/VM

Figure A-2
Object-Based and Object-Oriented Programming Languages

- Distributed   Object-oriented languages emphasizing distributed objects

- Frame-based   Languages supporting frame theory

- Hybrid   Object-oriented extensions to traditional languages

- Smalltalk-based   Smalltalk and its dialects

- Ideological   Application of object-oriented features to other domains

- Miscellaneous   Object-oriented languages that do not fit any other category

Figure A-2 provides the names of many of these important object-based and object-oriented programming languages, and the Classified Bibliography offers references to sources of information for most of them.

Notes

Preface

Mills, H. 1985. *DPMA and Human Productivity*. Houston, TX: Data Processing Management Association.

The First Section: Concepts

Wagner, J. 1986. *The Search for Signs of Intelligent Life in the Universe*. New York, NY: Harper and Row, p. 202. By permission of ICM, Inc.

Chapter 1: Complexity

[1]   Brooks, F. April 1987. No Silver Bullet: Essence and Accidents of Software Engineering. *IEEE Computer*, vol. 20 (4), p. 12.

[2]   Peters, L. 1981. *Software Design*. New York, NY: Yourdon Press, p. 22.

[3]   Brooks. No Silver Bullet, p. 11.

[4]   Parnas, D. July 1985. Why Software Is Unreliable. *Software Aspects of Strategic Defense Systems.* Victoria, Canada: University of Victoria, Report DCS-47-IR.

[5]   Peter, L. 1986. *The Peter Pyramid.* New York, NY: William Morrow, p. 153.

[6]   Courtois, P. June 1985. On Time and Space Decomposition of Complex Structures. *Communications of the ACM,* vol. 28 (6), p. 596.

[7]   Simon, H. 1982. *The Sciences of the Artificial.* Cambridge, MA: The MIT Press, p.218.

[8]   Ibid., p. 217.

[9]   Ibid., p. 221.

[10] Ibid., p. 209.

[11] Gall, J. 1986. *Systemantics: How Systems Really Work and How They Fail.* 2nd ed. Ann Arbor, MI: The General Systemantics Press, p. 65.

[12] Miller, G. March 1956. The Magical Number Seven, Plus or Minus Two: Some Limits on Our Capacity for Processing Information. *The Psychological Review,* vol. 63 (2), p. 86.

[13] Simon. *Sciences,* p. 81.

[14] Dijkstra, E. 1979. Programming Considered as a Human Activity. *Classics in Software Engineering.* New York, NY: Yourdon Press, p.5.

[15] Parnas, D. December 1985. Software Aspects of Strategic Defense Systems. *Communications of the ACM,* vol. 28 (12), p. 1328.

[16] Tsai, J., and Ridge, J. November 1988. Intelligent Support for Specifications Transformation. *IEEE Software,* vol. 5 (6), p. 34.

[17] Langdon, G. 1982. *Computer Design.* San Jose, CA: Computeach Press, p. 6.

[18] Miller. Magical Number, p.95.

[19] Shaw, M. 1981. *ALPHARD: Form and Content.* New York, NY: Springer-Verlag, p. 6.

[20] Stein, J. March 1988. Object-Oriented Programming and Database Design. *Dr. Dobb's Journal of Software Tools for the Professional Programmer,* No. 137, p.18.

[21] Peters. *Software Design.*

[22] Yau, S. and Tsai, J. June 1986. A Survey of Software Design Techniques. *IEEE Transactions on Software Engineering,* vol. SE-12 (6).

[23] Teledyne Brown Engineering. *Software Methodology Catalog,* Report MC87-COMM/ADP-0036. October 1987. Tinton Falls, NJ.

[24] Sommerville, I. 1985. *Software Engineering.* 2nd ed. Workingham, England: Addison-Wesley, p. 68.

[25] Yourdon, E., and Constantine, L. 1979. *Structured Design.* Englewood Cliffs, NJ: Prentice-Hall.

[26] Myers, G. 1978. *Composite/Structured Design.* New York, NY: Van Nostrand Reinhold.

[27] Page-Jones, M. 1988. *The Practical Guide to Structured Systems Design.* Englewood Cliffs, NJ: Yourdon Press.

[28] Wirth, N. January 1983. Program Development by Stepwise Refinement. *Communications of the ACM,* vol. 26 (1).

[29] Wirth, N. 1986. *Algorithms and Data Structures.* Englewood Cliffs, NJ: Prentice-Hall.

[30] Dahl, O., Dijkstra, E., and Hoare, C. A. R. 1972. *Structured Programming*. London, England: Academic Press.

[31] Mills, H., Linger, R., and Hevner, A. 1986. *Principles of Information System Design and Analysis*. Orlando, FL: Academic Press.

[32] Jackson, M. 1975. *Principles of Program Design*. Orlando, FL: Academic Press.

[33] Jackson, M. 1983. *System Development*. Englewood Cliffs, NJ: Prentice-Hall.

[34] Orr, K. 1971. *Structured Systems Development*. New York, NY: Yourdon Press.

[35] Goldberg, A. 1984. *Smalltalk-80: The Interactive Programming Environment*. Reading, MA: Addison-Wesley, p. 80.

[36] Petroski, H. 1985. *To Engineer Is Human*. St Martin's Press: New York, p. 40.

[37] Mostow, J. Spring 1985. Toward Better Models of the Design Process. *AI Magazine*, vol. 6 (1), p. 44.

[38] Eastman, N. 1984. Software Engineering and Technology. *Technical Directions*, vol. 10 (1): Bethesda, MD: IBM Federal Systems Division, p. 5.

[39] Brooks. No Silver Bullet, p. 10.

Chapter 2: The Object Model

[1] Rentsch, T. September 1982. Object-Oriented Programming. *SIGPLAN Notices*, vol. 17 (12), p. 51.

[2] Wegner, P. June 1981. *The Ada Programming Language and Environment*. Unpublished draft.

[3] Abbott, R. August 1987. Knowledge Abstraction. *Communications of the ACM*, vol. 30 (8), p. 664.

[4] Ibid., p. 664.

[5] Shankar, K. 1984. Data Design: Types, Structures, and Abstractions. *Handbook of Software Engineering*. New York, NY: Van Nostrand Reinhold, p. 253.

[6] *Macintosh MacApp 1.1.1 Programmer's Reference*. 1986. Cupertino, CA: Apple Computer, p. 2.

[7] Bhaskar, K. October 1983. How Object-Oriented Is Your System? *SIGPLAN Notices*, vol. 18 (10), p. 8.

[8] Stefik, M., and Bobrow, D. Winter 1986. Object-Oriented Programming: Themes and Variations, *AI Magazine*, vol. 6 (4), p. 41.

[9] Yonezawa, A., and Tokoro, M. 1987. Object-Oriented Concurrent Programming: An Introduction, in *Object-Oriented Concurrent Programming*. Cambridge, MA: The MIT Press, p. 2.

[10] Levy, H. 1984. *Capability-Based Computer Systems*. Bedford, MA: Digital Press, p. 13.

[11] Ramamoorthy, C., and Sheu, P. Fall 1988. Object-Oriented Systems. *IEEE Expert*, vol. 3 (3), p. 14.

[12] Myers, G. 1982. *Advances in Computer Architecture*. 2nd ed. New York, NY: John Wiley and Sons, p. 58.

[13] Levy. *Capability-Based Computer*.

[14] Kavi, K., and Chen, D. 1987. Architectural Support for Object-Oriented Languages. *Proceedings of the Thirty-second IEEE Computer Society International Conference.* IEEE.

[15] *iAPX 432 Object Primer.* 1981. Santa Clara, CA: Intel Corporation.

[16] Dally, W. J., and Kajiya, J. T. March 1985. An Object-Oriented Architecture. *SIGARCH Newsletter,* vol. 13 (3).

[17] Dahlby, S., Henry, G., Reynolds, D., and Taylor, P. 1982. The IBM System/38: A High Level Machine, in *Computer Structures: Principles and Examples.* New York, NY: McGraw-Hill.

[18] Dijkstra, E. May 1968. The Structure of the "THE" Multiprogramming System. *Communications of the ACM,* vol. 11 (5).

[19] Pashtan, A. 1982. Object-Oriented Operating Systems: An Emerging Design Methodology. *Proceedings of the ACM '82 Conference.* ACM.

[20] Parnas, D. 1979. On the Criteria to Be Used in Decomposing Systems into Modules, in *Classics in Software Engineering.* New York, NY: Yourdon Press.

[21] Liskov, B., and Zilles, S. 1977. An Introduction to Formal Specifications of Data Abstractions. *Current Trends in Programming Methodology: Software Specification and Design,* vol. 1. Englewood Cliffs, NJ: Prentice-Hall.

[22] Guttag, J. 1980. Abstract Data Types and the Development of Data Structures, in *Programming Language Design.* New York, NY: Computer Society Press.

[23] Shaw. Abstraction Techniques.

[24] Nygaard, K., and Dahl, O-J. 1981. The Development of the Simula Languages, in *History of Programming Languages.* New York, NY: Academic Press, p. 460.

[25] Atkinson, M., and Buneman, P. June 1987. Types and Persistence in Database Programming Languages. *ACM Computing Surveys,* vol. 19 (2), p. 105.

[26] Rumbaugh, J. April 1988. Relational Database Design Using an Object-Oriented Methodology. *Communications of the ACM,* vol. 31 (4), p. 415.

[27] Chen, P. March 1976. The Entity-Relationship Model – Toward a Unified View of Data. *ACM Transactions on Database Systems,* vol. 1(1).

[28] Barr, A., and Feigenbaum, E. 1981. *The Handbook of Artificial Intelligence.* Vol. 1. Los Altos, CA: William Kaufmann, p. 216.

[29] Stillings, N., Feinstein, M., Garfield, J., Rissland, E., Rosenbaum, D., Weisler, S, Baker-Ward, L. 1987. *Cognitive Science: An Introduction.* Cambridge, MA: The MIT Press, p. 305.

[30] Rand, Ayn. 1979. *Introduction to Objectivist Epistemology.* New York, NY: New American Library.

[31] Minsky, M. 1986. *The Society of Mind.* New York, NY: Simon and Schuster.

[32] Jones, A. 1979. The Object Model: A Conceptual Tool for Structuring Software. *Operating Systems.* New York, NY: Springer-Verlag, p. 8.

[33] Stroustrup, B. May 1988. What Is Object-Oriented Programming? *IEEE Software,* vol. 5 (3), p. 10.

[34] Cardelli, L., and Wegner, P. On Understanding Types, Data Abstraction, and Polymorphism. December 1985. *ACM Computing Surveys,* vol. 17 (4), p. 481.

[35] DeMarco, T. 1979. *Structured Analysis and System Specification.* Englewood Cliffs, NJ: Prentice-Hall.

[36] Yourdon, E. 1989. *Modern Structured Analysis.* Englewood Cliffs, NJ: Prentice-Hall.

[37] Gane, C., and Sarson, T. 1979. *Structured Systems Analysis.* Englewood Cliffs, NJ: Prentice-Hall.

[38] Ward, P., and Mellor, S. 1985. *Structured Development for Real-Time Systems.* Englewood Cliffs, NJ: Yourdon Press.

[39] Hatley, D., and Pirbhai, I. 1988. *Strategies for Real-Time System Specification.* New York, NY: Dorset House.

[40] Jenkins, M., and Glasgow, J. January 1986. Programming Styles in Nial. *IEEE Software,* vol. 3 (1), p. 48.

[41] Bobrow, D., and Stefik, M. February 1986. Perspectives on Artificial Intelligence Programming. *Science,* vol. 231, p. 951.

[42] Dahl, O., Dijkstra, E., and Hoare, C. A. R. 1972. *Structured Programming.* London, England: Academic Press, p. 83.

[43] Shaw, M. October 1984. Abstraction Techniques in Modern Programming Languages. *IEEE Software,* vol. 1 (4), p. 10.

[44] Berzins, V., Gray, M., and Naumann, D. May 1986. Abstraction-Based Software Development. *Communications of the ACM,* vol. 29 (5), p. 403.

[45] Abelson, H., and Sussman, G. 1985. *Structure and Interpretation of Computer Programs.* Cambridge, MA: The MIT Press, p. 126.

[46] Ibid., p. 132.

[47] Seidewitz, E., and Stark, M. 1986. Towards a General Object-Oriented Software Development Methodology. *Proceedings of the First International Conference on Ada Programming Language Applications for the NASA Space Station.* NASA Lyndon B. Johnson Space Center, TX: NASA, p. D.4.6.4.

[48] Ingalls, D. The Smalltalk-76 Programming System Design and Implementation. *Proceedings of the Fifth Annual ACM Symposium on Principles of Programming Languages.* ACM, p. 9.

[49] Gannon, J., Hamlet, R., and Mills, H. July 1987. Theory of Modules. *IEEE Transactions on Software Engineering,* vol. SE-13 (7), p. 820.

[50] Date, C. 1986. *Relational Database: Selected Writings.* Reading, MA: Addison-Wesley, p. 180.

[51] Liskov, B. May 1988. Data Abstraction and Hierarchy. *SIGPLAN Notices,* vol. 23 (5), p. 19.

[52] Britton, K., and Parnas, D. December 8, 1981. *A-7E Software Module Guide.* Washington, D.C. Naval Research Laboratory, Report 4702, p. 24.

[53] Stroustrup, B. 1988. Private communication.

[54] Myers, G. 1978. *Composite/Structured Design.* New York, NY: Van Nostrand Reinhold, p. 21.

[55] Liskov, B. 1980. A Design Methodology for Reliable Software Systems, in *Tutorial on Software Design Techniques.* 3rd ed. New York, NY: IEEE Computer Society, p. 66.

[56] Zelkowitz, M. June 1978. Perspectives on Software Engineering. *ACM Computing Surveys,* vol. 10 (2), p. 20.

[57] Parnas, D., Clements, P., and Weiss, D. March 1985. The Modular Structure of Complex Systems. *IEEE Transactions on Software Engineering,* vol. SE-11 (3), p. 260.

[58] Britton and Parnas. *A-7E Software*, p. 2.

[59] Parnas, D., Clements, P., and Weiss, D. 1983. Enhancing Reusability with Information Hiding. *Proceedings of the Workshop on Reusability in Programming*, Stratford, CT: ITT Programming, p. 241.

[60] Meyer, B. 1988. *Object-Oriented Software Construction*. New York, NY: Prentice Hall, p. 47.

[61] Cox, B. 1986. *Object-Oriented Programming: An Evolutionary Approach*. Reading, MA: Addison-Wesley, p. 69.

[62] Danforth, S., and Tomlinson, C. March 1988. Type Theories and Object-Oriented Programming. *ACM Computing Surveys*, vol. 20 (1), p. 34.

[63] Liskov. 1988, p. 23.

[64] As quoted in Liskov. 1980, p. 67.

[65] Zilles, S. 1984. Types, Algebras, and Modelling, in *On Conceptual Modeling: Perspectives from Artificial Intelligence, Databases, and Programming Languages*. New York, NY: Springer-Verlag, p. 442.

[66] Borning, A., and Ingalls, D. 1982. A Type Declaration and Inference System for Smalltalk. Palo Alto, CA: Xerox Palo Alto Research Center, p. 134.

[67] Wegner, P. October 1987. Dimensions of Object-Based Language Design. *SIGPLAN Notices*, vol. 22 (12), p. 171.

[68] Tesler, L. August 1981. The Smalltalk Environment. *Byte*, vol. 6 (8), p. 142.

[69] Borning and Ingalls. Type Declaration, p. 133.

[70] Thomas, D. March 1989. What's in an Object? *Byte*, vol. 14 (3), p. 232.

[71] Lim, J., and Johnson, R. April 1989. The Heart of Object-Oriented Concurrent Programming. *SIGPLAN Notices*, vol. 24 (4), p. 165.

[72] Ibid., p. 165.

[73] Black, A., Hutchinson, N., Jul, E., Levy, H., and Carter, L. July 1986. *Distribution and Abstract Types in Emerald*. Report 86-02-04. Seattle, WA: University of Washington, p. 3.

[74] Proceedings of the ACM SIGPLAN Workshop on Object-Based Concurrent Programming. April 1989. *SIGPLAN Notices*, vol. 24 (4), p. 1.

[75] Atkinson, M., Bailey, P., Chisholm, K., Cockshott, P., and Morrison, R. 1983. An Approach to Persistent Programming. *The Computer Journal*, vol. 26 (4), p. 360.

[76] Khoshafian, S., and Copeland, G. November 1986. Object Identity. *SIGPLAN Notices*, vol. 21 (11), p. 409.

[77] *Vbase Technical Overview*. September 1987. Billerica, MA: Ontologic, p. 4.

[78] Stroustrup, B. November 1987. Possible Directions for C++. *Proceedings of the USENIX C++ Workshop*. Santa Fe, NM, p. 14.

[79] Meyer. *Object-Oriented Software*, p. 233.

[80] Robson, D. August 1981. Object-Oriented Software Systems. *Byte*, vol. 6 (8), p. 74.

Chapter 3: Classes and Objects

[1] Lefrancois, G. 1977. *Of Children: An Introduction to Child Development.* 2nd ed. Belmont, CA: Wadsworth, p. 244–246.

[2] Nygaard, K., and Dahl, O-J. 1981. The Development of the Simula Languages, in *History of Programming Languages.* New York, NY: Academic Press, p. 462.

[3] Halbert, D., and O'Brien, P. September 1988. Using Types and Inheritance in Object-Oriented Programming. *IEEE Software*, vol. 4 (5), p. 73.

[4] Smith, M., and Tockey, S. 1988. *An Integrated Approach to Software Requirements Definition Using Objects.* Seattle, WA: Boeing Commercial Airplane Support Division, p. 132.

[5] Cox, B. 1986. *Object-Oriented Programming: An Evolutionary Approach.* Reading, MA: Addison-Wesley, p. 29.

[6] MacLennan, B. December 1982. Values and Objects in Programming Languages. *SIGPLAN Notices*, vol. 17 (12), p. 78.

[7] Brodie, M., and Ridjanovic, D. 1984. On the Design and Specification of Database Transactions, in *On Conceptual Modeling: Perspectives from Artificial Intelligence, Databases, and Programming Languages.* New York, NY: Springer-Verlag, p. 288.

[8] Lippman, S. 1989. *C++ Primer.* Reading, MA: Addison-Wesley, p. 185.

[9] *Macintosh MacApp 1.1.1 Programmer's Reference.* 1986. Cupertino, CA: Apple Computer, p. 4.

[10] Khoshafian, S., and Copeland, G. November 1986. Object Identity. *SIGPLAN Notices*, vol. 21 (11), p. 406.

[11] Ibid., p. 406.

[12] Ingalls, D. 1981. Design Principles behind Smalltalk. *Byte*, vol. 6 (8), p. 290.

[13] Gall, J. 1986. *Systemantics: How Systems Really Work and How They Fail.* 2nd ed. Ann Arbor, MI: The General Systemantics Press, p. 158.

[14] Seidewitz, E., and Stark, M. 1986. Towards a General Object-Oriented Software Development Methodology. *Proceedings of the First International Conference on Ada Programming Language Applications for the NASA Space Station.* NASA Lyndon B. Johnson Space Center, TX: NASA, p. D.4.6.4.

[15] *Webster's Third New International Dictionary of the English Language,* unabridged. 1986. Chicago, Illinois: Merriam-Webster.

[16] Meyer, B. 1987. *Programming as Contracting.* Report TR-EI-12/CO. Goleta, CA: Interactive Software Engineering.

[17] Snyder, A. November 1986. Encapsulation and Inheritance in Object-Oriented Programming Languages. *SIGPLAN Notices*, vol. 21 (11).

[18] LaLonde, W. April 1989. Designing Families of Data Types Using Exemplars. *ACM Transactions on Programming Languages and Systems*, vol. 11 (2), p. 214.

[19] Rumbaugh, J. April 1988. Relational Database Design Using an Object-Oriented Methodology. *Communications of the ACM*, vol. 31 (4), p. 417.

[20] Lieberman, H. November 1986. Using Prototypical Objects to Implement Shared Behavior in Object-Oriented Systems. *SIGPLAN Notices*, vol. 21 (11).

[21] Brachman, R. October 1983. What IS-A Is and Isn't: An Analysis of Taxonomic Links in Semantic Networks. *IEEE Computer*, vol. 16 (10), p. 30.

[22] Micallef, J. April/May 1988. Encapsulation, Reusability, and Extensibility in Object-Oriented Programming Languages. *Journal of Object-Oriented Programming*, vol. 1 (1), p. 15.

[23] Snyder. Encapsulation, p. 39.

[24] Cardelli, L., and Wegner, P. On Understanding Types, Data Abstraction, and Polymorphism. December 1985. *ACM Computing Surveys*, vol. 17 (4), p. 475.

[25] As quoted in Harland, D., Szyplewski, M., and Wainwright, J. October 1985. An Alternative View of Polymorphism. *SIGPLAN Notices*, vol. 20 (10).

[26] Kaplan, S., and Johnson, R. July 21, 1986. *Designing and Implementing for Reuse.* Urbana, IL: University of Illinois, Department of Computer Science, p. 8.

[27] Deutsch, P. 1983. Efficient Implementation of the Smalltalk-80 System, in *Proceedings of the 11th Annual ACM Symposium on the Principles of Programming Languages*, p. 300.

[28] Ibid., p. 299.

[29] Duff, C. August 1986. Designing an Efficient Language. *Byte*, vol. 11 (8), p. 216.

[30] Stroustrup, B. 1988. Private communication.

[31] Stroustrup, B. November 1987. Possible Directions for C++. *Proceedings of the USENIX C++ Workshop.* Santa Fe, New Mexico, p. 8.

[32] Keene, S. 1989. *Object-Oriented Programming in Common Lisp.* Reading, MA: Addison-Wesley, p. 44.

[33] Winston, P., and Horn, B. 1989. *Lisp.* 3rd ed. Reading, MA: Addison-Wesley, p. 510.

[34] Keene, p. 11.

[35] Micallef, J. April/May 1988. Encapsulation, Reusability, and Extensibility in Object-Oriented Programming Languages. *Journal of Object-Oriented Programming*, vol. 1 (1), p. 25.

[36] Snyder. Encapsulation, p. 41.

[37] Vlissides, J., and Linton, M. 1988. Applying Object-Oriented Design to Structured Graphics. *Proceedings of USENIX C++ Conference.* Berkeley, CA: USENIX Association, p. 93.

[38] Meyer, B. 1988. *Object-Oriented Software Construction.* New York, NY: Prentice Hall, p. 274.

[39] Keene. *Object-Oriented Programming*, p. 118.

[40] Snyder. Encapsulation, p. 43.

[41] Hendler, J. October 1986. Enhancement for Multiple Inheritance. *SIGPLAN Notices*, vol. 21 (10), p. 100.

[42] Booch, G. 1987. *Software Components with Ada.* Menlo Park, CA: Benjamin/Cummings.

[43] Stroustrup, 1987, p. 3.

[44] Stroustrup, B. 1988. Parameterized Types for C++. *Proceedings of USENIX C++ Conference.* Berkeley, CA: USENIX Association, p. 1.

[45] Ibid.

[46]   Meyer, B. November 1986. Genericity versus Inheritance. *SIGPLAN Notices*, vol. 21 (11), p. 402.

[47]   Stroustrup. 1988, p. 4.

[48]   Robson, D. August 1981. Object-Oriented Software Systems. *Byte*, vol. 6 (8), p. 86.

[49]   Goldberg, A., and Robson, D. 1983. *Smalltalk-80: The Language and Its Implementation*. Reading, MA: Addison-Wesley, p. 287.

[50]   Ingalls, D. August 1981. Design Principles behind Smalltalk. *Byte*, vol. 6 (8), p. 286.

[51]   Stevens, W., Myers, G., and Constantine, L. 1979. Structured Design, in *Classics in Software Engineering*. New York, NY: Yourdon Press, p. 209.

[52]   Page-Jones, M. 1988. *The Practical Guide to Structured Systems Design*. Englewood Cliffs, NJ: Yourdon Press, p. 59.

[53]   Meyer. 1987, p. 4.

[54]   Halbert, D., and O'Brien, P. September 1988. Using Types and Inheritance in Object-Oriented Programming. *IEEE Software*, vol. 4 (5), p. 74.

[55]   Sakkinen, M. December 1988. Comments on "the Law of Demeter" and C++. *SIGPLAN Notices*, vol. 23 (12), p. 38.

[56]   Lea, D. August 12, 1988. *User's Guide to GNU C++ Library*. Cambridge, MA: Free Software Foundation, p. 12

[57]   Ibid.

[58]   Meyer. 1988, p. 332.

[59]   Wirth, N. 1986. *Algorithms and Data Structures*. Englewood Cliffs, NJ: Prentice-Hall, p. 37.

[60]   Keene. *Object-Oriented Programming*, p. 68.

[61]   Parnas, D., Clements, P., and Weiss, D. 1989. Enhancing Reusability with Information Hiding. *Software Reusability*. New York, NY: ACM Press, p. 143.

Chapter 4: Classification

[1]   As quoted in Swaine, M. June 1988. Programming Paradigms. *Dr. Dobb's Journal of Software Tools*, No. 140, p. 110.

[2]   Michalski, R. and Stepp, R. 1983. Learning from Observation: Conceptual Clustering, in *Machine Learning: An Artificial Intelligence Approach*. Palo Alto, CA: Tioga, p. 332.

[3]   Darwin, C. 1984. *The Origin of Species. Vol 49 of Great Books of the Western World*. Chicago, IL: Encyclopedia Britannica, p. 207.

[4]   *The New Encyclopedia Britannica*. 1985. Chicago, IL: Encyclopedia Britannica. vol. 3, p. 356.

[5]   May, R. September 16, 1988. How Many Species Are There on Earth? *Science*, vol. 241, p. 1441.

[6]   As quoted in Lewin, R. November 4, 1988. Family Relationships Are a Biological Conundrum. *Science*, vol. 242, p. 671.

[7]   *The New Encyclopedia Britannica*, vol. 3, p. 156.

[8]   Descartes, R. 1984. *Rules for the Direction of the Mind. Vol. 31 of Great Books of the Western World.* Chicago, IL: Encyclopedia Britannica, p. 32.

[9]   Shaw, M. May 1989. Larger Scale Systems Require Higher-Level Abstractions. *SIGSOFT Engineering Notes,* vol. 14 (3), p. 143.

[10]   Goldstein, T. May 1989. The Object-Oriented Programmer. *The C++ Report,* vol. 1 (5).

[11]   Coombs, C., Raiffa, H., and Thrall, R. 1954. Some Views on Mathematical Models and Measurement Theory. *Psychological Review,* vol. 61 (2), p. 132.

[12]   Flood, R., and Carson, E. 1988. *Dealing with Complexity.* New York, NY: Plenum Press, p. 8.

[13]   Birtwistle, G., Dahl, O-J., Myhrhaug, B., and Nygard, K. 1979. *Simula begin.* Lund, Sweden: Studentlitteratur, p. 23.

[14]   Heinlein, R. 1966. *The Moon Is a Harsh Mistress.* New York, NY: The Berkeley Publishing Group, p. 11.

[15]   Sowa, J. 1984. *Conceptual Structures: Information Processing in Mind and Machine.* Reading, MA: Addison-Wesley, p. 16.

[16]   Lakoff, G. 1987. *Women, Fire, and Dangerous Things: What Categories Reveal About the Mind.* Chicago, IL: The University of Chicago Press, p. 161.

[17]   Wegner, P. 1987. The Object-Oriented Classification Paradigm, in *Research Directions in Object-Oriented Programming.* Cambridge, MA: The MIT Press, p. 480.

[18]   Aquinas, T. 1984. *Summa Theologica. Vol. 19 of Great Books of the Western World.* Chicago, IL: Encyclopedia Britannica, p. 71.

[19]   Stepp, R., and Michalski, R. February 1986. Conceptual Clustering of Structured Objects: A Goal-Oriented Approach. *Artificial Intelligence,* vol. 28 (1), p. 53.

[20]   Maier, H. 1969. *Three Theories of Child Development: The Contributions of Erik H. Erickson, Jean Piaget, and Robert R. Sears, and Their Applications.* New York, NY: Harper and Row, p. 111.

[21]   Lakoff. *Women, Fire,* p. 32.

[22]   Minsky, M. 1986. *The Society of Mind.* New York, NY: Simon and Schuster, p. 199.

[23]   *The Great Ideas: A Syntopicon of Great Books of the Western World.* 1984. *Vol. 1 of Great Books of the Western World.* Chicago, IL: Encyclopedia Britannica, p. 293.

[24]   Stepp, p. 44.

[25]   Lakoff. *Women, Fire,* p. 7.

[26]   Ibid., p. 16.

[27]   Meyer, private communication.

[28]   Shlaer, S., and Mellor, S. 1988. *Object-Oriented Systems Analysis: Modeling the World in Data.* Englewood Cliffs, NJ: Yourdon Press, p. 15.

[29]   Ross, R. 1987. *Entity Modeling: Techniques and Application.* Boston, MA: Database Research Group, p. 9.

[30]   Coad, P., and Yourdon, E. 1990. *Object-Oriented Analysis.* Englewood Cliffs, NJ: Prentice-Hall, p. 62.

[31]   Arango, G. May 1989. Domain Analysis: From Art Form to Engineering Discipline. *SIGSOFT Engineering Notes,* vol. 14 (3), p. 153.

[32] Moore, J., and Bailin, S. 1988. *Position Paper on Domain Analysis*. Laurel, MD: CTA Incorporated, p. 2.

[33] Abbott, R. November 1983. Program Design by Informal English Descriptions. *Communications of the ACM*, vol. 26 (11).

[34] Saeki, M., Horai, H., and Enomoto, H. May 1989. Software Development Process from Natural Language Specification. *Proceedings of the 11th International Conference on Software Engineering*. New York, NY: Computer Society Press of the IEEE.

[35] McMenamin, S., and Palmer, J. 1984. *Essential Systems Analysis*. New York, NY: Yourdon Press, p. 267.

[36] Ward, P., and Mellor, S. 1985. *Structured Development for Real-time Systems*. Englewood Cliffs, NJ: Yourdon Press.

[37] Seidewitz, E., and Stark, M. August 1986. *General Object-Oriented Software Development*, Report SEL-86-002. Greenbelt, MD: NASA Goddard Space Flight Center, p. 5-2.

[38] Seidewitz, E. 1990. Private communication.

[39] Goldberg, A. 1984. *Smalltalk-80: The Interactive Programming Environment*. Reading, MA: Addison-Wesley, p. 77.

[40] Thomas, D. May/June 1989. In Search of an Object-Oriented Development Process. *Journal of Object-Oriented Programming*, vol. 2 (1), p. 61.

[41] Stroustrup, B. 1986. *The C++ Programming Language*. Reading, MA: Addison-Wesley, p. 7.

[42] Halbert, D., and O'Brien, P. September 1988. Using Types and Inheritance in Object-Oriented Programming. *IEEE Software*, vol. 4 (5), p. 75.

[43] Stefik, M., and Bobrow, D. Winter 1986. Object-Oriented Programming: Themes and Variations, *AI Magazine*, vol. 6 (4), p. 60.

[44] Stefik and Bobrow. Object-Oriented Programming, p. 58.

[45] Jackson, M. 1983. *System Development*. Englewood Cliffs, NJ: Prentice-Hall.

[46] Ibid., p. 4.

[47] Adams, S. July 1986. MetaMethods: The MVC Paradigm, in *HOOPLA: Hooray for Object-Oriented Programming Languages*. Everette, WA: Object-Oriented Programming for Smalltalk Applications Developers Association, vol. 1 (4), p. 6.

[48] Russo, V., Johnston, G., and Campbell, R. September 1988. Process Management and Exception Handling in Multiprocessor Operating Systems Using Object-Oriented Design Techniques. *SIGPLAN Notices*, vol. 23 (11), p. 249.

[49] Englemore, R., and Morgan, T. 1988. *Blackboard Systems*. Wokingham, England: Addison-Wesley, p. v.

The Second Section: The Method

Petroski, H. 1985. *To Engineer is Human*. New York, NY: St Martin's Press, p. 73.

Chapter 5: The Notation

[1]   Shear, D. December 8, 1988. CASE Shows Promise, but Confusion Still Exists. *EDN*, vol. 33 (25), p. 168.

[2]   Whitehead, A. 1958. *An Introduction to Mathematics*. New York, NY: Oxford University Press.

[3]   Defense Science Board. *Report of the Defense Science Board Task Force on Military Software*. September 1987. Washington, D.C.: Office of the Undersecretary of Defense for Acquisition, p. 8.

[4]   Kleyn, M., and Gingrich, P. September 1988. GraphTrace – Understanding Object-Oriented Systems Using Concurrently Animated Views. *SIGPLAN Notices*, vol. 23 (11), p. 192.

[5]   Weinberg, G. 1988. *Rethinking Systems Analysis and Design*. New York, NY: Dorset House, p. 157.

[6]   Aho, A., Hopcroft, J., and Ullman, J. 1974. *The Design and Analysis of Computer Programs*. Reading, MA: Addison-Wesley, p. 2.

[7]   Buhr, R. August 22, 1988. *Machine Charts for Visual Prototyping in System Design*. SCE Report 88-2. Ottawa, Canada: Carleton University.

Chapter 6: The Process

[1]   Druke, M. 1989. Private communication.

[2]   Jones, C. September 1984. Reusability in Programming: A Survey of the State of the Art. *IEEE Transactions on Software Engineering*. vol. SE-10 (5).

[3]   Curtis, B. May 17, 1989. *. . . But You Have to Understand, This Isn't the Way We Develop Software at Our Company*. MCC Technical Report Number STP-203-89. Austin, TX: Microelectronics and Computer Technology Corporation, p. x.

[4]   Heinlein, R. 1966. *The Moon Is a Harsh Mistress*. New York, NY: The Berkeley Publishing Group, p. 290.

[5]   Boehm, B. August 1986. A Spiral Model of Software Development and Enhancement. *Software Engineering Notes,* vol. 11 (4), p. 22.

[6]   Bailin, S. 1988. *Remarks on Object-Oriented Requirements Specification*. Laurel, MD: CTA Incorporated, p. 1.

[7]   Brownsword, L. 1989. Private communication.

[8]   Beck, K., and Cunningham, W. October 1989. A Laboratory for Teaching Object-Oriented Thinking. *SIGPLAN Notices*, vol. 24 (10).

Chapter 7: Pragmatics

[1]   Dijkstra, E. May 1968. The Structure of the "THE" Multiprogramming System. *Communications of the ACM,* vol. 11 (5), p. 341.

[2]   Kishida, K., Teramoto, M., Torri, K., and Urano, Y. September 1988. Quality Assurance Technology in Japan. *IEEE Software*, vol. 4 (5), p. 13.

[3]   Hawryszkiewycz, I. 1984. *Database Analysis and Design*. Chicago, IL: Science Research Associates, p. 115.

[4]   Boehm, B. August 1986. A Spiral Model of Software Development and Enhancement. *Software Engineering Notes*, vol. 11 (4), p. 23.

[5]   Hatley, D., and Pirbhai, I. 1988. *Strategies for Real-Time System Specification*. New York, NY: Dorset House, p. 27.

[6]   Mellor, S., Hecht, A., Tryon, D., and Hywari, W. September 1988. Object-Oriented Analysis: Theory and Practice, Course Notes, in *Object-Oriented Programming Systems, Languages, and Applications*. San Diego, CA: OOPSLA'88, p. 1.3.

[7]   Yourdon, E. 1989. *Modern Structured Analysis*. Englewood Cliffs, NJ: Prentice-Hall.

[8]   DeMarco, T. 1979. *Structured Analysis and System Specification*. Englewood Cliffs, NJ: Prentice-Hall.

[9]   Gane, C., and Sarson, T. 1979. *Structured Systems Analysis*. Englewood Cliffs, NJ: Prentice-Hall.

[10] Ward, P., and Mellor, S. 1985. *Structured Development for Real-time Systems*. Englewood Cliffs, NJ: Prentice-Hall.

[11] Hatley and Pirbhai. *Strategies for Real-Time*.

[12] DeMarco, T. 1987. Private communication.

[13] Shlaer, S., and Mellor, S. 1988. *Object-Oriented Systems Analysis: Modeling the World in Data*. Englewood Cliffs, NJ: Yourdon Press.

[14] Coad, P. Summer 1989. OOA: Object-Oriented Analysis. *American Programmer*, vol. 2 (7–8).

[15] Smith, M., and Tockey, S. 1988. *An Integrated Approach to Software Requirements Definition Using Objects*. Seattle, WA: Boeing Commercial Airplane Support Division, p. 133.

[16] Marca, D., and McGowan, C. 1988. *SADT™: Structured Analysis and Design Technique*. New York, NY: McGraw-Hill.

[17] Alford, M. 1983. Derivation of Element-Relation-Attribute Database Requirements by Decomposition of System Functions, in *Entity-Relationship Approach to Software Engineering*. Amsterdam, The Netherlands: Elsevier Science Publishers.

[18] Stoecklin, S., Adams, E., and Smith, S. 1987. *Object-Oriented Analysis*. Tallahassee, FL: East Tennessee State University.

[19] Page-Jones, M. 1988. *The Practical Guide to Structured Systems Design*. Englewood Cliffs, NJ: Yourdon Press. pp. 261–265.

[20] Stefik, M., and Bobrow, D. Winter 1986. Object-Oriented Programming: Themes and Variations, *AI Magazine*, vol. 6 (4), p. 41.

[21] Meyer, B. 1988. *Object-Oriented Software Construction*. New York, NY: Prentice Hall, p. 340.

[22] As quoted in Sommerville, I. 1989. *Software Engineering*. 3rd ed. Wokingham, England: Addison-Wesley, p. 546.

[23] As quoted in Zelkowitz, M. June 1978. Perspectives on Software Engineering. *ACM Computing Surveys*, vol. 10 (2), p. 204.

[24] Showalter, J. 1989. Private communication.

[25] Davis, A., Bersoff, E., and Comer, E. October 1988. A Strategy for Comparing Alternative Software Development Life Cycle Models. *IEEE Transactions on Software Engineering*, vol. 14 (10), p. 1456.

[26] Lang, K., and Peralmutter, B. November 1986. Oaklisp: an Object-Oriented Scheme with First-Class Types. *SIGPLAN Notices*, vol. 21 (11), p. 34.

[27] Meyrowitz, N. November 1986. Intermedia: The Architecture and Construction of an Object-Oriented Hypermedia System and Applications Framework. *SIGPLAN Notices*, vol. 21 (11), p. 200.

[28] Schmucker, K. 1986. *Object-Oriented Programming for the Macintosh*. Hasbrouk Heights, NJ: Hayden, p. 11.

[29] Simonian, R., and Crone, M. November/December 1988. InnovAda: True Object-Oriented Programming in Ada. *Journal of Object-Oriented Programming*, vol. 1 (4), p. 19.

[30] Pascoe, G. August 1986. Elements of Object-Oriented Programming. *Byte*, vol. 11 (8), p. 144.

[31] Russo, V., and Kaplan, S. 1988. A C++ Interpreter for Scheme. *Proceedings of USENIX C++ Conference*. Berkeley, CA: USENIX Association, p. 106.

[32] Kempf, R. October 1987. Teaching Object-Oriented Programming with the KEE System. *SIGPLAN Notices*, vol. 22 (12), p. 11.

The Third Section: Applications

Minsky, M. April 1970. Form and Content in Computer Science. *Journal of the Association for Computing Machinery*, vol. 17 (2), p. 197.

Chapter 8: Smalltalk: Home Heating System

[1] White, S. October 1986. Panel Problem: Software Controller for an Oil Hot Water Heating System. *Proceedings of COMPSAC*. New York, NY: Computer Society Press of the IEEE. pp. 276–277.

[2] Kerth, N. Private communication.

[3] *Pluggable Gauges Version 1.0 User Manual*. 1987. Cary, NC: Knowledge Systems.

Chapter 9: Object Pascal: Geometrical Optics Construction Kit

[1] Sears, F., Zemansky, M., and Young., H. 1987. *University Physics*. 7th ed. Reading, MA: Addison-Wesley, p. 887.

[2] Sears, Zemansky, and Young. *University Physics*, p. 890.

[3] *Inside Macintosh*, Vol. 1–5. 1988. Reading, MA: Addison-Wesley.

[4] Scheifler, R., and Gettys, J. 1986. The X Window System. *ACM Transactions on Graphics*, vol. 63.

[5] *Open Look Graphical User Interface Functional Specification.* 1990. Reading, MA: Addison-Wesley.

[6] Durant, D., Carlson, G., and Yao, P. 1987. *Programmer's Guide to Windows.* Berkeley, CA: Sybex.

[7] *IBM Operating System/2 Seminar Proceedings, IBM OS/2 Standard Edition Version 1.1, IBM Operating System/2 Update, Presentation Manager.* April 1988. Boca Raton, FL: International Business Machines.

[8] *MacApp: The Expandable Macintosh Application,* version 2.0B9. 1989. Cupertino, CA: Apple Computer.

[9] *MacApp,* p. 2.

[10] *Inside Macintosh.*

[11] *OSF/Motif Style Guide, Version 1.0.* 1989. Cambridge, MA: Open Software Foundation.

Chapter 10: C++: Problem Reporting System

[1] Levy, P. 1989. Private communication.

[2] Date, C. 1981. *An Introduction to Database Systems.* Vol. 1. Reading, MA: Addison-Wesley, p. 4.

[3] Date. *An Introduction,* p. 10.

[4] Hawryszkiewycz, I. 1984. *Database Analysis and Design.* Chicago, IL: Science Research Associates, p. 425.

[5] Wiorkowski, G., and Kull, D. 1988. *DB2 Design and Development Guide.* Reading, MA: Addison-Wesley, p. 29.

[6] Date. *An Introduction,* p. 63.

[7] Wiorkowski and Kull. *DB2 Design,* p. 2.

[8] Date. *An Introduction.* p. 237.

[9] Date. *An Introduction.* p. 238.

[10] Wiorkowski and Kull. *DB2 Design.* p. 15.

[11] Date, C. 1986. *Relational Database: Selected Writings.* Reading, MA: Addison-Wesley, p. 461.

[12] *Oracle for Macintosh: References, Version 1.1.* 1989. Belmont, CA: Oracle, p. 5–118.

[13] Hawryszkiewycz. *Database Analysis.* p. 431.

Chapter 11: Common Lisp Object System: Cryptanalysis

[1] Meyer, C., and Matyas. 1982. *Cryptography.* New York, NY: John Wiley and Sons, p. 1.

[2] Erman, L., Lark, J., and Hayes-Roth, F. December 1988. ABE: An Environment for Engineering Intelligent Systems. *IEEE Transactions on Software Engineering*, vol. 14 (12), p. 1758.

[3] Nii, P. Summer 1986. Blackboard Systems: The Blackboard Model of Problem Solving and the Evolution of Blackboard Architectures. *AI Magazine*, vol. 7 (2), p. 46.

[4] Englemore, R., and Morgan, T. 1988. *Blackboard Systems.* Wokingham, England: Addison-Wesley, p. 16.

[5] Ibid., p. 19.

[6] Ibid., p. 6.

[7] Ibid., p. 12.

[8] Nii. Blackboard Systems, p. 43.

[9] Englemore and Morgan. *Blackboard Systems,* p. 11.

Chapter 12: Ada: Traffic Management System

[1] *Rockwell Advanced Railroad Electronic Systems.* 1989. Cedar Rapids, IA: Rockwell International.

[2] Murphy, E. December 1988. All Aboard for Solid State. *IEEE Spectrum*, vol. 25 (13), p. 42.

[3] Murphy. All Aboard.

[4] Tanenbaum, A. 1981. *Computer Networks.* Englewood Cliffs, NJ: Prentice-Hall.

Afterword

Lefrancois, G. 1977. *Of Children: An Introduction to Child Development, Second Edition.* Belmont, CA: Wadsworth, p. 371.

Appendix

[1] Wulf, W. January 1980. Trends in the Design and Implementation of Programming Languages. *IEEE Computer*, vol. 13 (1), p. 15.

[2] Birtwistle, G., Dahl, O-J., Myhrhaug, B., and Nygard, K. 1979. *Simula begin.* Lund, Sweden: Studentlitteratur.

[3] Schmucker, K. 1986. *Object-Oriented Programming for the Macintosh.* Hasbrouk Heights, NJ: Hayden, p. 346.

[4] Ingalls, D. The Smalltalk-76 Programming System Design and Implementation. *Proceedings of the Fifth Annual ACM Symposium on Principles of Programming Languages*, ACM, p. 9.

[5] Borning, A., and Ingalls, D. 1982. Multiple Inheritance in Smalltalk-80. *Proceedings of the National Conference on Artificial Intelligence.* Menlo Park, CA: AAAI.

[6] Goldberg, A., and Robson, D. 1989. *Smalltalk-80: The Language.* Reading, MA: Addison-Wesley.

[7] Goldberg, A. 1984. *Smalltalk-80: The Interactive Programming Environment.* Reading, MA: Addison-Wesley.

[8] Krasner, G. 1983. *Smalltalk-80: Bits of History, Words of Advice.* Reading, MA: Addison-Wesley.

[9] Schmucker, K. August 1986. Object-Oriented Languages for the Macintosh. *Byte*, vol. 11 (8), p. 179.

[10] *Macintosh Programmer's Workshop Pascal 3.0 Reference.* 1989. Cupertino, CA: Apple Computer.

[11] Stroustrup, B. 1986. *The C++ Programming Language.* Reading, MA: Addison-Wesley, p. 4.

[12] Gorlen, K. 1989. An Introduction to C++, in *UNIX System V AT&T C++ Language System, Release 2.0 Selected Readings.* Murray Hill, NJ: AT&T Bell Laboratories, p. 2-1.

[13] *UNIX System V AT&T C++ Language System, Release 2.0 Product Reference Manual.* 1989. Murray Hill, NJ: AT&T Bell Laboratories.

[14] *UNIX System V AT&T C++ Language System, Release 2.0 Selected Readings.* 1989. Murray Hill, NJ: AT&T Bell Laboratories.

[15] *UNIX System V AT&T C++ Language System, Release 2.0 Release Notes.* 1989. Murray Hill, NJ: AT&T Bell Laboratories.

[16] *UNIX System V AT&T C++ Language System, Release 2.0 Library Manual.* 1989. Murray Hill, NJ: AT&T Bell Laboratories.

[17] Keene, S. 1989. *Object-Oriented Programming in Common Lisp.* Reading, MA: Addison-Wesley, p. 215.

[18] Bobrow, D. 1990. Private communication.

[19] Bobrow, D., DeMichiel, L., Gabriel, R., Keene, S., Kiczales, G., and Moon, D. September 1988. Common Lisp Object System Specification X3J13 Document 88-002R. *SIGPLAN Notices*, vol. 23.

[20] *Reference Manual for the Ada Programming Language.* February 1983. Washington, D.C.: Department of Defense, Ada Joint Program Office, p. 1-3.

[21] Ibid.

[22] Saunders, J. March/April 1989. A Survey of Object-Oriented Programming Languages. *Journal of Object-Oriented Programming*, vol. 1 (6).

[23] Ibid., p. 6.

Glossary

abstract class A class that has no instances. An abstract class is written with the expectation that its subclasses will add to its structure and behavior, usually by completing the implementation of its (typically) incomplete methods.

abstraction The essential characteristics of an object that distinguish it from all other kinds of objects and thus provide crisply-defined conceptual boundaries relative to the perspective of the viewer; the process of focusing upon the essential characteristics of an object. Abstraction is one of the fundamental elements of the object model.

active object An object that encompasses its own thread of control.

actor An object that can operate upon other objects but is never operated upon by other objects. In some contexts, the terms *active object* and *actor* are interchangeable.

agent An object that can both operate upon other objects and be operated upon by other objects. An agent is usually created to do some work on behalf of an actor or another agent.

aggregate class A class that is constructed primarily by inheriting from other classes and rarely adds its own structure and behavior.

algorithmic decomposition The process of breaking a system into parts, each of which represents some small step in a larger process. The application of structured design methods leads to an algorithmic decomposition, whose focus is upon the flow of control within a system.

base class The most generalized class in a class structure. Most applications have many such base classes. Some languages define a primitive base class, which serves as the ultimate superclass of all classes.

behavior How an object acts and reacts, in terms of its state changes and message passing.

blocking object A passive object whose semantics are guaranteed in the presence of multiple threads of control.

cardinality The number of instances that a class may have; the number of instances that participate in a using class relationship.

class A set of objects that share a common structure and a common behavior. The terms *class* and *type* are usually (but not always) interchangeable; a class is a slightly different concept than a type, in that it emphasizes the importance of hierarchies of classes.

class category A collection of classes, some of which are visible to other class categories, and others of which are hidden.

class diagram Part of the notation of object-oriented design, used to show the existence of classes and their relationships in the logical design of a system. A class diagram may represent all or part of the class structure of a system.

class structure The "kind of" hierarchy of a system; a graph whose vertices represent classes and whose arcs represent relationships among these classes. The class structure of a system is represented by a set of class diagrams.

class utility A collection of free subprograms.

class variable A placeholder for part of the state of a class. Collectively, the class variables of a class constitute its structure. A class variable is shared by all instances of the same class.

client An object that uses the resources of another, either by operating upon it or by referencing its state.

concurrency The property that distinguishes an active object from one that is not active. Concurrency is one of the fundamental elements of the object model.

concurrent object An active object whose semantics are guaranteed in the presence of multiple threads of control.

constructor An operation that creates an object and/or initializes its state.

container class A class whose instances are collections of other objects. Container classes may denote homogeneous collections (all of the objects in the collection are of the same class) or heterogeneous collections (each of the objects in the collection may be of a different class, although all must share a common superclass). Container classes are most often defined as generic or parameterized classes, with some parameter designating the class of the contained objects.

destructor An operation that frees the state of an object and/or destroys the object itself.

dynamic binding Binding denotes the association of a name (such as a variable declaration) with a class; dynamic binding is a binding in which the name/class association is not made until the object designated by the name is created (at execution time).

encapsulation The process of hiding all of the details of an object that do not contribute to its essential characteristics; typically, the structure of an object is hidden, as well as the implementation of its methods. The terms *encapsulation* and *information hiding* are usually interchangeable. Encapsulation is one of the fundamental elements of the object model.

field A repository for part of the state of an object; collectively, the fields of an object constitute its structure. The terms *field, instance variable, member object* and *slot* are interchangeable

free subprogram A procedure or function that serves as a nonprimitive operation upon an object or objects of the same or different classes. A free subprogram is any subprogram that is not a method of an object.

friend A method typically involving two or more objects of different classes, whose implementation for any one class may reference the private parts of all the corresponding classes that are also friends.

function In the context of a requirements analysis, a single, outwardly visible and testable behavior.

generic function An operation upon an object. A generic function of a class may be redefined in subclasses; thus, for a given object, it is implemented through a set of methods declared in various classes related via their inheritance hierarchy. The terms *generic function* and *virtual function* are usually interchangeable.

generic class A class that serves as a template for other classes, in which the template may be parameterized by other classes, objects, and/or operations. A generic class must be instantiated (its parameters filled in) before objects can be created. Generic classes are typically used as container classes. The terms *generic class* and *parameterized class* are interchangeable.

hierarchy A ranking or ordering of abstractions. The two most common hierarchies in a complex system include its class structure (the "kind of" hierarchy) and its object structure (the "part of" hierarchy); hierarchies may also be found in the module and process architectures of a complex system. Hierarchy is one of the fundamental elements of the object model.

identity The nature of an object that distinguishes it from all other objects.

implementation The inside view of a class, object, or module, including the secrets of its behavior.

information hiding The process of hiding all the details of an object that do not contribute to its essential characteristics; typically, the structure of an object is hidden, as well as the implementation of its methods. The terms *encapsulation* and *information hiding* are usually interchangeable.

inheritance A relationship among classes, wherein one class shares the structure or behavior defined in one (single inheritance) or more (multiple inheritance) other classes. Inheritance defines a "kind of" hierarchy among classes in which a subclass inherits from one or more superclasses; a subclass typically augments or redefines the existing structure and behavior of its superclasses.

instance Something you can do things to. An instance has state, behavior, and identity. The structure and behavior of similar instances are defined in their common class. The terms *instance* and *object* are interchangeable.

instance variable A repository for part of the state of an object. Collectively, the instance variables of an object constitute its structure. The terms *field, instance variable, member object,* and *slot* are interchangeable.

instantiation The process of filling in the template of a generic or parameterized class to produce a class from which one can create instances.

interface The outside view of a class, object, or module, which emphasizes its abstraction while hiding its structure and the secrets of its behavior.

iterator An operation that permits the parts of an object to be visited.

key abstraction A class or object that forms part of the vocabulary of the problem domain.

levels of abstraction The relative ranking of abstractions in a class structure, object structure, module architecture, or process architecture. In terms of its "part of" hierarchy, a given abstraction is at a higher high level of abstraction than others if it builds upon the others; in terms of their "kind of" hierarchy, high-level abstractions are generalized, and low-level abstractions are specialized.

mechanism A structure whereby objects work together to provide some behavior that satisfies a requirement of the problem.

member function An operation upon an object, defined as part of the declaration of a class; all member functions are operations, but not all operations are member functions. The terms *member function* and *method* are usually interchangeable. In some languages, a member function stands alone and may be redefined in a subclass; in other languages, a member function may not be redefined, but serves as part of the implementation of a generic function or virtual function, both of which may be redefined in a subclass.

member object A repository for part of the state of an object; collectively, the member objects of an object constitute its structure. The terms *field, instance variable, member object,* and *slot* are interchangeable.

message An operation that one object performs upon another. The terms *message, method,* and *operation* are usually interchangeable.

metaclass The class of a class; a class whose instances are themselves classes.

method An operation upon an object, defined as part of the declaration of a class; all methods are operations, but not all operations are methods. The terms *message, method,* and *operation* are usually interchangeable. In some languages, a method stands alone and may be redefined in a subclass; in other languages, a method may not be redefined, but serves as part of the implementation of a generic function or a virtual function, both of which may be redefined in a subclass.

mixin A class that embodies a single, focused behavior, used to augment the behavior of some other class via inheritance; the behavior of a mixin is usually orthogonal to the behavior of the classes with which it is combined.

modifier An operation that alters the state of an object.

modularity The property of a system that has been decomposed into a set of cohesive and loosely coupled modules. Modularity is one of the fundamental elements of the object model.

module A unit of code that serves as a building block for the physical structure of a system; a program unit that contains declarations, expressed in the vocabulary of a particular programming language, that form the physical realization of some or all of the classes and objects in the logical design of the system. A module typically has two parts: its interface and its implementation.

module architecture The hierarchy of modules that form the physical structure of a system; a graph whose vertices represent modules and whose arcs represent relationships among these modules. The module architecture of a system is represented by a set of module diagrams.

module diagram Part of the notation of object-oriented design, used to show the allocation of classes and objects to modules in the physical design of a system. A module diagram may represent all or part of the module architecture of a system.

monomorphism A concept in type theory, according to which a name (such as a variable declaration) may only denote objects of the same class.

object Something you can do things to. An object has state, behavior, and identity; the structure and behavior of similar objects are defined in their common class. The terms *instance* and *object* are interchangeable.

object diagram Part of the notation of object-oriented design, used to show the existence of objects and their relationships in the logical design of a system. An object diagram may represent all or part of the object structure of a system, and primarily illustrates the semantics of key mechanisms in the logical design. A single object diagram represents a snapshot in time of an otherwise transitory event or configuration of objects.

object model The collection of principles that form the foundation of object-oriented design; a software engineering paradigm emphasizing the principles of abstraction, encapsulation, modularity, hierarchy, typing, concurrency, and persistence.

object structure The "part of" hierarchy of a system; a set of graphs whose vertices represent objects and whose arcs represent relationships among those objects. An object diagram may represent all or part of the object structure of a system.

object-based programming A method of programming in which programs are organized as cooperative collections of objects, each of which represents an instance of some type, and whose types are all members of a hierarchy of types united via other than inheritance relationships. In such programs, types are generally viewed as static, whereas objects typically have a much more dynamic nature, which is somewhat constrained by the existence of static binding and monomorphism.

object-oriented analysis A method of analysis in which requirements are examined from the perspective of the classes and objects found in the vocabulary of the problem domain.

object-oriented decomposition The process of breaking a system into parts, each of which represents some class or object from the problem domain. The application of object-oriented design methods leads to an object-oriented decomposition, in which we view the world as a collection of objects that cooperate with one another to achieve some desired functionality.

object-oriented design A method of design encompassing the process of object-oriented decomposition and a notation for depicting both logical and physical as well as static and dynamic models of the system under design; specifically, this notation includes class diagrams, object diagrams, module diagrams, and process diagrams.

object-oriented programming A method of implementation in which programs are organized as cooperative collections of objects, each of which represents an instance of some class, and whose classes are all members of a hierarchy of classes united via inheritance relationships. In such programs, classes are generally viewed as static, whereas objects typically have a much more dynamic nature, which is encouraged by the existence of dynamic binding and polymorphism.

operation Some action that one object performs upon another in order to elicit a reaction. All of the operations upon a specific object may be found in free subprograms and member functions or methods. The terms *message, method,* and *operation* are usually interchangeable.

parameterized class A class that serves as a template for other classes, in which the template may be parameterized by other classes, objects, and/or operations. A parameterized class must be instantiated (its parameters filled in) before instances can be created. Parameterized classes are typically used as container classes; the terms *generic class* and *parameterized class* are interchangeable.

passive object An object that does not encompass its own thread of control.

persistence The property of an object by which its existence transcends time (i.e., the object continues to exist after its creator ceases to exist) and/or space (i.e., the object's location moves from the address space in which it was created). Persistence is one of the fundamental elements of the object model.

polymorphism A concept in type theory, according to which a name (such as a variable declaration) may denote objects of many different classes that are related by some common superclass; thus, any object denoted by this name is able to respond to some common set of operations in different ways.

private A declaration that forms part of the interface of a class, object, or module; what is declared as private is not visible to any other classes, objects, or modules.

process architecture The hierarchy of processes that form the physical structure of a system; a graph whose vertices represent processors and devices and whose arcs represent connections among these processors and devices. The process architecture of a system is represented by a set of process diagrams.

process diagram Part of the notation of object-oriented design, used to show the allocation of processes to processors in the physical design of a system. A process diagram may represent all or part of the process architecture of a system.

protected A declaration that forms part of the interface of a class, object, or module, but that is not visible to any other classes, objects, or modules except those that represent subclasses.

protocol The ways in which an object may act and react, constituting the entire static and dynamic outside view of the object; the protocol of an object defines the envelope of the object's allowable behavior.

public A declaration that forms part of the interface of a class, object, or module, and that is visible to all other classes, objects, and modules that have visibility to it.

round-trip gestalt design A style of design that emphasizes the incremental and iterative development of a system, through the refinement of different yet consistent logical and physical views of the system as a whole; the process of object-oriented design is guided by the concepts of round-trip gestalt design; round-trip gestalt design is a recognition of that fact that the big picture of a design affects its details, and that the details often affect the big picture.

selector An operation that accesses the state of an object but does not alter that state.

sequential object A passive object whose semantics are guaranteed only in the presence of a single thread of control.

server An object that never operates upon other objects, but that is only operated upon by other objects.

slot A repository for part of the state of an object; collectively, the slots of an object constitute its structure. The terms *field, instancevariable, member object,* and *slot* are interchangeable

state One of the possible conditions in which an object may exist, characterized by definite quantities that are distinct from other quantities; at any given point in time, the state of an object encompasses all of the (usually static) properties of the object plus the current (usually dynamic) values of each of these properties.

state space An enumeration of all the possible states of an object. The state space of a software object encompasses an indefinite yet finite number of possible (although not always desirable nor expected) states.

state transition diagram Part of the notation of a class diagram, used to show the state space of an instance of a given class, the events that cause a transition from one state to another, and the actions that result from a state change.

static binding Binding denotes the association of a name (such as a variable declaration) with a class; static binding is a binding in which the name/class association is made when the name is declared (at compile time) but before the creation of the object that the name designates.

strongly typed A characteristic of a programming language, according to which all expressions are guaranteed to be type-consistent.

structure The concrete representation of the state of an object. An object does not share its state with any other object, although all objects of the same class do share the same representation of their state.

structured design A method of design encompassing the process of algorithmic decomposition.

subclass A class that inherits from one or more classes (which are called its immediate *superclasses*).

subsystem A collection of modules, some of which are visible to other subsystems and others of which are hidden.

superclass The class from which another class inherits (which is called its immediate *subclass*).

synchronization The concurrency semantics of an operation. An operation may be simple (only one thread of control is involved), synchronous (two processes rendezvous), balking (one process rendezvous with another only if the second process is already waiting), timeout (one process rendezvous with another, but will wait for the second process only for a specified amount of time), or asynchronous (the two processes operate independently).

thread of control A single process. The start of a thread of control is the root from which independent dynamic action within a system occurs; a given system may have many simultaneous threads of control, some of which may dynamically come into existence and then cease to exist. Systems executing across multiple CPUs allow for truly concurrent threads of control, whereas systems running on a single CPU can only achieve the illusion of concurrent threads of control.

timing diagram Part of the notation of an object diagram, used to show the dynamic interactions among various objects in an object diagram.

type The definition of the domain of allowable values that an object may possess and the set of operations that may be performed upon the object. The terms *class* and *type* are usually (but not always) interchangeable; a type is a slightly different concept than a class, in that it emphasizes the importance of enforcing the type of the object.

typing The enforcement of the class of an object, which prevents objects of different types from being interchanged or, at the most, allows them to be interchanged only in very restricted ways. Typing is one of the fundamental elements of the object model.

use To reference the outside view of an abstraction. A using relationship implies the ability to send messages along the path between two objects.

visibility The ability of one abstraction to see another and thus reference resources in its outside view. Abstractions are visible to one another only where their scopes overlap.

virtual function An operation upon an object. A virtual function may be redefined by subclasses; thus, for a given object, it is implemented through a set of methods declared in various classes that are related via their inheritance hierarchy. The terms *generic function* and *virtual function* are usually interchangeable.

Classified Bibliography

This classified bibliography is divided into eleven sections, labeled from A to K. References at the ends of chapters to items appearing in the bibliography take the form [<label> <year>]. For example, Brooks [H 1975] refers to his 1975 book, *The Mythical Man-Month,* in section H (Software Engineering) of the bibliography.

A. Classification

Aquinas, T. *Summa Theologica. Vol. 19 of Great Books of the Western World.* Chicago, IL: Encyclopedia Britannica.

Aristotle. *Categories. Vol. 8 of Great Books of the Western World.* Chicago, IL: Encyclopedia Britannica.

Classification Society of North America. *Journal of Classification.* New York, NY: Springer-Verlag.

Coombs, C., Raiffa, H., and Thrall, R. 1954. Some Views on Mathematical Models and Measurement Theory. *Psychological Review* vol. 61 (2).

Courtois, P. June 1985. On Time and Space Decomposition of Complex Structures. *Communications of the ACM* vol. 28 (6).

Darwin, C. *The Origin of Species. Vol. 49 of Great Books of the Western World.* Chicago, IL: Encyclopedia Britannica.

Descartes, R. *Rules for the Direction of the Mind. Vol. 31 of Great Books of the Western World.* Chicago, IL: Encyclopedia Britannica.

Flood, R., and Carson, E. 1988. *Dealing with Complexity.* New York, NY: Plenum Press.

Lakoff, G. 1987. *Women, Fire, and Dangerous Things: What Categories Reveal About the Mind.* Chicago, IL: The University of Chicago Press.

Lefrancois, G. 1977. *Of Children: An Introduction to Child Development.* 2nd ed. Belmont, CA: Wadsworth.

Lewin, R. 4 November 1988. Family Relationships Are a Biological Conundrum. *Science* vol. 242.

Maier, H. 1969. *Three Theories of Child Development: The Contributions of Erik H. Erickson, Jean Piaget, and Robert R. Sears, and Their Applications.* New York, NY: Harper and Row.

May, R. 16 September 1988. How Many Species Are There on Earth? *Science* vol. 241.

Michalski, R., and Stepp, R. 1983. Learning from Observation: Conceptual Clustering, in *Machine Learning: An Artificial Intelligence Approach.* ed. R. Michalski, J. Carbonell, and T. Mitchell. Palo Alto, CA: Tioga.

Miller, G. March 1956. The Magical Number Seven, Plus or Minus Two: Some Limits on Our Capacity for Processing Information. *The Psychological Review* vol. 63 (2).

Minsky, M. April 1970. Form and Content in Computer Science. *Journal of the Association for Computing Machinery* vol. 17 (2).

Minsky, M. 1986. *The Society of Mind.* New York, NY: Simon and Schuster.

Moldovan, D., and Wu, C. December 1988. A Hierarchical Knowledge-Based System for Airplane Classification. *IEEE Transactions on Software Engineering* vol. 14 (12).

Newell, A., and Simon, H. 1972. *Human Problem Solving.* Englewood Cliffs, New Jersey: Prentice-Hall.

Papert, S. 1980. *Mindstorms: Children, Computers, and Powerful Ideas.* New York, NY: Basic Books.

Plato. *Statesman. Vol. 7 of Great Books of the Western World.* Chicago, IL: Encyclopedia Britannica.

Siegler, R., and Richards, D. 1982. The Development of Intelligence, in *Handbook of Human Intelligence.* ed. R. Sternberg. Cambridge, London: Cambridge University Press.

Simon, H. 1982. *The Sciences of the Artificial.* Cambridge, MA: The MIT Press.

Sowa, J. 1984. *Conceptual Structures: Information Processing in Mind and Machine.* Reading, MA: Addison-Wesley.

Stepp, R., and Michalski, R. 1986. Conceptual Clustering of Structured Objects: A Goal-Oriented Approach. *Artificial Intelligence* vol. 28 (1).

Stevens, S. June 1946. On the Theory of Scales of Measurement, *Science* vol. 103 (2684).

Stillings, N., Feinstein, M., Garfield, J., Rissland, E., Rosenbaum, D., Weisler, S., and Baker-Ward, L. 1987. *Cognitive Science: An Introduction.* Cambridge, MA: The MIT Press.

B. Object-Oriented Analysis

Arango, G. May 1989. Domain Analysis: From Art Form to Engineering Discipline. *SIGSOFT Engineering Notes* vol. 14 (3).

Bailin, S. 1988. *Remarks on Object-Oriented Requirements Specification.* Laurel, MD: Computer Technology Associates.

Bailin, S., and Moore, J. 1987. *An Object-Oriented Specification Method for Ada.* Laurel, MD: Computer Technology Associates.

Borgida, A., Mylogoulos, J., and Wong, H. 1984. Generalization/Specialization as a Basis for Software Specification, in *On Conceptual Modeling: Perspectives from Artificial Intelligence, Databases, and Programming Languages.* ed. M. Brodie, J. Mylopoulos, and J. Schmidt. New York, NY: Springer-Verlag.

Cernosek, G., Monterio, E., and Pribyl, W. 1987. *An Entity-Relationship Approach to Software Requirements Analysis for Object-Based Development.* Houston, TX: McDonnell Douglas Astronautics.

Coad, P. Summer 1989. OOA: Object-Oriented Analysis. *American Programmer* vol. 2 (7-8).

Coad, P., and Yourdon, E. 1990. *Object-Oriented Analysis.* Englewood Cliffs, NJ: Prentice-Hall.

Dahl, O-J. 1987. Object-Oriented Specifications, in *Research Directions in Object-Oriented Programming.* ed. B. Schriver and P. Wegner. Cambridge, MA: The MIT Press.

DeMarco, T. 1979. *Structured Analysis and System Specification.* Englewood Cliffs, NJ: Prentice-Hall.

EVB Software Engineering. 1989. *Object-Oriented Requirements Analysis.* Frederick, MD.

Gane, C., and Sarson, T. 1979. *Structured Systems Analysis.* Englewood Cliffs, NJ: Prentice-Hall.

Hatley, D., and Pirbhai, I. 1988. *Strategies for Real-Time System Specification.* New York, NY: Dorset House.

Iscoe, N. 1988. *Domain Models for Program Specification and Generation.* Austin, TX: University of Texas.

Iscoe, N., Browne, J., and Werth, J. 1989. *Modeling Domain Knowledge: An Object-Oriented Approach to Program Specification and Generation.* Austin, TX: The University of Texas.

Marca, D., and McGowan, C. 1988. *SADT™: Structured Analysis and Design Technique.* New York, NY: McGraw-Hill.

McMenamin, S., and Palmer, J. 1984. *Essential Systems Analysis.* New York, NY: Yourdon Press.

Mellor, S., Hecht, A., Tryon, D., and Hywari, W. September 1988. Object-Oriented Analysis: Theory and Practice, Course Notes, from *Object-Oriented Programming Systems, Languages, and Applications.* San Diego, CA: OOPSLA'88.

Moore, J., and Bailin, S. 1988. *Position Paper on Domain Analysis.* Laurel, MD: Computer Technology Associates.

Page-Jones, M., and Weiss, S. Summer 1989. Synthesis: An Object-Oriented Analysis and Design Method. *American Programmer* vol. 2 (7-8).

Saeki, M., Horai, H., and Enomoto, H. May 1989. Software Development Process from Natural Language Specification. *Proceedings of the 11th International Conference on Software Engineering.* New York, NY: Computer Society Press of the IEEE.

Shemer, I. June 1987. Systems Analysis: A Systemic Analysis of a Conceptual Model. *Communications of the ACM* vol. 30 (6).

Shlaer, S., and Mellor, S. 1988. *Object-Oriented Systems Analysis: Modeling the World in Data.* Englewood Cliffs, NJ: Yourdon Press.

Shlaer, S., and Mellor, S. July 1989. An Object-Oriented Approach to Domain Analysis. *Software Engineering Notes* vol. 14 (5).

Shlaer, S., and Mellor, S. Summer 1989. Understanding Object-Oriented Analysis. *American Programmer* vol. 2 (7-8).

Stoecklin, S., Adams, E., and Smith, S. 1987. *Object-Oriented Analysis.* Tallahassee, FL: East Tennessee State University.

Sully, P. Summer 1989. Structured Analysis: Scaffolding for Object-Oriented Development. *American Programmer* vol. 2 (7-8).

Tsai, J., and Ridge, J. November 1988. Intelligent Support for Specifications Transformation. *IEEE Software* vol. 5 (6).

Veryard, R. 1984. *Pragmatic Data Analysis.* Oxford, England: Blackwell Scientific Publications.

Ward, P. March 1989. How to Integrate Object Orientation with Structured Analysis and Design. *IEEE Software* vol. 6 (2).

Weinberg, G. 1988. *Rethinking Systems Analysis and Design.* New York, NY: Dorset House.

C. Object-Oriented Applications

Abdali, K., Cherry, G., and Soiffer, N. November 1986. A Smalltalk System for Algebraic Manipulation. *SIGPLAN Notices* vol. 21 (11).

Almes, G., and Holman, C. September 1987. Edmas: An Object-Oriented, Locally Distributed Mail System. *IEEE Transactions on Software Engineering* vol. SE-13 (9).

Anderson, D. November 1986. Experience with Flamingo: A Distributed, Object-Oriented User Interface System. *SIGPLAN Notices* vol. 21 (11).

Archer, J., and Devlin, M. 1987. *Rational's Experience Using Ada for Very Large Systems.* Mountain View, CA: Rational.

Bagrodia, R., Chandy, M., and Misra, J. June 1987. A Message-Based Approach to Discrete-Event Simulation. *IEEE Transactions on Software Engineering* vol. SE-13 (6).

Barry, B. October 1989. Prototyping a Real-Time Embedded System in Smalltalk. *SIGPLAN Notices* vol. 24 (10).

Barry, B., Altoft, J., Thomas, D., and Wilson, M. October 1987. Using Objects to Design and Build Radar ESM Systems. *SIGPLAN Notices* vol. 22 (12).

Bezivin, J. October 1987. Some Experiments in Object-Oriented Simulation. *SIGPLAN Notices* vol. 22 (12).

Bhaskar, K., and Peckol, J. November 1986. Virtual Instruments: Object-Oriented Program Synthesis. *SIGPLAN Notices* vol. 21 (11).

Bjornerstedt, A., and Britts, S. September 1988. AVANCE: An Object Management System. *SIGPLAN Notices* vol. 23 (11).

Bobrow, D., and Stefik, M. February 1986. Perspectives on Artificial Intelligence Programming. *Science* vol. 231.

Boltuck-Pasquier, J., Grossman, E., and Collaud, G. August 1988. Prototyping an Interactive Electronic Book System Using an Object-Oriented Approach. *Proceedings of ECOOP'88: European Conference on Object-Oriented Programming.* New York, NY: Springer-Verlag.

Bonar, J., Cunningham R., and Schultz, J. November 1986. An Object-Oriented Architecture of Intelligent Tutoring Systems. *SIGPLAN Notices* vol. 21 (11).

Booch, G. 1987. *Software Components with Ada: Structures, Tools, and Subsystems.* Menlo Park, CA: Benjamin/Cummings.

Borning, A. October 1981. The Programming Language Aspects of ThingLab, a Constraint-Oriented Simulation Laboratory. *ACM Transactions on Programming Languages and Systems* vol. 3 (4).

Bowman, W., and Flegal, B. August 1981. ToolBox: A Smalltalk Illustration System. *Byte* vol. 6 (8).

Britcher, R., and Craig, J. May 1986. Using Modern Design Practices to Upgrade Aging Software Systems. *IEEE Software* vol. 3 (3).

Britton, K., and Parnas, D. December 8, 1981. *A-7E Software Module Guide*, Report 4702. Washington, D.C.: Naval Research Laboratory.

Bruck, D. 1988. Modeling of Control Systems with C++ and PHIGS. *Proceedings of USENIX C++ Conference.* Berkeley, CA: USENIX Association.

Budd, T. January 1989. The Design of an Object-Oriented Command Interpreter. *Software – Practice and Experience* vol. 19 (1).

Call, L., Cohrs, D., and Miller, B. October 1987. CLAM – an Open System for Graphical User Interfaces. *SIGPLAN Notices* vol. 22 (12).

Caplinger, M. October 1987. An Information System Based on Distributed Objects. *SIGPLAN Notices* vol. 22 (12).

Cargill, T. November 1986. Pi: A Case Study in Object-Oriented Programming. *SIGPLAN Notices* vol. 21 (11).

Cmelik, R., and Genani, N. May 1988. Dimensional Analysis with C++. *IEEE Software* vol. 5 (3).

Cointe, P., Briot, J., and Serpette, B. 1987. The Formes System: A Musical Application of Object-Oriented Concurrent Programming, in *Object-Oriented Concurrent Programming.* ed. Yonezawa and M. Tokoro. Cambridge, MA: The MIT Press.

Coutaz, J. September 1985. Abstractions for User Interface Design. *IEEE Computer* vol. 18 (9).

Dasgupta, P. November 1986. A Probe-Based Monitoring Scheme for an Object-Oriented Operating System. *SIGPLAN Notices* vol. 21 (11).

Davidson, C., and Moseley, R. 1987. *An Object-Oriented Real-Time Knowledge-Based System.* Albuquerque, NM: Applied Methods.

Dietrich, W., Nackman, L., and Gracer, F. October 1989. Saving a Legacy with Objects. *SIGPLAN Notices* vol. 24 (10).

Dijkstra, E. May 1968. The Structure of the "THE" Multiprogramming System. *Communications of the ACM* vol. 11 (5).

Durand, G., Benkiran, A., Durel, C., Nga, H., and Tag, M. 9 March 1988. *Distributed Mail Service in CSE System.* Paris, France: Synergie Informatique et Development.

Englemore, R., and Morgan, T. 1988. *Blackboard Systems.* Wokingham, England: Addison-Wesley.

Epstein, D., and LaLonde, W. September 1988. A Smalltalk Window System Based on Constraints. *SIGPLAN Notices* vol. 23 (11).

Ewing, J. November 1986. An Object-Oriented Operating System Interface. *SIGPLAN Notices* vol. 21 (11).

Fenton, J., and Beck, K. October 1989. Playground: An Object-Oriented Simulation System with Agent Rules for Children of All Ages. *SIGPLAN Notices* vol. 24 (10).

Fischer, G. 1987. *An Object-Oriented Construction and Tool Kit for Human-Computer Communication.* Boulder, CO: University of Colorado Department of Computer Science and Institute of Cognitive Science.

Foley, J., and van Dam, A. 1982. *Fundamentals of Interactive Computer Graphics.* Reading, MA: Addison-Wesley.

Frankowski, E. 20 March 1986. *Advantages of the Object Paradigm for Prototyping.* Golden Valley, MN: Honeywell.

Freburger, K. October 1987. RAPID: Prototyping Control Panel Interfaces. *SIGPLAN Notices* vol. 22 (12).

Funk, D. 1986. Applying Ada to Beech Starship Avionics. *Proceedings of the First International Conference on Ada Programming Language Applications for the NASA Space Station.* Houston, TX: NASA Lyndon B. Johnson Space Center.

Garrett, N., and Smith, K. November 1986. Building a Timeline Editor from Prefab Parts: The Architecture of an Object-Oriented Application. *SIGPLAN Notices* vol. 21 (11).

Goldberg, A. 1978. *Smalltalk in the Classroom.* Palo Alto, CA: Xerox Palo Alto Research Center.

Gorlen, K. December 1987. An Object-Oriented Class Library for C++ Programs. *Software – Practice and Experience* vol. 17 (12).

Gray, L. 1987. *Transferring Object-Oriented Design Techniques into Use: AWIS Experience.* Fairfax, VA: TRW Federal Systems Group.

Grimshaw, A., and Liu, J. October 1987. Mentat: An Object-Oriented Macro Data Flow System. *SIGPLAN Notices* vol. 22 (12).

Grossman, M., and Ege, R. October 1987. Logical Composition of Object-Oriented Interfaces. *SIGPLAN Notices* vol. 22 (12).

Gutfreund, S. October 1987. ManiplIcons in ThinkerToy. *SIGPLAN Notices* vol. 22 (12).

Harrison, W., Shilling, J., and Sweeney, P. October 1989. Good News, Bad News: Experience Building a Software Development Environment Using the Object-Oriented Paradigm. *SIGPLAN Notices* vol. 24 (10).

Ingalls, D., Wallace, S., Chow, Y., Ludolph, F., and Doyle, K. September 1988. Fabrik: A Visual Programming Environment. *SIGPLAN Notices* vol. 23 (11).

Jacky, J., and Kalet, I. November 1986. An Object-Oriented Approach to a Large Scientific Application. *SIGPLAN Notices* vol. 21 (11).

Jerrell, M. October 1989. Function Minimization and Automatic Differentiation using C++. *SIGPLAN Notices* vol. 24 (10).

Johnson, R., and Foote, B. June/July 1988. Designing Reusable Classes. *Journal of Object-Oriented Programming* vol. 1 (2).

Jones, M., and Rashid, R. November 1986. Mach and Matchmaker: Kernel and Language Support for Object-Oriented Distributed Systems. *SIGPLAN Notices* vol. 21 (11).

Kay, A., and Goldberg, A. March 1977. Personal Dynamic Media. *IEEE Computer.*

Kerr, R., and Percival, D. October 1987. Use of Object-Oriented Programming in a Time Series Analysis System. *SIGPLAN Notices* vol. 22 (12).

Kuhl, F. 1988. *Object-Oriented Design for a Workstation for Air Traffic Control.* McLean, VA: The MITRE Corporation.

LaPolla, M. 1988. *On the Classification of Object-Oriented Design: The Object-Oriented Design of the AirLand Battle Management Menu System.* Austin, TX: Lockheed Software Technology Center.

Lea, D. 12 August 1988. *User's Guide to GNU C++ Library.* Cambridge, MA: Free Software Foundation.

Lea, D. 1988. The GNU C++ Library. *Proceedings of USENIX C++ Conference.* Berkeley, CA: USENIX Association.

Ledbetter, L., and Cox, B. June 1985. Software-ICs. *Byte* vol. 10 (6).

Lee, K., and Rissman, M. February 1989. *An Object-Oriented Solution Example: A Flight Simulator Electrical System.* Pittsburgh, PA: Software Engineering Institute.

Lee, K., Rissman, M., D'Ippolito, R., Plinta, C., and Van Scoy, R. December 1987. *An OOD Paradigm for Flight Simulators,* Report CMU/SEI-87-TR-43. Pittsburgh, PA: Software Engineering Institute.

Levy, P. 1987. *Implementing Systems Software in Ada.* Mountain View, CA: Rational.

Linton, M., Vlissides, J., and Calder, P. February 1989. Composing User Interfaces with InterViews. *IEEE Computer.* vol. 22 (2).

Liu, L., and Horowitz, E. February 1989. Object Database Support for a Software Project Management Environment. *SIGPLAN Notices* vol. 24 (2).

Locke, D., and Goodenough, J. 1988. *A Practical Application of the Ceiling Protocol in a Real-Time System,* Report CMU/SEI-88-SR-3. Pittsburgh, PA: Software Engineering Institute.

Madany, P., Leyens, D., Russo, V., and Campbell, R. 1988. A C++ Class Hierarchy for Building UNIX-like File Systems. *Proceedings of USENIX C++ Conference.* Berkeley, CA: USENIX Association.

Madduri, H., Raeuchle, T., and Silverman, J. 1987. *Object-Oriented Programming for Fault-Tolerant Distributed Systems.* Golden Valley, MN: Honeywell Computer Science Center.

Maloney, J., Borning, A., and Freeman-Benson, B. October 1989. Constraint Technology for User Interface Construction in ThingLab II. *SIGPLAN Notices* vol. 24 (10).

McDonald, J. October 1989. Object-Oriented Programming for Linear Algebra. *SIGPLAN Notices* vol. 24 (10).

Meyrowitz, N. November 1986. Intermedia: The Architecture and Construction of an Object-Oriented Hypermedia System and Applications Framework. *SIGPLAN Notices* vol. 21 (11).

Miller, M., Cunningham, H., Lee, C., and Vegdahl, S. November 1986. The Application Accelerator Illustration System. *SIGPLAN Notices* vol. 21 (11).

Mohan, L., and Kashyap, R. May 1988. An Object-Oriented Knowledge Representation for Spatial Information. *IEEE Transactions on Software Engineering* vol. 14 (5).

Mraz, R. December 1986. *Performance Evaluation of Parallel Branch and Bound Search with the Intel iPSE Hypercube Computer.* Wright-Patterson Air Force Base, Ohio: Air Force Institute of Technology.

Muller, H., Rose, J., Kempf, J., and Stansbury, T. October 1989. The Use of Multimethods and Method Combination in a CLOS-Based Window Interface. *SIGPLAN Notices* vol. 24 (10).

Murphy, E. December 1988. All Aboard for Solid State. *IEEE Spectrum* vol. 25 (13).

NeXT Embraces a New Way of Programming. 25 November 1988. *Science* vol. 242.

Orden, E. 1987. Application Talk. *HOOPLA: Hooray for Object-Oriented Programming Languages* vol. 1 (1). Everette, WA: Object-Oriented Programming for Smalltalk Application Developers Association.

Oshima, M., and Shirai, Y. July 1983. Object Recognition Using Three-Dimensional Information. *IEEE Transactions on Pattern Analysis and Machine Intelligence* vol. 5 (4).

Page, T., Berson, S., Cheng, W., and Muntz, R. October 1989. An Object-Oriented Modeling Environment. *SIGPLAN Notices* vol. 24 (10).

Pashtan, A. 1982. Object-Oriented Operating Systems: An Emerging Design Methodology. *Proceedings of the ACM '82 Conference.* New York, NY: Association of Computing Machinery.

Piersol, K. November 1986. Object-Oriented Spreadsheets: The Analytic Spreadsheet Package. *SIGPLAN Notices* vol. 21 (11).

Plinta, C., Lee, K., and Rissman, M. 29 March 1989. A Model Solution for C3I: Message Translation and Validation. Pittsburgh, PA: Software Engineering Institute.

Pope, S. April/May 1988. Building Smalltalk-80-based Computer Music Tools. *Journal of Object-Oriented Programming* vol. 1 (1).

Rockwell International. 1989. *Rockwell Advanced Railroad Electronic Systems.* Cedar Rapids, IA.

Rubin, K., Jones, P., Mitchell, C., and Goldstein, T. September 1988. A Smalltalk Implementation of an Intelligent Operator's Associate. *SIGPLAN Notices* vol. 23 (11).

Ruspini, E., and Fraley, R. 1983. ID: An Intelligent Information Dictionary System, in *Entity-Relationship Approach to Software Engineering.* ed. C. Davis et al. Amsterdam, The Netherlands: Elsevier Science.

Russo, V., Johnston, G., and Campbell, R. September 1988. Process Management and Exception Handling in Multiprocessor Operating Systems Using Object-Oriented Design Techniques. *SIGPLAN Notices* vol. 23 (11).

Sampson, J., and Womble, B. 1988. *SEND: Simulation Environment for Network Design.* Dallas, TX: Southern Methodist University.

Scaletti, C., and Johnson, R. September 1988. An Interactive Environment for Object-Oriented Music Composition and Sound Synthesis. *SIGPLAN Notices* vol. 23 (11).

Schoen, E., Smith, R., and Buchanan, B. December 1988. Design of Knowledge-Based Systems with a Knowledge-Based Assistant. *IEEE Transactions on Software Engineering* vol. 14 (12).

Schulert, A., and Erf, K. 1988. Open Dialogue: Using an Extensible Retained Object Workspace to Support a UIMS. *Proceedings of USENIX C++ Conference.* Berkeley, CA: USENIX Association.

Scott, R., Reddy, P., Edwards, R., and Campbell, D. 1988. GPIO: Extensible Objects for Electronic Design. *Proceedings of USENIX C++ Conference.* Berkeley, CA: USENIX Association.

Smith, R., Barth, P., and Young, R. 1987. A Substrate for Object-Oriented Interface Design. *Research Directions in Object-Oriented Programming.* Cambridge, MA: The MIT Press.

Smith, R., Dinitz, R., and Barth, P. November 1986. Impulse-86: A Substrate for Object-Oriented Interface Design. *SIGPLAN Notices* vol. 21 (11).

Sneed, H., and Gawron, W. 1983. The Use of the Entity/Relationship Model as a Schema for Organizing the Data Processing Activities at the Bavarian Motor Works, in *Entity-Relationship Approach to Software Engineering.* ed. C. Davis et al. Amsterdam, The Netherlands: Elsevier Science.

Snodgrass, R. 1987. An Object-Oriented Command Language, in *Object-Oriented Computing: Implementations* vol. 2. ed. G. Peterson. New York, NY: Computer Society Press of the IEEE.

Sridhar, S. September 1988. Configuring Stand-Alone Smalltalk-80 Applications. *SIGPLAN Notices* vol. 23 (11).

Stokes, R. 1988. Prototyping Database Applications with a Hybrid of C++ and 4GL. *Proceedings of USENIX C++ Conference.* Berkeley, CA: USENIX Association.

Szcur, M., and Miller, P. September 1988. Transportable Applications Environment (TAE) PLUS: Experiences in "Object"ively Modernizing a User Interface Environment. *SIGPLAN Notices* vol. 23 (11).

Szekely, P., and Myers, B. September 1988. A User Interface Toolkit Based on Graphical Objects and Constraints. *SIGPLAN Notices* vol. 23 (11).

Tanner, J. 1 April 1986. *Fault Tree Analysis in an Object-Oriented Environment.* Mountain View, CA: IntelliCorp.

Temte, M. November/December 1984. Object-Oriented Design and Ballistics Software. *Ada Letters* vol. 4 (3).

Tripathi, A., and Aksit, M. November/December 1988. Communication, Scheduling, and Resource Management in SINA. *Journal of Object-Oriented Programming* vol. 1 (4).

Tripathi, A., Ghonami, A., and Schmitz, T. 1987. Object Management in the NEXUS Distributed Operating System. *Proceedings of the Thirty-second IEEE Computer Society International Conference.* New York, NY: Computer Society Press of the IEEE.

Ursprung, P., and Zehnder, C. 1983. HIQUEL: An Interactive Query Language to Define and Use Hierarchies, in *Entity-relationship Approach to Software Engineering.* ed. C. Davis et al. Amsterdam, The Netherlands: Elsevier Science.

van der Meulen, P. October 1987. INSIST: Interactive Simulation in Smalltalk. *SIGPLAN Notices* vol. 22 (12).

Vernon, V. September/October 1989. The Forest for the Trees. *Programmer's Journal* vol. 7 (5).

Vines, D., and King, T. 1987. *Experiences in Building a Prototype Object-Oriented Framework in Ada*. Minneapolis, MN: Honeywell.

Vlissides, J., and Linton, M. 1988. Applying Object-Oriented Design to Structured Graphics. *Proceedings of USENIX C++ Conference*. Berkeley, CA: USENIX Association.

Volz, R. Mudge, T., and Gal, D. 1987. Using Ada as a Programming Language for Robot-Based Manufacturing Cells, in *Object-Oriented Computing: Concepts* vol. 1. ed. G. Peterson. New York, NY: Computer Society Press of the IEEE.

Walther, S., and Peskin, R. October 1989. Strategies for Scientific Prototyping in Smalltalk. *SIGPLAN Notices* vol. 24 (10).

Weinand, A., Gamma, E., and Marty, R. September 1988. ET++ – An Object-Oriented Application Framework in C++. *SIGPLAN Notices* vol. 23 (11).

White, S. October 1986. Panel Problem: Software Controller for an Oil Hot Water Heating System. *Proceedings of COMPSAC*. New York, NY: Computer Society Press of the IEEE.

Wirfs-Brock, R. September 1988. An Integrated Color Smalltalk-80 System. *SIGPLAN Notices* vol. 23 (11).

Yoshida, N., and Hino, K. September 1988. An Object-Oriented Framework of Pattern Recognition. *SIGPLAN Notices* vol. 23 (11).

Yoshida, T., and Tokoro, M. 31 March 1986. *Distributed Queueing Network Simulation: An Application of a Concurrent Object-Oriented Language*. Yokohama, Japan: Keio University.

Young, R. October 1987. An Object-Oriented Framework for Interactive Data Graphics. *SIGPLAN Notices* vol. 22 (12).

D. Object-Oriented Architectures

Athas, W., and Seitz, C. August 1988. Multicomputers: Message-Passing Concurrent Computers. *IEEE Computer* vol. 21 (8).

Dahlby, S., Henry, G., Reynolds, D., and Taylor, P. 1982. The IBM System/38: A High Level Machine, in *Computer Structures: Principles and Examples*. ed. G. Bell and A. Newell. New York, NY: McGraw-Hill.

Dally, W., and Kajiya, J. March 1985. An Object-Oriented Architecture. *SIGARCH Newsletter* vol. 13 (3).

Fabry, R. 1987. Capability-Based Addressing, in *Object-Oriented Computing: Implementations* vol. 2. ed. G. Peterson. New York, NY: Computer Society Press of the IEEE.

Flynn, M. October 1980. Directions and Issues in Architecture and Language. *IEEE Computer* vol. 13 (10).

Harland, D., and Beloff, B. December 1986. Microcoding an Object-Oriented Instruction Set. *Computer Architecture News vol.* 14 (5).

Iliffe, J. 1982. *Advanced Computer Design.* London, England: Prentice/Hall International.

Intel. 1981. *iAPX 432 Object Primer.* Santa Clara, CA.

Ishikawa, Y., and Tokoro, M. March 1984. The Design of an Object-Oriented Architecture. *SIGARCH Newsletter* vol. 12 (3).

Kavi, K., and Chen, D. 1987. Architectural Support for Object-Oriented Languages. *Proceedings of the Thirty-second IEEE Computer Society International Conference.* New York, NY: Computer Society Press of the IEEE.

Lahtinen, P. September/October 1982. A Machine Architecture for Ada. *Ada Letters* vol. 2 (2).

Lampson, B., and Pier, K. January 1981. A Processor for a High-Performance Personal Computer, in *The Dorado: A High Performance Personal Computer,* Report CSL-81-1. Palo Alto, CA: Xerox Palo Alto Research Center.

Langdon, G. 1982. *Computer Design.* San Jose, CA: Computeach Press.

Levy, H. 1984. *Capability-Based Computer Systems.* Bedford, MA: Digital Press.

Lewis, D., Galloway, D., Francis, R., and Thomson, B. November 1986. Swamp: A Fast Processor for Smalltalk-80. *SIGPLAN Notices* vol. 21 (11).

Mashburn, H. 1982. The C.mmp/Hydra Project: An Architectural Overview, in *Computer Structures: Principles and Examples.* ed. G. Bell and A. Newell. New York, NY: McGraw-Hill.

Myers, G. 1982. *Advances in Computer Architecture,* 2nd ed. New York, NY: John Wiley and Sons.

Rattner, J. 1982. Hardware/Software Cooperation in the iAPX-432. *Proceedings of the Symposium on Architectural Support for Programming Languages and Operating Systems.* New York, NY: Association of Computing Machinery.

Rose, J. September 1988. Fast Dispatch Mechanisms for Stock Hardware. *SIGPLAN Notices* vol. 23 (11).

Samples, D., Ungar, D., and Hilfinger, P. November 1986. SOAR: Smalltalk Without Bytecodes. *SIGPLAN Notices* vol. 21 (11).

Soltis, R., and Hoffman, R. 1987. Design Considerations for the IBM System/38, in *Object-Oriented Computing: Implementations* vol. 2. ed. G. Peterson. New York, NY: Computer Society Press of the IEEE.

Thacker, C., McCreight, E., Lampson, B., Sproull, R., and Boggs, D. August 1979. *Alto: A Personal Computer,* Report CSL-79-11. Palo Alto, CA: Xerox Palo Alto Research Center.

Ungar, D. 1987. *The Design and Evaluation of a High-Performance Smalltalk System.* Cambridge, MA: The MIT Press.

Ungar, D., Blau, R., Foley, P., Samples, D., and Patterson, D. March 1984. Architecture of SOAR: Smalltalk on a RISC. *SIGARCH Newsletter* vol. 12 (3).

Ungar, D., and Patterson, D. January 1987. What Price Smalltalk? *IEEE Computer* vol. 20 (1).

Wah, B., and Li, G. April 1986. Survey on Special Purpose Computer Architectures for AI. *SIGART Newsletter,* no. 96.

Wulf, W. January 1980. Trends in the Design and Implementation of Programming Languages. *IEEE Computer* vol. 13 (1).

Wulf, W., Levin, R., and Harbison, S. 1981. *HYDRA/C.mmp: An Experimental Computer System*. New York, NY: McGraw-Hill.

E. Object-Oriented Databases

Alford, M. 1983. Derivation of Element-Relation-Attribute Database Requirements by Decomposition of System Functions, in *Entity-Relationship Approach to Software Engineering*. ed. C. Davis et al. Amsterdam, The Netherlands: Elsevier Science.

Atkinson, M., Bailey, P., Chisholm, K., Cockshott, P., and Morrison, R. 1983. An Approach to Persistent Programming. *The Computer Journal* vol. 26 (4).

Atkinson, M., and Buneman, P. June 1987. Types and Persistence in Database Programming Languages. *ACM Computing Surveys* vol. 19 (2).

Atkinson, M., and Morrison, R. October 1985. Procedures as Persistent Data Objects. *ACM Transactions on Programming Languages and Systems vol.* 7 (4).

Bachman, C. 1983. The Structuring Capabilities of the Molecular Data Model, in *Entity-Relationship Approach to Software Engineering*. ed. C. Davis et al. Amsterdam, The Netherlands: Elsevier Science.

Batini, C., and Lenzerini, M. 1983. A Methodology for Data Schema Integration in the Entity-Relationship Model, in *Entity-Relationship Approach to Software Engineering* ed. C. Davis et al. Amsterdam, The Netherlands: Elsevier Science.

Beech, D. 1987. Groundwork for an Object Database Model, in *Research Directions in Object-Oriented Programming*. ed. B. Schriver and P. Wegner. Cambridge, MA: The MIT Press.

Beech, D. September 1988. Intensional Concepts in an Object Database Model. *SIGPLAN Notices* vol. 23 (11).

Bertino, E. 1983. Distributed Database Design Using the Entity-Relationship Model, in *Entity-Relationship Approach to Software Engineering*. ed. C. Davis et al. Amsterdam, The Netherlands: Elsevier Science.

Blackwell, P., Jajodia, S., and Ng, P. 1983. A View of Database Management Systems as Abstract Data Types, in *Entity-Relationship Approach to Software Engineering*. ed. C. Davis et al. Amsterdam, The Netherlands: Elsevier Science.

Bloom, T. October 1987. Issues in the Design of Object-Oriented Database Programming Languages. *SIGPLAN Notices* vol. 22 (12).

Bobrow, D., Fogelsong, D., and Miller, M. 1987. Definition Groups: Making Sources into First-class Objects, in *Research Directions in Object-Oriented Programming*. ed. B. Schriver and P. Wegner. Cambridge, MA: The MIT Press.

Brathwaite, K. 1983. An Implementation of A Data Dictionary to Support Databases Designed Using the Entity-Relationship (E-R) Approach, in *Entity-Relationship Approach to Software Engineering*. ed. C. Davis et al. Amsterdam, The Netherlands: Elsevier Science.

Breazeal, J., Blattner, M., and Burton, H. 28 March 1986. *Data Standardization Through the Use of Data Abstraction.* Livermore, CA: Lawrence Livermore National Laboratory.

Brodie, M. 1984. On the Development of Data Models, in *On Conceptual Modeling: Perspectives from Artificial Intelligence, Databases, and Programming Languages.* ed. M. Brodie, J. Mylopoulos, and J. Schmidt. New York, NY: Springer-Verlag.

Brodie, M., and Ridjanovic, D. 1984. On the Design and Specification of Database Transactions. *On Conceptual Modeling: Perspectives from Artificial Intelligence, Databases, and Programming Languages.* ed. M. Brodie, J. Mylopoulos, and J. Schmidt. New York, NY: Springer-Verlag.

Carlson, C., and Arora, A. 1983. UPM: A Formal Tool for Expressing Database Update Semantics, in *Entity-Relationship Approach to Software Engineering.* ed. C. Davis et al. Amsterdam, The Netherlands: Elsevier Science.

Casanova, M. 1983. Designing Entity-Relationship Schemes for Conventional Information Systems, in *Entity-Relationship Approach to Software Engineering.* ed. C. Davis et al. Amsterdam, The Netherlands: Elsevier Science.

Cattell, R. May 1983. *Design and Implementation of a Relationship-Entity-Datum Data Model,* Report CSL-83-4. Palo Alto, CA: Xerox Palo Alto Research Center.

Chen, P. March 1976. The Entity-Relationship Model – Toward a Unified View of Data. *ACM Transactions on Database Systems* vol. 1 (1).

Chen, P. 1983. ER – A Historical Perspective and Future Directions, in *Entity-Relationship Approach to Software Engineering.* ed. C. Davis et al. Amsterdam, The Netherlands: Elsevier Science.

Claybrook, B., Claybrook, A., and Williams, J. January 1985. Defining Database Views as Data Abstractions. *IEEE Transactions on Software Engineering* vol. SE-11 (1).

Date, C. 1981, 1983. *An Introduction to Database Systems.* Reading, MA: Addison-Wesley.

Date, C. 1986. *Relational Database: Selected Writings.* Reading, MA: Addison-Wesley.

Date, C. 1987. *The Guide to the SQL Standard.* Reading, MA: Addison-Wesley.

D'Cunha, A., and Radhakrishnan, T. 1983. Applications of E-R Concepts to Data Administration, *Entity-Relationship Approach to Software Engineering.* ed. C. Davis et al. Amsterdam, The Netherlands: Elsevier Science.

Duhl, J., and Damon, C. September 1988. A Performance Comparison of Object and Relational Databases Using the Sun Benchmark. *SIGPLAN Notices* vol. 23 (11).

Harland, D., and Beloff, B. April 1987. OBJEKT – A Persistent Object Store with an Integrated Garbage Collector. *SIGPLAN Notices* vol. 22 (4).

Hawryszkiewycz, I. 1984. *Database Analysis and Design.* Chicago, IL: Science Research Associates.

Hull, R., and King, R. September 1987. Semantic Database Modeling: Survey, Applications, and Research Issues. *ACM Computing Surveys* vol. 19 (3).

Jajodia, S., Ng, P., and Springsteel, F. 1983. On Universal and Representative Instances for Inconsistent Databases, in *Entity-Relationship Approach to Software Engineering.* ed. C. Davis et al. Amsterdam, The Netherlands: Elsevier Science.

Ketabchi, M., and Berzins, V. January 1988. Mathematical Model of Composite Objects and Its Application for Organizing Engineering Databases. *IEEE Transactions on Software Engineering* vol. 14 (1).

Ketabchi, M., and Wiens, R. 1987. Implementation of Persistent Multi-User Object-Oriented Systems. *Proceedings of the Thirty-second IEEE Computer Society International Conference.* New York, NY: Computer Society Press of the IEEE.

Kim, W., Ballou, N., Chou, H., Garze, J., Woelk, D., and Banerjee, J. September 1988. Integrating an Object-Oriented Programming System with a Database System. *SIGPLAN Notices* vol. 23 (11).

Kim, W., Banerjee, J., Chou, H., Garza, J., and Woelk, D. October 1987. Composite Object Support in an Object-Oriented Database System. *SIGPLAN Notices* vol. 22 (12).

Kim, W., and Lochovsky, K. 1989. *Object-Oriented Concepts, Databases, and Applications.* Reading, MA: Addison-Wesley.

Laenens, E., and Vermeir, D. August 1988. An Overview of OOPS+, An Object-Oriented Database Programming Language. *Proceedings of ECOOP'88: European Conference on Object-Oriented Programming.* New York, NY: Springer-Verlag.

Larson, J., and Dwyer, P. 1983. Defining External Schemas for an Entity-Relationship Database, in *Entity-Relationship Approach to Software Engineering.* ed. C. Davis et al. Amsterdam, The Netherlands: Elsevier Science.

Maier, D., and Stein, J. 1987. Development and Implementation of an Object-Oriented DBMS, in *Research Directions in Object-Oriented Programming.* ed. B. Schriver and P. Wegner. Cambridge, MA: The MIT Press.

Margrave, G., Lusk, E., and Overbeek, R. 1983. Tools for the Creation of IMS Database Designs from Entity-Relationship Diagrams, in *Entity-Relationship Approach to Software Engineering.* ed. C. Davis et al. Amsterdam, The Netherlands: Elsevier Science.

Mark, L., and Poussopoulos, N. 1983. Integration of Data, Schema, and Meta-schema in the Context of Self-documenting Data Models, in *Entity-Relationship Approach to Software Engineering.* ed. C. Davis et al. Amsterdam, The Netherlands: Elsevier Science.

Marti, R. 1983. Integrating Database and Program Descriptions using an ER Data Dictionary, in *Entity-Relationship Approach to Software Engineering.* ed. C. Davis et al. Amsterdam, The Netherlands: Elsevier Science.

Merrow, T., and Laursen, J. October 1987. A Pragmatic System for Shared Persistent Objects. *SIGPLAN Notices* vol. 22 (12).

Mitchell, J., and Wegbreit, B. 1977. Schemes: A High-Level Data Structuring Concept, in *Current Trends in Programming Methodology: Data Structuring* vol. 4. ed. R. Yeh. Englewood Cliffs, NJ: Prentice-Hall.

Morrison, R., Atkinson, M., Brown, A., and Dearle, A. April 1988. Bindings in Persistent Programming Languages. *SIGPLAN Notices* vol. 23 (4).

Moss, E., Herlihy, M., and Zdonik, S. September 1988. Object-Oriented Databases, Course Notes, from *Object-Oriented Programming Systems, Languages, and Applications.* San Diego, CA: OOPSLA'88.

Nastos, M. January 1988. Databases, Etc. *HOOPLA: Hooray for Object-Oriented Programming Languages* vol. 1 (2). Everette, WA: Object Oriented Programming for Smalltalk Application Developers Association.

Navathe, S., and Cheng, A. 1983. A Methodology for Database Schema Mapping from Extended Entity Relationship Models into the Hierarchical Model, in *Entity-Relationship Approach to Software Engineering*. ed. C. Davis et al. Amsterdam, The Netherlands: Elsevier Science.

Ontologic. 1987. *Vbase Technical Overview*. Billerica, MA.

Oracle. 1989. *Oracle for Macintosh: References, Version 1.1*. Belmont, CA.

Penny, J., and Stein, J. October 1987. Class Modification in the GemStone Object-Oriented DBMS. *SIGPLAN Notices* vol. 22 (12).

Peterson, R. 1987. Object-Oriented Database Design, in *Object-Oriented Computing: Implementations* vol. 2. ed. G. Peterson. New York, NY: Computer Society Press of the IEEE.

Sakai, H. 1983. Entity-Relationship Approach to Logical Database Design, in *Entity-Relationship Approach to Software Engineering*. ed. C. Davis et al. Amsterdam, The Netherlands: Elsevier Science.

Skarra, A., and Zdonik, S. November 1986. The Management of Changing Types in an Object-Oriented Database. *SIGPLAN Notices* vol. 21 (11).

Skarra, A., and Zdonik, S. 1987. Type Evolution in an Object-Oriented Database, in *Research Directions in Object-Oriented Programming*. ed. B. Schriver and P. Wegner. Cambridge, MA: The MIT Press.

Smith, D., and Smith, J. 1980. Conceptual Database Design, in *Tutorial on Software Design Techniques*, 3rd ed. ed. P. Freeman and A. Wasserman. New York, NY: Computer Society Press of the IEEE.

Smith, J., and Smith, D. Database Abstractions: Aggregation and Generalization. *ACM Transactions on Database Systems* vol. 2 (2).

Smith, K., and Zdonik, S. October 1987. Intermedia: A Case Study of the Differences Between Relational and Object-Oriented Database Systems. *SIGPLAN Notices* vol. 22 (12).

Stein, J. March 1988. Object-Oriented Programming and Database Design. *Dr. Dobb's Journal of Software Tools for the Professional Programmer*, no. 137.

Teorey, T., Yang, D., and Fry, J. June 1986. A Logical Design Methodology for Relational Databases Using the Extended Entity-Relationship Model. *ACM Computing Surveys* vol. 18 (2).

Thuraisingham, M. October 1989. Mandatory Security in Object-Oriented Database Systems. *SIGPLAN Notices* vol. 24 (10).

Veloso, P., and Furtado, A. 1983. View Constructs for the Specification and Design of External Schemas, in *Entity-Relationship Approach to Software Engineering*. ed. C. Davis et al. Amsterdam, The Netherlands: Elsevier Science.

Wiebe, D. November 1986. A Distributed Repository for Immutable Persistent Objects. *SIGPLAN Notices* vol. 21 (11).

Wiederhold, G. December 1986. Views, Objects, and Databases. *IEEE Computer* vol. 19 (12).

Wile, D., and Allard, D. May 1982. Worlds: an Organizing Structure for Object-bases. *SIGPLAN Notices* vol. 19 (5).

Zdonik, S., and Maier, D. 1990. *Readings in Object-Oriented Database Systems*. San Mateo, CA: Morgan Kaufmann.

Zhang, Z., and Mendelzon, A. 1983. A Graphical Query Language for Entity-Relationship Databases, in *Entity-Relationship Approach to Software Engineering.* ed. C. Davis et al. Amsterdam, The Netherlands: Elsevier Science.

F. Object-Oriented Design

Abbott, R. November 1983. Program Design by Informal English Descriptions.*Communications of the ACM* vol. 26 (11).

Abbott, R. August 1987. Knowledge Abstraction. *Communications of the ACM* vol. 30 (8).

Alabios, B. September 1988. Transformation of Data Flow Analysis Models to Object-Oriented Design. *SIGPLAN Notices* vol. 23 (11).

Beck, K., and Cunningham, W. October 1989. A Laboratory for Teaching Object-Oriented Thinking. *SIGPLAN Notices* vol. 24 (10).

Berard, E. 1986. *An Object-Oriented Design Handbook.* Rockville, MD: EVB Software Engineering.

Berzins, V., Gray, M., and Naumann, D. May 1986. Abstraction-Based Software Development. *Communications of the ACM* vol. 29 (5).

Booch, G. September 1981. Describing Software Design in Ada. *SIGPLAN Notices* vol. 16 (9).

Booch, G. March/April 1982. Object-Oriented Design. *Ada Letters* vol. 1 (3).

Booch, G. February 1986. Object-Oriented Development. *IEEE Transactions on Software Engineering* vol. 12 (2).

Booch, G. 1987. *On the Concepts of Object-Oriented Design.* Denver, CO: Rational.

Booch, G. Summer 1989. What Is and What Isn't Object-Oriented Design. *American Programmer* vol. 2 (7-8).

Booch, G., Jacobson, I., and Kerth, N. September 1988. Specification and Design Methodologies in Support of Object-Oriented Programming, Course Notes, from *Object-Oriented Programming Systems, Languages, and Applications.* San Diego, CA: OOPSLA'88.

Boyd, S. July/August 1987. Object-Oriented Design and PAMELA™. *Ada Letters* vol. 7 (4).

Bruno, G., and Balsamo, A. November 1986. Petri Net-Based Object-Oriented Modelling of Distributed Systems. *SIGPLAN Notices* vol. 21 (11).

Buhr, R. 1984. *System Design with Ada.* Englewood Cliffs, NJ: Prentice-Hall.

Buhr, R. 22 August 1988. *Machine Charts for Visual Prototyping in System Design.* SCE Report 88-2. Ottawa, Canada: Carleton University.

Buhr, R. 14 September 1988. *Visual Prototyping in System Design.* SCE Report 88-14. Ottawa, Canada: Carleton University.

Buhr, R. 1989. *System Design with Machine Charts: A CAD Approach with Ada Examples.* Englewood Cliffs, NJ: Prentice-Hall.

Buhr, R., Karam, G., Hayes, C., and Woodside, M. March 1989. Software CAD: A Revolutionay Approach. *IEEE Transactions on Software Engineering* vol. 15 (3).

Bulman, D. August 1989. An Object-Based Development Model. *Computer Language* vol. 6 (8).

Cherry, G. 1987. *PAMELA 2: An Ada-Based Object-Oriented Design Method.* Reston, VA: Thought**Tools.

Cherry, G. 1990. *Software Construction by Object-Oriented Pictures.* Canandaigua, NY: Thought**Tools.

Clark, R. June 1987. Designing Concurrent Objects. *Ada Letters vol.* 7 (6).

Comer, E. July 1989. *Ada Box Structure Methodology Handbook.* Melbourne, FL: Software Productivity Solutions.

Constantine, L. Summer 1989. Object-Oriented and Structured Methods: Towards Integration. *American Programmer* vol. 2 (7-8).

CRI, CISI Ingenierie, and Matra. 20 June 1987. *HOOD: Hierarchical Object-Oriented Design.* Paris, France.

Cunningham, W., and Beck, K. November 1986. A Diagram for Object-Oriented Programs. *SIGPLAN Notices* vol. 21 (11).

Davis, N., Irving, M., and Lee, J. *The Evolution of Object-Oriented Design from Concept to Method.* 1988. Surrey, United Kingdom: Logica Space and Defence Systems Limited.

Felsinger, R. 1987a. *Integrating Object-Oriented Design, Structured Analysis/Structured Design, and Ada for Real-time Systems.* Mt. Pleasant, SC.

Felsinger, R. 1987b. *Object-Oriented Design, Course Notes.* Torrance, CA: Data Processing Management Association.

Firesmith, D. May 6, 1986. *Object-Oriented Development.* Fort Wayne, Indiana: Magnavox Electronic Systems Co.

Gane, C. Summer 1989. Object-Oriented Data/Process Modeling. *American Programmer* vol. 2 (7-8).

Giddings, R. May 1984. Accommodating Uncertainty in Software Design. *Communications of the ACM* vol. 27 (5).

Gomaa, H. September 1984. A Software Design Method for Real-Time Systems. *Communications of the ACM* vol. 27 (9).

Gouda, M., Han, Y., Jensen, E., Johnson, W., and Kain, R. November 1977. Towards a Methodology of Distributed Computer System Design. *6th Texas Conference on Computing Systems.* New York, NY: Association of Computing Machinery.

Grosch, J. December 1983. Type Derivation Graphs – A Way to Visualize the Type Building Possibilities of Programming Languages. *SIGPLAN Notices* vol. 18 (12).

Harel, D. 1987. Statecharts: A Visual Formalism for Complex Systems. *Science of Computer Programming* vol. 8.

Harel, D. May 1988. On Visual Formalisms. *Communications of the ACM* vol. 31 (5).

Jackson, M. Summer 1989. Object-Oriented Software. *American Programmer* vol. 2 (7-8).

Jacobson, I. August 1985. *Concepts for Modeling Large Real-Time Systems.* Academic dissertation. Stockholm, Sweden: Royal Institute of Technology, Department of Computer Science.

Jacobson, I. October 1987. Object-Oriented Development in an Industrial Environment. *SIGPLAN Notices* vol. 22 (12).

Jamsa, K. January 1984. Object-Oriented Design vs. Structured Design – A Student's Perspective. *Software Engineering Notes,* vol. 9 (1).

Jones, A. 1979. The Object Model: A Conceptual Tool for Structuring Software, in *Operating Systems.* ed. R. Bayer et. al. New York, NY: Springer-Verlag.

Kadie, C. 1986. *Refinement Through Classes: A Development Methodology for Object-Oriented Languages.* Urbana, IL: University of Illinois.

Kaplan, S., and Johnson, R. 21 July 1986. *Designing and Implementing for Reuse.* Urbana, IL: University of Illinois, Department of Computer Science.

Kay, A. August 1969. *The Reactive Engine.* Salt Lake City, Utah: The University of Utah, Department of Computer Science.

Kelly, J. 1986 A Comparison of Four Design Methods for Real-Time Systems. *Proceedings of the Ninth International Conference on Software Engineering.* New York, NY: Computer Society Press of the IEEE.

Kent, W. 1983. Fact-Based Data Analysis and Design, in *Entity-Relationship Approach to Software Engineering.* ed. C. Davis et al. Amsterdam, The Netherlands: Elsevier Science.

Ladden, R. July 1988. A Survey of Issues to Be Considered in the Development of an Object-Oriented Development Methodology for Ada. *Software Engineering Notes* vol. 13 (3).

Lieberherr, K., and Riel, A. October 1989. Contributions to Teaching Object-Oriented Design and Programming. *SIGPLAN Notices* vol. 24 (10).

Liskov, B. 1980. A Design Methodology for Reliable Software Systems, in *Tutorial on Software Design Techniques.* 3rd ed. ed. P. Freeman and A. Wasserman. New York, NY: Computer Society Press of the IEEE.

Mannino, P. April 1987. A Presentation and Comparison of Four Information System Development Methodologies. *Software Engineering Notes,* vol. 12 (2).

Masiero, P., and Germano, F. July 1988. JSD As an Object-Oriented Design Method. *Software Engineering Notes* vol. 13 (3).

Meyer, B. March 1987. Reusability: The Case for Object-Oriented Design. *IEEE Software* vol. 4 (2).

Meyer, B. 1988. *Object-Oriented Software Construction.* New York, NY: Prentice Hall.

Meyer, B. 1989. From Structured Programming to Object-Oriented Design: The Road to Eiffel. *Structured Programming* vol. 10 (1).

Mills, H. June 1988. Stepwise Refinement and Verification in Box-Structured Systems. *IEEE Computer* vol. 21 (6).

Mills, H., Linger, R., and Hevner, A. 1986. *Principles of Information System Design and Analysis.* Orlando, FL: Academic Press.

Minkowitz, C., and Henderson, P. March 1987. *Object-Oriented Programming of Discrete Event Simulation Using Petri Nets.* Stirling, Scotland: University of Stirling.

Mostow, J. Spring 1985. Toward Better Models of the Design Process. *AI Magazine* vol. 6 (1).

Moulin, B. 1983. The Use of EPAS/IPSO Approach for Integrating Entity Relationship Concepts and Software Engineering Techniques, in *Entity-Relationship Approach to Software Engineering.* ed. C. Davis et al. Amsterdam, The Netherlands: Elsevier Science.

Mullin, M. 1989. *Object-Oriented Program Design with Examples in C++.* Reading, MA: Addison-Wesley.

Nielsen, K. March 1988. *An Object-Oriented Design Methodology for Real-Time Systems in Ada.* San Diego, CA: Hughes Aircraft Company.

Nielsen, K., and Shumate, K. August 1987. Designing Large Real-Time Systems with Ada. *Communications of the ACM* vol. 30 (8).

Nies, S. 1986. The Ada Object-Oriented Approach. *Proceedings of the First International Conference on Ada Programming Language Applications for the NASA Space Station.* Houston, TX: NASA Lyndon B. Johnson Space Center.

Ossher, H. 1987. A Mechanism for Specifying the Structure of Large, Layered, Systems, in *Research Directions in Object-Oriented Programming.* ed. B. Schriver and P. Wegner. Cambridge, MA: The MIT Press.

Parnas, D. 1979. On the Criteria to be Used in Decomposing Systems into Modules. *Classics in Software Engineering,* ed. E. Yourdon. New York, NY: Yourdon Press.

Parnas, D., Clements, P., and Weiss, D. March 1985. The Modular Structure of Complex Systems. *IEEE Transactions on Software Engineering* vol. SE-11 (3).

Pasik, A., and Schor, M. January 1984. Object-Centered Representation and Reasoning. *SIGART Newsletter,* no. 87.

Rajlich, V., and Silva, J. 1987. *Two Object-Oriented Decomposition Methods.* Detroit, Michigan: Wayne State University.

Ramamoorthy, C., and Sheu, P. Fall 1988. Object-Oriented Systems. *IEEE Expert* vol. 3 (3).

Reenskaug, T. August 1981. User-Oriented Descriptions of Smalltalk Systems. *Byte* vol. 6 (8).

Reiss, S. 1987. An Object-Oriented Framework for Conceptual Programming, in *Research Directions in Object-Oriented Programming.* ed. B. Schriver and P. Wegner. Cambridge, MA: The MIT Press.

Richter, C. August 1986. An Assessment of Structured Analysis and Structured Design. *Software Engineering Notes,* vol. 11 (4).

Rine, D. October 1987. A Common Error in the Object Structure of Object-Oriented Methods. *Software Engineering Notes* vol. 12 (4).

Ross, R. 1987. *Entity Modeling: Techniques and Application.* Boston, MA: Database Research Group.

Rosson, M., and Gold, E. October 1989. Problem-Solution Mapping in Object-Oriented Design. *SIGPLAN Notices* vol. 24 (10).

Rumbaugh, J. April 1988. Relational Database Design Using an Object-Oriented Methodology. *Communications of the ACM* vol. 31 (4).

Sahraoui, A. 1987. *Towards a Design Approach Methodology Combining OOP and Petri Nets for Software Production.* Toulouse, France: Laboratoire d'Automatique et d'analyses des systemes du C.N.R.S.

Sakai, H. 1983. A Method for Entity-Relationship Behavior Modeling, in *Entity-Relationship Approach to Software Engineering.* ed. C. Davis et al. Amsterdam, The Netherlands: Elsevier Science.

Seidewitz, E. May 1985. *Object Diagrams.* Greenbelt, MD: NASA Goddard Space Flight Center.

Seidewitz, E., and Stark, M. 1986. Towards a General Object-Oriented Software Development Methodology. *Proceedings of the First International Conference on Ada Programming Language Applications for the NASA Space Station.* Houston, TX: NASA Lyndon B. Johnson Space Center.

Seidewitz, E., and Stark, M. August 1986. *General Object-Oriented Software Development,* Report SEL-86-002. Greenbelt, MD: NASA Goddard Space Flight Center.

Seidewitz, E., and Stark, M. July/August 1987. Towards a General Object-Oriented Design Methodology. *Ada Letters* vol. 7 (4).

Seidewitz, E., and Stark, M. 1988. *An Introduction to General Object-Oriented Software Development.* Rockville, MD: Millennium Systems.

Shilling, J., and Sweeney, P. October 1989. Three Steps to Views: Extending the Object-Oriented Paradigm. *SIGPLAN Notices* vol. 24 (10).

Shumate, K. 1987. *Layered Virtual Machine/Object-Oriented Design.* San Diego, CA: Hughes Aircraft Company.

Smith, M., and Tockey, S. 1988. *An Integrated Approach to Software Requirements Definition Using Objects.* Seattle, WA: Boeing Commercial Airplane Support Division.

Stark, M. April 1986. *Abstraction Analysis: From Structured Analysis to Object-Oriented Design.* Greenbelt, MD: NASA Goddard Space Flight Center.

Strom, R. October 1986. A Comparison of the Object-Oriented and Process Paradigms. *SIGPLAN Notices* vol. 21 (10).

Teledyne Brown Engineering. October 1987. *Software Methodology Catalog,* Report MC87-COMM/ADP-0036. Tinton Falls, NJ.

Thomas, D. May/June 1989. In Search of an Object-Oriented Development Process. *Journal of Object-Oriented Programming* vol. 2 (1).

Wahl, S. 13 December 1988. Introduction to Object-Oriented Software. *C++ Tutorial Program of the USENIX Conference.* Denver, CO: USENIX Association.

Wasserman, T., Pircher, P., and Muller, R. December 1988. *An Object-Oriented Structured Design Method for Code Generation.* San Francisco, CA: Interactive Development Environments.

Wasserman, A., Pircher, P., and Muller, R. Summer 1989. Concepts of Object-Oriented Structured Design. *American Programmer* vol. 2 (7-8).

Webster, D. December 1988. Mapping the Design Information Representation Terrain. *IEEE Specturm* vol. 21 (12).

Williams, L. 1986. *The Object Model in Software Engineering.* Boulder, CO: Software Engineering Research.

Wirfs-Brock, R., and Wilkerson, B. October 1989. Object-Oriented Design: A Responsibility-Driven Approach. *SIGPLAN Notices* vol. 24 (10).

Yau, S., and Tsai, J. June 1986. A Survey of Software Design Techniques. *IEEE Transactions on Software Engineering* vol. SE-12 (6).

Zachman, J. 1987. A Framework for Information Systems Architecture. *IBM Systems Journal* vol. 26 (3).

Zimmerman, R. 1983. Phases, Methods, and Tools – A Triad of System Development, in *Entity-Relationship Approach to Software Engineering.* ed. C. Davis et al. Amsterdam, The Netherlands: Elsevier Science.

G. Object-Oriented Programming

Adams, S. July 1986. MetaMethods: The MVC Paradigm. *HOOPLA: Hooray for Object-Oriented Programming Languages* vol. 1 (4). Everette, WA: Object-Oriented Programming for Smalltalk Applications Developers Association.

Agha, G. October 1986. An Overview of Actor Languages. *SIGPLAN Notices* vol. 21 (10).

Agha, G. 1988. *Actors: A Model of Concurrent Computation in Distributed Systems.* Cambridge, MA: The MIT Press.

Agha, G., and Hewitt, C. 1987. Actors: A Conceptual Foundation for Concurrent Object-Oriented Programming, in *Research Directions in Object-Oriented Programming.* ed. B. Schriver and P. Wegner. Cambridge, MA: The MIT Press.

Aksit, M., and Tripathi, A. September 1988. Data Abstraction Mechanisms in Sina/st. *SIGPLAN Notices* vol. 23 (11).

Albano, A. June 1983. Type Hierarchies and Semantic Data Models. *SIGPLAN Notices* vol. 18 (6).

Almes, G., Black, A., Lazowska, E., and Noe, J. January 1985. The Eden System: A Technical Review. *IEEE Transactions on Software Engineering* vol. SE-11 (1).

Althoff, J. August 1981. Building Data Structures in the Smalltalk-80 System. *Byte* vol. 6 (8).

Ambler, A. 1980. Gypsy: A Language for Specification and Implementation of Verifiable Programs, in *Programming Language Design.* ed. A. Wasserman. New York, NY: Computer Society Press.

America, P. 1987. POOL-T: A Parallel Object-Oriented Language, in *Object-Oriented Concurrent Programming.* ed. Yonezawa and M. Tokoro. Cambridge, MA: The MIT Press.

Apple Computer. 1989. *MacApp: The Expandable Macintosh Application,* version 2.0B9. Cupertino, CA.

—— *Macintosh Programmer's Workshop Pascal 3.0 Reference.* Cupertino, CA.

AT&T Bell Laboratories. 1989. *UNIX System V ATT C++ Language System, Release 2.0 Library Manual.* Murray Hill, NJ.

—— *UNIX System V ATT C++ Language System, Release 2.0 Product Reference Manual.* Murray Hill, NJ.

—— *UNIX System V ATT C++ Language System, Release 2.0 Release Notes.* Murray Hill, NJ.

—— *UNIX System V ATT C++ Language System, Release 2.0 Selected Readings.* Murray Hill, NJ.

Attardi, G. 1987. Concurrent Strategy Execution in Omega, in *Object-Oriented Concurrent Programming.* ed. Yonezawa and M. Tokoro. Cambridge, MA: The MIT Press.

Bach, I. November/December 1982. On the Type Concept of Ada. *Ada Letters* vol. II (3).

Badrinath, B., and Ramamritham, K. May 1988. Synchronizing Transactions on Objects. *IEEE Transactions on Computers* vol. 37 (5).

Ballard, M., Maier, D., and Wirfs-Brock, A. November 1986. QUICKTALK: A Smalltalk-80 Dialect for Defining Primitive Methods. *SIGPLAN Notices* vol. 21 (11).

Beaudet, P., and Jenkins, M. June 1988. Simulating the Object-Oriented Paradigm in Nial. *SIGPLAN Notices* vol. 23 (6).

Bennett, J. October 1987. The Design and Implementation of Distributed Smalltalk. *SIGPLAN Notices* vol. 22 (12).

Bergin, J., and Greenfield, S. March 1988. What Does Modula-2 Need to Fully Support Object-Oriented Programming? *SIGPLAN Notices* vol. 23 (3).

Bhaskar, K. October 1983. How Object-Oriented Is Your System? *SIGPLAN Notices* vol. 18 (10).

Birman, K., Joseph, T., Raeuchle, T., and Abbadi, A. June 1985. Implementing Fault-tolerant Distributed Objects. *IEEE Transactions on Software Engineering* vol. SE-11 (6).

Birtwistle, G., Dahl, O-J., Myhrhaug, B., and Nygard, K. 1979. *Simula begin.* Lund, Sweden: Studentlitteratur.

Black, A., Hutchinson, N., Jul, E., and Levy, H. November 1986. Object Structure in the Emerald System. *SIGPLAN Notices* vol. 21 (11).

Black, A., Hutchinson, N., Jul, E., Levy, H., and Carter, L. July 1986. *Distribution and Abstract Types in Emerald.* Report 86-02-04. Seattle, WA: University of Washington.

Blaschek, G. 1989. Implementation of Objects in Modula-2. *Structured Programming* vol. 10 (3).

Blaschek, G., Pomberger, G., and Stritzinger, A. 1989. A Comparison of Object-Oriented Programming Languages. *Structured Programming* vol. 10 (4).

Block, F., and Chan, N. October 1989. An Extended Frame Language. *SIGPLAN Notices* vol. 24 (10).

Bobrow, D. November 1984. *If Prolog Is the Answer, What Is the Question?* Palo Alto, California. Xerox Palo Alto Research Center.

Bobrow, D. 1985. An Overview of KRL, a Knowledge Representation Language, in *Readings in Knowledge Representation.* ed. R. Brachman and H. Levesque. Los Altos, CA: Morgan Kaufmann.

Bobrow, D., DeMichiel, L., Gabriel, R., Keene, S., Kiczales, G., and Moon, D. September 1988. Common Lisp Object System Specification X3J13 Document 88-002R. *SIGPLAN Notices* vol. 23.

Bobrow, D., Kahn, K., Kiczales, G., Masinter, L., Stefik, M., and Zdybel, F. August 1985. *COMMONLOOPS: Merging Common Lisp and Object-Oriented Programming,* Report ISL-85-8. Palo Alto, CA: Xerox Palo Alto Research Center, Intelligent Systems Laboratory.

Borgida, A. January 1985. Features of Languages for the Development of Information Systems at the Conceptual Level. *IEEE Software* vol. 2 (1).

Borgida, A. October 1986. Exceptions in Object-Oriented Languages. *SIGPLAN Notices* vol. 21 (10).

Borning, A., and Ingalls, D. 1982a. A Type Declaration and Inference System for Smalltalk. Palo Alto, CA: Xerox Palo Alto Research Center.

Borning, A., and Ingalls, D. 1982b. Multiple Inheritance in Smalltalk-80. *Proceedings of the National Conference on Artificial Intelligence.* Menlo Park, CA: AAAI.

Bos, J. September 1987. PCOL – A Protocol-Constrained Object Language. *SIGPLAN Notices* vol. 22 (9).

Briot, J., and Cointe, P. October 1989. Programming with Explicit Metaclasses in Smalltalk. *SIGPLAN Notices* vol. 24 (10).

Buzzard, G., and Mudge, T. 1987. Object-Based Computing and the Ada Programming Language, in *Object-Oriented Computing: Concepts* vol. 1. ed. G. Peterson. New York, NY: Computer Society Press of the IEEE.

Canning, P., Cook, W., Hill, W., and Olthoff, W. October 1989. Interfaces for Strongly-Typed Object-Oriented Programming. *SIGPLAN Notices* vol. 24 (10).

Caudill, P., and Wirfs-Brock, A. November 1986. A Third Generation Smalltalk-80 Implementation. *SIGPLAN Notices* vol. 21 (11).

Chambers, C., Ungar, D., and Lee, E. October 1989. An Efficient Implementation of Self, a Dynamically-Typed Object-Oriented Language Based on Prototypes. *SIGPLAN Notices* vol. 24 (10).

Clark, K. December 1988. PARLOG and Its Application. *IEEE Transactions on Software Engineering* vol. 14 (12).

Cleaveland, C. 1980. Programming Languages Considered as Abstract Data Types. *Communications of the ACM.*

Connor, R., Dearle, A., Morrison, R., and Brown, A. October 1989. An Object Addressing Mechanism for Statically Typed Languages with Multiple Inheritance. *SIGPLAN Notices* vol. 24 (10).

Conroy, T., and Pelegri-Llopart, E. 1983. An Assessment of Method-lookup Caches for Smalltalk-80 Implementations, in *Smalltalk-80: Bits of History, Words of Advice.* ed. G. Krasner. Reading, MA: Addison-Wesley.

Cointe, P. October 1987. Metaclasses Are First Class: the ObjVlisp Model. *SIGPLAN Notices* vol. 22 (12).

Corradi, A., and Leonardi, L. December 1988. The Role of Opaque Types in Building Abstractions. *SIGPLAN Notices* vol. 23 (12).

Cox, B. January 1983. The Object-Oriented Pre-compiler. *SIGPLAN Notices* vol. 18 (1).

Cox, B. October/November 1983. Object-Oriented Programming in C. *Unix Review.*

Cox, B. January 1984. Message/Object Programming: An Evolutionary Change in Programming Technology. *IEEE Software* vol. 1 (1).

Cox, B. February/March 1984. Object-Oriented Programming: A Power Tool for Software Craftsmen. *Unix Review.*

Cox, B. 1986. *Object-Oriented Programming: An Evolutionary Approach.* Reading, MA: Addison-Wesley.

Cox, B., and Hunt, B. August 1986. Objects, Icons, and Software-ICs. *Byte* vol. 11 (8).

deJong, P. October 1986. Compilation into Actors. *SIGPLAN Notices* vol. 21 (10).

Deutsch, P. August 1981. Building Control Structures in the Smalltalk-80 System. *Byte* vol. 6 (8).

Deutsch, P. 1983. Efficient Implementation of the Smalltalk-80 System. *Proceedings of the 11th Annual ACM Symposium on the Principles of Programming Languages.* New York, NY: Association of Computing Machinery.

Dewhurst, S., and Stark, K. 1989. *Programming in C++.* Englewood Cliffs, NJ: Prentice Hall.

Diederich, J., and Milton, J. May 1987. Experimental Prototyping in Smalltalk. *IEEE Software* vol. 4 (3).

Dixon, R., McKee, T., Schweizer, P., and Vaughn, M. October 1989. A Fast Method Dispatcher for Compiled Languages with Multiple Inheritance. *SIGPLAN Notices* vol. 24 (10).

Dony, C. August 1988. An Object-Oriented Exception Handling System for an Object-Oriented Language. *Proceedings of ECOOP'88: European Conference on Object-Oriented Programming.* New York, NY: Springer-Verlag.

Duff, C. August 1986. Designing an Efficient Language. *Byte* vol. 11 (8).

Dussud, P. October 1989. TICLOS: An Implementation of CLOS for the Explorer Family. *SIGPLAN Notices* vol. 24 (10).

Eccles, J. 1988. Porting from Common Lisp with Flavors to C++. *Proceedings of USENIX C++ Conference.* Berkeley, CA: USENIX Association.

Edelson, D. September 1987. How Objective Mechanisms Facilitate the Development of Large Software Systems in Three Programming Languages. *SIGPLAN Notices* vol. 22 (9).

Endres, T. May 1985. Clascal – An Object-Oriented Pascal. *Computer Language* vol. 2 (5).

Filman, R. October 1987. Retrofitting Objects. *SIGPLAN Notices* vol. 22 (12).

Finzer, W., and Gould, L. June 1984. Programming by Rehearsal. *Byte* vol. 9 (6).

Foote, B., and Johnson, R. October 1989. Reflective Facilities in Smalltalk-80. *SIGPLAN Notices* vol. 24 (10).

Freeman-Benson, B. October 1989. A Module Mechanism for Constraints in Smalltalk. *SIGPLAN Notices* vol. 24 (10).

Fukunaga, K., and Jirose, S. November 1986. An Experience with a Prolog-Based Object-Oriented Language. *SIGPLAN Notices* vol. 21 (11).

Goldberg, A. August 1981. Introducing the Smalltalk-80 System. *Byte* vol. 6 (8).

Goldberg, A. September 1988. Programmer as Reader. *IEEE Software* vol. 4 (5).

Goldberg, A., and Kay, A. March 1976. *Smalltalk-72 Instruction Manual.* Palo Alto, CA: Xerox Palo Alto Research Center.

Goldberg, A., and Kay, A. 1977. *Methods for Teaching the Programming Language Smalltalk*, Report SSL 77-2. Palo Alto, CA: Xerox Palo Alto Research Center.

Goldberg, A., and Pope, S. Summer 1989. Object-Oriented Programming Is Not Enough. *American Programmer* vol. 2 (7-8).

Goldberg, A., and Robson, D. 1983. *Smalltalk-80: The Language and Its Implementation.* Reading, MA: Addison-Wesley.

Goldberg, A., and Robson, D. 1989. *Smalltalk-80: The Language.* Reading, MA: Addison-Wesley.

Goldberg, A., and Ross, J. August 1981. Is the Smalltalk-80 System for Children? *Byte* vol. 6 (8).

Goldstein, T. May 1989. The Object-Oriented Programmer. *The C++ Report* vol. 1 (5).

Gonsalves, G., and Silvestri, A. December 1986. Programming in Smalltalk-80: Observations and Remarks from the Newly Initiated. *SIGPLAN Notices* vol. 21 (12).

Gorlen, K. 1989. An Introduction to C++, in *UNIX System V ATT C++ Language System, Release 2.0 Selected Readings.* 1989. Murray Hill, NJ: ATT Bell Laboratories.

Gougen, J., and Meseguer, J. 1987. Unifying Functional, Object-Oriented, and Relational Programming with Logical Semantics, in *Research Directions in Object-Oriented Programming*. ed. B. Schriver and P. Wegner. Cambridge, MA: The MIT Press.

Graube, N. August 1988. Reflexive Architecture: From ObjVLisp to CLOS. *Proceedings of ECOOP'88: European Conference on Object-Oriented Programming.* New York, NY: Springer-Verlag.

Hagmann, R. 1983. Preferred Classes: A Proposal for Faster Smalltalk-80 Execution, in *Smalltalk-80: Bits of History, Words of Advice.* ed. G. Krasner. Reading, MA: Addison-Wesley.

Hailpern, B., and Nguyen, V. 1987. A Model for Object-Based Inheritance, in *Research Directions in Object-Oriented Programming*. ed. B. Schriver and P. Wegner. Cambridge, MA: The MIT Press.

Halbert, D., and O'Brien, P. September 1988. Using Types and Inheritance in Object-Oriented Programming. *IEEE Software* vol. 4 (5).

Halstead, R. 1987. Object-management on Distributed Systems, in *Object-Oriented Computing: Implementations* vol 2. ed. G. Peterson. New York, NY: Computer Society Press of the IEEE.

Harland, D., Szyplewski, M., and Wainwright, J. October 1985. An Alternative View of Polymorphism. *SIGPLAN Notices* vol. 20 (10).

Hendler, J. October 1986. Enhancement for Multiple Inheritance. *SIGPLAN Notices* vol. 21 (10).

Hines, T., and Unger, E. 1986. *Conceptual Object-Oriented Programming*. Manhattan, Kansas: Kansas State University.

Ingalls, D. The Smalltalk-76 Programming System Design and Implementation. *Proceedings of the Fifth Annual ACM Symposium on Principles of Programming Languages*, New York, NY: Association of Computing Machinery.

Ingalls, D. August 1981a. Design Principles Behind Smalltalk. *Byte* vol. 6 (8).

Ingalls, D. August 1981b. The Smalltalk Graphics Kernel. *Byte* vol. 6 (8).

Ingalls, D. 1983. The Evolution of the Smalltalk Virtual Machine, in *Smalltalk-80: Bits of History, Words of Advice.* ed. G. Krasner. Reading, MA: Addison-Wesley.

Ingalls, D. November 1986. A Simple Technique for Handling Multiple Polymorphism. *SIGPLAN Notices* vol. 21 (11).

Ishikawa, Y., and Tokoro, M. 1987. Orient84/K: An Object-Oriented Concurrent Programming Language for Knowledge Representation, in *Object-Oriented Concurrent Programming*. ed. Yonezawa and M. Tokoro. Cambridge, MA: The MIT Press.

Jackson, M. May 1988. Objects and Other Subjects. *SIGPLAN Notices* vol. 23 (5).

Jacky, J., and Kalet, I. September 1987. An Object-Oriented Programming Discipline for Standard Pascal. *Communications of the ACM* vol. 30 (9).

Jacobson, I. November 1986. Language Support for Changeable, Large, Real-Time Systems. *SIGPLAN Notices* vol. 21 (11).

Jeffery, D. February 1989. Object-Oriented Programming in ANSI C. *Computer Language*.

Jenkins, M., and Glasgow, J. January 1986. Programming Styles in Nial. *IEEE Software* vol. 3 (1).

Johnson, R. November 1986. Type-Checking Smalltalk. *SIGPLAN Notices* vol. 21 (11).

Johnson, R., Graver, J., and Zurawski, L. September 1988. TS: An Optimizing Compiler for Smalltalk. *SIGPLAN Notices* vol. 23 (11).

Kaehler, T. November 1986. Virtual Memory on a Narrow Machine for an Object-Oriented Language. *SIGPLAN Notices* vol. 21 (11).

Kaehler, T., and Patterson, D. 1986. *A Taste of Smalltalk*. New York, NY: W. W. Norton.

Kaehler, T., and Patterson, D. August 1986. A Small Taste of Smalltalk. *Byte* vol. 11 (8).

Kahn, K., Tribble, E., Miller, M., and Bobrow, D. November 1986. Objects in Concurrent Logic Programming Languages. *SIGPLAN Notices* vol. 21 (11).

Kahn, K., Tribble, E., Miller, M., and Bobrow, D. 1987. Vulcan: Logical Concurrent Objects, in *Research Directions in Object-Oriented Programming*. ed. B. Schriver and P. Wegner. Cambridge, MA: The MIT Press.

Kaiser, G., and Garlan, D. October 1987. MELDing Data Flow and Object-Oriented Programming. *SIGPLAN Notices* vol. 22 (12).

Kalme, C. 27 March 1986. *Object-Oriented Programming: A Rule-Based Perspective*. Los Angeles, CA: Inference Corporation.

Kay, A. *New Directions for Novice Programming in the 1980s*. Palo Alto, CA: Xerox Palo Alto Research Center.

Keene, S. 1989. *Object-Oriented Programming in Common Lisp*. Reading, MA: Addison-Wesley.

Kelly, K., Rischer, R., Pleasant, M., Steiner, D., McGrew, C., Rowe, J., and Rubin, M. 30 March 1986. *Textual Representations of Object-Oriented Programs for Future Programmers*. Palo Alto, CA: Xerox AI Systems.

Kempf, J., Harris, W., D'Souza, R., and Snyder, A. October 1987. Experience with CommonLoops. *SIGPLAN Notices* vol. 22 (12).

Kempf, R. October 1987. Teaching Object-Oriented Programming with the KEE System. *SIGPLAN Notices* vol. 22 (12).

Khoshafian, S., and Copeland, G. November 1986. Object Identity. *SIGPLAN Notices* vol. 21 (11).

Kilian, M. April 1987. *An Overview of the Trellis/Owl Compiler*. Hudson, MA: Digital Equipment Corporation.

Kimminau, D., and Seagren, M. 1987. *Comparison of Two Prototype Developments Using Object-Based Programming*. Naperville, IL: AT&T Bell Laboratories.

Koshmann, T., and Evens, M. July 1988. Bridging the Gap Between Object-Oriented and Logic Programming. *IEEE Software* vol. 5 (4).

Koskimies, K., and Paakki, J. July 1987. TOOLS: A Unifying Approach to Object-Oriented Language Interpretation. *SIGPLAN Notices* vol. 22 (7).

Knowledge Systems Corporation. 1987. *PluggableGauges Version 1.0 User Manual*. Cary, NC.

Knudsen, J. August 1988. Name Collision in Multiple Classification Hierarchies. *Proceedings of ECOOP'88: European Conference on Object-Oriented Programming*. New York, NY: Springer-Verlag.

Knudsen, J., and Madsen, O. August 1988. Teaching Object-Oriented Programming Is More than Teaching Object-Oriented Programming Languages. *Proceedings of ECOOP'88: European Conference on Object-Oriented Programming*. New York, NY: Springer-Verlag.

Krasner, G. August 1981. The Smalltalk-80 Virtual Machine. *Byte* vol. 6 (8).

Krasner, G., ed. 1983. *Smalltalk-80: Bits of History, Words of Advice.* Reading, MA: Addison-Wesley.

Krasner, G., and Pope, S. August/September 1988. A Cookbook for Using the Model-View-Controller User Interface Paradigm in Smalltalk-80. *Journal of Object-Oriented Programming* vol. 1 (3).

Kristensen, B., Madsen, O., Moller-Pedersen, B., and Nygaard, K. 1987. The BETA Programming Language, in *Research Directions in Object-Oriented Programming.* ed. B. Schriver and P. Wegner. Cambridge, MA: The MIT Press.

LaLonde, W. April 1989. Designing Families of Data Types Using Exemplars. *ACM Transactions on Programming Languages and Systems* vol. 11 (2).

LaLonde, W., Thomas, D., and Pugh, J. November 1986. An Examplar Based Smalltalk. *SIGPLAN Notices* vol. 21 (11).

Lang, K., and Peralmutter, B. November 1986. Oaklisp: an Object-Oriented Scheme with First Class Types. *SIGPLAN Notices* vol. 21 (11).

Laursen, J., and Atkinson, R. October 1987. Opus: A Smalltalk Production System. *SIGPLAN Notices* vol. 22 (12).

Lieberherr, K., and Holland, I. March 1989. Formulations and Benefits of the Law of Demeter. *SIGPLAN Notices* vol. 24 (3).

Lieberherr, K., and Holland, I. September 1989. Assuring Good Style for Object-Oriented Programs. *IEEE Software* vol. 6 (5).

Lieberherr, K., Holland, I., Lee, G., and Riel, A. June 1988. An Objective Sense of Style. *IEEE Computer* vol. 21 (6).

Lieberman, H. November 1986. Using Prototypical Objects to Implement Shared Behavior in Object-Oriented Systems. *SIGPLAN Notices* vol. 21 (11).

Lieberman, H. 1987. Concurrent Object-Oriented Programming in Act 1, in *Object-Oriented Concurrent Programming.* ed. Yonezawa and M. Tokoro. Cambridge, MA: The MIT Press.

Lieberman, H., Stein, L., and Ungar, D. May 1988. Of Types and Prototypes: The Treaty of Orlando. *SIGPLAN Notices* vol. 23 (5).

Lim, J., and Johnson, R. April 1989. The Heart of Object-Oriented Concurrent Programming. *SIGPLAN Notices* vol. 24 (4).

Linowes, J. August 1988. It's an Attitude. *Byte* vol. 13 (8).

Lippman, S. 1989. *C++ Primer.* Reading, MA: Addison-Wesley.

Liskov, B., Atkinson, R., Bloom, T., Moss, E., Schaffert, C., Scheifler, R., and Snyder, R. 1981. *CLU Reference Manual.* New York, NY: Springer-Verlag.

Liskov, B., Snyder, A., Atkinson, R., and Schaffert, C. 1980. Abstraction Mechanisms in CLU, in *Programming Language Design.* ed. A. Wasserman. New York, NY: Computer Society Press.

Lujun, S., and Zhongxiu. August 1987. An Object-Oriented Programming Language for Developing Distributed Software. *SIGPLAN Notices* vol. 22 (8).

MacLennan, B. 1987. Values and Objects in Programming Languages,, in *Object-Oriented Computing: Concepts vol.* 1. ed. G. Peterson. New York, NY: Computer Society Press of the IEEE.

Madsen, O. 1987. Block Structure and Object-Oriented Languages, in *Research Directions in Object-Oriented Programming*. ed. B. Schriver and P. Wegner. Cambridge, MA: The MIT Press.

Madsen, O., and Moller-Pedersen, B. August 1988. What Object-Oriented Programming May Be – And What It Does Not Have To Be. *Proceedings of ECOOP'88: European Conference on Object-Oriented Programming*. New York, NY: Springer-Verlag.

Madsen, O., and Moller-Pedersen, B. October 1989. Virtual Classes: A Powerful Mechanism in Object-Oriented Programming. *SIGPLAN Notices* vol. 24 (10).

Marcus, R. November 1985. Generalized Inheritance. *SIGPLAN Notices* vol. 20 (11).

Markowitz, V., and Raz, Y. 1983. Eroll: An Entity-Relationship, Role-Oriented Query Language, in *Entity-Relationship Approach to Software Engineering*. ed. C. Davis et al. Amsterdam, The Netherlands: Elsevier Science.

Mellender, F. October 1988. An Integration of Logic and Object-Oriented Programming. *SIGPLAN Notices* vol. 23 (10).

Methfessel, R. April 1987. Implementing an Access and Object-Oriented Paradigm in a Language That Supports Neither. *SIGPLAN Notices* vol. 22 (4).

Meyer, B. November 1986. Genericity versus Inheritance. *SIGPLAN Notices* vol. 21 (11).

Meyer, B. February 1987. Eiffel: Programming for Reusability and Extendability. *SIGPLAN Notices* vol. 22 (2).

Meyer, B. November/December 1988. Harnessing Multiple Inheritance. *Journal of Object-Oriented Programming* vol. 1 (4).

Micallef, J. April/May 1988. Encapsulation, Reusability, and Extensibility in Object-Oriented Programming Languages. *Journal of Object-Oriented Programming* vol. 1 (1).

Minsky, N., and Rozenshtein, D. October 1987. A Law-Based Approach to Object-Oriented Programming. *SIGPLAN Notices* vol. 22 (12).

Minsky, N., and Rozenshtein, D., October 1989. Controllable Delegation: An Exercise in Law-Governed Systems. *SIGPLAN Notices* vol. 24 (10).

Miranda, E. October 1987. BrouHaHa – A Portable Smalltalk Interpreter. *SIGPLAN Notices* vol. 22 (12).

Mittal, S., Bobrow, D., and Kahn, K. November 1986. Virtual Copies: At the Boundary Between Classes and Instances. *SIGPLAN Notices* vol. 21 (11).

Moon, D. November 1986. Object-Oriented Programming with Flavors. *SIGPLAN Notices* vol. 21 (11).

Mossenbock, H., and Templ, J. 1989. Object Oberon – A Modest Object-Oriented Language. *Structured Programming* vol. 10 (4).

Mudge, T. March 1985. Object-Based Computing and the Ada Language. *IEEE Computer* vol. 18 (3).

Nierstrasz, O. October 1987. Active Objects in Hybrid. *SIGPLAN Notices* vol. 22 (12).

Novak, G. June 1983. Data Abstraction in GLISP. *SIGPLAN Notices* vol. 18 (6).

Novak, G. Fall 1983. GLISP: A Lisp-Based Programming System with Data Abstraction. *AI Magazine* vol. 4 (3).

Nygaard, K., and Dahl, O-J. 1981. The Development of the Simula Languages, in *History of Programming Languages*. ed. R. Wexelblat. New York, NY: Academic Press.

Nygaard, K. October 1986. Basic Concepts in Object-Oriented Programming. *SIGPLAN Notices* vol. 21 (10).

Object-Oriented Programming Workshop. October 1986. *SIGPLAN Notices* vol. 21 (10).

O'Brien, P. 15 November 1985. *Trellis Object-Based Environment: Language Tutorial.* Hudson, MA: Digital Equipment Corporation.

Olthoff, W. 1986. *Augmentation of Object-Oriented Programming by Concepts of Abstract Data Type Theory: The ModPascal Experience.* Kaiserslautern, West Germany: University of Kaiserslautern.

Osterbye, K. June/July 1988. Active Objects: An Access-Oriented Framework for Object-Oriented Languages. *Journal of Object-Oriented Programming* vol. 1 (2).

Paepcke, A. October 1989. PCLOS: A Critical Review. *SIGPLAN Notices* vol. 24 (10).

Parc Place Systems. 1988. *The Smalltalk-80 Programming System Version VI 2.3.* Palo Alto, CA.

Pascoe, G. August 1986. Elements of Object-Oriented Programming. *Byte* vol. 11 (8).

Pascoe, G. November 1986. Encapsulators: A New Software Paradigm in Smalltalk-80. *SIGPLAN Notices* vol. 21 (11).

Perez, E. September/October 1988. Simulating Inheritance with Ada. *Ada Letters* vol. 8 (7).

Peterson, G. ed. 1987. *Object-Oriented Computing Concepts.* New York, NY: Computer Society Press of the IEEE.

Pinson, L., and Wiener, R. 1988. *An Introduction to Object-Oriented Programming and Smalltalk.* Reading, MA: Addison-Wesley.

Pohl, I. 1989. *C++ for C Programmers.* Redwood City, CA: Benjamin/Cummings.

Pokkunuri, B. November 1989. Object-Oriented Programming. *SIGPLAN Notices* vol. 24 (11).

Pountain, D. August 1986. Object-Oriented FORTH. *Byte* vol. 11 (8).

Proceedings of ECOOP'88: European Conference on Object-Oriented Programming. August 1988. New York, NY: Springer-Verlag.

Proceedings of OOPSLA'86: Object-Oriented Programming Systems, Languages, and Applications. November 1986. *SIGPLAN Notices* vol. 21 (11).

Proceedings of OOPSLA'87: Object-Oriented Programming Systems, Languages, and Applications. October 1987. *SIGPLAN Notices* vol. 22 (12).

Proceedings of OOPSLA'88: Object-Oriented Programming Systems, Languages, and Applications. September 1988. *SIGPLAN Notices* vol. 23 (11).

Proceedings of OOPSLA'89: Object-Oriented Programming Systems, Languages, and Applications. October 1989. *SIGPLAN Notices* vol. 24 (10).

Proceedings of the ACM SIGPLAN Workshop on Object-Based Concurrent Programming. April 1989. *SIGPLAN Notices* vol. 24 (4).

Proceedings of the USENIX Association C++ Workshop. November 1987. Berkeley, CA: USENIX Association.

Proceedings of the Workshop on Data Abstraction, Databases, and Conceptual Modelling. 1980. *SIGPLAN Notices* vol. 16 (1).

Pugh, J. March 1984. Actors – The Stage is Set. *SIGPLAN Notices* vol. 19 (3).

Rathke, C. 1986. *ObjTalk: Repräsentation von Wissen in einer objektorientierten Sprache* Stuttgart, West Germany: Institut für Informatik der Universität Stuttgart.

Rentsch, T. September 1982. Object-Oriented Programming. *SIGPLAN Notices* vol. 17 (12).

Rettig, M., Morgan, T., Jacobs, J., and Wimberly, D. January 1989. Object-Oriented Programming in AI. *AI Expert*.

Robson, D. August 1981. Object-Oriented Software Systems. *Byte* vol. 6 (8).

Rumbaugh, J. October 1987. Relations as Semantic Constructs in an Object-Oriented Language. *SIGPLAN Notices* vol. 22 (12).

Russo, V., and Kaplan, S. 1988. A C++ Interpreter for Scheme. *Proceedings of USENIX C++ Conference*. Berkeley, CA: USENIX Association.

Sakkinen, M. August 1988. On the Darker Side of C++. *Proceedings of ECOOP'88: European Conference on Object-Oriented Programming.* New York, NY: Springer-Verlag.

Sakkinen, M. December 1988. Comments on "the Law of Demeter" and C++. *SIGPLAN Notices* vol. 23 (12).

Saltzer, J. 1979. Naming and Binding of Objects, in *Operating Systems.* ed. R. Bayer et. al. New York, NY: Springer-Verlag.

Sandberg, D. November 1986. An Alternative To Subclassing. *SIGPLAN Notices* vol. 21 (11).

Sandberg, D. October 1988. Smalltalk and Exploratory Programming. *SIGPLAN Notices* vol. 23 (10).

Saunders, J. March/April 1989. A Survey of Object-Oriented Programming Languages. *Journal of Object-Oriented Programming* vol. 1 (6).

Schaffert, C., Cooper, T., Bullis, B., Kilian, M., and Wilpolt, C. November 1986. An Introduction to Trellis/Owl. *SIGPLAN Notices* vol. 21 (11).

Schaffert, C., Cooper, T., and Wilpolt, C. November 25, 1985. *Trellis Object-Based Environment: Language Reference Manual.* Hudson, MA: Digital Equipment Corporation.

Schmucker, K. 1986a. MacApp: An Application Framework. *Byte* vol. 11 (8).

Schmucker, K. 1986b. Object-Oriented Languages for the Macintosh. *Byte* vol. 11 (8).

Schmucker, K. 1986c. *Object-Oriented Programming for the Macintosh.* Hasbrouk Heights, NJ: Hayden.

Schriver, B., and Wegner, P. eds. 1987. *Research Directions in Object-Oriented Programming.* Cambridge, MA: The MIT Press.

Seidewitz, E. October 1987. Object-Oriented Programming in Smalltalk and Ada. *SIGPLAN Notices* vol. 22 (12).

Shafer, D. 1988. *HyperTalk Programming.* Indianapolis, IN: Hayden Book.

Shah, A., Rumbaugh, J., Hamel, J., and Borsari, R. October 1989. DSM: An Object-Relationship Modeling Language. *SIGPLAN Notices* vol. 24 (10).

Shammas, N. October 1988. Smalltalk a la C. *Byte* vol. 13 (10).

Shan, Y. October 1989. An Event-Driven Model-View-Controller Framework for Smalltalk. *SIGPLAN Notices* vol. 24 (10).

Shaw, M. 1981. *ALPHARD: Form and Content.* New York, NY: Springer-Verlag.

Shibayama, E. September 1988. How to Invent Distributed Implementation Schemes of an Object-Based Concurrent Language – A Transformational Approach. *SIGPLAN Notices* vol 23 (11).

Shibayama, E., and Yonezawa, A. 1987. Distributed Computing in ABCL/1, in *Object-Oriented Concurrent Programming*. ed. Yonezawa and M. Tokoro. Cambridge, MA: The MIT Press.

Shopiro, J. 13 December 1988. Programming Techniques with C++. *C++ Tutorial Program of the USENIX Conference*. Denver, CO: USENIX Association.

Simonian, R., and Crone, M. November/December 1988. InnovAda: True Object-Oriented Programming in Ada. *Journal of Object-Oriented Programming* vol. 1 (4).

Software Productivity Solutions. 1988. *Classical-Ada User Manual*. Melbourne, FL.

Snyder, A. February 1985. *Object-Oriented Programming for Common Lisp*. Report ATC-85-1. Palo Alto, CA: Hewlett-Packard.

Snyder, A. November 1986. Encapsulation and Inheritance in Object-Oriented Programming Languages. *SIGPLAN Notices* vol. 21 (11).

Snyder, A. 1987. Inheritance and the Development of Encapsulated Software Components, in *Research Directions in Object-Oriented Programming*. ed. B. Schriver and P. Wegner. Cambridge, MA: The MIT Press.

Stankovic, J. April 1982. Software Communication Mechanisms: Procedure Calls Versus Messages. *IEEE Computer* vol. 15 (4).

Stefik, M., and Bobrow, D. Winter 1986. Object-Oriented Programming: Themes and Variations, *AI Magazine* vol. 6 (4).

Stefik, M., Bobrow, D., Mittal, S., and Conway, L. Fall 1983, Knowledge Programming in Loops. *AI Magazine* vol. 4 (3).

Stein, L. October 1987. Delegation Is Inheritance. *SIGPLAN Notices* vol. 22 (12).

Stroustrup, B. January 1982. Classes: An Abstract Data Type Facility for the C Language. *SIGPLAN Notices* vol. 17 (1).

Stroustrup, B. October 1986. An Overview of C++. *SIGPLAN Notices* vol. 21 (10).

Stroustrup, B. 1986. *The C++ Programming Language*. Reading, MA: Addison-Wesley.

Stroustrup, B. November 1987. Possible Directions for C++. *Proceedings of the USENIX C++ Workshop*. Santa Fe, NM: USENIX Association.

Stroustrup, B. November 1987. The Evolution of C++. *Proceedings of the USENIX C++ Workshop*. Santa Fe, NM: USENIX Association.

Stroustrup, B. May 1988. What Is Object-Oriented Programming? *IEEE Software* vol. 5 (3).

Stroustrup, B. August 1988. A Better C? *Byte* vol. 13 (8).

Stroustrup, B. 1988. Parameterized Types for C++. *Proceedings of USENIX C++ Conference*. Berkeley, CA: USENIX Association.

Suzuki, N. 1981. Inferring Types in Smalltalk, *Proceedings of the 8th Annual Symposium of ACM Principles of Programming Languages*. New York, NY: Association of Computing Machinery.

Suzuki, N., and Terada, M. 1983. Creating Efficient Systems for Object-Oriented Languages. *Proceedings of the 11th Annual ACM Symposium on the Principles of Programming Languages*. New York, NY: Association of Computing Machinery.

Symposium on Actor Languages. October 1980. *Creative Computing*.

Tektronix. 1988. *Modular Smalltalk.*

Tesler, L. August 1986. Programming Experiences. *Byte* vol. 11 (8).

The Smalltalk-80 System. August 1981. *Byte* vol. 6 (8).

Thomas, D. March 1989. What's in an Object? *Byte* vol. 14 (3).

Tieman, M. 1 May 1988. *User's Guide to GNU C++.* Cambridge, MA: Free Software Foundation.

Tokoro, M., and Ishikawa, Y. October 1986. Concurrent Programming in Orient84/K: An Object-Oriented Knowledge Representation Language. *SIGPLAN Notices* vol. 21 (10).

Touati, H. May 1987. Is Ada an Object-Oriented Programming Language? *SIGPLAN Notices* vol. 22 (5).

Tripathi, A., and Berge, E. An Implementation of the Object-Oriented Concurrent Programming Language SINA. *Software – Practice and Experience* vol. 19 (3).

Ungar, D. September 1988. Are Classes Obsolete? *SIGPLAN Notices* vol. 23 (11).

Ungar, D., and Smith, R. October 1987. Self: The Power of Simplicity. *SIGPLAN Notices* vol. 22 (12).

U. S. Department of Defense. February 1983. *Reference Manual for the Ada Programming Language.* Washington, D.C.: Ada Joint Program Office.

van den Bos, J., and Laffra, C. October 1989. PROCOL: A Parallel Object Language with Protocols. *SIGPLAN Notices* vol. 24 (10).

Vaucher, J., Lapalme, G., and Malenfant, J. August 1988. SCOOP: Structured Concurrent Object-Oriented Prolog. *Proceedings of ECOOP'88: European Conference on Object-Oriented Programming.* New York, NY: Springer-Verlag.

Warren, S., and Abbe, D. May 1980. Presenting Rosetta Smalltalk. *Datamation.*

Watanabe, T., and Yonezawa, A. September 1988. Reflection in an Object-Oriented Concurrent Language. *SIGPLAN Notices* vol 23 (11).

Wegner, P. October 1987. Dimensions of Object-Based Language Design. *SIGPLAN Notices* vol. 22 (12).

Wegner, P. January 1988. Workshop on Object-Oriented Programming at ECOOP 1987. *SIGPLAN Notices* vol. 23 (1).

Wiener, R. June 1987. Object-Oriented Programming in C++ – A Case Study. *SIGPLAN Notices* vol. 22 (6).

Williams, G. Summer 1989. Designing the Future: The Power of Object-Oriented Programming. *American Programmer* vol. 2 (7-8).

Wilson, R. 1 November 1987. Object-Oriented Languages Reorient Programming Techniques. *Computer Design* vol. 26 (20).

Winston, P., and Horn, B. 1989. *Lisp.* 3rd ed. Reading, MA: Addison-Wesley.

Wirfs-Brock, R. and Wilkerson, B. September 1988. An Overview of Modular Smalltalk. *SIGPLAN Notices* vol. 23 (11).

Wirth, N. June 1987. Extensions of Record Types. *SIGCSE Bulletin* vol. 19 (2).

Wirth, N. July 1988a. From Modula to Oberon. *Software – Practice and Experience* vol. 18 (7).

Wirth, N. July 1988b. The Programming Language Oberon. *Software – Practice and Experience* vol. 18 (7).

Wolf, W. September 1989. A Practical Comparison of Two Object-Oriented Languages. *IEEE Software* vol. 6 (5).

Yokote, Y., and Tokoro, M. November 1986. The Design and Implementation of Concurrent Smalltalk. *SIGPLAN Notices* vol. 21 (11).

Yokote, Y., and Tokoro, M. October 1987. Experience and Evolution of Concurrent Smalltalk. *SIGPLAN Notices* vol. 22 (12).

Yonezawa, A., and Tokoro, M. eds. 1987. *Object-Oriented Concurrent Programming.* Cambridge, MA: The MIT Press.

Yonezawa, A., Briot, J., and Shibayama, E. November 1986. Object-Oriented Concurrent Programming in ABCL/1. *SIGPLAN Notices* vol. 21 (11).

Yonezawa, A., Shibayama, E., Takada, T., and Honda, Y. 1987. Modelling and Programming in an Object-Oriented Concurrent Language ABCL/1, in *Object-Oriented Concurrent Programming.* ed. Yonezawa and M. Tokoro. Cambridge, MA: The MIT Press.

Yourdon, E. February 1990. Object-Oriented COBOL. *American Programmer* vol. 3 (2).

Zave, P. September 1989. A Compositional Approach to Multiparadigm Programming. *IEEE Software* vol. 6 (5).

H. Software Engineering

Abelson, H., and Sussman, G. 1985. *Structure and Interpretation of Computer Programs.* Cambridge, MA: The MIT Press.

Appleton, D. 15 January 1986. Very Large Projects. *Datamation.*

Aron, J. 1974a. *The Program Development Process: The Individual Programmer.* Vol. 1. Reading, MA: Addison-Wesley.

Aron, J. 1974b. *The Program Development Process: The Programming Team.* Vol. 2. Reading, MA: Addison-Wesley.

Ben-Ari, M. 1982. *Principles of Concurrent Programming.* Englewood Cliffs, NJ: Prentice-Hall.

Boehm, B. August 1986. A Spiral Model of Software Development and Enhancement. *Software Engineering Notes,* vol. 11 (4).

Boehm-Davis, D., and Ross, L. October 1984. *Approaches to Structuring the Software Development Process,* Report GEC/DIS/TR-84-B1V-1. Arlington, VA: General Electric.

Booch, G. 1986. *Software Engineering with Ada.* Menlo Park, CA: Benjamin/Cummings.

Brooks, F. 1975. *The Mythical Man-Month.* Reading, MA: Addison-Wesley.

Brooks, F. April 1987. No Silver Bullet: Essence and Accidents of Software Engineering. *IEEE Computer* vol. 20 (4).

Curtis, B. 17 May 1989. . . . .*But You Have To Understand, This Isn't The Way We Develop Software At Our Company.* MCC Technical Report Number STP-203-89. Austin, TX: Microelectronics and Computer Technology Corporation.

Dahl, O., Dijkstra, E., and Hoare, C. A. R. 1972. *Structured Programming.* London, England: Academic Press.

Davis, A., Bersoff, E., and Comer, E. October 1988. A Strategy for Comparing Alternative Software Development Life Cycle Models. *IEEE Transactions on Software Engineering* vol. 14 (10).

Davis, C., Jajodia, S., Ng, P., and Yeh, R. eds. 1983. *Entity-Relationship Approach to Software Engineering.* Amsterdam, The Netherlands: Elsevier Science.

DeMarco, T., and Lister, T. 1987. *Peopleware.* New York, NY: Dorset House.

DeRemer, F., and Kron, H. 1980. Programming-in-the-Large versus Programming-in-the-Small. *Tutorial on Software Design Techniques* 3rd ed. ed. P. Freeman and A. Wasserman. New York, NY: Computer Society Press of the IEEE.

Dijkstra, E. 1979. Programming Considered as a Human Activity, in *Classics in Software Engineering.* ed. E. Yourdon. New York, NY: Yourdon Press.

Dijkstra, E. 1982. *Selected Writings on Computing: A Personal Perspective.* New York, NY: Springer-Verlag.

Dowson, M. August 1986. The Structure of the Software Process. *Software Engineering Notes,* vol. 11 (4).

Dreger, B. 1989. *Function Point Analysis.* Englewood Cliffs, NJ: Prentice-Hall.

Eastman, N. 1984. Software Engineering and Technology. *Technical Directions* vol. 10 (1). Bethesda, MD: IBM Federal Systems Division.

Foster, C. 1981. *Real-Time Programming.* Reading, MA: Addison-Wesley.

Freeman, P. 1975. *Software Systems Principles.* Chicago, IL: Science Research Associates.

Freeman, P., and Wasserman, A. eds. 1983. *Tutorial on Software Design Techniques* 4th ed. New York, NY: Computer Society Press of the IEEE.

Glass, R. 1982. *Modern Programming Practices: A Report from Industry.* Englewood Cliffs, NJ: Prentice-Hall.

Glass, R. 1983. *Real-Time Software.* Englewood Cliffs, NJ: Prentice-Hall.

Hansen, P. 1977. *The Architecture of Concurrent Programs.* Englewood Cliffs, NJ: Prentice-Hall.

Hoare, C. April 1984. Programming: Sorcery or Science? *IEEE Software* vol. 1 (2).

Holt, R., Lazowska, E., Graham, G., and Scott, M. 1978. *Structured Concurrent Programming.* Reading, MA: Addison-Wesley.

Humphrey, W. 1989. *Managing the Software Process.* Reading, MA: Addison-Wesley.

Jackson, M. 1975. *Principles of Program Design.* Orlando, FL: Academic Press.

Jackson, M. 1983. *System Development.* Englewood Cliffs, NJ: Prentice-Hall.

Jensen, R., and Tonies, C. 1979. *Software Engineering.* Englewood Cliffs, NJ: Prentice-Hall.

Jones, C. September 1984. Reusability in Programming: A Survey of the State of the Art. *IEEE Transactions on Software Engineering.* vol. SE-10 (5).

Kishida, K., Teramoto, M., Torri, K., and Urano, Y. September 1988. Quality Assurance Technology in Japan. *IEEE Software* vol. 4 (5).

Lammers, S. 1986. *Programmers at Work.* Redmond, WA: Microsoft Press.

Ledgard, H. Summer 1985. Programmers: The Amateur vs. the Professional. *Abacus* vol. 2 (4).

Linger, R., and Mills, H. 1977. On the Development of Large Reliable Programs, in *Current Trends in Programming Methodology: Software Specification and Design* vol. 1. ed. R. Yeh. Englewood Cliffs, NJ: Prentice-Hall.

Linger, R., Mills, H., and Witt, B. 1979. *Structured Programming: Theory and Practice*. Reading, MA: Addison-Wesley.

Liskov, B., and Guttag, J. 1986. *Abstraction and Specification in Program Development*. Cambridge, MA: The MIT Press.

Lorin, H. 1972. *Parallelism in Hardware and Software*. Englewood Cliffs, NJ: Prentice-Hall.

Martin, J., and McClure, C. 1988. *Structured Techniques: The Basis for CASE*. Englewood Cliffs, NJ: Prentice-Hall.

Mascot, Version 3.1, The Official Handbook of. June 1987. London, England: Crown Copyright.

Mellichamp, D. 1983. *Real-Time Computing*. New York, NY: Van Nostrand Reinhold.

Mills, H. November 1986. Structured Programming: Retrospect and Prospect. *IEEE Software* vol. 3 (6).

Munck, R. 1985. Toward Large Software Systems That Work. *Proceedings of the AIAA/ACM/NASA/IEEE Computers in Aerospace V Conference.* Menlo Park, CA: AIAA.

Myers, G. 1978. *Composite/Structured Design*. New York, NY: Van Nostrand Reinhold.

Newport, J. 28 April 1986. A Growing Gap in Software. *Fortune.*

Office of the Under Secretary of Defense for Acquisition. September 1987. *Report of the Defense Science Board Task Force on Military Software.* Washington, D.C.

Orr, K. 1971. *Structured Systems Development*. New York, NY: Yourdon Press.

Page-Jones, M. 1988. *The Practical Guide to Structured Systems Design*. Englewood Cliffs, NJ: Yourdon Press.

Parnas, D. July 1985a. Why Conventional Software Development Does Not Produce Reliable Programs. *Software Aspects of Strategic Defense Systems*, Report DCS-47-IR. Victoria, Canada: University of Victoria.

Parnas, D. July 1985b. Why Software is Unreliable. *Software Aspects of Strategic Defense Systems*, Report DCS-47-IR. Victoria, Canada: University of Victoria.

Parnas, D. December 1985. Software Aspects of Strategic Defense Systems. *Communications of the ACM* vol. 28 (12).

Peters, L. 1981. *Software Design*. New York, NY: Yourdon Press.

Pressman, R. 1987. *Software Engineering: A Practitioner's Approach*. 2nd ed. New York, NY: McGraw-Hill.

Ramamoorthy, C., Garg, V., and Prakask, A. July 1986. Programming in the Large. *IEEE Transactions on Software Engineering* vol. SE-12 (7).

Ross, D., Goodenough, J., and Irvine, C. 1980. Software Engineering: Process, Principles, and Goals. *Tutorial on Software Design Techniques.* 3rd ed. ed. P. Freeman and A. Wasserman. New York, NY: Computer Society Press of the IEEE.

Sommerville, I. 1989. *Software Engineering*. 3rd ed. Wokingham, England: Addison-Wesley.

Spector, A., and Gifford, D. April 1986. Computer Science Perspective of Bridge Design. *Communications of the ACM* vol. 29 (4).

Stevens, W. Myers, G., and Constantine, L. 1979. Structured Design, in *Classics in Software Engineering.* ed. E. Yourdon. New York, NY: Yourdon Press.

The Software Trap: Automate – Or Else. 9 May 1988. *Business Week.*

U. S. Department of Defense. 30 July 1982. *Report of the DoD Joint Service Task Force on Software Problems.* Washington, D.C.

Vick, C., and Ramamoorthy, C. 1984. *Software Engineering.* New York, NY: Van Nostrand Reinhold.

Vonk, R. 1990. *Prototyping.* Englewood Cliffs, NJ: Prentice-Hall.

Ward, P., and Mellor, S. 1985. *Structured Development for Real-Time Systems: Introduction and Tools.* Englewood Cliffs, NJ: Yourdon Press.

Wegner, P. 1980. *Research Directions in Software Technology.* Cambridge, MA: The MIT Press.

Wegner, P. July 1984. Capital-intensive Software Technology. *IEEE Software* vol. 1 (3).

Wirth, N. 1986. *Algorithms and Data Structures.* Englewood Cliffs, NJ: Prentice-Hall.

Yeh, R. ed. 1977. *Current Trends in Programming Methodology: Software Specification and Design.* Englewood Cliffs, NJ: Prentice-Hall.

Yourdon, E. 1975. *Techniques of Program Structure and Design.* Englewood Cliffs, NJ: Prentice-Hall.

Yourdon, E. 1979. ed. *Classics in Software Engineering.* New York, NY: Yourdon Press.

Yourdon, E. 1989a. *Modern Structured Analysis.* Englewood Cliffs, NJ: Prentice-Hall.

Yourdon, E. 1989b. *Structured Walkthroughs.* Englewood Cliffs, NJ: Prentice-Hall.

Yourdon, E. August 1989. The Year of the Object. *Computer Language* vol. 6 (8).

Yourdon, E. Summer 1989. Object-Oriented Observations. *American Programmer* vol. 2 (7-8).

Yourdon, E., and Constantine, L. 1979. *Structured Design.* Englewood Cliffs, NJ: Prentice-Hall.

Zave, P. February 1984. The Operational versus the Conventional Approach to Software Development. *Communications of the ACM* vol. 27 (2).

Zelkowitz, M. June 1978. Perspectives on Software Engineering. *ACM Computing Surveys* vol. 10 (2).

I. Special References

Rand, Ayn. 1979. *Introduction to Objectivist Epistemology.* New York, NY: New American Library.

Gall, J. 1986. *Systemantics: How Systems Really Work and How They Fail.* 2nd ed. Ann Arbor, MI: The General Systemantics Press.

Gleick, J. 1987. *Chaos.* New York, NY: Penguin Books.

Heinlein, R. 1966. *The Moon Is a Harsh Mistress.* New York, NY: The Berkeley Publishing Group.

Hofstadter, D. 1979. *Gödel, Escher, Bach: An Eternal Golden Braid.* New York, NY: Vintage Books.

Inside Macintosh Volumes 1-5. 1988. Reading, MA: Addison-Wesley.

Meyer, C., and Matyas. 1982. *Cryptography.* New York, NY: John Wiley and Sons.

Peter, L. 1986. *The Peter Pyramid.* New York, NY: William Morrow.

Petroski, H. 1985. *To Engineer Is Human.* New York, NY: St. Martin's Press.

Sears, F., Zemansky, M., and Young., H. 1987. *University Physics.* 7th ed. Reading, MA: Addison-Wesley.

Wagner, J. 1986. *The Search for Signs of Intelligent Life in the Universe.* New York, NY: Harper and Row.

Whitehead, A. 1958. *An Introduction to Mathematics.* New York, NY: Oxford University Press.

J. Theory

Aho, A., Hopcroft, J., and Ullman, J. 1974. *The Design and Analysis of Computer Programs.* Reading, MA: Addison-Wesley.

Almarode, J. October 1989. Rule-Based Delegation for Prototypes. *SIGPLAN Notices* vol. 24 (10).

Appelbe, W., and Ravn, A. April 1984. Encapsulation Constructs in Systems Programming Languages. *ACM Transactions on Programming Languages and Systems* vol. 6 (2).

Averill, E. April 1982. Theory of Design and Its Relationship to Capacity Measurement. *Proceedings of the Fourth Annual International Conference on Computer Capacity Management* . San Francisco, CA: Association of Computing Machinery.

Barr, A., and Feigenbaum, E. 1981. *The Handbook of Artificial Intelligence.* Los Altos, CA: William Kaufmann.

Bastani, F., and Iyengar, S. March 1987. The Effect of Data Structures on the Logical Complexity of Programs. *Communications of the ACM* vol. 30 (3).

Bastani, F., Hilal, W., and Sitharama, S. October 1987. Efficient Abstract Data Type Components for Distributed and Parallel Systems. *IEEE Computer* vol. 20 (10).

Belkhouche, B., and Urban, J. May 1986. Direct Implementation of Abstract Data Types from Abstract Specifications. *IEEE Transactions on Software Engineering* vol. SE-12 (5).

Bensley, E., Brando, T., and Prelle, M. September 1988. An Execution Model for Distributed Object-Oriented Computation. *SIGPLAN Notices* vol. 23 (11).

Berztiss, A. 1980. Data Abstraction, Controlled Iteration, and Communicating Processes. *Communications of the ACM.*

Bishop, J. 1986. *Data Abstraction in Programming Languages.* Wokingham, England: Addison-Wesley.

Boehm, H., Demers, A., and Donahue, J. October 1980. *An Informal Description of Russell.* Technical Report TR 80-430. Ithaca, NY: Cornell University.

Borning, A., Duisberg, R., Freeman-Benson, B., Kramer, A., and Woolf, M. October 1987. Constraint Hierarchies. *SIGPLAN Notices* vol. 22 (12).

Boute, R. January 1988. Systems Semantics: Principles, Applications, and Implementation. *ACM Transactions on Programming Languages and Systems* vol 10. (1).

Brachman, R. October 1983. What Is-a Is and Isn't: An Analysis of Taxonomic Links in Semantic Networks. *IEEE Computer* vol. 16 (10).

Brachman, R., and Levesque, H. eds. 1985. *Readings in Knowledge Representation.* Los Altos, CA: Morgan Kaufmann.

Bruce, K., and Wegner, P. October 1986. An Algebraic Model of Subtypes in Object-Oriented Languages. *SIGPLAN Notices* vol. 21 (10).

Cardelli, L., and Wegner, P. December 1985. On Understanding Types, Data Abstraction, and Polymorphism. *ACM Computing Surveys* vol. 17 (4).

Claybrook, B., and Wyckof, M. 1980. Module: an Encapsulation Mechanism for Specifying and Implementing Abstract Data Types. *Communications of the ACM.*

Cline, A., and Rich, E. December 1983. *Building and Evaluating Abstract Data Types*, Report TR-83-26. Austin, TX: University of Texas, Department of Computer Sciences.

Cohen, A. January 1984. Data Abstraction, Data Encapsulation, and Object-Oriented Programming. *SIGPLAN Notices* vol. 19 (1).

Cohen, N. November/December 1985. Tasks as Abstraction Mechanisms. *Ada Letters* vol. 5 (3-6).

Cohen, P., and Loiselle, C. August 1988. Beyond ISA: Structures for Plausible Inference in Semantic Nets. *Proceedings of the Seventh National Conference on Artificial Intelligence.* Saint Paul, MN: American Association for Artificial Intelligence.

Cook, W., and Palsberg, J. October 1989. A Denotational Semantics of Inheritance and Its Correctness. *SIGPLAN Notices* vol. 24 (10).

Courtois, P., Heymans, F., and Parnas, D. October 1971, Concurrent Control with "Readers" and "Writers." *Communications of the ACM* vol. 14 (10).

Danforth, S., and Tomlinson, C. March 1988. Type Theories and Object-Oriented Programming. *ACM Computing Surveys* vol. 20 (1).

Demers, A., Donahue, J., and Skinner, G. Data Types as Values: Polymorphism, Type-Checking, Encapsulation. *Proceedings of the Fifth Annual ACM Symposium on Principles of Programming Languages.* New York, NY: Association of Computing Machinery.

Dennis, J., and Van Horn, E. March 1966. Programming Semantics for Multiprogrammed Computations. *Communications of the ACM* vol. 9 (3).

Donahue, J., and Demers, A. July 1985. Data Types Are Values. *ACM Transactions on Programming Languages and Systems* vol. 7 (3).

Eckart, J. April 1987. Iteration and Abstract Data Types. *SIGPLAN Notices* vol. 22 (4).

Embley, D., and Woodfield, S. 1988. Assessing the Quality of Abstract Data Types Written in Ada. *Proceedings of the 10th International Conference on Software Engineering.* New York, NY: Computer Society Press of the IEEE.

Ferber, J. October 1989. Computational Reflection in Class-Based Object-Oriented Languages. *SIGPLAN Notices* vol. 24 (10).

Gannon, J., Hamlet, R., and Mills, H. July 1987. Theory of Modules. *IEEE Transactions on Software Engineering* vol. SE-13 (7).

Gannon, J., McMullin, P., and Hamlet, R. July 1981. Data Abstraction Implementation, Specification, and Testing. *ACM Transactions on Programming Languages and Systems vol.* 3 (3).

Gardner, M. May/June 1984. When to Use Private Types. *Ada Letters* vol. 3 (6).

Goguen, J., Thatcher, J., and Wagner, E. 1977. An Initial Algebra Approach to the Specification, Correctness, and Implementation of Abstract Data Types, in *Current Trends in Programming Methodology: Data Structuring* vol. 4. ed. R. Yeh. Englewood Cliffs, NJ: Prentice-Hall.

Graube, N. October 1989. Metaclass Compatibility. *SIGPLAN Notices* vol. 24 (10).

Gries, D., and Prins, J. July 1985. A New Notion of Encapsulation. *SIGPLAN Notices* vol. 20 (7).

Grogono, P., and Bennett, A. November 1989. Polymorphism and Type Checking in Object-Oriented Languages. *SIGPLAN Notices* vol. 24 (11).

Guttag, J. 1980. Abstract Data Types and the Development of Data Structures, in *Programming Language Design.* ed. A. Wasserman. New York, NY: Computer Society Press of the IEEE.

Hammons, C., and Dobbs, P. May/June 1985. Coupling, Cohesion, and Package Unity in Ada. *Ada Letters* vol. 4 (6).

Harrison, G., and Liu, D. July/August 1986. Generic Implementations Via Analogies in the Ada Programming Language. *Ada Letters* vol. 6 (4).

Hayes, P. 1981. The Logic of Frames, in *Readings in Artificial Intelligence.* ed. B. Webber and N. Nilsson. Palo Alto, CA: Tioga.

Hayes-Roth, F. July 1985. A Blackboard Architecture for Control. *Artificial Intelligence* vol. 26 (3).

Hayes-Roth, F., Waterman, D., and Lenat, D. 1983. *Building Expert Systems.* Reading, MA: Addison-Wesley.

Haynes, C., and Friedman, D. October 1987. Embedding Continuations in Procedural Objects. *ACM Transactions on Programming Languages and Systems* vol. 9 (4).

Henderson, P. February 1986. Functional Programming, Formal Specification, and Rapid Prototyping. *IEEE Transactions on Software Engineering* vol. SE-12 (2).

Herlihy, M., and Liskov, B. October 1982. A Value Transmission Method for Abstract Data Types. *ACM Transactions on Programming Languages and Systems* vol. 4 (4).

Hesselink, W. January 1988. A Mathematical Approach to Nondeterminism in Data Types. *ACM Transactions on Programming Languages and Systems* vol. 10 (1).

Hibbard, P., Hisgen, A., Rosenbers, J., Shaw, M., and Sherman, M. 1981. *Studies in Ada Style.* New York, NY: Springer-Verlag.

Hilfinger, P. 1982. *Abstraction Mechanisms and Language Design.* Cambridge, MA: The MIT Press.

Hoare, C. October 1974. Monitors: An Operating System Structuring Concept. *Communications of the ACM* vol. 17 (10).

Hoare, C. 1985. *Communicating Sequential Processes.* Englewood Cliffs, NJ: Prentice/Hall International.

Hogg, J., and Weiser, S. October 1987. OTM: Applying Objects to Tasks. *SIGPLAN Notices* vol. 22 (12).

Jajodia, S., and Ng. P. 1983. On Representation of Relational Structures by Entity-Relationship Diagrams, in *Entity-Relationship Approach to Software Engineering.* ed. C. Davis et al. Amsterdam, The Netherlands: Elsevier Science.

Johnson, C., 1986. Some Design Constraints Required for the Assembly of Software Components: The Incorporation of Atomic Abstract Types into Generically Structured Abstract Types. *Proceedings of the First International Conference on Ada Programming Language Applications for the NASA Space Station.* Houston, TX: NASA Lyndon B. Johnson Space Center.

Knight, B. 1983. A Mathematical Basis for Entity Analysis, in *Entity-Relationship Approach to Software Engineering.* ed. C. Davis et al. Amsterdam, The Netherlands: Elsevier Science.

LaLonde, W., and Pugh, J. August 1985. Specialization, Generalization, and Inheritance: Teaching Objectives Beyond Data Structures and Data Types. *SIGPLAN Notices* vol. 20 (8).

Leeson, J., and Spear, M. March 1987. Type-Independent Modules: The Preferred Approach to Generic ADTs in Modula-2. *SIGPLAN Notices* vol. 22 (3).

Lenzerini, M., and Santucci, G. 1983. Cardinality Constraints in the Entity-Relationship Model, in *Entity-Relationship Approach to Software Engineering.* ed. C. Davis et al. Amsterdam, The Netherlands: Elsevier Science.

Levesque, H. July 1984. Foundations of a Functional Approach to Knowledge Representation. *Artificial Intelligence* vol. 23 (2).

Lindgreen, P. 1983. Entity Sets and Their Description, in *Entity-Relationship Approach to Software Engineering.* ed. C. Davis et al. Amsterdam, The Netherlands: Elsevier Science.

Liskov, B. 1980. Programming with Abstract Data Types, in *Programming Language Design.* ed. A. Wasserman. New York, NY: Computer Society Press of the IEEE.

Liskov, B. May 1988. Data Abstraction and Hierarchy. *SIGPLAN Notices* vol. 23 (5).

Liskov, B., and Scheifler, R. July 1983. Guardians and Actions: Linguistic Support for Robust, Distributed Programs. *ACM Transactions on Programming Languages and Systems* vol. 5 (3).

Liskov, B., and Zilles, S. 1977. An Introduction to Formal Specifications of Data Abstractions, in *Current Trends in Programming Methodology: Software Specification and Design* vol. 1. ed. R. Yeh. Englewood Cliffs, NJ: Prentice-Hall.

Lucco, S. October 1987. Parallel Programming in a Virtual Object Space. *SIGPLAN Notices* vol. 22 (12).

Maes, P. October 1987. Concepts and Experiments in Computational Reflection. *SIGPLAN Notices* vol. 22 (12).

Mark, L. 1983. What is the Binary Relationship Approach?, in *Entity-Relationship Approach to Software Engineering.* ed. C. Davis et al. Amsterdam, The Netherlands: Elsevier Science.

Markowitz, V., and Raz, Y. 1983. A Modified Relational Algebra and Its Use in an Entity-Relationship Environment, in *Entity-Relationship Approach to Software Engineering.* ed. C. Davis et al. Amsterdam, The Netherlands: Elsevier Science.

Matsuoka, S., and Kawai, S. September 1988. Using Tuple Space Communication in Distributed Object-Oriented Languages. *SIGPLAN Notices* vol. 23 (11).

McAllester, D., and Zabih, F. November 1986. Boolean Classes. *SIGPLAN Notices* vol. 21 (11).

McCullough, P. October 1987. Transparent Forwarding: First Steps. *SIGPLAN Notices* vol. 22 (12).

Mealy, G. 1977. Notions, in *Current Trends in Programming Methodology: Data Structuring* vol. 4. ed. R. Yeh. Englewood Cliffs, NJ: Prentice-Hall.

Merlin, P., and Bochmann, G. January 1983. On the Construction of Submodule Specifications and Communication Protocols. *ACM Transactions on Programming Languages and Systems* vol. 5 (1)

Meyer, B. 1987. *Programming as Contracting*, Report TR-EI-12/CO. Goleta, CA: Interactive Software Engineering.

Minoura, T., and Iyengar, S. January 1989. Data and Time Abstraction Techniques for Multilevel Concurrent Systems. *IEEE Transactions on Software Engineering* vol. 15 (1).

Murata, T. 1984 Modeling and Analysis of Concurrent Systems, in *Software Engineering.* ed. C. Vick and C. Ramamoorthy. New York, NY: Van Nostrand Reinhold.

Mylopoulos, J., and Levesque, H. 1984. An Overview of Knowledge Representation. *On Conceptual Modeling: Perspectives from Artificial Intelligence, Databases, and Programming Languages.* ed. M. Brodie, J. Mylopoulos, and J. Schmidt. New York, NY: Springer-Verlag.

Nakano, R. 1983. Integrity Checking in a Logic-Oriented ER Model, in *Entity-Relationship Approach to Software Engineering.* ed. C. Davis et al. Amsterdam, The Netherlands: Elsevier Science.

Newton, M., and Watkins, J. November/December 1988. The Combination of Logic and Objects for Knowledge Representation. *Journal of Object-Oriented Programming* vol. 1 (4).

Nii, P. Summer 1986. Blackboard Systems: The Blackboard Model of Problem Solving and the Evolution of Blackboard Architectures. *AI Magazine* vol. 7 (2).

Ohori, A., and Buneman, P. October 1989. Static Type Inference for Parametric Classes. *SIGPLAN Notices* vol. 24 (10).

Pagan, F. 1981. *Formal Specification of Programming Languages.* Englewood Cliffs, NJ: Prentice-Hall.

Parent, C., and Spaccapieta, S. July 1985. An Algebra for a General Entity-Relationship Model. *IEEE Transactions on Software Engineering* vol. SE-11 (7).

Parnas, D. 1977. The Influence of Software Structure on Reliability, in *Current Trends in Programming Methodology: Software Specification and Design* vol. 1. ed. R. Yeh. Englewood Cliffs, NJ: Prentice-Hall.

Parnas, D. 1980. Designing Software for Ease of Extension and Contraction, in *Tutorial on Software Design Techniques.* 3rd ed. ed. P. Freeman and A. Wasserman. New York, NY: Computer Society Press of the IEEE.

Parnas, D., Clements, P., and Weiss, D. 1983. Enhancing Reusability with Information Hiding. *Proceedings of the Workshop on Reusability in Programming,* Stratford, CT: ITT Programming.

Pattee, H. 1973. *Hierarchy Theory.* New York, NY: George Braziller.

Peckham, J., and Maryanski, F. September 1988. Semantic Data Models. *ACM Computing Surveys* vol. 20 (3).

Pedersen, C. October 1989. Extending Ordinary Inheritance Schemes to Include Generalization. *SIGPLAN Notices* vol. 24 (10).

Peterson, J. September 1977. Petri Nets. *Computing Surveys* vol. 9 (3).

Reed, D. September 1978. *Naming and Synchronization in a Decentralized Computer System*. Cambridge, MA: The MIT Press.

Robinson, L., and Levitt, K. 1977. Proof Techniques for Hierarchically Structured Programs, in *Current Trends in Programming Methodology: Program Validation* vol. 2. ed. R. Yeh. Englewood Cliffs, NJ: Prentice-Hall.

Ross, D. July/August 1986. Classifying Ada Packages. *Ada Letters* vol. 6 (4).

Ruane, L. January 1984. Abstract Data Types in Assembly Language Programming. *SIGPLAN Notices* vol. 19 (1).

Rumbaugh, J. September 1988. Controlling Propagation of Operations Using Attributes on Relations. *SIGPLAN Notices* vol. 23 (11).

Shankar, K. 1984. Data Design: Types, Structures, and Abstractions, in *Software Engineering*. ed. C. Vick and C. Ramamoorthy. New York, NY: Van Nostrand Reinhold.

Shaw, M. 1984. The Impact of Modeling and Abstraction Concerns on Modern Programming Languages. *On Conceptual Modeling: Perspectives from Artificial Intelligence, Databases, and Programming Languages*. ed. M. Brodie, J. Mylopoulos, and J. Schmidt. New York, NY: Springer-Verlag.

Shaw, M. October 1984. Abstraction Techniques in Modern Programming Languages. *IEEE Software* vol. 1 (4).

Shaw, M. May 1989. Larger Scale Systems Require Higher-Level Abstractions. *SIGSOFT Engineering Notes* vol. 14 (3).

Shaw, M., Feldman, G., Fitzgerald, R., Hilfinger, P., Kimura, I., London, R., Rosenberg, J., and Wulf, W. 1981. Validating the Utility of Abstraction Techniques, in *ALPHARD: Form and Content*. ed. M. Shaw. New York, NY: Springer-Verlag.

Shaw, M., Wulf., W., and London, R. 1981. Abstraction and Verification in ALPHARD: Iteration and Generators, in *ALPHARD: Form and Content*. ed. M. Shaw. New York, NY: Springer-Verlag.

Sherman, M., Hisgen, A., and Rosenberg, J. 1982. A Methodology for Programming Abstract Data Types in Ada. *Proceedings of the AdaTEC Conference on Ada*. New York, NY: Association of Computing Machinery.

Siegel, J. April 1988. Twisty Little Passages. *HOOPLA: Hooray for Object-Oriented Programming Languages* vol. 1 (3). Everette, WA: Object Oriented Programming for Smalltalk Application Developers Association.

Stefik, M., Bobrow, D., and Kahn, K. January 1986. Integrating Access-Oriented Programming into a Multiparadigm Environment. *IEEE Software* vol. 3 (1).

Strom, R., and Yemini, S. January 1986. Typestate: A Programming Language Concept for Enhancing Software Reliability. *IEEE Transactions on Software Engineering* vol. SE-12 (1).

Stubbs, D., and Webre, N. 1985. *Data Structures with Abstract Data Types and Pascal*. Monterey, CA: Brooks/Cole.

Swaine, M. June 1988. Programming Paradigms. *Dr. Dobb's Journal of Software Tools*, no. 140.

Tabourier, Y. 1983. Further Development of the Occurrences Structure Concept: The EROS Approach, in *Entity-Relationship Approach to Software Engineering*. ed. C. Davis et al. Amsterdam, The Netherlands: Elsevier Science.

Tanenbaum, A. 1981. *Computer Networks*. Englewood Cliffs, NJ: Prentice-Hall.

Throelli, L. October 1987. Modules and Type Checking in PL/LL. *SIGPLAN Notices* vol. 22 (12).

Tomlinson, C., and Singh, V. October 1989. Inheritance and Synchronization with Enabled-sets. *SIGPLAN Notices* vol. 24 (10).

Toy, W. 1984. Hardware/Software Tradeoffs, in *Software Engineering*. ed. C. Vick and C. Ramamoorthy. New York, NY: Van Nostrand Reinhold.

Vegdahl, S. November 1986. Moving Structures between Smalltalk Images. *SIGPLAN Notices* vol. 21 (11).

Wasserman, A. 1980. Introduction to Data Types, in *Programming Language Design*. ed. A. Wasserman. New York, NY: Computer Society Press of the IEEE.

Weber, H., and Ehrig, H. July 1986. Specification of Modular Systems. *IEEE Transactions on Software Engineering* vol. SE-12 (7).

Wegner, P. 6 June 1981. *The Ada Programming Language and Environment*. Unpublished draft.

Wegner, P. 1987. On the Unification of Data and Program Abstraction in Ada, in *Object-Oriented Computing: Concepts* vol 1. ed. G. Peterson. New York, NY: Computer Society Press of the IEEE.

Wegner, P. 1987. The Object-Oriented Classification Paradigm, in *Research Directions in Object-Oriented Programming*. ed. B. Schriver and P. Wegner. Cambridge, MA: The MIT Press.

Wegner, P., and Zdonik, S. August 1988. Inheritance as an Incremental Modification Mechanism or What Like Is and Isn't Like. *Proceedings of ECOOP'88: European Conference on Object-Oriented Programming*. New York, NY: Springer-Verlag.

Weihl, W., and Liskov, B. April 1985. Implementation of Resilient, Atomic Data Types. *ACM Transactions on Programming Languages and Systems vol.* 7 (2)

Weller, D., and York, B. May 1984. A Relational Representation of an Abstract Type System. *IEEE Transactions on Software Engineering* vol. SE-10 (3).

White, J. July 1983. On the Multiple Implementation of Abstract Data Types within a Computation. *IEEE Transactions on Software Engineering* vol. SE-9 (4).

Wirth, N. December 1974. On the Composition of Well-structured Programs. *Computing Surveys* vol. 6 (4).

Wirth, N. January 1983. Program Development by Stepwise Refinement. *Communications of the ACM* vol. 26 (1).

Wirth, N. April 1988. Type Extensions. *ACM Transactions on Programming Languages and Systems* vol. 10 (2).

Wolf, A., Clarke, L., and Wileden, J. April 1988. A Model of Visibility Control. *IEEE Transactions on Software Engineering* vol. 14 (4).

Woods, W. October 1983. What's Important About Knowledge Representation? *IEEE Computer* vol. 16 (10).

Zilles, S. 1984. Types, Algebras, and Modelling, in *On Conceptual Modeling: Perspectives from Artificial Intelligence, Databases, and Programming Languages*. ed. M. Brodie, J. Mylopoulos, and J. Schmidt. New York, NY: Springer-Verlag.

Zippel, R. June 1983. Capsules. *SIGPLAN Notices* vol. 18 (6).

K. Tools and Environments

Andrews, T., and Harris, C. 1987. *Combining Language and Database Advances in an Object-Oriented Development Environment.* Billerica, MA: Ontologic

Corradi, A., and Leonardi, L. 1986. *An Environment Based on Parallel Objects.* Bologna, Italy: Universita' di Bologna.

Deutsch, P., and Taft, E. June 1980. *Requirements for an Experimental Programming Environment,* Report CSL-80-10. Palo Alto, CA: Xerox Palo Alto Research Center.

Diederich, J., and Milton, J. October 1987. An Object-Oriented Design System Shell. *SIGPLAN Notices* vol. 22 (12).

Durant, D., Carlson, G., and Yao, P. 1987. *Programmer's Guide to Windows.* Berkeley, CA: Sybex.

Erman, L., Lark, J., and Hayes-Roth, F. December 1988. ABE: An Environment for Engineering Intelligent Systems. *IEEE Transactions on Software Engineering* vol. 14 (12).

Ferrel, P., and Meyer, R. October 1989. Vamp: The Aldus Application Framework. *SIGPLAN Notices* vol. 24 (10).

Fischer, H., and Martin, D. 1987. *Integrating Ada Design Graphics into the Ada Software Development Process.* Encino, CA: Mark V Business Systems.

Goldberg, A. 1984a. *Smalltalk-80: The Interactive Programming Environment.* Reading, MA: Addison-Wesley.

Goldberg, A. 1984b. The Influence of an Object-Oriented Language on the Programming Environment, in *Interactive Programming Environments.* ed. B. Barstow. New York, NY: McGraw-Hill.

Goldstein, I., and Bobrow, D. March 1981. *An Experimental Description-Based Programming Environment,* Report CSL-81-3. Palo Alto, CA: Xerox Palo Alto Research Center.

Gorlen, K. May 1986. *Object-Oriented Program Support.* Bethesda, MD: National Institute of Health.

Hecht, A., and Simmons, A. 1986. Integrating Automated Structured Analysis and Design with Ada Programming Support Environments. *Proceedings of the First International Conference on Ada Programming Language Applications for the NASA Space Station.* Houston, TX: NASA Lyndon B. Johnson Space Center.

Hedin, G., and Magnusson B. August 1988. The Mjolner Environment: Direct Interaction with Abstractions. *Proceedings of ECOOP'88: European Conference on Object-Oriented Programming.* New York, NY: Springer-Verlag.

Hudson, S., and King, R. June 1988. The Cactic Project: Database Support for Software Environments. *IEEE Transactions on Software Engineering* vol. 14 (6).

International Business Machines. April 1988. *Operating System/2 Seminar Proceedings, IBM OS/2 Standard Edition Version 1.1, IBM Operating System/2 Update, Presentation Manager.* Boca Raton, FL.

Kant, E. 26 March 1987. *Interactive Problem Solving with a Task Configuration and Control System.* Ridgefield, CT: Schlumberger-Doll Research.

Kleyn, M., and Gingrich, P. September 1988. GraphTrace – Understanding Object-Oriented Systems Using Concurrently Animated Views. *SIGPLAN Notices* vol. 23 (11).

Laff, M., and Hailpern, B. July 1985. SW-2 – An Object-Based Programming Environment. *SIGPLAN Notices* vol. 20 (7).

MacLenna, B. July 1985. A Simple Software Environment Based on Objects and Relations. *SIGPLAN Notices* vol. 20 (7).

Marques, J., and Guedes, P. October 1989. Extending the Operating System to Support an Object-Oriented Environment. *SIGPLAN Notices* vol. 24 (10).

Minsky, N., and Rozenshtein, D. February 1988. A Software Development Environment for Law-Governed Systems. *SIGPLAN Notices* vol. 24 (2).

Moreau, D., and Dominick, W. 1987. *Object-Oriented Graphical Information Systems: Research Plan and Evaluation Metrics.* Lafayette, LA: University of Southwestern Louisiana, Center for Advanced Computer Studies.

Nakata, S., and Yamazak, G. 1983. ISMOS: A System Based on the E-R Model and its Application to Database-Oriented Tool Generation, in *Entity-Relationship Approach to Software Engineering.* ed. C. Davis et al. Amsterdam, The Netherlands: Elsevier Science.

Nye, A. 1989. *Xlib Programming Manual for Verison 11.* Newton, MA: O'Reilly and Associates.

O'Brien, P., Halbert, D., and Kilian, M. October 1987. The Trellis Programming Environment. *SIGPLAN Notices* vol. 22 (12).

Open Look Graphical User Interface Functional Specification. 1990. Reading, MA: Addison-Wesley.

OSF/Motif Style Guide, Version 1.0. 1989. Cambridge, MA: Open Software Foundation.

Penedo, M., Ploedereder, E., and Thomas, I. February 1988. Object Management Issues for Software Engineering Environments. *SIGPLAN Notices* vol. 24 (2).

Reenskaug, T., and Skaar, A. October 1989. An Environment for Literate Smalltalk Programming. *SIGPLAN Notices* vol. 24 (10).

Rosenplatt, W., Wileden, J., and Wolf, A. October 1989. OROS: Toward a Type Model for Software Development Environments. *SIGPLAN Notices* vol. 24 (10).

Russo, V., and Campbell, R. October 1989. Virtual Memory and Backing Storage Management in Multiprocessor Operating Systems Using Object-Oriented Design Techniques. *SIGPLAN Notices* vol. 24 (10).

Scheifler, R., and Gettys, J. 1986. The X Window System. *ACM Transactions on Graphics* vol. 63.

Schwan, K., and Matthews, J. July 1986. Graphical Views of Parallel Programs. *Software Engineering Notes,* vol. 11 (3).

Shear, D. 8 December 1988. CASE Shows Promise but Confusion Still Exists. *EDN* vol. 33 (25).

Sun Microsystems. 29 March 1987. *NeWS Technical Overview* Mountain View, CA.

Tarumi, H., Agusa, K., and Ohno, Y. 1988. A Programming Environment Supporting Reuse of Object-Oriented Software. *Proceedings of the 10th International Conference on Software Engineering,* New York, NY: Computer Society Press of the IEEE.

Taylor, R., Belz, F., Clarke, L., Osterweil, L., Selby, R., Wileden, J., Wolf, A., and Young, M. February 1988. Foundations for the Arcadia Environment. *SIGPLAN Notices* vol. 24 (2).

Tesler, L. August 1981. The Smalltalk Environment. *Byte* vol. 6 (8).

Vines, D., and King, T. 1988. *Gaia: An Object-Oriented Framework for an Ada Environment*. Minneapolis, MN: Honeywell.

Vines, P., Vines, D., and King, T. 1988. *Configuration and Change Control in Gaia*. Minneapolis, MN: Honeywell.

Weinand, A., Gamma, E., and Marty, R. 1989. Design and Implementation of ET++, a Seamless Object-Oriented Application Framework. *Structured Programming* vol. 10 (2).

Wiorkowski, G., and Kull, D. 1988. *DB2 Design and Development Guide*. Reading, MA: Addison-Wesley.

Index

Object Diagram
Illustrates the object structure, including the specification of individual objects and their relationships.

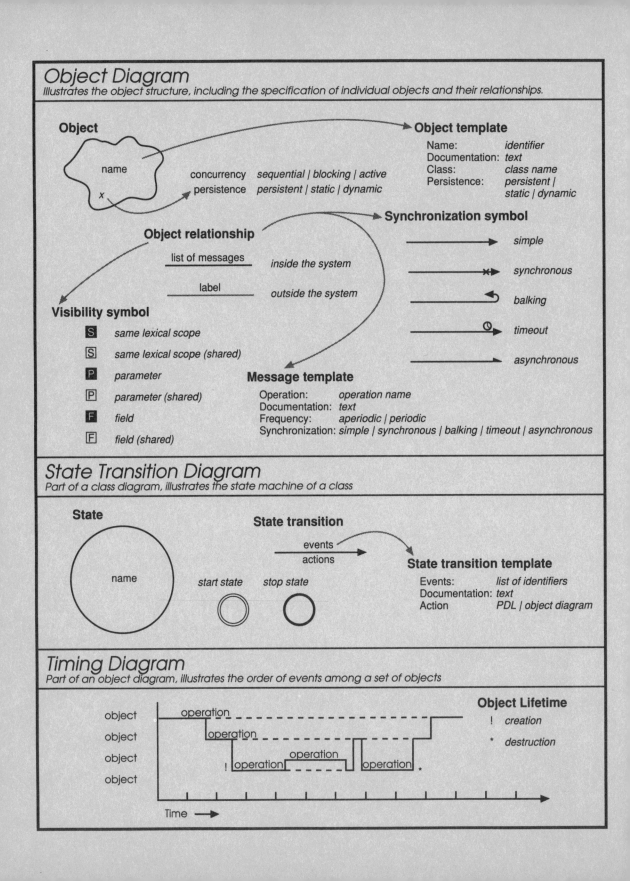

Object

name

x

concurrency   *sequential | blocking | active*
persistence   *persistent | static | dynamic*

Object template

Name: *identifier*
Documentation: *text*
Class: *class name*
Persistence: *persistent |*
                static | dynamic

Object relationship

list of messages   *inside the system*

label   *outside the system*

Synchronization symbol

simple
synchronous
balking
timeout
asynchronous

Visibility symbol

S   *same lexical scope*
S   *same lexical scope (shared)*
P   *parameter*
P   *parameter (shared)*
F   *field*
F   *field (shared)*

Message template

Operation: *operation name*
Documentation: *text*
Frequency: *aperiodic | periodic*
Synchronization: *simple | synchronous | balking | timeout | asynchronous*

State Transition Diagram
Part of a class diagram, illustrates the state machine of a class

State

name

start state   *stop state*

State transition

events
actions

State transition template

Events: *list of identifiers*
Documentation: *text*
Action   *PDL | object diagram*

Timing Diagram
Part of an object diagram, illustrates the order of events among a set of objects

object   operation
object   operation
object   operation   operation   operation
object

Time →

Object Lifetime

!   *creation*
*   *destruction*